HORSE GUARDS

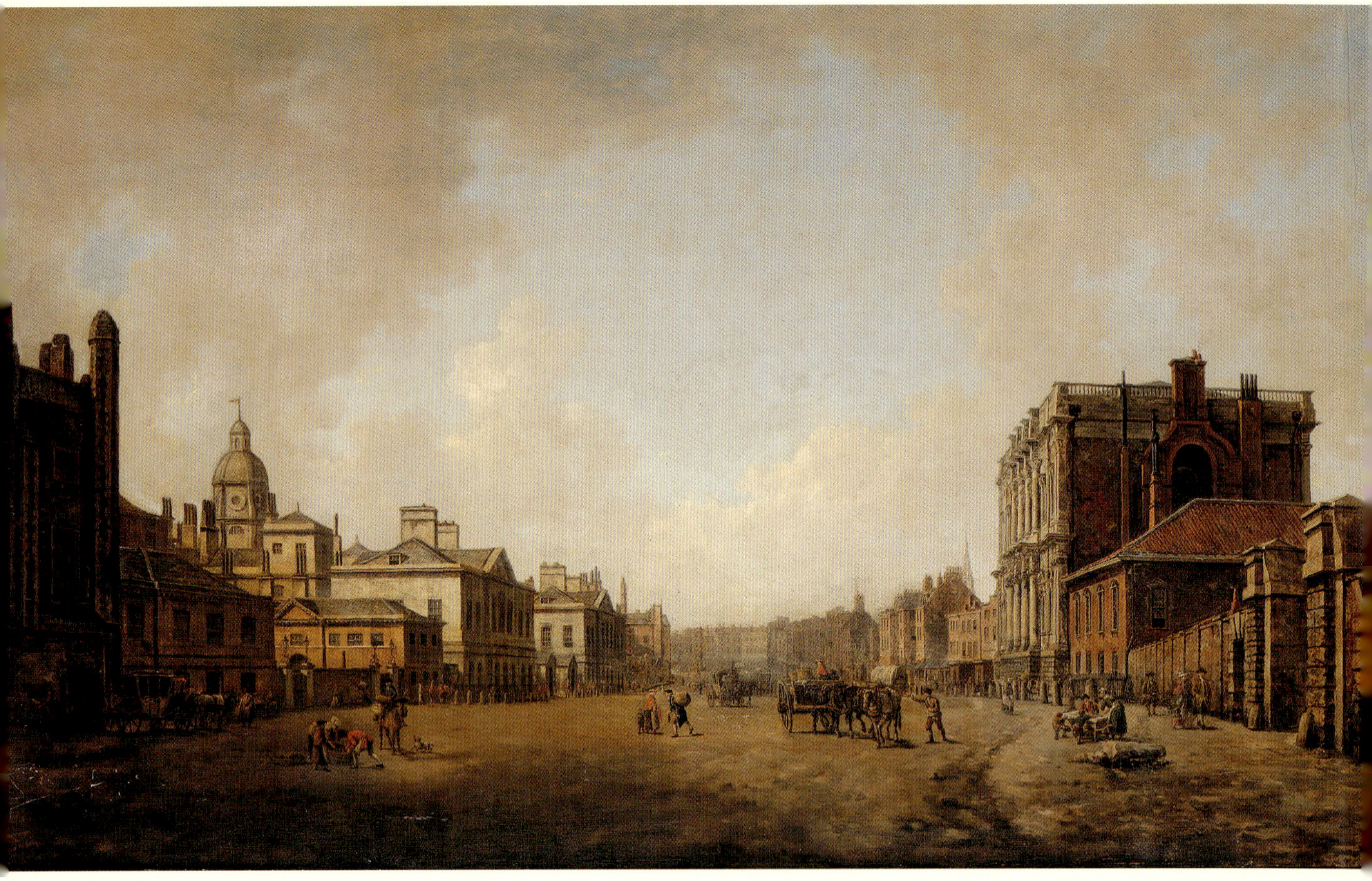

HORSE GUARDS

BARNEY WHITE-SPUNNER

Pictures researched by
SARAH JACKSON AND ANNABEL MERULLO

MACMILLAN

This book is dedicated to all those Household Cavalrymen who have lost their lives whilst serving their country

First published 2006 by Macmillan
an imprint of Pan Macmillan Ltd
Pan Macmillan, 20 New Wharf Road, London N1 9RR
Basingstoke and Oxford
Associated companies throughout the world
www.panmacmillan.com

ISBN-13: 978-1-4050-5574-1
ISBN-10: 1-4050-5574-X

Copyright © Major General Barney White-Spunner and the Household Cavalry Museum Trust Ltd

The right of Barney White-Spunner to be identified as the author of this work has been asserted by him in accordance with the Copyright, Designs and Patents Act 1988.

All rights reserved. No part of this publication may be reproduced, stored in or introduced into a retrieval system, or transmitted, in any form, or by any means (electronic, mechanical, photocopying, recording or otherwise) without the prior written permission of the publisher. Any person who does any unauthorized act in relation to this publication may be liable to criminal prosecution and civil claims for damages.

1 3 5 7 9 8 6 4 2

A CIP catalogue record for this book is available from the British Library.

Map artwork by Reginald Piggott

Colour Reproduction by Aylesbury Studios Bromley Ltd
Printed and bound in Great Britain by
Butler & Tanner Ltd, Frome

Page ii. The Horse Guards by W. Marlow, which hangs in the officers' mess at Windsor.

Contents

List of Maps vii

Acknowledgements viii

Author's Note xi

Part One
ROYAL GUARD AND STANDING ARMY
1660–1685

One – The King's Life Guard *4*
Two – Unton Croke's Regiment of Horse *39*
Three – The Tangier Horse *67*

Part Two
DIVIDED LOYALTIES
1685–1701

Four – Sedgemoor and James II's Reforms *86*
Five – The Glorious Revolution and War in Ireland *112*
Six – Flanders Fields *141*

Part Three
A PATTERN ESTABLISHED
1701–1763

Seven – Policing London and War in Spain *160*
Eight – Germanic Order *185*
Nine – The War of the Austrian Succession *197*
Ten – The Seven Years War *223*

Part Four
THE FIRST GREAT CHANGE
1763–1816

Eleven – The King's Peace and the Revolutionary's War *252*

Twelve – Fashion in Windsor and Campaigning in Spain *273*

Thirteen – Defeating Napoleon *303*

Part Five
ORNAMENTAL EXTRAVAGANCE
1816–1902

Fourteen – Ceremonial Frustration *346*

Fifteen – Small Wars in Africa *384*

Sixteen – The Boer War *409*

Part Six
'THE ORDERED PAST BEHIND US LIES'
1902–1939

Seventeen – Policing the Empire and Trench Warfare in Europe *434*

Eighteen – The End in France and Reorganisation *473*

Part Seven
THE SECOND GREAT CHANGE
After 1939

Nineteen – The Second World War: the Middle East *500*

Twenty – The Second World War: Europe *531*

Twenty-One – Withdrawal from Empire *552*

Epilogue – The Household Cavalry Today *567*

List of Illustrations *586*

Bibliography *595*

Notes and References *598*

Index *607*

Maps

Sedgemoor, 6 July 1685 *91*

Ireland, 1690 *125*

Flanders, 1689–1697 *145*

The Royals in Portugal and Spain, 1704–1710 *173*

War of the Austrian Succession, 1742–1746 *199*

The Seven Years War, 1756–1763 *227*

Warburg, 31 July 1760 *241*

Revolutionary Wars, 1793–1795 *267*

The Peninsula, 1809–1814 *289*

Fuentes de Oñoro, 5 May 1811 *293*

Waterloo: French Invasion of Belgium, 15–17 June 1815 *317*

Waterloo: The Household and Union Brigades' Charge *324*

The Crimea, 1854–1856 *373*

Balaclava, 25 October 1854 *375*

Egyptian Campaign, 1882 *393*

Sudan Campaign, 1884–1885 *393*

South Africa Operations, 1899–1900 *419*

Western Front, 1914–1918 *457*

First Battle of Ypres, October–November 1914 *461*

Middle East during the Second World War *507*

North Africa during the Second World War and The Western Desert *521*

North-west Europe, June 1944–May 1945 and Italy, 1943–1945 *541*

Acknowledgements

So many different and kind people have helped with this book that it is difficult to acknowledge them all as fully as I would like and they deserve. First, I am much indebted to Her Majesty The Queen for her kind permission to draw so extensively on both the Royal Archive at Windsor and on The Royal Collection for illustrations. Secondly, I owe a particular debt to Michael Sissons, my agent, and to Colonel Hamon Massey, whose idea it was to write a full history of the four regiments that comprise the Household Cavalry as part of the project to relaunch our museum in 2007. I also owe it to Michael that he shared his inspiration with Jeremy Trevathan of Pan Macmillan, who has so patiently supported and edited the book and who is largely responsible for it appearing today in what I hope is at least a vaguely readable form. Particular and special thanks also to Sarah Jackson and Annabel Merullo who have proved the most diligent, enthusiastic and inspired picture researchers and who have produced the wonderful illustrations that you are about to enjoy. Thank you also to Helen Campbell for her most careful copy-editing.

Next I must thank those who have done so much to help with the research. Three people stand out. Ben Weinstein, a PhD student at Cambridge when I met him, but now teaching at Newcastle University, was an exceptional research assistant, and I am so grateful to Neil McKendrick and Dean Godson for introducing me to him. He could not have worked without the very generous support of Major Paddy Kersting and Corporal Major Chris Hughes, both late of The Blues and Royals, who have been respectively Curator and Assistant Curator of the Household Cavalry Museum. Sadly, Chris Hughes died before this book reached publication. I am also much indebted to two historians to have been allowed to use their, as yet, unpublished work. First, Doctor Brigitte Mitchell's study of Windsor as a garrison town from 1815 to 1855, prepared for her PhD, was both invaluable and fascinating; secondly, the life of Major General John Brocklehurst, Lord Ranksborough, by Jean Bray, Archivist at Sudeley Castle, is a most thoroughly researched and interesting manuscript which I hope will soon be published. I am very grateful to them both.

I am also much indebted to all those who have helped point me in the right direction for research or advised me on how to handle this fascinating subject. Particular thanks are due to Professor John Childs of Leeds University, without whose exceptional trilogy of studies on the Stuart army I would have been completely lost and whose research in this area is unique; to Doctor Gary Sheffield for all his help with the chapters on the First World War; to Christopher Hibbert for his advice on sources and to Johnnie Watson, past Household Cavalry historian, for all his counsel. Particular thanks also to Pamela Clark and her staff at the Royal Archive for their help and their ideas.

Numerous generous people have either lent me their family papers or allowed me access to their private archives. I would like to thank in particular Lieutenant Colonel Gordon Birdwood for copying me the papers of his grandfather, Field Marshal Lord Birdwood; to Lord Northampton and his archivist, Peter McKay, for their help with the Compton archive; to the Duke of Rutland and Bob Webster for allowing me such complete access to the Granby papers at Belvoir; to Brigadier Valerian, Duke of Wellington, for copying me his papers and diaries; to Colonel James Hamilton-Russell for trusting me with his late father's letters, which were some of the most moving documents I read in my research. Thanks also to my great friend Johnny Shaw for allowing me to use the diaries and letters of his late father, Major John Shaw, known to my generation of Household Cavalrymen as 'the Major', and regarded by many of us as one of the most hospitable and approachable officers of his generation. Thanks also to Colonel David Smiley, one of the best known and bravest Household Cavalrymen of this century, for all his advice on the chapters on the Second World War, as well as to Colonel 'G' (Gerrard) Leigh, who fought with both him and the Duke of Wellington; to Johnny Seyfried, who accompanied me around Normandy and to Major General Sir Roy Redgrave.

Thanks also to Brigadier Andrew Parker Bowles, my ex-commanding officer, for his advice and proof reading and for access to his most interesting photograph albums and to Richard Onslow for copying me his information about his ancestor who commanded the Horse Grenadiers, and who seems to have taken almost as much hunting leave whilst serving as he did. I am also much indebted to John Lange, Director of the Household Cavalry Museum, for all his support; to my friend David Waterhouse, our Museum Appeal Director, for keeping me so amused during my research, and to Lieutenant Colonel Stuart Sibley who is now the curator.

Lastly, but most importantly, particular thanks and love to my wife, Moo, and my three children, Letty, Christy (who has asked me to point out that he is a boy) and Mouse, who put up with me spending endless evenings, weekends and holidays, which I should have rightly spent with them, engaged instead on this totally absorbing project.

Barney White-Spunner

Illustration Acknowledgements

Many of the photographs reproduced in this book are the result of extensive research in the Household Cavalry Museum at Combermere Barracks, Windsor, and The Royal Collection.

We would especially like to thank John Lange, Director of the Household

Cavalry Museum; Lieutenant Colonel Stuart Sibley, Curator of the Household Cavalry Museum; Major Paddy Kersting, former Curator of the Household Cavalry Museum; and photographer, Derek Askem.

We are most grateful to the many people who willingly offered their support and advice. Our particular thanks go to Lord Patrick Beresford, Colonel 'G' Gerrard Leigh, Brigadier Andrew Parker-Bowles, Colonel David Smiley, Mrs Robert Spencer Churchill and Brigadier Valerian, the Duke of Wellington, for unique access to their personal albums. We would also like to thank Colonel Simon Doughty, Camilla Seymour, Emma Gormley of the House of Commons, Major General Peter Grant-Peterkin, Sergeant-at-Arms, House of Commons, General Lord Guthrie, Colonel of the Life Guards, the late Corporal Major Chris Hughes, Jonathan Marsden and Cristina Robbins of The Royal Collection, Richard Onslow, Jane Wellesley, Colonel Hamon Massey, formerly Silver Stick and Lieutenant Colonel commanding the Household Cavalry, and Colonel Paddy Tabor, Silver Stick-in-Waiting and Lieutenant Colonel commanding the Household Cavalry.

Every effort has been made to trace the copyright holders. However, if we have omitted anyone we apologise and will if informed make corrections to any future editions. Those listed in the List of Illustrations have kindly granted us permission to reproduce photographs.

Sarah Jackson and Annabel Merullo

Mrs Albert Broom was the Household Brigade photographer between 1904 and 1939 and was presented with the badge of the 1st Life Guards in 1914 by Quarter Master Wragg. The postcards that she and her daughter sold in her booth, seen here in 1916 at the Exhibition of Women at War Work, would have been taken as the regiment went off to the front and capture many poignant moments, especially those taken at Waterloo Station with families and young wives.

Author's Note

This has been the most enjoyable book to write. The story is so absorbing, and draws together so many separate strands of British history, that I could have spent decades in research and written at least ten volumes. Sadly, had I done so, my publishers, Macmillan, might have justifiably refused to publish it and I doubt many of you would have bought it. Inevitably, therefore, I have had to cut an awful lot out. I am particularly conscious that I have not written as much about the post-1945 history of either The Life Guards or The Blues and Royals as I have prior to that date. This is partly because it is a period which has already been well covered by Willie Lloyd and Johnnie Watson in their excellent books (see Bibliography), partly because many of those who served then are still in the process of writing their memoirs so that all the necessary material is not yet available, and partly because, having served through many of the more recent events myself, I am too close to them to form an objective perspective. I therefore decided that it was for the next generation of Household Cavalry historians to take a more detached view. My apologies, therefore, to those readers who feel that I have not written enough about them, but I offer instead an Epilogue, which is in effect an essay on the Household Cavalry post-1960 and as we are today.

Secondly, although every attempt has been made to verify the accuracy and authenticity of all the material used, it is probably inevitable in a book that covers such an extended period of history, in both the general and the particular, that there will be the odd mistake. I have also used many first hand accounts by ex-Household Cavalrymen, and, literate as our soldiers have undoubtedly been over the centuries, I can not guarantee that the letter or diary entry scribbled in the guttering light of a candle in a bivouac in Spain or Flanders is as accurate in terms of dates and events as the more balanced and polished histories written afterwards. Generally, I have gone with what people in the regiments wrote at the time but acknowledge that in doing so I leave myself open to correction by more experienced historians.

Thirdly, being soldiers, we like to get the detail correct, but one thing I could get no agreement on was whether we were 'T'he Life Guards or 't'he Life Guards, or whether in the past we had been 'T'he Blues or 't'he Blues, 'T'he Royals or 't'he Royals. Every account is different. The truth is that our forebears were less obsessed with the definite article than we are, and so it does not really matter. However, I have adopted the following protocol that will, I hope, satisfy most critics. Prior to 1922, I refer to 't'he Life Guards on the grounds that the name 'Life Guards' was not an official title – the component parts of what is now 'T'he Life Guards being either troops of Horse Guards or Horse Grenadiers, or subsequently 1st Life Guards or 2nd Life Guards with no article at all. Post-1922 I refer to 'T'he Life Guards. For The Blues and The Royals, which were both technically nicknames, but so widely used that they almost came to form official titles, I have used 'The' throughout, and, post-1969, refer to 'The Blues and Royals' as that is now part of our official designation. Should any ex-Household Cavalry readers disagree with my solution I would be grateful if you would simply swallow your indignation and not bother to write to me about it.

The many changes in name, organization and structure can be confusing for the reader to follow. The chart below is designed to be a quick guide to the main events, which will hopefully make the text easier to follow.

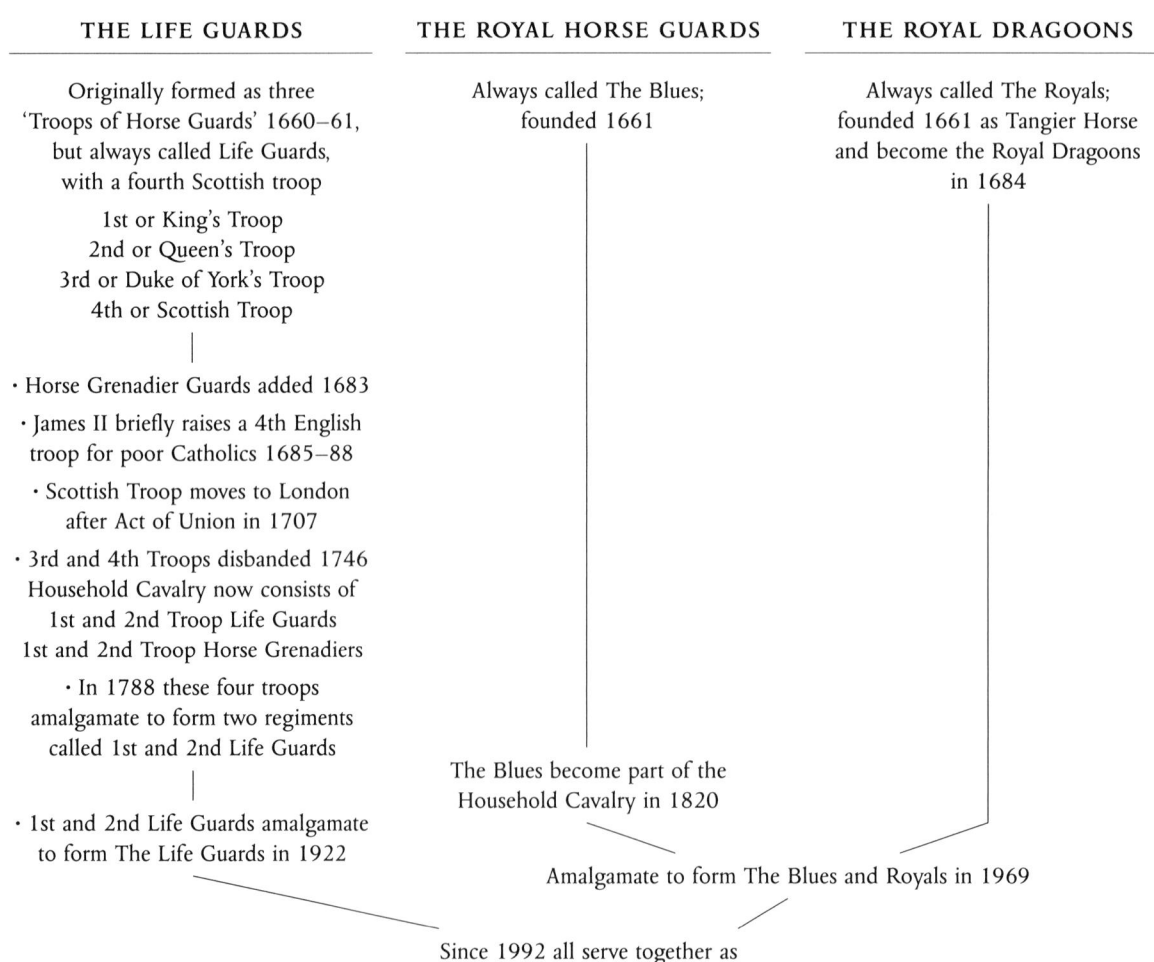

THE LIFE GUARDS	THE ROYAL HORSE GUARDS	THE ROYAL DRAGOONS
Originally formed as three 'Troops of Horse Guards' 1660–61, but always called Life Guards, with a fourth Scottish troop	Always called The Blues; founded 1661	Always called The Royals; founded 1661 as Tangier Horse and become the Royal Dragoons in 1684

1st or King's Troop
2nd or Queen's Troop
3rd or Duke of York's Troop
4th or Scottish Troop

· Horse Grenadier Guards added 1683
· James II briefly raises a 4th English troop for poor Catholics 1685–88
· Scottish Troop moves to London after Act of Union in 1707
· 3rd and 4th Troops disbanded 1746
Household Cavalry now consists of
1st and 2nd Troop Life Guards
1st and 2nd Troop Horse Grenadiers
· In 1788 these four troops amalgamate to form two regiments called 1st and 2nd Life Guards

· 1st and 2nd Life Guards amalgamate to form The Life Guards in 1922

The Blues become part of the Household Cavalry in 1820

Amalgamate to form The Blues and Royals in 1969

Since 1992 all serve together as
· The Household Cavalry Regiment in Windsor
with two squadrons of The Life Guards and two squadrons of The Blues and Royals
· The Household Cavalry Mounted Regiment in Knightsbridge
with one squadron of The Life Guards and one squadron of The Blues and Royals

Ranks

Officers: Senior to Regimental Level

Field Marshal – A largely honorific title, conferred on the most senior officers like Wellington or Royal Princes.

General – Usually commanding an army.

Lieutenant General – Usually commanding a corps of about 30,000 to 40,000 troops, like Buller in 1899.

Major General – Usually commanding a division, of about 10,000 troops, or, in the eighteenth century, a 'line'. Major General Richard Onslow, for example, commanded the 2nd Line of Cavalry. At one point Major Generals also commanded brigades.

Brigadier or (formerly) Brigadier General – Usually commanding a brigade of about 3,000 to 4,000 troops, like Dundonald in South Africa. It was also, confusingly, a non-commissioned officer's rank in the Life Guards prior to 1788.

Colonel – A staff rank, not normally commanding troops, although the Household Cavalry is an exception as today the Silver Stick is a colonel.

Officers: Serving with Regiments

Colonel – The Colonel did not actually command a regiment after 1660 although he drew the pay and enjoyed the privileges of the office. He was, however, always involved in the detail of who was commissioned, what the regiment did, what uniforms they wore, etc. In the Household Cavalry the colonels were, after the Popish Plot, called Gold Sticks and one was always on duty near the King called The Gold Stick in Waiting. Originally the most senior troop in The Blues & The Royals was known as The Colonel's Troop, and commanded by a captain-lieutenant.

Lieutenant Colonels – Because the colonels were too senior or busy to run their regiments on a daily basis, they appointed a lieutenant colonel to do it for them, usually known as 'The Commanding Officer'. In the Household Cavalry he usually also deputized as being responsible for the Monarch's personal security, and was known as the Silver Stick. The one on duty was known as The Silver Stick in Waiting.

The Lieutenant Colonel's troop was the second most senior in the regiment and, again, often commanded by a captain-lieutenant to leave the lieutenant colonel free to command the regiment.

Majors – The lieutenant colonel's second in command and right-hand man, who carried out much of the daily administration. His troop was the third most senior. More recently it has been normal practice for majors to command squadrons and therefore there are several in a regiment.

Captains – Commanded troops and, after the Crimea, when the basic cavalry sub-unit was changed to a squadron of two troops, a squadron, although more recently squadrons have been commanded by majors.

Lieutenants – Lieutenants originally acted as the second in command of a troop and did much of the captain's work for him. Since the mid-nineteenth century they have commanded troops in a squadron.

Cornets – Cornets were 2nd lieutenants and still are in The Blues and Royals. Originally they carried the Troop Standard (or flag), but this was soon relegated in the Household Cavalry to non-commissioned officers. Confusingly, cornets in the Life Guards originally acted as second in command of the troop and equated to majors in the rest of the army. This practice ceased in 1788. 2nd lieutenants in the Life Guards were called sub-lieutenants from 1788, and are today referred to as 2nd lieutenants, in common with the rest of the army.

Life Guard Officers' Ranks Prior to 1788

Prior to 1788 the Life Guards ran a thoroughly confusing system of officers ranks, which was designed to demonstrate their distance from the ordinary army. They were referred to by both their Life Guard rank and their army rank, such as 'Captain & Colonel', for example. The ranks below captain equated as follows:

Life Guards	Army
Cornet	Major
Guidon	Captain
Exempt	Captain/Lieutenant
Brigadier	Cornet/2nd Lieutenant
Sub-Brigadier	No real equivalent

Non-Commissioned Officers' Ranks

The Household Cavalry still has different non-commissioned ranks from the rest of the army. They are as follows:

Household Cavalry	Army
Regimental Corporal Major	Regimental Sergeant Major
Squadron Corporal Major	Sergeant Major
Staff Corporal	Staff or Colour Sergeant
Corporal of Horse	Sergeant
Lance Corporal of Horse	Corporal
Lance Corporal	Lance Corporal

Household Cavalry non-commissioned officers also still wear badges of rank senior to the actual rank they hold, which is a throwback to the old status of the Life Guards, and all wear a crown to show their link to the Monarch.

Note: Where it has been possible to check, all dates given are according to the Gregorian calendar.

HORSE GUARDS

Given by His Ma:tie to ỹ Right Hoble William Lord Viscount Dangan of Clean, the day of 1674.

Part One

ROYAL GUARD AND STANDING ARMY

1660–1685

Chapter One

THE KING'S LIFE GUARD

CHARLES II LANDED AT DOVER at about noon on 25 May 1660. He was greeted by General Monck, the man who had made his Restoration possible, 'with all imaginable love and respect', according to Samuel Pepys,[1] who rowed ashore at the same time as the King, escorting one of Charles's footmen and, more importantly, his favourite dog. After the formalities were completed it became apparent that the royal party was too large to be accommodated in Dover, and so the King set out for Canterbury where he spent his first night on English soil since his flight after the Battle of Worcester in 1651. The following day he started for London, accompanied by his two brothers, James, Duke of York, later to reign from 1685 to 1688 as King James II, and Richard, Duke of Gloucester, who was to die of smallpox within the year. 'Infinite the crowd of people and the gallantry of horsemen, citizens, and noblemen of all sorts'[2] who cheered them on their way. Accorded the singular, if uncomfortable, honour of riding on the back of the King's coach were Monck and Lord Gerard of Brandon, one of Charles's closest associates in exile, and the man to whom he had entrusted his personal security.

Brandon led a band of about 600 Cavalier gentlemen, most of whom had joined Charles in exile in France, and later Holland, either because they could not countenance living under the Commonwealth, or to escape Cromwell's vengeance, or because many had been bankrupted by the civil wars of the English Revolution. They now rode behind the royal party as they wound their way through the Kentish lanes, acting as a genuine escort but also as courtiers sharing in the good fortune of their newly restored King.

Mingled among them were a few personal followers of the Duke of York, more Cavaliers, who had recently fought with him against the Commonwealth at Dunkirk in the untidy and ultimately fruitless battles of 1659. Most of those who had acted as York's personal guard in that campaign had,

---

Page 2. King Charles II in his Garter robes in 1674, a portrait which hangs in the officers' mess in Windsor.

Louis XIV of France (*left*). Charles II envied his power and the splendour of his court. From 1670 he made a series of treaties with Louis taking French money in exchange for a promise to convert to Roman Catholicism. He was particularly envious of Louis XIV's royal guards, the Maison Militaire du Roi, who can be seen below escorting the French King in 1662 at a 'carousel' (a parade of cavalry horses). The Life Guards were modelled partly on them and partly on Cromwell's Life Guard.

however, remained in Holland. Many of them, like their master, were Roman Catholics.

Preceding the cortège was General Monck's own 'life guard', a more sober, disciplined group, in the manner of regular soldiers, uniformly dressed in red, wearing 'front and back' armour. They had been Cromwell's bodyguard, and many of them, including their famous captain, Sir Philip Howard – knighted later that very day by the King at Canterbury, probably as a precaution, and from a sense of relief – had once fought against those same Cavaliers who now pressed up behind the royal carriage to their rear.

It was a strange cavalcade, indicative of the conflicting pressures and concerns that had forced Parliament to ask for Charles's return, and which were to be played out, often very dramatically, in the events of the next twenty-eight years. Each of these three distinct groups who accompanied the King to London through the spring sunshine were destined to form troops of life guards, to be the first regiment in the English, and thereafter British, regular army, and to be an integral part, not only of the turbulent story of the coming decades but also of our continuing history.

CHARLES MUST HAVE HAD mixed thoughts as he entered the capital four days later, on his thirtieth birthday, approaching Whitehall Palace along the Strand and passing close to the site of his father's execution. He had last been in London eighteen years before in January 1642. Then he had experienced his father's shame and frustration at his inability to arrest the five treasonous members of Parliament (Pym, Hampden, Holles, Haselrig and Bulstrode) who had triggered the crisis. Not only had they been forewarned of his approach and fled, but, more importantly, there had been no military force in London on which the King could rely. Now the London crowds were shouting for his son. These were the same people who had turned the Royalists back from the city after the Battle of Edgehill, who had provided regiments for Parliament's service, who had cheered Cromwell, and who had looked on, admittedly in silence, as Charles I's head was struck off on a cold January morning just eleven years previously. Only one year earlier, Monck's bodyguard, who were even now escorting him, would gladly have done the same to him. The difference that a loyal body of regular troops would have made in 1642 was a lesson that was not lost on Charles II, and it had been reinforced during his stay at the court of Louis XIV.

Louis had himself experienced the dangers of a weak monarchy during his chronically unstable childhood and had concluded that an effective body of royal guards, owing their loyalty and, perhaps more importantly, their livelihood to the throne, was indispensable to the machinery of absolutism that he went on to effect so successfully. His father, Louis XIII, had established an enormous guard force that protected both his person and his residences and formed the core of his army at large. The Mousquetaires de la Garde were an elite regiment within the elite, the 'children of the best families of France, equipped with a blue casaque, and distinguished by silver crosses'.[3] They consisted of two companies, the Mousquetaires Noirs and the Mousquetaires Gris, according to the colour of their horses. Disbanded during the endless Frondes, or revolts against the monarchy between 1648 and 1653, when their exploits provided exciting material for Dumas, they were re-created by Louis XIV in 1657, after he had finally established his authority. 'He who [amongst them] hath not made two or three campaigns by the time he is eighteen years of age, is esteemed a *person lasche* – that is, of a soft education and small repute,' wrote the diarist John Evelyn,[4] revealing something of the violence that prevailed in mid-seventeenth-century France. Thereafter Louis never ventured far without his guards, and even had four of them follow his coach when he was hunting. The Venetian Ambassador commented in 1683 that 'his Majesty never goes from one apartment to another without guards being placed in the corridors, on the stairs, and in the communicating passages'.[5]

The kings of England never enjoyed the luxury of such a force. Henry VII established the Yeomen of the Guard after Bosworth in 1485, and although they fought well for him, wearing the white and green Tudor livery, at the Battle of Stoke the following year, they were never more than royal gaolers and security guards. Henry VIII eventually reduced them and in 1520 changed their uniforms to the famous red that they wear today. Later he set up a corps of gentlemen pensioners, adopting the French concept of training sons of noble families in the arts of war. It was an unsuccessful experiment, and the pensioners ultimately developed into the Corps of Gentlemen at Arms, whose role was largely ceremonial.

So when matters deteriorated for Charles I in 1639, there was no reliable force that he could deploy. The Yeomen of the Guard and the gentlemen pensioners were incapable of forming the nucleus of an army around which trained bands of militiamen could muster, or of protecting the King himself. This uncomfortable reality was brought home starkly in the Bishop's War of 1639, the conflict that began the English civil wars when Charles was humiliatingly forced to back down in the face of a vastly superior Scottish army at Kelso, and again the following year at Newburn, after which Newcastle and Durham were lost.

By the time the English civil wars had started in earnest in 1642, Charles I had to make do with what he could muster as an army, but he had at least formed a regiment of mounted King's life guards, divided into two troops, 'The King's and The Queene's Troopes', complemented by troops to protect other members of the Royal Family. The Royalist order of battle at Leicester in 1645 shows not only 'The King's Life Guards of Horse' commanded by Charles's cousin, Lord Bernard Stuart, which totalled 130 horsemen but also a troop of 130 life guards for Prince Rupert and another of 'above 100 gentlemen etc. and reformados for Prince Maurice'.[6]

These life guard troops acquitted themselves well in the early stages of the war. Richard Symonds, a staunch Royalist from Essex, served as a trooper in the King's Troop from 1643 until 1645 and kept a detailed diary, much of it a list of marches and camps and – Symonds being something of a snob – details of who was knighted, which lords attended the King, and the owners of various estates and their income. However, we do get from him a sense of a competent and cohesive unit as we follow, in his pages, the troops progress through the battles in the West Country to the Royalist nemesis at Naseby some two years later.

The life guards often found themselves in the midst of savage fighting, and suffered significant casualties. They were a regiment of horse, in other words cavalry, but were not averse to dismounting and closing in hand-to-hand fighting, particularly if the King himself was threatened; Charles I was personally brave, so he often was. Each troop carried its own standard, a type of flag that indicated the presence of an important personage. The King's Troop carried the King's 'colours' – a square flag, with the cross of St George on the left and a gold lion rampant on a red background on the right, under the motto 'Dieu et mon Droit'. The colours always remained near the King in battle, and were withdrawn if the fighting became too intense for fear they might be lost. This was the first 'royal standard' to be carried by the life guards, a custom that continues to this day. The men seem mostly to have been educated and of some standing, like Symonds, who ended his days as an official in the Court of Chancery, although a Royalist trooper was hanged near Huntingdon for stealing the plate from the local church. Another well-known life guard, the wonderfully named Troilus Turberville, was knighted by the King for leading a crucial charge at Edgehill in 1642, the first major battle, and was rewarded further, strangely, with a doctorate in civil law from Oxford for the same deed.

As the wars progressed with myriad battles in the mid-1640s, an ongoing disagreement developed between the King and his nephew Prince Rupert, who commanded the Royalist cavalry, over the command of the life guards. In November 1644 Prince Rupert 'because the King would not give him command over the guards, did give the king his command, and asked to leave the kingdom. The King consented; he required a passe, and the King denyed, because he would be not seene to consent to his going'. Such rows were commonplace and eventually 'His highnes yeilded to the King's resolucion'. Unsurprisingly, in the resulting confusion matters started to go wrong in the face of Parliament's efficient 'new model army'.

Symonds claimed that they fought valiantly at Naseby on 14 June 1645, the last major battle of the civil war and the one which sealed the Royalists' fate, although he admits that they had to flee from the field. 'The horse escaped to Leicester this afternoon, and were persued by a body of the enemyes horse and loose scowters, to Great Glyn, and there the Earle of Lichfield [as Lord

Bernard Stuart had become] charged their loose men with halfe a score of horse and beate them back.' Unfortunately for Symonds, the Parliamentarian Colonel Okey, who commanded the regiment of dragoons who charged them, also left an account of the battle that was less complimentary. He wrote that he 'charged the King's Regiment of horse, who faced about and run away and never made any stay until they came to Leicester, which was about 15 miles from the place where we fought . . . we took between four and five thousand men with as many horse, all their ordinance, bag and baggage. I lost but one man and had but three wounded.'[7] His account may, no doubt, be exaggerated in the exhilaration of victory for we know that the Royalist life guards were not totally destroyed, as they continued to fight on throughout 1645. The truth of what happened at Naseby probably lies somewhere between the two accounts.

Distinguished as their conduct may have been, the Royalist life guard troops drifted away when Charles finally capitulated in 1646 in the face of the revived Parliamentarian army and a lack of funds. Many went to France, to join the court in exile, of whom we will shortly hear rather more, and of those who stayed behind like Symonds, many surrendered to Parliament by asking to 'compound for delinquency'. So unsurprisingly, the dominant 'life guard model' that emerged after the civil wars ended in 1651 was not the King's but Cromwell's, and ironically, it was ultimately to them that Charles II would look for the model for his own guards.

THE EARLY HISTORY OF the Parliamentarian life guard was hardly distinguished. It was originally formed in August 1642 to protect the Earl of Essex, the Lord General, or parliamentary commander, at the time and was recruited from the young gentlemen of the Inns of Court. Sir Philip Stapleton, Member of Parliament for Boroughbridge, was Captain. The historian Clarendon, who obviously held Yorkshiremen in low regard, wrote that he, 'according to the education of that county, spent his time in those delights which horses and dogs administer'.[8] He had no military experience, but recruited a lieutenant, Adam Bainham, who was considered to be something of a military paragon. However, Stapleton's scrutiny of his credentials cannot have been that thorough. When Essex's life was threatened by a party of Royalist horse early in the campaign, Bainham ordered the life guard to 'wheel about', omitting the elementary precaution of first checking which way they were facing. 'Our own gentlemen not well understanding the difference between wheeling about, and shifting for themselves, their backs now towards the enemy, whom they thought to be close in the rear, retired to the army in a very dishonourable manner,' wrote a trooper, Edmund Ludlow,[9] who was eventually to go on to command his own regiment, sign Charles I's death warrant, and become Cromwell's Lord Lieutenant in Ireland and a noted diarist.

The Parliamentary Life Guard started the Civil War equipped as cuirassiers with heavy plate armour – but this was soon abandoned. The only other regiment so equipped was Sir Arthur Haselrig's 'Lobsters', prompting a rare joke from Charles I that if 'Sir Arthur had been victualled as well as fortified, he might have stood a siege'.

By 1644 armour had virtually disappeared from the battlefield. Instead troopers in regiments of Horse wore a helmet and 'front and backs' or breast and back plates, sometimes with arm and hand protection. The fronts were 'proofed' by firing a musket ball at them and the mark can still be clearly seen on this example, which is in the Household Cavalry Museum. The 'front and backs' or cuirasses worn by the Household Cavalry today are very similar.

The Parliamentarian life guard was originally equipped in the style of cuirassiers with heavy plate armour and helmets similar to those of the European cavalry who fought in the Thirty Years War from 1618 onwards. It was, however, now becoming generally accepted that armour restricted movement and was not that effective against musket fire. All that was actually required was a 'pot', or iron skullcap worn under a wide-brimmed hat, and front and back breastplates. Only one other regiment apart from the Lord General's Life Guard wore complete armour. They were Sir Arthur Haselrig's 'Lobsters', a source of amusement for both sides, prompting a rare joke from Charles I that 'if Sir Arthur had been victualled as well as fortified, he might have stood a siege'.[10] Edmund Ludlow found his armour so cumbersome that he was unable to remount when he was knocked off his horse in a skirmish.

The life guards soon changed their dress and tactics, and, determined to acquit themselves better, charged bravely at Edgehill in October 1642, their next engagement. We get the first indications at this time of the strong puritan streak that was to develop and dominate their character over the coming decade. 'The Lord General's troop consisting mostly of gentlemen, yea, and very many of them most pious and gracious gentlemen, carried themselves most valiantly,' wrote the sanctimonious John Vicars.[11] Yet they were still not taken seriously, and at the unsatisfactory stand-off at Turnham Green at the end of 1642, where the Royalists were rebuffed from London by trained bands of civilian militia, it was noted that 'too many gentlemen volunteers generally attached themselves to the Commander-in-Chief's Life Guard when they proposed to take part in an engagement'.[12]

On the formation of Parliament's new model army in 1644, Essex stood down as Commander-in-Chief and Lord General, to be replaced by Sir Thomas Fairfax in 1645. The life guard was radically reorganized at the same time. Many of the original members – the band of gentlemen – like Ludlow, departed to found their own regiments in the army and were replaced by officers and soldiers selected less for their standing in society and more for their professionalism and sound puritan credentials, epitomized by the stout and unpopular Charles d'Oyley, who was brought in to command them. The troopers were paid the considerable bounty of 3s. a day – more than less favoured regiments – and they fought very effectively at Naseby. Their extra pay and standing in the army attracted many of the most able and intelligent puritan volunteers, and unsurprisingly, from being one of the least zealous units in Parliament's original army, they became one of the most efficient in the new model. But they were also one of the most uncompromising and extreme in their puritanism and this was, temporarily, to be their undoing.

In 1647, with the war effectively won, Parliament's attention was centred elsewhere and it began to neglect its army, which not unnaturally objected. It was the life guards who led the army delegation that complained about their pay, that they were 'in worse condition than the enemies whom they have

The Parliamentary victory over the Royalists at the Battle of Naseby in 1645, when the King's Life Guard fled, demonstrated the value of the army reforms initiated by Fairfax

and Cromwell. The future organization, equipment and tactics of both the Life Guards
and The Blues were based on those of Cromwell's regiments of Horse.

subdued' and 'become a scorn and reproach to the disaffected', and that the army leadership was not sticking to the puritan principles upon which their soldiers fought. They posed a real threat to Fairfax and Cromwell – his Lieutenant General of the Horse – in this, and to Parliament's authority.

Consequently no provision was made for the life guards when the new army establishment was introduced on 19 February 1648. This was not well received and the troops refused to disband. Their ringleader was Private William Clarke, who carried off the colours, refused to surrender them, and was subsequently sentenced to death. That the Leveller John Lillburne championed the life guards says something for how extreme they had become. 'Upon pretence of easing the charge of the Commonwealth', he wrote in *England's New Chaines Discovered*, 'the life-guard must be disbanded, because consisting of discerning men, faithful to their country and former promises . . . the designe being by weeding the choisest and best resolved men, to make the army wholly mercinary, slavish and the executioners of a few mens lusts and lawless pleasures'.[13] Their extreme puritanism was to be matched by only one other regiment in the new model army, Berry's Horse, of whom we will shortly be hearing much more.

When Cromwell departed for his ruthless and bloody campaign in Ireland in 1648 he quickly re-formed a bodyguard for himself, taking care to recruit a better class of trooper – 'His life-guard consisting of 80 gallant men, the meanest whereof a commander or esquire in stately habit . . .'[14] Quite a few stayed on in Ireland, forming a life guard for Ireton, Cromwell's successor as Commander-in-Chief there, and subsequently received land grants under the Cromwellian settlement. Others returned with Cromwell himself, and became his life guard when he formally took over as Lord General and Commander-in-Chief from Fairfax in 1650. They served him well in September 1651 at Worcester, where Charles II, now leading the Royalist cause in his dead father's place, was routed. Ironically Captain Charles Howard, later to be made Earl of Carlisle by Charles II, commanded them. He also led them at various public ceremonies during the ensuing Commonwealth, including Cromwell's installation as Lord Protector in 1653 – incongruously the first 'coronation' in which troops ultimately to form the Household Cavalry participated.

In 1656 the twin threats posed by sporadic Royalist uprisings, such as Penruddock's in Wiltshire the previous year, and the military fiasco of the Commonwealth's expedition against the Spanish in the Caribbean, led Cromwell to increase the life guard to 160, drafting in extra men from other regiments of horse. It also suited his status as Lord Protector and de facto monarch to have an elitist guard bound personally to him. They were divided into eight squadrons, commanded by Captain Beake, who was married to Cromwell's' niece, paid at the extremely generous rate of 4s. 6d. per day and had 'very good horses'. There were still undesirables among them, and some were subsequently laid off as suspected Anabaptists. One, Thomas Buttevant, was discovered spreading seditious pamphlets with the Fifth Monarchists;

Oliver Cromwell re-formed the Life Guard as his bodyguard during his bloody campaign in Ireland, restoring their elite status and paying them much more than troopers in other regiments of Horse. His niece's husband, Captain Beake, commanded them.

another was the entertaining Leveller William Howard, who petitioned Charles II on the Levellers' behalf, saying of Cromwell that by 'peeping a little (now and then, as I had opportunity) under the vizard of the imposter, got such glimpses, though but imperfect ones, of his ugly face, concealed under the painted pretences of sanctity'.[15] He was destined, despite his Anabaptist beliefs, to become Lord Howard of Escrick.

THE FINAL TRANSFORMATION to the troop that escorted Monck to greet Charles II at Dover occurred after Cromwell's death in September 1658. His son Richard, who succeeded him briefly as Lord Protector, proved ineffectual, and throughout 1659 a struggle for political power developed between Parliament and the army. Monck, an ex-Royalist officer who had subsequently fought for Parliament, was among the more conservative in the senior army leadership and was at this stage still commanding the army in Scotland, a position he had occupied since 1645. He had raised and trained his own regiments in Scotland, to one of which we will soon return, and had achieved a reputation as a good tactician and competent administrator. In December 1659, alarmed that the more extreme generals such as John Lambert were in danger of forcing Parliament to establish a puritan military regime, he moved his force to Coldstream, on the border between England and Scotland, and let it be known that he supported the sovereignty of Parliament and was opposed to any further military adventurism. Parliament now ordered Cromwell's life guard, commanded by the ineffectual Arthur Evelyn, to protect them in Westminster, but as they formed up to face Lambert's followers, Evelyn allowed himself to be persuaded by his lieutenant, Cathness, a Lambert supporter, to side with the rebels.

Thus in December 1659 the life guard marched north to join Lambert, who was preparing to oppose Monck as he advanced south from Coldstream, but, as they neared Newcastle, Lambert's army began to desert. The reputation of Monck's force of about 6,000 well-trained troops, and his own men's lack of pay, made Lambert's prospects seem doubtful. Many of the life guard went over to Monck, and were with him as he arrived in London in February 1660. Monck reorganized them once more, increased their number to 200, renamed them 'The General's Life Guard', and introduced more reliable officers such as Captain Philip Howard, whom we have already seen leading them at the Restoration. The re-formed life guard, together with his efficient Scottish regiments, were to give Monck the force and authority he needed in London and the south of England as he orchestrated the Restoration through Parliament. Under the arrangements made for disbanding the Commonwealth army later that summer, the life guard and one of these regiments were to be left until last. The strange events of that winter were to ensure that they remained in being, as they do to this day.

KING CHARLES II's return to London was possible because of the four conditions he agreed with Parliament's representatives, enshrined in the Declaration of Breda. The first three were a free and general pardon for all those who had opposed the monarchy (excepting the regicides); a 'liberty to tender consciences', or, in other words, a degree of religious toleration; third, the disposal of lands that had changed hands during the interregnum was to be decided in Parliament. Lastly, and most importantly for this story, although control of the army technically passed into the King's hands, Parliament agreed to vote money to pay the men off and disband them. In May 1660 the army stood at approximately 40,000 and was costing £55,000 a month, a considerable expense, but one that Parliament — which recent experience had made nervous of independent military forces, and which still regarded a Stuart monarchy with its own army as decidedly dangerous — was determined to meet. Charles II might have wanted to retain an element of the standing army, but it was clearly unacceptable to Members of Parliament who persuaded Monck that the army should withdraw from politics in return for receiving their arrears of pay.

Yet the situation was not quite as simple as it seemed. There were, in effect, three British armies in existence in 1660. First, there were the remnants of the Royalist army which had fought, unsuccessfully, with the Spanish for Dunkirk in 1657–8. When Cromwell signed an alliance with Louis XIV in 1655, Charles II had pledged to help the new hosts of his exiled court, the Spanish Netherlands, in their war with the French. He had equipped three regiments, which included a life guard of about fifty men, which fought under Charles's brother James, Duke of York. They had been decisively defeated by the great French Marshal, Turenne, who had 6,000 of Cromwell's Commonwealth soldiers under his command, at the Battle of the Dunes in June 1658. Although Cromwell had gained Dunkirk, about 2,500 of the defeated Royalist army now remained in Holland, including those who had been the Duke of York's Life Guard. Second, Dunkirk was now garrisoned by 10,000 Commonwealth troops, who were costing £10,000 each month, and, worryingly, their loyalty to the new monarch, whose army they had so recently defeated, was of necessity uncertain. Finally, there was the main Commonwealth army, now commanded by Monck, whose overall loyalty either to him or to the Restoration was also questionable. Would such a well-trained force, many of whom had been, in effect, regular soldiers for eighteen years, now agree to disband peacefully when recent experience had revealed their power over the government currently presiding in London?

That they eventually did so was due to a combination of Monck's leadership, generous demobilization terms and, in many cases, a desire to retire to a more congenial life, prompted by the bewildering speed of change in political fortunes and cynicism for their Parliamentary masters, who had sold out the cause for which they had sacrificed so much. The Committee of the Army put detailed proposals to the House of Commons on 30 August 1660. All officers and soldiers who had been serving on 25 April 1660, and who had not since deserted, would receive full arrears of pay and a bonus of an extra week's pay from the King. Parliament subsequently passed two acts, one for the 'Speedy Provision of Money for Disbanding and paying off the Forces of this Kingdom by land and sea', which provided £560,000 through a poll bill, and a second act which fixed a tight programme for the demobilization process.

Three regiments at a time were to be paid off, in an order to be determined by the Privy Council. The King's unofficial bodyguard in exile, Lord Gerard's Cavaliers, were particularly, and rather offensively, included, but exceptions were made for Monck's Life Guard and for the two other regiments which had accompanied him from Scotland. One, a regiment of foot, which would later become the Coldstream Guards, need not concern us further, but the other was Colonel Unton Croke's Regiment of Horse, which performed an important role policing Bristol and the West Country. They were not spared as such, but were to be left until last. The Duke of York's Life Guard was also exempted and was to be added to the Dunkirk garrison. At the same time Parliament relaxed the Apprenticeship Laws to ease demobilized soldiers into learning a trade. 'You shall have this captain turned a shoemaker; the lieutenant a baker; this a brewer; that a haberdasher . . .' Pepys noted disapprovingly in his diary entry for 9 November 1663. By December 1660 the Commonwealth army had ceased to exist, save for Monck's Life Guard and regiments. The final bill was £835,819, of which Charles had to find the balance from his own purse. Much of it was spent immediately on drink. So riotous was the behaviour of the newly demobilized, that orders were issued in December banning all former officers and soldiers from coming within 20 miles of London.

Various other garrisons, twenty-eight in total across the country, remained and were manned on a different basis from the regular army – they were to continue throughout the coming reign. The Cromwellian garrison in Dunkirk was also left alone, its loyalty still uncertain, and remained as something of an embarrassment until 1662 when Charles sold the port to Louis XIV. Those who wanted to, came back to England, where they were subsequently incorporated into Lord Wentworth's Regiment of Foot Guards, whilst many who did not, went either into the French army or to the English regiments that Charles had by then offered as part of his marriage settlement to his father-in-law, the King of Portugal, to assist him in his war of independence with Spain. In return he received Bombay and Tangier, of particular importance to our story.

But what of King Charles's and the Duke of York's companions who had returned from exile, of Monck's Life Guard and regiments, so purposefully left until last on the roster for disbandment? The final months of 1660 were full of plots, rumours of plots and a genuine fear within Parliament for the King's safety, for were Charles now to lose his life the fragile Restoration settlement would inevitably collapse. In January 1661 a serious riot broke out in London. It was spurred on by an obscure wine cooper called Thomas Venner,[16] the leader

George Monck. Parliamentary Commander in Scotland, whose support for the exiled Stuarts made the Restoration possible. Ennobled as Duke of Albemarle, he remained Commander-in-Chief of Charles II's army. The Third Troop of Life Guards, who protected him, were found from Cromwell's Life Guard, and led by Sir Philip Howard.

of a group of around fifty Fifth Monarchists. They believed, rather unhelpfully just after the Restoration, that all earthly kings were evil, and that all earthly authority was 'Babylon'. They vowed not to sheathe their swords until they had established the universal monarchy of Christ on earth, and until 'the kings of the earth should be bound in chains, and the nobles in fetters of iron'.

On 6 January 1661 Venner and his associates broke into St Paul's and demanded of an unfortunate night watchman whether he was for the King. He replied that he was for King Charles, whereupon the Fifth Monarchists shot him through the head, declaring that they were only for King Jesus. Sixteen of the trained bands of civilian militiamen were called from the Royal Exchange, but they ran away. The Lord Mayor came next, with his private guards, who forced the rebels to withdraw to Caen Wood, near Highgate, killing a constable en route. Sir Thomas Sandys, with 100 of Monck's Life Guard, arrived next, but was beaten back with the loss of twenty men, although it transpired subsequently that many of these had fallen into a gravel pit. The following day Venner's band reappeared in the city, causing general mayhem before being run to earth in an alehouse in Wood Street, Cheapside, by the Duke of York, some of his companions and the rest of Monck's much-reduced Life Guard. It was left to nine of these, led by Colonel Corbet, to enter the house and kill the rebels, whilst the rest of their party 'did a little desert him and retreated to the upper end of Cheape Side, calling out for foote, which does a little staine on their redd scarves'.[17] Two of them, Captains Doughty and Madan, were wounded, and all Venner's followers were killed; only one tried to surrender but he was stabbed by a companion. Venner himself was badly wounded, but was kept alive long enough to be publicly hanged.

The Duke of York now seized an opportunity for which he, King Charles and, almost certainly, Monck – by now ennobled as the Duke of Albemarle – had been waiting for several months. As early as August 1660, while Parliament was passing its acts to disband the army, Charles had drawn up proposals for a force of royal guards, consisting of two regiments of horse and two regiments of foot, at an annual cost of £118,529. Monck's regiments may well have been retained until such an opportunity presented itself, and that is exactly what Venner had ironically now given the King. Conveniently, Parliament had been dissolved on 29 December 1660. The Duke of York wrote in plain terms to the Lord Chancellor and Council, wondering that 'the King's chief counsellors, who had been eye-witnesses of the insurrections and rebellions in the time of King Charles I, and what he suffered for want of good guards, should now be so careless of the King's safety as not to have advised him to secure himself from such dangers for the future'.[18] The Council, thoroughly alarmed, agreed, and suggested to the King that he retain Albemarle's regiments in his own service.

It was a masterstroke of opportunism, which showed the Duke of York at his most able and most politic, and which not only created the permanent royal guard force, but also led to the establishment of the English and Scottish stand-

James, Duke of York, dressed as Mars, God of War. A competent military administrator, it was James who created the first Army Board in 1670 as well as being Lord High Admiral. He was also very attached to the colour yellow – creating a very gauche yellow standard for his troop of Life Guards.

ing armies, and thereafter the British army. Had the Duke acted a few weeks earlier, Parliament, which would have then still been in session, might have insisted on the disbandment of the final regiments. Had the Venner riots occurred a few months later, a more confident Council might have seen them for the inconsequential and localized disturbance they were. James kept not only Albemarle's Life Guard and his Regiment of Foot – the precursor to the Coldstream Guards – but also Unton Croke's Regiment of Horse – officially disbanded a few weeks earlier but, mysteriously, still intact in Bath – and took the opportunity to establish officially the assorted groups of Cavaliers who had been in exile with him and the King.

ON 26 JANUARY 1661 the King signed the order for the creation of three 'Troopes of Guards', though historically, and for reasons of precedence, it is generally assumed that the 'Life Guards', as such, existed as a regiment from the Restoration. The 1st Troop was to be 'His Majesties own Troope of Guards', consisting of ten officers, four corporals and 200 'private gentlemen' or non-commissioned officers; the second 'His Highness Royall the Duke of Yorke his Troope of Guards'; and the third was to be a formal retention of 'His Grace the Duke of Albemarle his Troope of Guards'. The latter troops were much the same as the King's Troop but had only seven officers and 150 private gentlemen. On the same day Unton Croke's Regiment of Horse, loyal to Albemarle, was established as the Royal Regiment of Horse, to which we will shortly return, and his Regiment of Foot as the 2nd Foot Guards. In addition another regiment of Foot Guards, the 1st Guards, were raised under Colonel John Russell, partly from ex-Cavaliers and partly from those Commonwealth soldiers who did not want to stay in Dunkirk.

By the end of the month King Charles had succeeded in creating the guard force that he had planned the previous August. He now had two regiments of horse, the three troops of the King's, York's and Albemarle's Guards – which, taken together, constituted a regiment – and the Royal Regiment of Horse Guards. He also had two regiments of foot, the 1st and 2nd Foot Guards. It is too far-fetched to suggest that the Venner riots were in any way contrived, but it is certainly fair to say that both the royal brothers were, at the very least, expedient in their reaction to them.

The three 'troopes of guards' were, confusingly, called horse guards, but they acted as, and have always subsequently been known as, Life Guards, so that is how we will refer to them from now on. Each troop was very different. The King's Troop was made up almost entirely of those Cavalier gentlemen who had accompanied the King in exile, and was consequently very much of the French *mousquetaire* model, with men who were of 'good family', and, after recent wars, extensive military experience. Given that there were only a few places for officers, many had to be content to fill the lower ranks as private gentlemen. It was normal to find baronets and colonels as corporals, and from this derived the custom of referring to Life Guard officers by two ranks, the first being their regimental position and the second their army rank. Lord Gerard, for example, would be referred to as 'Captain and Colonel'. This system was later formalized, as it had been in the French *mousquetaires*, and a royal warrant of 12 September 1666 laid down that 'as to the Horse, that the three troops of Guards take place before all others' and established that officer ranks in the Life Guards were superior to equivalent ranks in the rest of the army. This lasted, to the occasional irritation of other regiments of horse, until the troops of Life Guards became regiments in the regular army in 1788.

Lord Gerard certainly deserved the honour of being Captain of the King's Troop. His support for the Royalist cause had been steadfast, both during the civil wars and later with Charles II in exile, but he was less successful as a peacetime commander. The son of a large landowner at Halsall in Lancashire, he was among the most dashing and inspiring of the senior Royalist officers and was one of the first to declare for Charles I, whom he joined shortly after the commencement of war at Shrewsbury in 1642 with a troop of horse that he had raised himself. He commanded a brigade of infantry at Edgehill, and was later severely wounded at Rowton Heath. He ended the first civil war as Lieutenant General in Wales, under Prince Rupert. He went into exile after Charles I's execution, and raised a troop to guard Charles II in 1657. A confirmed Protestant, and close friend of Charles II's illegitimate son the Duke of Monmouth, he was chosen by the King during the Exclusion Crisis in 1679 to tell Monmouth 'out of his great tenderness he gave him till to-night to begone'. Gerard was subsequently created Earl of Macclesfield. Given his strong opposition to Catholicism and his consequent support for the exclusion of the Duke of York from the accession, he was, not unnaturally, much out of favour when the latter became James II. Declared an outlaw and exiled again, he fled to Holland and was instrumental in William III's accession in the Glorious Revolution of 1688. Returning to England, he became Lord Lieutenant of an enormous expanse of Wales and the Marches and was buried in Westminster Abbey when he died in 1693. His wife was French – we know little of her except that Charles disliked her as she gossiped to his Queen, Catherine of Braganza, about his mistress, Lady Castlemaine, and that she was once set upon by an undiscerning London mob, who mistook her for the unpopular Duchess of Portsmouth, another of the King's mistresses.

Lord Gerard's lieutenant was Randolph Egerton, another distinguished Cavalier and Charles I's first general of horse. His position in the troop is indicative of its status – whilst Egerton had been a general in the Royalist army, he was still only a lieutenant in the Life Guards. He was also buried in Westminster Abbey. Another lieutenant was Sir Thomas Sandys, a baronet from Kent and a rather unattractive friend of Monmouth, who was later associated with the

Charles II's court was much more relaxed and informal than Louis XIV's, and from 1662 the Life Guards became increasingly involved in its life, being on duty during royal visits and balls.

The Life Guards escorted Charles II to his wedding to the Portuguese Princess, Catherine of Braganza in May 1662. Part of her dowry was Tangier, which The Royals were raised to garrison.

Charles II enjoyed a series of beautiful mistresses, such as Barbara Palmer (née Villiers), Duchess of Cleveland (*right*) and Louise de Kéroualle, Duchess of Portsmouth (*below right*), in marked contrast to his brother James, Duke of York, whose first wife Anne Hyde (*below*), and mistresses were considered so ugly that it was joked that they had been imposed on him as a penance by his priests.

mugging of Sir John Coventry, of which more later. A third was Lord Gerard's younger brother, Sir Gilbert Gerard, who spent most of his service using his proximity to the King to petition for various grants of land that might be forthcoming. At one point he suggested an investigation of land and property that might belong to the King, if he could keep two-thirds of any successful claims. The King didn't buy it, but did recommend him to be given grants of land by the Diocese of Peterborough.

The fourth lieutenant was perhaps the most entertaining. Colonel Thomas Panton, another senior Royalist commander, held two commissions, being also a company commander in the Foot Guards, and drew pay from both. An inveterate gambler, one evening he won enough money to give him the substantial amount of £1,500 a year for life. He never gambled himself again, but ran a gaming house called Piccadilly Hall. Streets around Haymarket still bear his name and are testament to its profitability.

The Cornet – the officer responsible for the colour – was Edward Stanley, son of the Earl of Derby whose French wife famously defended the family seat, Latham House, during the civil wars. The corporals were also men of considerable substance. Francis Lovelace, one-time Governor of New York, with New Jersey thrown in for good measure, Charles Scrimshaw and Edward Roscarrick had all been well-known colonels and were given their places as a reward for their service to the Royalist cause.

The Duke of York's Troop was different. It was in existence in Dunkirk in January 1661, and was consequently brought over en masse to join the few officers who had accompanied the Duke at the Restoration. Smaller, and not quite as select as the King's Troop, it was commanded by Sir Charles Berkeley who was also in command during the 1659 campaign. From Bruton, in Somerset, he was another of those knighted on the day of the Restoration. He later became Lord Fitzhardinge, and subsequently Earl of Falmouth. He was held in high regard by both the King and the Duke of York, who wrote to his brother when Charles wanted to make him Lord Privy Purse, 'But, Sir, I must have your promise . . . that if ever you have occasion for an army again I may have him with me, believing him to be the best commander of an army in the world.' Yet he was not always the most tactful. When the Duke of York announced his marriage to Anne Hyde, Berkeley 'deliberately slandered the lady', saying that she had been his own mistress. Confronted by a furious Duke of York, his excuse was that he was trying to prevent an unsatisfactory marriage. He had a point. Not only did many think it unsuitable that the heir to the throne should marry a commoner whose father, Clarendon, was a less than universally popular First Minister, but Anne was also plain. The Duke of York had a strange penchant for ugly women. One of his more self-effacing mistresses, Catherine Sedley, once remarked, 'what he saw in any of us I cannot tell. We were all plain, and if any of us had wit, he would not have understood it.'[19] Even his brother thought that he must be a remorseless masochist, and that most of the women whom he bedded were so ugly that his priests must have imposed them upon him as a penance. Whatever, Berkeley's tactlessness was forgiven, and he survived to have his brains blown out while standing beside the Duke of York during a naval battle with the Dutch in 1665. Pepys regarded him as one of the worst of Restoration courtiers, writing that 'Sir Charles Berkeley's greatness is only in his being pimp to the King'.

The 3rd Troop, the Duke of Albemarle's, was different again. Although the newly created Duke had purged his officers in 1659, the soldiers were still largely those recruited by Cromwell in 1656. It was, in effect, the old Lord Protector's Life Guard with a new master, which many of the more puritan men must have found uncomfortable. But it offered a job and status at a very difficult time, when most of their contemporaries had been demobilized. Many of them were also from rich, land-owning families, Cromwell having expunged the Anabaptists and Levellers, and they were of a class that had decided that the Restoration offered the best chance of a stable future.

The redoubtable Sir Philip Howard remained the troop's Captain, and quickly became one of the leading society figures in Restoration London. He was slightly 'alternative' by the standards of the time, wearing Turkish clothes at home and employing guitar players who entertained him while he dressed. His mistress was the well-known actress Betty Hall, who played at the King's Playhouse, and whom Pepys found 'a mighty pretty wench' when he sat next to her at a performance, though he did add 'my wife will not think so'.[20] Pepys was a great admirer of Howard's, 'one of the finest persons that I ever saw in my life'. He was a firm Protestant, as one would expect of a Captain of the Lord General's Life Guard, and was much engaged with Albemarle in outing various plots against the King in the early 1660s. Pepys particularly objected to his continual response of 'Damn me!' during a particular Anabaptist's drawn-out confession, noting that it was 'a fine way of rhetorique to persuade a Quaker or Anabaptist from his persuasion'. Howard remained an active soldier, taking a full part in the Dutch war of 1666. His Chaplain in the troop was the Rev. Thomas Gumball, who wrote a celebrated biography of Albemarle, and the Surgeon was John Troughback, a well-known surgeon for Parliament in the civil wars. When Albemarle died in 1670 the troop became the Queen's Troop, and, much to the Duke of York's chagrin, took precedence over his troop, which reverted to being the third in precedence.

All three troops were strictly structured along new model army lines, a direct reflection of Albemarle's 3rd Troop. The King's Troop had more officers, with the other two having a captain, paid £546 per year; four lieutenants at £274; a cornet at £255; a quartermaster at £164; a chaplain at £121; a surgeon, who was allowed a second horse to carry his chest of implements, at £146; four corporals at £128 each; four trumpeters at £91 each; a kettle-drummer at £91 and 200 private gentlemen, or 150 in the 2nd and 3rd Troops, at £73. There was also an adjutant per troop, although from 1679 there was just one for all three.

The adjutant was a commissioned officer, paid £127 per year, performing the functions now associated with regimental sergeant majors. The pay was generous compared with contemporary equivalents. Lawyers in 1660 were averaging £154 per year and 'Eminent Clergymen' got around £72, or roughly the same as the private gentlemen. 'Lesser Clergymen' only warranted £50, and 'Freeholders of the lesser sort' were calculated to average only £55.[21] It must have been something of a relief to the King to be able to pay anyone. He had been chronically short of funds in exile, and although he was never to have enough to satisfy his aspirations during his reign, the early years of the Restoration must have seemed bountiful. On receiving his first grant from Parliament to equip his return to London, he opened the chest of money and invited his family and courtiers to view it before it was distributed.

A fourth Scottish troop of Life Guards was raised three months later in Edinburgh, on 2 April 1661. The armies in Ireland and Scotland remained legally independent from the English army after the Restoration. Although the few troops that Monck had left behind in Scotland when he marched south had been disbanded, a new, smaller force of around 1,200 was now being raised of which this troop, and an accompanying regiment of Foot Guards, formed the core. Its original role, different to its English counterparts', was less the protection of the monarch and more to assist the executive – the Lord High Commissioner and Parliament – 'against disobedient persons'. Its first Captain was the Earl of Newburgh, and it was officially and ponderously titled 'His Majesty's Troop of Guards in Scotland'. Its officers and soldiers were paid considerably less than their brethren in London, which must have rankled, but otherwise its establishment was very similar and it was, similarly, recruited from the Scottish nobility and gentry. Although it existed only briefly, being incorporated into the English troops after the Act of Union in 1707, it achieved much in its fifty-odd years, seeing action under Monmouth against the Covenanters in 1679, and acting as escort to the Duke of York when he was sent from London to Scotland as Lord Commissioner in the 1680s, hopefully to defuse the Exclusion Crisis.

The formal inclusion of drummers and trumpeters in the Life Guards establishment was another Cromwellian legacy, although both sides used drummers in the civil wars. The drums were lightweight, unlike their modern silver equivalents, and were carried mounted in regiments of horse. They had a practical function in that they kept time, and together with the trumpeters were an essential means of communication. However, their ceremonial appeal was already manifest in 1660 and at Charles II's coronation the Life Guard drummers and trumpeters led each troop.

The Life Guards' musicians, together with those of the Foot Guards, doubled up as the King's court musicians, and consequently wore expensive red and gold royal livery with velvet jockey caps (then costing 13s. each), a version of which is still in use today. The King paid for these himself, and detailed accounts exist from the various lucky drapers and tailors in the 'Royal Wardrobe Books', as the King's personal accounts were known. Some of the musicians had been in exile with him, and many had long records of service. John Mauggeridge, for example, was Master Kettle Drummer of the King's Troop in the 1660s and was still recorded as being fitted for a new uniform under William III in the 1690s. He was a busy man as he was also a Master Drummer in the Foot Guards, and volunteered for Monmouth's controversial Dutch expedition in February 1673, for which he claimed a brand-new uniform. He was given the further privilege of being allowed to sell off his old uniform when he received a new one, as he did every two years, at a cost to the King, in 1674, of £52 17s. 8d. The drapers' bills contain many interesting asides, which shed light on both the King's private and diplomatic life. There are, for example, bills for 'Furniture for His Majesty's New Yacht at Chatham', for a 'large bedd for His Majesty's use at Newmarket' and for 'Her Majesty's Dogg two large Ticken cushions filled with the best feathers 18 shillings'. Then there are those for 'William Hester his Majesty's Rattkiller in Ordinary his livery', and 'The Strewer of Herbes his Livery', and for presents to the Basha of Algiers, the Dye of Tripoli and several to the Bey of Tunis.[22]

Each troop had a standard, which it was the cornet's job to carry, and which was also paid for from the Royal Wardrobe. The King's Troop standard had changed since the civil wars. It was now crimson damask, much like modern Household Cavalry standards, and carried the royal cypher, with two Cs reversed and interlaced and the royal motto 'Dieu et Mon Droit', as on Charles I's standard. Underneath were three small crowns, representing England, Scotland and Ireland. The standard of the Queen's Troop was similar, but bore her initials and motto 'Una Salus Ambobus' – One hope for both. The Duke of York's Troop standard was at first similar to these, but became radically different. At a review in 1684 we hear that it was now a very un-British yellow, with a large monogram 'JDY' (James Duke of York) carried gauchely under a crown. No wonder there were those who despaired of James ever becoming a king.

Yet if the structure and organization of the troops of Life Guards were Cromwellian, their spirit and method of employment were most definitely French, derived from Louis XIV's *mousquetaires* in particular. The concept of the aristocracy and gentry publicly committing to the service and protection of the monarch was understandably attractive to two brothers raised during the civil wars, and was one they regarded as essential to establish the royal prerogative. Consequently the system of purchase was introduced whereby officers and the private gentlemen had to buy their right to a position so near the throne. Ironically, it was a system that Louis XIV ended in the mid-1660s, but by then it had taken firm root within Charles II's four regiments and was to remain a feature of the British armies until the Cardwell reforms in the late nineteenth century. It certainly ensured that the guards were officered by men of wealth and property, and it was popular with the officers themselves, as it meant their commission was an investment that they could sell when they retired; the money for commissions went to the holder, not to the Crown.[23]

Yet it had many disadvantages too. Apart from the obvious problem of excluding those with potential military talent but lacking funds, it led to officers regarding their commissions as business opportunities and abusing their positions to recoup at least some of their initial investment. Lord Gerard, for example, rapidly took this sort of abuse to ridiculous extremes. On 24 September 1666 the King was surprised to find that his troop appeared unwilling to escort him on a visit to Audley End where he stayed when racing at Newmarket. It transpired that the men were five months behind in their pay, 'the rolls being in Lord Gerard's hands', and Sir Stephen Fox, the Paymaster General, had rapidly to find £2,100 to make good the arrears. Gerard had hit upon a profitable scheme whereby his men's pay was invested, with the connivance of a crooked agent called William Carr, and not until he had derived sufficient interest did he pay the private gentlemen, months late. Charles was slow to take action, but the matter came to a head when, in July 1667, William Carr disappeared to Calais with a further £1,630 which had been advanced by Sir Stephen out of his own pocket. Gerard refused to pay it back, and furthermore refused to allow the matter to go to court, claiming his privilege as a peer. Ultimately Carr was discovered and put in the pillory. Gerard's position was untenable, even by the lax standards of the time, and furthermore the King was fed up with his wife's gossip about Lady Castlemaine. Gerard's exit was a dignified one and in September 1668 he sold the Captaincy of the King's Troop to the King's illegitimate son, the Duke of Monmouth, for a sum thought to be around £12,000. Various attempts were made to fix the prices at which commissions should change hands, but there was no regular tariff in the Life Guards until fixed by George I in 1720.

Another unintended effect of the purchasing of commissions was that officers and often private gentlemen took the view that, as they had paid large sums for their position, they need not be as rigorous in the observance of their duty as the Crown had intended. Contrary to the French model, whereby the scions of the great families of France were bound into a strict court routine, English Guards officers perfected a system of deputyship, whereby they appointed others to carry out their duties while they spent their time far more agreeably. From this, much to the bewilderment of continental observers and the disappointment of the Duke of York, developed a reliance on non-commissioned officers – the corporals and the specialist officers such as the adjutant – who dealt with day-to-day administration. Officers were only present for major escorts or parades. It is ironic that what was initially viewed as a serious weakness in the Guards was to lead to the formalization of the role of non-commissioned officers throughout the British army, which was to develop into one of its greatest strengths.

One pastime that officers particularly enjoyed was politics. Of 188 officers who served in the four standing regiments in the 1660s, eighty-nine held seats in the House of Commons at various times and a further sixty-one were peers. Although this was not quite what the King had in mind, it helpfully established a Royalist block in Parliament, since army officers tended to vote in the Crown's favour. It was perhaps naïve of the King and the Duke of York to think that the French model would work in England, with a monarchy more familiar and conditional than Louis XIV's glittering autocracy. However, to their credit, once they realized their officers would interpret matters in their own way, they adjusted their expectations and worked the system that emerged to the advantage of the Crown. So, for instance, official sanction was given to the lengthy leave some officers required to run their estates. Sir Thomas Armstrong, an important Irish landowner, was allowed to 'repair into our Kingdome of Irelande for his own private affairs for six months', taking three servants from his troop, all of whom were to be paid while they were away.[24]

As for the lower ranks, since entry into the Life Guards was seen as an attractive proposition, even as a private gentleman, positions changed hands for around £100 well into the next century. Yet in the first heady days of the Restoration, with countless ex-officers in circulation, and many families ruined in the civil wars, places were over-subscribed. There were countless applications to the King from men like 'Hugh, son of Sir T. Redmaine, late Governor of Pontefract Castle, [who] petitions for a place in the Life Guards, or to be Page of the backstairs. His father died in the King's father's service, and his widow and six children are left destitute', or Stephen Caslee who 'petitions to be appointed surgeon in the Life Guards'. He was not taken on. More realistic, perhaps, were those like Lieutenant Colonel Thomas Cropper who wrote that 'he served the late King till taken prisoner at Bridgwater, and since His Majesty's return has been at great charge to fit himself with a horse and handsome equipage to maintain himself in the Guards'.

Each private gentleman had to supply his own horse, forage it out of his pay and buy his own uniform and weapons. Horses were in short supply in Restoration England – so many were lost in the civil wars – and were consequently expensive. There is a sad petition from 'Philip, younger son of Sir T. Fetherstonhaugh of Kirkoswald, for a horse so that he may once more serve in His Majesty's Guards. His father lost £10,000 and was beheaded'. He received a horse and arms in 1662, but the horse died and he was 'disbanded'. Later the Crown bought horses in bulk, and sold them on to potential recruits at £15, and by 1697 regulations were introduced whereby all army horses became Crown property. Private gentlemen also had to provide ornate saddlery. A 'saddle of coloured velvett with stirrop leathers, woollen webb girthes, covers and serge saddle cloathes lyned and bound' cost £3 17s. Even everyday saddles used for exercise, called 'watering saddles' cost £1, and a 'Bitt with silver and gilt Bosses' cost 8s. Other stable equipment was relatively cheap, and surprisingly similar to any one might find in a modern stable.[25]

Captain Thomas Lucy of The Blues, in the less decadent style of dress preferred
for portraits at the time, and showing, to the right, his black groom.
Lucy was later killed at the Siege of Limerick.

Private gentlemen also had to provide their own elaborate uniform, the design for which was decided in January 1661, based partly on that in use by Albemarle's Troops, partly on the dress of the former royal life guard in the civil wars and partly on what Gerard and his companions had acquired in Holland. Armour was restricted to the now standard front and back breast plates, which were burnished in the King's and Duke of York's Troop and were a more utilitarian black in Albemarle's. A 'pot' was still worn on the head under a wide-brimmed felt hat, decorated with feathers specially imported from France for the coronation and exempted from customs duty, and pistol-proof helmets were still required, though seldom worn.[26] The coats were red – not only the old royal colour, but also the colour widely used in the new model army because it was one of the cheapest dyes. Coats were richly decorated with gold lace facings, and sometimes worn with short red cloaks. Breeches and boots were of soft, buff-coloured leather, as were gauntlets. All ranks wore wide waist sashes, the officers' being generously fringed. The officers were further distinguished by wearing a shoulder knot or epaulette on their right shoulder, and by carrying canes – soon formalized according to appointment.

This uniform may have looked very fine in the great coronation procession, but it was not universally popular, with either the public or the Life Guards themselves, who thought it too elaborate and decadent. The days when people would have their portraits painted in full regimental uniform were still some way off, and if they did appear in uniform most chose to be styled in a plainer buff coat, as in the magnificent portrait of Captain Thomas Lucy by Kneller.[27] Sir Ralph Verney was more forthright: 'Grosveneur tells me you designe a Souldiers sute, which noe man living would weare but you ... You may almost as well waere a Canonicall Coate, and thinke how many wold laugh at that, & soe they will at the King's livery.'[28] There is no record of the Life Guards being required to use certain specified tailors (until the funeral of Queen Caroline in 1737), so there must also have been a considerable divergence of patterns within the very broad regulations issued. Swords were of a standard cavalry model, long and straight with a black leather scabbard, carried on a buff sword belt. Two pistols were carried, with 14-inch barrels, and a carbine, mounted on a belt with a swivel hook so that it could be brought quickly off the shoulder and into action. The Life Guards always had modern flintlocks instead of the older and more cumbersome firelocks, and these were issued centrally from the Ordnance.

The first major public demonstration of this new Life Guard was at King Charles's splendid coronation on 23 April 1661. He rode in state from the Tower of London to Westminster under four huge triumphal arches erected by Peter Mills, the city surveyor, and accompanied by all three troops. The kettle-drummers and trumpeters led the glittering procession, of which Pepys wrote, 'so glorious was the show with gold and silver that we were not able to look at it – our eyes at last being so overcome with it', which is unsurprising given

Charles II's state entry into the City of London on 22 April 1661, prior to his coronation. The Drummers and Trumpeters of the Life Guards lead the procession, followed by Albemarle's Troop. The King is centre right on a grey horse, followed by his troop, and James, Duke of York, rides in front of his troop to the left of the painting, having just passed through the left-hand arch. This was not the first coronation in which the Life Guards participated, having already escorted Oliver Cromwell when he was installed as Lord Protector eight years earlier.

that he had arrived at Westminster Abbey at 4 a.m. to be sure of his seat. The Duke of York followed, escorted by his troop, then the King with his troop, followed by Albemarle and his at the rear. It was a display designed to demonstrate the splendour and power of the restored monarchy, and it was the first occasion on which the reformed Life Guards participated in state ceremonial. It was, as such, partially successful – Pepys reports 'a great many gallants, men and women . . . would have us drink the King's health' – but the future employment of this new body of guards, both the Life Guards and their counterparts in the two regiments of Foot Guards, was to be less popular.

THE LIFE GUARDS' duties in those early days involved a mixture of escorting the royal family or Albemarle – whose life could have been threatened by those who thought he had betrayed the Commonwealth – at ceremonial functions in London and acting as a military reserve to assist constables in quelling disturbances in London. They lived, and stabled their horses, in pubs around Whitehall. The King's Troop were situated around the Strand, St Clement's, Drury Lane, Holborn, Long Acre, Covent Garden and St Martin's Lane, whilst the Duke of York's Troop were in Horseferry, Millbank, Petty France and St James's Street. Albemarle's Troop stayed in Tothill Street, King Street, Haymarket and Piccadilly, and Charing Cross except for the Chequer and Star Inns, which were reserved for the 'Orderlie men' of The Blues, (see pp. 70–1).[29] There was nothing new in this – Cromwell had stabled his Life Guard in the same area – yet Parliament would soon come to think, after the first heady days of the Restoration, that having such regular troops readily available to the King in the capital was too redolent of French absolutism, particularly as Charles travelled with an escort of Life Guards to open Parliament in February 1670.

Escort duties could be onerous, for the King and the Duke of York travelled frequently, particularly to Windsor and Newmarket. When the entire court moved to Windsor, for example, all three troops would be required. Detailed orders were issued for these journeys, which specified routes and lodgings to be used. A quartermaster would be sent on ahead to find accommodation and stabling in 'Staynes, Egham, Chersey, Waybridge, Laleham, Uxbridge, Hillingdon and divers', the large area covered reflecting the difficulty in finding sufficient room for so large an escort. Every order finishes, 'and the officers are to take care that the Gentlemen of ye said party satisfy their Land Lords for themselves and their Horses and behave themselves Orderly', which was indicative of a growing problem to which we will shortly return.[30] On those occasions when the King and Queen travelled with the Duke of York, a composite escort of 180 was created on a rota system, with each of the three troops supplying sixty men.

The Council was keen that the King should always travel with an escort. In August 1663, for example, the King and Queen went to Bath for a fortnight's stay because the Queen's health necessitated getting out of a hot and unpleasant London. An escort of 200 accompanied them, with four companies of Foot Guards sent on ahead to provide security in Bath. The escort must have been a pleasant one, and the return journey turned into a royal progress, with the King and Queen staying at Badminton, where they were entertained by the Marquess of Worcester, at Longleat by Sir James Thynne, at Marlborough by Lord Seymour, at Newbury by Sir Thomas Doleman, at Cornbury by Lord Chancellor Clarendon, and finally at Oxford where they were hosted by the University. The Life Guards stayed in local pubs. A purported conversation between the King and Clarendon, upon the King's intention of travelling to visit his sister, perhaps shows the royal attitude: 'I suppose you will go with a light train?' asked Clarendon. 'I intend to take nothing but my night bag,' replied the King. 'You will surely not go without forty or fifty horse?' exclaimed Clarendon. 'I count that as part of my night bag,' retorted the King.[31]

Apart from mounting the guard, escorting the Royal Family and acting as an early prototype of the Metropolitan Police, the Life Guards were also increasingly involved with many other aspects of royal and London life. In May 1662 they officiated at the King's marriage to the Portuguese Princess Catherine of Braganza in Portsmouth, the first of many royal weddings in which they were to participate over the centuries. The 1st Troop escorted the King from London to Guildford and the 2nd Troop took him on from there to the south coast. The 3rd Troop had been sent on ahead, and was drawn up in Portsmouth for his arrival. A royal review of the guards was subsequently held in Hyde Park, after the royal couple's return to London, and created a considerable stir, it being reported that 'the horse and foot were in such exquisite order, that t'is not easie to imagine anything so exact; which is the more credible, if you consider that there were but few of that great body who had not formerly been Commanders'.[32] It was obviously considered a useful exercise, not least to show the guards off to Parliament and the London population, and was repeated in July 1663 and at regular intervals thereafter. Pepys found it less impressive. 'Methought all these gay men are not the soldiers that must do the King's business, it being such as these that lost the old King all he had and were beat by the most ordinary fellows that could be,' he wrote in his diary entry for 4 July 1663, but Pepys never really rated Charles II and his republican upbringing probably militated against him ever supporting the Life Guards. Historically, it was the first time the Guards had been formally reviewed, and was, as such, the precursor of many future reviews that today are represented by the annual Queen's Birthday Parade, or Trooping the Colour, which takes place every year in June in London. The Life Guards were also present for the first time at a court ball on 22 February 1664, partly for security and partly for the impressive spectacle they created, which was, once again, to be a precedent for many future royal functions.

A further duty was to escort visiting royalty or important ambassadors, another task that has continued to this day, although the first such occasion was hardly auspicious. On 30 September 1661, Count Brahe, the Swedish Ambassador, was to make his official arrival in London, and a royal coach with a troop of Life Guards was sent to meet him. For some inexplicable reason, the Ambassadors of France and Spain arrived at Tower Wharf at the same time, accompanied by their own escorts, who were, according to contemporary custom, armed. While Brahe set off in front, with his Life Guard escort, a desperate race for second place developed between the French and Spaniards. The French soon got the better of the Spaniards who, not to be outdone, proceeded to hamstring two of the French carriage horses. A fight broke out between the rival parties, which the local mob soon joined, lobbing bricks at random at anyone they perceived to be foreign. Several people were killed, and the Life Guards only restored order with difficulty. Now hopelessly handicapped, the embarrassed French Ambassador suffered the indignity of arriving at Whitehall a poor third, drawn by two remaining horses, and cheered on by an enormous crowd.

A sadder duty was to escort the coffin of General Monck, the Duke of Albemarle, when he died in January 1670. Subsequently his 3rd Troop became the Queen's Troop and took precedence over the Duke of York's, to James's chagrin.

Chapter Two

UNTON CROKE'S REGIMENT OF HORSE

By the second year of his reign Charles II had, in his troops of Life Guards and Foot Guards, both an effective guard for himself and his court, providing security and an element of pageantry, and a force of loyal troops in his capital. The Royalist Restoration Parliament was, for the time being, acquiescent, if not actually supportive of the Guards, and the King met the annual expenses from his own pocket. As we have seen, in January 1661 the Venner riots allowed the King also to retain the two regiments that had supported Monck so strongly in 1660. On 26 January he established Monck's Regiment of Foot as the 2nd Regiment of Foot Guards – the Coldstream Guards – and Colonel Unton Croke's Regiment of Horse was formally raised as the Royal Regiment of Horse Guards.

The King had, in fact, formed a close relationship with Unton Croke's troops at the Restoration, even though they were stationed in the West Country, and he replaced some of the Commonwealth officers with his own supporters whom he wanted to reward. It was not enough to save the regiment from temporary disbandment, however, and early in December 1660 they were paid off under the Parliamentary demobilization scheme at Bath. However, the soldiers did not actually disperse, adding weight to the theory that the King and the Duke of York were determined to preserve them as part of the permanent force they had planned in detail the previous August. No sooner had the Venner riots provided the necessary opportunity than they were moved as a regiment to London and held their first parade in their new guise in Tothill Fields, now Vincent Square, on 6 February 1661.

The Royal Regiment of Horse Guards, also known as the Royal Horse Guards, have since their formation always been called The Blues after the colour of their uniform, and, it is simpler if we refer to them as such from now on. The Blues would not become formally part of the Household Cavalry until after Waterloo, nearly 150 years later, but they were always very close to the monarch, were to be the largest regiment in the English army as it developed, and would carry out many of the same tasks as the Life Guards. It is ironic that they were to become so closely associated with the monarchy, as they were originally among the most extreme puritan regiments of the New Model Army, and it is still not entirely clear why they were singled out for special royal attention so soon after the Restoration, or why Monck placed so much confidence in them.

Sir Arthur Haselrig – he of 'Haselrig's Lobsters' fame (see p. 11) – raised The Blues from the northern counties on 29 August 1650, together with the Coldstream Guards, as part of extra forces Cromwell needed for his invasion of Royalist Scotland. There were six troops of fifty men each, one commanded by Haselrig himself and the others by a Major Sanderson, and Captains Robert Hutton, John Ogle, Edward Fenwick and Manuel Dowsson. They wore blue coats from the start, and are recorded as having carried a blue standard fringed with gold: in Cromwell's army the colour of the standard always matched that of the uniform. There is no reason to suggest why blue was chosen other than that it was the only cloth available locally when the regiment was being equipped.

The Blues' first action was in February 1651 near Stirling, where they dismounted as the Scots retreated into a bog and pursued them on foot. Dowsson and a party of his troopers were captured, and later murdered by the Scots, and Unton Croke took his place. Croke came from Oxfordshire, and seems to have been a typical Parliamentarian, as opposed to Cromwellian, officer, a factor that would prove very significant for his regiment. His father was a lawyer and the family lived at Marston; Fairfax had used their house as his headquarters during the siege of Oxford when Croke had distinguished himself as a lieutenant by stealing some Royalist horses from Magdalen Meadows. Within two months of joining The Blues he and his troop had distinguished themselves further by effectively putting down an insurrection by the Earl of Eglinton at Dumbarton.

The regiment remained in Scotland throughout 1651, taking part in the brutal pillage of Dundee. That summer Haselrig was replaced by James Berry, a friend and strong supporter of Cromwell, who had commanded Cromwell's own troop, in his regiment of Ironsides, as his 'Captain Lieutenant' – the officer who ran the troop on a daily basis. Berry, a dedicated republican, had been a clerk in an ironworks in Shropshire and numbered the extreme puritan preacher, Richard Baxter, among his closest friends. He had tried to persuade Baxter to become Chaplain to his new regiment, but perhaps luckily for The Blues, Baxter refused on the grounds that Berry attended church and was therefore a 'Congregationalist', an accusation he also levelled at Cromwell. Beyond that, Berry was an efficient soldier, who had distinguished himself at the Battle of Gainsborough in 1643 when he killed the Royalist general Charles Cavendish 'with a short thrust under his short ribs', as Cromwell wrote in his dispatch after the battle.[1] His highly efficient command of The Blues made them one of the most trustworthy Cromwellian regiments and probably ensured that they were useful to Monck, thus, ironically, guaranteeing their survival at the Restoration.

Berry wasted no time in introducing to his new regiment the strict disciplinary code prevalent in Cromwell's Ironsides. A fine of 12d. was levied for swearing, the stocks were used to punish drunkenness, and two soldiers convicted of robbing fellow countrymen near Dundee of 7s. 6d. were led to the gallows with ropes around their necks, given thirty lashes apiece and made to beg forgiveness from their victims on their knees. Berry also introduced Cromwell's high standards of administration. Each troop had a lieutenant, a cornet, two corporals, two trumpeters and a quartermaster. Each soldier's equipment cost £5, and consisted of iron front and back armour, a 'pot' to cover his skull, a sword, a pair of pistols, which were expensive at 38s., with holsters a further 3s. 4d., a sword and saddlery. Pay was 2s. 6d. per day, but from that the soldiers had to provide for themselves and their horses. The regiment also had a surgeon, and two 'surgeon's mates', and, of course, a chaplain. It was the typical New Model Army structure, which, as we have seen with the post-Restoration organization of the Life Guards, was to endure well into the next century as the most efficient method of running a regiment of horse.

Berry also introduced Cromwell's own methods of horse management, something in which the cavalry of both sides in the civil wars had been found wanting. In 1645 Berry had to demobilize eight of his troopers in the Ironsides because horses could not be found for them, perhaps mindful of Cromwell's reply when ordered to charge again with his exhausted regiment at the second Battle of Newbury, 'you may have of their skins, but you can have no service'.[2] By 1650 the average price paid for a horse had gone up to around £10, and Cromwell introduced a system whereby each county produced a levy for the army, but even that did not produce enough beasts. Horse care therefore became one of the main factors in determining a regiment's usefulness, and given the extent to which Berry's Blues would be used in the coming decade, they must have achieved particularly high standards, a tradition which they have maintained, on and off, for most of their history.

In 1653 The Blues moved to England and played a major role in Cromwell's seizure of power and establishment as Lord Protector that December. Thereafter they were widely dispersed around the country, with troops at Exeter, Newark, Bristol and Marlborough, engaged in keeping the peace and preventing Royalist uprisings. This they did most efficiently, subduing the Rufford Abbey plot near Newark and the Wagstaffe rebellion, with house-to-house fighting in South Molton, in 1654. The latter action was undertaken by Croke's Troop, and Cromwell singled him out for praise. Berry had his own troop at Ludlow, from where he petitioned Cromwell to allow him to rebuild the castle, which would 'one of these days, I feare, fall down and knocke somebody on the head'.[3] He was made Major General of Wales and the Border Counties in

October 1655, while still retaining command of The Blues, and thus formed part of the military administration of England that was to prove so unpopular and ultimately lead to the dissolution of the Commonwealth. Berry later became a Member of the Upper House in Cromwell's second Parliament, leaving the running of his regiment to Unton Croke. His religious views seem to have become more extreme, to the extent that his old friend Richard Baxter complained that he was corrupted by Cromwell and came to 'look down on puritans of the old type'.[4]

In 1657 The Blues returned to Scotland, where Monck was now Major General. He used them to suppress the rise of Quakerism, which was concerning him. It was probably his first encounter with the regiment, and they seem to have made a favourable impression, despite the fact that he thought that they had become badly infected with Quakerism themselves. Monck wrote to Cromwell complaining that three officers in the regiment were Quakers 'and where they are (as I am informed) the greatest part of their troops are Quakers. Truly I thinke they will prove a very dangerous people, should they increase in your army, and be neither fitt to command nor obey, but ready to make a distraction in the army, and to mutiny uppon very slight occasion'.[5] Monck's judgement was, predictably, fairly accurate. Quakerism had penetrated deeply throughout all ranks. Cornet Ward, in Berry's own troop, was exposed as being a 'perfect Quaker' and was cashiered for harbouring a radical Quaker preacher, John Hall, in his troop and for rather tactlessly telling the clergy in Aberdeen that they were 'upholders of the kingdom of Satan and of darkness'.

Despite this tendency, Monck seems to have formed a strong respect for Croke, whose troop was noted as being clear of the affliction, and who commanded while Berry discharged his duties in the Marches. In 1658 The Blues were back in England, helping to ensure Richard Cromwell succession to his father as Lord Protector. Croke, now promoted to Major, and his troop were pelted with 'caret and turnip tops' by the students in Oxford while escorting the Vice Chancellor of the University.[6] Croke remained in Oxford, becoming Sheriff of the county and a Member of Parliament in 1658.

In the confused struggle between the army and Parliament in 1658 that led to Richard Cromwell's resignation of the Protectorate in May, Berry, predictably, backed the army against Parliament, and was one of those who supported Lambert's rebellion, with which the Cromwellian Life Guards also sided (see p. 16). Berry was promptly cashiered, but Croke, ever the opportunist and in effective command, was more circumspect. He was at Old Sarum at the time of Lambert's revolt, and was in communication with Haselrig, the effective leader of the parliamentary rump, who urged him to declare for Parliament. The army had already sacked Captains Dutton and Hacoridge, two troop commanders, for not supporting Lambert. There must have been considerable support for Parliament among the other officers for in December the regiment made an extraordinary declaration at Warminster. They declared that 'liberty of conscience, as to spirituals, for all the Lord's people' was a 'fundamental from which we will not swerve'; second, that 'we cannot willingly suffer our liberties, our estates nor persons to be disposed of by any but our just, legal, and due representative in Parliament'; third, that a 'free regulated Commonwealth' was the only acceptable form of government, and, interestingly, they renounced 'any king, single person, or House of Peers, particularly against Charles Stuart and his family', words which they must have recalled with a wry smile only a year later. They concluded by saying that they had no malice against their errant fellow soldiers now in revolt.[7]

Thus with Lambert's revolt defeated by Monck, and with Parliament restored late in December, The Blues were seen as one of the most trustworthy regiments. On 10 January 1660, Croke had his command of the regiment confirmed by Parliament, and troops were given to George Sedascue, who had been Adjutant General until sacked by Lambert; to Nathaniel Whetham, who was Governor of Portsmouth and had helped Haselrig persuade Croke to support Parliament; to David Gascoyne and Noel Boteler, both loyal lieutenants, and to Thomas Randall. They were sent back to the West Country – always, with its large cloth-working population, liable to be the most puritan of strongholds – with Croke's Troop stationed at Exeter, and were responsible to Monck for security there during the Restoration.

What had made Croke abandon his old patron Berry and turn to Parliament during the chaotic days following Richard Cromwell's abdication? Natural opportunism certainly – a quality Monck had noted in Croke back in 1657 – but there must have been more to turn the other officers, particularly Boteler, whose father had been Major, under Berry, before Croke and was guilty of some of the worst excesses in suppressing the South Molton revolt. Perhaps there was a lot more to Quakerism than Monck had realized, and perhaps the army's strong opposition to that sect had influenced the regiment. The wording of the Warminster Declaration is notable for its emphasis on 'liberty of conscience', and it is possible, as so often in the late 1650s, after nearly eighteen years of bloodshed, that the soldiers felt the principles for which they had sacrificed so much were being ignored in the struggle for power.

Croke may also have seemed to Monck to be an officer whose background made him a safe choice. He was, after all, from a 'good' Oxfordshire family, and very much of the class of Protestant squireachy from which the majority of the Parliamentary commanders had been recruited before the army became so extreme. Berry, the sometime clerk in a Shropshire ironworks, would not, for example, have been thought fit to command a regiment in 1642. Monck, the son of a West Country squire, would have identified as much with Croke's background during the turmoil of 1659 as he would with his undoubted efficiency. And Croke may also have felt that Berry had become so extreme in his religious and social views that he was no longer comfortable in supporting him.

The treatment of the senior officers in the regiment after the Restoration was indicative of how well known it had become. Opportunist as he may have been, Croke was too closely associated with the Commonwealth to continue as Colonel. He was replaced by the Royalist Colonel Daniel O'Neill that summer, and was arrested on suspicion of sedition, being bound over to keep the peace under a penalty of £4,000. He also had to surrender the lands near Salisbury that had belonged to Thomas Mompesson, and which had been granted to him by Parliament after the West Country rising. That apart, he continued to live peacefully in Oxford, dying in 1693, survived by his three daughters. Sir Arthur Haselrig, one of the few Parliamentarians whom Charles II was not prepared to forgive, was imprisoned in the tower and died there on 7 January 1661. Berry was also arrested, and kept as a prisoner for several years in Scarborough Castle. After his release, his friend Richard Baxter wrote, 'he became a gardener, and lived in a safer state than all his greatness'.[8]

Yet his greatness lived on in the regiment that he had done so much to create. Although Monck soon replaced officers nominated by Parliament, the vast majority of the soldiers remained under O'Neill, to be disbanded at Bath in December and re-raised, as the Royal Regiment of Horse Guards, that cold February day in 1661. It was therefore through them, and Monck's Troop of Life Guards, that the discipline and standards of Berry, and therefore of Cromwell's Ironsides, came to be the model of the Royalist army, and of the English army thereafter. There is a certain paradox in realizing that Parliament saw Cromwell's army as a threat which could menace their control of the state, for he had created a degree of military professionalism which later served that same Parliament and state very well indeed. It was an army that valued its own professional standards, happy thereafter to act as instructed by its political masters and never again to threaten the Crown or Parliament.

The officers whom Monck put in over the Cromwellian veterans were nearly all men who had fought for the King in the civil wars. At forty-eight, Daniel O'Neill was himself a veteran of Newbury, Marston Moor and Naseby, and had been Charles I's Groom of the Bedchamber. He was also a close friend of Charles II and had fought alongside him at Worcester in 1651. One of the old Irish aristocracy, he was the nephew of the famous Irish commander Owen O'Neill, and had been a useful bridge between his peers and the new Anglo-Irish. Clarendon gives a partly complimentary portrait of him, describing him as a man who was 'a great observer and discerner of men's natures and humours and very dextrous in compliance where he found it useful'.[9] He made a dramatic escape from Parliamentary captivity and joined Charles II in exile, where he was a particular favourite of the Princess Royal, and eventually married her governess, who was created Countess of Chesterfield. In August 1661 he became the Captain of the King's Own Troop and, as such, lieutenant colonel, or commanding officer, of the regiment. The man who has most famously been associated with the re-formed regiment, Aubrey de Vere – 20th Earl of Oxford,

The famous siege of Basing House during the Civil Wars. Several of the first officers in the Life Guards and The Blues had distinguished themselves in similar incidents such as the siege of Beeston Castle.

Monck holds an 'Orders Group'. It was his confidence in Unton Croke in 1660 that led to the survival of his Regiment of Horse, who would, early in 1661, become the Royal Horse Guards, always known as The Blues.

a staunch Royalist, a professional soldier and a grandee whose position gave him considerable standing – was put in above him as Colonel.

Oxford was also half Dutch. His mother was Beatrice de Banck, who came from Friesland where Aubrey was educated after his father, also a professional soldier, was mortally wounded in 1632 while in Dutch service at one of the endless sieges of Maastricht. Aubrey succeeded to the title at the age of six, and was later commissioned into the English regiment of foot that was serving with the Dutch during the Thirty Years War. He appears to have remained in Holland during the civil wars, only returning to England in 1651, after which he became involved in successive Royalist plots. He had his estates sequestrated, and in 1654 was imprisoned in the Tower for allegedly plotting against Cromwell. However, he was never brought to trial. He was released, only to be arrested again for his involvement in Sir George Booth's rising in 1659. He was one of the six peers who went to The Hague to petition Charles II to return in early May 1660, and consequently rather hoped to be made Lord Chamberlain in the scramble for position at the Restoration. He lost out to Lord Lindsay, and may have been made Colonel of The Blues by way of consolation. The appointment may also have had something to do with the fact that he was a great favourite of the Duchess of Cleveland, yet another of Charles II's mistresses. Oxford was then courting the Earl of Bristol's daughter, although he never actually married her. Bristol was 'in high favour' with the Duchess,[10] and he obviously wanted a successful son-in-law. Although his daughter eventually married the Earl of Sunderland, he lobbied hard for Oxford. The Oxford family livery colour was blue, and The Blues were often referred to thereafter as 'the Oxford Blues', but this is pure coincidence. There are no accounts showing new uniforms being issued in 1661, and the troopers simply continued to wear the same coats as they had under the Commonwealth.

Oxford was also made Lord Lieutenant of Essex, and awarded the Garter. During Charles II's reign other considerable honours were to come his way. Described by Macaulay as a man of loose morals, but of inoffensive temper and of courtly manners, he must have fitted in well at the Restoration court, where he was apparently a major figure. A couple of good portraits of him remain, showing him to be a tall, distinguished, slightly disdainful-looking man. Pepys was not a fan, complaining that he had violent parties at his house, one of which had to be broken up by the Guard. Pepys was also scandalized by seeing Oxford driving in the park in a hackney coach wearing his Garter Robes. There was a popular story, totally unsubstantiated, that he married an actress in secret and asked a trumpeter and kettle-drummer of The Blues to act as parson and clerk.

Oxford did not have much to do with the regiment on a daily basis, preferring to live in London and to attend at court. However, he served The Blues very well by his rigid adherence to his Protestant principles which he ensured were also present in his officers, and which must have made it easier for the remaining puritan and Quaker soldiers. Although initially he worked closely with the Duke of York as the army was built up, he was more a friend of Monmouth, at least until the latter's disgrace. He subsequently refused to support the Duke of York when, as James II, he attempted to catholicize the army establishment, being temporarily replaced as Colonel and forced to resign all his other offices. He threw in his lot with William and Mary, and positioned The Blues fortuitously in the aftermath of the Glorious Revolution. He remained as Colonel until his death in 1703, having been in office for forty-two years, less the nine months in 1688 when he had been replaced by James II's son, the Duke of Berwick. It is also greatly to his credit that he formed an implacable hatred of Charles II's favourite, the Duke of Buckingham, who swore that 'he would for ever be his enemy, and do him all the mischief he could', to which Oxford replied that 'he neither cared for his friendship nor feared his hatred',[11] a judgement that was to prove remarkably accurate.

The other officers in the eight troops reflected Oxford's Protestant sympathies. After the King's Own Troop, under Daniel O'Neill, was Oxford's Own Troop. His Captain Lieutenant was Sir Thomas Armstrong, whose father had served with Oxford in Holland. He had acted as Oxford's messenger between the Royalist plotters in England and the court in exile during the Commonwealth, a particularly dangerous occupation that must have left its mark. Described as a 'lewd and beggarly fellow of no religion or morals', and as 'a lewd bully and gamester',[12] we have already seen him taking six months off to attend to his estates in Ireland. He became a very close friend of Monmouth, which was ultimately to lead to his grisly end.

Other troops were very much family affairs. The Major who commanded the third most senior troop after the King's and the Colonel's was Sir Francis Wyndham, whose father had so bravely defended Dunster in the civil wars and who had effected Charles II's escape after Worcester. In his troop the Cornet was his brother Charles. The 4th Troop was commanded by one of Prince Rupert's cavalry commanders, Francis Lord Hawley, who was to succeed Daniel O'Neill as Lieutenant Colonel in 1664. A Member of Parliament, and later Governor of Deal Castle, Hawley did not have a very good public image, and was thought of as something of a placeman who amassed offices. He is satirized as 'Sergeant Buffoon & Commissioner for the sale of Fee Farm Rents', in the 'Sarcastical List', a spoof highlighting the patronage inherent in the system of granting army commissions and other public appointments.[13]

The 5th Troop was entirely officered by the Compton brothers. Their father, the Earl of Northampton, had been a staunch Royalist and was killed at Hopton Heath rather than suffer the indignity of surrendering to the 'rebels'. He had six sons, three of whom were commissioned into The Blues. Sir Charles Compton was the Captain; it had been he who, with six men in disguise, had taken Beeston Castle, by pretending to bring in supplies, and who had so nearly captured Compton House in Warwickshire. Sadly he was killed falling from his horse very soon after joining the regiment. His place was taken by his brother Francis, who was to be one of The Blues' most distinguished commanding officers (as opposed to colonels), and was later made a general. The third brother was Henry Compton, who served as a Cornet for a few months, before taking holy orders and eventually becoming Bishop of London. He was to be tutor to Princess Anne, later Queen Anne, and James II loathed him for his uncompromising opposition to Roman Catholicism, complaining that he preached more like a colonel than a bishop. Sir Edward Bret, Sir Henry Wroth and John, later Lord, Fretchville commanded the other troops.

So what role did The Blues fulfil, with no wars to fight and with the King's security well covered by the Life Guards and Foot Guards? Although intended to be the core of a future army, they were to spend the first twenty-five years of their existence effectively as police. England in 1660 was not entirely the happy, relaxed country rejoicing in the Restoration of its merry monarch that popular history may have us suppose. Over 11 per cent of the population of the British Isles had been killed between 1642 and 1650. Put in perspective, this is proportionately five times British losses in the First World War. The effect of this destruction had been devastating in large areas, and although Cromwell's strict policies had suppressed much of the violence, there was still considerable unrest in many places, together with crime, smuggling and frequent outbreaks of civil disorder.

Consequently The Blues' duties remained much as they had been under the Commonwealth. The troops were generally widely dispersed, but not always in the south of England, with troops frequently stationed in the London suburbs. There was usually a troop in Southwark, near the Tower, from where it was possible to get to Dover and Portsmouth without having to pass through London. A snapshot in spring 1670 shows the King's Troop at Canterbury, the Colonel's at Reading, Sir Francis Wyndham's at Salisbury, Sir Edward Brett's moving from Watford and Rickmansworth to Hammersmith, Lord Fretchville's at York, Sir Francis Compton's at Uxbridge and Colebrooke, Sir Henry Jones's moving from Bromley in Kent to Islington, and Sir Thomas Armstrong's at Farnham. Apart from general preservation of the peace, the troops were charged in particular with arresting highwaymen, who posed a serious problem on the approaches to London. We find Compton's Troop, for example, posted to Bagshot, where they were to 'send partyes constantly to patroll in the day time for the secureing the Highwayes from Robberys and Dissorders'.[14] Regular duties included escorting pay from the Navy Pay Office in Broad Street to the fleet anchored at Portsmouth, a chore that was generally entrusted to a corporal with a few men. The escort of prisoners, and rounding-up of remaining Cromwellians whom the King and Clarendon would not pardon, were also part of their remit. This was not always well received, and it took two troops to secure three ex-Cromwellian officers in Coventry in January 1662 when the locals rioted to prevent their arrest. Some of the soldiers must have found this

Aubrey de Vere, Earl of Oxford,
'the noblest subject in England', who was
Colonel of The Blues from 1661 until 1705,
except for a short break of nine months in 1688.

The Compton brothers officered the
5th Troop of The Blues. Francis, on the left,
was to be Oxford's lieutenant colonel from 1685
and commanded the regiment at Sedgemoor and
in Ireland. Henry, in the middle, became Bishop
of London, and tutor to the future Queen Anne.
Charles, on the right, distinguished himself in the
Civil War but was killed falling from a horse
soon after the Restoration.

Sir Francis Compton

Henry Compton
afterwards Bishop of London
Sons of the 2nd Earl of Northampton Officers in the 5th Troop of Blues 1661

Sir Charles Compton

particularly hard, but there is no record of any of them refusing a duty or mutinying, something which happened on several occasions in the Foot Guards.

York was considered to be particularly republican, with regular political rallies in the Dissenters' Meeting Houses. In 1664 fifteen 'republicans' were executed after trial by a special commission, and thereafter a troop of The Blues was stationed in the city almost permanently, with an increased establishment of eighty men. In 1665 Lord Hawley's Troop were carrying out this duty and had to be complemented with three companies of Foot Guards to maintain order. They did a good job, and received favourable press reports when they handed over to Fretchville's Troop that September; perhaps this was not unconnected with Hawley's having sent a drummer round asking all tradesmen and innkeepers to submit bills for money owing by his soldiers to him before they left. Fretchville's Troop still had to deal with considerable unrest. His Lieutenant, Sir Thomas Carnaby, was killed later that year and was buried in York Minster.

Another frequent duty was to assist in the destruction of illegal tobacco crops. This was a matter of some importance to the King, a substantial part of whose income was made up of customs revenues. Gloucestershire seems to have been something of a hotbed for this contraband. 'There are diverse persons in and about Wynchcombe, and severall other places in the County of Gloucester and Worcester, and in the Counties and places adjacent,' says one order to Sir Charles Wyndham's Troop, 'who take the libertie and boldnesse upon them to plant, set and sow Tobacco, contrary to the Acts of Parliament'. The troop was to assist Charles Osborne, Surveyor General of His Majesty's Customs, to 'pick up and destroy all tobacco so planted, set or sown'.[15]

These duties meant that The Blues, unlike the Life Guards and the Foot Guards, were constantly on the move. They lived and stabled their horses in inns, which must have become tedious and repetitive, particularly for those who wanted some stability after eleven years of campaigning. Nor was it a way of life that greatly appealed to the officers. Although for major operations such as York – where Lord Hawley was present personally – senior officers were often absent and a system of duty officers was developed. From 1662 we find instructions being sent from London to the captain of the troop 'or in his absence the officer in Chieff commanding that Troop'.[16] Nevertheless, it was a way of life that offered regular employment and a certain stability at a very uncertain time, and the regiment had maintained its professional pride. In 1668 Prince Cosmo of Tuscany paid a visit to the English court and came across 'a troop of Horse, excellently mounted, of the Royal Regiment of my Lord Aubrey de Vere, Earl of Oxford'. They had been sent to meet him at Basingstoke as he made his way to London. The Prince then dismounted and 'inspecting every file of the company, the officers of which wore a red sash with gold tassels'.[17] He was highly impressed.

Accepted and popular as the Life Guards and The Blues may have been in the heady days of the early 1660s, when there was general relief at the stability of a restored monarchy, and when Parliament was generally not in session, this happy situation was not destined to last. As Charles II's reign progressed, and his relations with Parliament worsened, so his new regiments became increasingly associated with what the opposition saw as an attempt to impose a French-inspired absolutist system of monarchy. The open Catholicism of the Duke of York, heir to the throne – the King's marriage having failed to produce any children – heightened these fears. They were not without justification, for as early as 1670 Charles II had made his 'Secret' Treaty of Dover with Louis XIV whereby the French agreed to provide him with what was to amount to £123,664 each year. Much of this money went towards paying his guards, who were costing him £283,000 per year by the time of his death,[18] amongst other pressing priorities. In return Charles II would announce his conversion to Catholicism when the time was right.

It was, on reflection, a quite extraordinary arrangement for the King to have made, and one that left him vulnerable at home when it became general knowledge,[19] which of course it did. Pepys heard rumours of the deal, noting that 'this is a thing which will make the Parliament and Kingdom mad, and will turn to our ruin – for this money the King shall wanton away his time in pleasures and think nothing of the main till it be too late'.[20] As the details slowly and inevitably leaked, so the Guards became even more unpopular, and they were to become the specific target of Shaftesbury and the anti-monarchist faction in Parliament as the anti-Catholic feeling increased. They were not helped in this by their own behaviour.

Whereas in 1665 65 per cent of the 210 Guards officers had fought in the civil wars, this figure dropped appreciably as age and the attraction of a more settled life opened up vacancies for younger candidates. Although The Blues, deployed more or less permanently outside London, generally kept out of trouble, the Life Guards found that it was difficult to maintain discipline with their private gentlemen living in small groups in the pubs of central London. There was also no effective military law in England until Parliament passed the Mutiny Act of 1689. Even if there had been, it is doubtful whether the private gentlemen, who considered themselves part of the court and therefore subject to the royal prerogative, would have paid any attention to it. The Duke of York had drawn up a collection of 'Articles and Rules of War' in 1666, which he tried unsuccessfully to have turned into an act of Parliament. The Articles stated that no civilian magistrate could imprison an officer or soldier except for high treason or murder, but Parliament insisted that soldiers should be subject to common law just as everybody else was. Even so, the magistrates were reluctant to act against soldiers without first receiving their commanding officer's permission, and in the case of Michael Hall, a private gentleman in the Life Guards, who was arrested in 1675 for an offence against Henry Richards, the Privy Council had to be asked to adjudicate.

As Charles II's reign progressed, and his relations with Parliament worsened, a propaganda war broke out between those who associated him and our regiments with a French-inspired, Catholic-style and absolutist monarchy and those who saw Charles as the exact opposite, as above, where he rests one triumphant foot on the back of a three-headed monster emblazoned with a fleur-de-lis, as Britannia and an angel look on approvingly.

It was not surprising that the Life Guards therefore considered themselves somewhat above the law, and from the late 1660s there are numerous examples of appalling behaviour which not only antagonized the Londoners, whom they were intended to police, but also increased criticism in Parliament. Among the endless instances of indebtedness, fighting, drunkenness and duelling there are some more lurid instances. A Mr Remington complained that a Life Guard man had offered to whisper something in his ear but instead bit his nose off. Another hired the maid of a certain Mr De La Noy, against whom he held a grudge, to burn down De La Noy's house. This she successfully did, and was duly convicted, whilst the Life Guard was acquitted.

These cases excited public interest. The assault on Sir John Coventry particularly provoked, not least because it implicated Monmouth, Charles II's illegitimate son, who had bought Gerard's Captaincy of the King's Troop. Coventry was a country Member of Parliament who opposed the court party, and had the temerity to sneer at the actresses Nell Gwynne and Moll Davies, well known as the King's mistresses, during a debate in 1670 as to whether theatres should be taxed. Shortly thereafter he was waylaid by four Life Guards – Sandys, O'Brien, Reeves and Parry – near Suffolk Street, where he was thrown to the ground and had his nose slit. The Life Guards were acting on Monmouth's instructions, a fact publicly announced by the Member of Parliament and poet Andrew Marvell, a persistent critic of the Life Guards in Parliament. The outrage was so great that Parliament subsequently passed the 'Coventry Act', which made malicious wounding a capital crime, though none of the Life Guards was ever convicted. Shortly afterwards Monmouth, out on the town with Monck's son, who had just succeeded as Duke of Albemarle, and a party of Life Guards, drunkenly attacked a beadle who stopped them, forcing him to his knees and then murdering him as he begged for his life. Again this atrocity went unpunished, something which did nothing for the Life Guards' reputation and created an unfortunate precedent for members of the regiment to misuse their close associations with members of the Royal Family.

MONMOUTH'S ASSOCIATION WITH the Life Guards was to prove a mixed blessing. Born in Rotterdam in 1649, Monmouth was both acknowledged and adored by the King. He was handsome and charming, and a great success with women, and had married Anne Scott, Countess of Buccleuch, one of the richest heiresses in the country. He was also a Protestant. He was, in short, all the things that the Duke of York was not. But he was also 'brainless, ungovernable, vain and ambitious'[21] and lived in the expectation that the King might legitimize him and therefore his claim to the throne.

He was not inefficient as a military commander by contemporary standards, and did something to rectify some of the administrative chaos that Gerard and his crooked agent, Carr, had left and which had done so much to damage the

Life Guards' reputation. For not only had Gerard misappropriated large amounts of their pay, but he had also allowed the strength of the troops to drop, declaring what were known as 'false musters', whereby he drew pay for established posts that he left unfilled, and kept the money for himself. Soon after he took over Monmouth was ordering fifty sets of fronts and backs and 200 carbines, all of which had been deficient. He was installed at a grand review in Hyde Park on 16 September 1670, for which the King had presented him with a very smart new saddle. 'I took a hackney-coach and saw it all,' recorded Pepys, 'and indeed it was mighty noble, and their firing mighty fine, and the Duke of Monmouth in mighty rich clothes; but the well-ordering of the men I understand not.' Yet Monmouth became more than just Captain of the King's Troop, for in 1674 he was made Commander-in-Chief, a post which had been vacant since Albemarle's death in 1670, and the Life Guard troops were instructed to obey orders issued by him.[22] His appointment was hotly contested by the Duke of York, who saw him as an obvious rival for the throne and had coveted the position for himself. Consequently the loyalty of two of the troops of Life Guards became polarized, the King's Troop supporting Monmouth as their Captain and the Duke of York's naturally supporting their patron. Uninvolved, and in keeping with their Commonwealth tradition, the Queen's Troop maintained a degree of sober detachment, remaining under Sir Philip Howard's erratic but effective command until his death in 1685, the same year as the King.

In the early 1670s the King's favour was firmly behind Monmouth, who attempted to instil some uniformity into the army, issuing the first Standing Orders in August 1674 that, ironically coming from his hand, forbade drunkenness and bad language.[23] The Duke of York had suffered an initial reverse in 1667 when Parliament voted to exclude all Catholic officers from the army. Both he and the King had tried their utmost to prevent this bill becoming law, but it was passed by one vote that September. On the 26th all Catholic officers and soldiers were dismissed, with eighty-seven of the Life Guards included, many from the Duke of York's Troop. It was an unnecessary and venal move, which showed how rapidly deep-rooted Parliamentary fears of Charles II's leanings towards the French Catholic monarchy had grown. Most of those dismissed were loyal primarily to the Crown at this stage, but religion was a still stronger tie, and there is only evidence that three members of the Duke of York's Troop took the oaths of Allegiance and Supremacy, thus allowing their continued employment. The dismissals caused real hardship. One cannot help but feel for those who, after eighteen years of war and dislocation, felt that they had achieved at least some stability, only now to find themselves with no means of support. In one petition to the King from some of these dismissed private gentlemen they 'beg him to find them bread; they spent their youth and blood, and underwent all hardships short of death, for His Majesty and his Father, and now a fate worse than death awaits them, they being made incapable of employment'.[24]

The Duke of Monmouth and Buccleuch, Charles II's adored son (*right*), was the eldest of fourteen illegitimate children. Charming, ambitious and unprincipled, he would later tragically overestimate both his father's and the public support for his cause and damage his reputation by being linked to the Rye House plot. He became Colonel of the First Troop in 1670.

A Protestant and a competent military commander, the portrait below commemorates his role as commander of the English auxiliary force against the Dutch in 1672–3, and particularly his heroic part in the siege of Maastricht.

Charles II tried his best, making specific arrangements for many of the men to enter French service, where Sir George Hamilton, of the King's Troop, led an English Catholic regiment. He eventually became a Marshal of France and was killed in French service in 1676. (He was, incidentally, married to the sister of the famous Sarah Jennings, later Duchess of Marlborough.) Only two junior officers in The Blues were affected, evidence of their continuing puritanism and Oxford's careful screening of candidates. However, the regiment suffered a further indignity when twenty-four Protestant officers, who had been fighting in Portuguese service since the sale of Dunkirk to Louis XIV, now returned to England, and The Blues were instructed to take three into each troop. Nicholas Rendarvy, Theodore Russell and William Armstrong went to the King's Troop, by now under Lord Hawley, a highly unpopular move with the existing officers.[25] One of these officers, William Littleton, would become Major by 1688 and will play a rather fuller role in our story.

A few of the dismissed officers quietly made their way back over the next few years, when the atmosphere had become less hysterical, and they were useful when the English army was increased in 1673 prior to the Third Dutch War. Some, like Sir Henry Jones, one of the two Blues officers dismissed, and who had gone to Spain in 1667, actually raised a regiment for service against the Dutch that fought at Maastricht in 1673. He was killed during the siege, which may have been timely, as the Test Acts were applied stringently on the army's return and many officers were forced out for a second time.

For the next six years Monmouth's star was firmly in the ascendant. He still enjoyed his father's favour and his moderate success as a field commander offset, at least to some extent, the arrogance of his behaviour. Although some of the Life Guards had fought as seamen in the Second Dutch War of 1665, and seen action at the Battle of Lowestoft, where the unfortunate Sir Charles Berkeley was killed – making it technically their first battle honour – it was not until Monmouth raised troops to fight alongside the French in the Third Dutch War that they had their first experience of land warfare as a body. Fifty men from each troop served under the command of Lord Duras, who ranks, against a rich field, as one of the most extraordinary Life Guards officers of the period. He was French and Catholic and, as such, appealed strongly to the Duke of York. His chief claim to military ability seems to have rested on his being the nephew of Louis XIV's great Marshal, Turenne, which judging from his future career we can safely assume was the sum of his military qualifications. He became a firm friend and confidant of the Duke of York in the 1650s, and had succeeded, after Berkeley's death, as Captain of his troop. Somewhat prophetically, Monmouth did not like him, as Duras, later to become Marquis de Blanquefort and, in England, the Earl of Feversham, was to command James II's army against him at Sedgemoor.

Monmouth seems to have kept his distance from his Life Guards during the campaign. Arriving at the French camp at Charleroi on 1 May 1672, they took part in the successful march up the Rhine to take Utrecht that summer, fighting directly under Louis XIV. They spent that winter in Paris, where they were reported as being very popular with the Queen and the ladies of the court (history does not, perhaps fortunately, relate exactly why), while Monmouth returned home. The following spring they were present at the Siege of Maastricht, and fought with some distinction on foot in the trenches. In one instance the Dutch blew a mine under their section of trench, and followed it up with a vigorous assault. Monmouth personally led the counter-attack, and distinguished himself along with twelve private gentlemen. They all lost their carbines in this incident, and a subsequent order for their replacement shows that one was a Pursell, another a Throckmorton and a third an O'Brien, all well-known Catholic names; it is possible that they were among those who, like Henry Jones, had left in 1667, only to return when the fuss over Catholics serving in the forces had died down.[26] O'Brien, one of those who mugged Coventry, was killed in the incident.

The Blues, hardly surprisingly for a puritan regiment with a half-Dutch and strongly Anglican colonel, regarded a war on behalf of Catholic France against Protestant Holland with distaste and produced very few troops. Indeed, so enraged was Henry Jones when his personal appeal to his old troop produced only a handful of volunteers that he 'sur le champ put out one of those that stayed out of the troop'.[27] Instead, The Blues' main part in the war involved rounding up deserters from other regiments and from the navy, manned by a draft. It never seems to have occurred to anyone that they should have been deployed as a regiment. Instead, new regiments were raised specifically for the campaign. Jones, therefore, was recruiting for his own regiment of light horse, which he led at Maastricht, where he was killed in the same incident in which Monmouth distinguished himself. A total of nine new regiments were raised in 1672,[28] most subsequently disbanded when the unpopular war was concluded in February 1674 with the Treaty of Westminster, leaving the French to fight on against the Dutch until 1678. The Life Guards returned home, having lost fifty men, who were not replaced. Charles II carried out a general reduction in the army that year, including ten men from each troop in The Blues. Oxford, demonstrating a surprisingly modern attitude, directed that these should not be 'effective men', but rather the officers' servants and grooms.

Charles had, predictably, been forced into these reductions by Parliament, who never supported a war whose prosecution seemed directly opposed to what they perceived as the national interest, and which cost English lives in support of the hated French monarchy. After peace was concluded they presented the King with a 'Quest of Grievances', which listed, among other things, their opposition to the Guards. 'According to the laws of the land the King hath no guards but those called gentlemen pensioners and the Yeomen of the Guard,' ran the Quest, and 'that ever since this Parliament, although there have been so many sessions, they never settled the Life Guard by Act of Parliament

A naval battle against the Dutch during the Second Dutch War. The Life Guards had their first experience of combat in such a battle fighting under James Duke of York's command.

Sir Charles Berkeley, Captain of the Second Troop, was killed along with 2,000 other British soldiers and seamen.

– nay, they have been so far from it, that whensoever they have been so much as mentioned in the House of Commons, they would never in the least take any favourable notice of them, always looking upon them as a number of men unlawfully assembled, and in no respect fit to be the least countenanced by the Parliament of England.'

The Quest went on to say that they were 'a vast charge to the Kingdom', that 'Guards or Standing Armies are only in use where princes govern by fear, rather than by love, as in France, where the government is arbitrary', and that 'the Life Guard is a place of refuge and retreat for Papists . . . and a school and nursery for men of debauched and arbitrary principles, and favourers of the French government, as did plainly appear in the case of Sir John Coventry'. It concluded by calling on the King to disband the Life Guards, though not, interestingly, The Blues, who seem to have been perceived as doing useful police work, and thus to save 'some Hundreds of Thousands of Pounds per annum, which would in a few years enable him to pay his debts, without burdening the good people with taxes to that end'.[29]

It was hardly a very warm homecoming for the heroes of Maastricht, although the reductions Charles II made were the least he could get away with. Yet Parliament was unable to force through disbandment. Although the King's finances were badly stretched by the recent war, he had agreed a further deal with Louis XIV who was to continue his subsidies, despite England's withdrawal from the war, in return for which the King prorogued Parliament. It did not meet again for four years, but in that period Charles II, urged on by Danby, his First Minister, underwent something of a Damascene conversion. He may have been motivated by a desire to extract himself from what was rapidly becoming an unworkable European policy, or by a genuine dislike of war, something of which he had seen far too much; it was probably a more calculated consideration as to how he could pass the throne on to his brother, the Duke of York, and a realization that he would never win popular support for his succession as long as he was seen to be so closely associated with France, Popery and absolutism. In November 1677 the Duke of York's eldest daughter, Mary, raised as a Protestant, married her cousin William of Orange, who was the Dutch Stadtholder and son of Charles I's daughter Princess Mary. Although the Duke of York, whose first wife Anne Hyde had died in 1671, had slightly complicated matters in 1673 by marrying a Catholic princess, Mary of Modena, he had still not produced an heir with her and there was therefore a reasonable expectation that any child of William and Mary's would one day rule as a Protestant. When Parliament met in 1678, the King announced that he was now to support Holland in its struggle with France, at which point Louis XIV promptly cut off his subsidies.

This was a change in policy which was to have very profound implications for the Life Guards and The Blues, and the French wars that would ultimately result lasted on and off for the next 137 years. The initial implications, however, were at home. Although Parliament authorized funds for an army of 30,000 men to deploy to Flanders to assist William, and twenty new regiments were duly raised, Louis XIV did yet another deal with the cash-strapped Charles II. As a result the army was withdrawn, and Charles received more money for persuading the Dutch to agree to a negotiated settlement. Neither regiment was directly involved in this charade, although individuals volunteered, like Sir Thomas Armstrong who commanded a new regiment of horse and took Richard Bings, Quartermaster of the King's Troop, as his Major.

Yet their role at home suddenly seemed to both the King and, this time, Parliament to have become considerably more important. Parliament's views were divided; some undoubtedly believed in the existence of a 'Popish' plot to assassinate the now pro-Dutch Charles and replace him with his Catholic brother; indeed several Members, like Shaftesbury, were responsible for spreading such rumours. The King's safety consequently assumed even more importance. Others still distrusted a Stuart monarchy with a large guard force, fearing that it would either be used against them – which it duly was when Charles moved Parliament to Oxford in 1684 – or, more frighteningly, devolve upon the Duke of York when he inherited, which was again to prove to be the case.

The King himself was always careful of his own security and, however relaxed his court, he took this increasingly seriously as the potential threats to his life multiplied throughout his reign. Three significant developments resulted from this. First, the Life Guards started to mount a permanent guard of fifty private gentlemen, called the King's Life Guard, at the entrance to Whitehall Palace. A new gatehouse was completed in 1664 at a cost of £4,000 to house them, which included stabling, and this building came subsequently to be known as the 'Horse Guards'. It stood for ninety years until it finally collapsed from neglect. It was on the same site now occupied by the current Horse Guards, which replaced it in the 1750s, from where the present Queen's Life Guard continue to perform the same daily duty. The King's Life Guards' duties do not appear to have been prescribed in any detail, although they probably doubled up as the escort when the King travelled locally within London. There was also a permanent guard of Foot Guards in the Horse Guards building, which developed into more of a headquarters and rallying point for the Life Guard troops distributed in the local inns nearby. The Guard also had a second useful function in that they provided a ready body of soldiers in central London to respond to riots and civil disturbances, and they earned considerable praise for their assistance in the Great Fire of 1666. Consequently, when Whitehall Palace burned to the ground in 1698, the Guard remained in the old Horse Guards while the court removed itself to Kensington Palace and St James's Palace. The Horse Guards building also served as the entrance to the King's private St James's Park, and the Guard restricted access to those who enjoyed his permission to use it. In time this became a peculiar and much sought-after privilege, protected by a password that was changed weekly.

The second development was the King's insistence, after the events of 1678 and the hysteria engendered by Titus Oates, a populist preacher who was later exposed as a charlatan, but who persuaded many that there was a 'Popish Plot' to kill the King, that the captain of one of the troops of Life Guards should now accompany him at all times. This was to be 'attendance on the King's person on foot, wheresoever he walks, from his rising to his going to bed; and this is performed by one of the three Captains, who always waits immediately next to the King's own person, before all others'. Interestingly, and probably necessarily, he was excluded from the King's bedchamber. He carried, as a sign of his office, 'an ebony staff or truncheon, with a gold head, engraved with His Majesty's cypher and crown', and was subsequently called the 'Gold Stick-in-Waiting'. Hardly surprisingly the captains, of whom Monmouth was, as Captain of the King's Troop, the first to hold the office, found this an exceedingly tedious chore that severely restricted their freedom. Consequently they delegated the task to the next most senior officer in the troop and we soon find that 'near him attends another principal Commissioned Officer, with an ebony staff and silver head', afterwards styled the 'Silver Stick-in-Waiting', 'who is ready to relieve the Captain on occasions'.[30] In today's Household Cavalry, colonels of the respective regiments are still referred to as the Gold Sticks and take turns to attend the Queen – though now only on ceremonial occasions – and the regular serving officer who commands the Household Cavalry is known as the Silver Stick. Even though Titus Oates was subsequently exposed as a fraud, the custom continued, and probably owed as much to the King imitating Louis XIV as it did to fears for his own safety.

The third development, and one which was ultimately to be of great significance in the history of the Life Guards, was another direct imitation of Louis XIV. In December 1676 Louis had added a troop of 154 *grenadiers à cheval* to his already impressive Maison Militaire du Roi, a somewhat bizarre innovation that incorporated grenade throwing – the latest military technology[31] – within his Household Cavalry. It was not the most inspired of military experiments, and the French abandoned the hand grenades after more casualties were caused to themselves than to the enemy at Steenkirk in 1690, but not before Charles II had excitedly copied them. Grenadier companies were eventually attached to the Foot Guards, and to the battalions of infantry raised subsequently, and were to become an elite force within each formation, but in 1678 the King now had the perfect excuse to create his own Horse Grenadier Guards. A detachment of three officers, three sergeants, three corporals, two drummers, two hautboys and eighty private gentlemen were added to the King's Troop, and sixty men to the other two troops. In 1702 a similar detachment was added to the Scottish Troop.

Mary of Modena (*right*), the Duke of York's second wife, whom he married in 1673. Initially barren, in 1688 she gave birth to a son, making the heir to the throne a Roman Catholic.

The hysteria aroused by frauds such as Titus Oates, who preached that there was a 'Popish Plot' to kill Charles II, and who is shown in the pillory (*below*) led directly to the creation of the posts of Gold Stick and Silver Stick to oversee the King's safety, which was paramount and to the raising of the Horse Grenadiers.

The Horse Grenadiers were briefly disbanded after one of the more violent anti-militarist outcries in Parliament in 1680, but were reintroduced during renewed fears for the King's safety in 1683. They were, in various forms, to remain an integral part of the Household Cavalry until they formed the core of the reconstituted regiments of Life Guards in 1788. They should not be confused with the 1st Foot Guards, who were much later to assume the title Grenadier Guards, which they still hold. The idea was that they would act as mounted infantry in battle, much as dragoons would do (see p. 81). Detailed drill movements, translated from the French and practised on field days, were hideously complicated and involved throwing the grenades by ranks on foot, followed by falling in with much 'huzzaing', before mounting to fire their pistols and 'fusils'.[32] That splendid cynic, Sir Ralph Verney, summed up the attitude of contemporary officers in 1680, writing, 'I do not understand How the Granadiers can Doe any considerable Execution with fflying Hand Granadoes on Horseback which makes me wonder that his Majesty can have so great a ffancy for that sort of souldiering.'[33]

Militarily, Horse Grenadiers ranked below the Life Guards; their commissions were cheaper, they were paid less, and their soldiers were not proper private gentlemen who bought their places but 'effective men', recruited like those in other regiments. They were, in effect, much like the dragoon regiments created at the same time and of which we will shortly hear more. Nor were the original officers of quite the same social stature as their Life Guard contemporaries; John Parker and Thomas Gray became lieutenants in the King's Troop detachment, Richard Potter and Robert Dixon in the Queen's Troop and Anthony Heyford and John Vaughan in the Duke of York's Troop. Their uniform was another bizarre concoction, modelled on the *grenadiers à cheval*. 'The King', John Evelyn noted in his diary, 'has now augmented his Guards with a new sort of dragoons who carry granadoes and were habitted after the Polish manner, with long peaked caps, very fierce and fantastical.'[34] Unlike the Life Guards, the Horse Grenadier Guards were, from August 1683, all quartered centrally in the Royal Mews[35] at Charing Cross, on the site of the National Gallery, including extra stabling for 222 horses.

During the events of 1678 Monmouth gradually fell out of favour, possibly because the King realized that he must now work to facilitate his brother's succession, and partly because Monmouth himself was beginning to prove unreliable. His return from Maastricht in 1674 had been celebrated with a re-creation of the siege in Windsor Great Park, where a model of the fortress was built and duly stormed by the Life Guards. John Evelyn noted 'being night it made a formidable show, and was really very divertisant'.[36] However, in 1676 Monmouth had his powers as Commander-in-Chief limited by the necessity of securing the signature of the Secretary at War (see p. 70–1) on all his orders. Monmouth was predictably furious, and asked to be made a general by way of compensation. Charles yielded, but referred to Monmouth in the commissioning document as his 'natural' son, at the insistence of the Duke of York.

Monmouth was still trusted sufficiently to command the forces sent to Scotland in 1677 to suppress the Covenanters' Rebellion, although this may have been a device to get him out of the way, much as for the Duke of York during the worst years of the Exclusion Crisis. Monmouth finally defeated the Covenanters at the Battle of Bothwell Bridge, near Glasgow, on 22 June 1679. Over 1,200 Covenanters were captured and a further 800 killed. It was a bloody result, but an effective one, which ended a revolt that threatened the Stuart right to govern in Scotland. The Scottish Troop of Life Guards, under the command of the Duke of Montrose, were with Monmouth, as, almost certainly, were the troops of The Blues stationed in York, although annoyingly there is no War Office order to substantiate this. Had there been, it would have been the regiment's first attributable action since its formation.

On his return to London Monmouth courted Shaftesbury and the Whigs – as those opposed to the Duke of York's succession were coming to be known – setting himself up as an alternative successor to the throne. Convinced of his own popularity in both Parliament and the country, he toured England generally creating a nuisance, and getting himself arrested for affray. In November 1679 Charles II, at the Duke of York's insistence, dismissed Monmouth as Captain of the King's Troop, replacing him with his friend Albemarle, and exiled him to Holland, where he stayed briefly, returning to England soon afterwards with the King's connivance, if not his official sanction.

Still unable to accept his changed position, Monmouth continued scheming and was strongly implicated, if not actually a prime mover, in the disastrous Rye House Plot of the spring of 1683. This was a bizarre scheme to abduct and kill the King and the Duke of York as they returned from Newmarket to London, and, or so the plotters thought, ensure Monmouth's succession. The plotters chose a spot near Hoddesdon in Hertfordshire where the road narrowed as it passed the Rye House, inhabited by a maltster's widow who had subsequently remarried Richard Rumbold, one of the guards around the scaffold at Charles I's execution. The idea was to shoot the Life Guard escort first, and then the King and the Duke. At the same time detailed plans were made to disarm the scattered groups of Life Guards and the King's Guard in London, which was, if nothing else, testament to their perceived loyalty and effectiveness.

The popular version of the story is that the King and the Duke of York left Newmarket early because of a fire; it is more likely that the plot was discovered. On investigation, not only was Monmouth found to be heavily involved, but four Life Guards were party to it as well. One of the chief conspirators was Sir Thomas Armstrong, late of The Blues and recently transferred to the Life Guards as Captain Lieutenant in Monmouth's own troop. In the strange, almost schoolboy series of code names the plotters used, Armstrong was known as 'the

Player', the Duke of York was code-named 'Slavery', and muskets were 'goose-quills'. Armstrong fled to Holland, where he was eventually arrested at Leyden and handed over to the Government. No royal prerogative would save him now, and he was hanged, drawn and quartered without even the dignity of a trial. One part of his quartered corpse was displayed in Stafford, where he had been Member of Parliament. In a bizarre and unpleasant twist he was accused of having been a spy in Cromwell's pay in the 1650s, and his dangerous journeys to the court in exile in Holland as Oxford's messenger were portrayed as an attempt to kill the King.

The King seemed unable to accept that his son was implicated and Monmouth lay low, with his father's connivance. He was discovered by a party of Life Guards, curiously out of touch with the King's wishes. Colonel Edward Griffin, of the King's Troop and acting Silver Stick, rushed to report to Charles II that he had seen Monmouth, to which the King is reputed to have replied, 'Odds fish, you are a fool! James is at Brussels.' Thereafter Charles II 'could never bear the sight of [Griffin] again',[37] blaming him for the fact that Monmouth did then have to flee abroad. Old loyalties die hard, and his freedom to escape may not have been unconnected with the fact that it was another group of private gentlemen of the Life Guards who came across him as he was making his getaway. 'L. came to me at 11 at night,' Monmouth, captured after Sedgemoor, wrote in his diary, 'and told me that 29 [the plotters strange way of referring to the King] could never be brought to believe I knew anything of that part of the plot which concerned Rye House. I went to E. and was in some danger of being discovered by some of Oglethorpe's men, who met me accidentally at the back door of the garden.'[38] Major Theophilus Oglethorpe had commanded the advance guard under Monmouth with such success at Bothwell Bridge.

Of the other plotters, Monmouth's close friend Lord Grey, who had already challenged the Duke of Albemarle to a duel and crossed Patrick Sarsfield, later to be one of the Life Guards' best-known officers, got his guards drunk and escaped to Europe; he lived to command Monmouth's cavalry at Sedgemoor. Lord Russell and Algernon Sidney were both executed, escorted to the scaffold by the Life Guards. Their executions were possibly unnecessary and did nothing for the Stuarts' reputation. The Rye House Plot was always seen for what it was, an amateur affair that had no chance of success – characteristics that also marked Monmouth's subsequent attempt to claim the throne in 1685. Russell's and Sidney's deaths made a deep and unpleasant impact on the Protestant squirearchy, which they would remember four years later.

Chapter Three

THE TANGIER HORSE

By 1685, when Charles II died, his Guards were deeply unpopular with Parliament not only because they were seen as a tool of repressive, French-style absolutism, but also because they were expensive, badly behaved, and some of them had now shown themselves to be politically unreliable. These misgivings, freely aired by Shaftesbury and his Whig supporters, possibly masked a deeper fear, less easy to articulate.

Since 1660, the Stuarts had carefully developed a military bureaucracy, designed not only to administer their small force of permanent guards, the garrisons and the troops serving overseas, but also to enable the rapid expansion of the army as had been required for the two Dutch wars and for the subsequent deployment to Flanders in 1678. The administration of the navy, at the same time, had been much improved, and it too was now a well-organized, and vastly more expensive, standing force, as devotees of Pepys's diary will know only too well. Much of the inspiration behind these developments came from the Duke of York, the most influential figure in the army leadership after Albemarle's death, despite Monmouth's pretension to be Commander-in-Chief. By the time the Duke acceded to the throne as James II in 1685, he had built up a centralized army bureaucracy, based largely in the Horse Guards building, which provided a tolerably efficient administrative system, and which, though hampered by the problems of patronage and corruption, probably functioned as well as anything that has taken its place since. The fact that the Life Guards and The Blues were subject to these bureaucrats was not always welcome, but it provided the template for the administration of the English, and later the British, army; in other words, the Ministry of Defence was born alongside the Household Cavalry.

It was still, in many ways, a reflection of the Commonwealth system, although financial management had never been Cromwell's strong point. It was the Stuarts' Crown servants who refined the basic Commonwealth model, copying once more the reforms that Louis XIV introduced into the French army. There were effectively four main departments: the Secretary at War, the Paymaster General, the Commissary General of the Musters and the Judge

Old Horse Guards in the late seventeenth century. The building, opposite Whitehall Palace and the gateway to St James's Park, was the focal point for the dispersed troops of Life Guards who lived in nearby inns. The first mounted guard was positioned here to protect Charles II after the Restoration.

William Blathwayt, Secretary at War 1683–1704, who developed the military bureaucracy necessary to support the Stuart armies. Working from Horse Guards, Blathwayt's power centred on his control of the sale of commissions, the granting of leave and his authority for troop movements. His sons and grandson later joined the Life Guards.

Advocate General. A Scout Master General, responsible for intelligence, was added in 1664, and an Adjutant General in 1673.[1] These officials operated nominally under the Commander-in-Chief, which was a straightforward matter when Albemarle held the post, as his authority was absolute; he was trusted by Parliament and depended on by the King. After his death the system faltered. Monmouth was nominally Captain General, but was in effect too busy enjoying himself or campaigning to take much of an interest in administration. In reality it was the Duke of York, also Lord High Admiral, who thereafter assumed control. To that end he established an 'Army Board', which met for the first time on 5 August 1670. He chaired it himself, and Mathew Locke, the Secretary at War, took the minutes. Present were the Captains of the three troops of Life Guards (Monmouth, Sir Philip Howard and Duras), Oxford as Colonel of The Blues, together with Lord Craven as Colonel of the 2nd Foot Guards and Sir Charles Lyttelton, Colonel of the Duke of York's Lord High Admiral's Regiment, the prototype of the Royal Marines. Interestingly, there was no representation from the Ordnance, then functioning as a separate department responsible for the supply of armour and weapons. The Army Board spent most of their time debating how to prevent 'false musters' (of which more below) and do not appear to have met regularly thereafter, particularly as the Duke of York's position became more difficult towards the end of the 1670s.

Consequently it was the Secretary at War who ran the day-to-day administration of the army. It was he who devised and signed the movement orders of the troops based, probably, on fairly scant guidance from the court and probably rather more on his own intuition, liaison with local authorities and the realization that even The Blues needed to move regularly to prevent too familiar relationships with locals, many of whom would also object to the burden of having troops billeted on them for too long. Interestingly, his carefully worded instructions, of which thousands survive,[2] always placed troops under the command of local magistrates; this may have been a precaution against the military playing for power, as in 1659, or it may have reflected the Parliamentary fear that the army should always be subject to civil law. Bearing in mind that the Secretary was a royal, as opposed to a Parliamentary servant, and a civilian as opposed to a military appointment, it established a valuable precedent whereby troops in Britain are subject to the common law in the manner in which they conduct operations (as opposed to their individual conduct off duty, as discussed earlier).

Getting orders to the Life Guards in London was relatively easy as these did not vary greatly from day to day and were largely decided by the routine of the court. It was more complicated for the widely dispersed Blues, and a system of 'orderly men' was developed whereby each troop maintained two 'orderly', or in other words reliable, soldiers who were not inclined to get drunk, at two specified pubs in Whitehall, the Chequer and Star Inns. Their job was to relay the carefully worded orders from the Secretary's office to wherever their troop was based. These specified not only where the troop was to move, but also what route it was to take, and, working from a master list of 'approved' inns formalized in 1686,[3] where it was to stay en route. A typical move of a troop of The Blues from Hounslow Heath to Northampton, for example, had them covering approximately 10 miles per day, stopping at Barnet, St Albans and Hatfield on the first night, then Dunstable, then Stony Stratford, arriving in Northampton five days later. As the army expanded the system was extended to other regiments, and proved remarkably reliable, even during the rapid expansion of 1678 and what amounted to a contemporary version of a general mobilization as necessitated by Monmouth's landings in 1685. There was no operational role for Oxford or a regimental headquarters' staff, and The Blues did not have an adjutant until 1684, when it became apparent prior to a royal review on Putney Heath that the regiment had for the twenty-three years of its existence been little more than a series of independent troops. This officer's role was, yet again, a direct imitation of Louis XIV's Maison Militaire du Roi, hence the French title for the post.

There were three highly distinguished holders of the office of Secretary at War during Charles II's reign, of whom the last, William Blathwayt, who was in office from August 1683 until 1704, was perhaps the greatest. He was responsible for instituting many of the administrative procedures which endured for generations, and developed the power of his office so that he came to exercise fairly tight control on the sale of commissions, officers' leave – except that of the Life Guards – and, critically, regimental seniority. This was important not just because of the connected issues of pride and position but because the most recently raised regiments tended to be disbanded the soonest, with the consequent devaluing of commissions for which the holders might have paid a considerable amount of money. One of the reasons why commissions in the Life Guards and The Blues were so valued, apart from their prestige and the close association with the court, was because it was clear that neither regiment was ever going to be disbanded, making them a very sound investment. This was something of which Blathwayt, who had himself purchased his position from his predecessor, Mathew Locke, would have been keenly aware. It was the financial implications of regimental seniority, rather than the more romantic notion of jealousy and position, that made this such an important issue. Furthermore, those in the more senior regiments were more likely to survive any action. Since the civil wars, regiments disbursed into battle from a marching formation, turning right or left in turn. So the regiment at the front of a march always found itself on the right flank, the second regiment on the left, and the most junior regiments, in other words those last in the march order, took up the middle – usually the most dangerous position. The obvious precedence of the Life Guards ensured the superiority of the cavalry over the infantry, something that the social status they had achieved in the civil wars had already ensured.

The Commissary General of the Musters acted as the Chief of Staff to the Secretary at War, being responsible for the organization of regiments and for supervising the raising and disbanding of those units needed in 1667, 1673 and 1678. His recruiting instructions were fairly vague. It was particularly difficult for infantry regiments, who frequently had to resort to press gangs, much as the navy did. It was a problem for neither the Life Guards nor The Blues, both of which had a queue of candidates willing to purchase places. Both regiments recruited all over the British Isles, rather than in specific geographical areas, as most other regiments did. Annoyingly, we do not have detailed nominal roles until the next century, so we know little of individual soldiers, but we can deduce matters indirectly. There was, for example, no age limit. The civil war veterans were largely kept on the books and were paid until they died, providing them with a form of pension. Neither was it uncommon for them to stay on the books even after they were dead. As early as 1663, Charles II expressed his annoyance to Lord Gerard that so many dead men remained on the books of the King's Troop. The extra pay was, of course, forming part of Gerard's illicit income (see p. 30). Frequent attempts were made to clamp down on these 'false musters', although in particular cases false musters were authorized for soldiers who had given particularly valuable service. We find Blathwayt, for example, writing in 1689 to Marlborough, who was then Commander-in-Chief, requesting that a 'Mr Henry Wood who was a real sufferer in the time of King Charles the first and has served ever since ye restauration in the Horse Guards [Life Guards] and Royal Regiment of Horse [Blues] being become thorrough Age and infirmity unable to perform his duty, was by the late King's order allowed duty free upon the Muster Rolls.'[4]

The rudiments of a pension system had in fact been in operation since the time of Elizabeth I. Every time the Stuart army expanded after 1660 there was, for example, an allowance made by the Commissary General for Pension Payments, producing pension rates varying between 6d. and 2s. per day depending on rank and service. In the Life Guards and The Blues, where most officers had private means, the system did not always apply, although a system for providing lump sums for widows and orphans existed. The system for ordinary soldiers in The Blues was less satisfactory. They could either apply to stay on the musters, as with the aged Henry Wood, or else apply to their home parish for subsistence, though this was hardly ever generous. An Invalid Fund was also established to provide for those injured, and 8d. from every £1 of pay was deducted to pay for this. Finally, in 1681 Kilmainham Hospital was set up in Dublin to provide for military pensioners, followed by the Royal Hospital in Chelsea three years later. This was financed by a levy of 1s. per £1 on the sale of commissions, and soldiers admitted were allowed to continue to receive one-third of their pay. It may have been a rudimentary system but by contemporary standards it was adequate, and is again evidence that even by 1685 the administration of the English army was not quite as arbitrary and chaotic as popular history would have us believe, a theme that recurs fairly consistently as this story unfolds.

Pay itself was the responsibility of the Paymaster General. There were five of these officials in Charles II's reign, the most famous of whom was Sir Stephen Fox, in office from 1661 until 1676. Although he became immensely rich in that time, there is evidence that the system he operated was basically effective. When the Treasury was late in issuing him with necessary funds, he simply borrowed the money from himself and charged a healthy rate of interest. Consequently pay appears to have been issued to regiments fairly regularly, something that certainly did not happen in the navy. Any problems tended to occur at the regimental level between the colonel and his civilian agent – men like Carr – employed as paymasters. The Treasury issued the money to Fox, who duly passed it on to the Life Guards and Blues roughly every six to eight weeks. The colonels deducted official 'off reckonings' for clothing and equipment, which amounted to about 6d. per day, before passing on the remainder to the troop officers for distribution. From this the soldiers had to pay for their food and accommodation and provide for their horse. Given that a private gentleman was paid 4s. per day, he actually received 3s. 6d., whereas a soldier in The Blues, on 2s. 6d. per day, received 2s. – though for The Blues, being rarely in London, food and accommodation were cheaper. The provision of horses posed more of a problem. It became apparent that expecting soldiers to provide their own was unsustainable and the regiments started to build up troop funds for horse purchase. Deductions were again made for this, although they were not formalized until the 1730s.

This increasingly efficient bureaucracy was not, of course, just there for the Life Guards, The Blues and the Foot Guards. Its principal function was, in many ways, to enable the rapid expansion and contraction of the entire army in time of war. There were also two other important elements of the army that it had to administer. The first of these were the permanent garrisons, exempted from the reductions of 1660. They equated approximately to the modern Territorial Army and, interesting as they are, they are not really relevant to this story. However, the second element, the management of the overseas garrisons, most certainly is, for it was from Tangier that the third component regiment of what today forms the Household Cavalry was drawn.

This third component started life as the Tangier Horse. Tangier was given to Charles II by his father-in-law as part of Catherine of Braganza's dowry, along with Bombay, which, in the long run, was an altogether more profitable gift. The Portuguese were probably fairly relieved to be rid of Tangier, despite its value as a base from which to dominate the Mediterranean. Relations with the local Moorish kings had not been easy, and it was a price worth paying for English support in Portugal's long-running war of independence from Spain. Charles II duly sent several regiments, grouped into a brigade, to assist the Portuguese. Those Protestant officers who were forced on The Blues in 1667 came from this brigade, when they disbanded. For the English, Tangier seemed a valuable addition. Admiral Blake had already shown under the Commonwealth what an English fleet operating in the Mediterranean could achieve, and the opportunity to get one over the Dutch in Mediterranean trade was very popular in the City. There was also a growing problem with Barbary pirates intercepting English merchant ships and taking their white-skinned crew and passengers back to sell as slaves in the North African markets. For over sixty years these attacks had become increasingly daring and raids on coastal villages around the British Isles were not uncommon. On 20 June 1631, for example, two Algerian galleys had crept into Baltimore harbour in County Cork and taken virtually the whole population back to the slave market in Algiers. (As a satisfactory, though totally unconnected, aside it is pleasing to note that one of the most attractive girls, an O'Driscoll, was sold to a local bey or chieftain and stabbed him in the middle of his seraglio.) By 1661 there were estimated to be 30,000 British slaves in Algiers alone and there was considerable pressure on the Council to do something about it.

Occupation of Tangier required a garrison. No sooner was Charles's marriage treaty signed than Pepys's patron, Lord Sandwich, who as Edward Montague had been the Commonwealth General-at-Sea, sailed into the harbour to prevent a Dutch or Spanish coup de main while troops were assembled. Charles II appointed Henry Mordaunt, Earl of Peterborough, as Governor and instructed him to raise a force. He wanted 500 Horse, but the Council baulked at the cost, so he was limited to 100. His commission from the King was signed on 6 September 1661,[5] and on 21 October his new troop paraded for the first time on St George's Fields, which ran along what is now Kennington Road in London. There were a hundred 'well appointed' horsemen, wearing long, collarless, full-skirted scarlet coats over doublets of buff, leather breeches and high boots reaching above the knee. They had low-crowned, broad-brimmed hats, and were issued with fronts and backs and 'pots'. Each carried a brace of pistols, a carbine and a long straight sword. It was, in other words, a re-created troop of Cromwellian horse, and any uniform less suited to the steamy heat of Tangier would be hard to find. We do not know in detail where the 100 men and horses came from, but many seem to have been recruited direct from the remaining troops in Dunkirk and Flanders, in other words those who did not go off to serve in Portugal and who were not incorporated in the Guards regiments in England. Although there would have been no shortage of volunteers from among Cromwell's disbanded troopers, most of these had now been paid off for over a year and would have dispersed. To get a force of the necessary size together in four weeks suggests that at least a proportion of them were already serving. The Major, Tobias Bridges, who was effectively the commanding officer, whilst Peterborough and his successors as Governor became colonels by virtue of their position, had served with the Commonwealth forces in Flanders and was an experienced officer. It is likely that he brought some of his existing soldiers with him.

They sailed in three ships on 15 January 1662, together with three regiments of foot, making a total force of 3,000, and arrived on 29 January. The remaining Portuguese promptly fled. It must have been a slightly forlorn party who put into the North African shore. Most had been fighting for some time, and by volunteering to serve in what would inevitably be a dangerous and unhealthy post they were, in effect, admitting that the opportunity to live a normal life had passed them by. The Tangier Horse generally behaved better than the three infantry regiments over the coming years, but even so it suffered from its fair share of drunkenness and poor discipline. Given the environment in which the men found themselves, this is hardly surprising. The local Moorish King, Abdul Ghailan, had not been consulted on the change of ownership and, unsurprisingly, he took considerable exception to it. The next twenty years were a continual struggle not only against disease and dreadful administration, but also against the King's skilful local forces who had recently bettered the Al Rashid dynasty of Morocco, leaving him free to confront the English against whom he promptly declared a jihad. His Arab troops, reinforced by local Berbers, were well armed and equipped, and specialized in irregular tactics from which the English eventually learned quite a lot that would prove useful in the Irish wars of the 1690s. By the time Ghailan mounted his first attack in May the Tangier Horse had already lost twenty horses, and faced him in very reduced circumstances. It was a bloody encounter, with the infantry losing 350 men after they fell for an Arab ploy of pretending to withdraw, luring them from their lines into a trap wherein they were surrounded and slaughtered: they blamed the Horse for not supporting them properly. Subsequently a second troop was raised, mounted on imported Portuguese horses and manned by converted infantrymen, but it proved unsustainable.

Peterborough's task was, therefore, a formidable one. Not only did he have to fight Abdul Ghailan, but he also had to start work on an artificial sea wall – a mole – to enable shipping to use the harbour, and to prise funds from a reluctant Council in England. He was not equal to it, and retired with a generous pension of £1,000 per year in May 1663. The altogether more capable Lord Teviot, an experienced soldier and competent administrator, replaced him as Governor and Colonel of the troop. He emerges as an attractive and sympathetic character, and is one of the first of many subsequent British public servants to make a real effort to understand the new country to which he was posted. He studied and respected Islam – something of a first for a generation who regarded many of their fellow-Christians as beyond redemption – and learned the native tactics. He also quickly got to grips with what had become a shambolic and dispirited garrison. The fortifications were extended and improved, and when Ghailan attacked again in June he was repulsed, not least because Teviot had noticed that the Arabs used barking dogs to alert them to

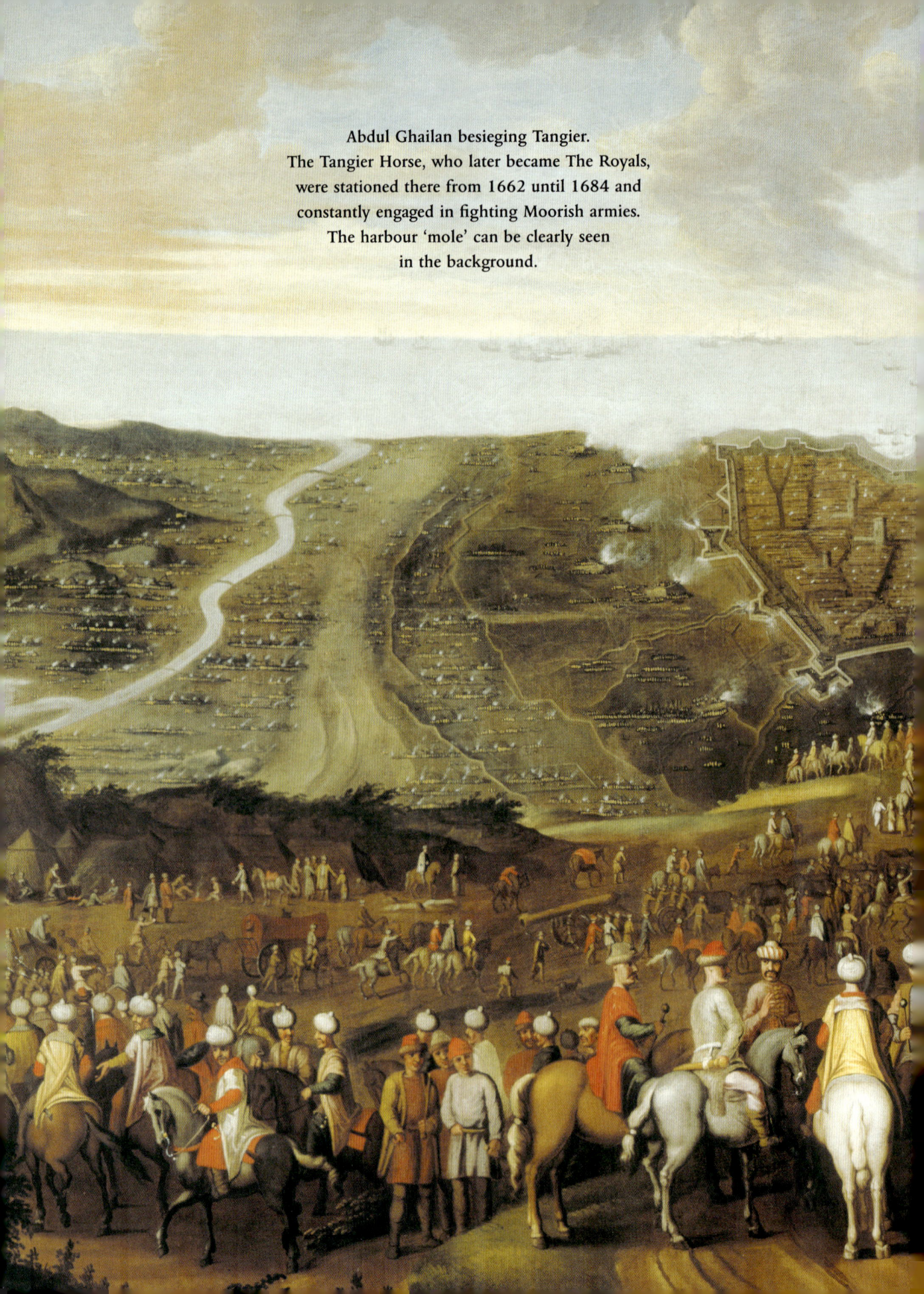

Abdul Ghailan besieging Tangier.
The Tangier Horse, who later became The Royals,
were stationed there from 1662 until 1684 and
constantly engaged in fighting Moorish armies.
The harbour 'mole' can be clearly seen
in the background.

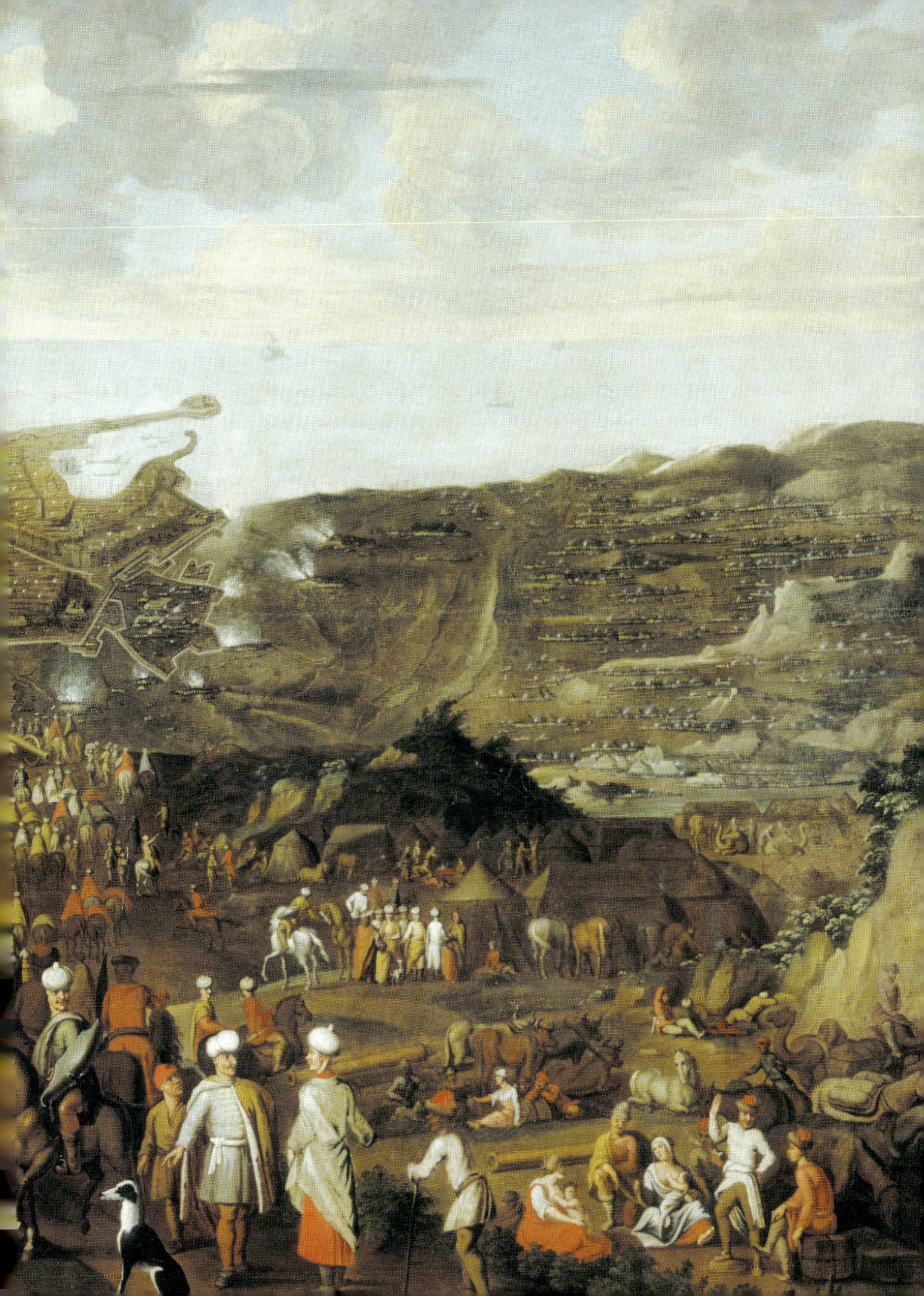

his movements. He copied the idea, using the same principle as the Romans with their geese. He further avoided another of Ghailan's traps, so the Arab reserves were themselves pounded by artillery, instead of cutting up vulnerable infantry. To cap it all, Teviot had the bodies of the enemy dead washed and sent back to Ghailan in clean linen.

The result was a truce, with a welcome limit of 10 miles agreed from the city walls to give the English officers an area in which to hunt and to start some limited local trading. Teviot then returned to England, forcing £30,000 for the mole out of the Council and bringing back 500 extra men, of whom 100 went to the Tangier Horse. They were now subdivided into three smaller troops, with Teviot as Colonel of one, Bridges of the second and Edward Witham of the third. Teviot also brought out two new young officers from his native Scotland, Cornets Mackenzie and Leslie. It was to prove a brief high point in the fortunes of the regiment, now 150 strong, particularly when Witham foiled a further attack by Ghailan in February 1664 by sallying out with his troop and seizing the King's famous red standard without the loss of a single man. His success was not destined to last, however. In May Ghailan attacked again in force. This time he got the better of Teviot, successfully luring him into one of his favourite traps. He separated him and the infantry from the horse, and Teviot and 400 soldiers were killed. It marked the beginning of one of the lowest points in the garrison's fortunes, even though renewed fighting with the Al Rashids meant that Ghailan was unable to follow up his victory.

The next ten years are notable for a succession of ineffective Governors, reductions in the garrison to save money, arrears of pay and almost constant drunkenness. By 1668 the Tangier Horse were reduced to thirty soldiers, and the more able officers like Witham returned home. Lord Middleton, who took over in October 1669, had made an attempt to restore morale, but, unable to secure funds from England, he lost heart and, in 1675, died after falling drunk from his horse. Only the infighting between the Al Rashids and Ghailan prevented a total Moorish victory, but by 1673 a new rival, Malis Ismail, had eleminated them both. Lord Inchiquin, who took over from Middleton, proved unequal to him. In September 1675 Ismail surprised a foraging party escorted by 100 foot and eighteen of the Tangier Horse under Mackenzie. All were killed except Mackenzie, who was captured and sold into slavery for a year. He was eventually ransomed for 400 guns and resumed command of the troop in 1676, later returning with them to England. He is, as far as it is possible to ascertain, the only officer in the regiment's history to have been enslaved. Inchiquin, showing doubtful leadership qualities, promptly cut the troops' pay by 6d. a day after this debacle, and they were not sorry to see him return to England in 1676.

Inchiquin left the garrison quite literally in a state of mutiny, a situation that still pertained when his successor, Lord Fairborne, arrived. He had the ringleaders shot but, with the Tangier Horse now down to an effective strength of ten horses, faced a hopeless situation. Securing a truce with Ismail, he sent Mackenzie to buy Spanish horses, which were better suited to the climate. He also secured recruits from England, so that when the truce ended in 1678 and Ismail attacked in force he was just able to hold the town. This attack saw one of the first uses of chemical weapons, Ismail's so-called 'stinck pots', which the Arabs threw into the English fortifications and which 'upon its breaking makes a suddaine flame and from them proceeds such a stinck that men are suffocated with it'.[6] But Fairborne realized that he could not hold out without major reinforcements, and in London the Government finally agreed a viable force to defeat Ismail. A substantial number of troops were dispatched under the experienced Lord Ossory, including several officers who had fought in France and three new troops to reinforce the Tangier Horse, commanded by Charles Nedby, John Coy and Thomas Langston, all of whom had served in Sir Henry Jones's Regiment of Light Horse at Maastricht and consequently probably had soldiers with strong Catholic sympathies. Being short of horses, they purchased some from both the Life Guards and The Blues, paying £20 for the former and £17 for the latter, which is perhaps a comment on the standard of horseflesh in the respective regiments. In addition Fairborne acquired a further 200 Spanish horses, although their feet rotted on the boat from Spain and they could not be shod for several months.

Thus reinforced, Fairborne mounted a major offensive on 27 October 1680. It was particularly well planned, with Mackenzie leading the Tangier Horse in a diversionary attack and sailors from the fleet used as auxiliaries, mounted on draft horses from the still unfinished mole. Although they lost 500 out of their 3,000 men, it was a complete victory. The Horse lost three officers and seventeen men, and forty horses. It was to be the last battle in Tangier. Although Ismail was comprehensively defeated, Charles II had run out of money and a hostile Parliament was not minded to support the increasingly expensive garrison. In July 1683 a Royal Commission was dispatched to Tangier, led by Lord Dartmouth and with Samuel Pepys as a member, to decide what to do with it.

Pepys's account of his visit, to which he devoted a separate volume of his diary, reveals much of what life was like for the troops during the twenty-odd years of garrison life. Though not Pepys at his most vivid, lacking the immediacy of his earlier volumes, his account does give us some idea of the stifling heat in October, the discomfort of being bitten by endless insects, and the real boredom of garrison life. He took a violent and understandable dislike to Colonel Sir Percy Kirke, the garrison commander – although, typically, he took a fancy to his wife. Kirke he portrays as a drunk and a bully, owing £1,500 to traders in the town and causing 'a sergeant to be tied to a post, then beaten by himself as long as he could do it; then by another; and all for bidding a servant of his to go to his mistress, Mrs. Collier'. 'To show how little he makes of drunkenness', Pepys continues '. . . I have seen, as he has been walking with me in the street, a soldier reel on him as drunk as a dog . . . He hath only laughed at him and cried "The fellow hath got a good morning's draft already!"' Furthermore Kirke was said 'to have got his wife's sister with child . . . And that while he is with his whores at his little bathing house which he has furnished with jade a-purpose there, his wife, whom he keeps by in awe, sends for her gallants and plays the jade by herself at home.'

Despite these unattractive sybaritic tendencies, Pepys's account of Kirke's brutality rings true. Tangier was under martial law, and whereas in England soldiers could only be sentenced to more severe punishments by a civil magistrate, in Tangier the Governor could order executions. Theft and insubordination were punishable by flogging, 'riding the wooden horse' or imprisonment and during the life of the garrison successive Governors made good use of all three. Pepys was also scandalized by the scale of false musters. Kirke claimed for 700 out of a total strength of 2,700, extreme even by Lord Gerard's standards. In addition he found the garrison militarily inefficient. 'To the fields over Fountain Fort', he notes on 10 October, 'the first time; seeing the Moors' sentries and people rating at the stockades. The folly of this place, being overlooked everywhere!' The Horse could only mount eighty-two of their 194 soldiers for the parade to welcome Dartmouth, which was indicative of how quickly things had deteriorated, even so soon after Fairborne's victory. Dartmouth's instructions were plain, and it was hardly surprising that the decision was taken to evacuate. 'It is', Pepys noted in conclusion, 'a place of the World I would last send a young man to but to Hell.'

The remaining soldiers of the Tangier Horse embarked on the ship *Charles* on 1 February 1684. Furious that the miserly Government had ordered their horses to be left behind, they were forced to sell them in Spain at a far cheaper rate than they would have commanded in England. Dartmouth supported them, noting they could buy two or three dragoons' horses apiece in England for the value of their Spanish horses, which may have said much for the quality of dragoons' mounts. It does, however, also say something about their future employment, for the decision had previously been taken to reorganize the remaining four troops (Mackenzie's, Nedby's, Langston's and Coy's) into dragoons, to be the core of a new regiment being formed with Lord Churchill as Colonel. Hard as it was to leave their horses behind, the future must have suddenly looked considerably brighter for many of the men, with employment under an already well-established Colonel and on good rates of pay.

How many of the Tangier Horse were Catholic? We do not know, but certainly a fair number of those who had originally been in Sir Henry Jones's Light Horse were. Parliament always suspected the Tangier garrison of being a hotbed of Catholicism, and Pepys makes reference to a Catholic church and being shown round by a 'Popish Friar', presumably not there to minister to the Moors. This strong Catholic tendency was further complicated by the fact that many of the men, having served overseas for so long, now saw themselves as professional soldiers, whose primary loyalty was to the King as their employer rather than to a Parliamentary idea of Anglican-based Englishness which favoured the landed classes and changed to suit the prevailing wind. It was a combination of these pressures that would cause the new regiment so much trouble four years later.

Two new troops were raised in England and by 1 May 1684 the new regiment, called 'Our Owne Royall Regiment of Dragoones', was formally taken on to the establishment with six troops of fifty men each. New equipment was issued and a proper regimental staff added, including a major, an adjutant, a surgeon, a quartermaster and a gunsmith. Each troop had a captain, a lieutenant, a cornet, a quartermaster, two sergeants, three corporals, two drummers and two 'Hautbois' or trumpeters. In addition each troop had a crimson standard with its own device, modelled on the symbols of successive English kings, depicted in gold. New red coats were issued, faced with blue, and the annual cost of each troop was estimated at £2,200, evidence of Churchill's careful administration. He was yet to reach the height of his power, but as a close friend of the Duke of York he had recently been ennobled, and successfully commanded operations in France under Turenne between 1672 and 1678. A similar mark of favour was that the Lieutenant Colonel was Lord Cornbury, grandson of Charles II's first Chancellor, and consequently nephew to the now deceased Duchess of York, mother of the future Queens Mary and Anne. Cornbury was destined to play a central, and somewhat bizarre, role in the events of the next three years, and because of both him and Churchill the new regiment would do so as well.

They were to have several changes of name during their long life, but all were variations on the theme of 'Royal' and 'Dragoons' – the King's Own Royal Regiment of Dragoons, the Royal Regiment of Dragoons, the 1st Royal Dragoons, and finally the Royal Dragoons. However, in the army they were always known simply as The Royals, which is how we shall refer to them from now on.

Dragoons were mounted infantry who used horses to move around the battlefield but fought on their feet when they got to the point of action. They rode smaller horses than proper horse regiments, ostensibly so that they were easier to get on and off, but also because they were cheaper. Dragoons had been used very effectively in the civil wars, attracting some of the most able soldiers and being well represented in Cromwell's order of battle. His first regiment, commanded by Colonel Okey, was 1,000 strong, and it was they who put the King's Life Guard to flight at Naseby. Okey himself went on to be one of Cromwell's senior officers and was eventually executed in 1662. Socially and militarily it was difficult to know whether dragoons should be classed as Horse or Foot. They were paid less than the Horse, with a private soldier receiving 1s. 4d. per day as opposed to 2s. 6d., but that was a lot more than the 10d. which an infantry private received. In addition The Royals had to provide all their own horses, which put them in a class above the average

By 1685, when he died, Charles II had isolated the opposition so that
the throne passed peacefully to his Catholic brother James, Duke of York.
During his last parliament, which met in Oxford, The Blues deployed
as a regiment for the first time to deter trouble.

infantryman, though officers were not required to purchase their commissions on formation. Blathwayt came up with a typically British compromise, saying that when they were in the field with their horses they should be counted as a regiment of Horse, and take precedence over all other regiments except the Life Guards and The Blues, but when they were in barracks they should be counted as infantry and take precedence as the senior regiment of that arm. It was all fairly meaningless. Eventually all dragoon regiments became fully-fledged cavalry regiments and The Royals took precedence accordingly. There had in fact been other regiments of dragoons created during the various army expansions in the 1660s and 70s, even one called the Royal Dragoons, but none had survived parliamentary scrutiny in England, although in 1681 a regiment had been raised in Scotland. This was afterwards known as the 2nd Dragoons or the Scots Greys, not after the subsequent colour of their horses but after the drab grey material chosen by Sir Thomas Dalyell for their uniform in preference to the Stuart red. What was different about them, and now Churchill's new regiment, was that they were destined to be permanent, and to fight regularly alongside each other in the coming centuries.

Their first public appearance was at the Putney Heath Review in September 1684, and they took their place as the third most senior regiment in the army, after the Life Guards and The Blues. It was the first time that all three of the regiments which today comprise the Household Cavalry paraded together. What a change it must have been for Mackenzie, the professional soldier from Scotland who had followed Lord Teviot out to Tangier twenty years before, had been captured and enslaved by the Moors and seen his soldiers decimated by disease, by his own Government and enemy action, to find himself now at the head of the 3rd Troop (after the Colonel's and Lieutenant Colonel's – the Major, Hugh Sutherland, does not appear to have had a troop). From Putney Heath the Royals moved to Berkshire, to be engaged in much the same policing duties as The Blues, but the death of Charles II in February 1685 saw them being recalled to London. It was an event which was to bring about a very considerable change for all three regiments.

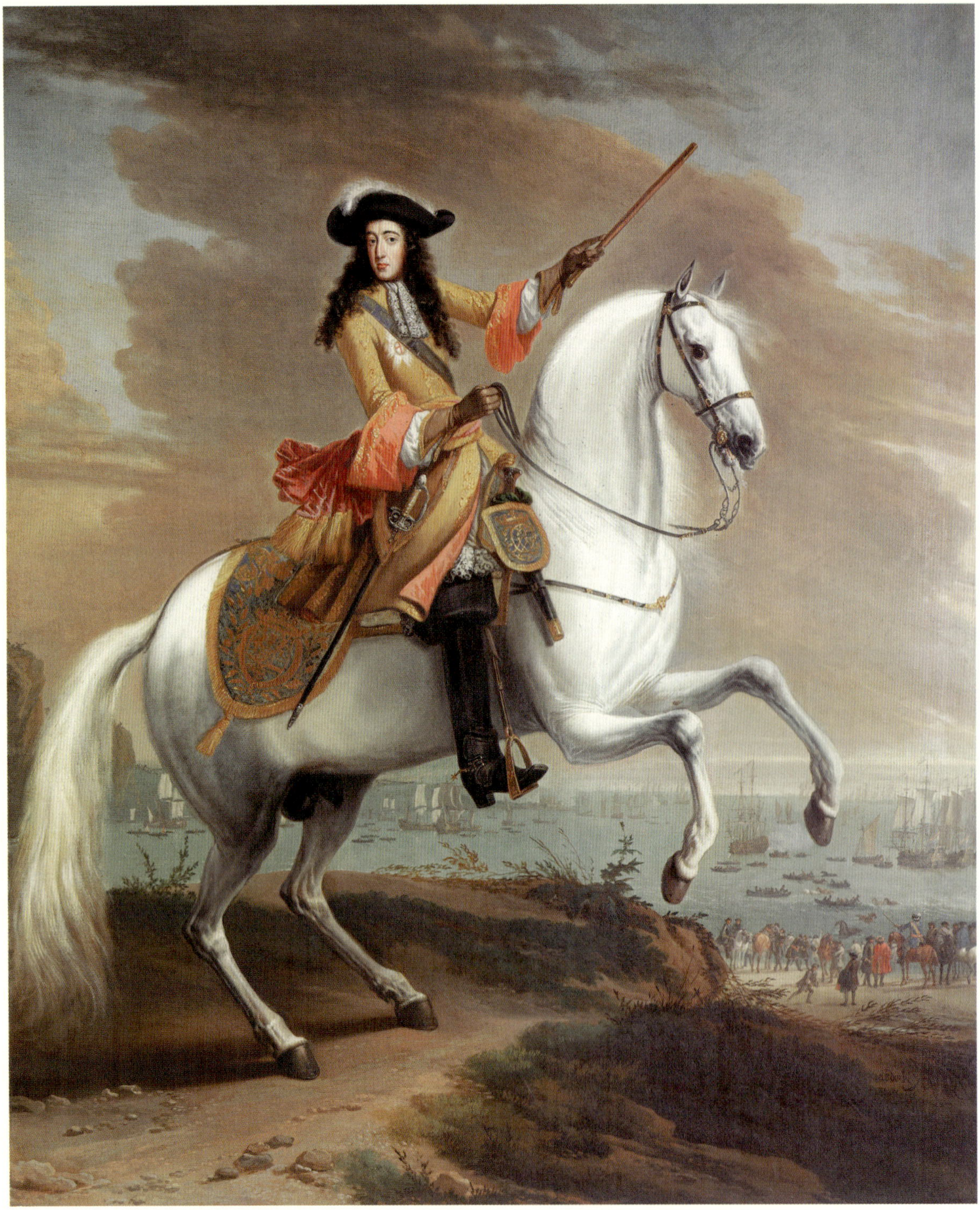

Part Two

DIVIDED LOYALTIES

1685–1701

Chapter Four

SEDGEMOOR AND JAMES II'S REFORMS

THE NIGHT OF SUNDAY, 5 July 1685 was a memorable if uncomfortable one for Sir Francis Compton. Promoted to Lieutenant Colonel of The Blues only four days before – Oxford himself had wanted to command but the King thought it more important he continued his duties as Lord Lieutenant in Essex – Compton was now commanding 100 soldiers of his own regiment and fifty from The Royals, as part of a cavalry screen deployed to give early warning of any move by Monmouth and his rebel forces out of Bridgwater, a few miles to his front. His screen was centred on the small Somerset village of Chedzoy, in the middle of Sedgemoor, a wet, barren area crossed by deep drainage ditches called 'rhynes'. A mile to his left, covering the rough track that led south out of Bridgwater towards Westonzoyland, was a second outpost of forty private gentlemen of Captain Upcott's 2nd Troop of Life Guards. Between them forty musketeers from the Foot Guards manned the walls of an old sheepfold, so placed as to provide a refuge for the cavalry if they were surprised. Left again, and several miles to the south, Captain Coy's Troop of The Royals secured the crossing over the River Parrett at Barrow Bridge, a route by which Monmouth could outflank the Royalist army. Between Compton's screen and Bridgwater itself, a mobile patrol of Life Guards under Major Theophilus Oglethorpe, a Yorkshire Catholic who had previously served with Sir Henry Jones's Horse in France and as a Captain with the Tangier Horse, and who was now Major of the 2nd Troop, probed north-east of the town to give early warning of any attempt by the rebels to break out towards Bristol.

Behind the screen, to the south, six battalions of Royalist infantry, three of Foot Guards and three from Tangier, were camped in tents, their front protected by a particularly deep ditch, the Bussex Rhyne, which consequently meant that it lay between them and Compton's force. To the left of the infantry was the

---

Page 84. William of Orange landing at Torbay, 1688.

Royalist artillery, whilst behind them, in the village of Westonzoyland, was the headquarters of the Earl of Feversham, the newly appointed Commander-in-Chief, whom we last saw as Lord Duras leading the Life Guard contingent under Monmouth in France ten years previously (see p. 56). He was now considered even more irresolute, having been hit on the head by a falling timber during the Temple Fire of 1679. Still Captain of the 3rd Troop of Life Guards, he had marched from London with a composite group of fifty private gentlemen and twenty Horse Grenadiers from each of the three troops on 20 June.[1] With him now was the rest of the Horse. This consisted of six troops of The Blues (with the 7th Troop forward with Compton and the 8th, Slingsby's, left behind in London escorting pay), the remainder of The Royals (less a few who were guarding the guns), and those Life Guards and Horse Grenadiers not deployed forward under Oglethorpe and Upcott.

The forthcoming battle was to be the first time that all three regiments were in action together. It was also only the third time that all eight troops of The Blues had operated as one regiment since 1661, the previous occasions being in 1681 when Blathwayt collected them to police the area around Oxford, where Charles II's last Parliament had met, and in 1684 at the Putney Heath review.

The Blues and The Royals had already been fighting in the West Country for three weeks. Four troops of The Blues who had been in the Home Counties – Wyndham's, Sandys', Littleton's and Parsons' – were ordered to form an advance force 'to be commanded by our Trusty and wellbeloved John Ld Churchill in all things according to the Rules and Discipline of War'.[2] On 15 June, two days after news of Monmouth's landing had reached London, they had been ordered to meet Churchill, rapidly promoted to Brigadier, in Salisbury, where they also met up with four troops of The Royals.[3] The Royals' other two troops, Mackenzie's and Langston's, had already been sent to Carlisle to assist in the suppression of Argyll's rebellion; timed to coincide with Monmouth's, this had been quickly put down and Argyll executed. The two troops left Waltham Abbey and Hoddesdon on 20 and 21 April and arrived in Carlisle on 10 and 12 May, covering a distance of 290 miles in twenty days, an average of 20 miles a day. It was an impressive piece of mobilization, which demonstrated the sophistication of Blathwayt's growing administrative machine in Whitehall.

Churchill pressed on to the West Country, leaving Feversham to bring up the main body of the infantry with the Life Guards and the remaining three troops of The Blues a few days later. Monmouth had landed at Lyme Regis on 11 June, and had made fairly good progress inland. James II and Blathwayt's initial reaction had been to send Albemarle, at that point still Commander-in-Chief, to assume command of the local militia to confront Monmouth's forces at Axminster but this was not a success. The militia, many of whose colleagues had already sided with Monmouth, refused to fight, and Monmouth got to Axminster first. He wrote to Albemarle, cheekily signing himself 'James R', and urged his erstwhile drinking partner to join him. Albemarle refused, but without troops could do nothing until Churchill arrived. He withdrew, while Monmouth proceeded to Taunton, intending to take Bristol.

On 21 June Churchill reached Chard by way of Sherborne and Yeovil, and learned that Monmouth had already made for Taunton. If there was a campaign plan, it seems to have been to prevent Monmouth taking Bristol and heading north, where he could reach the strongly Protestant areas of Cheshire and possibly join with Argyll's forces. Consequently Churchill's immediate aim was to discover the whereabouts of Monmouth's forces. To that end he dispatched a troop of The Blues under Lieutenant Philip Munnocks towards Taunton. They came across some of Monmouth's Horse at Ashill and Munnocks was killed, thus becoming the regiment's first recorded war casualty. Both The Blues and The Royals then kept pace with Monmouth's force as it slowly made its way to Bridgwater and then on to Shepton Mallet, harassing the stragglers, reporting back their movements and preventing reinforcement.

Meanwhile Feversham, in an unusual fit of energy, had reached Bristol with the main body of the troops on 23 June, thus blocking Monmouth's route north over the River Avon. With Churchill on his eastern flank, and his route north blocked, Monmouth was now effectively trapped against the Bristol Channel. To have any chance of success he had to break out across the Avon and so he made for Keynsham, a few miles east of Bristol, where there was a bridge. He reached it on 25 June, taking Feversham by surprise, and that night his cavalry camped north of the river. However, his inexperienced officers failed to get sufficient troops across the Avon to hold the bridge, and they neglected to post sentries, taking advantage of comfortable beds in the town instead. Feversham was now aware of Monmouth's forces in the area, but not of their exact location. He sent Major Oglethorpe, who had been scouting on the flank of the army, with a mixed party of Life Guards, Horse Grenadiers – which included Patrick Sarsfield – and Blues to scout and report back. Oglethorpe rode straight into Keynsham that night, unaware that the rebels held it. His troops, led by Lieutenant Parker and the Horse Grenadiers, were in the town's centre before realizing with a shock that they were surrounded. In the confusion, and with many of Monmouth's troops still asleep, Oglethorpe, who was following with the detachment of Blues, cut his way through to save Parker, and brought him out with only six casualties. Two men were killed, and four wounded, including Lord Newburgh who was shot in the stomach but survived, and Sarsfield who was wounded in the hand.

Monmouth jumped to the conclusion that Oglethorpe was the advance guard of Feversham's army, and thus failed to seize the advantage and push across the river and continue north. It was a mistake that was to cost him his campaign and subsequently his life. Turning south, he made for Bath, hoping to find it evacuated by Feversham. His expectation was fulfilled, but the townspeople shut the gates and shot his messenger. He continued further south,

The Right Honble LEWIS Earle of Feversham, Viscount Sondes, Baron of Holdenby & Throwley, Captain of his Maties first Troops of Guards, Lord of ye Bed-Chamber to ye King, Lieutent. Genll. of his Maties Armie, Knt of ye most noble Order of ye Garter, & Chamberlain to ye Queen Dowager.

J. Riley pinx. J. Smith ex. J. Beckett f.

Louis Duras, Earl of Feversham, a favourite of James II, who was
Colonel of the King's Troop of Life Guards and who commanded the royal forces
at Sedgemoor. His only claim to any military qualification was that
he was a nephew of the great French Marshal Turenne.

heading inexorably away from his areas of likely support, and Feversham, who had by now linked up with Churchill, caught up with him again at the village of Philip St Norton, between Bradford and Westbury. Here the Foot Guards bravely tried to force the rebels out of the village, but this time the rebels defended rather better, and the Foot Guards took over thirty casualties, needing Parker and Vaughan and their Horse Grenadiers to rescue them – sadly, there is no record as to whether they used their grenades. The Blues and The Royals both skirmished indecisively with Monmouth's horse outside the village, and by the late afternoon they had broken off in heavy rain. Monmouth escaped, making for Frome, while Feversham and the Royal army repaired to the comforts of Bradford. Oglethorpe, rapidly becoming the hero of this campaign, continued to shadow the rebels. At Frome Monmouth heard of the depressing failure of Argyll's rebellion and of an ambush of an anticipated supply of arms and ammunition by the now reinvigorated militia under Lord Pembroke. His heart must have been heavy as he retraced his route towards Bridgwater, the strongly puritan town that had received him so rapturously the week before, and which he reached on 3 July. En route his soldiers sacked Wells Cathedral, which did little to help their cause locally.

Climbing the tower of Bridgwater Church on the afternoon of Sunday, 5 July, Monmouth realized that even the snail-like Feversham had finally trapped him. No doubt urged on by Churchill, he had now brought the Royalist army from Bradford and Monmouth could see it clearly, to the east of the town, drawing up in positions across Sedgemoor. Churchill's cavalry dispositions meant that his routes north and south were cut off. The only possibility open to him was to cross the Royal lines, slip behind Feversham and try once again to break for the north. Encouraged by a local man, Robert Godfrey from Sutton Mallet, who both knew a short cut across the Bussex Rhyne and testified that the Royalist army was drunk, Monmouth resolved to slip out of Bridgwater under cover of darkness. His horse, under Lord Grey, would cut round Compton's post at Chedzoy, cross the rhyne and set fire to Westonzoyland as Feversham and his troops slept off their excesses. They would then turn back against the Royalist infantry, trapping them against the Bussex Rhyne and Monmouth's infantry, who would have come out of Bridgwater and drawn up, facing them, at first light. The plan was well conceived, and might have worked with well-trained troops. An officer in The Blues, writing in 1718, with a perspective that probably enabled him to relate events more truthfully than in the immediate aftermath, admitted that 'on Sunday night most of the officers were drunk and had no matter of apprehension of the enemy'.[4] Another first-hand account of the battle was written by Edward Dummer, a gunner with the artillery train, whose diary entry for 6 July records a supine mood 'and a preposterous confidence of ourselves with an undervaluing of the Rebells that many days before had made us make such tedious marches had put us into the worst circumstances of surprize'.[5]

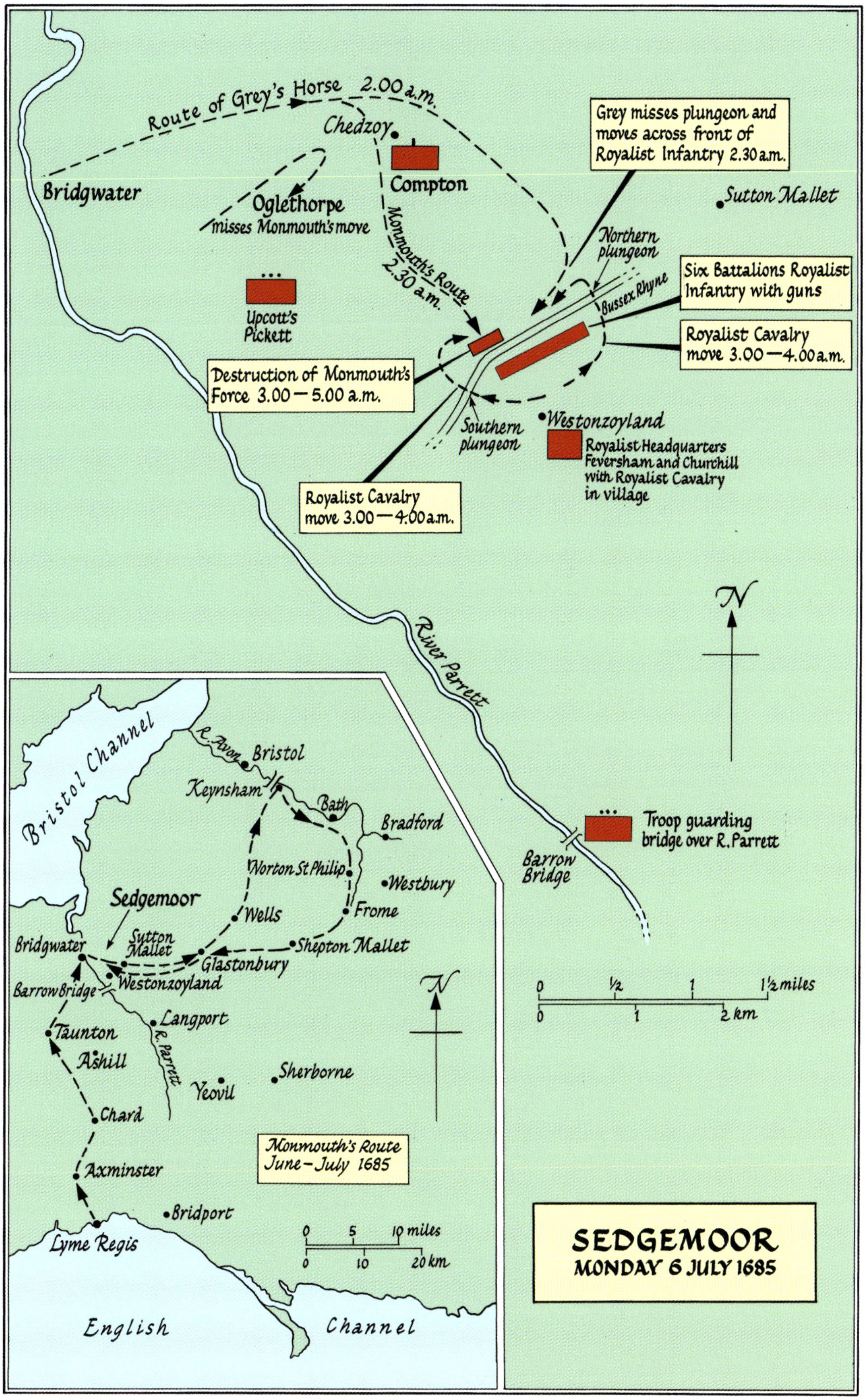

Route of Grey's Horse 2.00 a.m.
Chedzoy
Compton
Bridgwater
Oglethorpe
misses Monmouth's move
Monmouth's Route
2.30 a.m.
Grey misses plungeon and moves across front of Royalist Infantry 2.30 a.m.
Sutton Mallet
Northern plungeon
Bussex Rhyne
Six Battalions Royalist Infantry with guns
Royalist Cavalry move 3.00 — 4.00 a.m.
Upcott's Pickett
Destruction of Monmouth's Force 3.00 — 5.00 a.m.
Southern plungeon
Westonzoyland
Royalist Headquarters Feversham and Churchill with Royalist Cavalry in village
Royalist Cavalry move 3.00 — 4.00 a.m.
N
River Parrett
Troop guarding bridge over R. Parrett
Barrow Bridge
0 ½ 1 1½ miles
0 1 2 km
Bristol Channel
R. Avon
Bristol
Keynsham
Bath
Bradford
Norton St Philip
Westbury
Sedgemoor
Wells
Frome
Bridgwater
Sutton Mallet
Shepton Mallet
Glastonbury
Westonzoyland
Barrow Bridge
Langport
Taunton
R. Parrett
Ashill
Sherborne
Yeovil
Chard
Monmouth's Route June – July 1685
Axminster
Bridport
Lyme Regis
0 5 10 miles
0 10 20 km
English Channel
SEDGEMOOR
MONDAY 6 JULY 1685

The sad fact for Monmouth was that his army were almost totally untrained, poorly armed, and had only four light artillery pieces. He also had few experienced officers. For example, Lord Grey of Warke, who had been heavily implicated in the Rye House Plot and who had duelled with Patrick Sarsfield, commanded the cavalry. He had already fled in the face of the barely threatening militia near Bridport, and his disastrous command of the horse in the coming battle would ensure that Monmouth's plan would fail from the outset. The foot were mostly West Country puritans – Monmouth's choice of Dorset for his landfall had been intentional. West Countrymen were sufficiently frightened of James II's Catholicism to risk everything in rebellion, but, on top of inadequate weapons, there was no plan, or time, to train them.

Monmouth's campaign presumed that James II was so unpopular, and he, Monmouth, so well loved, that the country would immediately rise up to support him. In particular he thought that the army, especially the Life Guards, from loyalty, and The Blues, from conviction, would come over to him rather than fight for their Catholic King. With those two regiments on his side and the militia ambivalent, his rebellion might have succeeded. Monmouth seems to have misunderstood that his undoubted popularity and his creditable military performance in France and Scotland in the 1670s had been superseded by irritation at the Exclusion Crisis and by the incredibly inept Rye House Plot. The Life Guards, ironically from Oglethorpe's Troop, might then have allowed him to slip quietly away, but he should have noted rather better the behaviour of Colonel Griffin, the Silver Stick, who so infuriated Charles II by revealing that Monmouth was in hiding in London; loyalty to the Crown was a stronger tie than personal loyalty to a man who had been a partially successful Gold Stick.

Beyond that, Monmouth never presented as a credible candidate to the country at large. Although he had been in exile in Holland, William of Orange asked him to leave when James II succeeded, and he enjoyed no Dutch military support in his rebellion. William of Orange had no interest in upsetting his father-in-law at that stage, and actually sent troops to help him. Furthermore, by the summer of 1685 James II, though a Catholic, had not substantially altered the delicate religious status quo in England, and his heir remained his Protestant daughter, Mary. Any successful Protestant rebellion against the Stuarts would probably have sprung up at the time of Titus Oates and the Exclusion Crisis, when Shaftesbury's Whigs enjoyed so much popular support. It was the Life Guards who had helped Charles II defuse it then and, ironically, it was those same regiments that were now to frustrate Monmouth's ambition.

Nothing, therefore, could have been further from the staunchly Protestant conscience of Sir Francis Compton, as he drew his blue cloak around him that moonless and foggy Sunday night, than to side with Monmouth. Feversham had ridden up to see him and had left at 11 p.m., retiring to bed in Westonzoyland, confident that any rebel movement would be spotted by the ever-enthusiastic Oglethorpe or would run into his cavalry pickets. Early on the Monday morning Monmouth set out. Oglethorpe missed him, lingering too far from the town to see any movement clearly. Compton, whom Grey deliberately tried to bypass, nearly missed him too. Monmouth got most of his horse past them and down to the Bussex Rhyne and had almost succeeded, when, at 2 a.m., a shot rang out and alerted Compton. Some said later that a Monmouth supporter, Captain Hucker, realizing his interests would be best served by changing allegiance, fired it on purpose. The tail end of Grey's column clashed with Compton's forces. Compton was shot in the chest and handed over command to Captain Sandys, who immediately pursued Grey, inflicting several casualties before withdrawing to Westonzoyland. Grey, meanwhile, approaching the Bussex Rhyne, could not find the route that Godfrey had assured him would be easy to spot. Grey could have located it, had he taken more care, but instead he panicked and rode along the rhyne across the face of the now thoroughly alert Royalist infantry, six battalions of whom stood in line. The rebels' horse promptly broke and fled towards Bridgwater, led by Grey himself, just as Monmouth led his infantry into position as planned.

Feversham was also now finally awake, and showed sound military sense in dispatching the Life Guards, Horse Grenadiers and Captain Adderley's Troop of The Blues round to the left of his infantry, to cross the rhyne by the next ford and to come round on Monmouth's right. At the same time he sent the ubiquitous Oglethorpe with Upcott's detachment, who had sensibly withdrawn once they realized that they were outflanked, and Sandys around the other end, so that they came round the right of the Royalist line and were positioned to hit Monmouth from his left.

Meanwhile Churchill took direct command of the infantry, who were suffering serious casualties from Monmouth's small field guns, which were firing at the Royal Scots, the Dumbartonshire regiment. With great difficulty in the dark, Churchill brought up three Royalist guns. In the best traditions of the warrior-priest, the Bishop of Winchester, who was visiting the camp, attached his coach horses to the guns, dragged them to the front and directed their fire. There could be no clearer signal to Monmouth that the Protestant Church saw his rebellion as nothing but an unwelcome threat to the established order. Once the good Bishop had silenced Monmouth's guns, Churchill crossed the rhyne on the right, taking with him a troop of The Royals, joined with Oglethorpe's party and charged and killed the crews. At the same time the Life Guards and Horse Grenadiers charged from the opposite end of the line, while the Royalist infantry scrambled across the rhyne as best they could and finished off the rebels in hand-to-hand fighting. Over 300 of them died in the last hour, just as it was getting light, and long after Grey and Monmouth had fled. They had no bayonets or pikes to form squares against well-trained cavalry, and probably would not have known how to, even if they had. Their total casualties were estimated at 1,500, although Judge Jeffreys would see to it that the overall toll was considerably higher in the coming weeks. The Royalist casualties were

The Battle of Sedgemoor depicted on playing cards. The rebel horse miss the north plungeon and ride across the front of the, by now, alert Royalist army (*above left*). The rebel and Royalist infantry clash across the Bussex Rhyne (*above right*). Churchill's quick action in putting the rebels' artillery out of action ensures the defeat of their infantry (*left*).

250, of whom fifty were killed, mostly from the Dumbartonshire Regiment, according to Feversham.[6] Only one officer was killed, and Compton's wound proved not to be severe, as he had been wearing his front and back plates.

Oglethorpe was chosen, predictably, to carry the good news to James II in London, for which he was knighted and promoted to Colonel. Feversham moved ominously into Bridgwater. The same captain in The Blues who admitted that many officers had been drinking the night before the battle, wrote that

> The Earl of Feversham march'd away from Sedgemore with many poor prisoners tied together like slaves, & making a halt at the first great Sign-Post that stood cross the Road, he commanded four or five of the poor wretches to be hang'd upon it, & would have gone on in that way of Arbitrary Execution, if The Bishop of Bath & Wells – as the better soldier & better lawyer too – had not come up and expostulated with him, 'My Lord, you don't know what you do; This is murder in the Law and your Lordship may be called to account for it. These poor Rogues, now the Battel is over, must be tried before they can be put to death.'[7]

Two days later Feversham departed for London with the Life Guards, Horse Grenadiers and the Foot Guards, while The Blues and The Royals were left to police a sour and dispirited West Country, and to become unwilling assistants in Judge Jeffreys' Bloody Assizes during which some 150 were condemned to death and 800 transported to slavery in the West Indies; many of those who suffered under Jeffreys might have preferred to have been summarily hanged by Feversham. One direct result was that no Dorset jury would ever again convict on a capital charge.

Feversham himself was made a Knight of the Garter as a reward for his services and was advanced from Captain of the 3rd Troop of Life Guards to the 1st Troop in place of the uncomfortable Albemarle. Albemarle retired from public life, but did quite well two years later when, as chief promoter of a scheme to raise a sunken Spanish treasure ship, he netted £90,000; sadly, he did not have long to spend it as he died the following year, without issue. Churchill, to whom James II probably realized he owed rather more, took over the 3rd Troop. Cornbury, who had been present at Sedgemoor, became Colonel of The Royals in his place, though he did not spend much time with them, an oversight for which he would pay dearly in 1688. Sir Philip Howard, that redoubtable ally of Monck, and still Colonel of the troop he had commanded in the 1650s, had died on 10 February 1685, four days after Charles II. In Howard's place James II appointed his illegitimate nephew, George Fitzroy, Duke of Northumberland, and Charles II's son by the Duchess of Cleveland. A good-looking and genial man, described by John Evelyn as 'of all His Majesty's children the most accomplished and worth knowing',[8] Northumberland had served with the French in Luxembourg and was an accomplished horseman. He played little part in politics, preferring to live in the country where he 'courted the neighbouring gentry rather than the acquaintance of the nobility',[9] and he caused a minor scandal in 1686 by marrying a poulterer's daughter from Bracknell. He was Gold Stick-in-Waiting for James II's coronation but otherwise played little part in the life of his troop, whose Lieutenant Colonel was Sir John Fenwick, whilst Captain Upcott had commanded the detachment which served at Sedgemoor.

Monmouth was captured, with Grey, on 9 July: he was discovered hiding in a ditch in the New Forest, dressed as a shepherd. He was taken to London, escorted by a troop of The Royals, and condemned to death. James II, his natural uncle, granted him an interview where he pleaded unsuccessfully for his life. When he realized that his death was inevitable, he drafted a final declaration which included, 'I declare that the title of King was forced upon me and that it was very much contrary to my opinion when I was proclaimed.'[10] He was put to death on 15 July on Tower Hill, making him the only Gold Stick, to date, to be executed. Before his execution, in front of a silent crowd, he proclaimed that he died with a clear conscience having wronged no man; he then turned to the executioner and reputedly said to him, 'Do not hack at me as you did my Lord Russell,' but it was in vain. After seven blows with the axe the nervous man had to sever Monmouth's head with a knife. Possibly having learnt from the popular revulsion at Russell's and Sidney's deaths after the Rye House Plot, James II pardoned Grey in exchange for £40,000. Grey would survive, to be promoted in the peerage by William III and to serve as Lord Privy Seal before his death in 1702.

Thereafter James II learned all the wrong lessons from Sedgemoor. First, although his easy victory had undoubtedly shown the value of a professional army, and that the militia were not to be trusted, he now came to believe that his throne depended on the rapid expansion of that army. He had started raising new regiments as the threat from Monmouth became apparent, and he did not stop once he was defeated. He inherited an army of approximately 7,500 men, consisting of the Household troops, namely the Life Guards and the two regiments of Foot Guards, as well as The Blues, The Royals, two other regiments of horse[11] and five of foot, including those Tangier regiments incorporated in the regular army, much as The Royals had been. Its annual cost was £283,000. By 1688 it had increased to 25,000 men and cost over £900,000.[12] This was not abnormal by European standards. It was roughly equivalent to the combined Danish and Norwegian army of 32,000 men, and was easily dwarfed by Louis XIV's massive force of over 100,000. However, it was deeply unpopular in England, not only with Parliament, who still instinctively distrusted Stuarts with a large standing force and who preferred reform of the militia, but also with the luckless villages on which the new regiments were billeted. Their attitude was well summed up by Mr Thomas Coningsby, speaking in debate on 16 November, who said, 'the guards I am not against.

A private gentleman of the Life Guards after Sedgemoor. Sedgemoor was the first occasion when our regiments fought together, and showed the advantages of a regular, well-trained army. Had the regiments gone over to Monmouth, the result would have been very different.

Feversham's harsh treatment after Sedgemoor of those who had fought for Monmouth disgusted The Blues and The Royals, who remained policing the dispirited West Country throughout the summer and autumn of 1685. This mural depicts the destitute from the battle being comforted by Alice Lisle.

These showed themselves useful in Venner's business and the late rebellion. I am not against them. I speak only to those that have been raised.'[13]

Parliament also objected strongly to James's second move towards greater emancipation of Catholics, permitting them, for instance, to be commissioned into the army. He misjudged the strong support that he received from both Parliament and the army during the Sedgemoor campaign as an acceptance of his Catholic sympathies. James II was acceptable as a Catholic King provided that he had a good Protestant heir and did not attempt to catholicize the English establishment. This is exactly what he now proceeded to do. He had begun commissioning Catholic officers in the summer of 1685, and refused to make them resign, in line with the Test Acts, when Parliament requested it. On 23 November he 'dispensed' sixty-eight Catholic officers from the provisions of the Test Act, and subsequently used his influence with the judiciary to obtain a ruling that he had a right to appoint Catholics to both civil and military posts in defiance of the acts. There was little Parliament could do. James II enjoyed an income of £1,700,000, meaning that he could afford the expense of his increased forces without asking Parliament for money. Consequently he prorogued it on 30 November 1685 and it was not to meet again in his reign.

Both the King's policies were to cause particular problems for the Life Guards as well as for The Blues and The Royals. First, the army's larger size meant that many who considered buying a private gentleman's place in the Life Guards now went for a commission in one of the new regiments instead, leading to a shortage of suitable applicants. John Chitham, for example, who started as a Captain in Tangier and became progressively a private gentleman and a Brigadier in the Life Guards, now became a Lieutenant in the newly raised Earl of Peterborough's Horse. 'Any bankrupt merchant,' wrote an anonymous author in 1687, 'a virulent French Huguenot, a valet de chambre or an little broken tradesman that can now advance but £60 gets in to be a life guard man' and 'many that would otherwise reckon it a great honour to guard their prince's person do not covet being ranked with such scandalous fellows'.[14] This opinion is borne out by the experience of a penniless Lincolnshire baronet, Sir Baptiste Wray, who tried through Lord Ailesbury to obtain a Cornetcy for his son. James II, bizarrely, referred Ailesbury to his confessor, Father Petre, who was unable to help as the position had already been promised to Solomon de Faubert, an exiled Huguenot, for £500. Generally these newcomers remained in the minority, and there were still many men like Thomas Ward, an ex-schoolmaster with a keen interest in religion, who entered into a detailed correspondence with Dr Tenison, the Archbishop of Canterbury, before Tenison discovered 'to his infinite annoyance, that the grave theologian with whom he had been contending was in fact a layman . . . and actually a trooper in the Horse Guards'.[15]

Second, in May 1686 the King created a troop specifically for Catholics, the 4th Troop of Life Guards, in which the private gentlemen did not have to purchase their positions. His idea was 'to have the gentlemen troopers of Roman Catholics, out of charity towards poor country gentlemen of that persuasion charged with children and not able to put them into the world'. Its Captain was Henry Jermyn, recently created Lord Dover, who sadly frustrated James II's high-minded design from the outset by requiring substantial bribes for places. One poor Catholic gentleman seeking a place for his son, from whom Dover's secretary, Mr Mollins, had demanded 50 guineas, petitioned the King, who refused to believe Dover was capable of such behaviour. The petitioner was not to be moved. Ailesbury tells us, 'to end the gentleman took courage and told the King that above half the troop were French Huguenots and it was actually so; for if a Turk had come, the fifty guineas had been acceptable to that Lord the Captain'.[16] He must have been right, as in 1688 only half the troop was to stay loyal to James, although to be fair to him that did include Dover who would fight for him at the Boyne. Its most distinguished lieutenant was Patrick Sarsfield.

The total number of Catholic officers in the three regiments prior to 1685 was very small, probably around the army average of 1 or 2 per cent, and did not increase much over the next three years, even in the supposedly Catholic 4th Troop; by 1688 there were only about 100 Catholic officers in the whole army, which, given that the Catholic gentry only numbered about 7 per cent of the population, is hardly surprising. However, many of these came to occupy important positions. There was, for example, a definite Catholic clique in The Royals, many of whom had returned from Tangier. Some, like John Chappell, who had first been commissioned into the Tangier garrison and had later found a vacancy in the horse, transferred to notably Catholic regiments such as Sir Edward Hales's. Chappell was later to fight for James II in Ireland. Others, such as the Major, the Irishman Robert Clifford, who joined as second-in-command in October 1685, were well-known Catholics. Clifford had in fact attempted to abduct a wealthy widow, a certain Mrs Siderfin, to which end he was helped by Patrick Sarsfield; sadly, Mrs Siderfin was unimpressed with her suitor and both Clifford and Sarsfield were arrested. The Major of The Blues, Walter Littleton, of Pillaton in Staffordshire, an experienced soldier who had fought with Sir Henry Jones's Horse in France, was also a Catholic, and a few others, such as Philip Lawson, of Brough Hall in Yorkshire, slipped in as a junior officer, but Oxford's policy remained firmly to commission Protestants.

What was emerging more strongly than Catholicism, and bound officers more closely to the Crown than may have been apparent to either King or Parliament, was a degree of military professionalism and financial dependence on the Crown as their employer. The return of the Tangier garrison had brought an influx of officers who had lived for years by the profession of arms, and many whom they joined had fought in the European campaigns either against or, later, with the Dutch. Initially, these men, like Kirke (the ex-Governor of Tangier so despised by Pepys, see pp. 79–80), Churchill, Coy and Langston,

The vulgar yellow standard and guidon (*above left*) carried by James, Duke of York's Troop, had thankfully been replaced by a more royal red damask by his coronation. The Royal Dragoons guidon and troop standards (*above right*) had devices modelled on the symbols of successive Kings of England. The red damask standard (*below*) is from the later period of William and Mary.

sympathized with James II's army reforms, and they also respected him as someone who himself had extensive military experience.

The King had realized the value of the Putney review in practising the rapid assembly of forces and drilling the normally widely dispersed troops in regimental formations. He therefore now instigated an annual army camp on Hounslow Heath. The first one took place at the end of June 1686 and lasted for six weeks. Blathwayt again carefully planned the arrival of the troops, no mean feat given how quickly the army was expanding. The Royals, for example, started to move up from the West Country in May,[17] totalling 400 when they had all arrived, against The Blues' 450. After them the next largest regiment of horse was the Queen's Regiment, with 360 men, whilst the newer regiments could only muster 240 each.[18] The administration and training in the camp were both thoroughly prepared, and personally supervised by the King who now had the perfect opportunity to shape the army as he had always wanted, and as he had tried to do in the previous decade before his exile. He also realized that however successful it had been at Sedgemoor, there was much still to be improved. A contemporary account of James's coronation procession describes in glorious detail how finely dressed the three troops of Life Guards were, noting that the officers were distinguished from the private gentlemen by the number and size of the feathers in their hats and the amount of taffeta ribbon in their horses' tails, blue for the 1st Troop, green for the 2nd and, of course, James II's favourite yellow for the 3rd. Each troop carried two flags, a square standard and a longer, fork-tailed guidon (which they would continue to do until 1788) although the same witness tells us that, thankfully, the dreadful yellow standard had now been replaced with a more suitable one of crimson damask.[19] Overall it sounds more like a Pony Club fancy dress competition than a military parade and it is difficult not to sympathize with the King in his realization that something more workmanlike was now needed. There was also a continuing problem with false musters throughout the army. Lord Cornbury was known to be a particular offender in The Royals, though he did not go as far as Lieutenant George Butler in Sir John Reresby's Independent Company in York, who actually sold his soldiers by accepting bribes for discharging them. When asked to explain himself, he shrugged and said that everyone was doing the same thing.[20] The infantry regiments also suffered badly from desertion, especially as the increase in their number led to more widespread use of press gangs to recruit unwilling men. It was a problem that affected The Blues and The Royals only much later in the following century, and then only very infrequently.

The Blues and The Royals, therefore, as the core of the Horse, were now at the centre of a vigorous package of reforms driven through by the King and assisted by Churchill and the Tangier veterans. The emphasis at Hounslow was to make them act as regiments, or 'squadrons' of half regiments, rather than as troops,[21] although it was always accepted that when not campaigning they would continue to operate as independent troops policing the countryside. The

THE CA
on Honflow

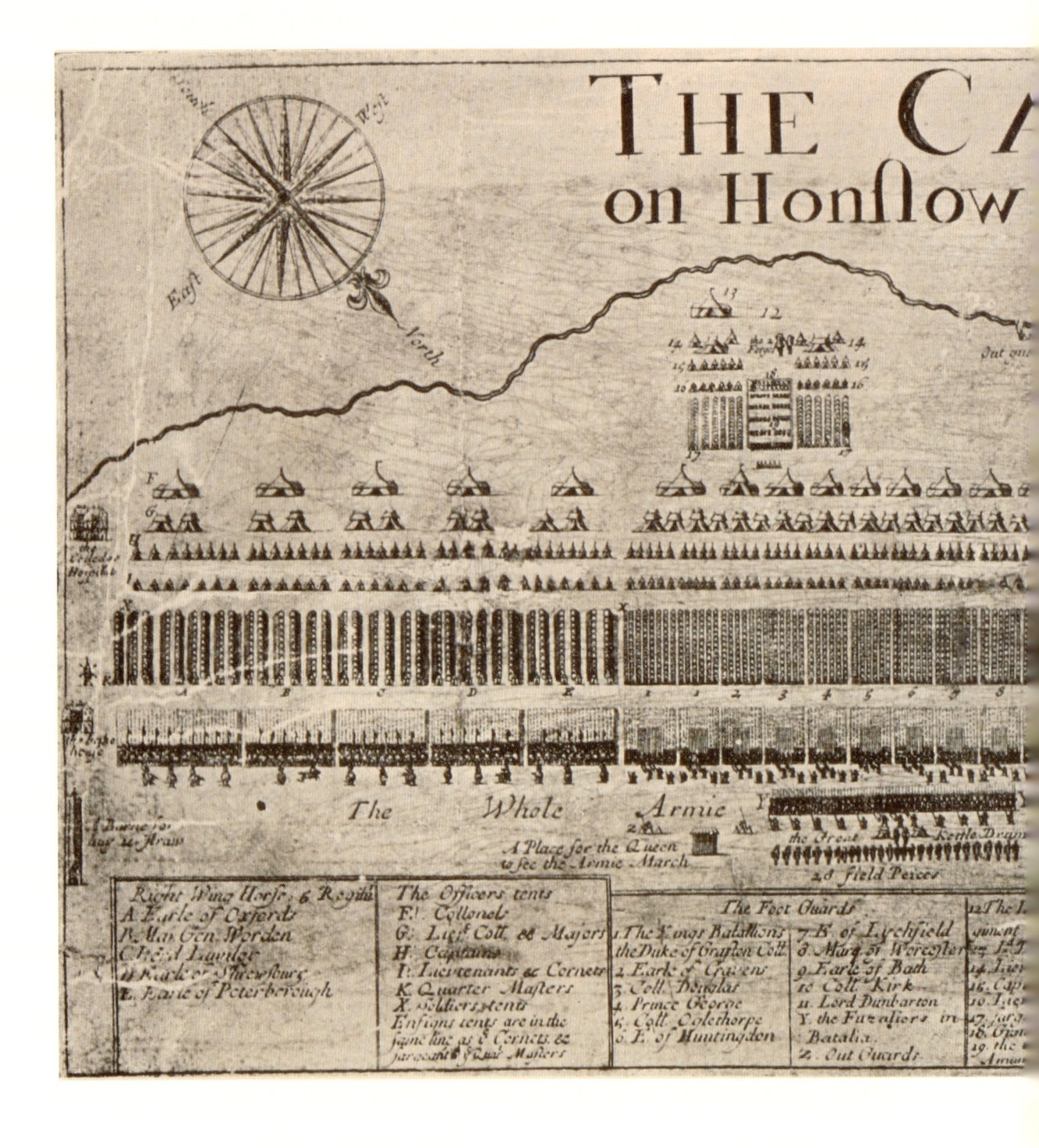

Right Wing Horse, 6 Regitt	The Officers tents		The Foot Guards	
A. Earle of Oxfords	F. Collonel	1. The Kings Batallions the Duke of Grafton Coll.	7. E. of Lychfield	12. The
B. Maj. Gen. Worden	G. Lieut. Coll. & Majors	2. Earle of Cravens	8. Marq. of Worcester	gument 13.
C. Br. A Lawiler	H. Captains	3. Coll. Douglas	9. Earle of Bath	14. Lieu
D. Earle of Shrewsbury	I. Lievtenants & Cornets	4. Prince George	10. Coll. Kirk	15. Cap
E. Earle of Peterborough	K. Quarter Masters	5. Coll. Colethorpe	11. Lord Dunbarton	16. Lieu
	X. Soldiers tents	6. E. of Huntingdon	Y. the Fuzasiers in Batalia	17. Surj
	Ensigns tents are in the same line as y Cornets & Serieants & Q. Masters		Z. Out Guards	18. Gun 19. the Amm

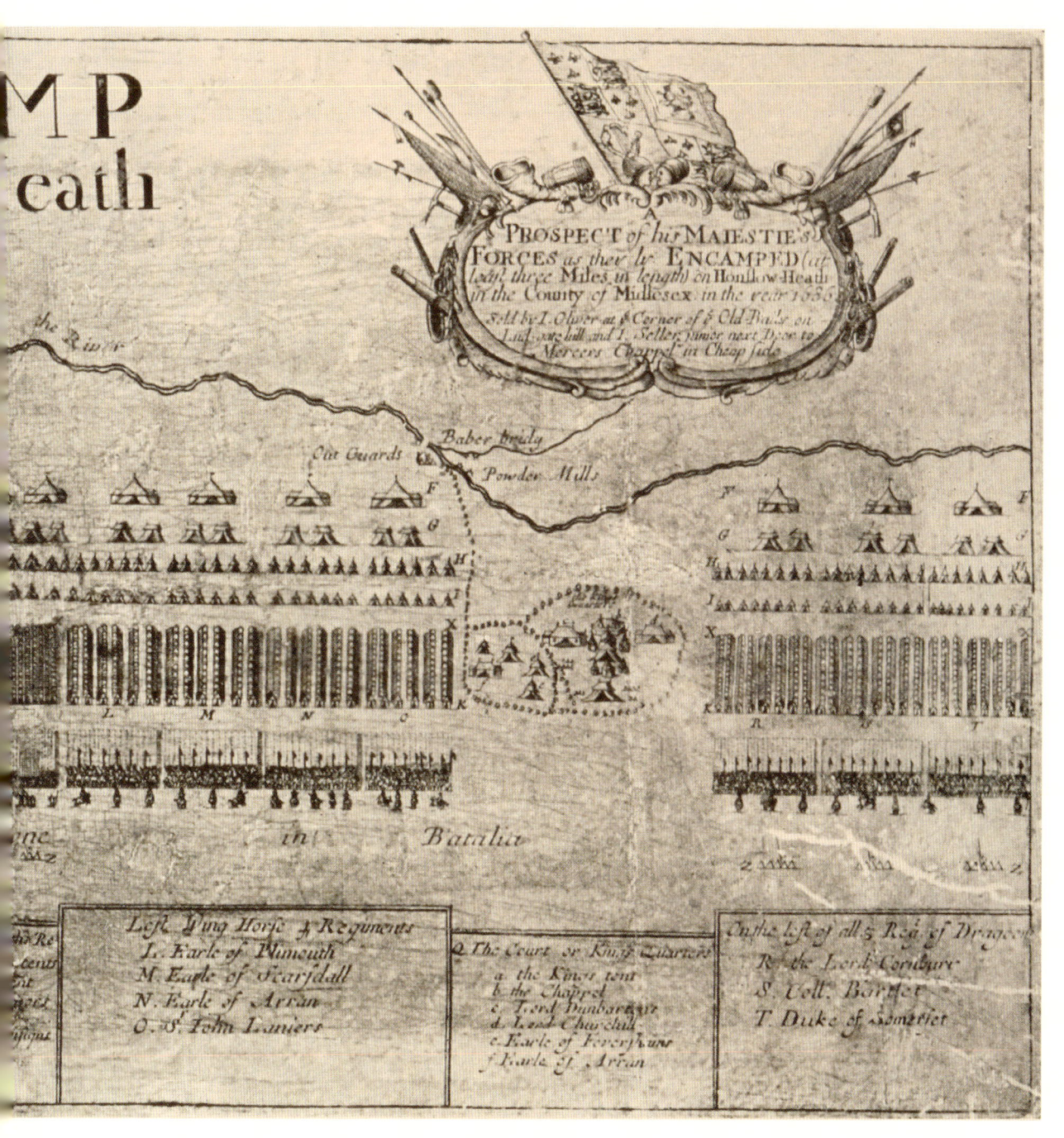

James II's army reforms after Sedgemoor included staging annual army manoeuvres on Hounslow Heath. Sir John Reresby regretted taking his wife and daughter to watch, as the tents were full of 'lewd women'.

Life Guards, with the Horse Grenadiers, were also present and now totalled fifty-eight officers and 1,052 private gentlemen. They appointed Peter Smith 'Marshal' to the four troops and the ever-enthusiastic Oglethorpe was made Adjutant.

The first problem for the regiments was a complete lack of generally accepted training tactics; none had really been needed before Sedgemoor. The methods employed at Hounslow were therefore a mixture of rapid improvisation derived from senior officers' experience in Tangier and, more importantly, what Feversham and those with experience in Europe had picked up from Louis XIV's marshals, though the French approach was largely based on siege craft. Several English tactical manuals competed with each other, such as Richard Elton's *Complete Body of the Art Military*, originally published in 1650, and reprinted unaltered as late as 1668. The Earl of Orrery wrote about tactics for the Horse 'with judgements founded upon the miserable and disorderly skirmishes which passed for battles in Ireland'.[22] In 1675, Charles II had published an 'Abridgement of English Military Discipline', which tried to learn lessons from the Third Dutch War, and to introduce very regulated, French-style commands. It can't have been much used by the army, who were still largely using Civil War tactics by the start of the Hounslow Camps. An attempt was now made to standardize. A mock fort about the size of Sheerness was built on the Heath, and was regularly stormed, much to the delight of many spectators who came out from London to watch, although Sir John Reresby regretted taking his wife and daughter as the tents were full of 'lewd women . . . to debauch the soldiers'.[23] A set of 'Orders and Regulations for the Horse' was also issued.[24] These did not really deal with tactics as such, but covered procedures in camp: how to post guards, how a regiment was to form up to march, how senior officers were to be guarded when campaigning (a major general, for example, was to have twelve dragoons under a 'serjant'), and, most importantly, how foraging was to be conducted. It was also the first time it was formally noted that officers did not take an interest in the day-to-day management of their troops, and that this was the corporal's job, with only one out of the troop lieutenant, cornet and quartermaster required to be present. Captains were expected to inspect their troops and drill them every three to four days.

The orders also introduce the idea of 'brigades', or groups of several regiments, normally commanded by a major general and not a brigadier, which term was, confusingly, used for both a senior officer and now for corporals in the Life Guards who wanted rank that showed their special status, equivalent to junior officers in the rest of the army rather than to other non-commissioned officers. Even Oxford joined in the general mood of improvement; noticing that each troop in The Blues had different uniforms, he detailed a standard pattern, selected one type of cloth from Mr Munnocks, a woollen draper in the Strand, and ordered all officers to use them. The result was heavy on gold lace, two rows for captains and one for lieutenants and cornets, and feathers, reflecting current French fashions, but at least the regiment now looked the same. It is nice to reflect that Munnocks was probably the father of the officer killed at Ashill (see p. 88), showing Oxford's human side and why he was held in such high affection by the regiment for so long. It is also clear that whereas the senior positions in the regiment continued to be filled by landed families, who could afford the substantial cost of those commissions, many junior officers, who bore the brunt of the daily administration, were now being recruited from more humble backgrounds, something of a throwback to the regiment's early days in the 1650s.

Detailed ration and forage allowances were also worked out, and were to stay in use for decades. Each horse received 'Two trusses of good new hay weighing 64 lbs. each for each horse per week and a Truss of straw at 36 lbs.', and 'a sufficient supply of good sweet oats', for which 10d. per day was stopped from The Royals' pay, with a further 5½d. stopped for 'one pound and a half averdupois weight of good wholesome bread'. The horses were tethered in troop lines to stakes, one of which was carried by each soldier. Sea coal was delivered for cooking, presumably to the relief of the owners of the local woods, and instructions were issued for brewing beer. Detailed orders were prepared for a military hospital and for the surgeons to 'keep the sick from rambling or the healthfull from coming to them without permission'.[25]

There were few changes to the weapons or equipment used by the regiments. The Royals were only recently kitted out as dragoons and both the Life Guards and The Blues continued to carry the heavy civil war pattern sword, a pair of pistols and a flintlock carbine; these were now introduced to other regiments as well, although they did not become universal throughout the army until 1702. In 1685 James II had also introduced a policy of trumpeters riding grey horses, the supply of horses being by then sufficiently replenished to allow that luxury, and of the Life Guards' trumpeters wearing red as opposed to white feathers in their hats. Trumpeters played a vital role in the new regimental tactics that were developing at the Hounslow Camps, as trumpeting was the only means of communicating. Traditionally trumpeters had no weapons, a throwback to the Middle Ages when they were used in parleying, and the idea now was to protect them by making them distinguishable. The fashion of using black trumpeters seems to have started at about the same time. One hopes that this was due to their musical talent, but it is difficult, though distasteful, not to conclude that it was also something of a joke to see black men on grey horses as opposed to white soldiers on black horses. There had been black servants in British households for several decades, a result of interests in the West Indies and Tangier. The great portrait of Captain Lucy of The Blues, painted by Kneller in 1680, shows him with a black groom holding his charger. There was also a precedent in the previous century, as one of the trumpeters shown in the Westminster Tournament Roll of Henry VIII in 1510 is black.[26] This was a tradition that was to continue in the Life Guards until well into the nineteenth century.²⁷ The Life Guards' trumpeters continued to be employed more at court than they were with the troops, and in 1672 Charles II employed the French Huguenot composer Cambert to become their director.

Annoyingly, there are no records in existence to tell us much about the lives of the soldiers at the time. Their pay had not increased since 1661, and was still 4s. a day for the private gentlemen of the Life Guards, 2s. 6d. for the soldiers in the Horse Grenadiers and The Blues and 1s. 6d. for The Royals. There are no very reliable figures for inflation, but prices are generally held to have remained fairly constant for the period.²⁸ These were therefore still reasonable rates, particularly when compared to the infantry, but still not generous, given that the men had to keep their horses as well, and money was often held back for forage, food, clothing and one-off charges such as for medicine for the regimental surgeon. What was left could be spent with the sutler, a sort of travelling shopkeeper who set up his business at Hounslow and provided food, drink and tobacco. There had been a well-established sutler with a coffee house in the Horse Guards building since 1661, and his business was well patronized not only by the Life Guards, but also by passers-by. The nomadic existence of The Blues and The Royals meant they had little use for one, but this would change during the campaigns of the next decade. There was still no minimum or maximum age limit, and we do not know how many soldiers were married. A proportion of the private gentlemen of the Life Guards, living semi-permanently in lodgings in London, undoubtedly were, but the lifestyle of The Blues and The Royals, and the presence of so many prostitutes on Hounslow Heath, possibly suggests that many of them were not.

There were, however, occasional applications made for widows' pensions, particularly for soldiers who had served in Tangier for a long period and who presumably married into the settler community there. Mary Helme, for example, a widow of a soldier in the Tangier Horse, who was a 'little crazed; her husband's four Troopers all killed and their horses' was awarded £4 per year, hardly a generous sum.²⁹ There was a naval pension system operating, and in 1685, presumably partly in gratitude for Sedgemoor, James II introduced an official pension scheme for the army. Soldiers had to have either twenty years' service or to have been disabled. Benefits were scaled, so that an ex-Life Guard received 1s. 6d. per day, whereas an infantry private only got 5d.; Edmund Serch, a Royal, unable to continue in service, received 40s. per year despite only four years' service in Tangier because he had 'been burst in the same service'.³⁰ Special payments were authorized for those who had been wounded during the Sedgemoor campaign; Edward Crooke, Oxenbridge Harwood and Rowland Lloyd, all of The Blues, received £30 8s. each, a substantial sum, and a further twelve soldiers received amounts from £5 to £20.³¹ In 1687 the Royal Hospital in Chelsea was opened, but was far too small, with only 472 spaces, having been designed for the much smaller army of Charles II.

There was little for James II's new regiments to do, when not in camp, and

One of James II's reforms was to mount trumpeters on grey horses. Later the idea of having black musicians became fashionable. This was partly because of their natural musical ability, but also because contemporary taste thought it amusing to have black men on grey horses – in contrast to white men on black ones.

consequently their behaviour was not good. This made them unpopular in areas where they were billeted, and Blathwayt was forced to tighten up disciplinary procedures. Regimental courts martial were introduced, and a superior military court, a standing court martial, was established at Horse Guards, largely because the King could not cajole civilian magistrates to be tougher with military miscreants. He wanted, for example, cases of desertion to be treated as felonies, but the magistrates would not comply. The new military courts proved far more willing to inflict corporal and capital punishment, which increased in severity from this time. Each regiment was supposed to have a marshal, responsible for enforcing discipline. This was a popular and lucrative post in infantry regiments, the marshal being allowed to keep three-quarters of the pay of prisoners in his charge. In the horse regiments it was never taken that seriously. The marshal's role in The Royals attracted 1s. a day, and was combined with that of quartermaster in the Colonel's Troop. Neither the Life Guards nor The Blues bothered to have a marshal at all, merely appointing someone when they needed to, like Peter Smith at Hounslow. Contrary to contemporary observers' complaints, neither The Blues nor The Royals had difficulty in recruiting good men, though there were persistent complaints about The Royals in the West Country, leading to the arrest of two trumpeters by civil magistrates, and their behaviour in Chester, later in the decade, would be widely criticized. Problems continued with the Life Guards, but arose more from their claustrophobic living conditions in London and from their status as private gentlemen, which commissioned officers in other regiments found difficult to understand. A private gentleman's pay, at 4s., was the same as a lieutenant's in a regiment of foot, and the brigadiers got the same as a lieutenant colonel. During the 1686 Hounslow Camp, Colonel John Culpepper, 'a man with an abominable temper', quarrelled with a private gentleman in the Life Guards and shot him with a blunderbuss. His victim must have said something fairly heinous, for he attracted little sympathy at Culpepper's trial, where fifty of his colleagues swore to the jury that Culpepper had been sleepwalking and that 'he was prone to those extravagances in his sleep which he much abhorred when awake'.[32] Duelling remained a persistent problem, but there was little appetite for removing officers' commissions, representing, as they did, a lifetime's investment, and nobody wanted to set a dangerous precedent.

Political dissent, however, was to be a very different matter. James II's willingness to remove officers whom he regarded as insufficiently Catholic was to trigger the conspiracy in the army, originally hatched in the Life Guards, The Blues and The Royals, which was to cost him his throne. The majority of officers in these same regiments, whose loyalty had ensured his victory over Monmouth, now sided with the Parliamentary faction which was determined to invite William of Orange to replace his father-in-law. By 1688 James II had partially succeeded in creating a large professional army mainly dependent on the throne for employment and generally loyal to him. He had also helped

The Duke of Berwick was James II's illegitimate son. He became briefly Colonel of The Blues for nine months in 1688 when Oxford refused to support the King's Catholic policies. Thereafter he commanded Jacobite armies in Ireland and Europe, fell deeply in love with Sarsfield's wife, and married her when Sarsfield was killed, bringing up his son as his own. He refused to command the army of his half-brother, the Old Pretender, in 1715, which many people thought led directly to the failure of the rebellion.

The 1688 plot to oust James II and replace him with his Protestant son-in-law, William of Orange, was hatched by senior officers of our regiments in London coffee houses – fashionable places to socialize.

create 'an officer corps that was substantially professional' and 'did not have the same tender regard for the laws and liberties of England as the gentry and aristocracy who had played at soldiers after the Restoration, whilst the Catholic officers had everything to gain by their overthrow'.[33] However, whilst many of the officers in his new regiments, both Catholic and Protestant, were to stay loyal to James, the likes of Oxford, Churchill, Compton, Langston and even Cornbury still identified with those laws and liberties, and when they felt they were irrevocably threatened they tried to bring their regiments behind Parliament in demanding his abdication.

Starting from Windsor on 16 August 1687, and escorted by the Life Guards, James II departed on a tour of England to rally support for his policy of 'liberty of conscience' towards Catholics, should he recall Parliament. He went first to Portsmouth and Southampton, then north by way of Gloucestershire to Chester and then back to Oxford, where he found the University hostile. The tour was not a success, though much enjoyed by the accompanying Life Guards, and the King remained blind to the level of opposition to his policies. He next ordered the Lords Lieutenant to appoint Catholics to public offices. At least half refused, and prominent amongst them was Oxford. 'The noblest subject in England, and as Englishmen loved to say, in Europe',[34] replied, 'I will stand by your Majesty against all enemies to the last drop of my blood. But this is a matter of conscience and I can not comply.' In February 1688 Oxford was sacked as Lord Lieutenant of Essex and as Colonel of The Blues. James II's natural son by Arabella Churchill, James FitzJames, the Duke of Berwick, took his place as colonel. Later that month there was widespread opposition among army officers to signing 'three questions', designed by James II to test the loyalty of officers and public officials.

The discontent among a few key senior army officers, which had been evident for some time, now began to develop into a conspiracy. It centred around two groups, who met in different London coffee houses. The 'Tangerines', as their name suggests, were all Tangier veterans, originally united by their common loathing of Lord Dartmouth and Samuel Pepys for having closed the colony. Prominent among them were Langston, the ex-Troop Captain of The Royals, who now commanded the newly raised Princess Anne's Regiment of Horse. Percy Kirke, the ex-Governor whose loathing of Pepys was mutually reciprocated, and Charles Trelawney were also included. Most importantly, Churchill was a member. He was by now the most influential senior officer in the army, partly because of the Sedgemoor campaign, and partly because of his closeness to the King. Cornbury was a member of the Tangerines and of the more aristocratic and political Treason Club, which met in the Rose Tavern in Russell Street. Other prominent officers in this group were Sir Francis Compton, Richard Savage and Lord Colchester, the Lieutenant Colonel to Dover in the 4th Troop of Life Guards. Thomas Langston acted as the go-between for the two groups. Cornbury would later be influential in getting the support of his cousin, Princess Anne, and her unathletic husband Prince George of Denmark. The members of these clubs were taking a substantial risk and knew it. Had events turned out differently they would certainly have paid with the loss of their commissions, a strong disincentive even to aristocrats like Cornbury whose family was not particularly rich, and who relied on his position as Colonel of The Royals for his livelihood, as his persistent efforts to return false musters attest.

Matters worsened at the Hounslow Camp that June. On arrival the King promptly questioned his officers, by regiment, on their support for the repeal of the Test Acts. He went so far as to call into his tent Captain Sandys of The Blues, who had taken over so effectively from the wounded Compton at Sedgemoor, 'and told him what a great commander he would be if he would but be a catholic. To which the Captain replied, in a big hoarse voice as he always spoke, "I understand Your Majesty well enough. I fear God and honour the King, as I ought, but I am not a man that is given to change". Which unexpected answer so stopped the King's mouth that he had not a word to say'. Later Sandys repeated his extraordinary conversation to Oxford, who told him not to resign his commission and that 'these things will not last long'.[35]

Much more seriously, on the morning of 10 June each regiment received a 'Circular to the sevl. Colnells of Horse, ffoot and Dragoons', informing them that 'it had pleased Almighty God about four of the clock this morning to bless his Maty. And his Royal Consort the Queen with the Birth of a Son'.[36] The baby was widely reputed to have been smuggled into the Queen's bed in a warming pan as she was known to be barren. Colonel Edward Griffin, fated to share so many of the later Stuarts' more intimate moments, and who, as Silver Stick-in-Waiting, had the dubious honour of being present at the birth, was later to swear that it was a real birth. The baby, now Prince of Wales, ensured a Catholic succession, frustrating all the hopes pinned on James II's Protestant daughter, Mary. During the Hounslow Camp the conspirators, minus Cornbury, who temporarily departed to get married to the enticingly rich Catherine O'Brien, advanced their opposition to the King's catholicizing ways into a definite plan to invite William of Orange and Mary to assume the throne. The presence of three regiments of the Anglo-Dutch Brigade, recently recalled by James II from Europe and presumably full of Dutch spies, probably helped. It was a considerable risk, not least because the Dutch were not popular among the soldiers; some of the older ones had, after all, fought three wars against them in the last thirty years. Furthermore, many of the recently commissioned officers were obviously loyal to the Crown. The case of the 'Portsmouth Six' helped change the mood that September. Six captains, refusing the King's demand that they accept Irish Catholics into their companies, lost their commissions, creating a degree of nervousness among many whose sympathies were firmly Protestant, but who could not afford a similar fate.

Chapter Five

THE GLORIOUS REVOLUTION AND WAR IN IRELAND

William of Orange, carried by a 'protestant wind' from Holland, finally landed at Torbay on 5 November 1688. James II had been led to believe by his incompetent ambassador in The Hague that Yorkshire was William's more likely landing place. His plan, therefore, was to secure London while assembling a field army that would march to meet the Dutch wherever they might be. Once it became clear that William was in the West Country, the army, in what was to become a well-established British military tradition, started to assemble on Salisbury Plain. The mobilization did not proceed nearly as smoothly as it had before Sedgemoor, although the plan was almost identical. An advance force of The Blues and The Royals, as supposedly the most reliable regiments, was to scout forward under General Lanier and make contact with the enemy, while Feversham and the King brought up the main body. Blathwayt was later to be accused by the Jacobites of being part of the conspiracy and it is difficult to conclude otherwise. He delayed the orders to The Blues by three days so they arrived late at Salisbury. He also failed to authorize the suspiciously centralized release of sufficient fronts and backs, probably at Compton's instigation. It must also be noted that Blathwayt was to serve William of Orange throughout his reign in the same office.

The atrocious weather that autumn was also partially responsible for the delay. Salisbury Plain was under several feet of snow and the roads were almost impassable. Many regiments had been marching around England since the Hounslow Camp, unsure of where they were to be billeted and short of tents. Morale was low and not improved by the arrival of new Catholic regiments from Ireland, seen as something of an insult to the loyalty of the English regiments and another strain on the administration. In addition, the Scottish Troop of Life Guards with their accompanying Horse Grenadiers were brought south to supplement the existing four troops. However, whatever chaos there ensued in assembling the army was to be rapidly overshadowed by the regiments' behaviour once they marched.

Militarily William's forces should have been easily outmatched by James II's army. He had only 11,000 foot and 3,660 horse; about 3,000 of these were English or Scottish, left over from the Anglo-Dutch Brigade, and, in an interesting precedent to British future practice, also included a West Indian regiment manned by blacks from the Dutch plantations. He had only twenty-one guns, unloaded at Exeter, and, importantly for our story, had with him both his Dutch Blue Guards, whose officers included fifty-four French Huguenots, and his Life Guard, which also had thirty-four Huguenot officers. Yet the conspirators had done their work well. Whilst Churchill stayed with James II, the majority of Lanier's force went over to William, and it was the disaffection of these regiments which started to undermine the morale of the King and the remainder of the army.

In individual regiments the scenes bordered on the farcical. On 9 November Cornbury and Compton announced that they had been ordered to disrupt the Dutch at Honiton and were to march immediately without the normal precautions of scouts and pickets, practised so laboriously at Hounslow. The Royals led the way from Salisbury, and The Blues brought up the rear. When they reached Axminster, on the Devon–Dorset border, Cornbury, in an extraordinary episode that revealed how little time he spent with his regiment, ordered the Major, Thomas Clifford, to take the regiment on to the Dutch camp. Clifford's old Catholic name might have struck a note of warning with Cornbury; moreover, he was widely known throughout the army as one of the most devoutly Catholic officers and intensely loyal to James. In a furious altercation in the centre of Axminster, Clifford demanded to see Cornbury's orders. Of course he had none, and appealed to the assembled regiment for support. It must have been a particularly difficult moment for the junior officers and troopers, unaware of the plotting of their leadership and mostly anxious simply to guarantee their positions. In the event only about a dozen agreed to go with Cornbury, who galloped off to join a sceptical William at Honiton while Clifford took the remainder back to Salisbury. In an almost exact replay of the same incident Walter Littleton refused Compton's orders for The Blues to desert, but Compton, a wiser officer who knew his soldiers well, followed his advice, possibly influenced by the fact that he was without armour, and retired to Salisbury to a frosty reception from Berwick and the King.

Meanwhile, matters had worsened in the Life Guards. The 2nd and 4th Troops had been sent on ahead to Salisbury, while the 1st, 3rd and Scots Troops escorted the King and the army's guns more slowly. The 4th Troop, James's well-intentioned attempt to help poor Catholic gentlemen, was ironically the first to desert, with Lord Colchester taking over sixty private gentlemen on 13 November, but the other half stayed loyal and fought the one single action of the whole campaign. It was commanded by that most interesting and distinguished Life Guardsman, Patrick Sarsfield. He was fighting from personal conviction as much as from loyalty to James II, being partly from the old Irish

William III departing from Hellevoetslouis on 19 October 1688. Blown by a 'Protestant wind' he landed at Torbay on 5 November 1688. Officers of The Royals, then The Blues and the Life Guards, led the mutiny in James II's army and went over to William – but left their regiments divided and untrusted by the new Dutch administration.

aristocracy on his mother's side, she being an O'Moore – his father's family were Anglo-Norman settlers – and therefore strongly Catholic. Sarsfield had been sent on a separate mission by Colchester, and was genuinely looking to disrupt a Dutch foraging party that had been reported between Bruton and Wincanton in Somerset. He had with him seventy Life Guards and fifty Horse Grenadiers under another strong Irish Catholic, Henry Luttrell. The Dutch were in fact a Scottish patrol from one of the Anglo-Dutch Brigade regiments under Lieutenant Campbell, recently commissioned from Sergeant, and an experienced soldier. Hearing of Sarsfield's approach along the Bruton Road, he laid a careful ambush. As Sarsfield appeared he stepped out into the road and halted him.

'Stand,' he said, 'for who are ye?'
'I am for King James,' replied Sarsfield. 'Who are you for?'
'I am for the Prince of Orange.'
'God damn you!' came the reply. 'I'll prince you,' whereupon a general mêlée broke out which resulted in Campbell and twelve of his Scots being killed and Sarsfield and Luttrell losing three dead with six taken prisoner. A local then announced that more Dutch were on the way and Sarsfield broke off the engagement. It was to be the first of many such actions he would fight over the next two years.[1]

There were also rumours of imminent desertion among the other troops. Feversham, as Gold Stick-in-Waiting and still Commander-in-Chief, told the King that 'though the private men were steady, the officers could not be relied upon'.[2] He actually proposed removing them and replacing them with the Brigadiers, not as revolutionary a move in the Life Guards as it would have been in any other regiment. He was right, for once, though neither he nor the King realized that Churchill would lead the defection. On 24 November Feversham rode out with the Duke of Grafton, Colonel of the Foot Guards, to join William. He took a few Life Guard officers with him, and a few Blues, including Cornet Compton, nephew of Sir Francis, 'with two or three subalterns and about ten troopers', which James II subsequently saw as an indication 'of a greater honour and fidelity in the common men than in the generality of the officers, who usually value themselves much for these qualifications'.[3] It was rumoured that Churchill had proposed taking James II with him as far as Warminster, where the army was supposed to be moving, but James had a bad nose bleed and could not travel.

Churchill, and Cornbury, received a decidedly cool welcome from William, who was never to trust Churchill fully. Churchill's desertion led to James's final loss of confidence in the army. At a disastrous Council of War he decided to retire to London, leaving Feversham with the bulk of the Horse with the curious strategy of lingering near Salisbury and Reading to exhaust the forage so as to deny it to William. In practice the army now started to disintegrate. Kirke, forward at Warminster, went over to William together with most of the

3rd Troop, who were with him under Churchill's Lieutenant Colonel, Edmund Maine, but the bulk of the 1st and 2nd Troops remained loyal. They escorted James back to London, and took charge of the Queen and the infant Prince of Wales to escort them to the coast so that they could embark for France on 6 December. Four days later the King himself decided to flee, and wrote to Feversham ordering him to offer no more resistance. Feversham subsequently wrote to William, saying that to avoid further bloodshed the army would no longer resist. The letter was signed by him as Colonel of the 1st Troop, by Sir John Fenwick, Lieutenant Colonel of the 2nd Troop, and, of course, by Oglethorpe, now promoted to Brigadier General. Sensible, almost inevitable, a move as it was, it left the Life Guards and the army confused and divided.

Worse was to come. James spent what would apparently be his last night in London on 11 December with Northumberland as Gold Stick-in-Waiting. The following morning Northumberland concealed James's flight for several hours to enable him to get safely to Sheerness. Here he took a ship for France, but was unluckily intercepted by piratical fishermen, who brought him ashore and handed him over to the local militia, who treated him roughly. Only after the local Lord Lieutenant got word to London was Feversham able to rescue him with 240 loyal Life Guards and Horse Grenadiers. Arriving early in the morning of 15 December, having shown uncharacteristic energy in riding through the night, Feversham scattered the militia and took James back to London, where he received a really popular reception. It must have been an extraordinary time, not least for the confused Life Guards. Here was their King, who had fled in the night, discarding the Great Seal in the Thames en route, roughed up by opportunistic fishermen, imprisoned by the militia, rescued by his guards and now mobbed in the streets of his capital, which his son-in-law with the bulk of his former army was now approaching. Fortunately, for probably the first time since he came to the throne, James II showed some wisdom, and when William sent Count Solmes with his Dutch Life Guard to demand his departure, he agreed, and the remnants of the 1st and 2nd Troops escorted him for the last time to Rochester, from where he left for France. The next time they would see him they would be in opposing armies.

The English army was now in chaos. Feversham's letter of 10 December to William of Orange formally ended all resistance, but the Secretary at War's department had actually ceased to issue instructions a week earlier. Until William imposed control the army was without instructions and, more importantly as far as the men were concerned, without pay. The Royals did not receive a single penny for the first three months of the year. Lieutenant Colonel Francis Russell, for instance, had to borrow £150 from his brother to pay for his troop's lodging. It was a dangerous situation. The loyalty of many regiments was still firmly with James II. There were also 2,820 Irish soldiers and 2,964 Scots billeted on reluctant English families. In Blathwayt's temporary absence, William's secretary, Constantine Huygens, ran the War Office, but was unable to cope. Blathwayt was back by the end of January 1689, enthusiastically attempting to re-establish some degree of control over the dispersed and demoralized regiments, and, by February, restoring pay. For William this was a matter of some urgency. He badly needed the English regiments restored to operational effectiveness quickly in order to fight the French in Europe. But to re-form the army he needed the acquiescence of Parliament, which met on 1 February 1689 and passed the Bill of Rights, that fundamental step in establishing Parliamentary control over the Crown, which specifically legislated against a standing army in peacetime. As the Bill of Rights was debated, William prematurely ordered some regiments to Holland. Unpaid and unwilling, they mutinied, alarming Parliament as much as the King. The resulting Mutiny Act made legal provision for wartime service and granted the Crown the right to enforce military discipline for short periods of one year, or exceptionally two years only, and was consequently to prove a useful mechanism for ensuring that the King called regular parliaments. For the time being, however, it allowed William to mobilize the English army against Louis XIV.

However, he was unsure of the regiments upon which he could rely. He had been, to put it mildly, unimpressed with the army's performance to date, and had not helped matters himself by tactlessly announcing a bounty for his Dutch regiments, unavailable to their English counterparts. Grateful as he undoubtedly was to Churchill and Cornbury, as a soldier he found their conduct despicable. On greeting Churchill, his commander Count Schomberg observed that he was the first general he had encountered who had deserted his post. A contemporary Life Guard records that thereafter, Churchill, unlike William's Dutch officers, never dined with the new King, but waited on him behind his chair. William did not trust the Life Guards, in particular, who were sent away from London and their duties passed to the Dutch Life Guard and Blue Guards. A specially established commission inspected every regiment to assess their effectiveness and loyalty.

The bitterly cold months of January, February and March 1689 were particularly difficult for all of our three regiments. The Life Guards were dispersed with the 1st Troop at Maidstone, the 2nd at Chelmsford and the 3rd at St Albans, and the confused Scots Troop at Bicester. The 4th Troop was, hardly surprisingly, disbanded on 1 January 1689, although the 'poor Catholics' were given their arrears of pay. Many had already left for Ireland, with Sarsfield and Luttrell, and were to form the core of two troops of Life Guards in James II's Irish army later that year. Feversham was arrested, thoroughly alarming the new King's supporters in London. William seems to have appreciated the implications for he was released soon afterwards, allegedly for the vital reason that the Queen Dowager 'could not enjoy her nightly game of basset without him'.[4] Feversham remained a reluctant supporter of the new regime, though he was later accused of refusing to pray for William's success in Ireland. He survived until 1709, being well received by Queen Anne, and finally earned a burial in

Westminster Abbey. He was replaced as Colonel of the 1st Troop by Richard Lumley, created Earl of Scarborough, who had raised an independent troop of horse in 1685 and fought at Sedgemoor. A convinced adherent of the Dutch intervention, he was dangerously open in his criticism of James II. Northumberland and his officers of the 2nd Troop presented William with an address stating their willingness to serve the new regime, but William considered Northumberland 'a great blockhead'[5] and replaced him with the Duke of Ormonde, grandson of Charles II's great Irish viceroy and a staunch Protestant, while Churchill was allowed to remain in the 3rd Troop.

Oxford was quickly reinstated as Colonel of The Blues, but his regiment was sent to kick their heels at Northampton. It was not a happy time for them and the future was very uncertain. Major Walter Littleton had been killed in a duel with Captain Adderley as a direct result of the fiasco outside Axminster. A regiment that had prided itself on its loyalty and its Protestantism now found itself doubted on both counts. However, Oxford and Compton played the new King well. On 1 February 1689 Parliament passed a vote to thank the army for having 'testified their sturdy adherence to the Protestant religion and being instrumental in delivering this country from popery and slavery.'[6] A copy was forwarded to Oxford by Blathwayt to be read at the head of his regiment. Gradually William came to realize that The Blues, part of the original army, were trustworthy, and by April he had exempted them from the Commission of Inspection.

The Royals, affected by William's scant regard for Cornbury as much as the Life Guards were by his view of Churchill, assembled around Farnham at the end of December, where Cornbury and his party rejoined them. Of the three regiments at the centre of the army conspiracy, The Royals were the worst affected by the fallout. Of twenty-five officers serving on 1 January 1688, only eight were still there a year later, and only four of the eight quartermasters. Cornbury himself was not to last much longer. Moving with the regiment to Newcastle, he found himself dismissed because his father, Lord Clarendon, flatly refused to support the new Government. His place was taken by Anthony Heyford, a professional officer and originally a Horse Grenadier, who had been a member of the army conspiracy, rather than by a peer or a prince, reflecting William's more utilitarian view of the role of colonels. Cornbury himself, however, was far from finished. He became Member of Parliament for Christchurch and Master of the Horse to Prince George of Denmark, husband of his cousin, the future Queen Anne. Later she would send him to govern New York and New Jersey, where he was very unpopular. New Yorkers accused him of being a transvestite, apparently lurking 'behind trees to pounce, shrieking with laughter on his victims', and of misappropriating £1,500 intended for rebuilding the harbour. They had their revenge when he left in 1708. In his official portrait he wears woman's clothing. It hangs in the New York Historical Society to this day, the only Colonel of The Royals to be depicted in female dress until the

Lord Cornbury was a particularly inept Colonel of The Royals and an even worse Governor of New York, where the colonists accused him of stealing public funds and of being a transvestite. When he left they got their own back by having his official portrait painted showing him in 'drag'.

Princess Royal became Colonel in 1998. Said to illustrate the worst form of the English aristocracy's 'arrogance, joined to intellectual imbecility',[7] Cornbury died penniless in 1723.

Throughout the army in general about a third of the officers remained to serve William, a third were to fight for James II in Scotland and Ireland and a third simply left. Some had, not unnaturally, gone quickly, like Clifford, who took with him Mackenzie and Lieutenants La Rue, Crawley, Burke and Hopkins, the core of the ex-Tangier Catholic clique. All Catholics were officially cashiered on 14 December 1688. Clifford was to become Sarsfield's cavalry commander in Ireland and would incur the undying odium of the Irish for allowing the Williamite forces to slip across the Shannon and take Limerick three years later. Others left simply because they were professional officers whose loyalty had been to the Crown and not based on religious conviction; Henry Cornwall, for example, Captain Lieutenant for Oxford and later Berwick in the Colonels' Troop of The Blues since 1682, left because his conscience would not permit him to break his oaths and fight against his old patron. And yet others went on to enjoy advancement: the Tangier veteran Coy, for example, took over Colonel Richard Hamilton's Regiment of Irish Horse that was later to become the very distinguished 4th (Royal Irish) Dragoon Guards.

THIS FRUSTRATING PERIOD came to an end on 22 March 1689 when James II landed at Kinsale in Ireland with nearly 18,000 men, financed and equipped by Louis XIV. William consequently committed the English and Dutch to the Grand Alliance with the Holy Roman Emperor against France, signed in Vienna on 12 May 1689. It must always have been his purpose to draw on England's reserves of manpower and money to help his struggle against Louis XIV, and whilst 1688 may have been a 'Glorious' or bloodless revolution for the Whig landowners whose power was consolidated in Parliament, it succeeded at the cost of the English army's blood. Eight years of sustained campaigning in Flanders were to follow, in a cause that was peripheral to English interests and subject to Dutch military leadership that was often less than effective.

The Life Guards, now reinstated as three troops, and the Scots Troop in Edinburgh, were recalled to London to participate in the coronation procession of 11 April 1689. There were to be no smart new uniforms this time. Instead, William took the opportunity to restructure the troops so they could be deployed almost immediately on operations. The brigadiers and sub-brigadiers were given the army rank of captains and lieutenants respectively, thus removing an anomaly that had caused considerable resentment, and an adjutant was added to each troop. On 23 April the 2nd Troop were ordered to Holland, together with The Blues, whose strength was re-established at 450 men by taking ninety soldiers from other regiments of horse. Churchill,

One of the greatest Life Guard officers, and a gifted tactician, Patrick Sarsfield fled to Ireland with James II in 1688. Preventing William III from taking Limerick in 1690 after the Boyne by destroying his siege artillery, Sarsfield fought on at Aughrim and Limerick, eventually negotiating the evacuation of the remainder of the Irish army to Europe – the original 'Wild Geese'.

elevated to the Earldom of Marlborough in the coronation honours, commanded the force; William had reluctantly realized the need to win over the English military leadership for the forthcoming campaign.

The force joined the Allied army of the sixty-nine-year-old Prince Waldeck, whose plan was to cross the River Sambre and attack the French army near Charleroi. For the majority of those in the English force it was the first time they had been overseas, let alone on a military expedition of that scale, and initially Blathwayt's machine proved unequal to the administrative task. Waldeck complained that they suffered from 'sickness, slackness, wretched clothing and the worst of shoes'.[8] By way of contrast Northumberland offered his services to the 2nd Troop, and was accepted by a sceptical William, who was surprised that he arrived at the docks with three gentlemen attendants, two footmen, a waggoner, a sumpter and three grooms. He was the model for the officer in Shadwell's play *The Volunteers*, who remarks, 'Why I carry two launderesses on purpose for my points and laces. Damn me – would you have a gentleman go undressed in camp?'

Waldeck moved in August, and found the French south of Charleroi at the small town of Walcourt. The engagement was a muddle, with, as so often happened later, the French engaging a party of Allied foragers. They then came upon the main Allied army, which withdrew under Churchill, whom we will now refer to as Marlborough, to establish a position on some high ground with a windmill east of the town. The French deployed to attack, whereupon Marlborough detached the Life Guards and The Blues, worked his way round to a flank and charged in so successful an action that it caused D'Humieres, the French general, to withdraw with 2,000 casualties. It was the first of many similar actions over the next ten years, and showed the determination and aggression that were to make Marlborough such a successful commander. Even Waldeck changed his tune, reporting to William that the English horse had 'behaved themselves very well . . . and showed great courage'.[9]

If all this activity was a jolt for the English after decades of policing and escort duties in England, then worse was to come. The situation in Ireland had so deteriorated that William now decided to withdraw much of the English force from the Low Countries and lead the army in Ireland himself. To date his troops already there under Marshal Schomberg, who had been so rude to Marlborough on his defection, had achieved nothing except the loss of half its strength through disease, largely dysentery, or the 'bloody flux' as it was known, over the winter of 1689/90. James II still held Dublin and the Irish army was becoming increasingly successful at raiding, often under Sarsfield's leadership. Consequently the 2nd Troop and The Blues returned from Holland a year after they had left, landing at Spithead on 11 May. There was no time to catch up with families or to re-equip, and The Blues marched immediately for Highlake in Cheshire, embarking for Ireland on 19 May. They joined Schomberg and the Dutch Blue Guards on their arrival at Lough Brickland in the Protestant heartland of County Down. (To avoid confusion, The Blues were often colloquially referred to as the Oxford Blues to distinguish them from their less than esteemed colleagues.) Oxford himself joined them in camp, and was to stay with the army during the summer, although effective command was firmly with Francis Compton.

The 2nd Troop of Life Guards remained in London, whilst the 1st, 3rd and Dutch Life Guards arrived in Ireland with William on 14 May. The Royals, who had been deployed during the summer of 1689 in Scotland against Dundee's forces following his victory at Killiecrankie, had arrived the previous October. Separated from the main army at Dundalk, and with a residue of experience from Tangier days, they did not suffer as badly from diseases as the rest of the troops. However, their equipment was worn out and they needed fresh recruits and horses, which were eventually raised in Hertford and joined them in May. By June William's army totalled over 36,000 men and there was sufficient grass to allow him to forage his horses. His plan was to march on Dublin and to force James II either to fight a pitched battle or flee. As William prepared his army to march south, many of the Life Guards, The Blues and The Royals faced a campaign against former friends and colleagues of only a few months before. Many in the two armies wore the same uniforms, particularly the red of James II's regiments. To avoid confusion, the Jacobite army copied the French custom of wearing a white cockade in their hats, mostly, given their chronic supply problems, made from paper, whilst, ironically given the future connotations of that colour, the Williamites wore sprigs of green.

The Irish Jacobite army that faced William was an equal match in numbers, but not in equipment, training or organization. An amalgamation of the original Irish army, many of whom had been interned on the Isle of Wight and had now returned, and that part of the English army still loyal to James II, it was commanded by the autocratic and elderly Richard Talbot, James's friend and colleague from the civil wars, whom he had made Earl of Tyrconnell and Lord Lieutenant of Ireland in 1687. There were able, energetic and professional officers, like Sarsfield and Luttrell, who had fought together in the 4th Troop, and the Tangier veterans Clifford had brought from The Royals, but Tyrconnell seemed to resent the threat they posed to his leadership. Consequently what fighting there had been during the latter part of 1689 and early 1690 had been uncoordinated, with no attempt made to attack Schomberg's disease-ridden forces when they were so vulnerable.

The armies were to meet first near Drogheda. Elements of The Blues and The Royals, forming an advance guard under Sir John Lanier, just as in November 1688, advanced to the River Boyne where James II had decided to make a stand to defend Dublin. James II himself had originally favoured making a stand further north, near Dundalk, but had been overruled by Tyrconnell and his French military adviser, Lauzun. Neither was particularly happy with the revised plan of a stand on the Boyne, both regarding it as still too risky to

IRELAND 1690
0 10 20 30 40 50 miles
0 10 20 30 40 50 km
Royals arrive October 1689
Lough Neagh
Belfast
Charlemont
Enniskillen
Sligo
Newry
Life Guards, Blues arrive May 1690
Dundalk
R. Shannon
1 July 1690 Boyne
Slane
Drogheda
Blues: Spring to Summer 1691
Irish
R. Boyne
R. Suck
Athlone 22 July 1691
Aughrim 12 July 1691
R. Liffey
Dublin 5 July 1690
Galway
Banagher
Blues: Winter 1690–91
Kilcommodon Hill SW of Aughrim
Birr Castle
Lough Derg
Sea
Silvermines Mts
CLARE
Killaloe Bridge
Sarsfield's Raid 11 August 1690
R. Nore
Carlow
Parteen
R. Shannon
Kilkenny
Limerick
3 Troop Life Guards and Blues: August 1690
Ballyneety Castle
R. Barrow
Cashel
Wexford
R. Suir
Clonmel
Waterford
R. Blackwater
Royals – in England August to October 1690
KERRY
Royals: Winter 1690–91
Cork
Kinsale
1 and 2 Troops Life Guards return to London Autumn 1690
Bantry Bay
Castlehaven
James II lands March 1689
N

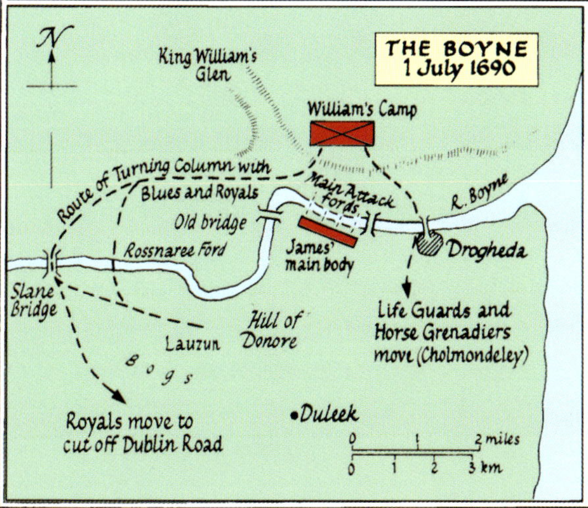
THE BOYNE 1 July 1690
N
King William's Glen
William's Camp
Route of Turning Column with Blues and Royals
Main Attack Fords
R. Boyne
Old bridge
Rossnaree Ford
James' main body
Drogheda
Slane Bridge
Hill of Donore
Lauzun
Life Guards and Horse Grenadiers move (Cholmondeley)
Bogs
Royals move to cut off Dublin Road
Duleek
0 1 2 miles
0 1 2 3 km

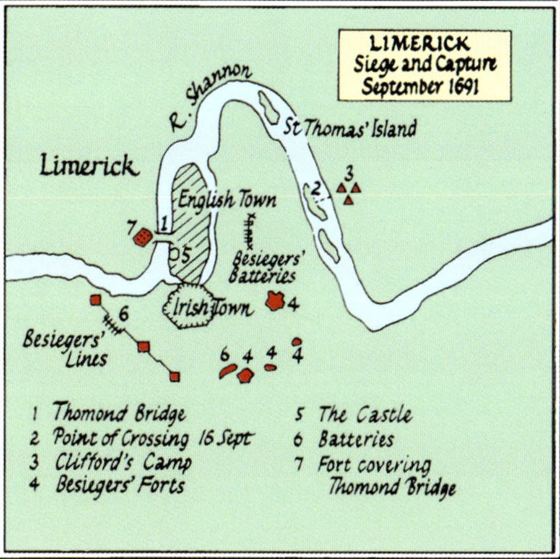
LIMERICK Siege and Capture September 1691
R. Shannon
St Thomas' Island
Limerick
English Town
Besiegers' Batteries
Irish Town
Besiegers' Lines
1 Thomond Bridge
2 Point of Crossing 16 Sept
3 Clifford's Camp
4 Besiegers' Forts
5 The Castle
6 Batteries
7 Fort covering Thomond Bridge

expose the poorly equipped and not very well-trained Irish army in a pitched battle against William III's Dutch and English regulars. James II, however, insisted he had to make a stand or else risk being 'driven fairly into the sea'. In the circumstances the Boyne was an adequate defensive position, and James II positioned his army on the southern bank in an attempt to make William III force a crossing in difficult and restricted terrain where his men had a chance of defeating him piecemeal. The right flank of the Irish army was the town of Drogheda, whose bridge was secured by Lord Iveagh with 1,300 men. From Drogheda upstream there were no crossing points until Oldbridge, where James II concentrated the bulk of his forces. He reasoned that this was the logical place for William to cross and to force the open battle that he wanted. The left flank of the Irish army, to the west, was protected by a flank guard of fewer than 500 under Sir Neal O'Neill, charged with guarding the ford at Rosnaree and the broken-down bridge at Slane. James himself was on Donore Hill, overlooking Oldbridge.

It was a reasonable assessment of the situation, but it did not allow for either the training achieved by William III's troops, of whom Dutch, Huguenot and English elements all had recent experience fighting the French, or William's own ability as a commander to think laterally. Expensive battles against Louis XIV had taught him that there was more value in utilizing space to outmanoeuvre the enemy than there was in attempting to destroy him in a confined area. On 30 June William rode down to join Lanier's force on the Boyne, escorted by a party of Life Guards, and slowly reconnoitred the Irish positions. Seeing the bulk of their forces drawn up between Oldbridge and Drogheda, he realized that James II had made two major mistakes. First, his left flank was dangerously open and vulnerable to an experienced force, and second, by concentrating on defeating the Williamites in the field, he had forgotten that his main objective in fighting a battle at all was to save Dublin. William never forgot that this was his strategic objective. However, he nearly got himself killed before he had a chance to do anything about it. Provocatively picnicking in a field in full view of the Irish positions, he was spotted by an Irish cavalry patrol, possibly led by Sarsfield, who opened fire on him with some light artillery pieces. The first shot killed a Life Guard and two horses, while the second hit the riverbank, but ricocheted, wounding William III in the shoulder. It was not enough to disable him, nor to frustrate his plan, which was to develop almost exactly as he predicted the following day.

A small English force, which included the Life Guards and the Horse Grenadiers, formed, unusually, into a separate regiment under Captain The Honourable George Cholmondeley, were placed under Lord Portland and instructed to cross the Boyne between Oldbridge and Drogheda to prevent Lord Iveagh's force from moving to link up with the main Irish army. Nothing more is recorded of the part this group played in the battle as the action took place elsewhere, so we can only assume that they were successful. The bulk of the English Horse, including The Blues and The Royals, under the command of Count Schomberg, son of the Dutch general, and the English infantry under General Douglas, were formed into a separate right wing. Their orders were to force a crossing of the Boyne to the west of the main Irish positions in the vicinity of Rosnaree and Slane. By 8 o'clock on the baking hot morning of 1 July they had reached the river and by 10 a.m. had forced a passage and scattered O'Neill's small guard force. James II immediately acted as William III had predicted. Fearing that the main attack was now coming on his left flank, he moved the bulk of his troops, under Lauzun and Sarsfield, from Oldbridge to face Schomberg and Douglas, leaving a disconsolate Tyrconnell guarding the main position with a much reduced force. Once the Irish had moved, William III's centre, consisting mostly of Dutch, Huguenot, Danish and local Protestant Irish infantry, closed to the river and forced a crossing at Oldbridge, which was where most of the fighting took place. Tyrconnell fought well, and his remaining horse caused considerable casualties to the Williamite infantry. The Duke of Berwick, so briefly a Colonel of The Blues, who was unhorsed and nearly killed in the resulting mêlée, led one of the charges. William III's general, Marshal Schomberg, was killed, unlamented by the English troops of whom so many had suffered as a result of his dreadful administration.

On his arrival on Donore Hill on the left flank, Sarsfield found a despondent King James. News of Oldbridge was filtering through, and he realized that he had been outwitted. His immediate reaction was to attack Count Schomberg and Douglas, and he ordered Sarsfield and Lauzun to do so, but a bog between the two forces made it virtually impossible. The Royals had already passed on south, behind Donore, to secure the road to Dublin, and James began to realize that the battle was lost. He fled to Dublin while he still could, leaving William III to lead the Enniskillen Regiment in a final assault, now well to the south of the river, which scattered the remaining Irish resistance.

The casualties at the Boyne were not severe, being estimated by William III's secretary as 1,000 on the Irish side and 500 of their own. There are no records of any member of our three regiments being among these, so it is probably safe to conclude that they escaped unharmed.[10] The political consequences, however, were far-reaching. James II stayed only briefly in Dublin, where he had arrived on the evening of the battle. He was offered supper by the beautiful Frances, Duchess of Tyrconnell, who had been previously married to the Catholic Life Guard George Hamilton, killed fighting under Louis XIV in 1676. Frances Tyrconnell was more popular than her husband, known throughout Ireland as 'lying Dick Talbot', but James refused her hospitality, reputedly saying, 'Madam, my breakfast today has been such as to leave me with no appetite for any other meal.'[11] Although much criticized for leaving the battlefield, he had been in the front line all day, losing the heel of a boot to one musket shot, while a second had shattered one of his pistols. What must have concerned

At the Battle of the Boyne, fought on 1 July 1690, William III outflanked
James II and opened the way to Dublin. It was not a spectacularly bloody battle,
and casualties in our regiments were minimal.

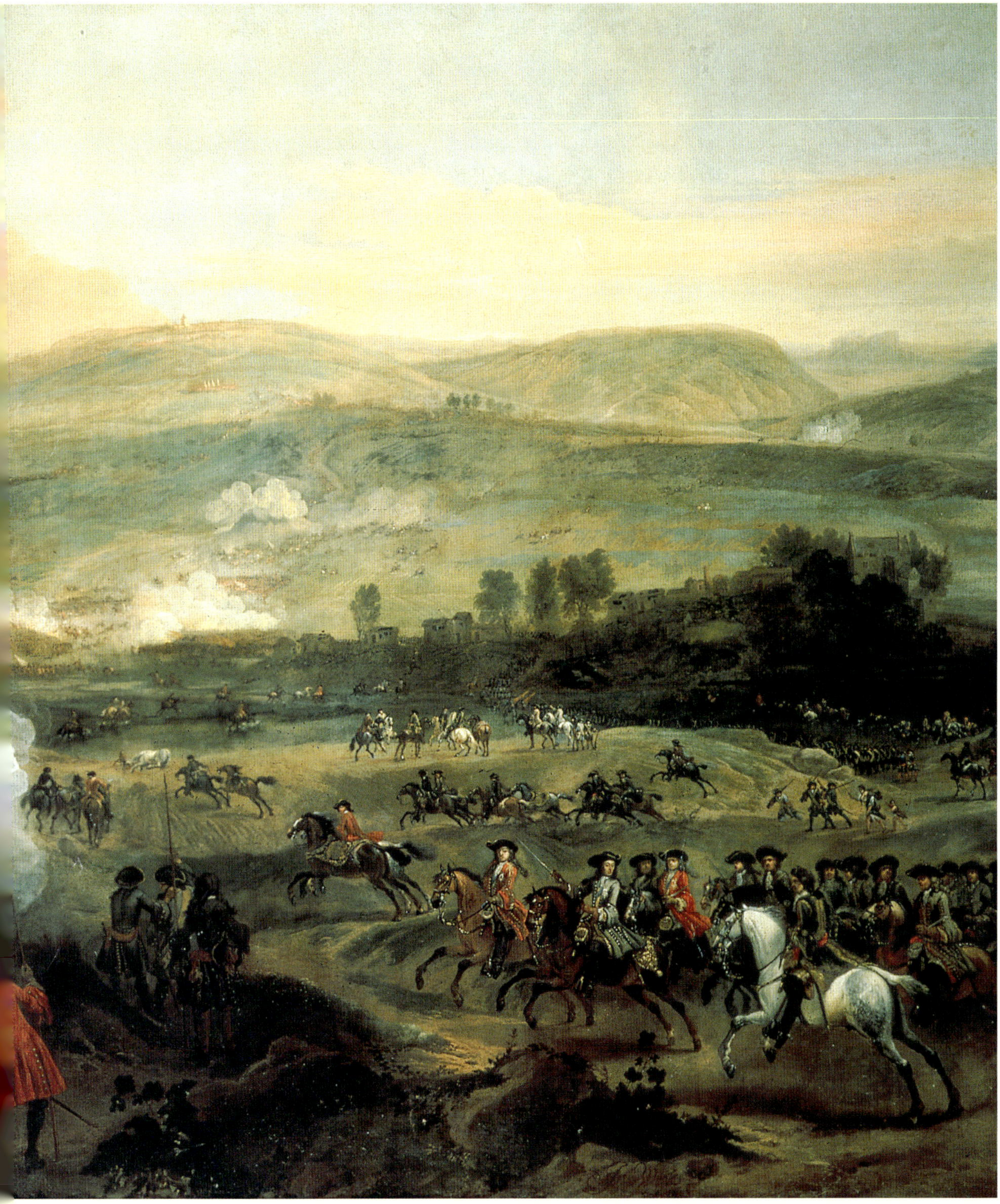

him more was that he had just squandered his main opportunity to recover not only Ireland but also the English throne. He left Dublin the following day, riding to Waterford, from where he sailed to Kinsale and thence to France, leaving Tyrconnell once again in control. The shattered Irish army slowly regrouped on Limerick, the port on the River Shannon in south-west Ireland. William has been criticized for not following up his victory on the Boyne more aggressively. He probably still did not trust his English troops not to go over to the Jacobites, demonstrated by his reliance on his Dutch troops for the main fighting at the Boyne.

Ormond, as Captain of the 2nd Troop, entered Dublin with the Life Guards and Dutch Guards on 4 July. William followed on the 5th, holding a service of thanksgiving in St Patrick's Cathedral, and a review of his army the following day, in which 273 private gentlemen of the Life Guards took part, together with ninety-five Horse Grenadiers and 145 Dutch Life Guards. The Blues numbered 368, and The Royals 406, both showing gaps in their establishment, of which more later (see pp. 172–5). On the 9th William left with the army for Limerick, sending Ormond to reduce Kilkenny, Clonmel and Waterford en route. The Royals went with him, creating such an impression on the terrified Governor of Waterford that he surrendered immediately.

Threats of a French invasion after the naval Battle of Beachy Head required William's temporary return to Dublin, and a portion of his army, including The Royals and two troops of Life Guards, to return home to prepare for operations in Flanders. A detachment of these men was to stay in London to guard the Queen. The Royals arrived in Hoylake in Cheshire on 5 August, a remarkably quick journey that was further evidence of the efficient Blathwayt machinery in Horse Guards, although shipping remained scarce. Only ten ships could be found and forty-two men and ninety horses remained behind in Ireland. The Royals stayed in the Welsh Marches until early September, by which time it was clear that a French invasion was not imminent, and they returned to Ireland once again. Anthony Heyford had died, apparently of natural causes, on 21 June and Edward Matthews, another professional officer destined to be an active colonel, took his place as Colonel. Heyford's widow was awarded a pension from the secret service fund, but probably more as recognition of her husband's valuable service than of any spying activity on his part.[12]

Meanwhile the remainder of William III's army finally arrived outside the walls of Limerick on 2 August to find a well-organized Irish defence. The French general, Boisselau, the Duke of Berwick and Sarsfield had set up a forward line of trenches which The Blues were involved in attempting to clear. William realized that he would need heavy siege artillery to take Limerick, and duly called forward his artillery 'train', which had been slowly following the army and had reached Cashel in County Tipperary.

What followed has become one of the most celebrated events of Irish history, and counts possibly as one of the most daring exploits ever carried out by a Life Guard officer, albeit one now fighting for one king against another. Sarsfield reckoned that if he could destroy the siege train before it reached Limerick there was a good chance that William would be unable to take the city that summer, giving James II time to organize fresh French troops and supplies for a renewed campaign in 1691. Learning of the siege train's progress from a Williamite deserter, and gaining Tyrconnell's reluctant permission, he gathered the best of the Irish cavalry, including those Life Guards and Royals who had remained loyal to James II, and slipped out of Limerick along the west bank of the River Shannon. Crossing the river over the ancient bridge at Killaloe, well north of the Williamite army, he rode through the night guided by a well-known highwayman and 'raparee' called Galloping Hogan. Choosing a remote route through the Silvermine Mountains, they intercepted the siege train near Ballyneety Castle without the Williamites realizing, despite intelligence reaching William III and Ginckel, who had taken over as army commander from Schomberg.

They were helped by the remarkably relaxed attitude of Captain Thomas Poultney, who was guarding the train with about eighty troopers from Colonel Villiers' regiment. It was not to be their finest hour. The train itself consisted of eight 16-pounder guns and about 100 wagons. There were a few fusiliers with the guns themselves, but most of Poultney's men had bedded down for the night some distance away, and he neglected to post sentries. Sarsfield's men surprised them on the night of 11 August, and although they only killed about twenty of the escort, they wrecked two guns completely, destroyed the carriages of the remaining six, and, most importantly, blew up the irreplaceable gunpowder. Poultney escaped across a cornfield without his boots, as, annoyingly for Sarsfield but importantly for William, did the Dutch Master Gunner Willem Meesters.[13]

Although the loss was made good throughout the winter, Sarsfield had achieved his aim of preventing an all-out attack on Limerick that summer. William III did attempt an assault, during which Captain Lucy of The Blues, whose portrait in his buff coat still hangs at Charlecote, was killed, but it failed, and very wet weather in late August forced him to abandon the siege. He returned to London, where his Life Guards had preceded him, leaving Ginckel with the considerable problem of accommodating and feeding the army throughout the winter. There was little more fighting, although Sarsfield slipped out of Limerick again to besiege Birr Castle, which the Williamite Sir Laurence Parsons was holding. General Kirke, the unattractive Governor of Tangier, headed a relief force that consisted of The Blues and the 3rd Troop of Life Guards, the only remaining Life Guards in Ireland. They raised the siege, and Sarsfield retired west across the Shannon at Banagher, but Kirke then destroyed all houses and crops around Birr, causing terrible suffering throughout the winter and resulting in the lasting enmity of the population and, consequently, much damage to the English reputation in Ireland.

The 3rd Troop returned to London in January 1691, whilst The Blues, in quarters around Birr and its neighbouring villages, and The Royals in County Cork, faced a miserable winter. The population, hardly surprisingly after Kirke's exploits, were hostile. There were frequent attacks by raparees, and bands of former Irish soldiers, part guerrilla fighters and part criminals desperate to feed themselves. During the course of the winter they captured over 1,000 horses from the English regiments, including, allegedly, twenty-two that were Sir John Lanier's own. William III had learnt from Schomberg's inactivity the previous winter, and constantly urged Ginckel to keep harassing the Irish, leading to several fruitless attacks. Morale was lifted temporarily by Marlborough's independent expedition to capture Cork and Kinsale in late September, in which his troop of Life Guards participated, and The Royals had a significant local success in December against a party of raparees who were attacking Castlehaven, killing over forty of them.

However, what both regiments were now facing was the need to organize themselves for protracted expeditionary operations, something of which the English army had precious little corporate memory and little supporting infrastructure. The Tangier Horse had always operated from a fixed base, and certainly The Blues' experience of policing the Home Counties was hardly preparation for what must have been an extraordinary two years, from Sedgemoor to Flanders to Ireland. Replacing men, horses and equipment, and maintaining morale, began to test the regimental organization severely. The nearest equivalent situation for them was the civil war, in which several officers and soldiers still serving had fought, including Compton, and it was to that system that they now returned, using areas of England as regimental depots in much the same way as the County Associations had supported Cromwell's army. The reason why both regiments appeared short of men at William III's Dublin Review was not casualties at the Boyne, as is often taken to be the case, but because troops were prudently left behind in England to organize new horses, or 'remounts' as they were termed, and recruits.[14] These troops were also responsible for collecting new equipment – there was no organization capable of collecting it from a combination of the Ordnance and selected regimental suppliers – and getting it out to Birr and to Cork. When The Royals were ordered back to Ireland in the autumn of 1690, Colonel Heyford had, for example, left a troop in Gloucester, who in May 1691 supplied the regiment not only with men and remounts but also with weapons, camp kettles, buckets, saddlery, belts and coats.[15]

Other customs, which were to become an accepted part of regimental and army life, also started to develop. Messes, the system by which different ranks pooled their ration allowance to eat together, which had started during the Hounslow Camps, became established and helped morale in the dangerous and uncomfortable conditions. Surprisingly good medical arrangements were also made, presumably as a result of the cost of Schomberg's maladministration the

Marshal Schomberg (*right*) was William's first commander in Ireland and ranks, amongst stiff competition, as the most incompetent of the group of Dutch favourites who were inflicted on the British army in the 1690s.

Godert De Ginckel (*below*) took over command of the English forces in Ireland at the beginning of 1691. Easily outclassing Schomberg, he was the victor at Athlone, Aughrim and Limerick.

James II left Ireland after the Boyne, leaving Richard Talbot, Earl of Tyrconnell (*below right*), as his Viceroy in Ireland. Known as 'lying Dick Talbot' it was Tyrconnell's scheming which did so much damage to the Jacobite cause and which infuriated Sarsfield.

previous winter. A base hospital was established in Dublin, a marching hospital was set up which followed the army the following summer, and both regiments had additional surgeons' mates appointed.[16]

By May 1691 Ginckel concluded there was sufficient grass to mobilize the army. The Irish, reinforced by French troops throughout the winter as Sarsfield had hoped, held the line of the River Shannon, with the major cities of Athlone and Limerick to the south. The addition of the French contingent was to cause considerable problems. It certainly gave a disciplined core to the Irish army, but the French troops never really integrated, and the Williamites hated their commander, St Ruth, particularly as he had been the general responsible for the persecution of the French Huguenots after the revocation of the Edict of Nantes. He was also a quarrelsome individual, who took his orders from Versailles rather than Tyrconnell or Berwick. Ginckel's campaign plan was to take Athlone first, to keep the Irish west of the river, and then swing south to take Limerick, whereupon, he correctly estimated, Irish resistance would collapse. The Royals continued suppressing raparees in Cork, with some success, while The Blues marched with Ginckel for Athlone.

They were not heavily engaged in the subsequent fighting, it being largely an infantry battle, but the city fell on 22 June, despite St Ruth and the French contingent being camped nearby. It was, however, a blow to St Ruth's Gallic pride, and his next decision, to face Ginckel in an open battle, was probably based largely on his desire to salvage his reputation. The decision was certainly fiercely contested by Berwick and Sarsfield, who realized that Ginckel's resupplied force of over 18,000 would easily outmatch them. The site St Ruth chose, near the village of Aughrim, was, however, a good one. His left flank, anchored on Aughrim village and the remains of its castle, in front of which was a bog crossed only by a narrow causeway, was defended by Major General Dominic Sheldon's division, whose dragoons were under the command of Henry Luttrell, the officer from the Catholic 4th Troop of Life Guards who had fought with Sarsfield in the skirmish at Wincanton. St Ruth's right was on the commanding ground of Kilcommodon Hill. Here he placed a second division of infantry, with beyond them his fourth and final division under Sarsfield consisting mainly of horse and dragoons. Ginckel, advancing south towards Galway from Athlone, had no real option but to attack the position, which he proceeded to do on the afternoon of Sunday, 12 July. He had decided that he would make feint attacks on the left, against Kilcommodon, and the centre, while developing his main attack on the right against Aughrim village. On his left, in other words opposite Sarsfield, he placed his Dutch, Danish and Huguenot horse. Next, in his centre and against the Irish centre, were the foreign infantry and then the English infantry, more or less opposite Aughrim village. On the far right was the English horse, with Compton and The Blues to their front.

Ginckel's first move was to send his foreign infantry against St Ruth's. They had some success in forcing the Irish infantry back on to Kilcommodon Hill, but were then charged successfully by Sarsfield and fell back. The foreign horse then engaged Sarsfield in one of the major cavalry engagements of the Irish war, pushing forward up the hill and gradually forcing the Irish horse back, but they had taken heavy casualties and were exhausted by the time they reached the second Irish line. The situation developed into stalemate. On the right, the English infantry had similar results, gaining some ground around Aughrim, but Luttrell's dragoons forced them back so that they maintained only a tenuous hold on the causeway across the bog, the only route by which the English Horse could advance. It was not going well for Ginckel, who could not afford a defeat. St Ruth had in fact declared that the day was his, and Ginckel knew he had but one last chance. He therefore took the risky gamble of sending forward the English horse on the right, the only one of his divisions yet to be engaged, to try to force the Aughrim village position and relieve the pressure on his infantry.

Major General Mackay, who commanded the English infantry, rode back to show the leading horse patrols the way forward. They were unenthusiastic at being asked to advance two abreast, which was all the causeway would allow, against entrenched infantry whom a whole English division had so far failed to clear. Beyond them, on the hill, were Luttrell's dragoons waiting to engage any that got through. Mackay, now in a fury, rode forward himself to prove the route, only for his horse to jump an unseen wall and for him to fall headlong into the bog. It was rumoured to be the only occasion on which the deeply religious Mackay was heard to swear. It was an inauspicious start for such a dangerous manoeuvre, and it was only by luck and the extraordinary bravery of Francis Compton and The Blues that it succeeded. Galloping forward two abreast along the causeway, they braced themselves for the inevitable hail of musket fire that would surely greet them from the Irish infantry still safely ensconced in the village and the castle. But no fire came. In one of those cock-ups that so characterize warfare, the Irish infantry, breaking into their reserve boxes of ammunition, found that they had been issued with English musket balls that were too large for their French flintlocks. All they could do was watch helplessly as Compton swept past. The Blues, unaware of their good fortune, charged right through the village, only to find that the two Irish regiments said to have been positioned on the road immediately behind Aughrim had moved to reinforce the centre and had not been replaced. The only Irish troops ahead of them were Luttrell's dragoons, whom they now quickly engaged. 'Sir Francis Compton, with my Lord of Oxford's Regiment, being one of the first that could be in a posture to engage, he fell a random in amongst the enemy, & charged them briskly with sword in hand & though his men were once or twice repulsed, they soon made good their party on that side though not without loss of several, both men and horses,' wrote the Rev. Doctor Story, a chaplain in the Williamite army, who witnessed the battle.[17]

Yet the outcome was still far from certain. There were only six squadrons of Horse with The Blues, and St Ruth still had Sarsfield's uncommitted reserve, which he now quickly led across Kilcommodon Hill to engage The Blues. At this point a stray English cannonball removed St Ruth's head, and the whole Irish force faltered. Sarsfield himself was still engaged on the right against the foreign Williamite Horse, and when he did arrive it was too late to reinvigorate them. Everywhere the Irish infantry were retreating, and Ginckel's forces were advancing unchecked up the hill. He gave what cover he could with his remaining regiments to allow as many of the infantry as possible to get away, but it was a hopeless task, and he must have realized then that Ireland was lost.

By now it was 8 p.m., a misty evening, and the defeat turned into a rout and slaughter as Ginckel's forces pursued the Irish fugitives. The scenes on Kilcommodon Hill, described by a Danish eyewitness, were horrific, and made worse by the fact that many of the Irish families had been camped behind the army. It seems the ferocity of the fighting unleashed the rage and emotions of the Huguenots turned out of France, the Protestants who had lost everything to the Jacobites, and the soldiers who had seen so many of their comrades killed. 'Terrible scenes followed as the English fell on the rear of the fugitives,' wrote Claudianus,[18]

> stricken with terror we saw them fleeing in all directions across the countryside into the mountains, bogs and wildernesses. Like mad people the women, children and waggoners filled every road weeping and wailing. Worse still was the sight . . . of the many men and horses too badly wounded to get away, who when attempting to rise fell back unable to bear their own weight. Some, mutilated and in great pain, begged to be put out of their misery, and others coughed up blood and threats, their bloodied weapons frozen in their hands as if in readiness for some future battle.

But there was to be no future battle. Aughrim had effectively ended Jacobite hopes in Ireland. The Irish had lost almost everything: artillery, gunpowder, muskets, food, forage and, most importantly, their leadership. Tyrconnell suffered a stroke the following month, unlamented by all except James II in Paris. St Ruth was dead, as were two brigadier generals and nine colonels. The most effective Irish major generals, Hamilton and Dorrington, were captured. Total Irish losses have never been properly established, with estimates between 4,000 and 7,000. The macabre body counters on Kilcommodon counted only 7,000 corpses in all, many of whom were from Ginckel's army. His foreign infantry and horse had suffered badly, and his total casualties were estimated at 3,000, making the lower Irish figure of 4,000 the more likely to be accurate. Sadly, among Ginckel's losses were too many of The Blues: one captain, two lieutenants, one cornet, forty-five privates killed and twenty-one wounded, with twenty-four horses killed. It was a fairly devastating tally for a regiment that had until then survived the campaign remarkably intact, and they were losses that would not be made up until the following year.

Yet there was still a small Irish force, concentrated under Berwick and Sarsfield in Limerick, which attempted to fight on, partly in the now almost incredible hope that the French, once more engaged against William III in Flanders, might send help, and partly in an attempt to negotiate decent surrender terms. Ginckel quickly captured Galway on 19 July and started to besiege Limerick on 25 August. He found it, as before, a tricky task. He needed to get troops across the Shannon if he was effectively to encircle the city, and yet if he did so he risked splitting his force and leaving himself vulnerable. With no bridge to allow the two parts of his army to reinforce each other quickly, he realized that he had to build one. There were few viable places, and the best site, upstream at Parteen, where the river was shallow and ran between two islands, was guarded by a strong Irish contingent of horse under our old friend Major Clifford, late of the Royal Dragoons.

Clifford's behaviour had become increasingly bizarre during the course of the campaign. He had failed to distinguish himself during the operations around Athlone, and at one point appeared every day, glass in hand, to drink the health of his English adversaries. It is evidence of how severe the Irish losses had been at Aughrim that Sarsfield now entrusted this key position to his old partner in crime, but it was to prove a fatal decision. On a particularly misty night Ginckel got a force of grenadiers across the river, which protected his engineers while they assembled a bridge of boats. They were discovered just before daylight, and urgent messages were sent to the sleeping Clifford, who refused to believe them. He 'seemed not to give credit to any such account, as not fearing that the enemy would dare undertake so perilous a passage',[19] and when he did it was too late. Ironically, the first complete English regiment across was The Royals, who had joined Ginckel from Cork, but history does not relate what Clifford's reaction was when he was told. Ginckel was now able to surround Limerick, and the French regarded Clifford's action, or lack of it, as treachery. Sarsfield was forced to lock his friend up in Limerick Castle to await court martial. It was never to take place, for his ineptitude had made Limerick indefensible and Sarsfield, by now effectively commanding the Irish forces, realized that surrender was inevitable.

In the circumstance, he cajoled relatively generous terms out of Ginckel, who did not want to spend another winter in Ireland and who believed that his job was done. The Treaty of Limerick, signed on 3 October, allowed whichever soldiers in the Irish army who so chose to leave Ireland for exile in France. Thus originated the Wild Geese, those Irishmen and English Catholics who were to fight for Louis XIV in the Irish Brigades against William III and Marlborough, and whose sad plight has given rise to so many songs and stories. There were dreadful scenes as they set sail from Ireland, most forced to abandon their families, destitute, on the quayside, having been promised they

Limerick fell in October 1692 after Clifford's incompetence when his old regiment, The Royals, surprised him as he guarded the ford over the River Shannon

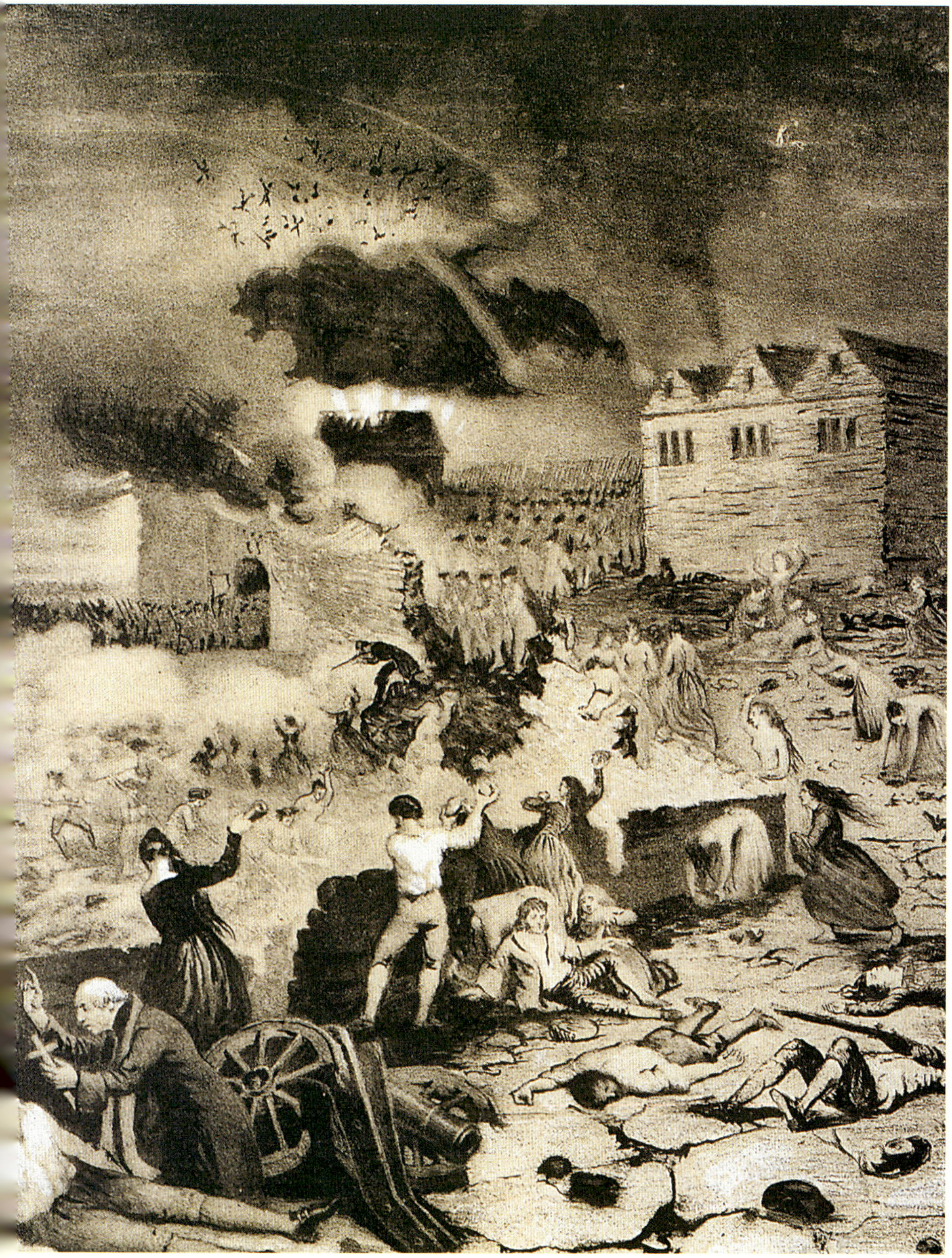

could accompany them. Many were also allegedly pressurized into signing up to French service by Sarsfield and his lieutenants. Eventually about 8,000 left, but, of those it is unclear how many were former Life Guards or Royals. Clifford, wisely, decided to stay in Ireland. Luttrell, who was accused of treason at Aughrim, and who was certainly corresponding with Ginckel's forces after the battle, went even further and announced that he was joining William's army. He lived until 1717 when he was assassinated in Dublin, not by some enraged Jacobite but by the husband of a woman he had been seeing. He was long regarded with particular loathing by Irish historians and as late as 1809 a popular poem ran:

> If heav'n be pleas'd, when mortals cease to sin –
> And hell be pleas'd when villains enter in –
> If earth be pleas'd, when it entombs a knave –
> All must be pleas'd – Now Luttrell's in his grave.

Sarsfield himself took his young wife to France. James II, ever fond of his Life Guards, created two troops from the Wild Geese; Berwick was Colonel of the 1st Troop and Sarsfield, whom James had created Earl of Lucan in 1690, of the 2nd. They functioned as an entity until at least 1695, and even at Culloden forty years later there were still references to them. Sarsfield fought as a Major General in French service against William III at Steenkirk and Landen where he was killed amidst the general slaughter on 29 July 1693. He left his nineteen-year-old widow three months pregnant with their son. She went on to marry the Duke of Berwick, that honourable, able, but ultimately tragic man, who was infatuated with her, much to James II's disgust; he did not approve of his son, albeit illegitimate, marrying a woman with no position or fortune. She died soon afterwards, aged twenty-four, and the heartbroken Berwick brought up Sarsfield's son as his own. He went on to become a Colonel in the Irish Brigades and a keen Jacobite plotter.

Chapter Six

FLANDERS FIELDS

For The Blues and The Royals the Treaty of Limerick offered an opportunity to go home. The Royals arrived back in England in January 1692, and were sent by Blathwayt to Leicester to resume their normal peacetime routine for two years. The Blues also returned in 1692, their headquarters now established in Westminster, and took over the duties normally performed by the Life Guards who, since June 1691, had been deployed fighting the French for William in Flanders. The Royals were not to become involved in that war until 1694 and The Blues were never involved at all. If Walcourt and Ireland had been a shock to The Blues, the ferocity of the fighting in Flanders was to verge on the horrific for the private gentlemen of the Life Guards, many of whom had purchased their places on the assumption of a more leisurely service. In terms of casualties it was to presage a future war just over two centuries away. From June 1691, when they fought at the Battle of Leuse, until the Peace of Ryswick six years later, the majority of the Life Guards were to be almost permanently deployed, acting either as William III's bodyguard, or with the combined troops of Horse Grenadiers as a regiment of horse. There is no accurate record of their total casualties, but the English army suffered heavily overall and, judging by the number of foreigners whom it was found necessary to recruit to fill gaps, the figure could have been as high as 200, or around 25 per cent of their combined strength.

It is not clear why the Life Guards were left overseas for so long. Few other regiments completed the full campaign, and they could have been relieved to carry out their traditional duties at home. William may have thought that many of them still harboured strong Jacobite sympathies and that they were best kept in Flanders where they would be unable to cause any trouble. After Aughrim he had come to trust The Blues completely, and knew that he could rely on Oxford and Compton to suppress any unrest in London, a confidence he did not, for example, extend to Marlborough and his 3rd Troop. It is impossible to ignore the fact that the Life Guards, of all the troops deployed, were kept the most heavily engaged in the war. Ironically, such Jacobite sympathies as eventually emerged did so in The Blues as well.

The Life Guards initially longed to get involved in the war. The events of 1690 and early 1691 had not been particularly satisfactory for them. Whilst they had proved themselves to William III's satisfaction at Walcourt, they had been left out of the action at the Boyne and sent back to England shortly thereafter. They knew that the King still did not fully trust them and they were not sanctioned to resume their former duties in London, which were now the preserve of the Dutch Guards. Instead they were banished to Cheshire with the Horse Grenadiers at Northampton. Several, like Sir James Hayes and Captain Thomas Smith, took leave to return to fight in Ireland, attaching themselves to other regiments. William also now created an entirely Dutch 4th Troop, which was unpopular with its English and Scottish counterparts as soldiers were posted into it on merit and not even the officers purchased their commissions. William's confidant, Monsieur Overkirke, commanded it and the best jobs tended to come its way. The soldiers were also known in London as bad payers. It came as something of a relief therefore when, in June 1691, the 3rd and 4th Troops were sent to Flanders via London, and even more so that they were to form a regiment together under Ormond with a detachment of Horse Grenadiers.

William III did, however, trust Ormond, who had won his respect in Ireland. It was his 2nd Troop that was left behind to guard the Queen, although in practice the troops cross-posted and by 1697 most had served for at least a year on active service. Ormond himself 'had the reputation of a very brave officer, though never that of a very able one'.[1] He was also thought to be 'more addicted to pleasure than business, and fond of splendour. Power was of no other use to him than as it raised his glory.'[2] He reflected his liking for splendour in commissioning in 1696, 'Two standards of white damask trimmed with gold fringe'[3] showing a highly dubious ceremonial taste which the Life Guards must have hoped had gone with James II. His administration was also at fault: in 1694 his preferred agent, a Mr Downes, absconded with £2,000 of the troop's money in cash.[4] Whatever his shortcomings, however, Ormond was undoubtedly a highly effective field commander, and the Life Guards owe him a considerable debt for so enhancing their reputation with the King that by 1697 he considered them to be as good as his Dutch Guards.

The Allied war aims were to prevent the increasing dominance of Catholic and absolutist France in Northern Europe in general, especially given Louis XIV's very public support for James II, and to prevent France from annexing the French-speaking lower part of the United Provinces in particular. Arriving in Flanders in June 1691, Ormond found that the French Marshal Luxemburg, who had seized the frontier fortress of Mons and was now threatening the gathering Allied army in Brussels, had outwitted William. William attempted to cut him off by manoeuvring behind him, but failed. Luxemburg retired to Mons and Tournai, and William to Brussels, from where he returned to England with Ormond, assuming the fighting was over and leaving a reduced army under

James, Second Duke of Ormond, Colonel of the Second Troop, had 'the reputation of a very brave officer, though never that of a very able one'. Despite that, he proved a competent commander in Flanders and ranks as one of the greater Gold Sticks.

Prince Waldeck. Waldeck, supposing that Luxemburg would also be seeking winter quarters, pushed forward to Leuse, near the French border, about 15 miles east of Tournai, to do the same. Luxemburg, however, moved forward to attack in early September, uncomfortable that Louis XIV would feel he had achieved little in a full campaigning season. He took Waldeck by surprise in a thick mist as his army was on its final day's march. Ten thousand French cavalry, including the Maison Militaire du Roi, fell on the Allied rear as they were crossing a bridge midway between Leuse and Cambron. The French trapped a large part of the Allied infantry against the river and killed 500 before the rest escaped and the Allied horse came up to counter-attack. The Life Guards were the only English regiment of Horse engaged, and were in some of the worst fighting. One private gentleman broke through the French ranks and was on the point of capturing Luxemburg before his bodyguard killed him. There was no more fighting after that, and the Life Guards were left in Flanders to endure the winter.

William III returned to Holland in March 1692, having secured funding from Parliament for 23,000 English troops. Ormond came with remounts and detachments from the other troops, so the Life Guards started that summer's campaign 600 strong. The job of guarding the Queen was given to the Scottish Troop. With Marlborough in one of his periodic disgraces and recently superseded as Captain of the 3rd Troop by Lord Colchester, command of the English contingent was given to yet another incompetent Dutchman, Count Solmes, whose chief claim to his position seems to have been an advanced degree of anglophobia. Luxemburg, whose victory at Leuse ensured he held Mons, opened the campaign season by once more surprising the Allies and taking Naumur, then conducting a flanking move to march on Brussels from the north-west. William marched out to meet him. Luxemburg halted his 115,000-strong force at the village of Steenkirk, about 20 miles north-west of Brussels, in thickly wooded country which he thought afforded adequate protection. To William, however, it offered an opportunity to attack in a place where Luxemburg would find his cavalry difficult to use. By chance William had discovered a French spy in his camp, and he now forced this man to write to Luxemburg saying that the troop movements that he would see the next day were only foraging parties and should not be taken seriously. Luxemburg fell into the trap and the following morning duly ignored reports of an Allied advance. He only realized his mistake when the Allied artillery barrage started, something which contemporary tactical rules demanded precede an infantry assault, but which forfeited all the surprise that William had gained.

Luxemburg quickly reorganized his forces, but already on the French right thirteen English battalions had forced back fifty-three French battalions which had been caught trying to deploy into battle formation. The first line of French troops had given way, and the second was on the point of doing so. William, commanding from the front, now sent back urgently to Solmes, in charge of

FLANDERS 1689–1697

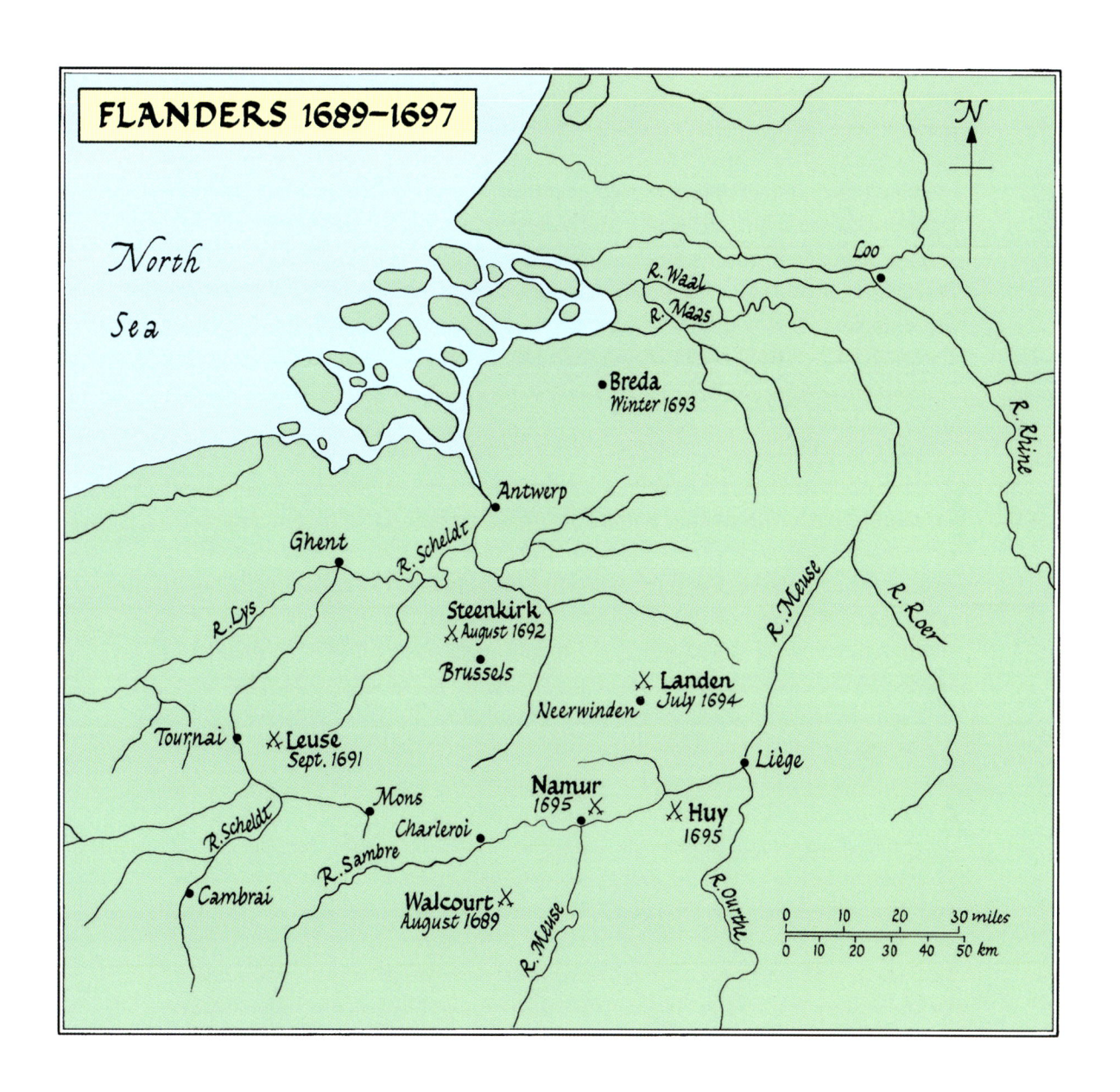

the reserves, for more infantry. For some reason Solmes had put the reserve infantry battalions behind the horse, so they could not get past them without a major reshuffle, awkward on the broken ground. He seems consequently to have decided it was too difficult to obey the King's demands, sending only some horse that could do little. Some infantry did eventually manage to get forward, but by then it was too late. Luxemburg had completed his reorganization and sent the French and Swiss infantry of the Maison Militaire du Roi to charge downhill to dislodge the increasingly hard-pressed English. The English line wavered and then broke. Both Sarsfield and Berwick took part in this charge. The Allied horse now came forward to cover their retreating infantry, and it was now that the Life Guards were most engaged. The Horse Grenadiers dismounted and, acting as dragoons, provided a rearguard action during which Lieutenant Colonel Cholmondeley, their commander, was wounded.

The total losses were severe. Of the 15,000 Allied troops engaged, over 3,000 were killed, 3,000 wounded and 1,300 taken prisoner. The Life Guards and Horse Grenadiers lost Brigadier Sooles, who was killed, and Colonel Staples, Captain Peavey, Captain Bennefield and Captain Jordan, all wounded in addition to Cholmondeley; there is no record of the non-commissioned casualties. The French suffered 7,000 casualties. Both armies were too badly broken for there to be any further fighting that summer. Solmes was execrated by everyone, dismissed by William and criticized in Parliament. He was rumoured to have held back the English reinforcements with the words, 'Damn the English! Since they are so fond of fighting, let them have a bellyful!'

Another depressing winter followed, made worse for the many wounded at Steenkirk by the abysmal English medical facilities. The Dutch had an adequate system in place, having learned that their traditional method of relying on nuns to care for the wounded was not a particularly good idea in Catholic areas where they tended to favour their French co-religionists over the Protestant Dutch and German soldiery. The English appear to have ignored the lessons learnt in Ireland, and no formal hospital system operated in Flanders. A contemporary report after Steenkirk tells of English soldiers 'lying with their wounds up and down the streets of Brussels'[5] and even Blathwayt, presumably partly responsible for medical organization, complained of the houses taken over by surgeons as 'miserable, under funded and badly in debt'. Some action was taken by the Princesse de Vaudemont, married to one of the Dutch generals and an early prototype of Florence Nightingale, who moved some of the worst cases into her palace. However, deaths from infection and from epidemics generally would have accounted for a good proportion of the total Life Guard casualties.

Losses were also occurring as private gentlemen were taken for commissions in other regiments. A general shortage of officers continued, and Members of Parliament aired the usual complaints that the army was reverting to the Cromwellian model of 'trumpeters and corporals',[6] rather than gentlemen, as

General Hugh Mackay showed The Blues the way forward at Aughrim, and fought with William's army in Flanders.

John Churchill became Colonel of the Third Troop of Life Guards in 1685 as a reward for the fundamental role he played at Sedgemoor. Initially a strong supporter of James II, whose patronage had advanced him, he turned to William of Orange in 1688. He was later elevated to Earl and later Duke of Marlborough, and commanded the Life Guards and The Blues at Walcourt in 1689 – but neither regiment served under him in his great campaigns in the War of the Spanish Succession.

officers who might not be sufficiently respectful to the divine rights of the propertied classes. Consequently the Life Guards, mostly men of at least some property, were much in demand elsewhere and the careers of several successful officers, such as Major General Henry Wood, started in the troops deployed in Flanders. But keeping up their own numbers was difficult for the Life Guards. The supply of would-be private gentlemen prepared to pay to serve in a war fought largely in the Dutch interest was not inexhaustible. In January 1693 the King ordered The Blues to send a draft over to make up the Life Guard numbers, a tactic used several times. Recruits were also found from the Dutch and French Huguenots, who William thought would make good officers and whom he wanted educated. There was no military academy at the time, William's plans for one having been thrown out by Parliament in 1689 in the same debate in which they discussed the licensing of hackney carriages, and furthermore he had always intended that the Life Guards should have an educational role. By 1697 there were 111 foreigners serving as private gentlemen. Soldiers for the line regiments were also hard to find, although a run of bad harvests in the 1690s and the resultant shortage of food swelled the recruiting officer's rolls.

The fourth year of the war, 1693, was to see even worse fighting. Ormond once again commanded a combined Life Guard and Horse Grenadier detachment, part of a total of 3,300 English horse and dragoons deployed. Yet the total Allied strength of 60,000 was still only half that of the French, and their numbers were further reduced by William's decision to dispatch the Duke of Wurtemberg with 14,000 men to protect Antwerp and the Scheldt estuary. Luxemburg's campaign plan that year was simple. He knew that his army was strong enough to destroy the Allies in a pitched battle and, if he could tempt William into the open from his prepared positions at Louvain, that he had a very good chance of winning the war. He did this by capturing the critical fortress of Huy on the River Meuse after a series of forced marches for which he would become famous and which once more took the Allies by surprise, and then threatening Liège. Were William to lose both, then the southern half of Flanders would be undefended. He marched south, and Luxemburg, again by forced marches, advanced to attack him on the march near Landen. William had chosen a curiously bad site for his camp, probably because he did not expect the French to come on him so soon. It was a triangular-shaped piece of ground, flanked by two streams which restricted movement on the flanks, and which presented a long front of 4 miles at its base and was therefore inevitably lightly defended. The key to the position was the small village of Neerwinden.

William realized he had been manoeuvred into an unfavourable position and was rumoured to have spent the night before the battle praying in his coach. He had, however, enough warning of Luxemburg's approach at least to make a plan, and for his troops to fortify their weak perimeter as best they could. The English infantry were now entrusted with the main positions, a striking change in William's attitude, perhaps brought about by their behaviour at

Steenkirk. The English horse and dragoons were stationed behind the infantry, in the area between the two streams, and divided into two wings. The Life Guards and Horse Grenadiers were on the left, under Ormond, who also had four other regiments.

Luxemburg split his force into three columns. One, on the left, would attack Neerwinden; a second, in the centre, commanded by Berwick, would attack the Allied centre, whilst a third column, on the right, would work its way round to the villages of Rumsdorp and Neerlanden. It was a simple design to cause maximum attrition and to rely on overwhelming force to annihilate William's army. Luxemburg was in no hurry, and his force stood for two hours in the early morning under fire from the Allied artillery while plans were perfected and ranks dressed, yet when the huge columns did move forward they could not penetrate the Allied line. The fighting was fiercest on the left where William positioned himself with the English Foot Guards, and in the centre, where Berwick was stranded as his men retreated, and where he was captured by Brigadier George Churchill, his cousin. On the right, four English infantry battalions held off sixteen French. Luxemburg decided therefore to concentrate his forces at one point, something he might have done to advantage earlier, and sent his reserves against the Foot Guards at Neerwinden. English casualties were already 4,000 out of the 14,000 who had been stationed there, and one can only imagine their feelings as they saw the French reserves, some 12,000 including both the horse and the infantry of the Maison Militaire du Roi, bearing down on them. It was too much, and despite bitter hand-to-hand fighting, William saw that he must withdraw.

The action now passed over to the horse and dragoons. The Duc de Montmorency, Luxemburg's son, rapidly enveloped the Allied right, mostly Dutch and German troops. It was again William himself who rescued the situation by riding over to Ormond and bringing up the division on the left. It did not save the day, but the shock of Ormond's charge stopped Montmorency's force and allowed the infantry to get away without being cut down. Ormond charged with the 1st Dragoon Guards and promptly had his horse shot from under him; he was being hacked at by a French horseman when 'a gentleman of the French guards perceiving his air of virtue & quality rode up and stopped the bloody villain's hand and asked his name & quality which he gave to the Duc d'Elbœuf, who was at the head of the cavalry there'.[7] William almost suffered a similar fate, and was only just saved by Lieutenant Hatton Compton of the 3rd Troop who rescued him from his captors with a few men and was instantly promoted to Colonel for his efforts.

It was a disastrous day, with over 12,000 Allied casualties as opposed to 8,000 French. Sarsfield had been killed in the centre, and Solmes also fell, unlamented by the English. Ormond, who was well treated by the French, had his wounds dressed with sugar and was taken to Namur in d'Elboeuf's coach before eventually being exchanged for Berwick. He returned to Brussels on

16 August, having paid the medical expenses of the other Life Guard prisoners he found in Naumur from his own pocket. Yet Luxemburg had no more reserves, while William still had Wurtemberg's force. He contented himself by taking Charleroi, while the Life Guards went into winter quarters at Breda. They rescued William once more before settling down for the winter, when a French patrol south-west of Brussels surprised him and seventeen French were killed. As he took up his winter residence at Loo he must have realized that any doubts he had entertained as to their Jacobite sympathies were now surely passed.

Landen was the last set-piece battle in the protracted war. In 1694 William assembled his largest army to date, totalling nearly 90,000 and including all four troops of Life Guards, the Horse Grenadiers and 800 Dutch horse guards. The Royals were now also deployed, arriving from the Midlands in May 1694. William for once nearly surprised Luxemburg by circumventing him to the north in an attempt to reach Dunkirk, but the great Marshal was too quick for him, realized what he was trying to do and forestalled him by marching 120 miles in six days and blocking his path. Thereafter the summer passed in watchful inactivity, and no major engagement ensued although The Royals were involved in several skirmishes, the first occasion of many in the course of its long history when the regiment would fight the French. The Royals' lack of experience over the last few years was evident in these engagements, as by the end of the war they had eighteen prisoners to redeem, more than any other English regiment of horse or dragoons. It did not seem to have any effect on Colonel Matthews' career, as he was soon made a Brigadier, commanding the Scots Greys and Fairfax's Dragoons as well as The Royals.

Despite Luxemburg's masterful move to counter William, energy seemed to have drained from the French campaign as they garrisoned an increasingly long line of frontier forts, either their own or those they had taken. The dreadful losses of Steenkirk and Landen, and the realization that the two armies were too evenly matched for either to strike a decisive blow, meant that the war was rapidly becoming one of constant manoeuvre with no appetite for a battle. Added to this was the effect in France of a declining economy, and a consequent shortage of money, and in England of a Parliament becoming increasingly exasperated at the cost in money and men, in that order, of their new King's European adventures. Neither King was helped by a run of bad harvests in the 1690s that caused famine and agricultural hardship. In September 1694 the Allies recaptured Huy, and the following January Luxemburg died, his place taken by the altogether less effective Villeroi. Queen Mary also died that winter. Her husband's long absences had obviously taken their toll on their relationship as he went hunting while she lay in state. It was not such a bad winter for the Life Guards, several of whose wives obtained permission from the Secretary at War to cross to Holland to be with them.

In the 1695 campaign William raised 88,000 men, of whom 30,000 were English, and retook Namur, a major setback for the French and possibly the biggest military reverse Louis XIV had suffered. Gradually, now, the war seemed to be going the Allies' way, and success at Namur placated Parliament who voted enough money for an even larger army in 1696. However, there was only minor fighting, and in 1697 what had become an increasingly pointless war was concluded by the Peace of Ryswick.

The Life Guards, excepting Overkirke's 4th Troop that stayed in Holland, arrived home in late October, and were disappointed to be sent not to London but to Chelmsford, Hertford and Ware. This was to prove a temporary solution, and when William III landed at Greenwich on 16 November he was met by the Earl of Scarborough and the 1st Troop who, correctly, escorted him into London. Although the Dutch Guards remained in London for the time being, the Life Guards gradually took over duties in the city from The Blues. On 17 November they moved first into Holborn and St Giles while The Blues vacated their old quarters. The 1st Troop was to be billeted around Lincoln's Inn, the second in Piccadilly and Knightsbridge, and the third in Westminster. The unfortunate Blues were ordered to move to the Birmingham area, which must have caused dismay among the officers after five years of enjoying the delights of London. Someone, probably Oxford, approached his old friend Blathwayt, whose grandsons were later to serve in the regiment, to seek a less remote posting, as two days later the orders were miraculously changed to the city of Oxford. Later they were sent further away from London, first to Worcestershire and Shropshire and then to the West Country, before resuming their traditional stations in the Thames Valley in 1700.

It seems that they had not enjoyed a particularly happy time standing in for the Life Guards. The camaraderie and efficiency that had distinguished the regiment on its return from Ireland proved impossible to maintain as the troops were once more separated throughout London, and the drafts to support the Life Guards on operations had taken many of their best soldiers. There were instances of desertion, which had previously been highly unusual, and Anthony Wright, the twenty-year-old Trumpeter of the King's Troop, ran off with his silver trumpet. Compton himself had acquired a house in Kew, but he soon found the cost of maintaining a London lifestyle on his army pay to be exorbitant. In 1693 he approached his nephew, now Earl of Northampton, for a guarantee against a loan for £1,000 he had taken from a George Bond, saying that 'I intend to sell and dispose of my Leftenant Collonels place in the Right Hon. The Earl of Oxford's regiment of horse . . . within three months . . . and out of the money arising thereby . . . discharge the said George Bond'.[8] Luckily he did not, and was to continue in office for a further nineteen years. He demonstrated his considerable stamina yet again by marrying, in 1699 when he was seventy, a girl of seventeen.

The behaviour of the officers was also a cause for concern, and with little to distract them apart from boring routine escorts, they soon returned to the favourite seventeenth-century pastime of duelling. One of the most celebrated

By the end of the European Wars William III had finally come to trust the Life Guards and The Blues, despite an alleged Jacobite conspiracy against him nurtured in The Blues in 1696.

The 1697 Treaty of Ryswick concluded William III's war with Louis XIV, which had become increasingly unpopular in England.

incidents was when Captain George Kirke killed Conway Seymour in a duel in St James's Park. Seymour was not an attractive character, 'a new set-up, vain young fop, who made a great eclat about the town by his splendid equipage, not setting any bounds to his pompous living',[9] and both he and Kirke were drunk. Kirke was subsequently found guilty of manslaughter and burnt on the hand. He was also temporarily suspended from his commission but, as under James II, no one wanted to set a dangerous precedent by removing such a valuable investment permanently and by 1704 Kirke was the Major of the regiment.

More serious were the accusations that The Blues harboured Jacobite supporters. In early 1696 a plot was discovered to kill William III in the salubrious surroundings of Turnham Green as he returned from hunting in Richmond Park. It came to nothing, as the hunting expedition was cancelled, but in the subsequent investigations suspicion fell on three members of The Blues who were subsequently committed to Newgate on 10 March. The link between the conspirators and the regiment turned out to be an ex-trumpeter, Thomas Keyes, who, before he was executed, said in his evidence that the whole regiment was ready to rise up. It was fairly obviously a false statement, but unfortunately a certain trooper, Edward Bish, had been arrested the year before and made to stand in the pillory after riding through the streets drunk and shouting that King William was dead and he would kill anyone who denied it. Oxford and Compton were predictably horrified, and had an uncomfortable summer, while the King returned to the war, during which they found that the whole regiment was under suspicion.

Fortunately for them, but not for the Life Guards, when the King returned that autumn, suspicion now fell on Sir John Fenwick, an ex-Life Guard who had resigned in 1688, who Ministers felt was the inspiration behind the plot. He was summoned before the Justices and, in his confession, implicated rather too many of the Whig ministry for their own comfort. Although the King appeared remarkably unperturbed by the whole episode, Parliament was now determined to have Fenwick's head. He was duly made the subject of a Bill of Attainder and after a long and convoluted trial was finally convicted by both Houses on 11 January 1697. He went to his execution on Tower Hill in the coach of his brother-in-law, the Earl of Carlisle, and was escorted, ironically, by a troop of The Blues.

It was an awkward episode, which threatened to undo the good work of Oxford and Ormond, and make William doubt both regiments once again. The accusations of Jacobite sympathy were far-fetched, but there was undoubtedly a strong anti-Dutch sentiment in London, with which The Blues would have come regularly into contact in the course of their daily duties, and which could have been misread as sympathy for James II. However, Oxford, promoted to Lieutenant General in 1693, had ensured that the King maintained close links with The Blues, reviewing them periodically during his winter breaks in London. Also William respected him, probably because he was half Dutch. But, most importantly, the Life Guards had confirmed the King's opinion of them by their performance at Landen. It was fortunate, for no sooner had the Life Guards returned from Flanders than Parliament began a prolonged battle with the King to reduce the army to just 7,000 men – the original regiments raised before 1680 – echoing the calls that had been made in 1685. Twelve thousand troops were to be kept on in Ireland and 4,000 in Scotland. In all, fifty-two regiments had to go, but the army's senior regiments were safe, leaving the three English troops and the Scottish Troop of the Life Guards, The Blues, The Royals, the two Foot Guard battalions and eight other battalions as well as some militia. There was little support for the army among Members of Parliament; there were only, on average, thirty officers in Parliament during William III's reign, down from eighty-nine under James II. The old fears of a professional officer class owing allegiance to the Crown rather than to the English idea of liberty embodied by Parliament surfaced yet again. The method of disbandment was both cruel and inefficient. Regiments were paraded, ordered to hand over their weapons, given fourteen days' subsistence money and told to disperse in groups of not more than three. No provision was made to get them back to their homes, let alone to provide any training for alternative employment.

There were also some reductions in the pre-1680 regiments. Each of the Life Guard troops was reduced by twenty-five men to 175 in July 1698, and the Horse Grenadiers were reduced from 180 to 160. The Blues did worse. Between July 1698 and May 1700 Oxford received a series of letters from Blathwayt which all began, 'Whereas we have thought fit that the severall Troops of our Royal Regiment of Horse do consist of', and went on to reduce the troops from fifty 'private troopers', as they now came to be called, first to forty, then to thirty-six and finally to thirty. The King's direction was that 'in their reductions the best men be kept and those less fit for service be disbanded'. Those unfortunates were allowed to keep their horse if they had served over a year; otherwise they had to make do with just twelve days' pay. The King's chronic shortage of funds did not permit keeping them on as false musters the old method – though it was gradually to creep back into practice during Queen Anne's reign. The Royals were also reduced fairly savagely, being instructed in January 1699 to disband their 'two youngest troops', bringing them down from eight troops of sixty to six troops of forty-six. The officers in the two junior troops, Captains La Roque and Crofts, together with their lieutenants, cornets and quartermasters, were put on half pay. Yet most of the officers' places in the Life Guards, The Blues and the remaining six troops of The Royals were safe, proving to their holders why their commissions had been so expensive. The King's intention had been to pay the costs of the disbandment from forfeited Irish estates, but too many of these had already been given away, many to Dutch favourites, and he resorted to issuing rather dubious debentures in lieu, which immediately became heavily discounted and were

After Whitehall Palace burned to the ground in 1698, the Court moved to St James's and Kensington Palaces, although increasing use was made of Windsor (*above and below*) and Hampton Court, which meant the Life Guards were constantly on the move.

liable to speculation by bankers. The officers suffered less than their men, but those with debts, of whom there were many, faced ruin and, as a result, resentment against the King and his Dutch favourites grew. It was an astonishing way to treat an army that had believed it was defending England and the Protestant cause. It was also a dreadful waste. Louis XIV remained undefeated and within three years many of these men would need to be raised again to fight in the Wars of the Spanish Succession.

Parliament further stipulated there were to be no foreigners – including at this point Irishmen, who remained 'foreign' until 1801 – in the reduced army, a provision inserted deliberately to force the King to take his Dutch regiments off the English payroll. This was particularly annoying to William, who planned to include the Dutch Blue Guards and his 4th Troop in the surviving army, rather than have them paid in Holland. In 1699 they finally departed London, leaving the Life Guards alone once again to provide guards and escorts in the capital. Parliament further wanted to know the number of foreigners actually serving in the Life Guards. Their return under the Naturalization Act of 1698 shows forty in the 1st Troop alone, some of whom had served for up to seventeen years. Most of them were French Huguenots, and Parliament, whose motive was more the removal of the Dutch and in particular Overkirke's troop, seems to have been content for them to serve on, particularly as several had produced certificates showing they had received the sacrament according to the usage of the Church of England. The pattern was repeated in The Royals, who had six Huguenot officers, of whom only one, La Roque, was put on half pay – more likely an accident of his being in one of the two junior troops, and certainly the other officers put on half pay with him all had English names. It was a nice touch, which showed how closely the regiment had bonded in the difficult years since Sedgemoor.

A far more public aspect of this anti-Dutch feeling surfaced in March 1699 after the King persuaded Lord Scarborough to resign as Colonel of the 1st Troop in favour of his Dutch favourite, Arnold Joost van Keppel, to whom he had already given the very English title of Earl of Albemarle – insensitive, given its links with the great Monck, whose memory Parliament still revered. It was rumoured that Albemarle paid £12,000 for the privilege, money William badly needed. Whatever, it was a great injustice to Ormond who, senior by both military rank and social position, could reasonably have expected to be given the position. He consequently resigned, and was immediately supported by fifty Members of Parliament, who talked openly of introducing a bill excluding foreigners from any public office. Whilst William realized he had gone too far, it was too late to withdraw the offer. He subsequently engineered a rather clumsy compromise, whereby Ormond was to be considered senior to Albemarle when on military operations as long as he withdrew his resignation, which he duly did.

The remaining few years of William's reign saw a return to something like normality. The Life Guards were given new uniforms, at a cost of £100 for each officer and £40 for a private gentleman. Those wretched ribbons reappeared in their hats, again colour-coded with red for the 1st Troop, blue for the 2nd and yellow for the 3rd, which must have made the King wince when he reviewed them in Hyde Park on November 1699. Yet they made a favourable impression on the public and 'appeared to be the finest Body of Men and the compleatest Cloth'd and Accoutred, in the World'.[10] The *London Post* went further, writing that they 'are generally thought to be the finest Body of Horse in Europe'.[11] The Blues remained in the south of England and The Royals in Yorkshire, policing and escorting, and frequently arresting robbers and highwaymen, most of whom were old soldiers, recent comrades-in-arms, forced into a life of crime by an ungrateful Government.

One other very significant change noticed in the Hyde Park Review of 1699 was that all the Life Guards were riding black horses, the colour traditionally associated with both them and The Blues. There had been no prescribed colour in the years after the civil wars, due to the serious shortage of horses mentioned previously, and in the campaigns in Ireland and Flanders soldiers rode anything that could be obtained, often captured from the French. James II had ordained that trumpeters ride greys, but had gone no further. However, in one of William III's more inspired military reforms, he had introduced a breeding stock of black Gelderland horses to England to improve the quality of the army's remounts and these were now producing a regular supply. The Blues appear to have adopted them during the 1690s, and the Life Guards on their return from Europe. Their use thereafter was not consistent, with the Life Guards reverting to bays at one time and, of course, on campaign anything that moved was used, but the tradition of 'the Blacks' was established.

For the Life Guards the past decade had established a more important tradition. When the country was at war, their priority and preference would be to be involved in the field army, either protecting the monarch or fighting as a regiment in their own right, though it was not always to be so. When in 1701 England found herself once again at war with France, the Life Guards were not included in the force of eight cavalry regiments who sailed to Flanders under Marlborough. They were, in fact, to play no part in the Wars of the Spanish Succession, and were not present at the famous victories at Blenheim, Ramilles, Oudenarde and Malplaquet. Nor were The Blues. Continuing Jacobite threats, and Parliament's insistence on 'capping' the number of English troops in the Allied armies at 18,000, meant that they were destined to stay at home.

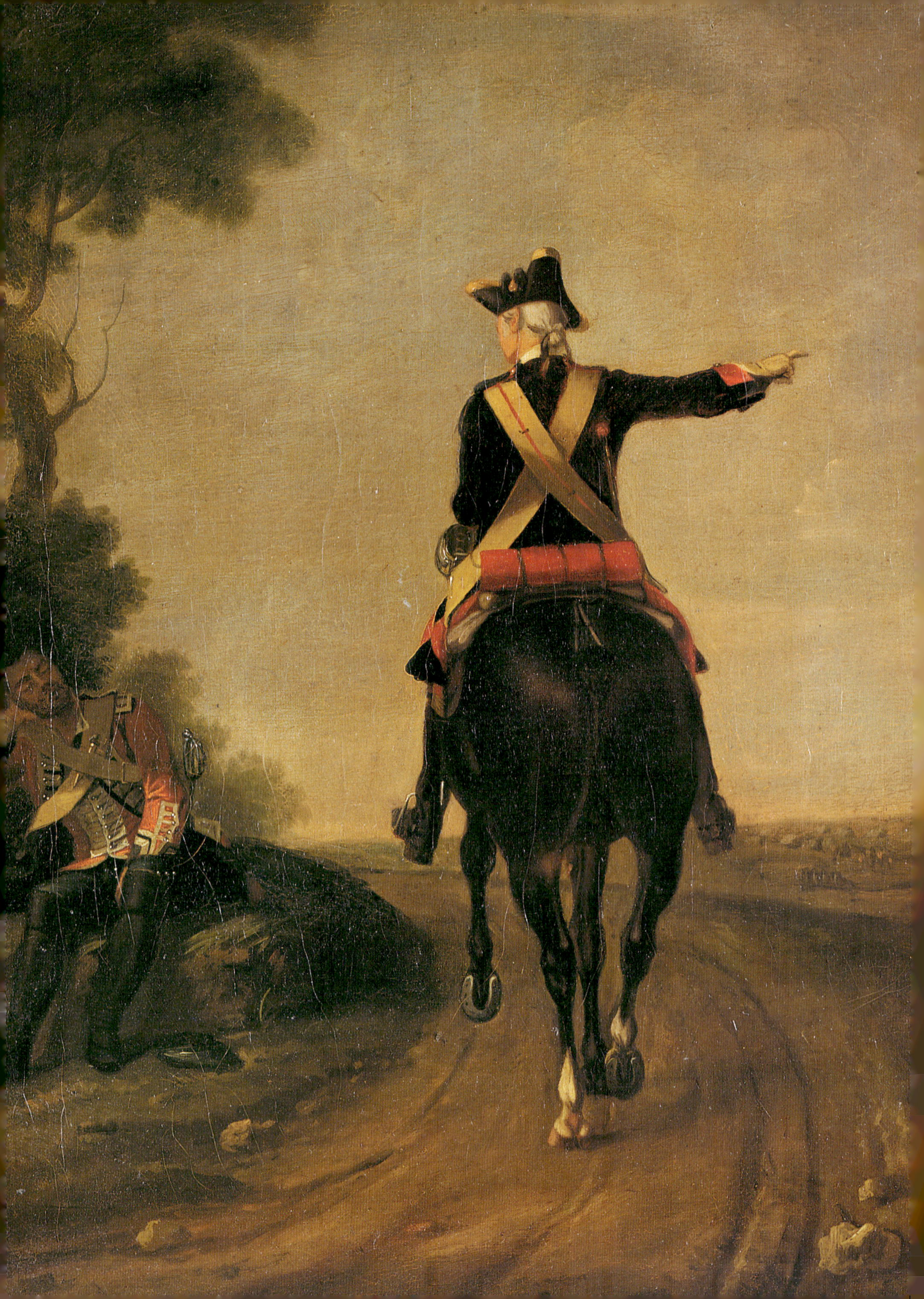

Part Three

A PATTERN ESTABLISHED

1701–1763

Chapter Seven

POLICING LONDON AND WAR IN SPAIN

JAMES II DIED IN FRANCE IN 1701. William III was killed in March the following year while riding at Hampton Court, when he was thrown from his horse after it stumbled on a molehill. His successor was his wife's sister, Anne, the second daughter of James II by his first wife Anne Hyde and a staunch Protestant, as was her Danish husband Prince George. Anne's only surviving son, the Duke of Gloucester, had died two years before, aged twelve, and she was not to produce another heir. Gloucester's death had led to the passing of the Act of Settlement, which laid down that only members of the Church of England could succeed to the English throne, and specifically limited Queen Anne's heirs to the Protestant Electress Sophia of Hanover, a granddaughter of King James I, and her son George who was an energetic opponent of France. Clear as these provisions were, the Jacobites still hoped that on Anne's death the English would reject the German-speaking Hanoverians in favour of James II's son, the Warming Pan baby, also called James and known to us as the Old Pretender. This Jacobite threat, first from the Old Pretender and subsequently from his son Charles Edward, the Young Pretender or, to the Scots, Bonnie Prince Charlie, was to dominate English politics until 1745 and the decisive battle at Culloden. It was therefore to have a considerable influence on the life and employment of our three regiments.

Excepting the deployment of The Royals to Flanders and subsequently Spain from 1702 until 1711, none of the regiments were to serve outside England from 1698 until 1742, a period consequently, but mistakenly, described as being 'not of a very interesting or important character'.[1] They were by no means unique in this. There were only 10,000 English troops in Marlborough's

---

Page 158. A Private of The Blues during the War of the Austrian Succession, showing his 'docked' horse's tail, which caused them so much misery in the hot summer of 1743.

army of 55,000 at Blenheim, about one-third of the number who fought in Iraq in 2003, the rest being Austrian, Dutch, Danish, Hanoverian, Hessian and Prussian. The remainder of the re-expanded English army was kept at home, both to meet the possible Jacobite threat and because, after its experience of William's European wars, Parliament imposed a tight cap on numbers. Whilst Marlborough honed his expeditionary force into the most effective English-led army yet to take the field, and in so doing had a major influence on the way the British army was subsequently to develop, most of that army was not to share in his glory. Although many individuals volunteered, and Marlborough took Mr Seignier, his trumpeter from the 3rd Troop as his personal trumpeter, the regiments were never to be involved as units.

Despite the pressures of this War of the Spanish Succession – always remote from London – and of the Jacobites, Queen Anne's court re-established a routine absent since the 1670s. Whilst Whitehall Palace had been destroyed by fire in 1698, the old Horse Guards building had, annoyingly for the Guards, survived in a just barely habitable state, ensuring its continued use. The Queen based herself at St James's Palace or Kensington when in London, but increasingly her time was spent at Hampton Court or Windsor. The Life Guards accompanied her, leaving enough private gentlemen to mount a guard twenty strong at Horse Guards, together with the Foot Guards. The Life Guards therefore became an increasingly integral part of court routine, which developed into that curious mixture of the formal and the informal which has been so characteristic of the British monarchy ever since. Queen Anne, whose mother came from an upper-class English family and lived much of her life in an ordinary house in Piccadilly, and who found nothing strange in observing the trial of Dr Sacheverell from the gallery of the House of Commons, or in lunching with City Aldermen, or in developing intimate friendships with Sarah Churchill and Abigail Masham, would take great exception should her ministers dare appear in anything but a full-bottomed wig when summoned to her presence in the middle of the night. It was a pattern of behaviour that slowly became apparent in the regiments as well.

Queen Anne's court was the political and social centre of an increasingly affluent England – an England of privilege and corruption, so effectively satirized by Alexander Pope and later by Hogarth – into which the Life Guards and, to a lesser extent, The Blues, became inextricably drawn. Queen Anne was the first of three queens to take a great personal interest in her Guards, and who liked to keep her Life Guards near her, partly for protection, partly for the status they conferred, and partly because she was genuinely fond of them. She was also a great believer in ceremonial and, after the rather dour days of William, the sight of a triumphant Queen, drawn in a state coach to St Paul's for the frequent thanksgiving services for her army's victories, escorted by the Life Guards, was immensely popular and established a pattern that has continued to this day. Perhaps the Life Guards blushed slightly at being asked to carry, in

Queen Anne's Court re-established a routine absent since the 1670s – a curious blend of the formal, as in the House of Lords (*above*), with the familiar, as in this group with her Knights of the Garter (*above right*). The Life Guards became increasingly involved in life at Court during her reign.

The Earl of Peterborough, charismatic Allied commander in Spain, who could 'make war without men and without money' and who 'had worked wonders with the troops'.

solemn procession on 3 January 1705, thirty-four French standards captured by others at Blenheim, but there was no doubting the patriotic demonstrations of support that the spectacle created. It all contributed to the image of an English-born Queen and staunch defender of the English Church, who believed that the English monarchy should make an impression. Her Guards were an integral part of that image. And, of course, in 1707, the Act of Union with Scotland made her a British Queen, and consequently the Scottish Troop of Life Guards moved from Edinburgh to London and became the 4th Troop of Life Guards. Their accompanying troop of Horse Grenadiers moved with them and were quartered in Kingston as the 2nd Troop of Horse Grenadiers.

There was more to the Life Guards' duties than guarding the Queen and providing her ceremonial, however. They still had to maintain public order in London. In the early years of Anne's reign this was an undemanding task as there was little to disturb the populace. The Triennial Act of 1694, requiring Parliament to sit at least once every three years, ensured the 25 per cent of the male population who had the vote – those men of property who tended to instigate disturbances – a regular vehicle through which to exercise their grievances. The small number of individuals directly committed to the war had little impact in the capital, although the Bank of England, founded in 1684, did finance it through loans. However, the economy was doing well and a run of good harvests meant England was exporting corn, ironically, to France, and wages rose consistently. Religious dissenters' aspirations were largely met through the Toleration Act of 1689.

However, with the Whigs forming a new Government in 1703, the tension between them and Tories in Parliament was another matter and was to spill over on to the London streets, most particularly after the abortive attempt at a landing in Scotland by the Young Pretender in 1708 in reaction to the Act of Union. Two Troops of Life Guards, the Horse Grenadiers and The Blues, had moved rapidly north to deal with this 'Jacobite Rising', but proved unnecessary as bad weather scattered the French fleet, and by August they were back in London for Queen Anne's celebrations to mark Marlborough's victory at Oudenarde. However, the Rising coincided with a new Land Tax imposed by the Whig Government, viewed as directly threatening Tory agricultural interests, and when the run of good harvests declined, the price of corn started to rise. Furthermore, the Government accepted a group of 10,000 Calvinist refugees from Bavaria, asylum seekers of the seventeenth century, regarded in London, quite unreasonably, as a threat to the established Church. Taken together, this combination of events was seen as an example of the arrogance and mismanagement of the Whig administration, which was thought not only to be profiting from the war but also to be ignoring traditional English interests.

In November 1709, Sir Samuel Garrard, the very Tory Lord Mayor of London, invited Dr Sacheverell, an 'over bearing, ill-natured, shallow, hard drinking, High Church, Oxford clergyman' to preach the annual sermon at St Paul's to commemorate Guy Fawkes's discovery and William III's landing. It was not the fact that Sacheverell preached for an hour and a half that caused consternation, but that he savaged the Whig administration, asserted that the Glorious Revolution of 1688 was 'odious' and claimed the Church of England was in dire peril from dissenters. They were brave words, however doubtful their source, and found an immediate public resonance. One hundred thousand copies of the sermon were printed and quickly sold out. The Whigs, predictably furious, unwisely accused Sacheverell of being a Jacobite and determined to impeach him. Worse, they took so long to bring him to trial that, when it finally started in late February 1710, he had become a public hero, the embodiment of the English Church against the dissident Whigs. He was carried to the Commons for his trial by a mob of 3,000, amidst cries of 'The Church in danger!' They quickly took the law into their own hands. Four dissenters' meeting houses were burnt that night, their contents piled into a bonfire in Lincoln's Inn Fields. Worse still, the Bank of England, symbol of the war, and the houses of the Lord Chancellor, the Lord Privy Seal and the Duke of Newcastle were threatened with destruction. Lord Sunderland, the Secretary of State, decided to request the Queen to deploy troops. The only soldiers immediately available were some Foot Guards and the Queen's Life Guard, commanded by Captain Samuel Horsey of the 4th Troop, recently moved to London. Conscious of the danger should he leave the Queen unguarded, Horsey initially refused to deploy, but the Queen, encouraged by the nervous Sunderland, insisted. Horsey then enquired, perfectly reasonably, whether he was to preach at the mob or fight them, receiving the wonderfully vague direction that he was to 'use his judgement and discretion' and 'to avoid violence except in cases of necessity'. There was no time to give him written orders and probably little inclination on Sunderland's part; he could later deny any involvement, should there be subsequent bloodshed. The Riot Act was still five years away. Horsey, realizing that he 'ventured his neck by going on verbal orders', quickly dispatched a Corporal and six Life Guards to the Bank of England, while he proceeded cautiously via Charing Cross towards the rioters.[2]

The Life Guards had no experience of riot control. The last time they had been similarly engaged in London was on Easter Monday 1668 when the London apprentices had rioted over the city's brothels – whether this was due to moral indignation at their presence or the high fees they charged was never made clear. There was no one still serving who had been present then, although some of the 4th Troop and 2nd Horse Grenadiers had been involved in disturbances in Edinburgh. Horsey, reputedly a fairly rough man, realized that he would probably lose his commission if his soldiers overreacted and he therefore resolved to use as little force as possible. On arrival in Lincoln's Inn Fields he ordered his men to ride amongst the mob and disperse them using the flats of their swords, which was remarkably successful. Only one rioter resisted and tried to push through the line of horses with his sword drawn. Captain Orrel of the Horse Grenadiers shouted at him, 'Do you know what you do in opposing the Guards? You are opposing the Queen's person!' to which he replied, 'Damn you! Are you against Sacheverell? I am for High Church and Sacheverell, and will lose my life in the cause.' He made a run at Orrel and was promptly recognized as a certain George Purchase, recently dismissed from the Life Guards for stealing horses and highly unpopular in the regiment. Richardson, a private gentleman in the 3rd Troop, tried to hit him with his sword, shouting, 'You rascal, have you a mind to kill my officer?' but he missed, hitting a wall instead and breaking his sword into several pieces. Purchase escaped into Long Acre, though he was subsequently arrested. He eventually received the Queen's pardon, as the judges at his trial could not decide his guilt.[3] Horsey's tactics had worked remarkably well. By 2 a.m. the following day the rioters had completely dispersed from Lincoln's Inn, Holborn and Blackfriars. No more meeting houses had been destroyed; the Bank was safe, as were the houses of the Whig ministers, and not a single shot had been fired. Only two people were killed, both by falling masonry. Horsey was rewarded with a promotion to Major in the 4th Troop. But he had achieved considerably more that night.

He had, probably unwittingly, set a precedent for restrained military operations against rioters which was to endure for most of the next century, and which, though broken during the industrial unrest of the early nineteenth century, has become the pattern for contemporary British policing. During the many ensuing riots in which the Life Guards and The Blues would become involved, both regiments, in common with the rest of the British army, would always interpret the Riot Act as literally as they could and would only use weapons if authorized by a magistrate in writing and then only in extremis. The principle of civilian magistrates' authority, on which Blathwayt had so firmly insisted, and which the Riot Act enshrined, allowed relations between the British military and the public to remain reasonably amicable, particularly in London. The Guards were never seen as the brutal oppressors of people's freedom that their equivalents were to be in other European states. Furthermore, they had the salutary example of Captain Porteous, accused of unnecessary harshness when escorting a convicted smuggler to his execution and lynched by the Edinburgh mob in 1736, to remind them what might happen should they overstep the mark.

The elections of 1711 and 1714 were particularly unruly and Life Guards, Horse Grenadiers and Blues were heavily involved in keeping the peace.[4] Violent crime and smuggling also increased between 1714 and the mid-1720s and kept them well occupied. So bad was it in London that in 1715 a regular Life Guard patrol was started on the road between St James' and Chelsea, as so many had been attacked in such close proximity to the palace.[5] Much of this violence was Jacobite-related. George I, Elector of Hanover, who had duly ascended the throne when Queen Anne died in August 1714, and the Whig

Government that had ensured his succession in the face of considerable Tory opposition, were highly unpopular throughout 1715. The situation was exacerbated by a very severe winter, a poor harvest and another Jacobite rebellion.

Many were to feel that, had a more competent commander than Lord Mar served the Old Pretender, the 1715 uprising might well have restored the Stuarts to the English throne. He never forgave his half-brother, The Blues' ex-Colonel, Berwick, now an experienced and competent commander, for declining to lead his forces. Berwick's presence might have made a difference, but he probably reached the conclusion that the expedition had little chance of success. None of our regiments played an active part in suppressing the Revolt, The Royals arriving just after the Jacobites had been defeated at Preston. The Life Guards, Horse Grenadiers and Blues were all kept near London to protect the court and Government, and the most exciting development for The Blues that year was the expansion of their area of responsibility to include Hampton and Teddington. More happily, the regiments survived the 1715 purge of suspected Jacobites in the army relatively unscathed. Given their recent history, George I's rather uncomplimentary view of his newly acquired army, and the fact that Ormond was the Old Pretender's co-conspirator in England, this was fortunate. They certainly fared better than the Foot Guards who lost three privates, hanged, drawn and quartered for Jacobite sympathies. Luckily Ormond, still the Tories' military hero, as opposed to the Whig Marlborough, whom the Life Guards now much disliked, had handed over as Colonel of the 2nd Troop in 1711, so when he fled to France the Life Guards could, for once legitimately, claim not to have been involved. The Blues enjoyed the added advantage of the Duke of Argyll as their Colonel, who, although heavily defeated by Mar at Sherrifmuir, was at least shown to be staunchly Whig, however unlucky or incompetent he may have been.

The passing of the Septennial Act in 1716, by which, in Dr Johnson's words, 'The Commons, chosen by the people for three years, chose themselves for seven', removed the frequency of electoral violence, though the tiresome policing duties continued well into the 1720s, throughout the troubles associated with the financial instability during the South Sea Bubble crisis and the half-hearted and inept Jacobite Atterbury Plot against the new King. Harvests improved and a gradual realization dawned that however irritating the German-speaking George I was, at least his First Minister, Walpole, was presiding over a period of prosperity and a rising standard of living.

WHILE THE LIFE GUARDS, Horse Grenadiers and Blues were so involved in keeping the peace for Queen Anne and George I, The Royals were taking part in the Allied operations against the French in Portugal and Spain, one of the most remarkable and historically unfamiliar campaigns in which the British army was ever engaged. It was remarkable for strangely conflicting reasons. It

Horse Guards was the official gateway into St James's Park (*above*), to which the Crown controlled access first by a password and later, from 1775, by issuing ivory passes that allowed carriages to pass through the archway.

The Life Guards became increasingly involved in keeping the peace in London during the eighteenth century, policing riots and disturbances resulting from incidents like the South Sea Bubble (*above right*) or during elections (*below right*).

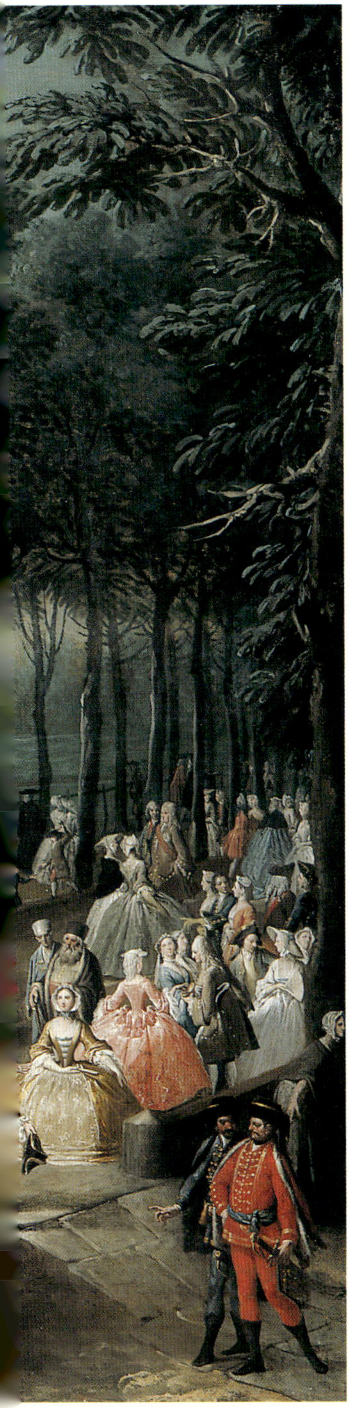

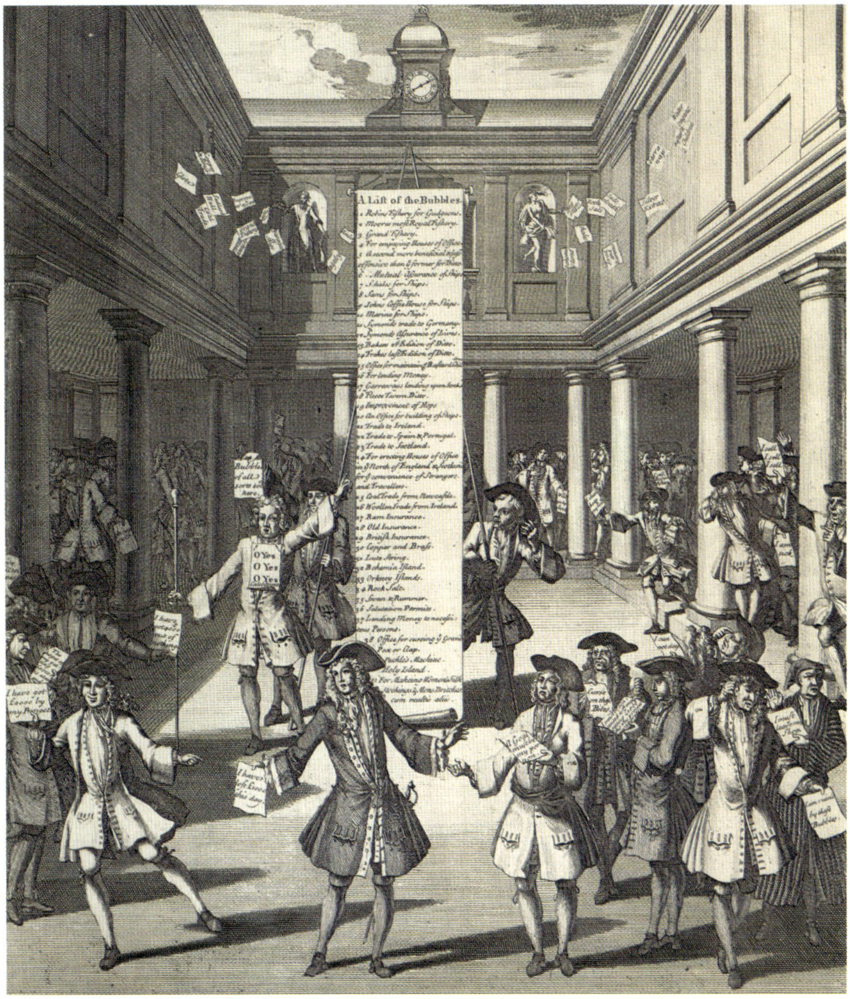
A List of the Bubbles

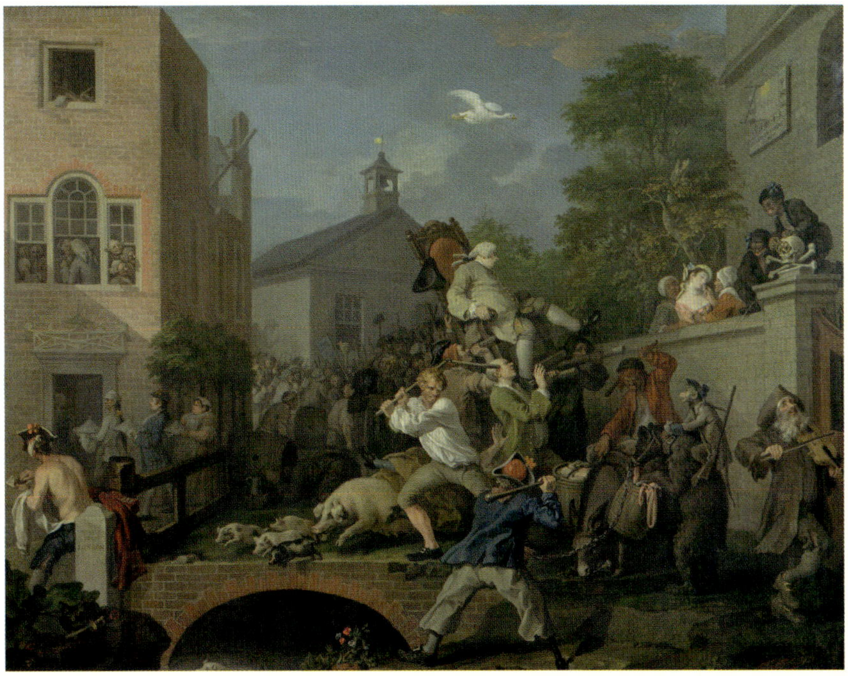

was extraordinarily violent and was of considerable strategic significance, yet attracted little official acknowledgement, being overshadowed by Marlborough's campaigns in Germany and Flanders. No battle honours were ever awarded for display on standards or colours, unlike for those who fought at Blenheim, Ramilles, Oudenarde and Malplaquet.

For The Royals the campaign was also particularly remarkable for the legacy of a very detailed correspondence between their new Colonel, Lord Raby, who replaced Matthews in May 1697 after his non-violent death, and his two Lieutenant Colonels serving successively in Spain, Killigrew and St Pierre.[6] Raby was a diligent and caring colonel, an experienced soldier who, as Thomas Wentworth, had joined the Life Guards in December 1688, fought with distinction at Steenkirk and Landen, and earned his promotion to Major of the 1st Troop. He was a good choice for Colonel of The Royals, his social rank bringing connections that neither the more humble Heyford nor Matthews could; he might actually have led the regiment directly in Spain had William III not sent him as Ambassador to Berlin as war broke out. Of more interest is that his correspondence gives a very detailed account of how a regiment organized itself on campaign, of senior officers' financial concerns, whom could they influence, who was to be commissioned, and where to find horses. By contrast, we also have the detailed diary of a private dragoon, writing for his son William 'that your children's children may see a little of a great deale what there grandfather have gone through.'[7] Annoyingly he never gives his name, so we shall refer to him as William's father. He was from Colchester, and joined Lieutenant Colonel Killigrew's Troop in The Royals in 1702, aged twenty-five. He was evidently a man of some education for he could write moderately well, and yet was not an officer or even a non-commissioned officer; in fact his comments are often very critical of the senior ranks, and this may reflect frustrated ambition, possibly due to lack of funds. He was writing after his discharge in 1713, and his recollection of earlier campaign years is consequently sketchy, and irritatingly much of the diary just lists towns, marches and other facts. However, his is one of the earliest accounts of a British campaign from the perspective of the lowest ranks and, in places, is both illuminating and amusing.

The regiment was first mobilized for the War of the Spanish Succession in the autumn of 1701 while it was in Yorkshire. The reductions of 1698 were reversed and positions were offered to the officers who had been put on half pay. With so many recently discharged soldiers around it was not difficult to fill the slots, and by March 1702 they were ready at Southwark to embark for Flanders. Captain Lieutenant Sheldon, in other words the Captain commanding Raby's own Troop, had never seen such a ship as was assigned to him. She had two feet of water in the hold, and only escaped sinking by being beached at low tide. When finally afloat she ran aground, and the Master was so out of control that he constantly fouled other vessels. Lighters had to be summoned to remove the horses that were in imminent danger of drowning. Eventually, the regiment moved to Essex and finally embarked from Harwich on 1 May. On arrival in Flanders they were in such a poor state that they had to rest for two weeks, with an extra forage allowance so that the unfortunate horses could recover.

The war in which they were engaged, the War of the Spanish Succession, started when the King of Spain died with no obvious heir. On his deathbed he left his substantial possessions, including large parts of Italy, the Spanish Netherlands and overseas colonies as well as Spain itself, to Philip of Anjou, the second son of Louis XIV's heir, and consequently to France. The Hapsburg Emperor, the Protestant German States and the English and Dutch, through William III, contested the terrible prospect of Bourbon French Catholic domination of Europe, and backed the Emperor's candidate, his son, Archduke Charles. On 7 September 1701 William III signed the Treaty of the Grand Alliance, which declared that the thrones of France and Spain would never be united. It was a declaration of war but hostilities had, in fact, already started. The French and combined Allied armies, under Marlborough's command, were already contesting control of the Flanders fortresses, and, once fit, The Royals were engaged in this skirmishing throughout 1702 and the early part of 1703. It never amounted to a major engagement, but they still lost fifteen men killed, ten taken prisoner and twenty horses. One of the casualties was Cornet Wentworth, a relation of Raby's, who was killed in action at Liège. His replacement was his nephew, a child far too young to fight, whose selection apparently spared the Colonel's family financial loss.

In May 1703 the Portuguese made alliance with England and the United Provinces and entered the war, nominally, against the French. This suited Marlborough, who wanted a second front to divert French attention from Flanders, and he agreed to part with 12,000 troops, including a regiment of dragoons to assist. The Royals, the largest dragoon regiment with eight troops, was chosen. It was thought undesirable to transport their horses to Portugal, so they were sold in Flanders, causing some hardship with the market saturated and prices low. The officers, who bore the financial burden, were further disadvantaged, as they also had to sell their camp kit, which commanded similarly low prices. Their situation was exacerbated by the Secretary at War straight away withholding the 7d. forage allowance from every man, and 1s. from every non-commissioned officer, despite the fact that it took some time to complete the sale of the horses. There followed a ghastly return voyage to England, during which they were held up on the Flemish coast for weeks in dreadful conditions, with men dying daily of disease. After direct complaints to Marlborough, he duly visited them and ordered a full allowance of rations, but the transport officials, 'agreeing with the reasonableness of the thing . . . gave good words to my Lord Duke and to us but did nothing'.[8]

It was a sad and dispirited regiment that finally arrived in Lisbon on 13 March 1704. They had been 'stowed like harrins together' on board ship and had endured 'bad weather, scarceness of victuals and the men were dirty and sick'. They had passed through England, on complicated orders drawn up by a War Office clerk who, obviously bored at the prospect of drafting so many similar orders to move troops from Flanders, has drawn an obscene cartoon in the margin of the War Office letter book.[9] On arrival they found that the cavalry commander, Harvey, had appropriated the best accommodation for his own Regiment of Horse and only left space for The Royals in the hospital alongside the sick. Eventually they settled for camping with the infantry, 'but', William's father noted, 'the weather was not knowne by the age of man, with raine and winds so we could keep no tent standing'. The Portuguese had provided only eighty horses instead of the 400-odd required; even these were half starved and scabby, as Harvey had already taken the best. However, they had at least brought decent equipment with them from England. They had complained at the quality of weapons issued in Flanders, particularly the swords, whose blades tended to smash on impact, and also the firearms. A grumpy Secretary of War had been forced to order an expensive reissue, and these now arrived together with 400 sets of saddlery and uniforms.[10] However, this was not sufficient to make them an effective regiment. The only satisfaction they gained that hot and uncomfortable summer, while Marlborough was winning the great victory at Blenheim, was for Captain Green, the senior officer on guard one day, to put Harvey's regiment in the most junior place, on the grounds that they were 'only an Irish regiment'. Harvey was gratifyingly furious.

The Duke of Berwick, the ex-Colonel of The Blues, and now commanding the combined French and Spanish Bourbon forces in Spain, advanced to attack the Portuguese and English in June but, restricting himself only to taking a few scattered fortresses, there was no serious engagement. By July both sides found it too hot and retired to summer quarters, The Royals moving up to Abrantes where they were finally given a further 118 new horses, 'all extraordinarily bad'. Captain Jason wrote to Raby, 'Pray God grant you may never see this hellish country, all are sick of it and everyone ill. Many say it is more unhealthy than the West Indies. They starve our horses first and then us.'[11] On 5 September Major St Pierre paraded the regiment and found only 276 fit men and horses. Forty-seven were sick and sixty had died since their arrival six months before. Disease was now resulting in a serious shortage of officers. There is a moving description of the funeral of Captain Peke, who died of fever at Abrantes and who was 'a young gentleman of 28 years, endowed with many good qualities, handsome in body and of a very clear understanding which had been much improved by his being bred in the university',[12] the last qualification being something of a novelty. Peke was not the only one to die, and Killigrew, the Lieutenant Colonel, faced a complicated problem finding replacements, fairly typical for many commanding officers. His first consideration had to be the value of the commission and the investment it represented,

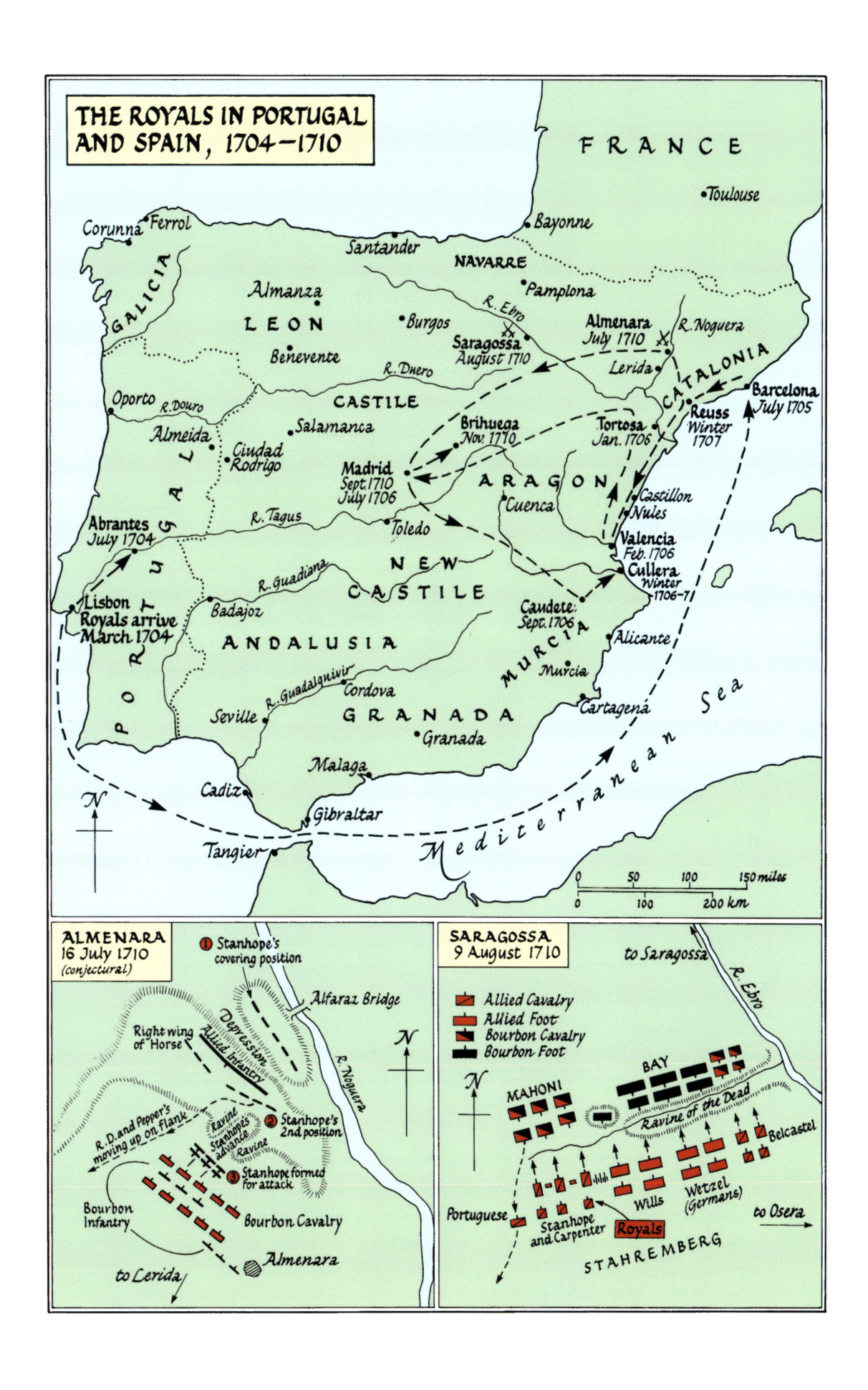

THE ROYALS IN PORTUGAL AND SPAIN, 1704–1710

hence the granting of Wentworth's vacancy to his juvenile relation. Yet at the same time a regiment on campaign had to have something approaching a full complement of officers for operations. The solution was not to bother too much about the more junior ranks, and The Royals were quite happy to take quartermasters as cornets, or to have a vacancy in one of those ranks; Raby thought you did not need both in a troop anyway. The quartermasters seem to have been able to find the price of a cornet's commission without too much trouble, which at £150 represented a considerable investment. Similarly sergeants, at a cost of £70, filled the quartermasters' vacancies, into which candidates normally bought directly at home.

There are several instances of serving officers with sons serving as non-commissioned officers, presumably because the family could not afford the investment represented by two commissions. Lieutenant Moore's son started as a private dragoon, becoming a non-commissioned officer and then a quartermaster after his father bought a place for him, and ended up as a lieutenant. One of Lieutenant Topham's sons, a corporal, deserted while his father was on leave. His brother, a quartermaster, subsequently sold his place, presumably in shame, although he may have had ulterior motives as he quickly became a Catholic and married his Spanish girlfriend. Poor Topham senior must have had rather a shock on his return.

It was very different for the senior ranks, and great care was taken to get the right people to buy in as lieutenants and captains. There are frequent references to men like Lieutenant Peers, 'a very pretty gentleman, heir to £1,500 a year and only 21 years of age',[13] being encouraged to buy in, when hopefully we can take pretty to mean suitable. Another was Lieutenant John Cope, a diligent and promising officer, who was to disappoint The Royals by being tempted by a place in Harvey's more expensive Horse and who would later be infamous for his defeat at Prestonpans in 1745. St Pierre, who replaced Killigrew as Lieutenant Colonel, wanted £4,000 for his place when he finally decided to sell, which makes one suspect that the profit on the position on active service was considerable. No one in the regiment could afford such an enormous sum and the place went to Captain Edward Montagu of Harvey's, a nephew of Lord Halifax.

Slightly more care was taken in finding horses than in acquiring privates. The horse problem rapidly became acute, and prevented not only the dragoons, who were still technically mounted infantry, from operating on horseback, but also the regiments of horse like Harvey's. By the end of 1704, the Secretary at War had instructed Ormond, Lord Lieutenant of Ireland, to acquire 500 horses and ship them to Portugal. A fourteen-two-hand 'good squat dragoon horse' was thought good value at £10, and if given an extra forage allowance for the three-week voyage to Lisbon would arrive reasonably fit. A 'hand' – or four inches – was the standard British horse measurement, which is still in use today. Ormond duly obliged, but his purchases were not well received. St Pierre wrote that 'the horses were mostly very old or very young, worth about 40s, many very unlucky or distempered and generally very poor'.[14] It was not until March 1706, after eighteen months of hard fighting, that The Royals were finally happy with their horses – partly captured from the French and partly native-bred Andalusians. It was quite typical of the time, and makes one sceptical of those stylized paintings of cavalry regiments charging into battle on beautifully matched horses. In reality such uniformity existed only in the artists' imaginations.

The problem of filling the ranks was met in two ways. First, as with the infantry battalions, The Royals were not averse to recruiting French prisoners of war, many of whom were happy, at least superficially, to change uniform, providing they were fed and paid. They would, of course, have been joining many compatriots, as the regiment still had a large Huguenot contingent; on mobilization in 1701 about a third of all officers were French. However, privates recruited in this way were apt to desert, so The Royals also reverted to the system employed in the Irish and Dutch Wars. Consequently, though all eight troops had deployed to Portugal in 1703, Killigrew now sent Captain Jason, together with Lieutenant Harris, Cornet Pulford and Quartermaster Barrett with four sergeants and four corporals back to the Midlands to recruit in the normal fashion 'by beat of drum'. They were moderately successful, it still being much easier to recruit for regiments of horse and dragoons, with their greater status and improved pay, than it was for the infantry. Tellingly, no officers were that keen to return home, which says much for morale after the previous depressing years, and Killigrew was obliged to choose them by lot. They returned with 141 recruits, mostly from Leicester, Oundle and Evesham, who, being countrymen should by rights have been good horsemen, but were found 'indifferent, many of them mere boys who had to be made servants and drummers',[15] whilst several were rejected for old age and other infirmities. Oddly, Jason had not weeded these out before going to the expense of bringing them over, which may have been connected with the bounty payable for each man they signed on.

By the time they arrived the regiment was already heavily engaged. In July 1705, preparing to fight under the energetic Huguenot, Ruvigny, now ennobled as Lord Galway and in command in Portugal, The Royals found themselves swiftly reassigned under Lord Peterborough in Barcelona. He had arrived with 6,000 fresh troops and instructions from Marlborough either to seize the key French port of Toulon, or to find another way to cause serious trouble in the western Mediterranean and force the French to withdraw troops from Flanders. Peterborough, accompanied by his Dutch counterpart Schartenbach and the Archduke Charles, contemplated an attack on Italy, but settled on taking Barcelona. Escorted by the fleet of the incomparable Admiral Sir Cloudesley Shovell, The Royals sailed from Lisbon by way of Gibraltar to arrive off Barcelona in the heat of August. They ran out of water for the horses on board and made an unscheduled stop at Valencia, from where word probably spread to the Bourbons that they were en route. Landing north of Barcelona, they were joined by local partisans, Catalonia being strongly in favour of the Hapsburgs, 'but the enemy sit all the straw and furrage for our horsses that they could on fire'.[16] By early September Peterborough felt strong enough to attack the well-fortified city. The Allied army, now nearly 9,000 strong, made a difficult night march, looping inland from their camp, and attacked the city in the south at the fortress of Mountjuich at dawn on 3 September. The Royals did not take part in storming Mountjuich, but were held in reserve to exploit any breakthrough, and were utilized to protect the army's flanks and communications. They were in fact, as Captain Benson wrote, 'used in Catalonia entirely as horse'. 'And,' he added 'the sword is the weapon we have to trust to. Those we have are useless.'[17] The idea of the dragoon as a mounted infantryman was beginning to disappear.

Barcelona duly fell on 28 September, which was fortunate for the Allies as 'it would have been impossible for us to have kept the field much longer, for there came down such heavy raines enough to drowne us', in the words of William's father. The regiment escorted Peterborough as he entered the town, where their main preoccupation was to stop the local Catalonian partisans lynching the Bourbon grandees. Peterborough now felt the initiative was with him and, overcoming Dutch reluctance, determined to press on to take Valencia and bring Aragon over to the Hapsburg cause. This he did in an extraordinarily effective campaign, always outnumbered by the French, but relying on speed, shock tactics and bluff, in which The Royals acted as the core of his force. Now better mounted, from October 1705 until February 1706, they led a remarkably successful campaign of rapid manoeuvre south along the Costa Dorada. In January they took Tortosa, at the mouth of the Ebro, deceiving a force four times as large into surrendering. Peterborough relied on the fact that Bourbon morale was low after Barcelona's fall, and used a complicated network of spies to spread confusion. Approaching Tortosa, he divided The Royals into three squadrons, disseminated the rumour that his force was far larger than it was, and ordered parts of the regiment to appear at different points on the heights above the town at the same time, thus convincing the nervous garrison that they were hopelessly outnumbered. The Royals had only one man slightly wounded in the whole operation.

Similar tactics ensured the rapid fall in succession of Castillon and Nules, which Peterborough heard was 'abounding in horses', once again badly needed by The Royals who were down to only 150 mounts by February. At Nules his bluff was nearly called, with a large French force in the neighbourhood, and the town only surrendered after he threatened to sack it. On 4 February he entered Valencia itself, defeating two Bourbon armies in the vicinity in quick succession by conducting a rapid night march with 400 dragoons, including The Royals and 800 foot. His tired but triumphant force finally paused for a short rest there. Killigrew found Valencia a very agreeable city, telling Raby that 'many of the servants, I believe, have slept in damask beds'. However, they were not always careful to pay for what they took. 'We seemed to be as welcome as water into a new ship,' noted William's father, 'but that was all one to us for we found that that would make us welcome, for their sheep, their horsses and piggs we did feed on and their wine we drunk on and that without being measured to us.'

Peterborough was one of a breed of seventeenth-century commanders who, like Marlborough, believed in taking risks. The Royals, used to Harvey's procrastination in Portugal and the ghastliness of the administration in Flanders, could hardly believe their luck. St Pierre found Peterborough 'the most extraordinary man I ever met who could make war without men and without money, who toiled indefatigably day and night and had worked wonders with the troops'.[18] Sadly, neither the Archduke Charles nor the Dutch shared Peterborough's qualities, and he was called back to face a reinforced French force, under Marshal de Tesse, who advanced from Madrid with plans to retake Barcelona. By 23 March de Tesse had reached the city with 12,000 men, linked up with the French fleet from Toulon and effectively split the Allies by trapping the Archduke in Barcelona. Peterborough and The Royals marched north but were unable to raise the siege on their own. Help arrived unexpectedly, as happened so often in this war, in the form of a fresh British fleet that dispersed the French fleet and landed five new British battalions. De Tesse, deprived of his maritime support, and with his troops suffering from disease, realized he was outmanoeuvred and slipped away quietly in the night, only to be relieved of command by a furious Louis XIV. The Royals tried to follow him in the van of Peterborough's force, so that the defeat could be turned into a rout, but they missed him. However, his departure left the way open to Madrid, and Galway, who had taken the fortress of Ciudad Rodrigo on the Portuguese frontier on 15 May, duly entered the capital from the west with his Allied and Portuguese force on 2 July. It was a bad few weeks for the Bourbons, with Marlborough's great victory at Ramillies on 23 May, and it allowed The Royals a break to reconstitute.

However, matters deteriorated rapidly after these Allied triumphs, and from July 1706 the fighting in Spain was to become increasingly confused and bloody. The Royals, 400-strong and in good spirits, left for Madrid with Peterborough and the Archduke Charles. The Archduke, however, insisted on going via Saragossa in an attempt to consolidate his hold on Aragon, and ignored increasingly urgent appeals for reinforcements from Galway, who was facing Berwick's growing strength in the north. By August Galway was forced to evacuate the capital after partisans loyal to the Bourbons cut his communications with his bases in Portugal, and he conducted a fighting withdrawal to meet up with Peterborough. A month of protracted skirmishing followed, as Berwick continually evaded Galway and Peterborough's attempts to draw him into pitched battle. Now acting truly as Horse, and often foremost in contact with the enemy as Peterborough's reconnaissance, these nasty skirmishes cost The Royals eighty men and 150 horses. By 28 September, after fighting a rearguard action and crossing three wide rivers, they reached Caudete, inland between Alicante and Valencia, with hardly a horse in the regiment still shod and the men 'naked'. Rations had dried up; in the previous three weeks they had received only four days' meat ration and no bread at all and had only survived by pillaging. Fortunately Berwick's force had also had enough, and he retired to winter in Madrid.

The Royals, still 300-strong, remained, however, one of the most complete and efficient units in the Allied army, and were therefore chosen to spend a cold and uncomfortable winter patrolling what was effectively No Man's Land, before a new offensive was launched under Galway in the following spring. Berwick fell back before them, and so, to compensate The Royals for their efforts that previous winter, Galway felt able to spare them and arranged their return to Cullera, on the coast, for a rest. It was lucky for them that he did, for shortly after their departure Berwick inflicted a serious defeat on Galway at Almanza on 14 April. The Portuguese had refused to fight and the British, Dutch and Huguenot forces were reduced to half their strength. The Allied horse was engaged only at the end of the battle and their repeated charges did prevent a catastrophe, but it was still a massive setback. The casualties included Killigrew, who had passed command of The Royals to St Pierre, who was killed leading a brigade in one such charge. Galway was forced to withdraw and desperately tried to shield the Hapsburg heartlands of Catalonia with his much-reduced force. Hopes were raised by rumours of the imminent arrival of Lord Rivers with an 8,000-strong British force, but the long sea voyage in cramped conditions, the diet of salt meat and the unsanitary conditions and subsequent disease had reduced their numbers by half on arrival. After the customary break for the hot weather, fighting resumed as a series of inconsequential engagements, costing The Royals a further twelve men killed, but there were no outright victories and by the following winter of 1707 it could be claimed that the Bourbon forces had been effectively kept at bay.

Another break, with the regiment quartered comfortably in Reus, allowed new swords and uniforms from England to be issued. The swords were considered good, but the blades were too short and were subsequently lengthened at the cost of 10s. each. The uniform was also satisfactory, although rats on the ships had eaten many of the boots and saddle panels. St Pierre found it difficult to extract money from Galway and, worse, discovered that he was withholding 4s. a week per head for bread and corn, 15d. a week more than he should have done, while the rations were never issued regularly. So it was a slightly better equipped but hungry regiment that awaited what they believed would be the inevitable Bourbon push into Catalonia in the spring of 1708. They quit their winter quarters and stood ready, hoping at least to have an

The Royals missed the Battle of Almanza on 25 April 1707, in which the Duke of Berwick, commanding the Bourbon forces in Spain, decisively defeated Galway (*right*), and for which he was rewarded by King Philip V of Spain (*below*).

opportunity to relieve Tortosa, which had been retaken the previous autumn. But there was no serious action, and The Royals were only involved in various raids and skirmishes. William's father did not approve of a Dutch raid against Berwick's camp at Cenco: 'having secured the sentinels and the gaurds, they went downe their lines and pulling up their tentpins and stabing the men as they lay asleep, sum turning out of their tent naked'. Berwick sent word the following day that he was relieved to hear that it had been the Dutch, as he could not believe The Royals 'could have been so barberous'.

The next two years were to be frustrating for The Royals. The Bourbons were too weak to attack, as Louis XIV withdrew many troops to Flanders, and the Allies were unable to reinforce themselves sufficiently to contemplate any serious offensive action. Some officers were replaced; St Pierre returned home on leave and was temporarily supplanted by Lieutenant Colonel Benson. Galway gave regular balls, during one of which Lieutenant John Cope was seduced into joining Harvey's, which he described as 'allowed by everybody to be the finest regiment in Europe'. The Royals were quietly offended, and not much consoled by the arrival of Mr Arundel, a rich relation of Raby's who quickly made a name for himself as arrogant, and who many of the long-serving junior officers realized would soon outrank them by purchasing a Captaincy. Endless letters were exchanged between Benson in Catalonia and Raby in Berlin discussing the minute details of the officer plot. Some of those who had been in Spain the longest were sent home, including Quartermaster Friday, the longest-serving member of the regiment at twenty-seven years. He had joined in Tangier in the 1680 draft, fought in the final actions there, served at Sedgemoor and in Ireland, had fought in Flanders in the 1690s and now in Flanders, Portugal and Spain in this war. He was so stiff from his wounds that he could no longer ride, and Benson was disturbed at his alcoholic intake of two bottles of Spanish wine a day, which was excessive even by contemporary standards. A place was found for him at the Royal Hospital in Chelsea.

By early 1710 the Allied armies had been finally reinforced and stood at 18,000 men, with 4,000 British troops. There were ten British squadrons of horse and dragoons, a squadron being taken as three to four troops. Major General Carpenter was posted in as 'cavalry' commander, a term now valid given that the employment of horse and dragoons was identical. Peterborough had been replaced by the competent and energetic Stanhope, but the Dutch had, as ever, circumscribed his authority by sending the cautious Stahremberg, who equalled him in authority. Stanhope quickly won two outstanding victories over the Bourbons, the first of which could have been decisive and ended the campaign in Spain. Surprising Philip of Anjou, now in command of the Bourbon forces, at Almenara, just north of Valencia on the River Noguera on 16 July, he had to await Stahremberg's permission to attack, which was not forthcoming until 6 p.m. Stanhope himself led a brilliant cavalry charge, with The Royals in the second rank, and broke the Bourbon cavalry who fled, quickly followed by their infantry. With sufficient daylight the cavalry could have turned a victory into a rout, but, wrote William's father, who rode in the charge, 'we advancing so fast after the enemy that our foot could not keep up with us likewise our traine [artillery] could not no way beare up with their canon to doe the enemie any damage'. As it was, Bourbon losses were still around 1,500 and a mass of equipment.

Even better was to come on 9 August at Saragossa. The Royals' approach march had been dreadful. The country, now comprehensively fought over for six years, was, unsurprisingly, barren. There was no water for two days, and the only wine on offer was sour. 'It is not to be conceived what we suffered,' wrote the Chaplain in biblical vein, 'smothered as we were with clouds of ashes.' Yet it was worth it, for the speed of their advance trapped the Bourbon forces against the River Ebro, south of Saragossa, on the site of an old Moorish battlefield called, ominously, the Ravine of the Dead. The Bourbon position was strong and their forces just outnumbered the Allies. Despite this Stanhope took the decision to press a deliberate attack which, though perhaps costly in casualties, would offer the opportunity of destroying the Bourbon force. The Royals were on the left flank in the second line, with eight Portuguese squadrons in the first line, opposing the Bourbon cavalry. Stanhope had also taken the precaution of placing four infantry battalions in amongst his cavalry, a tactic allegedly copied from Gustavus Adolphus, the great Swedish commander in the Thirty Years War and also recently used at Almanza. The battle started with an artillery duel, and in the late morning the Bourbon cavalry rode out to attack the Portuguese, who predictably fell back. They rallied, however, helped by the fire of the interlaced infantry, and The Royals and the second line now charged in their support. 'About 9 of the clock in the forenoon we had orders to goe to water our horsses . . . just then we received half a days bread, so we got a little bread and water before we engaged,' wrote William's father from the perspective of someone who had been starving for days, as had his horse.

> It was about 10 of the clock when the signal was blown up, at which time we mounted and advanced upon them sword in hand. Advancing likewise war the enemie to us and gave us the first fire, but by the blessing of God we gave them no liberty to let them fire again but ware upon them in a moment of time, cutting and hewing them downe sword in hand, for their firing at us first made their horses jarr.

The fighting was intense and hand-to-hand with swords. Lieutenant Vickers and Quartermasters Chatterton and Gunter were killed, as was Cornet Addison, whose squadron standard was lost, together with eleven others and twenty horses. Among the twenty-five wounded was the arrogant Lieutenant Arundel, who had fought so well that he dumbfounded his critics by earning promotion on merit from Stanhope.

The French cavalry tactic of firing pistols to disrupt an enemy charge had failed miserably. Their pistols were not powerful enough to cause real damage, and therefore had to be fired at close quarters. However, doing so agitated their horses and broke the close ranks they needed to prevent penetration by the enemy. They had little time to reorganize before The Royals were among them. The British horse and dragoons, at this time, were not using pistols or carbines at all on the battlefield, keeping them purely for guards and patrols. They copied Marlborough's tactic of a tight mass of horsemen advancing slowly at the trot, swords drawn, breaking into a gallop at the last moment and relying on speed and density to knock a hole in the enemy lines, break their formation and then cut them down singly.

Once their right flank collapsed under the Allied cavalry assault, the whole Bourbon army faltered and their infantry started to break. On their extreme right, their Irish Brigade Horse had re-attacked the Portuguese, who broke once more, but the Irish exuberance was too great and they pursued them right off the battlefield, returning to find their own army completely collapsed. It was a substantial victory. The Bourbons lost 7,000 men, 3,000 of whom were killed, and twenty-two guns. Philip of Anjou escaped with barely 8,000 men, whom he attempted to rally, but the way to Madrid was left open. Stahremberg cautioned against occupying the capital, arguing that it was easier taken than held. He proposed holding the passes on the Pyrenees, preventing supplies reaching Philip from France and forcing his eventual surrender. It was wise counsel, and Stanhope would have agreed with him if the political pressure had not been for a rapid occupation of Madrid. He entered the city with The Royals on 10 September, unopposed.

The result was an almost exact replay of the events of 1706. The Bourbon partisans cut off supply lines to Portugal, and the French pushed reinforcements over the Pyrenees. More importantly, they sent the great Marshal Vendôme as well. Stanhope rapidly became isolated and decided to fall back, once again, on Catalonia and to unite with Stahremberg's force. He left Madrid on 11 November in two columns, putting all his artillery, unwisely, in one column. He calculated that he had plenty of time to reach Catalonia, and was well able to withstand any Bourbon attack, but he had reckoned without Vendôme. A keen disciple of Luxemburg, the Marshal had learned the value of speed and surprise in the rather stately dance that passed as early-eighteenth-century warfare. He now totally surprised Stanhope by outmarching him and overhauling him. When the Allies occupied Brihuega on 26 November they found French troops on the ridge beyond the town the following morning. Stanhope was trapped, and with no artillery he could do nothing. William's father was sceptical as to how they had got into such a predicament. 'Our offecers proved our worst enemies for we lay there satterday and Sunday as pleased as could be, ateing and drinking and kept neither grandgaurd, pickqut or padrole. But our General said he was sure of it thare was no enemie naere us that could harm us.' He blamed the officers for wanting to wait for their baggage to catch up.

By 28 November 'our ammunition began to be wanting' and command within the British force was strained. Vendôme called on Stanhope to surrender. At first he refused, but after the French stormed the outer ramparts of the town he realized he had no option. He wrote to Stahremberg that he felt 'obliged in conscience to try to save so many brave men who had done good service to the Queen and will, I hope, live to do so again' and the battle was lost on 10 December. As it was, the initial defence cost The Royals forty more casualties, fighting, this time dismounted, inside the walls. Thus The Royals' war in Spain ended with the entire regiment prisoners of war. Twenty-three officers, sixteen sergeants, twenty-four corporals, sixteen drummers, one haut-boi, one gunsmith and 157 privates were taken, including Lieutenant Colonels Montagu and Benson. The war itself dragged on inconclusively, with neither side able to gain and maintain a decisive advantage. The Allies garrisoned Catalonia whilst the Bourbons held Madrid and the centre, until the Treaty of Utrecht ended hostilities in 1714.

The Royals were badly treated immediately after their capture, and had everything stolen except the 'poor clothes on their backs'. They were also mobbed and beaten up by locals as they marched via Madrid to Burgos, where they were to spend two years in captivity. 'It was deplorable enough for we were treated worse than dogs,' wrote William's father, strongly objecting to the fact that the officers kept their horses whilst the dragoons were forced to walk. They were probably paying the price of the locals' frustration at the pillaging and looting during six years of war. Their two years of mass captivity were a predictably depressing and worrying time. It is not so much the loneliness, inactivity or separation from families that dominates their correspondence, but finances. Initially these concerned the horses, which still, of course, belonged to the regiment, and a new batch of uniforms, ordered by Raby, which had arrived in the docks as they left Madrid. The latter were rapidly appropriated by Lepell's regiment, who were delighted with their windfall and masqueraded as The Royals for a number of years. Raby and Ellison were less than amused, and an anxious correspondence followed to make good the substantial financial loss. Later their concerns escalated. Would the regiment, ineffective as it now was, survive the cuts in the army that were bound to come at the end of the war? Should they be disbanded the financial loss would be severe, for the price of commissions in senior regiments such as theirs was always higher as they were generally thought to be safe from such threats.

The conditions in which they were held improved slightly after they quartered with poor families in Burgos, but 'the winter in year 1711 it went very hard for us, having no return of bills from England that we lived very hard, and our offecers would not lend us a penny,' complained William's father. 'We being there awhile there was offecers and serjant sent downe to us, Irish gentry, to inlist any of us as would go and indeed there was a pretty many that did inlist with them, to their shame.' But not as many as Vendôme had hoped, and he was irritated that not more would sign up for the French army as was the custom. Bad as matters were, it did not seem to prevent officers from arranging their own early release. Lieutenant Colonel Montagu was sent home soon after he was captured, and Benson, acting as second-in-command, was released so that he could sort out the regimental accounts. The French, who worked a similar system, obviously sympathized over the potential loss. Of the twenty-three officers taken only twelve, almost all cornets and quartermasters, who tended to be the oldest and the poorest, were with the 164 soldiers when they finally marched out of Burgos in September 1713. They eventually landed at Deal in January 1714, having marched 16 miles each day over the Pyrenees, first to Bordeaux, then to Bayennes and finally to Passages, where they were held in miserable conditions before boarding ship. Losses during the two years had been about a quarter of those taken, which was considered reasonable by contemporary standards, and, all importantly, left more than enough men to re-raise the regiment. There had been talk of making them part of the army in Ireland, which would have been most insulting, but Raby had lobbied well and the deciding issue remained regimental seniority. To have decided otherwise would have risked upsetting the whole delicate financial structure on which the British army was based, and no one wanted that, least of all those hardworking cornets and quartermasters who had mostly advanced themselves by a mixture of hard work and investment and who now returned home after ten years on continual operations or in captivity.

By 1715 the army was reduced to 15,000 men. Over half the infantry regiments were disbanded, three regiments of horse, and all dragoon regiments junior to the 6th, the Inniskillings. The Royals' establishment was cut back to its peacetime level of thirty-eight privates per troop, but the good news was that the War Office agreed to provide new horses and replace all the equipment lost at Brihuega, although Montagu and Benson fought an ongoing claim for years for £291 they had spent out of their own pockets to provide essentials in captivity. In May 1713 The Royals moved to the north of England and resumed their old duties.

Chapter Eight

GERMANIC ORDER

The Duke of Northumberland, as Gold Stick-in-Waiting, and the Life Guards and Horse Grenadiers en masse, met King George I as he landed at Greenwich on 18 September 1714. The Blues had moved to London and provided the guard in their absence. Splendid as the ensuing procession into London and the subsequent coronation may have been, George I did not find his newly acquired army particularly impressive, even though he had fought alongside them under Marlborough. He disapproved, for example, of the purchase system, unthinkable in Germany, and so disliked the idea of the private gentlemen. He also felt the British army was ill-disciplined. He therefore instituted a series of reforms, some of which his son would later complete, and most of which were to be applied army-wide. A few, however, were targeted specifically at the Life Guards and, whilst only partially successful in achieving short-term reform, would slowly reduce their privileges and eventually transform them, by 1788, into regular regiments. For example, the King thought their behaviour in London unacceptable. However Germanic his standards, he did have a point, for not only were there numerous cases of drunkenness and duelling, all avidly reported by the press, but magistrates still appeared unwilling to take action. While hardly a year went by without a serious incident or death, the verdicts on Life Guards accused of murder often cited self-defence. Furthermore, on the odd occasion when a conviction was handed down for manslaughter, an idiosyncrasy of the law allowed the prescribed punishment – to be burned on the hand – to be carried out with a cold iron. This was the fate of one Francis Chandler, who killed one bailiff when drunk in 1725 and another for good measure in 1726. The 1st Horse Grenadiers actually mutinied when three of them were 'picketed', or hung by their wrists with their feet over a sharpened stake, a punishment from which they believed they should be exempt, as were the Life Guards.[1]

Slack discipline was partly the product of life in a violent society, which early-eighteenth-century London certainly was, but it was also symptomatic of a deeper problem. Long years of peace had seen administration of the troops sadly neglected and had sapped their self-esteem. 'I passed some years in the

George I, who acceded in 1714, was not particularly impressed with his Life Guards.

most contemptible of human stations, that of a soldier in time of peace,' scoffed Dr Johnson, and his attitude probably represented popular feeling.[2] The worst affected was the 4th Troop, which may explain why their discipline was so weak. In 1713 the troop was reduced to petitioning Parliament as its Colonel, Lord John Ker, had dismissed men who had paid £100 for their posts with no compensation, had stolen their arms and equipment, and had then resold their places. In addition, he had been illegally stopping 4½d. daily from all his troop for six years 'which has not yet been accounted for'. Things did not improve much, and in March 1727, when Lord Shannon took over as Colonel, he 'found it in great want of all manner of necessarys and no fund to supply them . . . That all the accoutrements were worn out and the Arms by their long use rendered entirely unserviceable.' It subsequently transpired that the arms had not been renewed since 1678, a period of forty-nine years.[3]

Another problem was the growing rivalry between the Life Guards and the Horse Grenadiers, the latter claiming correctly that they performed exactly the same duties as the former but enjoyed much less advantageous terms. The tension had first become public in the 1690s, when the Life Guards had escorted Schomberg into London, whilst the Horse Grenadiers were ordered to escort his baggage. There were, however, some serious structural issues underlying the fairly widespread feuding that had developed by the time of George I's accession. The main issue was precedence. In 1712 a prolonged argument broke out as to whether Horse Grenadier officers could sit on courts martial of Life Guards – not that they were regular occurrences. One of Queen Anne's last acts, within three weeks of her death, was to decide that they could.[4] A more serious case was that of Lieutenant Colonel Turner, a Horse Grenadier, who petitioned the General Officers of the Army in 1722 regarding the seniority of Life Guards officers to other officers of the same rank in the army. His well-argued point was that as an experienced officer his position was constantly eroded by Life Guards who regarded him as junior, and, although this was not specified, inferior. The Board universally recommended to the King that the Life Guards officers should lose the privilege of being 'the eldest', and take army rank according to the date of their commissions as every other officer did. George I took five years to consider the point, but George II finally agreed on his accession.[5] The Horse Grenadiers further objected to the way Life Guards were treated as privileged beings in disciplinary matters, but did not put up much of a case. The picketing incident described above was atypical, and had the offenders been Royals dragoons then they would have been savagely flogged as would a soldier in any other regiment. In 1719 a court martial of five 'private men' of the Horse Grenadiers for publicly insulting Lord Albemarle sentenced one of them merely to apologize on his knees to the Earl. The Court appeared more concerned that Albemarle, as a peer, might be required to give evidence on oath.[6]

The Life Guards were also still finding it difficult to attract enough of the 'right quality' of private gentlemen. As we have seen, during William III's wars many of the most eligible privates benefited by gaining commissions in the newly raised regiments. Indeed, the King regarded the Life Guards as a breeding ground of potential officers for the rest of the army, much as Charles II had done. The resulting gaps in the ranks were filled with Huguenots, or men from other regiments, such as The Blues, who were excused the normal £100 fee. After the 1698 reductions some attempt was made to revert back, but large numbers of Huguenots lingered. Moreover, promoted men were often simply not replaced, of which the Colonels approved as they could draw 'false musters'. Approximately one-quarter of the Life Guards' officers whose commissions were confirmed on George I's accession were probably Huguenot. The supply of willing private gentlemen, keen for promotion as future officers and prepared to pay for the privilege, was fast drying up, and was replaced by a stock of men who saw the job as a continuing way of life with regular pay.

An analysis of the 1st Troop in 1736, whose nominal roll is preserved in the Household Cavalry Museum, shows that this pattern lasted until the Wars of the Austrian Succession in the 1740s, which was the next time the Life Guards were deployed on operations. The Colonel, Lord Cutherlough, formerly John Fane, had previously commanded the 1st Troop of Horse Grenadiers. He received an Irish peerage to give him sufficient status for this new position, although he held it only briefly before he succeeded his brother as Earl of Westmorland. The other senior officers were similarly well connected: the Lieutenant Colonel was Thomas Blathwayt, son of the great Secretary at War, who had originally been a Blue and who had held this position for nearly thirty years. The second Lieutenant Colonel was Lord Carpenter, and the Majors, Leighton and Driver, had bought their way in from other regiments. It was normal to deem a senior position in one of the Life Guard Troops as the pinnacle of a military career; preserved in the National Army Museum are the successive commissions of Edmund Smith, first commissioned into Lord Arran's Regiment under William III, later a Lieutenant in the Life Guards under Queen Anne – her childish signature is scratched on his commission parchment – and returned to a line regiment for a period during Marlborough's wars, before becoming a Major in the 2nd Troop in 1714.

The junior officers were old, unable to buy further progression, and not quite the young men about town of popular imagination. Their private gentlemen were even older, with an average age of thirty-five. The oldest was Mr Hodsall, who was sixty-nine and had joined, aged twenty, in 1687, two years after Sedgemoor. He was closely followed by Tavernor, aged fifty-six with twenty-three years' service, and Lafsall, a Huguenot aged fifty-six with twenty-eight years – and there were many more. The youngest private by far, who had just joined, was aged twenty-two. The average height of the troop was 5 feet 9 inches. Two widows occupied troop spaces and forty-five false musters were also included, whose pay was presumably going to Fane, out of an establishment of 135. The Drummer, Vandervand, and two of the four Trumpeters, Bullange and Gofsett, were probably German or Dutch. The average height of the horses was small at 15 hands, with the oldest aged twenty-five and the youngest seven.

It was this deep-grained institutionalization of the Life Guards that George I and George II tried, rather unsuccessfully, to improve. The rapid succession of colonels did not help and appointments now tended to be given to those in favour politically rather than to competent senior officers. With four troops of Life Guards and two of Horse Grenadiers there were plenty of positions on offer, and the Government utilized them to the full. The 1st Troop was not well served when Albemarle sold to another Dutchman, Lord Portland, for £10,000 in 1710. Portland subsequently passed the job on, at a profit, to Lord Ashburnham in 1713. More ludicrous was Ashburnham's successor, the Duke of Montagu, whose only military service consisted of a brief visit to the headquarters of his father-in-law, Marlborough, and of whom the Duchess of Marlborough wrote to her granddaughter, Diana Spencer: 'All my son-in-law's talents lie in things natural to boys of fifteen, and his is about two and fifty; to get people into his garden and wet them with squirts, or to invite people to his house and put things into their beds to make them itch, and twenty other such petty fancies.'[7] He served until August 1737, when he was relieved by the competent ex-Life Guards officer John, Lord Delawarr. A statesman and soldier, he commanded a brigade at Dettingen and became a lieutenant general. He was one of the great Gold Sticks, and we will be hearing more of him.

The 2nd Troop endured Northumberland for a few years after Ormond, who had relinquished his daily responsibilities after he was made Lord Lieutenant in Ireland, and then had another highly competent soldier in Algernon Seymour, Earl of Hertford and later Duke of Somerset. He had been chosen by Marlborough to carry home his dispatches after Oudenarde, reflecting the part he played in that battle, and subsequently commanded a regiment of foot. The 2nd Troop benefited considerably from his leadership, and in 1740 he went on to become Colonel of The Blues. The 3rd Troop was equally well served by Cholmondeley, who was given the position after his highly successful command of the 1st Troop of Horse Grenadiers and served until 1733. The 4th Troop, however, was disastrously served by John Ker, later Earl of Dundonald, and Lord Forester, as we have seen. Shannon succeeded in restoring some order and served until 1740.

The Blues also endured these political appointees. Oxford had died in 1703 to be replaced by the Duke of Northumberland, who took little interest in the regiment. He was replaced, briefly, in 1712 by Lord Rivers, commander of the ill-fated expedition to relieve Catalonia, who died within a year; the position was subsequently given to the brilliant and colourful Peterborough, back from leading The Royals in Spain. Peterborough, predictably, did not take to peacetime soldiering, and became decidedly eccentric. He took to doing his own shopping, in Fulham Market, often dressed in his regimental uniform with his Garter star, and was to be seen returning to his house in Parsons Green with a leg of mutton slung on either side of his saddle. This could possibly – following his wife's death – have been the result of his property being held until he managed to produce satisfactory accounts for his Spanish endeavours. Yet he was popular with the officers, who much enjoyed the racy literary parties at his villa, and who were sorry when he was appointed Ambassador to Vienna, although he decided to take himself off to Italy instead and was thereby censured. His place was then taken by John, 2nd Duke of Argyll, a brave and competent soldier and a valued subordinate of Marlborough's, who was given the position for his partial success against Mar, despite defeat at Sherrifmuir. Argyll was widely respected, even by Pope, whom he patronized, and who wrote of him:

> Argyll, the state's whole thunder born to wield
> And share alike the senate and the field.

Yet sadly, from 1715, there was too much senate and too few opportunities for Argyll to demonstrate his field qualities. He resigned, or was sacked, twice as Colonel, first in 1717, because he fell out with George I and second, having resumed office in 1733, because he opposed Walpole in 1740. He then resumed office for a month in 1742, probably to prove a point after Walpole's fall, but by then the regiment must have regarded him as a joke. In between Argyll's various tenures there was an even worse incumbent, the Duke of Bolton, who was Colonel from 1717 until 1733 but who was 'a dissatisfied man for being as proud as if he had any consequence, besides what his employments made him as vain as if he had some merit, and as necessitous as if he had no estate, so he was troublesome at court, hated in the country and scandalous in his regiment'.[8] He was best known in London for his very public attachment to the actress Lavinia Fenton, for whom he had fallen as she sang 'O ponder well, be not severe', using the stage name of Polly Peach. The justification for his appointment is revealed by the fact that he was dismissed for opposing the Excise Bill. Francis Compton had only died in February 1712, and it was he who had preserved the spirit of The Blues during Northumberland's tenure. It was his successors, George Fielding, Francis Byng and John Wyvilles, who maintained his discipline and tried to give some direction to their widely dispersed troops during the depressing era of Argyll and Bolton. Wyvilles had originally been a Troop Captain in The Royals in Spain, and had been prosecuted in unpleasant circumstances when his servant died having been flogged for stealing. He subsequently bought his way into The Blues and appears to have been a successful commanding officer, so perhaps he had mended his ways.

The reforms the early Hanoverians wanted to introduce were frustrated to

The Duke of Argyll who was Colonel of The Blues three times between 1715 and 1742.

The Horse Grenadiers were well regarded as soldiers and produced some competent officers such as General Richard Onslow, who commanded the 'Second Line of Cavalry' in the War of the Austrian Succession. Onslow retired to become Military Governor of Plymouth where he died of a heart attack whilst passing sentence at a Court Martial.

a degree, both by this succession of disinterested colonels and also because Walpole's policy of avoiding war, where possible, meant there was little operational urgency. George I did, however, manage to regulate the purchase system. He wanted to get rid of it altogether, but soon realized that was unworkable given the amount individuals invested in it. In 1719 he decreed that commissions could only be purchased by the rank below; in other words, a colonelcy could only be bought by a lieutenant colonel or a majority by a captain. Furthermore, a captaincy or senior rank could only be acquired by those who had already served ten years as a lieutenant. He specified that officers from other regiments were to be encouraged to buy into the Guards, and, most importantly, he fixed the prices of commissions. Prices were not given for the colonelcies of the Life Guards, Horse Grenadiers or Blues, as they were considered above trading, except at the King's instigation. The Royals' colonelcy was valued at £7,000. The table on p. 193 also shows the bewildering array of rank titles in the Life Guards, which, although apparently different to the rest of the army and mostly related to types of flag, were, in reality, the same. Lastly, a Board of General Officers was set up to supervise the new system.

George I also regulated the finances of the Life Guard troops, and not always to their advantage. Private gentlemen, who through 'old age, long service, and other infirmities and frequent accidents that happen render them unable to do further duty', were now to retire to the Royal Hospital to avoid the practice of retaining them on full pay in the troops. However, they were allowed 12d. a day, as opposed to the 5d. a day for ordinary pensioners, which was financed by two official 'false musters' on each troop's roll.[9] A new regulation was introduced in an attempt to improve the officers' rather poor record of duty time-keeping. From 1724 colonels had to send the Secretary of War a list of officers present every fourteen days and no officer was to be absent more than – a still generous – three months each year.[10]

A brave attempt was also made to regulate pay throughout the army and to standardize 'off reckonings', which had got as badly out of control in many regiments as they had in the 4th Troop. Marlborough had administered his deployed field forces very efficiently but, although he was Captain General, his writ did not necessarily apply to that large part of the army left in England. Some sensible improvements in the pay system had been introduced under William III, such as a One Day's Pay scheme, still in use in the British army today, whereby provision was made to fund Chelsea, Kilmainham and other facilities for pensioners. Regimental recruiting funds and remount funds had also been established – good ideas even if the rules for their use were interpreted fairly liberally. The Paymaster General, Ranelagh, had set a bad example, when justifying a misplaced £40,000 in his accounts, by telling Parliament that it was impossible to account for every penny and he preferred the generalist approach to book keeping.[11] Taking a private in The Royals as an example, the new rules now specified that from his weekly pay of 8s. 2d. he had to pay 5s. 3d. to the

First Troop of Horse Guards

	Price of Commissions
	£ s. d.
Captain & Colonel	
Lieutenant	4,000 — —
Cornet	3,400 — —
Guidon	3,200 — —
Exempt	1,600 — —
Brigadier	1,000 — —
Sub-Brigadier	500 — —
Adjutant	300 — —

2ᵈ Troop Ditto
3ᵈ Troop Ditto
4ᵗʰ Troop Ditto

First Troop of Horse Granadʳ Guards

	Price of Commissions
Captain & Colonel	
Lieutenant & Lt Colonel	3,600 — —
Major	2,900 — —
Lieutenant & Captain	2,000 — —
Guidon & Captain	1,600 — —
Sub-Lieutenant	900 — —
Adjutant	270 — —

2ᵈ Troop Ditto.

A document showing the prices for commissions in the Life Guards (First Troop of Horse Guards) and Horse Grenadier Guards as agreed by George I in 1719. Note the Life Guards' bewildering array of ranks, which remained in use until 1788.

landlord of whichever inn he was billeted to for food and lodging, 1s. 5d. for corn and 3d. to the farrier, leaving him 1s. 2d. for beer or to support his family if he had one. In the summer, when there was plenty of grass, forage money was reduced, although deductions of 1s. 9d. per week were still made from corporals, drummers and above to make good any troop clothing deficiencies, pay for medicine and other such general items. The deductions in The Blues were similar, except that all ranks contributed 6d. a week to the remount fund to buy new horses. Of course, being Horse, they were paid more.

Disciplinary regulations were also standardized, but remained no less harsh for that. In 1718 George I reissued the Articles of War, which now appear to have been applied by colonels in peacetime as well. There had always been severe physical punishment in the army, when deployed, as practised in garrisons like Tangier, but it was only during William III's campaigns that its use became more widespread. Perhaps it was necessary given the quality of men being drafted into the newly raised infantry battalions, or it may have been a reflection of German practice. Whatever the reasons, punishments handed down by courts martial became increasingly harsh, and were no longer equivalent to those awarded by magistrates. These punishments, however, were rarely applied to regiments of horse; the Life Guards and the Horse Grenadiers were exempt from being sentenced to physical punishment, hence the fuss when Fane picketed the three soldiers at Sevenoaks. No records survive to show that any member of The Blues was flogged during this period either, although privates were occasionally picketed. For The Royals, as a less privileged body, it was very different. Flogging was commonplace, as witnessed by the case of Private John Thorne from Frome, who deserted in peacetime and was sentenced to three lashes on his bare back for every private man and corporal in the regiment, so around 1,200 lashes. He was fortunate, in a way, as normally deserters were sentenced to death, though in practice usually pardoned and flogged instead.[12]

Finally, in 1729, George II attempted to improve and standardize the quality of recruits, horses and uniform, all still very much at the whim of the colonels. There were separate regulations for the Life Guards, but The Blues were now to have 'a new cloth coat well lined with serge, a new waistcoat, a new laced hat, a pair of new large buff gloves with stiff tops' every two years and new boots and saddles 'as they shall be wanting'. Horses were to be 15.1 to 15.2 hands, and 'not exceeding', which is much smaller than contemporary artists would have us believe. The Royals' horses were not to exceed 15 hands. Men were not to be less than 5 feet 10 inches 'in stockings'.[13]

Sensible and necessary as these reforms were, they did not exactly produce the efficient and well-administered army that the Georges sought. Whilst the Life Guards and Horse Grenadiers continued their traditional duties, neither The Blues nor The Royals found much to engage them. The Blues remained mostly in the Home Counties, with occasional forays north, and The Royals, in the north and Midlands, were regularly involved in tedious duties such as policing the races, and the Fair or the assizes in Nottingham. More insultingly, they had to vacate their normal lodgings during these events as the landlords could charge visitors more. Occasional anti-smuggling duties must have been more fun, but only after much patrolling to and fro. Some officers, realizing Walpole's policy of non-involvement on the Continent must inevitably end, gave some thought to how the army should be developing. Humphrey Bland, a lieutenant in The Royals, published a *Treatise on Discipline* in 1727, which became a standard work on tactics, but it must have been difficult to put into practice at Nottingham racecourse.

Regimental life in the 1730s was therefore somewhat dull. With no active service or prospect of army expansion, officers' progression in both The Blues and The Royals stagnated and the only available method of promotion was by purchase. However, more attractive prospects now existed for the adventurous young men who twenty years earlier would have competed for cornets' and quartermasters' places, such as in the army of the East India Company. The knock-on effect in the troops was that the social standing of the lower commissioned ranks, such as the quartermasters, declined. Only in the Life Guards and The Blues were they to remain 'King's Commissions'; the first army-wide officers' list, issued in 1740, did not even dignify quartermasters by name. Second, the cornets became increasingly old, and in many cases bitter at seeing younger men with money bypass them for captaincies and lieutenancies. When The Royals were finally mobilized in 1740, after the death of the Hapsburg Emperor Charles VI on 20 October that year, most of the cornets were over sixty, with one so palsied that he could not mount his horse and another too rheumatic to ride at all. It was not the best of starts for a British army that was soon to fight its first Continental war for thirty years.

The dead Emperor, who had no sons, had taken considerable trouble to ensure the smooth succession of his twenty-three-year-old daughter Maria Theresa to his huge dominions, which covered what today is Austria, Hungary, the Czech and Slovak Republics, northern Italy, a large portion of Germany and most of the Balkans. In 1713 he facilitated the signing of the 'Pragmatic Sanction' by the major European powers, which apparently guaranteed their support for Maria Theresa. His death still resulted in several conflicting claims for his throne, which continued, in theory, to be filled by election. The new King Frederick of Prussia, realizing he needed to expand at Austrian expense to become dominant in northern Germany, supported Charles Albert, Elector of Bavaria and Maria Theresa's main rival. Taking advantage of the prevailing uncertainty, he invaded the Austrian province of Silesia, defeating the Hapsburg army at Mollwitz on 10 April 1741. France, eager for an opportunity to counter Hapsburg power, mobilized in support of Charles Albert's claim, on the grounds that he was likely to prove a willing client of Louis XV. Popular opinion in England, fanned by resentment at continuing French support for the Jacobites and by growing commercial rivalry, was consequently strongly pro-Austrian, and Parliament voted an immediate grant of £3 million to Maria Theresa. However, a French threat to Hanover, and an adroit move by Frederick in placing a Prussian army on the Hanoverian border, forced George II to compromise. In the ensuing election he voted for Charles Albert, much to Parliamentary disgust. The Government's popularity declined rapidly, to the extent that Walpole, in power effectively since 1721, did badly in the 1741 elections. On 11 February 1742 he resigned, and with him went his policy of non-engagement. He was replaced by the more bellicose Lord Carteret, a great favourite of the King's, possibly because he could speak German, who took the European crisis as an opportunity to attack Britain's real enemy, France. In the spring of 1742 he guided a bill through Parliament offering Maria Theresa £5 million and an army of 16,000 troops. Logically George II and Carteret should have supported their fellow-Protestant, Frederick of Prussia, as Britain was later to do in the Seven Years War. But Frederick's real aim was to gain advantage against Austria, with French support, whilst the British goal was to attack France, as opposed to supporting Maria Theresa. The resulting misunderstanding, made worse by George II's intense personal dislike of Frederick, was one of the many contradictions of the muddled war which now engulfed Europe for the next four years.

Chapter Nine

THE WAR OF THE AUSTRIAN SUCCESSION

For the Life Guards, The Blues and The Royals, who were all, once again, destined to fight together, the war brought a frustrating period of home duty to an end. They had been preparing for their deployment since the Emperor's death two years before. The confusion and mistakes of the coming campaign were the result partly of the institutional problems outlined in the last chapter, partly of the failure to learn lessons from Marlborough's battles, particularly on logistics, and partly of official incompetence, though not quite to the extent that is often asserted. Sir William Yonge, the Secretary at War, had in fact mobilized the troops in the summer of 1740, when The Royals had moved from Worcestershire to join The Blues for training in Windsor Great Park, in General Honeywood's Brigade. The brigade dispersed that autumn, after George II's deal with Frederick the Great, but early in 1742 they were finally alerted for deployment. A dearth of forage in Flanders required both regiments to delay departure until the summer, and they arrived in August, together with the 3rd and 4th Troops of the Life Guards and the 2nd Troop of Horse Grenadiers. The 1st and 2nd Troops remained on duty in London, as did the 1st Troop of Horse Grenadiers.

The voyage from Gravesend to Ostend was dreadful. The wind 'blew very hard for two days together, when we were but a league from Ostend, but so much against us that we could not possibly get into harbour until it had ceased. I was a little cautious and asked several seamen before I would venture to call it a storm, lest I should discover either fear or ignorance, but they tell me that I may safely call it so', wrote Richard Davenport, who had paid £500 in May to be commissioned as a sub-brigadier, or cornet, in the 4th Troop of Life Guards, and who wrote regularly to his brother during the next four years.[1] Davenport is a good example of the sort of energetic young man from a respectable but modest background that saw a junior commission as a way of getting on in the world. He would have been unlikely to join the Life Guards had there been no war, and might very well have headed for India instead. Had he been richer or grander he might have progressed more rapidly to a more senior commission. From Gunnersbury in Middlesex, he had lost both his parents when he was in his teens, and he had been brought up together with his devoted brother John by his uncle, Ralph Marsh, a woollen draper in Aldgate. Richard had been introduced to the idea of joining the Life Guards by the Lieutenant Colonel of the 4th Troop, Francis Burton, who was engaged to a family friend. John Davenport went on to make a sizeable fortune, taking over his uncle's business and winning contracts to supply army clothing.

Another man who wrote a regular account of the coming campaign was Dr John Buchanan, Regimental Surgeon to The Blues, who had joined the regiment in 1733 and who now accompanied it on active service for the first time. His diary was largely designed to impress medical colleagues, and appears to have been written with possible publication in mind, but it does also give a colourful picture of regimental life.[2] He was happy to act as a vet as well, and there are frequent notes on how horses were treated. On the voyage over they coped rather better than the men, very few of whom had ever seen the sea, let alone sailed on it, and who were violently ill. Buchanan's remedy for them was to increase their liquid intake, from the regulation two quarts of small beer to three, which must have been popular with those well enough to enjoy it. He found that what upset the horses was not the swell but the intense heat generated by so many below decks on a wooden transport. 'When a horse sickens by heat . . . then it's absolutely necessary to bleed him immediately, or the consequence will be very bad; and some horses were lost for want of this help; if he cannot be conveniently blooded in the neck, let him be blooded in the mouth, when he has lost a sufficient quantity, rub the part with flour in order to stop it . . . a quart blood should be taken away the first halting day after landing.' They appear not to have mucked out en route, leaving the horses standing in their own dung, so that on arrival they nearly all lost their shoes. Fortunately they had several months to wait before they were to encounter the French; Carteret's enthusiasm had outpaced the Dutch, and the army now went into winter quarters at Ghent while a coalition was organized and the Dutch brought on side.

Davenport and the officers took over houses in the town. They rode, learned to skate on frozen canals, and bemoaned the lack of action. Constant rumours circulated of the King's imminent arrival, and of what the French might be up to. Once it was obvious that there was to be no action before the spring, several Life Guard officers sold their horses and returned to London, incurring the wrath of Lord Stair, newly arrived as Commander-in-Chief. Davenport busied himself learning his new profession and mastering French. Many wives had accompanied their husbands. 'Provisions are in plenty of all sorts, but the cooks of this place are the worst in the world and there are no English women but soldiers' wives. The wives of our men are above service and the wives of the foot soldiers, without excepting one that ever I saw, are as drunk as their

WAR OF THE AUSTRIAN SUCCESSION 1742–1746

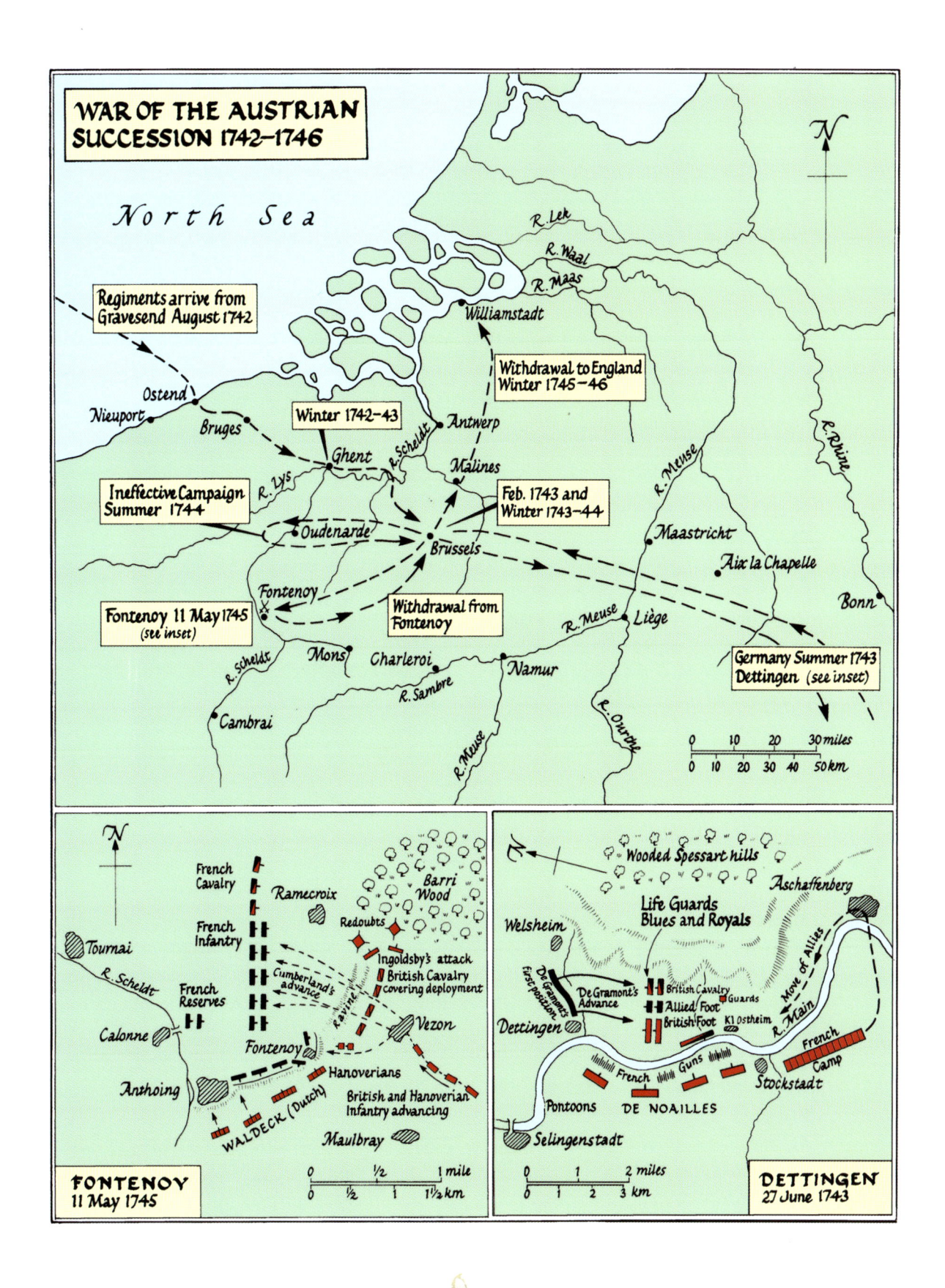

husbands.' Life for the soldiers was adequately comfortable, 'all are now in barracks, ordered to Boyle their kettle and mess regularly; al provisions being as good and as cheap as at home . . . two men lye in one bed on matrasses of coarse flax, are well enough covered, but have no curtains'. Buchanan found many of them fat and unfit, evidence of a lack of training, and had difficulty in getting officers to exercise the troops daily. There were several cases of the itch, which he blamed on the foot soldiers and dragoons who had used their transport ships before them, and colds and ague were common. Horses also got agues, a fact which at home, Buchanan wrote, would have been cured by drinking from the chalybeate water of Sunninghill Well in Windsor Forest.

Davenport, establishing what was to be a common theme of his correspondence, tried his hand with the local women, but 'I have not seen one that is so handsome as my laundress' sister . . . except at Bruges I was quartered upon a house where there was a very pretty woman. I made love to her in French . . . She seemed well pleased, perhaps though she might not understand me, I believe if I had not been ordered away . . . matters might have been brought to a happy conclusion'. Venereal disease was less common than generally supposed when British armies were in garrison but, Buchanan notes, 'it's a difficult task to cure the private men of the claps; when the painful symptoms abate they neglect taking medicines; let the running continue till it turns to a Glut, then say they were not well cured. Officers are more easily cured.' Fighting was a constant problem, although the Horse generally kept aloof from it. The Hungarian contingent was considered particularly troublesome, and the soldiers were amazed to witness a Hungarian having his head cut off 'at one cut with a seymeter for killing his comrade'.

Such prosaic details did little, however, to dent regimental pride. The regiments were reviewed by Lord Stair 'and accompanied by the Prince of H[e]ss; they both Expressed their Delight of the Beauty and Vigour and Exact Discipline of the Bold Britons who seemed worthy to be a shining pattern to the Best Forces in the whole world', wrote Edmund Cox, a troop quartermaster in The Blues, who also kept a detailed journal of the coming years,[3] although, irritatingly, he seems to have pioneered the Ten Year Diary approach by writing up successive decades on the same page. In February 1743 the majority of the army, including The Royals, started to move slowly into Germany, while the Life Guards and The Blues moved to Brussels to await the King's arrival. Davenport liked Brussels, which was emptier of troops and 'the women handsome and not virtuous'. He had now paid £1,000 for a lieutenancy and become Adjutant of his troop, but not without an anxious exchange of correspondence with John. They raised the money between them as a family investment by selling some bonds, but John was keen to get the contract for supplying the Life Guards' uniforms in return.

By the spring political negotiations were complete and in May the troops in Brussels moved to join the main Allied army in Germany at Hochst between

Trooper in the Blues
c.1742.

George II was the last British monarch to lead his army in person, at the Battle of Dettingen (*below*), an untidy skirmish south of Frankfurt in 1743. The Life Guards who escorted him during the day praised him for his bravery – but not his generalship.

Frankfurt and Mayence, or Mainz. George II duly arrived in early June from Hanover to take command, accompanied by his son, the Duke of Cumberland, and with Carteret in attendance. His presence caused a good deal of confusion. He outranked the fairly ineffective Austrian general, Aremberg, nominally Allied Commander-in-Chief, described by Smollet as 'a proud, rapacious glutton, without talent or sentiment'.[4] He did little to welcome his British allies, whose combined forces outnumbered his. He also put Stair, Commander-in-Chief of the British army, in a difficult position. Whilst he was a veteran of Marlborough's wars, his most valued experience was as a diplomat, having served as Ambassador to the French court from 1715 until 1720. Now old and irascible, he could not bear Aremberg and refused to speak to him, which Marlborough would have found unforgivable. Stair also found George II's constant interference intolerable, and their relationship was strained. Although they all accepted the need to march north to join the 6,000 Hanoverian and 6,000 Hessian troops, gathering at Hanau, just east of Frankfurt, and subsequently prevent the French army, under Noailles, from linking with their Bavarian allies, there was little agreement on how to do this. George II himself was driven partly by a personal desire to lead his troops in the field, much as William III had done. He prevented Stair from seizing an opportunity to attack Noailles in May when the French army were disadvantaged, as he would have missed the action. He was also keen to ensure the protection of Hanover. This in itself was becoming increasingly unpopular in England, and in Parliament. 'It is now but too evident', declared Pitt the Elder, 'that this great, this powerful, this formidable kingdom is considered only as a province of a despicable electorate',[5] which probably went some way to explaining why George II hated him so much.

Meanwhile the army of the great, powerful and formidable kingdom was marching along the River Main, partly excited at the prospect of action and partly fed up with double marches, bad provisions and worse lodging. Little about them would have been unfamiliar to Oxford or Francis Compton, for their equipment and tactics had scarcely changed in the past forty years. Apart from their coats being more dashing, and their hats and buttonholes more generously adorned with gold lace, the basic uniform and weaponry were much the same as in 1660. Each man carried a metal 'pot' to go under his three-cornered black hat, and a set of fronts and backs. The swords remained useless, and although the pistols' mechanisms were now more reliable, their penetrating power was sorely wanting. Each man carried twelve rounds of ammunition, as opposed to the infantry, who carried twenty-four. Also very familiar to Compton would have been the fact that after several weeks on the march they looked decidedly field-stained, camp kit strung off their horses, uniforms faded and patched, and mounted on horses of varying sizes and colours. Spades, picks, axes and shovels were carried and cloaks were rolled up on saddles, and tents and camp equipment followed in the baggage. What would have impressed Compton, however, was that not a single man or horse from the Life Guards or The Blues had been lost since they left Brussels. Heat was the main problem on the march. 'None of the officers were sicke', noted Buchanan, 'but their faces were red and hot, the skin peeling off; uncocking the hat would have proved a good preservative but was unmilitary. The men laye in Barns, haylofts etc. Officers set up their tent beds . . . in pitching tents Officers commonly assist their servants, in order to give them more time to take care of the horses, and have a particular pleasure in this kind of worke.' The families came too. 'Many tender women and young children marched with us . . . were never a horsebacke, nor carried in waggons. One of our Troopers wifes in Germany marched 36 hours with the child in her arms the fourth day after delivery.' Vermin was a problem, particularly when it got into the men's long hair, and the flies were dreadful, if the troops spent more than one day in the same place.

The horses suffered badly in the heat, especially with cracked heels, and Buchanan regretted the practice of docking their tails, as it prevented them from swishing away the flies. He blooded them frequently, which he thought improved their condition, but he noted that the French horses always looked healthier than the British, despite a lower forage allowance. Spring was always a difficult period for forage; the previous year's corn and hay was usually finished and horses relied on fresh grass, which supplied less energy than hard food, and required frequent rest days for grazing. The French army's foraging system was more efficient, relying on contractors – a reform Cumberland was to introduce to the British army the following year. Sore backs, a serious problem for the horses, were treated with a poultice made of dung mixed with soap and brandy.

By mid-June the troops had reached central Germany, and rumours circulated they were nearing the French, who apparently had 70,000 men, against the Allies' 30,000. Morale lifted when thirty French deserters came into the Life Guards' camp, some of whom were hussars mounted on 13.2-hand ponies. Davenport bought one of them, taking him up to six horses and three servants, 'a princely equipage' fit for his new rank and responsibility. Stair's original plan, before George II overruled him, had been to cross to the west bank of the Main and entice the French to attack. The army was seriously short of forage, as Davenport had noted, and, now it had joined up with the German troops, was too large to be supported by the country around Frankfurt. 'Our men & horse could stand it no longer for in three days they had but one feed of corn, & neither Hay nor Water,' wrote Edward Ingleton, a private, to his brother,[6] and Buchanan noted that 'we were sometimes disappointed by the Enemies Hussars surprising the bread waggons. Our Moroders had plundered and frightened the country people, that no provision was brought to camp. We were almost starving. Gin became a greater favourite than ever, was mixed with poor-sower Rhenish wine plundered from the neighbouring villages.'

George II had therefore decided that they should withdraw to the east bank, move north, and head for Hanau, where there was a stocked magazine. It was an obtuse tactic, for the east bank was dominated by thickly wooded hills, and movement was restricted to a narrow corridor along the river, which could easily be blocked. Noailles promptly took advantage, realizing that the Allies had fallen into a trap, and pushed his nephew, the Duc de Gramont, with 30,000 men across the river at Selingenstadt to occupy the valleys around the village of Dettingen, and so block the Allies' path. Meanwhile he came up on the west bank, deployed his artillery to fire across the river into the Allies' flank, and positioned troops to cross behind them and occupy Aschaffenberg, so that the Allies were surrounded on three sides. It was a supremely simple tactic, which Stair had foreseen, but by now he hardly participated in the King's councils with Aremberg and Cumberland.

The resultant Battle of Dettingen became famous as the last in which a British monarch led his troops in person. In truth, it was more of an untidy skirmish than a battle and was marked by the contrasting incompetence of Allied and French generalship. Frederick the Great described Noailles' tactics as worthy of the greatest captain and those of the Allies as beneath contempt, but he had a vested interest, and George II's dislike for him was fully reciprocated. However, it was a battle which revealed that thirty years of peace had not sapped the low-level ability of the British army. They averted disaster by their bravery as much as the French squandered their opportunity by lack of battlefield discipline. The Allied position on the morning of 27 June 1743 appeared desperate. They could only advance by attacking Gramont's now strongly defended position at Dettingen; they could not retreat because Noailles now held Aschaffenberg. To their right were the steeply wooded slopes of the Spessart Hills, which prevented any movement without completely losing formation and in which Gramont had positioned infantry, whilst to their left was an unfordable river across which the French batteries of large 18-pounder guns were already causing significant casualties. The day was only saved by the extraordinary conduct of Gramont who, apparently losing his nerve, left his fortifications at Dettingen and launched a series of attacks. By this time Stair had taken charge and formed the Allies into a hasty defensive position, with the main body in two lines; seven British battalions under General Clayton, an Austrian brigade and four British cavalry regiments, including the Life Guards, The Blues and The Royals, were in the front line, with five British infantry battalions, a Hanoverian brigade and the rest of the British cavalry in the second. The King's Life Guard, consisting of thirty-six men from the 3rd (Albemarle's) Troop, stayed with George II throughout.

The Allies had left Aschaffenberg at 1 a.m., and it was nearly midday by the time Stair had formed them into lines in front of Dettingen. No one passed any messages back, and the regiments had no idea what was happening. The fact that there was to be a major battle came as a surprise. By that time they had been under French artillery fire for nearly three hours, although it had caused only minor casualties. As they took up position, Major Jenkinson was surprised to see the corporal he had left with the troop's baggage ride up carrying a cannonball. 'Sir,' he said, 'see what great things they fire at us; if you don't order them to leave off they will beat all the Baggages to peices.'[7] The French attacks developed from midday, with the Gardes Françaises advancing against the British infantry, commanded by General Clayton, on the left of the first line. Volleys of disciplined musket fire beat them off and their units began to disintegrate. The cavalry of the Maison du Roi, the Life Guards' French equivalent, followed them up. Clayton called for cavalry support, and the 3rd Dragoons were dispatched, followed by two more regiments of dragoons and The Blues. A hand-to-hand cavalry battle ensued; The Blues found their pistols useless against the French breastplates, and most of the fighting was done with swords, many of which broke, leaving the frustrated soldiers to stab with hilts.

Meanwhile the Mousquetaires Noirs, deflected by the fire of Clayton's infantry, veered left and attacked the right of the British line, where they supposed George II to be. They were met almost head on by The Royals, who stopped them in their tracks. An unidentified sergeant killed the young French officer carrying their regimental colour; he had strapped himself to his horse and strapped the standard to his body so that it should not be seen to fall. By now the French attacks had faltered, and the Allies turned on the offensive. Those Life Guards not with the King had been waiting patiently on the extreme right, and were now ordered to charge the static remnants of the Gardes Françaises. Lord Craufurd, Colonel of the 2nd Horse Grenadiers and Brigade Commander, disliked the tone of the aide-de-camp who brought the message and replied, 'Mind, Sir; I shall obey orders when it suits most proper.' It clearly did suit him for, telling his men to forget their pistols and to trust to their swords, and with his trumpeter blowing 'Britons Strike Home', they charged and routed the remnants of the French. Craufurd was perhaps the most inspirational of the troop colonels of the day. Davenport wrote that 'he seemed to have no more concern than if it were at a review, which gave great spirit to the men, who, I really believe, would have followed him anywhere'. An experienced soldier who had fought on the Continent, Craufurd had been wounded in the thigh at Krotzka in 1739 and had been operated on by a surgeon in the French Maison du Roi. Thereafter he declined to sleep in houses on campaign, despite his pain, preferring to bivouac with his brigade. He finally died of his wound in 1749.

The French fell back on Dettingen and Noailles now failed to show the aptitude of a great captain, making no attempt to rally them. Hundreds were drowned trying to cross the Main, and the triumphant British infantry cut down many more on the banks. The cavalry started to pursue, but were called off in what was to prove one of George II's most surprising decisions on a day when he had made many. Noailles afterwards admitted that had he been

The Battle of Dettingen was fought on a narrow plain, with the Allies trapped by the French between the River Main and high wooded hills. Their victory was due to superior battlefield discipline and French mistakes, rather than any tactical brilliance on the part of their commanders.

vigorously pursued his army could have been decimated. It survived to gain its revenge two years later. It seems the King wanted to prove his personal bravery above all, which he undoubtedly did. Mr Kendal, of the 3rd Troop, was in his Life Guard during the battle. 'I was in the first rank next the King,' he wrote to his wife, 'Our Capt had his hat shot off, the man on my right hand had his horse shot & the man on my left was shot in the shoulder, & next to him shot dead. All the time the King was not at all concerned; the Duc d'Aremberg desired him to get out of danger: He made Answer, "Don't tell me of danger. I'll be even with them": he is certainly the bravest man I ever saw'.[8] Another account has him answering Aremberg, 'What do you think I am here for – to be a poltroon?'[9] Yet his bravery came at a cost: Colonel Russell, of the Foot Guards, wrote to his wife that 'the superior officers rode about bravely enough, and exposed themselves, but gave no sort of orders'.[10]

The French lost around 5,000 men and the Allies about 2,000. Our regiments escaped lightly, with seven killed in the Life Guards and Horse Grenadiers, eight in The Blues and only three in The Royals, despite their outstanding success against the Mousquetaires Noirs. Buchanan attributed this to wearing the fronts and backs, which were proof against French pistols and muskets, unless fired very close. The worst injuries were from the French artillery cannonade. Several officers were wounded, including Lord Albemarle. Major Johnston of the 3rd Troop was shot in the ankle and operated on by Buchanan, who wrote, 'I stitched the arterie and cut off the ankle . . ., leaving the amputation of the leg to a more convenient opportunity. It's surprising how some people bear pain better than others. This gentleman never changed his voice or altered his countenance.'

George II was generous in the flush of his victory. Trooper Brown of the 3rd Dragoons, who had been the first to go to Clayton's aid, was made a private gentleman in the Life Guards for recovering the regimental standard and receiving seven wounds in the process. Two privates in each Life Guard troop were given army commissions as a mark of respect for their gallantry, whilst The Royals adopted the colour black as their regimental colour. From then on they always had black candles in their messes, and all their regimental badges were backed with black felt, as they still are in The Blues and Royals today.

While George II dispensed honours and munched a leg of cold mutton, little was done for the wounded who were left where they fell until regimental surgeons could get up to them. 'We had no provision,' continued Buchanan, 'some men had not broke bread these eight and forty hours . . . the night passed amidst the groans of the dying, and the complaints of those who survived them.' The French recovered about 600 wounded after the Allies moved on. They were very well cared for by their surgeons and considered fortunate. Buchanan was particularly incensed that one of Colonel Beake's Troopers, whose leg was shot off by a cannonball and whom he patched up on the field, was just left to die.

Little was done to follow up the victory at Dettingen. The very able Saxe, who manoeuvred to prevent the main Austrian army under Prince Charles of Lorraine from joining the Allies in central Germany, replaced Noailles. Stair resigned, and George II returned home to a hero's welcome in November, and a *Te Deum* composed by Handel, while his army returned to winter quarters in Flanders. The Life Guards and The Blues went back to Brussels, from where Davenport's letters are more concerned with choosing a wife, news of friends, money and acquiring new uniforms than with the campaign. The strain of a second winter began to tell on the troops. 'Quarrel between our Regiment and Gen. Ligonier's; which began by a boxing match,' recorded Edmund Cox. 'Great numbers of both Regiments were Enga'd with Swords and Clubs; a great many was wound'd on both sides.'

Not only were the Allied troops becoming restive but the whole campaign now lacked focus. The events of 1743 had achieved little and it was clearly imperative for the British and Dutch to act in concert with the Austrians. The Austrian Commander-in-Chief, Prince Charles of Lorraine, consequently arrived in Brussels on 15 March 1744 to discuss plans for renewing the campaign that spring. He was escorted into the city by The Blues and reviewed the Life Guards and the Horse Grenadiers in front of the cathedral. 'In the evening there was great rejoicing as . . . ye town made him a present of Two Extream Large Barrels of Wine which was Drawn by six horses' and shared with the troops.' Field Marshal George Wade, famous for road-building in Scotland and subduing the Highland clans after the 1715 Rising, but now a tired seventy-three-year-old, had taken over from Stair, and hopes of concluding the war that summer were high as the Allies marched out of Brussels on 20 May, heading for Tournai and Lille. However, Aremberg, whom Prince Charles had left as his commander in the field, proved as intractable as ever. The Dutch generals prevaricated for, accurately, as they claimed, Holland was not at war with France and their troops were only acting as mercenaries for Maria Theresa. Wade told Carteret that he could only rely on his 22,000 British and 16,000 Hanoverian and Hessian troops. The French army, divided into two parts under Noailles – now partially rehabilitated – and Saxe, outmanoeuvred Wade at every turn, taking Coutrai, and forcing him to change his plans and besiege it. By November the army had spent six months marching and counter-marching around Flanders, without fighting a major battle and reducing the country to poverty. The regiments' attitude to the French, considered decent opponents after their treatment of the wounded at Dettingen, now hardened. 'Our Soldiers knowing we was in our Enemy's Country us'd it accordingly,' Cox continued, 'one instance I saw; which was in front of our Regiment an extream beautiful Nobleman's house with handsome out houses; pretty Gardens; a fine Widerness; a Mote round the House with draw Bridges. The House Well Furnish'd and everything compleat. About 3 in the morning they Brok down the Draw Bridges and went into the house . . . they plunder'd the house of

Although our regiments were shocked by the behaviour of the German and Austrian cavalry, they realized that they had much to learn from them in terms of organization and tactics. In particular, they were impressed with the Light Cavalry, such as this Hussar from the Karoly Regiment.

everything; they even destry'd the wenscoting, fine chairs . . . several villages round us was plunder'd in the same manner.' The soldiers were bored and desertion became common in the army; even The Blues had two deserters, highly unusual in the regiments of horse and the Highlanders. The two Blues were arrested and 'brought to the head of our Regiment to have the sentence of a Genl Court Martial put in Execution; one was to be hang'd', Cox records. Evidently the regiment thought this extreme 'as the Minister was praying to him; he Slipt in amongst the crowd and got clean off'. Drunkenness, however, was common throughout The Blues and The Royals, and was routinely dealt with by picketing, although the most notorious offender, Trooper Jeffard in Captain Shipman's Troop, had a convenient habit of falling 'into violent convulsive fitts' when tied up and so escaped punishment.

By November the army was back in winter quarters once more. Wade was made to resign, and Carteret, now elevated to Earl Granville, forced from office. Ligonier stood in as Commander-in-Chief, until it was decided, on 25 March 1745, to appoint Cumberland, with Ligonier as his mentor. Cumberland had fought bravely at Dettingen where he had been wounded in his ample thigh. It was felt that his Royal status would give him authority with the troublesome Austrians and Dutch and he was well regarded in the army. 'We have all been presented to the Duke and kissed his hand,' Davenport wrote. 'He receives everybody with great affability. We had the honour to pass before him in review in our new regimentals and furniture (which, by the way cost upwards of £70).'

Remembered, unfairly, for his army's behaviour after Culloden, and for his subsequent defeats in Germany, Cumberland was a more able soldier than his reputation suggests. On arrival in Flanders he set about a much-needed reorganization. He established a proper staff, on which several officers later to become closely connected with our regiments served, including Henry Seymour Conway. The Life Guards, Horse Grenadiers and Blues were put into a Household Cavalry Brigade under Lord Craufurd, the first time the term Household Cavalry appears to have been used in the army, whilst The Royals served in the second line, commanded by their Colonel, the dreaded Hawley, of whom we will shortly be hearing rather more, and Major General Richard Onslow, an ex-Horse Grenadier. An attempt was made to lease proper forage contracts and avoid a repetition of earlier troubles. Discipline was tightened up, not before time, and plundering was outlawed and looters hanged. Establishment tables were reviewed and deductions regularized. A proper military hospital was established, with detailed regulations for the care of the wounded. Weekly returns of those hospitalized were sent to Cumberland in person: the week the army eventually left Brussels the Life Guards had six men sick, The Blues seven and The Royals nine, which suggests that Buchanan's methods were paying off. Lastly, Cumberland proved an able diplomat, establishing a good working relationship with the aged Count Konigsegg, the new Austrian commander and a veteran of the Turkish wars, and with Prince Waldeck, the new Dutch commander, who was encouragingly impetuous.

It was, however, Cumberland's great misfortune that Saxe had also spent the last year reorganizing the French army. Whereas Cumberland's reforms were sensible and necessary, they were largely administrative and had not had time to take effect. Saxe, by contrast, had not only improved French organization over a period of eighteen months but had also developed their tactics. None of the various accounts of the winters our regiments spent in Flemish garrisons mentions a single training day, although parades and reviews were common. The prevailing sentiment, as personified by George II at Dettingen, was that, confronted by the French, British natural superiority would carry the day. Nothing had been done to replace useless swords, so many of which had shattered at Dettingen, or to acquire improved pistols. All these factors were to become tragically apparent at Fontenoy.

Cumberland was keen to get his army into the field early in 1745, but it was unable to move until mid-April. The Blues had enjoyed a party the night before they left Brussels, 'and we have many accidents nixt day and much confusion in passing the Gates. Attended with many inconveniences, carriages are overturned, broke down, men hurt and horses lame.'[11] Meanwhile Saxe, recovering from a severe illness, had stolen a march on Cumberland and, advancing in three columns, deceived the Allies into thinking he was going to take Mons, when in fact his objective was Tournai. Switching course abruptly, he besieged the key Dutch fortress on 28 April. His army was 90,000 strong against Cumberland's 50,000, many of whom, mainly Dutch and Austrian troops, remained on garrison duty. Cumberland's force now approached Tournai, intending to attack Saxe and relieve the siege, yet, despite the obvious threat posed by the French, they moved with little urgency. Taking eleven days to cover 48 miles, Cumberland was obliged to issue orders forbidding officers to go off for a day's hunting en route.[12] The Allies finally halted for thirty-six hours between the villages of Maubrai and Bougnies, only 10 miles from Saxe's camp, giving him ample warning of their intentions. Cumberland appears to have had no intelligence apparatus, and went forward himself to look for Saxe's positions with Konigsegg and Waldeck, which he found 3 miles east of Tournai, between the River Scheldt and Barri Wood, centred on the village of Fontenoy. Saxe had prepared his positions well and, perhaps not trusting the French infantry to withstand the concentrated British musket fire, had constructed a series of redoubts, reinforced with natural obstacles, which gave him considerable defence in depth.

Cumberland determined to attack, and now showed his inexperience. He decided that the main attack would be led by the British and Hanoverian infantry against the French centre around Fontenoy itself, the strongest part of their position. The Dutch would attack the French right wing, anchored on the hamlet of Anthoing on the Scheldt, whilst the cavalry would cover the

The Duke of Cumberland was not quite the ogre he was later to become known as because of his alleged excesses after Culloden. He was an energetic administrator, if outwitted tactically by Saxe, and he was well respected in the army.

An image of British Troops under Cumberland, an idealized view of what the army looked like in the Low Countries in the War of the Austrian Succession. The reality was a lot less glamorous.

Our regiments were all present at the Battle of Fontenoy on 11 May 1745, but only became engaged late in the day when they covered the infantry's retreat.

The War of the Austrian Succession was ended at the Peace of Aix-la-Chapelle in 1748 and a massive fireworks display, but our regiments' involvement ended at Fontenoy.

infantry's advance and be held in reserve to exploit any breakthrough. It was a supremely unoriginal plan, with no attempt at surprise, and pitted about 15,000 British infantry, advancing uphill, against approximately four times that number of French in fortified redoubts. A preliminary operation by the Household Cavalry brigade cleared the village of Vezon, a mile short of the French lines, and Cumberland set up his headquarters there. At 2 a.m. on 11 May the Household Cavalry filed through Vezon and took up position between it and Barri Wood. Craufurd had requested that the wood be cleared in advance, as it was clearly heavily defended – indeed, Saxe had constructed one of his most formidable redoubts, the Redoubt d'Eu, on its southern edge – but Cumberland refused. The folly of this decision now became evident as the wood was full of French skirmishers and cannon that harassed the cavalry and infantry forming up behind them. Cumberland changed his mind and gave the task of clearing the wood to Brigadier Ingoldsby on the right. Cumberland's orders were muddled, Ingoldsby was later to argue, and he was unsure what to do. So for two hours the infantry waited, endured the artillery fire, dressed their lines in full view of the French, and took heavy casualties. The Dutch attacked half-heartedly on their left, were quickly repulsed and thereafter refused to move. Ingoldsby reported Barri Wood clear, when it evidently was not. Cumberland finally lost patience and advanced with the Foot Guards, unsupported, and with the entire French effort against him.

The infantry attack at Fontenoy was one of those classically brave, but ultimately futile, British military episodes that have gone down in history. Cumberland reached the first French positions, unhinged Saxe's left, and beat off repeated cavalry attacks. For a period it seemed as if the whole French centre might crumple, but Cumberland was caught in the middle of a square of Foot Guards, and was unable to get word to the waiting cavalry to react. It was early afternoon by the time his orders reached them. The cavalry had been inactive all day in the baking heat, under artillery fire, taking some casualties, but basically untouched. But by then it was too late. The British infantry had been fought to a standstill and Saxe had brought up his reserves and more artillery. All the advancing cavalry could achieve was to cover the infantry as the remnants withdrew down the hill to the relative safety of Vezon. This was difficult, as thousands of Dutch and Austrian troops were now fleeing and there was very little room to manoeuvre. Eventually Craufurd got the majority of The Blues, who had been nearest Vezon, together with The Royals and the Scots Greys forward and established a screen to prevent the French cavalry from cutting down the retreating battalions. Craufurd's action stopped a defeat developing into a rout and definitely obstructed Saxe's pursuit of the remaining Allied right. 'The behaviour of The Blue Guards is highly to be commended which must in great measure be attributed to the conduct of their Major [Charles Jenkinson] and his care of them,' wrote Cumberland in his dispatch, but it could not disguise the Allies' decisive defeat. Louis XV had been present on the battlefield, the first time a French king had been in the field against the British since Poitiers in 1356, and Napoleon reckoned that Saxe's victory gave the Bourbons another forty years on the throne.

Craufurd's action allowed Cumberland to maintain that Fontenoy was not a total disaster, but the casualty figures were shocking. Total Allied losses were 7,545, with the British infantry losing one-third of its number. Cavalry casualties were low, at only 340, with The Blues the worst affected. Eleven men were killed and forty-nine wounded with seven missing when the regiment finally regrouped that night at Ath. In addition twenty-six had been taken prisoner. All, except three who died in captivity, were ransomed in August under the complicated terms of the Cartel of Frankfort. They had been well cared for, the French paying for surgeons, funeral expenses for the dead, candles, blankets and straw. Needless to say, all this was eventually recovered from their pay. Three of those killed in the battle, Ed Saunders, Andrew Farrier and Edward Anthony, had their wives with them, who were now returned to England with a lump sum as compensation. The new hospital was set up at Ath and Buchanan reported that it worked well, although he was again furious at the treatment of Corporal Orford of Sir James' Troop 'who was not dressed for ten days after I amputated his forearm . . . the part stunke abominaly, the dressings were almost rotted, a large discharge of sharp stinking water, and a long bare stump; but did well with proper care. He often imagined he wanted to stir the fingers of that hand, and in the night would often stir as if something had pricked them.' Again the fronts and backs had prevented many injuries from musketballs, although 'there were many contusions from spent balls', which, if not treated, could spread. Craufurd's advice at Dettingen was taken on board; most of the cavalry action had been with swords. Indeed, in the demands for stores, submitted after the battle, neither the Life Guards nor The Blues requested any pistol ammunition.[13] The worst injuries, again from cannonballs, had occurred during the initial French cannonade from Barri Wood. Davenport did not write much about the day, the Life Guards having been slightly out of the cavalry action, though he does list four friends suffering from artillery fire. Buchanan was also concerned about battle shock. 'Many were deeply concerned for the loss of the day; are morose and melancholy, require cheerfull company and a Glass of wine, or to be employed in some new enterprise.' He was called that evening to treat Cumberland, whom he bled 'by way of prevention' in case he should suffer from a fever brought on by depression and exhaustion, which had been troubling him throughout the war. 'Soldiers sometimes take a melancholy turn, become lowe spirited, senseless and childish, avoid company, cry or mutter to themselves, love to be solitary. Upon asking their case, they tell long stories about their past and present condition, are in great fear of being some way or other lost.'

Saxe was quick to turn tactical victory into operational success. With the Allies unable to field an effective army, he turned his attention to reducing the fortresses. Tournai and Ghent duly fell in June. The Dutch immediately garrisoned Mons, Ath, Naumur and Charleroi, thereby eliminating what little mobility their army had left. Cumberland withdrew to Brussels, whilst Saxe threatened Antwerp and took Ostend and Nieuport in August.

A more serious threat arose at home as, encouraged by Fontenoy, Charles Stuart, the Young Pretender, landed in western Scotland and fomented rebellion against the Hanoverians. Despite losing most of the arms and supplies transported from France when intercepted by HMS *Lion*, he had surprising success, outwitting John Cope, late of the Royal Dragoons, with what Crown forces were available, and he proclaimed himself King in Edinburgh on 16 September 1745. To make matters worse, Cope was subsequently defeated at Prestonpans with the loss of 1,300 men. The Government was forced to recall Cumberland's army and they sailed in October from Willemstadt to Newcastle, whence they marched west to meet the Jacobites at Derby. They missed them, but by then the Jacobite effort was spent and on 6 December they began their sad retreat through the Highlands, which was to culminate in their total defeat at Culloden the following April.

None of our regiments was involved in the Jacobite campaign. The Life Guards, serving in Flanders, were recalled to London to rejoin the 1st and 2nd Troops and to protect an increasingly nervous Government. Davenport complained of a bad journey, in which his troop lost fifteen horses, eventually arriving in Dartford in February. However, he had bought 'a great many drawings by the best Flemish masters for almost nothing' and was full of plans for the future and financial schemes. 'I am not very sorry we are coming home,' he writes, 'I begin to be tired of being abroad to so little purpose.' The Blues arrived at Gravesend in March, 'well pleased with seeing old England, and disembark our horses in good condition, having lost six by accidents whilst aboard'. They headed for their traditional area of operations in the Thames valley, while The Royals, who were at first sent north, were brought back to Hampshire. Though none of the regiments participated in the Jacobite campaign as formed units, several individual officers accompanied Cumberland north, the most prominent of whom was General Hawley, Colonel of The Royals. The regiment had not seen much of him in Flanders as he had commanded a brigade and then the first line of cavalry. In January 1746, when Cumberland was briefly recalled to London to plan against the possibility of a French invasion, Hawley was made temporary Commander-in-Chief in Scotland.

Hawley is probably the most unpleasant of the colonels of our regiments that we will encounter. He was a particular favourite of George I and George II, and was falsely rumoured to be George I's illegitimate son. However, as he himself wrote in his will, he 'began this world with nothing'. Originally commissioned in 1694, he had served in the dragoons throughout Marlborough's wars and commanded a dragoon regiment at Sheriffmuir in 1715. He became

The Old Horse Guards buildings (*inset*) was finally demolished in 1749 and replaced by William Kent's new Horse Guards (*above*), which was complete

by 1758. It was not to be everyone's taste but offered considerably better
accommodation for the King's Life Guard.

Colonel of The Royals in 1740, after Marlborough's resignation, and served until 1759. His soldiers knew him as 'Hawley the Hangman'. James Wolfe, the future victor of Quebec, served as his aide-de-camp and heartily loathed him. 'Hawley is expected in a few days, to keep us all in order . . . The troops dread his severity, hate the man, and hold his military knowledge in contempt.' Although Hawley undoubtedly fought bravely at Dettingen and Fontenoy, his performance in Scotland was lamentable. Never one to give respect to troops enlisted by force, as he supposed the Highlanders to be, he advanced with careless speed from Carlisle towards Stirling, which lay under siege, and encountered the Jacobite army near Falkirk. Resolving that such a rabble would not dare attack, he rode off to breakfast with Lady Kilmarnock while his army organized itself. Charles Stuart had other ideas, and prepared his men to attack. Hawley returned too late to prevent the Highlanders from forming up and, realizing the danger, immediately ordered three dragoon regiments to charge. They were cut down by fast and accurate musket fire and those who reached the Highlanders' line were dispatched with broadswords. The Highlanders then charged in their turn, routing Hawley's infantry and killing 400 of them. Seven guns were lost, together with 100 prisoners, and General Ligonier, the brother of the Commander-in-Chief, was killed. Cumberland was immediately sent back to Scotland, but Hawley's court connections were strong and he retained command of the cavalry. As such he was responsible for many of the atrocities committed after Culloden; it was his troops, no doubt partly driven by revenge, who were most diligent in the burning and killing for which Cumberland has taken much of the blame. Hawley also removed £600 worth of contents from a house he had requisitioned in Aberdeen and sent them to London on the same day that he sentenced Roger Weigh, of Wolfe's Regiment, to 1,200 lashes for stealing.

SAXE WAS NOT SLOW to seize the opportunity the Jacobite Revolt offered in Flanders. He took Brussels, with its garrison of 15,000 Dutch, in January 1746 and the main Dutch and Austrian supply depot at Vilvorden, for which he was rewarded with the use of the royal Château of Chambord for life. In October 1746 he decisively defeated the Allies, including a British detachment under Ligonier, at Rocoux near Liège. In 1747 he again defeated Cumberland at Laufeldt and sacked Bergen op Zoom. Peace was finally signed at Aix-La-Chapelle in 1748. None of our regiments was involved in this second part of the campaign in Europe, but they were to be very directly affected by the army reductions which inevitably followed the peace treaty.

This time the reductions were to be particularly severe. The war budget for 1747–8 amounted to £9.8 million, which was considered unaffordable. Pelham, now heading the Government, determined on immediate reductions, to take the army down from 50,000 to 18,850 men; at the same time the navy

A dragoon horse. Hawley's ideas envisaged creating Light Dragoon troops, an early version of Special Forces who would be used for raids and ambushes.

A view of the west front of the new Horse Guards, showing Horse Grenadiers – mounted in background – Blues in the foreground and Life Guards passing the time of day.

was reduced from 51,550 to 17,000 men. These reductions were not universally supported, and were opposed in particular by Pitt the Elder, who had served briefly in The Royals as a young man, and who realized that the 1748 treaty was only a brief interlude in the war with France. Nevertheless, they were carried through Parliament and supported by the King, who recognized the desirability of a comparable reduction in his Household Cavalry to show that he despised 'such grandeur as consists in nothing but expense'.[14] The decision to disband the 3rd and 4th Troops of Life Guards had already been taken and on Christmas Eve 1746, with Jacobite remnants still in the Highlands, the order was issued drafting twenty privates from each to the 1st and 2nd Troops, with the remainder to be pensioned off. The pension terms were relatively generous, with an immediate payment of £30 plus retention of all uniform and equipment. The horses were to be sold and the money put into a fund to supplement these payments. Officers went on to half pay, which many, like Davenport – by now bored and wanting time to pursue his commercial interests – were keen to do now that the war was over, but they also received an annuity taking their pay up to their previous rate. Davenport was in fact drawing pay from both his positions, in the 4th Troop and as a Brigadier in the 2nd Troop. Four privates from his troop, for whom no new place was found, continued to draw their pay up until 1760. The standards and drums were returned to the Royal Wardrobe.

The Household Cavalry now consisted of two troops of Life Guards and the two troops of Horse Grenadiers. The latter were retained as they were cheap, their entire establishment costing just over half what a Life Guard troop cost.[15] Furthermore, relying on enlisted men, they had maintained their strength during the war whilst the Life Guards had difficulty generating enough private gentlemen prepared to pay. The Horse Grenadiers had also proved themselves highly efficient, and produced several senior officers, such as the ample General Onslow, Colonel of the 1st Troop, who had commanded a division under Cumberland and who in 1747 would be made a lieutenant general and Governor of Plymouth.[16] Given the generous financial provision made, and the lack of comment in the press, it seems generally accepted that four troops of Life Guards were unsupportable, and the King's apparently magnanimous gesture to disband them was a skilful piece of royal public relations.

Chapter Ten

THE SEVEN YEARS WAR

THE HORSE GRENADIERS now took part in all royal escorts with the King's Life Guard, providing the advance and rear guards, whilst the Life Guard Troops always surrounded the King himself. To supplement them The Blues, most of whom had moved to Northampton in 1748, left a permanent detachment at Kingston, from where they could easily reach the various royal residences. This ensured their survival as the only regiment of horse left in the army after Pelham's cuts. All the others were transformed, much to their frustration, into Dragoon Guards, for which the establishments were so much cheaper. The suffix of 'Guards' did little to sweeten the pill. The Royals were cut down from 436 to 285 men, but because few cavalry regiments were actually disbanded they did not have to absorb spare officers and most of their officers kept their commissions.

Duties in London resumed a normal pattern, and the troops continued to occupy the same inns they had for nearly a century. However, the old Horse Guards building, which had so inconveniently survived the Whitehall fire of 1698, was nearing collapse. The Gold Stick-in-Waiting, and the Judge Advocate General, who had his office there, wrote jointly to the Secretary at War that 'it is not safe for the coaches of His Majesty and the Royal Family to pass under the gateway, and the men and horses doing duty there are in perpetual danger of losing their lives by the falling down of the buildings'.[1] In 1749 the old structure was demolished and a new building, designed by William Kent, began to arise in 1750. Kent's clean, classical style was not universally appreciated, and he also measured inaccurately, so the archway was too low for carriages to pass underneath.

> There see the Pile, in modern Taste,
> On top with tub-like Turret grac'd;
> Where the cramped Entrance, like some shed
> Knocks off the Royal Driver's head,

wrote Hogarth, rather unkindly. The Life Guards and Foot Guards moved back in 1758, and the ground under the arch was duly lowered to allow the King's coach to pass through, without fear of decapitation, in time for the State Opening of Parliament in 1762. It was still very narrow and even today Household Cavalry escorts passing through have to re-form so they are not squeezed out by the carriages. It was designed partly as the guardhouse to St James's Palace, still the main royal residence in London before Buckingham Palace was acquired, and partly as military headquarters. Lord Barrington, as Secretary at War, moved in, but the Commander-in-Chief, Ligonier, who did not like him much, preferred to work from Knightsbridge. The old custom of issuing a password to allow the favoured few access to St James's Park was replaced in 1775 by a system of ivory passes, which became seen as a sign of particular royal favour and were highly sought after.[2] They are still in use today, given to members of the Royal Family and senior Government figures who brave the crowds of tourists to drive through the archway.

Another innovation was the introduction of non-commissioned officers into the two troops of Life Guards. The Blues and The Royals had, of course, had non-commissioned rank since 1661, as had the Horse Grenadiers since their inception. However, it was thought that the Life Guards' private gentleman concept sat uneasily with ranks like sergeant (which, taken literally, meant servant), hence the bewildering variety of officer ranks the Life Guards had adopted. Now each troop was to have four quartermasters, non-commissioned, known as quartermaster corporals, and four corporals, who, to distinguish them from corporals in the rest of the army, would be known as 'Corporals of Horse Guards', but always referred to simply as 'Corporals of Horse'.

The eight years following the Peace of Aix-La-Chapelle were a dispiriting time for the army in general, as it reflected on what had been a fairly disastrous war. It had suffered three major defeats at the hands of Saxe for one fairly inconsequential victory. The English compared themselves most unfavourably with Frederick the Great's Prussians, and it was clear to men like Wolfe that the officers were inadequate. 'I am sorry to say that our method of training and instructing the troops is extremely defective,' he wrote, 'and tends to no good end. We are lazy in time of peace, and of course want vigilance and activity in war. Our military education is by far the worst in Europe.'[3] It was also clear to many that the war would soon resume and, in fact, had never really ended in India or the West Indies. The Treaty of Westminster in 1755 between Prussia and Britain, mutually guaranteeing their territory, drove France into alliance with Austria, and made the recurrence of war inevitable. The early years of the resulting Seven Years War went badly for Britain, who lost Minorca in 1756. Frederick the Great was defeated at Kolin in June 1757 and Cumberland surrendered to Richelieu at Klosterseven that September, leaving Hanover open to occupation. It was not, however, until Pitt returned to power in June 1757 that anyone in Government seriously addressed military reform. Pitt's main drive was later to be in America, India and the West Indies, but for now, despite his previous conviction that war in mainland Europe only benefited Hanover,

Horse Grenadier Guards uniforms in the 1st Troop c.1742 (*above left*) in 1747 (*above right*) and in 1760 (*right*). Horse Grenadiers gradually came to be used in the same way as the Life Guards during the eighteenth century, although they were paid less and enjoyed fewer privileges. The soldiers were enlisted as in the rest of the army.

he saw support for Protestant Prussia against the combined Catholic might of France and Austria as not only a diversionary tactic to occupy French forces away from other more important theatres, but also providing a clear moral case for war at home.

Some officers had been considering the reasons for recent defeats. One such was another Horse Grenadier, George Eliott. Unusually, he had been educated at a French military college, so 'knew his enemy', and had also served in the Prussian army as a young man, before buying a cornetcy in the 2nd Troop in 1739, possibly assisted by his uncle, the Colonel. He was wounded at both Dettingen and Fontenoy, and, again unusually, also maintained a commission as a field engineer. Purchasing a captaincy in 1745, a majority in 1749, and a lieutenant colonelcy in 1754, he did more than anyone both to train the Horse Grenadiers and, strongly influenced by the enigmatic Prussian cavalry commander, von Ziethen, to value light cavalry, so capable for reconnoitring and harassment. It was Eliott who raised the 15th Light Dragoons to fulfil these roles in the coming war, and who commanded them with such distinction, although it was, to give him his due, the dreaded Hawley, now comfortably ensconced as Governor of Portsmouth as well as remaining Colonel of The Royals, who raised the first British light cavalry units. He had been impressed with the French use of light cavalry during the last war, and realized how valuable 'Hussars' would have been in prosecuting the unfortunate Highlanders after Culloden. In 1756 he had written a paper on tactics, as all ambitious officers are inclined to do, proposing the addition of a troop of 'Light Dragoons' to each cavalry regiment, 'a very cheap and expeditious way of an augmentation to the Dragoons, which would not in any way hinder the raising of marines or filling up the foot, and would be of great service at this present juncture'. They would 'march with the van guard and to examine the Flanks, and the Rear of a Rearguard upon a retreat'. The troops would be sixty men strong, and wear green uniforms so that they were 'not to be discovered in ambuscades', with 'officers pick't out, who are proper for this sort of service'. Horses were to be of all colours except grey, which was too conspicuous, and to be no higher than 14.2 hands. They were to have speed and the strength to carry extra forage and equipment. For some reason Hawley thought the best source of these would be in Yorkshire, somewhere he clearly regarded as uncivilized, and, judging from the very carefully drawn illustrations which accompanied his proposal, where he believed the horses to have exceptional masculine endowments.

Cumberland, still Commander-in-Chief, liked Hawley's ideas, although the thought of green coats was clearly going too far, and in 1755 the troops were established with red ones. The Royals Light Troop was the first part of the regiment to see action in the new war, in a series of marine raids on the French coast, together with eight other light dragoon troops. These actions were designed to force the French to keep troops busy at home, and were more

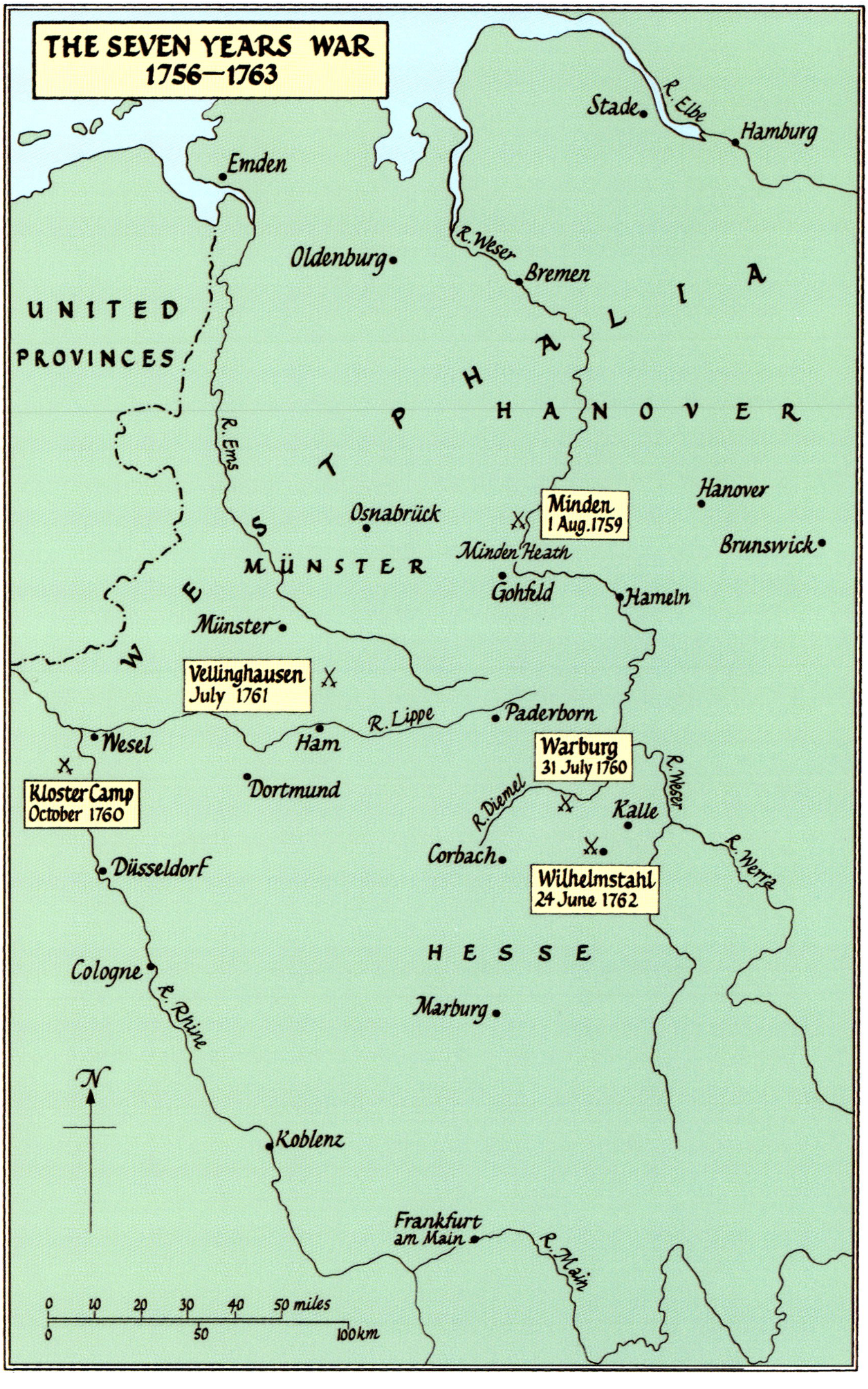

THE SEVEN YEARS WAR
1756–1763
R. Elbe
Stade
Hamburg
Emden
R. Weser
Oldenburg
Bremen
UNITED
PROVINCES
W E S T P H A L I A
H A N O V E R
R. Ems
Minden
1 Aug. 1759
Hanover
Osnabrück
Minden Heath
Brunswick
M Ü N S T E R
Gohfeld
Hameln
Münster
Vellinghausen
July 1761
R. Lippe
Paderborn
Wesel
Ham
Warburg
31 July 1760
Dortmund
R. Weser
Kloster Camp
October 1760
R. Diemel
Kalle
Corbach
R. Werra
Düsseldorf
Wilhelmstahl
24 June 1762
H E S S E
Cologne
R. Rhine
Marburg
N
Koblenz
Frankfurt
am Main
R. Main
0 10 20 30 40 50 miles
0 50 100km

successful than Walpole's unkind description of 'breaking windows with guineas' suggests. The first raid, commanded by The Royals' old Colonel, the 2nd Duke of Marlborough, was targeted at St-Malo, and was a masterpiece of combined naval and army planning, way in advance of its time. The fleet's guns silenced the French shore batteries, before the infantry secured the beaches. The cavalry landed, and the light troops quickly took St-Malo port, destroying over 100 ships before re-embarking in the face of a superior French force.

Overall it was considered a great success, and was repeated at Cherbourg, where twenty ships and 200 guns were destroyed, with the light troops exploiting down to the southern end of the Cotentin peninsula. Again they withdrew in the face of French opposition. The final raid was unsuccessful and the French caught a large infantry force again near St-Malo, taking nearly 1,000 prisoners. The Royals' Troop was lucky to escape back aboard their ship, and the raids were abandoned thereafter. The troops were to be more usefully employed by Prince Ferdinand of Brunswick, to whom Pitt had now entrusted command of the British, Hanoverian and Hessian troops, following Cumberland's disaster at Klosterseven. Seconded from Frederick the Great, Ferdinand's role was to protect Prussia, and therefore Hanover, from French attack, and The Blues and The Royals were now both to fight in Germany under Ferdinand. The Life Guards remained at home guarding the King.

Prince Ferdinand was a wise choice as commander. Well schooled by Frederick and described by Carlyle as 'a soldier of approved excellence', by June 1758 he had already reconstituted the remaining 30,000 Hanoverian troops, driven the French out of Hanover itself, pursued them to the Rhine, and defeated them again at Krefeldt. He then retired east of the river to await the 12,000 British reinforcements promised by Pitt. On 21 August 1758 they joined him at Munster, under the able command of Marlborough, who died of enteric fever within two months. Command devolved, fatefully, to Lord George Sackville with John Manners, Marquis of Granby, as second in command and general of cavalry, having only just assumed the Colonelcy of The Blues from the aged Ligonier. In his contingent were The Blues, still the largest cavalry regiment, together with the 1st and 3rd Dragoon Guards, Scots Greys and Inniskillings, all equipped similarly to The Blues, though still technically dragoons. In the coming war the distinction between horse and dragoons was finally to disappear, and the British cavalry would emerge, heavily influenced by Eliott and Granby, divided into heavy and light regiments. The Royals remained temporarily in England and only joined Granby in 1759, luckily without Hawley. He had handed over to one of the most distinguished colonels ever to be associated with the Household Cavalry, Henry Seymour Conway, who, after his time with The Royals, was to be Colonel of The Blues for twenty-five years. Hawley retired, unlamented, to Hartley Witney near Camberley, thereby establishing a trend for many future generations of senior officers.

For now, Granby was to dominate the stage.[4] Certainly the greatest colonel since Oxford, and probably the most important influence on the subsequent style and character of The Blues, Granby was as satisfactory as a man as he was competent and brave as a soldier. He also enjoyed the almost unique distinction of retaining his own regiment, under his command on active service, for five years. The eldest son of the Duke of Rutland, and consequently with considerable political influence, he was the first British commander since Marlborough who cared seriously for his soldiers' welfare and who understood morale. However, he cannot be called a great commander in the manner of Marlborough, or later Wellington, for logistics eluded him and even when he took over as Commander-in-Chief from Sackville after Minden, he was, in accordance with Pitt's policy, always under Prince Ferdinand's overall operational command. His importance as a general lies more in the character that he, and generals like Wolfe and Ligonier, established for the British army as a brave and efficient force which, when properly led, was unbeatable in war, if somewhat idle in peace. Nearly all the many portraits of Granby depict him in plain regimental uniform, with his weapons and front and back, either mounting his horse or helping the wounded: previously generals, and the French, preferred to be represented as latterday Roman emperors in allegorical settings. It was a precedent copied by many of his successors; Seymour Conway was even portrayed sitting alongside an artillery piece holding a private soldier's issued musket.

There was something very English and down to earth about Granby, which caught the public imagination at home. He was stout, and went bald when quite young, a natural state of which he was totally unashamed and, indeed, flaunted, rarely wearing a hat or a wig, which many Englishmen thought a nasty Continental habit. He was also compulsively generous – the number of pubs named after him, many of them started on money he gave to ex-soldiers, still testify to this today. He was devoted to his wife Frances Seymour, daughter of the Duke of Somerset, himself a previous Colonel of The Blues, who was as spendthrift as he was; on the day of their wedding he owed £7,000 and she £10,000, but they both agreed there was 'no use for money but in giving it away'. He was, very properly for a soldier, absorbed by operations but found peacetime service rather dull. He was not a particularly enthusiastic Commander-in-Chief and Master General of the Ordnance after the war, preferring to spend his time gambling or hunting. Indeed, he left an important hunting legacy in the Belvoir hounds, through which he helped to establish the famous black-and-tan English foxhound, and which he converted from stag to fox hunting. When he died, his executors sold forty-five horses and ninety couple of hounds to offset some of his debts. Granby remained, however, passionately interested in The Blues, and in the welfare of those who had fought with him in Germany. His papers at Belvoir contain lengthy and learned treatises from earnest artillery men, trying to interest him in devilish new explosives and guns, some of which remain unopened today, whilst petitions from old soldiers, or regimental

The Marquis of Granby, in one of many paintings by Reynolds, attired as
Colonel of The Blues and, characteristically, bald headed.

Granby was known throughout the army for his generosity, but he never managed to overcome the chronic supply problems during the Seven Years War that resulted from bureaucracy at Horse Guards.

Granby also lent money to his demobilized soldiers to start inns, which explains why there are so many named after him in England. Here the Royal Mail carriage leaves a Marquis of Granby pub in the 1850s.

correspondence, were replied to immediately. Such was his reputation as a benefactor that when the roof of the Fleet prison collapsed in 1768, and the authorities prevaricated, Lucius O'Bryan, a prisoner with no known connection to Granby, wrote to him on 22 August 1768 saying that 'your known generosity and humanity emboldens me to petition your Lordship in the behalf of myself and the rest of the unhappy sufferers . . . who are utterly destitute of any place to shelter themselves'.[5]

Granby was no military novice when he arrived in Munster. His early life had been conventional enough and included an education at Eton and Trinity College, Cambridge, an extended Grand Tour, and Parliamentary experience as the Whig Member for Grantham. In 1745 he had helped his father raise a volunteer regiment in Rutland, which, though limited to garrisoning Newcastle, was regarded as one of the most competent of its type.[6] Granby himself found garrison duties dull, and used his connections to arrange an attachment to Cumberland's staff in the Highlands, where he was involved in several skirmishes and was present at Culloden. In the meantime his regiment in Newcastle mutinied, for the Government had not paid them, a problem Granby initially put right out of his own pocket, learning an important lesson in morale. Thereafter he accompanied Cumberland back to Flanders, acting as his intelligence officer, a novelty for Cumberland who had evidently learnt from his disaster at Fontenoy. Granby was present at Cumberland's second great disaster, Laufeldt, where he grasped the effectiveness of the British cavalry under Ligonier, and where his brother Robert was captured. Robert, invited to dinner with Saxe, expressed to the great Marshal his sadness over the loss of so many men. 'Not above 11,000,' replied the imperturbable Saxe, a story which Granby found shocking. After the Peace of 1748 he lived on half pay, either at Rutland House, in Knightsbridge, or at Belvoir. His mobilization in 1758 was his first active service for over ten years, but his reputation in the army had remained high, with fifty-two officers volunteering to be his aide-de-camp; his initial choice was Lord Broome, later to be Lord Cornwallis, who would surrender the American colonies to Washington.

The fighting in Germany over the next four years is very confusing to follow and is best followed with the aid of the map on p. 227. Essentially the Allies were trying to prevent the French armies on the Rhine from marching east to take Hanover and Prussia, while looking for any opportunity to defeat them in a pitched battle. Ferdinand's policy, which would later become tediously familiar to future generations of Household Cavalrymen, was to hold the line of the River Weser, so most of the major engagements in the war were fought in a box bounded by the Rhine in the west, the Weser in the east, the River Main in the south and the sea in the north.

The autumn of 1758 was uneventful. The British lived in tents until November, and then retired to winter quarters in the villages around Munster and Paderborn. The soldiers were unimpressed, finding 'the meanest cottage in

England better Quarters than these villages'.[7] Richard Davenport, who had now purchased the lieutenant colonelcy of a regiment of dragoons, wrote to his brother that 'a man that has lived under canvas till 18 November is not apt to be dissatisfied that the house he comes into is not well built nor elegantly furnished. It is enough that he finds himself dry and warm . . . At the entrance into my house, on the right, there are four cows; on the left, three of my horses, between whom and my bedchamber there is a partition of lath and plaster, of which they now and then, in the night, kick a hat-full into the room.' The hospitals were still dreadful, a matter that Granby was to sort out, once Sackville had gone. Davenport soon found his attention drifting to his female companions. He would sit at his fireside drinking his customary bottle of red wine, while his eyes wandered to two maids 'who sit at a distance with their spinning wheels and laugh and say nothing. One of them is very well for a Frow [Frau] . . . but from that damned circumstance of being all on the same floor and somebody being forever in sight, there is no getting her long enough alone to quicken her circulation to a proper degree'.[8]

Ferdinand moved out of winter quarters in April 1759 to attempt a surprise attack on the French. They were divided into two armies. De Broglie commanded a southern army of 30,000 men near Frankfurt, whilst Contades had 50,000 men deployed along the Rhine from Wesel to Koblenz. Ferdinand's plan was to surprise de Broglie at Bergen, just north-east of Frankfurt, but he was beaten off by the superior French force and lost 2,000 men, including one trooper in The Blues killed, whilst two others lost their arms to French cannon fire. De Broglie gave Ferdinand the slip, joined forces with Contades, and advanced into Hesse. Kassel fell, requiring Ferdinand to fall back from Munster and concentrate on defending Minden and Hameln on the Weser to protect Hanover. On 10 July, however, he learned that Contades was behind him and had already captured Minden, and realized that Hanover would fall unless he could engage Contades in a pitched battle. It was an inauspicious start to the war.

Contades had paused at Minden, and divided his army, with de Broglie on the east bank of the Weser, and himself around Minden on the west bank. He seemed in no hurry to move, and was strongly positioned to the south of the town. Ferdinand's plan was to lure him out by offering him the apparent chance of destroying his army piecemeal, so he first sent a division under the Hanoverian general, Wagenheim, to within 600 yards of the north of the French positions as bait. He himself slipped round to the south-west with his main force, well out of contact, and bivouacked around Hille, while sending his nephew, known as 'the Hereditary Prince' (as heir to his brother, Ferdinand) and a competent general, south to the village of Gohfeld to feign a threat to the French rear. Contades, surprisingly, took the bait, ordering de Broglie back across the river to take up position opposite Wagenheim, and sending the Duc de Brissac with 8,000 men to intercept the Hereditary Prince. He then moved the main body of his force up to join de Broglie, forming up on his left, so that the full French force of 51,000 troops, including fifty-five squadrons of cavalry and 162 guns, was now exposed on Minden Heath, expecting to advance at dawn on 1 August to destroy a rather obviously weak Allied detachment. Ferdinand only heard of Contades' troop movements at 3 a.m., two hours after the French had set off. He immediately marched his army east, with the infantry in the centre, the Hanoverian cavalry in the lead and the British cavalry in the rear. The plan was that on reaching the French, the column would wheel left, so the cavalry would be on either flank with the infantry still central. The British cavalry were in two divisions, under Sackville's overall command. Sackville commanded the first line himself, which included The Blues, and Granby the second.

The troops had been expecting a battle for some time, and had saddled up every day at 1 a.m. to ensure they were ready by first light. All heavy baggage had been removed and they had lived off what could be carried by their horses since April. They were not necessarily uncomfortable; Davenport still had fourteen horses just for his personal possessions and five servants, but the strain of endless marching and uncertainty in recent weeks had been difficult. 'Our orders are never given till the moment they are to be executed,' Davenport complained in a letter from the camp at Hille. 'We have more lies in camp than you hear in a Coffee House and you know in London what we are doing just as well as we do upon the spot.' Ferdinand's policy of delaying orders till the last moment was necessitated by the active French intelligence network, so although The Blues knew they were very close to the French army, they did not realize just how close. The proximity of engagements in the Seven Years War in fact seems rather surprising today. The Blues posted mounted sentries, called vedettes, within 100 yards of Contades' patrols, and 'the officers bowed to one another at a distance', yet the French still seem to have been unaware of Ferdinand's strength.

The strain and lack of orders meant the day of the eventual battle started badly for The Blues. First, Sackville could not be found and, though the troops were fell-in in column and ready to move, they waited for him and then rushed to catch up the infantry. Granby himself was camping some way off, unaware of what was happening; he was not up until 5 a.m., and spent a frustrating hour galloping around to find Sackville. It was a hot morning, the dust from the marching army made it difficult to see, and no one really knew what was happening except Sackville, who had by now received Ferdinand's orders. As they emerged on to Minden Heath, they discovered they were more or less in the correct position, with the infantry on their left, and they took up position by a small wood, just in time to witness one of the most extraordinary manoeuvres of the war. Six battalions of British infantry wheeled right and started advancing on the French. It subsequently transpired that this was the result of a mistaken order. They marched on, unaware that the second line of infantry

The Blues were intensely frustrated at missing the opportunity to fight at the Battle of Minden in August 1759 and several were called to give evidence against Sackville at his court martial.

The Earl of Pembroke, who fought with the Light Dragoons in the Seven Years War, later became Colonel of The Royals.

was unable to support them as yet, but the effect on the French was devastating. The British infantry made directly for Contades' main force of forty battalions and fifty-five cavalry squadrons, took casualties from the French artillery, and were charged several times by their cavalry. They simply regrouped, delivered devastating volleys of musket fire, and continued their majestic march forward. Contades' force was thrown totally off balance; their carefully planned attack on what was supposed to be an isolated detachment had evaporated, and they began to panic. With thousands of them now milling around between the walls of Minden and the relentless British infantry, an ideal opportunity arose for the cavalry to attack and destroy Contades' force totally. This is exactly what Ferdinand ordered Sackville to do, no fewer than five times, but Sackville refused. He told Ferdinand's successive and increasingly frustrated aide-de-camps that their orders were not clear enough, and finally rode off to see Ferdinand himself. In the meantime, Ferdinand sent a message directly to Granby to move his second line, commenting, 'I know that at least he will obey me.' It was too much for The Blues to see their Colonel prepare to charge without them, and the commanding officer, Lieutenant Colonel Johnston, sent his Adjutant, Lieutenant Walsh, to ask Sackville's permission to accompany him, while the regiment prepared itself. The troops were wheeled left by quarter ranks, and the order was given to march. They set off at a brisk trot, the preferred pace for cavalry charges, which descended into chaos if any faster. Unfortunately Walsh met Sackville en route to Ferdinand, and was told that on no account could The Blues move, so he returned to halt them. In any event it was too late. As Ferdinand calmly remarked to Sackville, 'My Lord, the opportunity has now passed,' and Granby's line found that the French had retreated behind the fortifications of Minden. The German cavalry, masked from the main French force, had inflicted some casualties, as had the Allied artillery, but the chance of a decisive victory had been lost.

This does not seem to have bothered Sackville much; he arrived for dinner with Ferdinand that evening as though nothing had happened. The following day Ferdinand ordered 'it to be declared to Lieutenant General The Marquess of Granby that he is persuaded that, if he had the good fortune to have had him at the head of the cavalry of the Right Wing, his presence would have greatly contributed to make the decision of the day more complete and more brilliant'. Even Sackville realized the intended snub and, when Ferdinand refused to withdraw his comments, asked to be relieved of his command, which had been Ferdinand's intention anyway. Granby became the British Commander-in-Chief. Sackville returned to England and was subsequently court martialled. George II had wanted him shot, like the unfortunate Admiral Byng, who was executed for failing to relieve Minorca, and was disappointed he was merely found unfit ever to command again. He added a special rider, when confirming the sentence, stating that 'neither high birth nor great employments can shelter offences of such a nature, and seeing that they are subject to censure worse than death to a man who has any sense of honour, they may avoid the fatal consequences arising from disobedience of orders'.[9] This was to be read out at the head of every regiment in the army. The court martial was a difficult time for Granby, and for several officers of The Blues who were called to give evidence. It was awkward to have to criticize the Commander-in-Chief in an age when so much depended on preferment and patronage, particularly when he protested his innocence and tried to implicate other senior officers. Granby, while avoiding being too directly critical, encouraged his officers to speak plainly and discussed their evidence with them.[10] Their caution was justified as the King, initially so against Sackville, later decided that it was improper of the officers to have been so explicit and wanted them removed. Luckily he died before he could ensure his order was carried out.

Although they had not inflicted a decisive defeat on the French, the Allies had certainly saved Hanover, and forced Contades to retreat towards the Rhine. Minden surrendered, and there followed two months of pursuit and skirmishes through the dusty German lanes in a particularly hot summer, which turned into a wet and muddy autumn. Ferdinand, however, could not trap the French again and, when 12,000 troops were returned to Prussia after Frederick's defeat by the Russians, it became clear that the campaign in Germany would last at least another year. By December both the French and the Allies were more or less back where they started. The Blues, having been bridled and saddled by 2 a.m. almost every day since August, and their heavy baggage sent on to Osnabruck, were much looking forward to the winter break in campaigning. Although there had been no more major battles, there were constant engagements with French hussars, who were cunning and effective, and often harassed the foraging parties. Davenport summed up the feelings of many when he wrote congratulating his brother for securing the contract to provide uniforms for the Coldstream Guards and added, referring to the recent British naval victory at Quiberon Bay, 'You have so many healths to drink this Christmas that you must certainly be a very drunken crew. Under our circumstances, it is not convenient to be drunk, but had we wine, we should not throw it away.'

Once the men were established in their quarters, Johnston went home to acquire horses and recruits for The Blues. Interestingly, troopers' vacancies were largely filled by drafts from Dragoon Guards; the conditions of service in The Blues were so much better that even several sergeants volunteered. Granby, recovering from a bad fall, was looking forward to a couple of months with his family and hounds at Belvoir, but the King and the Prime Minister, Newcastle, felt that with too many officers in London, he should stay with the army on the Continent. Granby reluctantly agreed, and settled into a depressing winter dealing with a bad attack of glanders, which was killing many horses, and implementing some of the administrative improvements which he so badly wanted. Then he received the terrible news that his much-loved wife, Frances, had died of a sudden attack of St Anthony's Fire on 25 January 1760. Even the waspish Horace Walpole noted that theirs seemed to be a marriage made in heaven. A desperately sad Granby returned for her funeral, not the leave to which he had been so much looking forward. His depression was heightened by Sackville's court martial. He returned to Paderborn in April, to find that all his personal horses had died, and sent urgently to Belvoir for two good, aged horses of 16 hands 'as he has scarcely a horse to get upon'.[11]

Yet despite such a gloomy period in his personal life, Granby had achieved several effective reforms. While in England he had championed the idea of the light cavalry, even raising his own regiment from Rutland, the 21st Light Dragoons, or Royal Foresters, much on the lines he had in 1745. His relation Russell Manners, a cornet in The Blues, became the lieutenant colonel. Granby had also negotiated extra resources from Newcastle for better medical care, and a proper widows' fund, although he noted that 'a soldier's widow rarely remains so above twenty four hours'. Each cavalry troop was allowed four accompanying wives, who apparently fulfilled their functions on a collective basis. He could not, however, get to grips with the army's Byzantine logistics system, the inefficiencies of which were to cause the war to drag on for so long. Granby, as Commander-in-Chief, had no financial authority in the leasing of contracts, which was controlled by the Secretary at War's office, and was highly corrupt. The Hanoverian, and even the French, system was much simpler, leasing contracts for forage and other matters locally. Granby eventually persuaded Barrington to send out an officer to head a new logistic staff division; regrettably this was Colonel Pierson of the Foot Guards, and when George II heard of his appointment he countered it immediately, finding it totally unsuitable for a Guards officer to be so employed.

Granby was also showing real maturity as a field commander. He developed an excellent working relationship with Ferdinand, who was escorted by The Blues to receive the Order of the Garter from Granby on his return. He had also worked out how to play the King and Newcastle, both of whom could prove difficult masters. George II tended to restrict himself to trivia by this late stage in his life, telling Granby to improve his admittedly dreadful handwriting and to write in larger letters in darker ink. The King had also formed a particular attachment to The Blues, something shared by his grandson, the future George III. He therefore tried to influence Granby's thoughts on suitable candidates for regimental appointments, insisting that 'when there was a Cornetcy in the Horse they were the proper provision for his pages', and overruling Granby who wanted to put 'poor John Dodd's son' into Captain Lascelles' vacancy. The King had his way, and the page in question, known to Granby merely as a brother to Lord Torrington, eventually arrived in Paderborn to a frosty reception. Newcastle and Barrington, the Secretary at War, were more demanding. Newcastle, not unlike some future Prime Ministers, required endless information, and constantly pressed Granby for 'good news', while declining to send more troops or money. Granby's letters to him, though very difficult to read, are always polite, cooperative and very full. By April 1760 Newcastle had become impatient for a quick success against de Broglie, now French Commander-in-Chief in place of Contades. He wrote to Granby in late April saying that he had 'a force more than sufficient to deal with M. de Broglie: but for God's sake begin', which was at least clear political direction, if a little optimistic. Even after reinforcement the British contingent was still only 20,000 men in an Allied force which totalled about 90,000. That reinforcement included The Royals, who arrived in the autumn, and were driven mad by flies while being inspected by Prince Ferdinand. Both they and The Blues had the unpleasant task, before they left Paderborn, of press-ganging locals as recruits for the Prussian army. Davenport, who had spent the last month getting to know a 'young and handsome abbess' perhaps better than he should, wrote somewhat heartlessly that 'Before night they brought in 120 of all sorts, horribly frightened and expecting to be sent to the King of Prussia. I discharged all that looked old and locked up the rest for the night. All the following day . . . I had no peace for the crying of women and the squalling of children. If they had been English married women I believe that I would have made my conditions, but the married ones here have no signs of women but the mark of the sex, which is indeed in capitals.' Ultimately he did release all the married men.

The late spring finally arrived, and both The Blues and The Royals marched south from Paderborn with Granby to try to deliver what Newcastle demanded. Ferdinand's plan was to get between the main French army under de Broglie, concentrated around Kassel in Hesse, and their second army under St Germain at Dortmund. He failed, and the French linked up on 10 July, faced the Allies near Corbach and then attempted to outflank them once again with the ultimate aim of taking Hanover. The armies spent the next two weeks circling each other, with frequent skirmishes, during one of which Granby lost sixteen of his own horses, which had been turned out to grass for the night. He was particularly incensed because, in the still chivalrous manner in which enemy officers treated each other, two had been intended as presents for de Broglie, perhaps in gratitude for the special passport granted to Granby's French wine merchant to pass unmolested, with his valuable cargo, through de Broglie's lines. However, on 15 July at Emsdorff, the newly raised 15th Light Dragoons, who had only just arrived from England, under Eliott, routed a detachment, taking 1,600 prisoners but losing 129 men in the process.

Yet the superior French numbers were beginning to tell, and Ferdinand's army, on the move for ten weeks, was tiring. 'De Broglie with an incredible mob full double ours, whatever political falsifiers might say in England . . . And we have very little rest or belly provender . . . for never poor devils lived harder, or earned their pay more than we do . . .', wrote Lord Pembroke,[12] a future Colonel of The Royals. Ferdinand was seriously concerned about his communications back to the north, for which he relied heavily on the River Diemel.

He decided to fall back towards Kassel, with Granby commanding the rearguard. It was, as Pembroke continued, 'a very comical ugly operation, being kicked, then turning about to snarl and show your teeth', but by 27 July Ferdinand halted at Kalle, 10 miles before Kassel. De Broglie reviewed his tactics and now detached de Muy[13] with a reserve of approximately 25,000 troops to get behind the Allies, cross the Diemel and cut them off from Westphalia, while he diverted attention to the Allies' front. Ferdinand quickly detected de Muy and realized that de Broglie had become overconfident. De Muy might well cross the Diemel, but his men would soon be too far north to be adequately supported, and if Ferdinand moved quickly, he could cut them off and destroy them before de Broglie could react. Moving by night, and taking elaborate precautions to deceive de Broglie that he was still pinned down in front of Kassel, Ferdinand sent the Hereditary Prince with two columns to overtake de Muy, while Ferdinand himself, commanding one column of the infantry, and Granby with the cavalry and horse artillery, aimed for his centre. De Muy had halted for the night of 30 July on a ridge of high ground, facing east, with his right flank in Warburg and his left near the village of Ochsendorf, with the River Diemel to his rear. Early in the hot, stuffy, morning of 31 July, the Hereditary Prince, who had successfully crossed to the front of French undetected, opened his attack on de Muy's left. The Royals, under Lieutenant Colonel 'Irish' Johnston, so called to distinguish him from the Johnston commanding The Blues, made with his right-hand column for a tower-crowned hill just south of Ochsendorf. A thick mist helped, and the French were caught unawares to such an extent that Colonel Beckwith, commanding the British infantry within the Hereditary Prince's force, got a Grenadier regiment on top of the hill and held it against French counter-attacks. De Muy sent cavalry in support, including the Royal Piedmont regiment. As they formed up, they were charged by The Royals and broken, retreated in disorder and took no further part in the battle. It was an effective, well-managed cavalry operation, and it was The Royals' first regimental action for fifteen years.

The French left was now on the point of collapse and Ferdinand reasoned that if he struck at the centre and the right there was a chance of destroying de Muy's entire force. However, he was still some 5 miles from Warburg and his infantry were struggling to keep up the pace in the stifling weather. Fearing another missed chance, Ferdinand sent Granby ahead with his ten regiments of British cavalry and the Horse Artillery, to fix the French until he could bring up the main force. Granby, determined that there would be no repetition of Minden, advanced at a brisk trot. By 1 p.m., just as the mist was clearing, he had positioned his force parallel to the French, using the Warburg–Ochsendorf road as his axis. He had six regiments in his first line and had put The Blues in the centre, instead of the right, partly so he could ride at their head but also because he trusted James Johnston and wanted him close at hand to cope with the unexpected. It was to prove a sensible precaution. The

WARBURG 31 July 1760

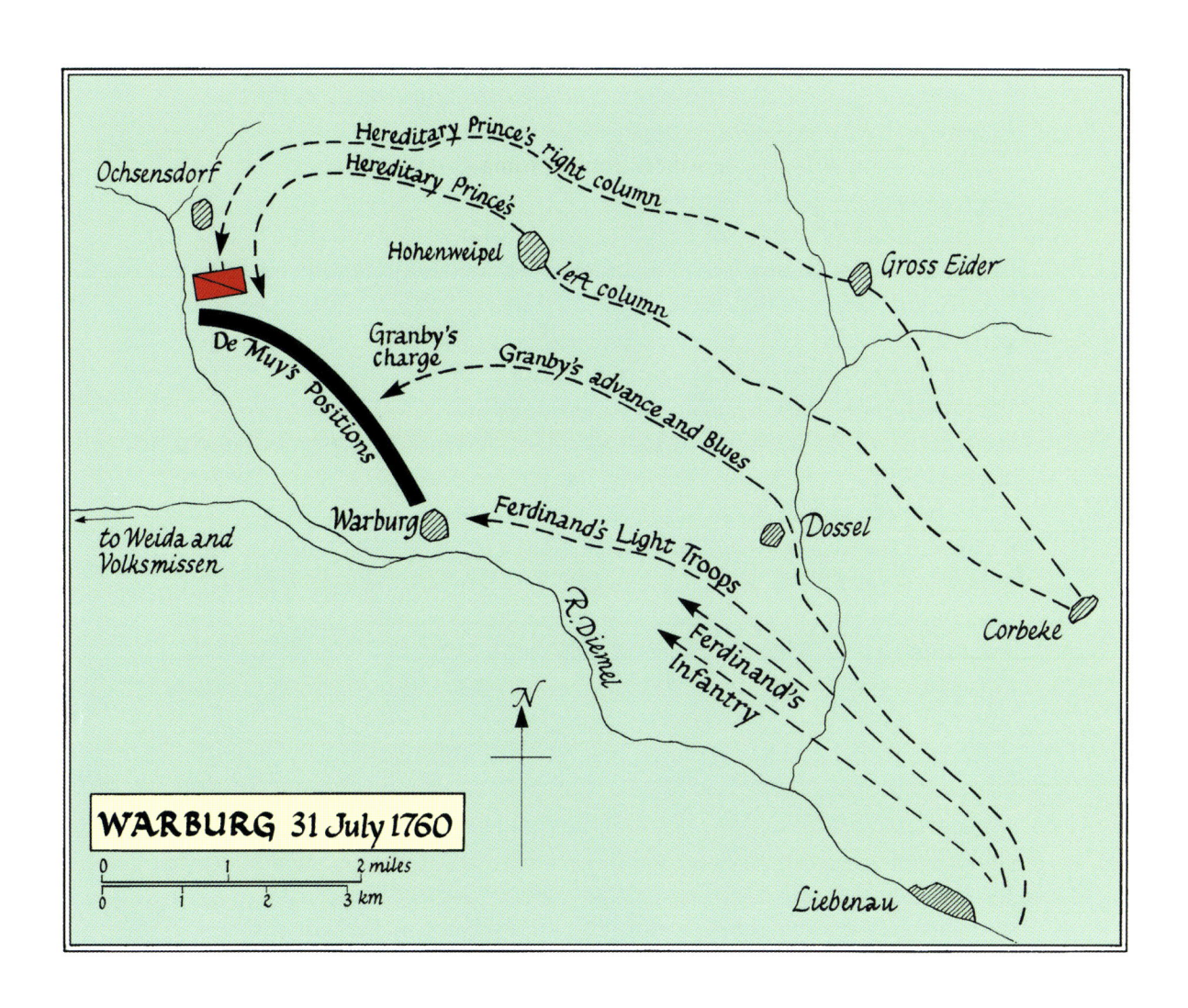

remaining four regiments formed the second line. The Horse Artillery kept up magnificently with the cavalry on the move forward – however neglectful Granby may have been later as Master General of the Ordnance, he had spent many months working out how best to use them in the field to provide the fire power and destructive force to support the 'shock action' of a cavalry charge. They were now positioned to cover the River Diemel.

Several remarkable aspects of the ensuing battle have passed into legend, but among these, Granby's extraordinarily effective tactical planning and control should not be overlooked. In the space of two hours he had advanced 5 miles with a force of about 8,000 men, maintained liaison with the Hereditary Prince's force some miles ahead, regrouped the artillery, and deployed them perfectly to support his plan. He subsequently exacted such control over the cavalry that he regrouped them twice after the confusion of a charge, belying the idea that the British cavalry were always out of control. Finally, and more remarkably, 8,000 British troops now routed a French force nearly three times as large.

As the mist cleared, Granby's trumpeters sounded 'To the Left Form Divisions' and the whole force pivoted left, moving from the three-man sections used for movement in column, to double-line divisions. The officers swung round to the front of their troops, their trumpeters alongside, with pairs of troops forming squadrons. Granby, who had been riding with The Blues in the centre, was now in front of, and central to the largest force of British cavalry that had taken the field since Marlborough's day. Pistols were checked, no doubt, for a final time, though there was to be little chance of using them; this was to be a charge reliant on speed and swords. Granby's trumpeter sounded 'Charge', and they did, galloping straight into the mass of thirty-eight French cavalry squadrons only a few hundred yards distant. The French wavered under the shock and started to break up; Granby regrouped the lines and charged again, this time wheeling left to come into the flank of the twenty-eight French infantry battalions, supported by 'a great number of cannon'.[14] This time the French broke and fled back towards the Diemel, where they encountered the pre-positioned Horse Artillery. Regrouping a second time, Granby led a third charge which turned into a general pursuit. Three French cavalry squadrons stood their ground, however, and now charged into the exposed right flank of the 1st Dragoon Guards, causing them to waver. Granby immediately sent Johnston and The Blues to their rescue, and the French squadrons were scattered.

Edmund Cox rode with The Blues in the charge. 'For we Rout'd all before us – Down precipices, over hollow ways we went like a torrant as the French General term'd it, which struck such a panick so that they [led] without firing a shot. The Marquis of Granby persued the enemy above 10 miles.' By the time Ferdinand came up with the main body of the Allied army it was all over. De Muy's force had ceased to exist; in the pursuit The Royals had charged the Swiss Planta regiment, who had surrendered to a man. Granby himself is reputed to have lost his hat and wig in the charge, but, more likely, he discarded them: he hated wearing them anyway and with his bald head was more visible as he rode forward. A French observer of the battle wrote that 'Lord Granby, at the head of his Blues, had his hat blown off; a big bald circle in his head rendering the loss more conspicuous. But he never minded; stormed on, bare bald head among the helmets and sabres.'[15] Horace Walpole, however, wrote that 'the Chronicle protests that [the victory] was achieved by Mylord Granby losing his hat, which he never wears.'[16] Whatever the circumstances, Granby now saluted Ferdinand bare-headed, highly unusual by contemporary custom. It was greatly appreciated by The Blues, who immediately copied him by similarly saluting their officers and discarding their hats in camp. The regiment has remained the only one in the British army to salute without headdress. Ferdinand would have been churlish to object. French losses were estimated at 8,000 and the threat to Westphalia and Hanover was once again removed. Allied losses were 1,200, of which a significant number were among the Grenadiers at Ochsendorf. The Royals had lost eight men killed, twelve wounded and thirty horses, while The Blues lost Cornet Cheney, six corporals and twenty-three private troopers. Granby was amused to find amongst de Muy's private correspondence a delicate letter to de Broglie's wife in Paris, which may have explained why de Broglie had been so ready to detach him from the main French army. Any levity or self-congratulation was to be short-lived, however, as news reached Granby that his eldest son, Lord Roos, had died suddenly while staying with his grandmother in Hill Street. And sadly, there was no letter home from Davenport to his brother John. 'Prepare yourself for the greatest shock,' wrote his close friend Eliott instead, 'our dear friend, your brother, was killed upon the spot, instantaneously, in the action of yesterday.'[17]

Though weakened by Warburg, de Broglie now occupied Kassel, while Ferdinand still felt too weak to force them out. In September he tried to take the old Prussian fortress of Wesel, on the Rhine, which the French had captured in 1757 and made into an important magazine. He dispatched the Hereditary Prince with 10,000 men, but their attack, near the Convent of Klostercamp, was beaten off when the infantry ran out of ammunition. The Blues were not involved, but The Royals were, and charged alongside the 10th Dragoons, Davenport's late regiment, with great distinction in support of the retreating infantry, destroying the Normandie Regiment. Their intervention could not, however, prevent an Allied retreat, and they themselves lost eight men killed, with four wounded, including 'Irish' Johnston, and twenty-eight men taken prisoner, among whom was Lieutenant Goldsworthy who would, much later, become Colonel.

By November the Allies were back in winter quarters and heartily fed up with a campaign of perpetual stalemate, whilst British forces achieved notable victories in India and Canada. The winter was wet and disease broke out in the garrison towns. By the end of November Granby had 4,000 men in hospital and needed 1,200 remounts to bring the cavalry up to strength. There was little comfort from London, where Ligonier wrote that apart from the Life Guards and Foot Guards, the only available troops were two regiments made up of old men and boys 'hardly able to manage their horses'. The Blues, in Osnabruck, were bored. 'We spend our time very stupidly here – no diversions but riding in the morning and billiards at noon,' wrote Cavendish Lester to his friend temporarily detached to Granby's staff in Paderborn, with the encouraging addendum, 'P.S. Your horses have all got mange.'[18]

ON 25 OCTOBER George II died, five days after reviewing the Life Guards and Horse Grenadiers in Hyde Park. Both regiments now went into mourning, their red coats faced with black and black crêpe around their swords, hats and sashes. They escorted the King's embalmed body to Westminster Abbey on 13 November through ranks of Foot Guards holding flaming torches, muffled drums beating slowly and bells tolling. It was, even the acerbic Walpole noted, 'a noble sight'.[19] Orders were issued by the Gold Sticks for the size of future royal escorts: for the Dukes of York and Cumberland and the royal princesses there were to be one officer, eight Life Guards and two Horse Grenadiers, who rode front and rear.

Granby ordered similar mourning in Germany, writing tactfully that 'no King ever lived more beloved, or died more sincerely regretted'.[20] However, it must have pained him to say so, for his problems with Colonel Pierson and the lack of logistic support threatened the army seriously, as was starkly evidenced in February 1761. Ferdinand and Granby had determined on a winter campaign to surprise de Broglie around Kassel. The Blues were involved in what began as a stroke of military genius, attacking the French at a time when all self-respecting armies were hunkered down for the winter, and many officers home on leave. De Broglie was driven back 50 miles and Kassel appeared to be on the point of falling, but the problems of movement and supply in the harsh German winter soon rendered the Allies ineffective. 'Roads, owing to alternate frost and thaw and the ceaseless passage of troops, were in such condition as almost to cancel any claim to that term,' with 'artillery and transport horses dying in their thousands. The roads between Beverungen, where the cargo boats from Bremen unloaded, to Warburg and beyond, were paved with dead horses.'[21] By March the allied infantry were down to a third of their effective strength, and by April they were forced back to winter quarters, while the French, whose competent system kept them well supplied from established magazines around Frankfurt, re-established control over Hesse.

Granby, still suffering from his bereavement, totally frustrated with the Government's unwillingness to address his supply problems and unsure of George III, who identified him too closely with the Newcastle administration which he had just got rid of, considered resignation. Questions were asked in Parliament as to why the British supply costs were six times those of the French, and why control was not passed from the Secretary at War to Granby in the field. 'These contractors dare not use the foreigners as they do us,' noted Pembroke, 'for, if they fail, they good-naturedly hang them.'[22] No such recourse was open to Granby, subject to the Byzantine procedures of the Civil Service in London. By 1 April 1761 the British cavalry were short of 504 men, about 10 per cent of their strength, had 489 sick, roughly another 10 per cent, and were short of 1,430 horses and, of those they had, 1,560 were sick or lame. On top of that the army's butchers' dogs were spreading rabies.

Louis XV poured more men into Germany, reinforcing de Broglie for another attempt to take Hanover and avenge his losses in the colonies. Ferdinand and Granby's task was to keep these large French armies tied down and, of course, to defend Hanover. They started the 1761 summer campaign with only 60,000 troops, the weakest yet, and 18,000 fewer than the Government insisted they had. De Broglie and the new French commander, Prince Soubise, had twice that number. The campaign was again marked by Ferdinand's skilful manoeuvring, which eventually forced a pitched battle at Vellinghausen, just east of Ham, where he engaged the two parts of the French army as one, and defeated Soubise before de Broglie could come to his assistance. It was an infantry battle, with The Blues and The Royals both present, but unable to take part due to the terrain. The tactical success was again due to Granby, however, whose successive infantry attacks and clever use of artillery forced the French to withdraw with heavy losses. The French lost 6,000 men, including three generals killed by the same cannonball as they conferred under a tree. Vellinghausen reaffirmed Granby as a popular hero. Walpole recorded that 'Lord Granby, to the mob's content, has the chief honour of the day . . . the French behaved to the mob's content too, that is shamefully . . . Mylord Granby is become nabob.'[23]

Yet the strategic situation was unchanged, and in the autumn stalemate still prevailed, although the French had become conscious of the enormous expense and their singular lack of success, despite vastly superior numbers. Choiseul, the War Minister, considered a treaty, but Pitt's terms were too tough and, reluctantly, he financed another campaign in 1762. However, the Duc de Broglie – the only French general in Germany with any skill – was sacked, apparently having fallen out with Louis XV's favourite, Madame de Pompadour, and command devolved on the inadequate Soubise. Granby used the possibility of peace to return home and spend a rather happier winter than he had been recently used to, hunting at Belvoir. At home the war was now deeply unpopular. Serious rioting broke out over a new ballot for the militia, and when the Coldstream Guards mustered in St James's Park to trawl for volunteers to serve with their 2nd Battalion in Germany, not a single man stepped forward. However, when the Government determined to oppose the French in Germany for

George III's coronation procession (*right*) approaching Horse Guards arch. The road had to be lowered to allow the state coach to pass through.

Trumpet banner, one of a pair called the Homeyer Banners. William Homeyer came to England with the Princess, later Queen Charlotte, as part of her marital entourage.

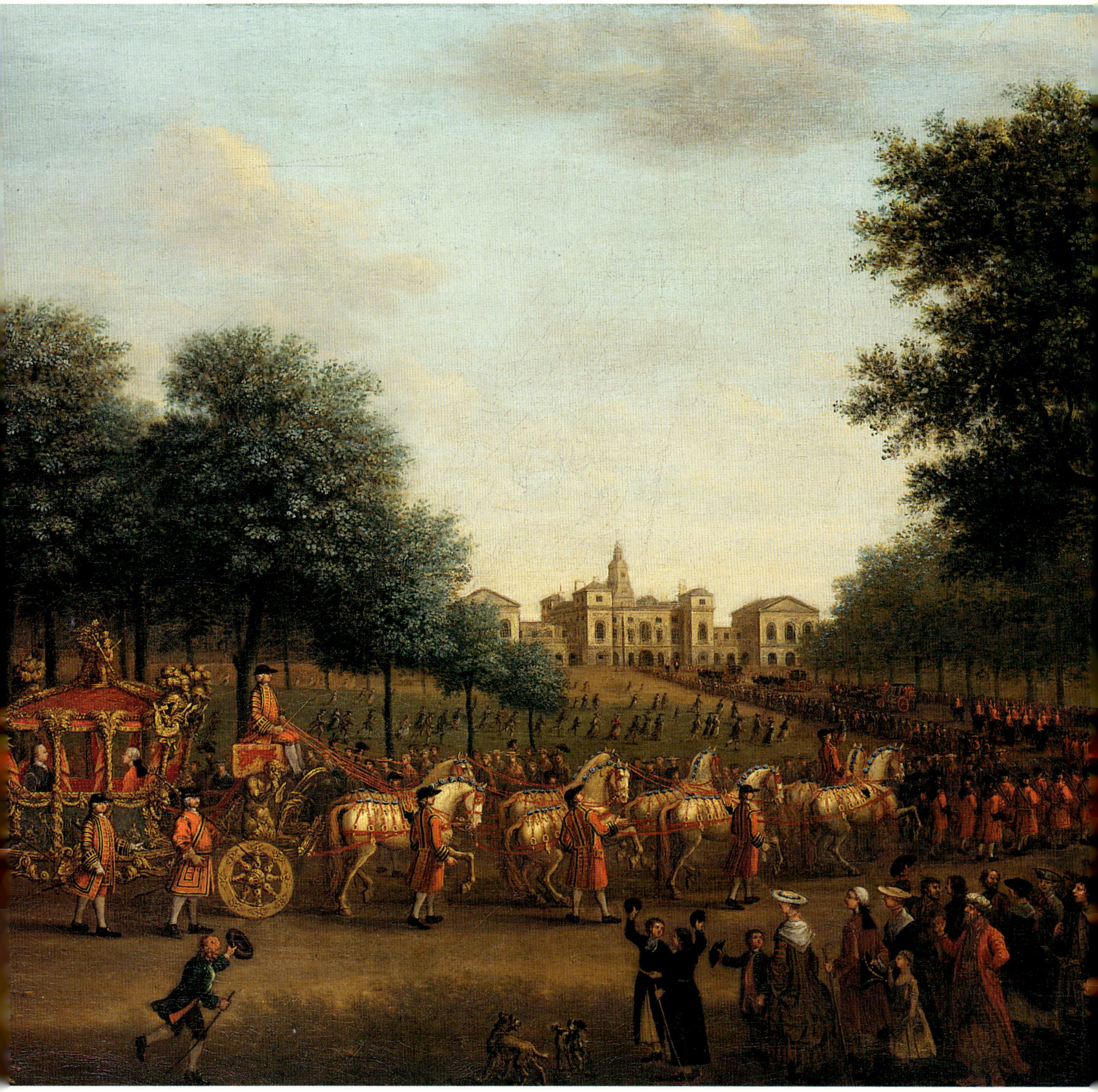

another year, they somehow found enough recruits to bring the British contingent more or less up to strength.

Granby returned heavy-hearted to The Blues in Paderborn, yet his and Ferdinand's combined experience was now to show. Determined finally to clear the French out of Hesse, the Allies, sensing both Soubise's weakness and French exhaustion, moved south over country that, by now, both The Blues and The Royals knew well. Soubise maintained his position and found himself enveloped by converging corps of the Allied army. As he withdrew from the trap, he detached de Stainville with a strong rearguard, who encountered Granby and The Blues, the 15th Light Dragoons and a small infantry force on 1 July near the village of Wilhelmstahl. The two cavalry regiments, realizing the French were forming up in the village, resolved to act before their positions were finished and immediately charged down the village high street, only four or five abreast, hemmed in by a stream, 'with such a continuance as did them an honour never to be forgot'.[24] The infantry then arrived and finished off the demoralized French. The action was a substantial success, destroying the French rearguard, with over 6,000 men taken prisoner, including three whole regiments, and, for almost the first time in the war, they had run out of ammunition as they employed their firearms as much as their swords. Their losses were incredibly slight, with one trooper and three horses killed, though sadly Harry Townshend, Granby's aide-de-camp from The Blues, wounded at Vellinghausen, was killed as well.

Soubise now withdrew from Hesse, taking up positions to the south along the River Ohm, near Marburg, and, finally, it seemed that peace might be signed by September. The Allies, thinking their job done, prematurely relaxed, when there ensued the nastiest incident in what was largely a gentlemanly war. Soubise suddenly attacked the Allied positions at Brucker Holz, inflicting 800 casualties to almost no gain. It was a strange move, with no obvious operational advantage, and seemed almost spiteful, for the war was nearly over, with no credit to Soubise. Ferdinand took advantage of Soubise's subsequent defeat to take Kassel, which surrendered on 1 November, and with its loss the war ended. The French threat to Hanover and Prussia had been removed, and finally the regiments, and Granby, could, in theory, return home.

Sadly it was not that simple, and, in a manner only the British army can achieve, the return journey was to drag on for months. The regiments finally moved in March 1763, marching by way of Holland, with no provision for rations or forage. Seymour Conway, temporarily in command as Granby was ill, had to apply to London for an increased allowance of 2d. per man per day, but the new Prime Minister, Bute, could not agree the expense. The Dutch, unhappy to have the British army marching through their country, were distinctly awkward, and the ferrymen went on strike. Granby, finally well enough to leave Warburg on 12 January, arrived in London to a hero's welcome, and accompanied the King to a review in Hyde Park in his honour. He was offered the Viceroyalty in Ireland, which he turned down, but was luckier than most of his regiment. As soon as The Blues reached home they were reduced from fifty-two to twenty-nine per men per troop. For those demobilized, the terms, almost identical to those William III had authorized in 1699, were not exactly generous. They were offered the value of their horses, if sold before returning to England – so avoiding the transport cost – generally raising about £7, as most of the horses were worn out. On top of that they were offered nine days' pay. Soldiers who had served less than a year were not allowed their horses and were just given eighteen days' pay in total. They were all allowed to retain their uniforms. The same terms applied to The Royals, who were reduced by over a third, to thirty men per troop. The Light Troop was removed and the men incorporated into one of the new light dragoon regiments. It was not a generous package, and showed scant regard for soldiers who had achieved so much, for the 1763 peace agreement secured India for the British Crown, as well as Tobago, Dominica, St Vincent and the Grenadines, Grenada and Minorca. Britain now effectively eclipsed France as the colonial power in the Americas, and, of course, French threats to Hanover and Prussia were removed. But the soldiers who had made it all possible were quickly forgotten, and Granby was soon dipping into his own pocket even more regularly, funding an ex-Blue to open an inn or subscribing £1,000 to an orphanage for children of soldiers killed in the wars. Although he could not prevent the reduction of The Blues, he could at least have them sent to Nottinghamshire, where he could keep an eye on them from Belvoir. They were not to return to southern England for forty years. Both they and The Royals had been subjected to the same savage pattern three times during the past sixty years. Men had been enrolled rapidly to fight in Europe, had been drastically decimated as soon as there was peace, and had been divided and posted around the country for civil policing duties. At no time was thought given to military training or administrative improvements in peacetime. When they were next mobilized, they would have to learn all the same lessons again.

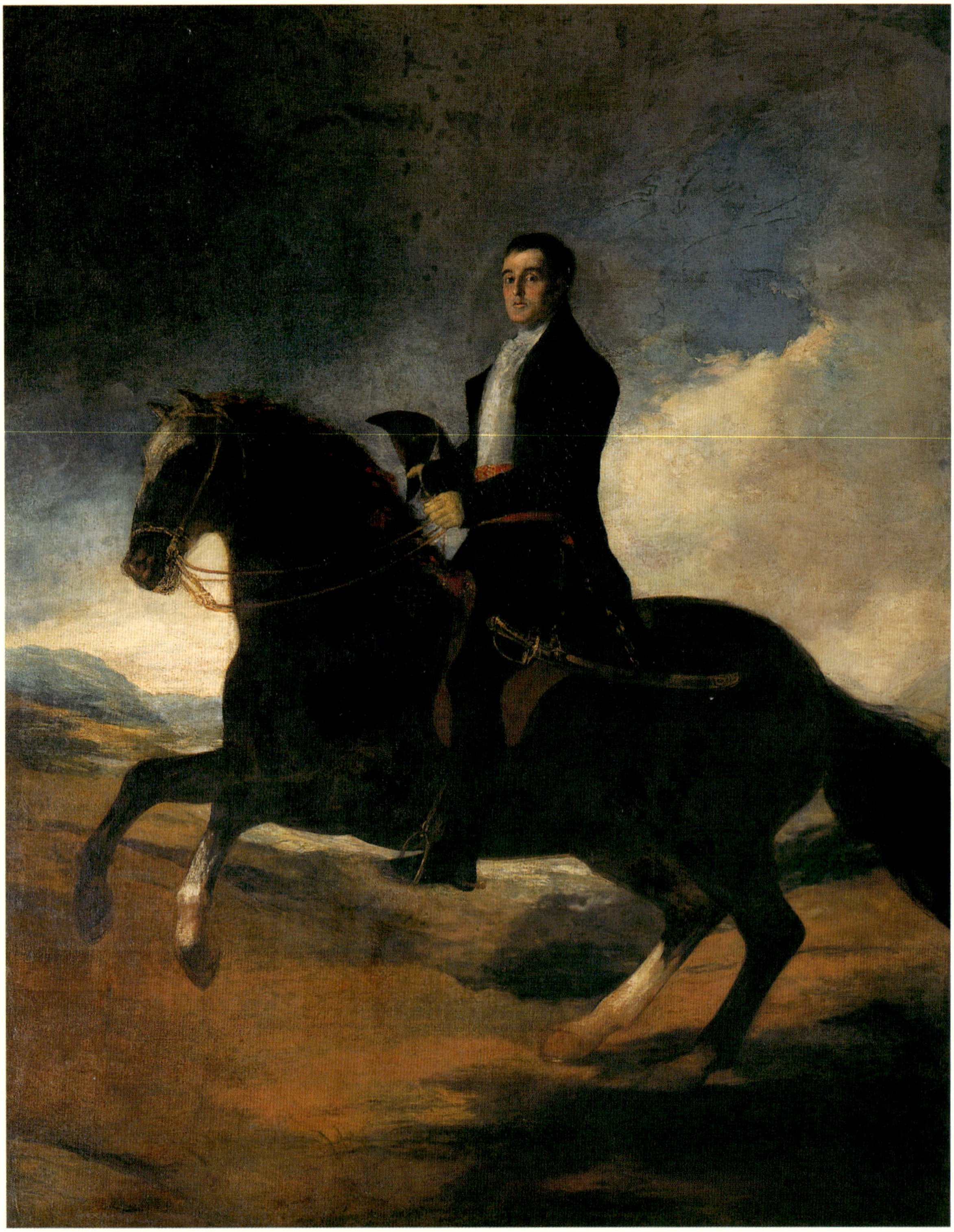

Part Four

THE FIRST GREAT CHANGE

1763–1816

Chapter Eleven

THE KING'S PEACE AND THE REVOLUTIONARY'S WAR

IN THE ELDER PITT'S view, the army reductions of 1763 doomed 'the bravest men the world ever saw to be sent to starve in country villages and forget their prowess'. It was to be thirty-one years before either The Blues or The Royals served overseas once more, and sixty-seven years for the Life Guards, who had to wait until 1812. There was little call for cavalry in the American War of Independence, which dominated British politics in the 1770s and shattered the good reputation the British army had acquired in the Seven Years War. The cavalry, who stayed at home, returned to normal peacetime policing duties, now more pressing in two particular spheres.

First, smuggling posed a serious threat to Government income, at a time when the exchequer relied on customs duties, and political pressure to arrest smugglers and impound their contraband increased. Nationally, about 40,000 people were engaged in smuggling of one sort or another in the 1760s. They traded mostly in everyday goods, and especially tea, rapidly establishing itself as a household drink, and not in the exotic items we now tend to associate with smuggling, such as brandy. Tea duty, until Pitt the Younger reduced it in 1784, was 119 per cent, and evading it could produce substantial profits.[1] The Blues and The Royals were to spend the years until Waterloo mounting endless anti-smuggling patrols, like their predecessors in the 1720s. Even when The Royals returned from the Peninsula in 1814, they were dispatched straight to the West Country on anti-smuggling duties, their troops spread as far apart as Exeter and Taunton. Generally the troop or squadron – now taken generically as being two troops – established its headquarters alongside the local magistrates', and mounted patrols to deter and, if possible, arrest smugglers.

Page 250. Wellington became Colonel of The Blues in 1813 and was their first Gold Stick. Initially he did not endear himself to the regiment, appropriating their quarters in Lisbon for some hussars and dispensing with the band.

The troops were not always popular locally, though attitudes gradually shifted in favour of the Government, as duties were reduced. From the regiments' perspective it was dull, repetitive work, and the necessarily scrappy deployment of troops made social cohesion and military discipline hard to sustain.

The maintenance of public order, the troops' other major duty, led to more immediate confrontations and, particularly in London, also heavily occupied the Life Guards. The social and economic upheaval of late-eighteenth-century Britain, of so much significance to our regiments, caused many riots, which it was the army's job to suppress. The first major skirmishes, after the Seven Years War, were the Weavers' Riots in 1765 and the Corn Riots of 1766. 'The present riotous assemblings on account of the high prices of corn,' wrote Barrington, still Secretary at War, have 'made it necessary for the Magistrates to call in a military force to their assistance.'[2] The troops were still under the control of magistrates and, as Dr Johnson succinctly put it, 'the magistrates dare not call the Guards for fear of being hanged. The Guards will not come, for fear of being given up to the blind rage of popular juries.'[3] Although the Wilkes Riots of 1768 and 1769 saw the Life Guards 'brought out ostentatiously each day',[4] by far the most serious altercations were the Gordon Riots of 1780. Reminiscent of the Sacheverell Riots seventy years earlier, they were apparently the London mob's reaction to the 1778 Catholic Relief Act, a fairly mild piece of legislation easing penalties on Roman Catholics, now the Jacobite threat had waned. On 2 June a crowd estimated at 50,000 met in St George's Fields, south of Westminster, at the instigation of Lord George Gordon, a strange figure whom history has judged misguided rather than malevolent, and his Protestant Association. With shouts of 'No Popery! We shall be burnt! Let us have the Protestant religion!' they marched on Parliament, and what probably started as a peaceful protest disintegrated into a week of the most violent rioting that London had seen. As so often happened, once the London mob was out of control, it was difficult to restrain, especially during this particularly hot June. The early ransacking of distilleries and breweries in the city only added fuel to the flames.

For the Life Guards it was a difficult time. They had plenty of experience of crowd control from the previous decade, but these riots were on a different scale, and the example of Captain Horsey was no doubt still firmly in their minds. In the first couple of days the crowds were relatively good-humoured, and at first the magistrates were very reluctant to call troops out. However, by the evening of 2 June a large number of peers and Members of Parliament were still barricaded in the Houses of Parliament and at 9 p.m. a decision was finally taken to ask for their assistance. Captain Topham formed up a detachment of Life Guards in Parliament Square. The crowd made way for them as they approached 'flourishing their swords in a menacing attitude',[5] but once they were drawn up there was little they could do. The crowd had not melted away in fear, and indeed were jeering at them and even throwing 'pieces of faggot which they had taken from a neighbouring bakers'. The Foot Guards

The Gordon Riots of 1780 were a difficult experience for the Life Guards, and made them highly unpopular in London.

The militia inspection camp of 1780 at Old Montague House. Eventually twenty regiments were deployed in the streets, and Hyde Park, where they mostly camped, looking like 'the field of Malplaquet before the battle', according to one contemporary with a surprisingly long memory.

fared worse in St Margaret's Street, hemmed in by the sheer mass of people, who amused themselves by 'knocking their hats off and poking sticks at their bottoms'.[6] Justice Addington, the Westminster magistrate who had called Topham out, now ordered him to charge through and open a passage to Westminster Hall. Simply walking forward had no impact, so Topham's Troop stepped back and then charged at the crowd 'in a full gallop, in order to give their career sufficient force to penetrate them. The consequence was that after the cavalry had passed through them, the mob lay in the most ludicrous manner one over another like a pack of cards.'[7] In the extraordinarily clever way in which horses avoid actually treading on people in such circumstances, the only accident was one broken leg, but the charge got nowhere near the Hall and its main effect was to reduce the crowd to 'paroxysms of infectious laughter' so that they could not get up from the ground.

Thereafter matters became more unpleasant. The Life Guards subsequently mounted a guard, full time, on the Houses of Parliament, and, as the crowds of the Protestant Association gave way to the mob, were required to use more force. Meanwhile the destruction in London spread. On the night of 5 June, a Life Guards' officer wrote, the city 'presented a dreadful scene of conflagration and bloodshed . . . many of the rioters were apprehended and sent to prison, but they were rescued and the prisons set on fire. The King's Bench prison, the Fleet Prison, the New Bridewell, St George's Fields and the new gaol were in flames at the same time.' The King was increasingly disillusioned with his ministers' apparent inability to restore order. At a stormy council meeting he asked the Attorney General if officers could legally use their own discretion in firing on the mob. The Attorney, Wedderburn, replied that they could, and the King immediately issued an order to Lord Amherst, the Commander-in-Chief, who subsequently directed the military 'to act without waiting for direction from the civil magistrates'. He also brought more troops into the city to back up the hard-pressed Guards. Eventually twenty regiments were deployed in the streets, and Hyde Park, where they mostly camped, looked like 'the field of Malplaquet before the battle', according to one contemporary with a surprisingly long memory.[8]

Despite the wide powers now available to them, only one really violent incident stands out where the Life Guards might possibly have been accused of excessive force. On Thursday, 8 June, Lieutenant Majoribanks and his detachment approached the Bank of England down Fleet Street to relieve the guard there. They were glimpsed by a mob 'bobbing proudly and complacently along',[9] who immediately charged them. Majoribanks' detachment carried muskets, but apparently had neither the time nor inclination to use them, and, according to an eyewitness, used their bayonets – no mean feat when mounted. More likely they used their swords. Whatever their tactic, they had soon killed twenty rioters, and a further thirty-five apparently died within the hour. While Majoribanks' action created a stir across the city – ghoulish crowds flocked to see the street awash with blood – it also helped to calm matters. London, by now, felt like a garrison town, the distilleries had been drunk dry, and the prisoners all released, and so an uneasy composure was restored. By Friday, a week after Gordon and his Protestant crowd had first approached Parliament, the worst was over. False rumours of summary trials and executions quickly circulated, and Amherst sensibly restored power to the civil authorities as soon as he felt secure. The Life Guards' annals record that 'the military were obliged to act with promptitude and decision and great numbers of the mob were killed; and many others, having broken into cellars and become intoxicated, perished in the flames'.[10] The official figures were 285 rioters killed, with twenty-five more hanged. Gordon was tried for treason, and acquitted. While Majoribanks was never brought to trial, for he had done nothing illegal, his actions soured relations between the Life Guards and the populace of London, and did little for the Life Guards' image, which was to have an important consequence eight years later.

Generally, however, the riots of the 1760s and 70s made the regiments even more wary of using force. From this period many kept a miniature copy of the Riot Act in their pistol cases, or screwed into a hollow in the butt of their pistols, to consult before any recourse to weapons.[11] When, for example, The Blues quelled a 'framework-knitters' riot' in Nottingham in 1783, they did so with no violence, despite arresting thirty-seven protesters. Furthermore, when assisting magistrates to maintain public order in Coventry and Loughborough in 1795, they were ordered not to 'repel force by force, unless in case of Absolute Necessity'. With the exception of the Burdett Riots in 1810, to which we will return later, that was to remain the regiments' prevailing attitude.

The Life Guards and the Horse Grenadiers were also involved in Parliamentary elections, more directly than was ideal for a body whose main task was to guard the King and the Royal Family. Suffrage in the 1770s was still dependent on individual worth and the Life Guards, generally men of some property, held nearly 300 votes in the Westminster Parliamentary constituency, a very sensitive one, given its position. In 1774 George III, never one to remain neutral in politics, pressured both Lord Delawarr, Colonel of the 1st Troop, and Lord Harrington, Colonel of the 2nd Troop of Horse Grenadiers, to order their men to vote for Lord North and the Government. More critically, he did so again in the more bitterly contested 1784 election, called to confirm the country's acceptance of Pitt the Younger's Government, which Fox and the Whigs believed had deviously achieved power the previous year with royal support. The Government, led by George III and Pitt, was determined to humiliate Fox with a defeat in the Westminster constituency, where he was standing against Admiral Hood and Sir Cecil Wray. The King insisted that 280 Life Guards and Horse Grenadiers voted for Wray, even though his manifesto included the closure of Chelsea Hospital, which provided for the retirement of many of the least wealthy Life Guards and the majority of Horse Grenadiers. 'All Horse

Guards, Grenadier Guards, Foot Guards and Blackguards, that have not polled for the destruction of Chelsea Hospital . . . are desired to meet at the Gutter Hole opposite the Horse Guards, where they will have a full bumper of knock-me-down and plenty of soapsuds before they go to poll for Sir C. Wray', read one of Fox's election posters.[12] To make matters worse, Admiral Hood sent a party of sailors to stop Fox's supporters getting to the polls. Ultimately Fox won, and he was not the only politician to feel it immoral to use military force and discipline for party ends. Many serving officers were still Members of Parliament; three Royals officers, Garth, Goldsworthy and Philipson, for example, sat throughout this period, the lax regimental attendance rules allowing them to do so. However, to use the military to create block votes was something, Walpole wrote, which his father 'would never have dared to do'.[13]

So apart from anti-smuggling duties, and a little riot control, there was not much for either The Blues or The Royals to do throughout a possibly rather depressing time, as they lost touch with their ex-comrades from Germany and watched the army, for which they had sacrificed so much, made into a laughing stock by the press. The Blues largely remained in the Midlands, their troops extended between Hertford, Peterborough, Stamford and Derby, with the odd foray to London when George III felt the need for a military review, largely ceremonial affairs with little military training involved. Otherwise they entertained themselves locally, much encouraged by Granby, and lapsed back to the pattern of the 1750s. Granby himself died, aged only forty-eight, at his house in Scarborough in 1770. His last few years as Commander-in-Chief and Master General of the Ordnance, cabinet posts he had assumed in 1766, had not been particularly happy. George III still resented his earlier support for Newcastle against Bute, and was always suspicious of his popularity with the mob, something upon which Granby occasionally played. When Grenville insisted on Granby's appointment as Commander-in-Chief, the King is reputed to have said, 'Lord Granby is so weak that the last man that sees him has him.'[14] Granby's behaviour in the Middlesex election, where his position was considered too pro-Wilkes, forced his resignation in January 1770, though he insisted on retaining the Colonelcy of The Blues, a position he did not consider a political post. He died hugely lamented by the regiment, though they were delighted that General Seymour Conway was appointed in his place. The Duke of Richmond, who had busily lined himself up for the post, was so upset to hear Seymour Conway had been offered it that he wrote the King a very intemperate letter, causing a rift that lasted for most of the monarch's remaining life. Richmond would ultimately win his prize, but not for twenty-five years.

Seymour Conway, an intensely political soldier, was a long-term Member of Parliament and later a cabinet minister. His relationship with George III was consequently far from easy. He had already been sacked as Colonel of The Royals in 1764 for voting against the Government on general warrants, and was later nearly dismissed from The Blues for his remarks on the Royal Marriages

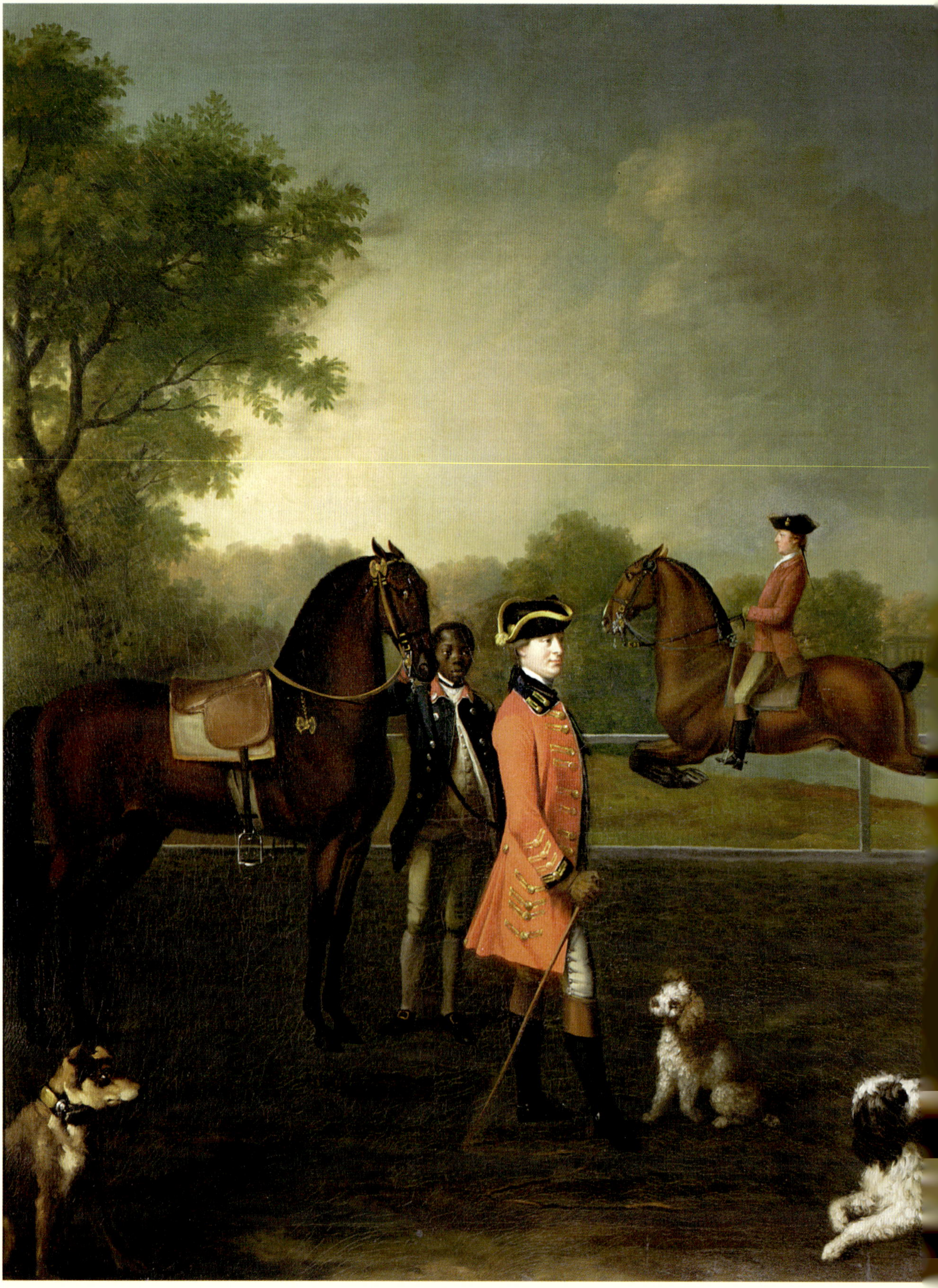

The Earl of Pembroke, Colonel of The Royals, who did so much to improve military equitation after the Seven Years War, in his menage at Wilton with his Riding Master and son Lord Herbert.

Act, and his less than energetic support for the American War. When George III vented his frustration on the regiment he had so long admired, by remarking at a Blackheath Review that he wished he 'could see The Blues behave as well as they used to do', Conway rounded on the King and, bravely, told him not to 'lay blame on the officers merely to mortify the Colonel'.[15]

Noteworthy incidents while The Blues were stationed in the Midlands included their first encounter with Freemasonry, later to enjoy strong support, particularly among the non-commissioned officers. Six officers were inducted to the St John Lodge, including Cornet Packe, who would, much later, be killed at Waterloo. Also during this time, The Blues built a Riding School at Nottingham for £400. They were the first regiment to have one, although it was The Royals who really advanced military horsemanship on a major scale. Their new Colonel, Lord Pembroke, had been appointed in 1764 to replace Seymour Conway. Pembroke had been an enthusiastic soldier in the Seven Years War, first buying a cornetcy in the King's Dragoon Guards, before transferring to Eliott's famous 15th Light Dragoons as Lieutenant Colonel in 1757. He had fought with Eliott's Troop throughout, and had not been impressed with their standard of horsemanship. In 1761 he published *Military Equitation*, which quickly became the standard work in what was not, admittedly, a particularly competitive market, but which eventually ran to three editions and was translated into several foreign languages. When he came to The Royals he brought the 15th Light Dragoons' Riding Master, John Floyd, with him. Floyd had been virtually raised by Pembroke as a son; a cornet in Eliott's Troop had died of wounds after Minden, leaving his eleven-year-old son both to inherit his rank and be cared for by the Lieutenant Colonel. Floyd proved a particularly adept horseman, and served with The Royals as their Riding Master from 1764 until 1775 when Pembroke chose him, slightly unusually, to escort his son on the Grand Tour. Between Pembroke and Floyd the standard of horsemanship in The Royals improved rapidly, and they acquired a reputation that lasted until mechanization in the 1940s. In the mid-eighteenth century The Royals, like The Blues, had black horses that were still, as dragoon horses, smaller than those of The Blues. Floyd, writing in 1780, reports that he has found 'the finest Regimental horse for an officer in the heavy cavalry I know of. I partly think he is too big for anything but The Blues. He is about 16 hands and a half high; rising six, of the blackest brown.'[16] Pembroke and Floyd's method was to encourage soldiers to be gentler with their horses and use persuasion rather than force. They also helped to stop the horrible, 'tidy' habit of docking, or cutting back to the stump, troop horses' tails, which stopped them swishing away flies, and had caused real misery in the hot Westphalian summers. Floyd accompanied The Royals from Scotland, where they were sent on return from Germany, on to Coventry, Dorset, Surrey, Suffolk, and York.

Two major influences were soon to coalesce and change this old-ordered world for ever. First, the rapidly developing economy was to force fundamental structural changes to the way the regiments were manned and organized, particularly the Life Guards. Second, by 1793 France had emerged as an extreme republican state, threatening Britain and her institutions in a far more menacing way than the Bourbons ever had. Reform of the army, for so long an afterthought, useful for tinkering in Europe or acquiring lucrative colonies, now became a matter of national survival. The Life Guards, The Blues and The Royals would consequently all emerge as very different organizations by 1815.

The first and most dramatic change was in the Life Guards. George III had never been fond of them. A down-to-earth and essentially unfussy man, he detested the restrictions they imposed on his freedom, and preferred to travel, as he frequently did to Windsor, accompanied just by one or two grooms. He also found them inefficient. In 1786 a madwoman had nearly stabbed him as he got out of his coach, and several further attempts on his life, a couple quite serious, meant the Government was concerned for his safety, despite his undoubted popularity. He also had to spend much time in London, and the Gordon riots had shown just how dangerous London could be. The Life Guards' reduction by two troops in 1745 had stretched them, and they had insufficient men both to perform their duties in London and be deployed in the Seven Years War. Now the King had little use for them, so, alienated from the people of London and the Whig opposition, they had little support when the question of 'economical reform' was debated at Westminster. Although Pitt the Younger was well established in power by 1788, a strong mood prevailed in Parliament, supported in the country, to reduce the Crown's considerable patronage and make royal appointments more accountable. It was not a parliamentary vote, however, but a royal decree on 18 June 1788 that abolished the two troops of horse guards (i.e. the Life Guards) and the two troops of Horse Grenadiers and replaced them with two regiments of Life Guards, manned similarly to the rest of the army, but remaining the most senior regiments, with direct access to the King through the Gold Sticks. From now on the men would be soldiers rather than private gentlemen. 'I have no doubt that Your Lordship will not regret the reduction of the Troops of Horse Guards and Horse Grenadiers as they were the most useless & the most unmilitary Troopes that ever were seen,' wrote the Duke of York to Earl Cornwallis in July 1788, 'I confess that I was a little sorry for the Horse Grenadiers because they were to a degree Soldiers, but the Horse Guards were nothing but a collection of London Tradespeople.'[17]

There were deeper reasons why the Life Guards suffered such a dramatic reorganization. British society in 1788 was very different to that in 1660. Then the pay and status of a private gentleman, attendant on the King, was hugely attractive, particularly for those who had lost everything in the civil wars. A century later it was no longer true. In 1660 £73 a year might have given a private gentleman the equivalent pay to 'Eminent Clergymen', but it had not increased since, and was now equivalent to bricklayers' and spinners' pay.

It certainly could not maintain a man and his horse from the country in an increasingly expensive London, and so over the years the Life Guards were recruited from native Londoners with alternative sources of income, whose part-time jobs as private gentlemen simply furthered family business interests, as we saw in the Davenport correspondence. Those who might once have joined to enhance their prospects now either became lawyers and Members of Parliament, or, increasingly, took positions in the rapidly expanding forces of the East India Company with its tempting lure of vast profits.

Another pressure for change came from those who just wanted the Life Guards to be something else entirely. Every other self-respecting European King or Emperor had a magnificent royal guard, imposing men chosen for their stature and soldierly qualities, which not only added considerable kudos but were also regarded as the elite of their army when in the field. The French Maison Militaire du Roi, soon to be transformed into Napoleon's Imperial Guard, was one example; others could be found in Russia, Prussia, Austria, Denmark, Spain and even Constantinople. The Life Guards had originally been the British mounted equivalent, but now, with The Blues almost permanently away from London, something more impressive than aged London merchants on indifferent and mismatched horses was required. Matters had, in fact, declined so badly that a story circulated in London in 1788 that the Queen had been forced to order her coachman to slow down en route to a levee as two of her Life Guard escort had fallen off. There was also a feeling that the officers were not up to scratch; between 1700 and 1749, there had been forty-three peers or peers' sons serving in the Life Guards; since 1750 there had only been seventeen, the majority of them colonels. Between 1800 and 1860, after the 1788 reforms had taken effect, that figure would rise to sixty.[18] This watershed came about despite the commissions remaining the most expensive in the army. The difference was that young men purchased them not for profit, but rather for the prestige of serving. The new regiments were seen, once again, as elite, rather than as a sort of upmarket city company. As proof of that, very soon, the cost of serving would far outweigh the pay.

Plans for the two new regiments were drawn up with care, and decent compensation was offered to those who lost their positions. The King had, in fact, decided on the changes in March, and the Secretary at War had been negotiating terms with the four respective Colonels – Lord Lothian and Lord Amherst for the Life Guards' troops and the Duke of Northumberland and Lord Howard de Walden for the Horse Grenadiers'. The majority of private gentlemen retired, and were compensated for their admittance money and received generous 'annuities for their lives'; the King personally approved their package and the large sum of £10,490 was set aside for the 1st Troop and £13,335 for the 2nd Troop. The Major of the 1st Troop, for example, who retired, was paid an annuity of £383 for life, drawn for him from the Paymaster General by the regimental agent. They were replaced partly by new recruits, but mostly by

King George III and Queen Charlotte driving through Deptford escorted by Horse Grenadiers in 1785. Rowlandson's irreverent view of royal escorts was widely shared and led to the disbandment of the old Life Guard troops in 1788.

Horse Grenadiers watching a parade. In 1788 the Horse Grenadier troops were merged with the Life Guards to form two regiments in the standing army.

private soldiers transferring from the Horse Grenadiers, with those from the 1st Horse Grenadier Troop going to the 1st Life Guards and the 2nd Troop to the 2nd Life Guards. It was this second Horse Grenadier troop that had retained the Scottish links of both the Scottish Horse Grenadiers and the 4th Troop of Life Guards, and the 2nd Life Guards were to retain this strong tradition until the 1920s.

Many Life Guards officers remained. The two Colonels, Lothian and Amherst, simply became Colonels of the 1st and 2nd Regiments of Life Guards and continued as Gold Sticks, though Lothian lost his position the following year when George III, recovered from his illness, discovered he had voted for the Regency Bill. Arrangements were made to preserve the value of the Horse Grenadier officers' commissions; some retired, some transferred to the new regiments, which had a much bigger officer establishment than the old troops had, and some went to other regiments in the army. In July 1788 a committee was established, consisting of Lothian, Amherst and, interestingly, Seymour Conway from The Blues, to draw up a price list for commissions. Pay rates were the highest in the army, with privates paid a total of 3s. 3d., made up of 1s. 6d. pay and subsistence, 1s. 3d. for their horse and 6d. for clothing, although that was still 9d. less than they had received 100 years earlier.

The two new regiments, 230-strong with four troops of fifty men each, took over a year to establish, and there were long debates over uniforms and customs. As ex-Horse Grenadiers outnumbered the private gentlemen, it was not surprising that some thought the new regiments resembled the Horse Grenadiers more than the original Life Guards. Certainly some items of Horse Grenadier uniform were retained, including the grenade badge, which is still to be found on Life Guards officers' cloaks today, and was used as a cap badge briefly in the 1830s with rather silly enormous bearskin hats. George III decided that sub-lieutenants would replace the rank of cornets, but otherwise the Life Guards' Byzantine rank structure was abolished and the new ranks were to correspond with the rest of the army's. Pages of regulations were generated over uniforms, and what to wear with what on which occasion, but to the casual observer in St James's Park the overall effect was very much the same. However, the privates, as they were now called, were younger and taller, most standing at 5 feet 11 inches or 6 feet, and their horses gradually became a uniform colour, dark bay for the 1st Life Guards and black for the 2nd Life Guards. During 1788 and 1789 they would also have noticed that, while the new regiments were forming up, it was The Blues, on a welcome sojourn from the Midlands, who mounted the King's Life Guard, which then consisted of three officers, a quartermaster, a trumpeter, four corporals and twenty-six privates.

Logically the whole army should now have been subject to a similar process of reform, but Pitt the Younger's administration was too preoccupied with rebuilding the navy to spare time and money for a service currently best employed in the colonies. Near-crises with Holland in 1787 and France in

1788 passed with no comprehension of the army's total inadequacy to fight in Europe. With the execution of Louis XVI and the threat to British interests posed by the new French regime, and the declaration of war in February 1793, it finally dawned on the Government just how bad matters were. Pitt the Younger candidly admitted that 'I distrust extremely any ideas of my own on military subjects.'[19] Not only was the small British expeditionary force he sent to Flanders in the spring of 1793 under George III's second son Frederick, Duke of York, 'the worst British army that had taken the field since Schomberg's in Ireland',[20] but its commander had no idea what to do, other than, as the nursery rhyme reminds us, to march its 10,000 men somewhat aimlessly around northern Europe. York was only twenty-eight, militarily inexperienced, and had originally been intended to command the Hanoverian and Hessian detachments under the Austrian commander, Coburg. However, Pitt's plan developed and York's force was now to include the British contingent within the larger army of a Grand Alliance of Russia, Prussia, Austria, Spain, Portugal, a medley of Italian states and Holland, which must surely, it was felt, prove overwhelming against the disorganized armies of the fledgling French Republic, now deprived of many of their officers. The Allies should have been able to field 350,000 men, against a French maximum of 270,000, and in theory should have been able to attack on four different fronts, but a lack of prior agreement on war aims led to confusion. Whilst Pitt saw the Low Countries as the critical theatre, the Russians and the Prussians were more concerned with the current revolt in Poland, which to them was a much more immediate threat. Austria was the only other major power interested in deploying an army to Holland, driven by a policy to extricate herself from the Austrian Netherlands in exchange for Bavaria rather than opposition to France, despite the imprisonment, and subsequent execution, of their Emperor's sister, Marie Antoinette. The story of the next two years was to be one of operational failure, Allied bickering and increasingly divergent British and Austrian war aims, only enlivened by a couple of stunning tactical successes.

Amherst, still Colonel of the 2nd Life Guards, was made Commander-in-Chief in February 1793. Both The Blues and The Royals were quickly augmented and embarked in June, after the customary pre-deployment royal review, as part of the 3,500 British cavalry. Both regiments left two troops behind to establish bases for recruitment and remounts, The Blues at Northampton and The Royals at Salisbury – some of the lessons of the Seven Years War had been learnt. The two new regiments of Life Guards were kept in London to protect the King and capital, an unpopular decision among them, as they had hoped that their reorganization would earn them a place in the expeditionary force. It was not to be the last time they would face this particular conundrum.

The Revolutionary Wars, as they came to be known, had begun with the French invasion of Belgium, threatening Holland. The Austrians had sent an army under Coburg, which met with some initial successes. So when The Blues, commanded by Lieutenant Colonel Sir Charles Turner, and The Royals, under Goldsworthy, disembarked at Ostend on 15 June, they marched to join the Allied army at Valenciennes, to which Coburg laid siege. It duly fell on 1 August, and the Allies now split, the Duke of York taking the British force with Dutch, Hanoverian and Hessian troops to capture Dunkirk, while Coburg laid siege to Le Quesnoy. Dunkirk was an ambitious and ultimately senseless goal. It was bound to prompt fierce French reaction, given its position and history, and, even if it had fallen, there was no plan to exploit its capture and no troops with which to do so. To be fair to York, he was acting under strict orders from London, which show Pitt at his most muddle-headed, and neither he nor anyone else realized just how determined the new Republican armies would be or how ruthlessly the Committee of Public Safety would push them. It seems to have dawned but slowly on the Allies that the new rulers of France did not enjoy the luxury of being able to negotiate; if they failed, so would the revolution.

Marshal Houchard, the French commander, decided to concentrate on York's force as he approached Dunkirk. Both The Blues and The Royals were in the cavalry screen, and were some of the first troops to encounter the French. The Blues were advancing along the sea when they were engaged by the French fleet; Lieutenant Board was knocked off his horse by a cannonball, and so severely injured that he died soon afterwards. The pressure from Houchard proved too great, and York withdrew, abandoning most of his supplies and all his heavy artillery which had only just arrived. He fell back towards Menin, pursued by Houchard, who subsequently defeated a second Allied force under the Prince of Orange. Both The Blues and The Royals were engaged in some nasty skirmishing throughout October, but there were no more decisive engagements and by November the British had retired to winter in Ghent. The campaign had achieved absolutely nothing; the Allies had made no progress into northern France and 'the most salutary illustration of the contrasting cultures of the two sides is that while the beaten Allied commanders retained their posts, Houchard was guillotined for failing to pursue the enemy with sufficient aggression'.[21]

No extra forces were sent to augment the British contingent during the winter, despite York's pleas, although The Blues' and The Royals' depot system worked well and some remounts and recruits arrived in Ostend in March. The Allies started the 1794 campaign 160,000 strong, against 250,000 mostly untrained, enforced French recruits, under Houchard's successor, Pichegru, the driven thirty-three-year-old son of a labourer, a good example of the new type of French general. The French were strung out in a line running roughly south from Dunkirk to Cambrai, and, as the events of April were to prove, could have been dealt with relatively easily by the more experienced Allies, if the Austrians had been minded to do so. Coburg's plan, however, was merely to cover his force from French attack, while he laid siege to Landrecies in the centre. The French, therefore, had time to organize and train, while the Allies were

REVOLUTIONARY WARS 1793–1795

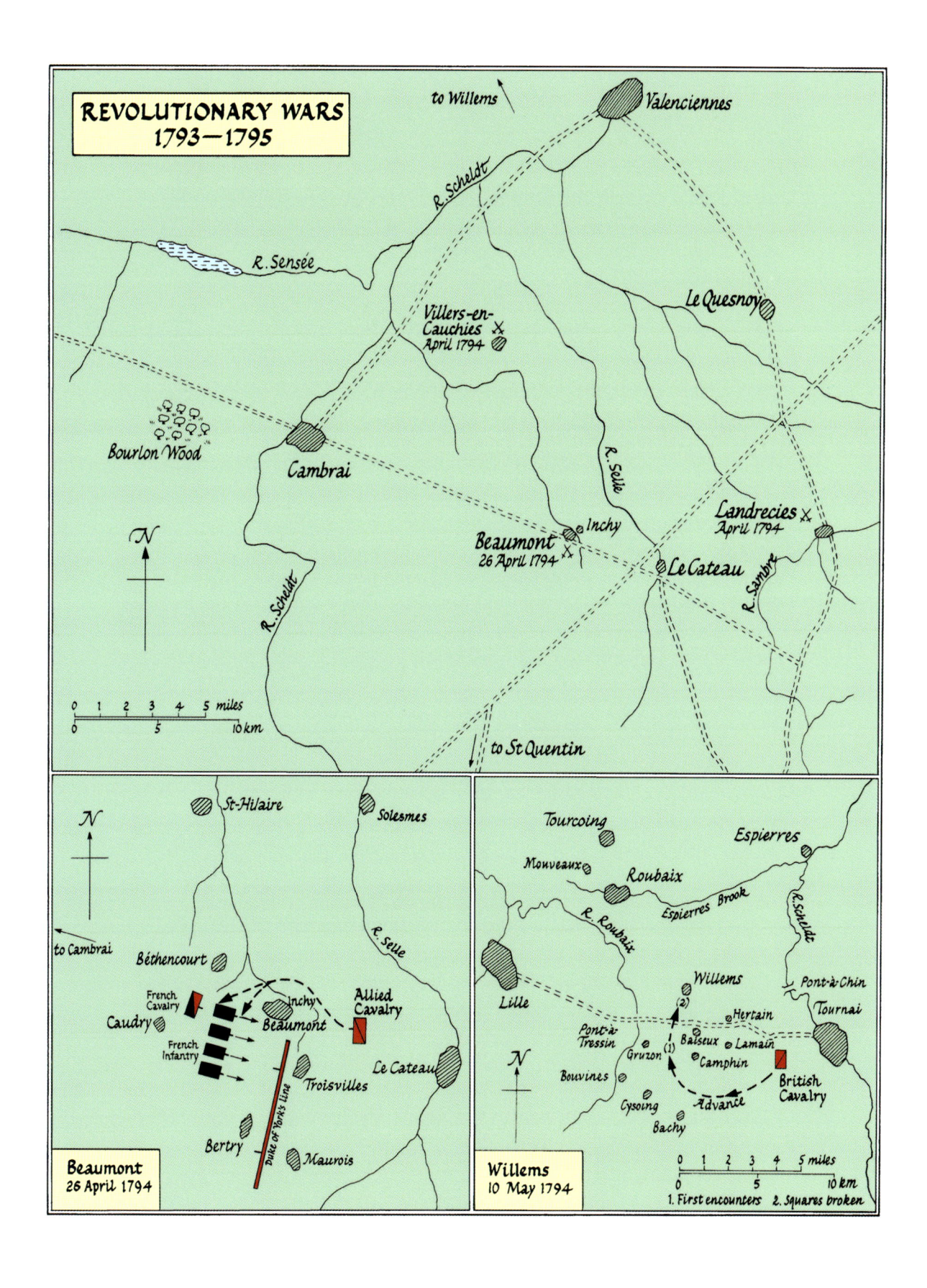

to Willems — Valenciennes

R. Scheldt

R. Sensée

Le Quesnoy

Villers-en-Cauchies ✕
April 1794

Bourlon Wood

Cambrai

R. Selle

Landrecies ✕
April 1794

Beaumont ✕
26 April 1794

Inchy

Le Cateau

R. Sambre

R. Scheldt

N

0 1 2 3 4 5 miles
0 5 10 km

to St Quentin

Beaumont — 26 April 1794

N

St-Hilaire

Solesmes

R. Selle

to Cambrai

Béthencourt

French Cavalry

Caudry

French Infantry

Inchy

Beaumont

Allied Cavalry

Le Cateau

Troisvilles

Duke of York's line

Bertry

Maurois

Willems — 10 May 1794

Tourcoing

Espierres

Mouveaux

Roubaix

Espierres Brook

R. Roubaix

Willems (2)

Pont-à-Chin

Lille

Pont-à-Tressin

Gruzon

Balsieux

Hertain

Lamain

Tournai

Bouvines

Camphin

British Cavalry

Cysoing

Bachy

Advance

N

0 1 2 3 4 5 miles
0 5 10 km

1. First encounters 2. Squares broken

tied up in old-fashioned siege tactics belonging to a previous age. The Duke of York commanded a corps of British, Hanoverian and Hessian troops, together with some Austrians, under Coburg, in the centre. The Blues and The Royals were brigaded with the 3rd Dragoon Guards under Major General Mansel, one of three British Heavy Cavalry brigades. Lord Pembroke died in January 1794 and Goldsworthy, now promoted to Lieutenant General, took over as Colonel of the Royals, and Garth became commanding officer for the remainder of the campaign.

Operations started in April, and after a short delay for the obligatory royal review, this time by the Hapsburg Emperor Francis, Coburg laid siege to Landrecies. Preliminary operations included attacking three outlying French divisions on 17 April, which, though successful, was not the decisive victory it could have been. Mansel's brigade had not engaged in action, although some thought they should have, and the cavalry were criticized for not properly exploiting the breakthrough achieved by the infantry. Coburg now pressed forward to Landrecies, and York's corps was put beyond the town to the west as a screen to prevent French reinforcements from getting through. On 23 April a large French force moved out from Cambrai, due west of Landrecies. York immediately dispatched his cavalry commander, the Austrian Lieutenant General Otto, with some light cavalry to investigate. They came across the French advance guard strung out along the River Selle, near the village of Villers-en-Cauchies, and, realizing they had achieved surprise, Otto called for support so he could attack. Mansel's brigade was duly dispatched and joined Otto's force on the night of 23 April. The plan was set for four squadrons of light cavalry to attack at dawn the following day, and though heavily outnumbered, to rely on shock and surprise to disorientate the French. Mansel's brigade was to follow up behind, exploit their anticipated success and come to their support if they got into difficulties. At first everything went exactly according to plan. The four light squadrons charged the unsuspecting French at dawn, driving their cavalry back across a sunken road into their massed ranks of infantry, who promptly broke and ran. The Light Dragoons and Hussars pursued them to the village of Bouchain, where they were confronted by a reserve with artillery. Mansel should have come to their assistance at this point, but there was no sign of him. Withdrawing to Villers, they discovered the French had reoccupied the village and got behind them. Undaunted, they charged again and broke through to find a shamefaced Mansel and his brigade. The chance of a decisive victory had been lost. Exactly what happened is unknown, and annoyingly neither regiment has left a first-hand account, but the London newspapers were clear that the fault was with Mansel,[22] and both regiments shared some of the subsequent bad feeling. The Duke of York's dispatch that evening, though it was written before he had seen Mansel, criticized him directly: 'had [the light cavalry] been properly supported, the entire destruction of the enemy must have been the consequence, but by some mistake General Mansel's brigade did not arrive in time'.[23] Mansel himself, already hurt by the criticism of his inaction on 17 April, now determined that he had to do something to redeem his shame.

His chance came two days later, at Beaumont, when the French, now reorganized, moved forward again to attack the Duke of York's screen under cover of thick fog. They secured a couple of hamlets in front of the Allied position, and, outnumbering York's corps by three to two, posed a serious threat both to his entrenched battalions and to Coburg still busy besieging Landrecies to his rear. However, as the fog cleared, York realized that their left flank, between the villages of Beaumont and Béthencourt, was unprotected. In a move that shows him maturing into an able and decisive tactical commander, York quickly dispatched the cavalry squadrons he had in reserve, behind his right wing under another Austrian, General Schwarzenberg, to loop round behind Beaumont village and attack the unprotected French flank. Schwarzenberg had with him Mansel's brigade, Vyse's brigade, six Austrian cuirassier squadrons from Zetchwitz's Regiment, the Archduke Ferdinand's Hussars, and the 16th Light Dragoons. He executed his move with considerable skill, using a stream valley for cover, and manoeuvred them into position north of the Beaumont to Cambrai road, where they formed from column into line behind a slight rise, still out of sight of the French. The Blues were in the first line with the Austrians under Mansel, the 3rd Dragoon Guards in the second and The Royals in the third; Vyse's brigade was in support. Before them, over the rise, were open cornfields with no hedges or obstacles to give the enemy cover or impede their movement.

The advance had hardly begun before they encountered the French cavalry, which had been held slightly back. Mansel, determined to redeem the shame of his previous mistake, and encouraged, no doubt, by the Duke of York's helpful comment as they passed him en route, 'Gentlemen, you must repair the disgrace of the 24th,' led The Blues and cuirassiers in an immediate charge. He had allegedly told his staff that he was so upset by the 'imputation on his character that he had declared that he would not return alive',[24] and so he duly fell, as, sadly, did his son. However, he achieved his object, as the French cavalry scattered and broke, leaving the French infantry vulnerable, busily engaged attacking the Allied positions to their front and completely unaware of the imminent threat. Infantry caught in the open by cavalry have little chance of survival unless they form squares, something Wellington was to develop into a fine art in the Peninsula. It was a manoeuvre quite beyond these poorly trained Republican conscripts. The British infantry, fighting hard in their trenches, reported seeing lines of Allied horsemen appear suddenly over a rise to their right, and the French battalions halt, waver and break up. The French artillery turned itself 90 degrees to the left and let off a few rounds, but Schwarzenberg's third line charged straight through them. At that point the whole French force broke and fled back towards Cambrai. They found little cover in the open cornfields, and the cavalry pursued them until their horses were blown. The French lost 5,000 men, thirty-two guns and General Chapuy,

The Allies consistently underestimated the determination of the French revolutionary commanders in the war of 1793–95.

The death of Major General Mansel at Beaumont in 1794. He was determined to redeem his disgrace, and was so upset by 'the imputation on his character that he had declared he would not return alive.'

Pichegru's deputy. The Allies lost only 150 men; of these fifteen were, sadly, from The Blues, including John Kipling, a troop quartermaster, a man in his mid-thirties who had bought his commission six years before. The regiment also lost twenty-five horses, whilst The Royals lost six men killed and thirteen wounded, and twenty-seven horses. They had, however, achieved a notable success. Landrecies, now deprived of its relief force, duly surrendered, and the Duke of York sent a laudatory message back to London, saying that all the regiments involved 'have acquired immortal honour to themselves'.[25]

Sadly, matters were not going so well for the Allies elsewhere. The Austrian commander of the Allies' northern army, Clairfayt, had been heavily defeated by a French army under Pichegru at Mouscron, near Tournai, on 28 April. This endangered the British base at Ostend, and Coburg therefore sent the Duke of York's corps to Clairfayt's aid, rather than pursue Chapuy's beaten force near Cambrai. The march was terrible, with torrential rain and thunderstorms and no dry clothes or rations, since all the heavy baggage had been lost. Nevertheless by 3 May they were in position around Tournai and the River Scheldt. The Duke of York again took up his position at the Allied centre, digging in west of Tournai, and his cavalry were once more in reserve. Ralph Dundas had taken over from Mansel and now commanded The Blues and The Royals. Pichegru, with 30,000 men, advanced in three columns across the deep and boggy plain between Lille and Tournai, and let his inexperience show by repeating Chapuy's mistake at Beaumont and leaving his right flank unprotected around the main Lille–Tournai road. Again, York, and General Harcourt, now commanding the British cavalry, saw their opportunity, and slipped the three heavy brigades round to the south. They harassed the French infantry, who formed pretty ineffective squares and tried to move north towards the village of Willems. French cavalry were dispatched to help them, but were seen off, and when the accompanying battery of British horse artillery engaged the rudimentary French squares, they broke. It was a repeat of Beaumont, the British cavalry pursuing them across the boggy plain, and killing up to 2,000 French and taking 400 prisoners and fourteen guns. British casualties were again very light, The Blues losing two men and four horses. Early on in the battle, the regiment had seen a French artillery team removing a gun from the village of Baisieux, and a detachment was ordered to capture it, which they duly did. A distinguished senior French officer tried to make good his escape on a grey horse, pursued by Private Joseph White, who demanded his surrender. The Frenchman turned on him and fought him single-handedly as the regiment looked on. White, to the cheers of his comrades, eventually ran his sword through the Frenchman's body, dismounted, and took his purse and watch as trophies. Years later, White, by then an Orderly Corporal at Windsor, consistently refused George III's rather unroyal attempts to persuade him to hand the watch over.

The battle at Willems saved Tournai and the Allied northern flank in much the same way that Beaumont had saved Landrecies and Coburg, but the

Austrians were unable to turn two such resounding tactical successes to any operational effect. Again, rather than pursue the battered French army, they waited a week for the Emperor to arrive in Tournai and drew up elaborate plans for an offensive that divided their already numerically inferior force into eight columns. None were consequently strong enough to do much damage on their own, and the staffwork and coordination required to bring them into action at the same time were quite beyond the capabilities of the Austrian headquarters. The Duke of York's corps moved into Roubaix, where Clairfayt's corps should have supported them, but he delayed. Pichegru, no doubt encouraged by the prospect of the guillotine should he fail a third time, realized York was vulnerable and immediately attacked him in force. York had to withdraw, and by 29 May the Allies were back where they had begun. The Emperor returned to Vienna, leaving something of a crisis in Austrian morale, and the Allied campaign effort lapsed.

For The Royals, who had been constantly on the move for two months, the rest in temporary quarters behind Tournai was welcome, and 'wine was cheap, eggs cost a half-penny a dozen, and occasional race-meetings afforded relaxation'.[26] On 14 June over 200 officers took part in one of these, riding their own horses; the Duke of York himself attended, and privates swamped the course, 'pints of gin in hand'. The French, too, were equally inactive for a period, although when they resumed the offensive, the Allies were ill-prepared. By July they had been forced back into The Netherlands, and the British force spent a miserable and cold winter retreating to the River Yssel. There was little forage or food, the population was distinctly hostile, and the Austrians were not prepared to fight.

The cavalry saw no action during this depressing time, which they spent in 'miserable villages which provide no comfort for the soldier',[27] and by March they had been forced back over the Ems into Germany. The French, having made peace with Prussia and wanting to avoid war in Westphalia, did not follow, and so the British withdrew to Hanover. Pitt wanted the infantry for his planned support for French Royalist uprisings in Brittany and La Vendée, but the cavalry remained until the autumn of 1795, probably because George III wanted British troops in Hanover and he distrusted the Prussians, but it made for a boring year for The Blues and The Royals. They occupied themselves by acquiring and schooling black Hanoverian horses, ideal for heavy cavalry, and offloaded their existing ones to the Light Dragoons. The Royals finally embarked by boat from Stade, at the mouth of the Elbe, in early November, with fourteen officers, 225 non-commissioned officers and men, 220 horses, twenty-two wives, eleven children and eight servants – entered in that order of priority in the manifest. The Blues travelled on the same shipping and finally reached Northampton in November, to find that they had a new Colonel. Seymour Conway had died that July, and was now replaced by the Duke of Richmond, who had long coveted the post.

Chapter Twelve

FASHION IN WINDSOR AND CAMPAIGNING IN SPAIN

WELLINGTON'S ACID COMMENT on the campaign of 1793–5, in which he commanded the 33rd Foot, was that the British army had learned 'what not to do, which is always something'. Whilst the cavalry had distinguished itself, the same could not be said of many of the hurriedly recruited infantry battalions, whose discipline was poor during that awful winter in Holland, or for the supply and medical arrangements. More importantly, a generation of officers, Wellington included, returned convinced that widespread reform was needed for any chance of defeating France, and this was before Napoleon had reorganized the French army himself. The Duke of York, who had proved a perfectly competent and occasionally inspired field commander, was to be made Commander-in-Chief in 1798, and, despite 'his gambling, his notorious womanizing, and the enormous expense of his racing stables',[1] he was to prove remarkably effective.

He began by procuring better weapons through the Ordnance. In 1796, new cavalry swords, heavy and light, were introduced to replace the old Seven Years War ones that were as useless in the Revolutionary War as they had been at Dettingen and Warburg. The new heavy cavalry sword issued to the Life Guards, The Blues and The Royals, was a derivation of the old sword with a stronger blade, a better edge – easier to sharpen – and an improved hilt. However, it was never as popular as the new light cavalry sword, a curved sabre-like affair, which many Household Cavalrymen were to carry instead of their issued heavy models. Both were thought to be too short, and indeed, importantly, were 6 inches shorter than the French heavy cavalry equivalent which was to lead to casualties in hand-to-hand fighting. A new carbine, the Nock Pattern Heavy Cavalry Carbine, was issued the same year, and was hung from a sling bar and placed in a holster at the front right side of the saddle. Henry Nock, the English gun-maker who cornered the Government market, also produced a new heavy cavalry pistol, with a 9-inch barrel – and later, a refined version for the Life Guards – which, through some genius of planning in the Ordnance

Department, required different cartridges to the carbine. The fronts and backs or cuirasses, as they were now called after the French, issued in Flanders, were cumbersome and afforded little protection against French musketry and were, therefore, abandoned for active service in the Peninsular War of the early 1800s, which had comparatively few heavy cavalry engagements. So when the Household Cavalry came up against the French cuirassiers, in good-quality steel, at Waterloo in 1815, they were vulnerable, whilst the cuirassiers were well protected. A board of generals also looked at uniform, and in all our regiments the old-fashioned but comfortable long coats, which had changed little since the mid-seventeenth century, were replaced with a tight-fitting waist-length tunic called a coatee. This was intended to be more practical, but inevitably commanding officers' desire for their men to look smart on parade meant that the coats were cut too tight and they became restrictive. New jackboots were also introduced, hollowed out behind the knee to make them easier to pull off, but, as we shall soon see, were considered to be of inferior quality by older soldiers. The old cocked hat was retained, but was now to be worn back to front as opposed to sideways, a reform of questionable practical value.

Perhaps the most significant of the ensuing reforms was the introduction of barracks, which allowed regiments to be stationed together in peacetime for collective training. The Life Guards, despite their reorganization in 1788, still lived in the same pubs in London as their forebears in 1660. Their quarters, as the King's Life Guard, had to be within easy riding distance of the various royal palaces and of Horse Guards, and so in 1798 it was determined that their headquarters at Knightsbridge would become proper barracks for the 1st Life Guards, whilst a temporary building was rented in King Street, off Portman Square, for the 2nd Life Guards. This was entirely unsuitable, and in 1812 a second new barracks in Albany Street, off Regent's Park, was controversially proposed. The more radical Members of Parliament felt the establishment of 'a Praetorian Camp in London grated the people's feelings' and the popular newspaper, *The Pilot*, wrote that they were 'likely to be converted into so many fortresses of the Crown, formidable to the freedom of the people'.[2] Whilst the timing was not ideal – the Duke of York was in one of his periodic bouts of unpopularity, and the Life Guards had been somewhat heavy-handed over the arrest of the radical Member of Parliament, Sir Francis Burdett, of which more later – ultimately the proposals were passed. Future generations of Life Guards would probably wish they had not been, as the resulting Regent's Park Barracks was cramped and uncomfortable, and remained in use as a cavalry barracks until 1945.[3]

The repercussions for The Blues were also significant, as they resulted in a permanent home in Windsor. George III had a particular liking for the regiment, as had his grandfather, and on their return from Hanover they provided his guard as he took his customary seaside holiday at Weymouth, for it was

The Life Guards after 1788, showing their ceremonial (*above left*) and stable dress (*above right*).

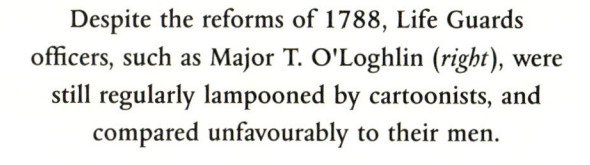

Despite the reforms of 1788, Life Guards officers, such as Major T. O'Loghlin (*right*), were still regularly lampooned by cartoonists, and compared unfavourably to their men.

feared that French privateers might kidnap him. In the summers of 1797, 1798 and 1799 they camped in Windsor Great Park, beside what is now Swinley Bottom on Ascot Racecourse, and in 1800 George III acquired 14 acres in Clewer, on the outskirts of the town, but close to the Castle. Over the next four years a permanent barracks was built, with sixty-two rooms for soldiers; eight soldiers shared a room, two to a bed until Wellington introduced single beds for the whole army in 1826.

Not only had The Blues now said goodbye for ever to their nomadic lifestyle, but the move to Windsor came during a period of fundamental change, which had developed over the previous two decades, and which also affected the Life Guards and The Royals. As with the Life Guards, Blues' officers no longer bought commissions as financial investments. Indeed, once the regiment was in Windsor, life rapidly became very expensive for the officers. Quite apart from the 1788 increase in the cost of commissions, the stagnating rates of pay and the cost of their two chargers and uniform, they now faced an expensive mess and social life, in which it was difficult not to participate. By the early nineteenth century their pay went nowhere near to meeting these costs. There had always been wealthy officers in The Blues, though by no means exclusively, and in the past those who could afford it had purchased more senior rank. Now even junior officers required a private income. The new class of officer bought a commission from a mixture of motives. First, there was a genuine desire, particularly during the French wars, to serve the country – a sort of social reimbursement by those for whom the industrial and agricultural revolutions had provided ample funds and time, and who had a vested interest in the stability of British society. Second, some sought prestige, court connections and social standing to match their newfound wealth. Third, and as always, there were those who loved the life and who scraped together the money to enable them to live it.

The officers now also adhered to a more sequential career pattern. The average age for cornets joining in the 1790s was eighteen, and they served for a period in that rank and then left, or else purchased their way up through the regiment. The old-style cornet in his fifties, often an ex-quartermaster or non-commissioned officer, who could not afford to progress, was now gone. Robert Hill, who later commanded the regiment at Waterloo, purchased a cornet's place, aged sixteen, in June 1794. In 1797 he purchased a lieutenancy, and a captaincy in 1800. He was major by 1805 and lieutenant colonel and commanding officer in 1813, aged thirty-five. Robert Packe, killed at Waterloo, purchased a cornetcy in 1799, aged eighteen, and was a major by 1813, aged thirty-two. Another change was that some were now buying quartermaster's positions – still King's commissioned officers in The Blues – in their late twenties and early thirties. Most remained quartermasters, serving for an average of about fifteen years, although some, like John Elley, were an exception. His father ran a pub, Furnival's Inn, and Elley had previously been apprenticed to a tanner. However, he soon tired of tanning and in 1790, aged seventeen, persuaded his father to buy him a quartermaster's commission. He spent four years as a troop quartermaster and did so well at Beaumont and Willems that he was 'gazetted' as a cornet, in other words promoted without purchase, and served throughout the long year in Holland and Hanover. In 1801 he became a captain, commanding a troop, and by 1808 was lieutenant colonel and commanding officer. He was well respected by Wellington, whom he served as Assistant Adjutant General of Cavalry in the Peninsula War. He filled the same role at Waterloo, was successively made a major and then a lieutenant general, and was finally knighted. On retirement he became Member of Parliament for Windsor and sat in Parliament until his death, aged sixty-six. The habit of officers progressing through the ranks by buying commissions in other regiments was also dying out and most now tended to stay in the regiment they originally joined. Of those joining The Blues in 1780s and 1790s, only nine transferred out, four of whom went to the Life Guards.

An effort was also made to improve officers' training. An introductory programme was arranged for young officers on joining. They had to pay 5 guineas to the Riding Master for instruction in military riding and breaking horses, and 2 guineas for sword and carbine instruction. They then studied a list of military books and manuals, including *Regulations for the Formation and Movement of the Cavalry*, and spent a year at regimental headquarters before joining a troop. By 1802 The Blues were even subscribing to a new military journal, *The British Military Library*, which included learned articles on French tactics and fortifications. Yet this programme was probably not very strictly observed. The problem that The Blues had, in common with many cavalry regiments, was that it was particularly difficult to attract cornets. Wartime usually produced enough volunteers, but peacetime service was considered boring and it was difficult to keep energetic young officers enthusiastic, especially when they had to pay out £1,200 for the privilege. As the Duke of Northumberland, then Colonel, wrote to Lieutenant Colonel Robert Hill, just before the regiment departed for the Peninsula, 'It is lucky that we have got cornets sufficient to compleat the two squadrons',[4] whilst in November 1813 Lord Harrington, Colonel of the 1st Life Guards, was forced to write to the Prince Regent 'to represent to HRH the impossibility I have experienced for a considerable time past of finding purchasers for cornetcies at the present regulated price of £1,200 and the necessity I have in consequence been lately under of exacting from officers quitting the Regiment by sale an agreement that their cornetcies shall be disposed of at half price'. He asks for the price of commissions to be reduced or 'I fear many cornetcies may remain vacant for years to come.'[5]

The type of soldier joining was also changing. They were younger; the average age for those joining in the 1780s and 1790s was nineteen, and though it was technically for life, most left within twenty years. The oldest serving man in the regiment at Waterloo, for example, was Joseph Holdsworth, who, at forty-two, was one of very few who had fought in Flanders in the 1790s. Desertion, never a serious problem in the cavalry, was almost unheard of, with only one or two recorded desertions between 1790 and 1815. The men were also now coming from different backgrounds. The growth of cities negated the old practice of regimental recruiting teams riding around country villages signing up bored farm labourers. Recruiters now concentrated on the industrial centres, where there was available manpower, particularly during lean times for manufacturers. In the 1780s, for example, 70 per cent of those joining The Blues were ex-weavers, put out of work through advancing technology. There was a broader spread of previous professions in the 1790s, but weaving still predominated. Recruitment was technically from all over the country, a Blues' tradition, as in the Life Guards and The Royals, and still is to this day, unlike other cavalry regiments who recruit from specific geographical areas. However, the Industrial Revolution meant that recruiting teams found the north of England the most fertile ground. One hundred and seventy-four soldiers joined the regiment between 1790 and 1799, an average of eighteen each year, and sixty-two of them were from industrial towns in Yorkshire. Height, appearance and character were important, and the vast majority of the men were over 5 feet 11 inches tall. Every recruit 'must produce testimonials on joining that prove their previous life to have been unimpeachable'.[6] A preference remained to recruit trumpeters from Germany and Holland where they were thought to have a better ear for martial music, and this trend continued when the regiment formed a full-time band under a Herr Stohwasser. Of six trumpeters recruited in the 1790s, two were German, two Dutch and the rest English. In the early 1800s the practice developed of recruiting boys as trumpeters and musicians, so that two privates are shown on the rolls in 1807 aged just seven and eight. One of the Life Guards trumpeters who blew the fatal charge at Waterloo was only thirteen. Soldiers very rarely changed troops, even when they were promoted, and they kept, where possible, the same horse all through their service. The most able were promoted to corporal within about five years. Those with an educated background were promoted more quickly, reflecting the amount of accounting work non-commissioned officers had to cope with. Thomas Bell, for example, a silversmith who joined, aged twenty-two, in 1806, had been promoted to corporal major by Waterloo. He died of his wounds on 12 July 1815.

On 25 March 1802 the Peace of Amiens was signed, ending the war with France. Britain relinquished her control over all the territories she had won, except Trinidad and Ceylon. Malta was returned to the Knights of St John of Jerusalem; Egypt and the Cape of Good Hope were given up. In return, the French agreed to evacuate Italy. The peace treaty marked the high point of Henry Addington's short, three-year ministry. He also did much to rationalize the nation's finances. In August 1802, Napoleon Bonaparte was elected First Consul for life and began to build up the French army despite the cessation of hostilities with Britain. In October, Napoleon organized an insurrection in Switzerland; Addington promised money and moral support to the Swiss if they chose to fight, and also delayed the evacuation of British troops from the various colonies that had been agreed in the peace treaty. However, he was both unwilling and unable to take any further action. Britain and France argued over the terms of the Peace of Amiens: neither side was keeping the terms of the treaty and it became clear that the war would be resumed. Unfortunately for Britain, Addington had been so convinced the peace would be permanent that he had reduced the size of both the army and the navy in an attempt to save money, and so when the war resumed on 18 May 1803, Britain was ill-prepared.

The regiment of Blues that moved into Clewer barracks in 1804 was therefore, as we have seen, very different to that which set out for Belgium ten years earlier. It was also, for the first time, a regiment that produced detailed standing orders to govern its daily activity and training. 'Stables parades', for example, happened four times a day, at 6 a.m. (or 7 a.m. in the winter), noon, 4 p.m. and 7 p.m. Horses were led out for water first thing and then fed. Oats and hay were issued and some hay chopped up to be fed as chaff. The morning was taken up with riding school, where a riding master, who was a quartermaster, supervised instruction. Field days, when the whole regiment paraded in marching order and rehearsed drills in Windsor Great Park or on Winkfield Plain, took place every Friday. After grooming the horses were always rugged up, summer and winter. Troop administration and running of the stables was very much the troop quartermaster's responsibility. He ensured horses were properly cared for and had their regimental number clipped with scissors under their saddle; later, this would be stamped on their feet when shoeing, as is still done today. He also had to maintain a Troop Book showing 'of the Corporals and Privates, who are the most active and intelligent in skirmishing and in the sword exercise', a 'list of married women who are considered as belonging to the troop', and who shared the troop accommodation with the men, and a list 'of malefactors together with punishments'. These ranged from 'Close confinement for 3 days' for being drunk and unfit for parade, to two extra guards for galloping a horse in the street. Soldiers' hair now had to be cut short in front and at the sides, 'the hair behind tied in a queue with black ribband the knot of which must come to the middle of the coat collar'.[7] Messes were now created for the corporals and in 1802, the senior Troop Corporal Major, Varley, was made Regimental Corporal Major, responsible for the mess and the overall conduct of the corporals. He was referred to as Mr Varley, in honour of his increased status, a custom still in use. The two regiments of Life Guards followed suit in 1805, with Mr Howarth assuming the appointment for the 1st Life Guards and Mr Easterby for the 2nd Life Guards.

Much work was also done to improve military equitation, even more necessary now that recruits tended to be from the industrial towns. William Tyndale, Major of the 1st Life Guards, took Lord Pembroke's and John Floyd's work and turned it into a series of specific lessons for training soldiers and horses.[8] His recommended course trained a recruit in equitation and stable duties within three months, and a young remount in ten weeks. His concept was that 'this work should be so plain and simple that the commander of a regiment of cavalry, though he may never have served before but in the infantry, shall have it in his power to say to his Riding master, "This, Sir, is the mode of instruction you are to adopt."' Tyndale bemoaned the English style of hunting riding of most officers, which was not well suited to the exactness required of modern cavalry. 'I cannot help observing', he continued, 'how few and trifling the instructions are which most regiments give a young officer, who though he may have led the field with fox hounds, and rode over turnpike gates in his native county, is in all probability totally unacquainted with the method of riding which is necessarily adopted in regiments of cavalry.' Wellington would come to sympathize with Tyndale in the Peninsula, but his work did some good at least. He also pioneered the idea of having two bits on a military bridle, or head kit as it is referred to. One was a light bridoon for watering and daily exercise, whilst the second was a strong curb bit that enabled his young recruits trained in just three months to stop. The style of the head kits was also developed so that after exercise or a march the bits and reins could be detached, leaving the horse in a head collar with attached chain, the so-called 'Bright Chain' still used by the Household Cavalry today, and by which it could be tethered to a stake in the field or, in barracks, to its stall ring.

George III took an enormous interest in his regiment once he had got them to Windsor. He appointed himself Captain of the King's Troop, a decision logically difficult to question however inconvenient, and had the Troop Orderly Corporal report to him daily in Windsor Castle. When he was at Windsor he would wear the regiment's blue uniform coat, with red facings and collar, the 'Windsor Uniform', as it came to be called, which members of the Royal Family still wear when at Windsor today. By this stage in his life the King was well past his first bout of madness, but was still decidedly eccentric. He was in the habit of walking over the Great Park to the barracks in the early morning and turning up unannounced for parade, which must have been rather testing for the commanding officer and officers, who now had to be rather more regular in their own attendance than they might otherwise have been. Should the commanding officer bring the regiment to attention to salute him, the King would say, 'No! No! No! Colonel, I am just Captain King.' On the other hand, if he ignored him, after a few minutes of drill the King would call out, 'No! No! Colonel, not like that. You do it this way.' On one occasion he arrived on the parade ground to find no officers at all, and went to the mess to investigate. The door was locked, so he went round

Duelling continued to be a serious problem amongst the officers. An officer in The Royals even challenged his Brigade Commander to a duel in Dundalk in 1809 – not a particularly inspired idea on their departure for the Peninsula.

All our regiments were badly affected by officers gambling, a fashionable contemporary evil that The Blues found a particular problem prior to the Peninsular War.

to the dining-room window where he found very bleary-eyed officers having breakfast in their nightcaps after a particularly heavy dinner the night before. He climbed through the window and gave them the benefit of his opinion on overindulging. He also gave the regiment a magnificent pair of silver kettle-drums at an elaborate parade prior to the annual Garter Service on St George's Day in 1805. Majors Elley and Miller escorted him on to the parade ground, wearing his regimental uniform, while the band played 'Britons, Strike Home', a very patriotic song popular until 'Rule Britannia' and the National Anthem became fashionable, and which went:

> Britons, Strike Home! Avenge your Country's Cause!
> Protect your King! Your Liberty! Your Laws!

The new drums were so heavy that the existing drum horses, used to the existing wood and canvas drums, were unable to carry them, and the riding master was sent off to locate more substantial animals, establishing the tradition of shire drum horses in the Household Cavalry. The drums are still in daily use.

The Blues also found that their popularity with George III and now permanent location at Windsor, where the court spent much of its time, made them rather fashionable. This had its disadvantages. Some officers wanted to join almost as an excursion, like Godfrey Meynell, already a captain in the Derbyshire Militia, who joined in February 1800 but left by July 1801. It also attracted several of the wrong sorts of people, and one of these was definitely deemed to be Edward Goulburn, who joined in 1803 and resigned in 1805 under something of a cloud. Goulburn's crime was that he wrote a highly satirical and, it has to be said, very entertaining poem sending up all the regiment's officers, that instantly became a bestseller in London. Called *The Blueviad*, and modelled on Pope's *Dunciad*, Goulburn sent up every officer from the Lieutenant Colonel, Dorrien, down to the cornets.

Goulburn seems to have made few friends in the regiment, and any he had he certainly lost once his poem was published. He reserved especial malice for John Horsley, the son of a city banker, who was called Bluster, and who:

> With looks ill-tempered, fraught with gloomy pride,
> Bluster next rears his gross and pampered hide.
> The face bespeaks the man, at once we see,
> The bloated remnants – of a debauchee.

After Goulburn left the regiment, Horsley saw him riding in London and shook his whip at him, not a very serious insult today, but in 1805 it was certainly taken as such. Goulburn immediately challenged Horsley, saying that his honour had been insulted, and demanded satisfaction in a duel. Duelling was still common, though, coming from Goulburn, who had very obviously

The Royals' uniform was changed in accordance with the prevailing fashion and the comfortable old-fashioned loose-fitting coats were replaced with tight coatees, and they now wore absurdly large cocked hats.

Henry Bernard Chalon, an officer of 1st Life Guards in 1796. After the creation of the two regiments of Life Guards in 1788 the old byzantine rank structure of the Life Guard troops was replaced.

insulted everyone, the challenge did seem a bit rich. Horsley consulted widely among his brother officers, whose advice was to decline Goulburn's challenge as unworthy. However, Goulburn then put up a series of placards around London calling Horsley a coward. The officers, led by the Duke of Richmond, then changed their tune and advised Horsley to fight Goulburn, but he still refused. It became such an issue in London that Richmond had to see the King at Weymouth. His view was that Horsley must resign, which he duly did, not having much option in the circumstances, but then, to the regiment's even more acute embarrassment, Horsley published his own version of what had happened, which also promptly became a bestseller. There was a similar incident in the Life Guards the following year, when Michael Lynch, a sub-lieutenant, brought an action against Alexis Thompson and other officers of the 2nd Life Guards for forcing him to resign his commission after he had refused a challenge from Captain Macnamara. The case was tried by Lord Ellenborough before a special jury, who found for Lynch, to whom they awarded £1,000 damages.

Goulburn's type was not the only one to leave in a hurry. Both the Life Guards and The Blues found there were several officers whose debts got out of hand. In Robert Hill's correspondence there are some sad letters from the parents of these miscreants that reflect the shame they felt at their sons' waste of the potential a place in either regiment offered. The unfortunate Mr Marsack, for example, writes sadly to Hill from his house at Caversham Park that his son must leave as he is inextricably involved with a gambling ring and 'had he grasped in his memory the principles I laid down for his guidance he would have pursued a very opposite course . . . his mother's mind is full of anxiety and foreboding evils'.[9] Entertaining as the whole *Blueviad* episode may have been for the chattering classes in London, and common as indebtedness was in early-eighteenth-century cavalry regiments, it was all pretty unedifying for the regiment as a whole, and the likes of Elley and Hill, who commanded in succession after the rather ineffective Dorrien, felt that all this gossip was obscuring a fighting tradition that included every campaign since 1660, except one. They were determined to tighten things up, and succeeded admirably, though they had to wait until 1812 for their next operational deployment.[10]

While the Life Guards reorganized themselves in London, and The Blues at Windsor, The Royals had, since 1795, enjoyed agreeable postings in Dorchester, West Sussex, Colchester, Woodbridge, York and Edinburgh, which they particularly enjoyed, before moving to Dundalk for a spell of Irish service in 1807. The social pressures outlined above similarly pertained to them, of course, though they were not always to be quartered together in the same barracks. They were also spared some of the more acute problems of Windsor, although they had their fair share of trouble, including an officer who challenged his brigade commander to a duel, not a particularly inspired idea, as the same brigade commander, General Sir John Slade, was to be the regiment's brigade commander in the Peninsula. The regiment's uniform was changed, in accordance with the prevailing fashion, and the comfortable old-fashioned loose-fitting coats were replaced with tight coatees, and they now wore absurdly large cocked hats instead of the helmets issued to the light cavalry.

Ralph Heathcote, who purchased a cornetcy in June 1806 for £735, and whose father had been George III's Minister Plenipotentiary to Hesse Cassel, gives us a good, if romantic, idea of what daily life was like in these various stations from his letters to his mother, who lived in Germany.[11] Either Heathcote was slightly priggish, or The Royals at the time were a model of virtue, which seems unlikely. Heathcote found his brother officers 'perfectly well bred, polite and gentlemanly men, some indeed far superior to most people I have seen . . . You would be astonished to hear that many of [them] know German and Italian: all know French'. He tells his mother of the excellent travelling library near the barracks in Edinburgh, of how 'drinking in the Mess is very uncommon' and how, after dinner at 5 p.m., for which, if you were late, you were fined a bottle of wine, no matter what your rank, the officers discussed politics, foreign travel and similar topics. The mess dinner was excellent and not expensive, and his lodging, coal, and candles were provided free, whilst he found his forage allowance of a guinea per horse per month quite adequate. He does describe his duties more accurately. Apart from parades and field days, not much was expected from him. His troop sergeant-major produced a list of words of command he should master before assuming control of his men, but advised there was no need to learn them, unless he was keen to, as the men knew what to do anyway. Officers, he wrote, 'are not teased with the minutiae of the service', and he preferred the German system whereby young officers were taught as privates before they were allowed to be commissioned. He did note, with some perception, that 'should the Government decide to send a force to the Continent it will do wonders and convince the foreign officers that the army of 1806 is no longer the same as that of 1793'.

His point was about to be proven. While The Royals were settling comfortably into Irish life in Dundalk, Sir John Moore's British Expeditionary Force to Spain was evacuating Corunna. The Royals expected to be called forward, but on marching to Cork they were stood down. However, the British Government's decision to re-engage in the Peninsula, and Wellington's victory at Talavera in July 1809, made their deployment only a matter of time. Eight troops, each augmented to eighty men, sailed on 2 September 1809, arriving in Lisbon ten days later after a quicker and easier voyage than the last time they had landed on the River Tagus, just over 100 years before.

The British engagement to help the Portuguese and Spaniards eject Napoleon's forces and brother, the impostor King Joseph, from the Peninsula was exactly the strategy Pitt the Younger had so long sought, and combined a realistic assessment of British military capability with an achievable strategic goal. Just as important, Britain now produced in Wellington an operational commander who understood that strategy. Like all great British commanders, he realized the British army lacked the strength to act unaided in Europe and operated best as part of a coalition. His genius, like Marlborough's, lay as much in convincing his coalition partners of his operational concept, and retaining their support as he executed it, as it did in tactics on the battlefield itself. The recent military reforms also rendered his 31,000 British troops, as Heathcote so perceptively noticed, considerably more battleworthy than they had been fifteen years earlier. The army drawn up by Wellington was formed into different organized units. A corps consisted of around 15,000 men, made up of divisions of approximately 7,000 men, each in turn made up of brigades of about 3,000 men, and each of those made up of regiments of either 500 cavalry or 1,000 infantry. Wellington initially had only one division of 3,000 cavalry in Portugal, commanded by Stapleton Cotton, later Viscount Combermere and Colonel of the 1st Life Guards, and after whom Clewer Barracks in Windsor was ultimately to be renamed. Cotton had four brigades under him, and The Royals were deployed in Slade's brigade with the 14th Light Dragoons and Bull's Troop of the Royal Horse Artillery, with whom they got on very well. The French had considerably more cavalry, and at first Wellington had to use his scarce resource carefully.[12]

The Peninsular War tactics are best explained in Wellington's dictum that 'as long as we continue in Portugal the contest must continue in Spain', while his ultimate aim was the defeat of the French forces and their ejection from the whole Iberian Peninsular. It is impossible to follow without a map, and the plan on p. 289 refers to these next stages. By the time The Royals arrived, most of the 31,000 British and 26,000 Portuguese forces were stationed around Lisbon and the Tagus valley, with some forces forward on the frontier. Furthermore, the installation of Joseph Bonaparte as King had so infuriated the Spanish peasantry that Wellington had at his disposal a new type of soldier, and the word 'guerrilla' entered into the vocabulary. The Spanish irregulars knew their homeland very well and hid in the hills, constantly raiding French convoys. Even messengers needed brigade-sized escorts to prevent successful ambushes, and through such ambushes, Wellington learned the contents of many of Napoleon's 'secret' communiqués.

Wellington had defeated Napoleon's Marshal Victor Perrin at Talavera in July 1809, but his Spanish allies' weakness, his own supply problems and a second French army to the north, under Soult, meant he felt unable to follow up his success. He consequently fell back towards Lisbon and the coast and the French did not pursue, preferring the softer option of invading Andalusia. It was not until 1810 that Massena finally invaded Portugal and attacked the British army, without whose support the Portuguese would have surrendered. By then Wellington was ready with a carefully planned operation to draw the French on to his prepared positions at Torres Vedras, force them to besiege it through the winter and stretch their long and tenuous supply lines back to

George III was particularly fond of The Blues, finding them a permanent home in Windsor and appointing himself a Captain in the regiment. He regularly wore their uniform, as here, which he adopted as court dress whilst at Windsor and which the royal family still wear as 'Windsor uniform'.

The Royals arrived on the River Tagus in Portugal in September 1809. They were to stay in the Peninsula for five years.

Spain, while local food and forage would have already been requisitioned or destroyed. His hope was that by the spring of 1811 Massena's army would be in no position to fight and could then be harassed and ultimately defeated, as it struggled back into Spain. It was a clever plan which was ultimately to work well, but first the Allies had to survive Massena's initial attack. This came in June 1810, as he advanced on the border fortress of Ciudad Rodrigo with 138,000 men.

Until then The Royals had found life remarkably pleasant. The horses had survived the sea voyage well, and they were quartered at Belem, described, predictably, by Heathcote as 'magnificent barracks and stables' where they 'enjoyed the luxuries of a delightful climate'. Wellington inspected them in October, writing, in a fit of rare generosity, that he 'had never seen a finer regiment. They are very strong, the horses in very good condition and the regiment apparently in high order.'[13] They moved forward up the Tagus valley in February 1810, in reaction to a false alarm, and remained around Belmonte, a small town about 30 miles west of the Spanish border. Massena took Ciudad Rodrigo, the fortress on the Spanish side of the border, on 10 July, and then besieged Almeida, its Portuguese counterpart, which fell, prematurely, on 26 August, after an ammunition explosion wrecked part of its defences. Wellington withdrew down the Mondego and Tagus valleys towards Torres Vedras, and The Royals had their first action, protecting the withdrawal and harassing the French advance cavalry patrols. On 28 August Major Dorville's squadron had success against a much larger French force, drawing special praise from Wellington. They were commended once more for holding a bridge over the River Criz near St Comba Dao in late September. Although not actually involved in the Battle of Busaco on 27 September, where Wellington made a stand against Massena, they were in action every day thereafter until the Allies finally slipped behind the prepared positions of Torres Vedras on 11 October.

Torres Vedras was a series of three lines of fortifications prepared by Wellington's engineers the previous winter. These ran between the Tagus and the sea, and were designed both to halt the French and to give the Allies a chance to refit in comparative safety. As a precaution, the third, and final, line, protected embarkation beaches near St Julian. Spanish and Portuguese troops and British Royal Marines manned the forts, allowing the field army to recuperate. And The Royals needed it. Torrential rain had overwhelmed the last few weeks of the withdrawal and many horses had lost shoes in the knee-deep mud and were lame, so by mid-October, 100 were useless. Twenty men had died in action and a further five from disease, and fifty-nine men are shown as sick on the return for 12 October. Private Helliar, in Captain Lamott's Troop, had been swept away in the River Maimoa, and the surgeon, Mr Steed, nearly drowned trying to save him. Lieutenant Colonel de Grey, the Commanding Officer, had been promoted to command a brigade in May, and the genial Wyndham took over and had, rather unfortunately, gone astray while inspecting troops and

THE PENINSULA
1809–1814
FRANCE
Toulouse
April 1814
Orthez
Bayonne
Santander
Corunna
R. Nive
Vitoria
June 1813
Logroño
Life Guards, Blues and Royals Route 1813
Burgos
R. Pisurga
R. Ebro
Lerida
Barcelona
Royals
Winter 1811–1812
R. Duero
Valladolid
Oporto
R. Douro
Salamanca
July 1812
Almeida
Busaco
Fuentes de Onoro
May 1811
Madrid
Mondego Valley
Life Guards and Blues
arrive Nov. 1812
R. Tagus
Talavera
27–28 July 1809
Abrantes
S P A I N
Torres Vedras
1810
R. Guadiana
Badajoz
Lisbon
Belem
Albuera
Royals Summer 1812
Zafra
Maguilla 1812
ANDALUSIA
Llerena
R. Guadalquivir
Royals arrive
September 1809
Cordova
PORTUGAL
Mediterranean Sea
Cadiz
N
0 50 100 150 200 miles
0 100 200 300 km

mistakenly ridden up to a French post and was captured. The regiment found Slade slow and tiresome as a brigade commander, and were particularly incensed that he had sequestered all the wine from the village of Leria, under the pretence that it was for The Royals, while drinking it all himself.

Slade, who kept a rather sketchy diary of his time in the Peninsula,[14] emerges as a complex character. He had spent much time in The Royals himself, and clearly liked them, but had been understandably upset by the duelling incident in Dundalk. He felt the regiment was now less disciplined and wrote that they are 'rather unruly'. However, he had a keen eye for interesting stories and details of life in Portugal. He mentions how gentlemanly the French cavalry were, noting that 'as a Corporal of the Royal Dragoons was posting his videttes [scouts] one morning, a French Dragoon galloped up to within twenty yards of him, dropped a cloak, a man of The Royals had lost the day before, and retired', perhaps also revealing the regard in which the French held the accuracy of the Nock heavy cavalry pistol at 20 yards. Slade thought little of the Portuguese.

> The men in Portugal are by no means good looking and the difference between them and the Spaniards is most marked. The Portuguese are short and fat in the extreme. The fair sex in Portugal have the same fault with the men – being very diminutive and corpulent. It is by no means uncommon to see a lover laying his head in the lap of his mistress, who is employed in taking the lice from his hair.

However, he approved of Portuguese oranges, oxen, partridges and pigs, but found their veneration for the Catholic Church astonishing. 'A regiment of Portuguese Infantry was standing in open column, the [consecrated] Host passed along their rear, on which they all went to the "right about", fell on one knee, their firelocks resting on the ground and their caps off' in respect.

During that winter, behind the lines of Torres Vedras, the lieutenants and cornets in The Royals formed a 'club'. The idea was to meet together and gossip about the goings-on in the regiment during the cold Iberian winter. Henry Stisted was appointed secretary. His job was to write the Club minutes, which are, in effect, a record of all that they got up to, officially and unofficially, between Torres Vedras and Waterloo. The resulting journal, quoted extensively here, therefore gives a very different view of the war to the drier official accounts. Some of it is, sadly, unquotable in a family history, but it does show that the regiment's main concerns were the hopeless Allied supply system, their promotion prospects, marriage possibilities, and the idiosyncrasies of senior officers, rather than the enemy. Some might argue that little has since changed.

By March 1811 the regiment had refitted. Wellington's plan had worked. Massena's supplies had diminished and he was forced to withdraw towards the Spanish frontier. The Royals marched out through Santarem, from where the

French had only recently withdrawn, and filed past Wellington as they rode over the town bridge. Captain Windsor had recently arrived with eighty remounts and 'Wellington was struck with the excellent condition of the horses, their coats so jet black and shining . . . there were not such grooms as The Royals were in those days.' Yet after a month harassing the retreating French, the horses 'exhibited the very sorrowful remains of their once boasted condition . . . their coats were long and brown and a parchment skin seem'd every instant to break'. The reasons, Stisted tells us, were '1st. the excessive hardships and fatigues, roads almost impassable, long marches, cold and wet bivouacs and 2nd. Mr House the Commissary!! Perhaps in the world there never existed a man so unfit for his place, so truly ignorant of his duty.' There are constant complaints about the uselessness of House, and the consequent shortage of forage, although it is hard to know how much it was really his fault and not the inevitable result of chronic difficulties of supply in a country now fought over for nearly four years. Stisted and the officers were also not that enamoured of their new commanding officer, Lieutenant Colonel Clifton, who had transferred from the 3rd Dragoons, something now quite unusual. The Royals would have preferred their senior major, Jervoise, to have been promoted in Wyndham's place. Known as 'Ben the Ruler', Clifton, who was to command until 1829, is portrayed as bad-tempered and crude, though it is clear he fairly soon earned the regiment's grudging respect.

The campaign of summer 1811 concentrated on pushing Massena back into Spain, but was only half successful. In December he was still in possession of Ciudad Rodrigo and Badajoz, both of which were to be stormed at great cost in early 1812. For The Royals it meant a summer of constant marches and skirmishing, and hunger.

> When the Regiment had been marching and fighting all day, and at night fall had put up in a wet camp, about half an hour afterwards Mr House would make his appearance, pitch his tent . . . he had his dinner cooked . . . would drink hot rum and water until comfortable. It was in vain that every night the poor officers and men . . . at every jingling of the mules bells thought that surely at last rations were arriv'd; but alas! Vain hopes! Mules would pass by with rum and corn and biscuit for Bull's artillery and the 14th but nothing for the poor Royals!

Remounts still arrived periodically from England and, just before the engagement at Fuentes de Oñoro – The Royals' only pitched battle that year – Cornet Sigismund Trafford wandered into the bivouac.

> About one o'clock a detachment of the regiment was seen to approach. At first it was thought to be Dorville's squadron . . . but upon examination it was found to be the remount from Lisbon, conducted by a young man of

> the name of Trafford . . . As soon as [Trafford] dismounted from his horse they took the opportunity of surveying him and of all the beings that ever join'd a regiment this was the most extraordinary. He was about 17 or 18 years of age, very tall, supported on the worst bandy legs it was possible to conceive . . . his face was long and pale . . . his dress was of the most shackling kind; an old neckcloth was loosely wound around the long neck and long jack boots sticking out of his overalls.

However, Trafford justified his extraordinary appearance a couple of days later at Fuentes de Oñoro.

Massena was determined to relieve the pressure on Almeida and Ciudad Rodrigo, the key fortresses on the main route from central Portugal to Salamanca and Madrid, which he saw as fundamental to the security of the French in Spain, and which he had taken at such cost the previous year. Consequently he decided he must rally his tired and hungry army, and surprise Wellington's force as it advanced over the border. He chose to attack at Fuentes de Oñoro, a small fortified town on the Portuguese frontier, and very nearly succeeded. Wellington admitted later it had been very close, and said that if Napoleon had been commanding as opposed to Massena, he would have lost. At dawn on 5 May, Massena's army fell on the 7th Division – a division was a group of two or more brigades – one of Wellington's less battle-hardened formations, and caught them unprepared. They were on the Allied flank, south of Fuentes and near the village of Nave de Haver. They retreated, in serious danger of being overrun by the French, and fell back to Pozo Bello, the next village north. Wellington brought Robert Craufurd's Light Division forward to deal with any further French advance, while the Allied cavalry made repeated charges into the French flank and the 7th Division extricated itself. The cavalry did particularly well, though it consisted of only two brigades against five French. 'We were but scattered drops amid their host and could not possibly arrest their progress' but they made repeated charges to assist the Light Division. The Royals found that on 5 May

> at half past three in the morning a heavy firing began on the right of the line; at half past four the piquets [troops] were driven in with considerable loss on the part of the infantry . . . Trafford much distinguished himself by a charge . . . the regiment continued the whole day drawn out in position. About 12 O'Clock the cannonade became extremely heavy, to which the regiment was expos'd for nearly four hours, altho' most fortunately every ball nearly went over the heads of the men. Several gallant charges were made during the course of the day, in one of which a Colonel Latour was taken prisoner and surrendered his sword to Gubbins [the club name for Lieutenant George Gunning in Captain Clark's Troop]. Steward the adjutant general had the impudence to declare that it was he who took the

Fuentes de Oñoro
5 May 1811

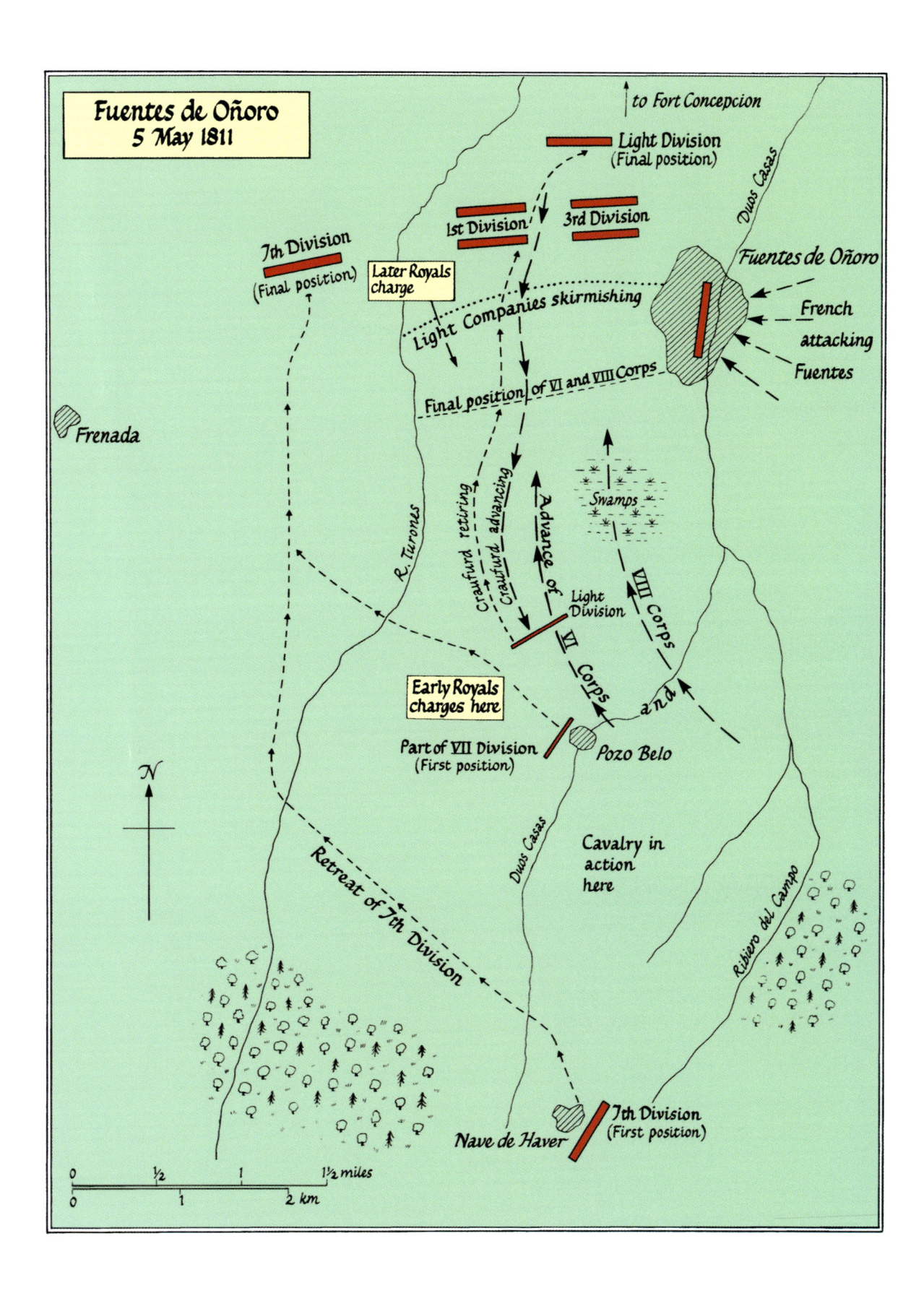

- to Fort Concepcion
- Light Division (Final position)
- 1st Division
- 3rd Division
- 7th Division (Final position)
- Later Royals charge
- Light Companies skirmishing
- Dos Casas
- Fuentes de Oñoro
- French attacking Fuentes
- Frenada
- Final position of VI and VIII Corps
- R. Turones
- Craufurd retiring
- Craufurd advancing
- Swamps
- Advance of Light Division
- VIII Corps
- VI Corps and
- Early Royals charges here
- Part of VII Division (First position)
- Pozo Belo
- N
- Dos Casas
- Cavalry in action here
- Retreat of 7th Division
- Ribiero del Campo
- Nave de Haver
- 7th Division (First position)
- 0 ½ 1 1½ miles
- 0 1 2 km

French colonel. The Secretary begs it may be known that the frenchman was knock'd off his horse in a charge with The Royals, and taken prisoner individually by the warrior Gubbins.

'Slade', adds the Secretary with some malice, 'behaved very well during the whole day except the mistake he made of ordering Bull to fire on the Brunswick Corps.' Slade himself, as always slightly immodest, thought he was in the thick of the fight all day. 'My favourite Dun mare Fidget was shot under me twice . . . and I mounted for a time the horse of my orderly dragoon. The scabbard of my sword was also shattered by a ball.' The Royals' losses were serious with four men killed, thirty-six wounded and eighteen horses killed and fifty-two wounded.

It seemed to the Allies that they had succeeded at Fuentes because Massena's army, and particularly his cavalry, were in such a poor state after their winter in front of Torres Vedras. 'Our men had evidently the advantage as individuals. Their broadswords, ably wielded, flashed over the Frenchmen's heads and obliged them to cower to the saddle bows.'[15] Another account has the French infantry half naked and without shoes, the artillery hardly able to find teams for their guns and the cavalry with hardly a horse capable of going at more than a walk.[16]

Massena's failure at Fuentes led to the fall of Almeida, though Wellington was furious its garrison escaped at night, and left the Allies free to concentrate on Badajoz. Slade's brigade was now put in reserve, and left under the Light Division outside Almeida. Here they were again attacked unexpectedly, this time by Marmont, with a vastly superior but not very motivated force. The Royals, covering the flank on which Marmont's attack fell, had what the Secretary called 'perhaps the narrowest escape the regiment ever had'. Dorville's squadron came into contact first and immediately charged the leading French patrols. They faltered, unclear as to what they were facing, and, assisted by the 14th Light Dragoons, Dorville made his escape but lost thirteen men, including his troop sergeant major with all the troop money and books. Marmont subsequently called off his attack, and lost the chance of destroying a British division.

From June The Royals were in reserve, and fairly inactive until September. It was a welcome break and they camped in a cork forest near Arronches. There was not much corn, and the horses fared badly in the heat, but the men made themselves comfortable, building huts of bark and boughs, there being very few tents in the Peninsula at this time. The local wine was strong and had to be diluted, which was fine until the local stream ran dry, leading to unsanitary conditions, so it was considered a good thing when the whole camp caught fire. Soup was served with hundreds of ants and flies floating on the surface. New clothing arrived in June, the first since their arrival in 1809, and they realized how scruffy they were, dressed in the likes of 'an old pair of yarn stockings with an old rusty spur at the heel, an old pair of shag breeches; . . . no old dustman in London ever wore so filthy or so dirty an apology for a hat, not a vestige of its former shape to be seen'. Those contemporary prints of pristine cavalrymen on finely matched horses charging into battle in perfect lines must have caused amusement when they got home.

The autumn of 1811 saw The Royals on the move again, as fresh attacks were expected on Wellington's forces, but despite Marmont's revitalization of the French army, and his joining forces with Soult, they were not to be in action again that year. In November they were sent back down to the coast near Oporto, an area which had so far been mercifully free of Allied troops, and enjoyed a relaxing winter. They would need it, for the campaign of 1812 would be their most taxing yet.

In January 1812 the French had 230,000 soldiers in Spain, so Wellington's small army of 60,000 should have been relatively easy to defeat. However, Napoleon had divided them into five different armies, each operating in a different part of the Peninsula, and ineffectively coordinated by his mild-mannered brother Joseph in Madrid. Napoleon himself was preoccupied in 1812 with his attack on Russia, and there was little attempt to enforce a coherent strategy on the competing army commanders. Wellington planned to take Ciudad Rodrigo and Badajoz, which he did in January and April 1812 respectively, defeat Massena decisively and liberate Madrid, all the while covering Soult's army in the south and preventing it from coming to Massena's aid. This last task he entrusted to General Rowland Hill, brother of Robert Hill in The Blues, and gave him a division of cavalry, under Erskine, consisting of two brigades, Long's and Slade's, which now consisted of the 3rd and 4th Dragoon Guards as well, of course, as The Royals.

Having been brought up to Ciudad Rodrigo in January in case they were needed, in February The Royals moved south with Hill's force, on a very long but attractive march, before it became too hot, and through a part of Portugal and Spain which seemed to the Secretary 'to hold its head up from the barbarism of the XIth and XIIth Centuries'. They were initially based on the borders of Portugal and Estremadura, with troops constantly detached for patrolling work, and watching for any move by Soult. He tried to join up with Massena in April, but the fall of Badajoz and Hill's quick thinking in destroying the bridge of boats over the Tagus at Almaraz stopped him. However, while Wellington was busy with Massena, Soult's cavalry were probing Hill's force and The Royals had several contacts. They thought little of Erskine, and were very fed up with Slade. Erskine was inexperienced and panicky 'in constant alarm of an attack on his cavalry screen'. Slade had got as bad. 'No sooner was it announced that the French were in motion, no matter where or at what distance, than an order was given to turn out. Jack [Slade] running about crying out, 'Haste, haste. Gallop. God damn you Corporal, tell those fellows to turn out . . . The consequence was that all was confusion.' By May the regiment had 180 men daily on 'picquet duty' in fixed positions acting as guards against surprise attack, thoroughly fed up, and surprisingly demoralized after their successes of 1811. Sadly, all this came to a head in one of the most disgraceful incidents of the Peninsular War, for which Slade must take most of the responsibility. Whilst British heavy cavalry under Le Marchant were earning lasting fame for their distinguished conduct at Salamanca, where Wellington decisively defeated Massena's army in July 1812, The Royals suffered the ignominy of defeat at Maguilla.

Hill had previously arranged with Wellington that he would launch an offensive against Soult in June, to deceive the French into believing that the main Allied thrust would be in the south. Slade's brigade led off on the road to Seville, with the aim of driving back the French cavalry screening force under Lallemand, Soult's infamous cavalry commander, to Fuente Ovejuna. D'Erlon, one of Soult's corps commanders and someone The Royals would soon meet again, had his headquarters there. Just after they had bivouacked on 11 June outside Llera, scouts brought word of a sizeable French cavalry force under Lallemand just over the hill. Slade bustled into action. 'Jack lost no time in the pursuit,' the Secretary tells us. 'The first thing he did was to take up his stirrup leathers full two holes. The next thing was to catch and make prisoner the arch rogue Lallemand himself. To this purpose he selected a determined man; The Great Gubbins.' The Warrior Gubbins was duly sent with Sergeant Hanship, 'the handsomest man in the whole regiment', and twelve soldiers in pursuit. 'However ridiculous, impossible and dangerous this order of Slade's was, it nevertheless flattered Gubbins. Away went the man of Kent. As he advanced the eyes of the whole brigade were fixed upon him. Never was man more important than Gubbins was at that moment.' Lallemand at first withdrew but, seeing that Gubbins was unsupported, turned and charged him with a full squadron. Poor Hanship and seven privates were killed, and Gubbins had to beat a hasty retreat.

Slade now 'resolved to chastise this insolence'. Instead of making a proper plan, 'he immediately pursued with the whole brigade at a hand canter'. He chased Lallemand for 12 miles, into the broken country around Maguilla. By the time The Royals and the 3rd Dragoons got there, their horses were blown and exhausted, as they were out of condition and had been fed mostly on green corn and hay. As Lallemand paused, Slade ordered a charge, despite warnings from Radclyffe and Eckersley of The Royals to be careful. As Lallemand's men fell back, a cry went up of 'Look to the right!' Lallemand's reserve, originally intended to cover his retreat, had now manoeuvred so they could take Slade's brigade in the flank, which they did. Even worse, the brigade panicked – it was now stifling hot, their horses were blown and their morale, sapped by Erskine's and Slade's numerous false alarms, was shaken. Someone, it is not known who, gave the order 'Threes About!' and the brigade turned tail and fled back towards Llera. Hulton, who had kept a squadron in reserve, charged the pursuing French

The three Hill brothers. Rowland, the eldest (*above left*), commanded a corps in the Peninsula and at Waterloo. Ennobled as Viscount Hill, he would later become Colonel of The Blues. The second brother, Robert (*above right*), joined the Blues in 1794 and commanded the regiment at Waterloo. His Silver Stick is seen below, together with a collection of sticks from the Household Cavalry Museum. Clement, the youngest brother (*right*), was Rowland's ADC at Waterloo. He was also in The Blues, later rising to the rank of Major General in the Madras Army. He died in India.

and bought some time, but 'not a man would face about; all galloped rearward as hard as their exhausted steeds could carry them, regardless of their officers'. At Valencia, 8 miles back, Slade finally halted them. Hill's carefully planned advance was in ruins. Slade's dispatch to him that evening was a masterpiece of double-speak: 'Nothing could exceed the gallantry displayed by both officers and men. The enemy brought up a support, and my troops being too eager in pursuit, we were obliged to fall back on Llera.' But Hill was not to be fooled and neither was Wellington, who was doubly furious as 'The Royals and the 3rd. DG were the best regiments of cavalry in the country . . . I do not wonder at the French boasting of it, it is the greatest blow they have struck.' The losses were dreadful: seventeen men were killed and fifteen wounded, and Lieutenant Windsor and forty-seven men were taken prisoner. One hundred and fifty out of 335 effective horses had been lost, forty of which died that night of exhaustion. Slade himself refused to accept any blame. He was required to make a full statement to Hill, which he copied into his diary, and which exonerates him and blames the men for being over-eager, which might have rung true as Wellington had frequently criticized the cavalry for their fox-hunting approach. 'The enemy defeat was complete,' he wrote, 'and I should in all probability have made two thirds Prisoners, had my people remained steady.' But Wellington was not taken in. He arranged with London to make Major General Henry Clinton, junior to Slade, a lieutenant general, which, by the odd rules of the time, precluded him from serving in the same theatre as any major generals senior to him. The snub was obvious and Slade resigned in high dudgeon, and, collecting his son from Lisbon, where he had just arrived to join the regiment, took him home with him.

The rest of that dreadfully hot summer in Estremadura was deeply depressing for The Royals. Disgraced at Maguilla, while the rest of the army was in high spirits and enjoying the comforts of Madrid, they moved to Albuera to patrol against any movement from Soult. The heat had reduced the Albuera brook to a trickle, and they had to dig holes in the dried-up swamps on its banks to get any water. Thousands of unburied and decaying bodies lay around from the Battle of Albuera the year before, and diseases soared. The Secretary rated 12 July as the worst day. The heat was unbearable, a fierce dry Sirocco wind blew, and the horses could not feed 'while a burning agony of thirst tormented them within and an oppressive atmosphere suffocated them without'. The men made shelters of their blankets and others 'laid gasping with their heads under their horses bellies . . . O ye cornets so snug this day at your depot in Canterbury . . . know that all the miseries you ever suffer'd . . . must all fall short of the horrors of the twelfth of July 1812!' Heat stroke was common and rapidly increased the sick toll. Even Dorville, now major after Jervoise's death, and renowned for his strength, was taken ill.

But there was consolation in that Soult's army was suffering as badly, and by September he had abandoned Andalusia and Estremadura, leaving Hill's army free to march to Madrid. They reached it just as Soult's and Joseph's forces combined to threaten the city with 60,000 men. Wellington had already returned to Portugal, and Hill had no option but to withdraw westwards, so no sooner had The Royals arrived than they were on the move again, on another retreat through the wet autumn weather, with morale now low. There was little fighting, but the army had suffered much in the last year, and discipline was difficult to maintain as they fell back to the Tormes and then to Agueda. Some of the horses simply couldn't cope, and were shot to prevent them falling into French hands. By December there were only 172 fit animals in the regiment, and dismounted men exceeded the mounted; they paraded each day at dawn and set off on foot so as not to fall behind. Ben the Ruler shared all these discomforts, though he annoyed the Secretary by finding time to shave every day. The retreat ended when the army was back behind the River Agueda, and Hill's troops were allocated quarters in the Tagus Valley. The Royals were quartered in the village of Sorez, which pleased them as it was miles from divisional headquarters at Alcantara, and while it was 'a miserable village in every respect', it was 'a paradise after the excessive hardships of the retreat as it very fortunately contained quantities of "long" forage [i.e. hay and straw], and before long the miserable skeletons of horses began to get the famine out of them'.

By December 1812 The Royals had been reduced to only ten effective officers; Ben the Ruler was still there, as was the Secretary, the Warrior Gubbins, Trafford, Hulton, Radclyffe, Eckersley, Clark and Heathcote. The rest had either been sent home sick or were prisoners. There were only 307 effective privates left, with sixty ill, twenty-six prisoners of war and 135 detached, mostly sent home unfit. It must have been a gloomy time, particularly as they were back where they had started in 1809. However, the strategic situation was better than they probably realized. The campaigns of 1812 had severely stretched the French, and concentrating their troops to force the Allies out of Madrid had obliged them to abandon large areas of southern Spain, including Andalusia. At the beginning of 1813, Wellington's efforts, and a growing Spanish guerrilla campaign, had left the French demoralized, short of men and supplies, and believing themselves abandoned by Napoleon, himself recovering from his disastrous Russian campaign. One more year's campaigning would see them forced out of Spain, and The Royals marching across Europe, now joined by detachments from the 1st and 2nd Life Guards and The Blues, who arrived in Portugal in November 1813 as part of Wellington's reinforcements.

It had been difficult to persuade the Prince Regent, now effectively on the throne while George III's mental state overwhelmed him, to agree to send them. He regarded both the Life Guards and The Blues as an essential part of his increasingly decorous court. At his celebrated fête, for example, on 19 June 1811, The Blues were on duty controlling the attendant crowds, the 1st Life Guards provided escorts for guests and the 2nd Life Guards were in Carlton

House, dismounted. The Blues were still not officially part of the Household Cavalry at this stage, but performed the same duties as the Life Guards, escorting the coffin of George III's favourite daughter, Princess Amelia, when she died in 1810, and providing the Prince Regent's escort when he opened Parliament in 1812. More seriously, there was concern at court about denuding London of its police force, for 1810 had seen some of the worst rioting in the city since 1780, over the attempted arrest of the radical Member of Parliament Sir Francis Burdett. He had fiercely condemned the abuse of flogging in the armed forces. After he announced that he would resist arrest, a large crowd duly gathered outside his house in Piccadilly to stop the Sheriff taking him to the Tower. Despite the Sheriff's advice, 'the two Regiments of Life Guards were then ordered out, the Riot Act was read, we were ordered to disperse the Mob, they fired on us, and shot my Right Hand Man through the thigh and wounded several others', wrote Henry Willis, a private in the 1st Life Guards. The Government overreacted and called in all troops within 100 miles of London. The next day they decided to break into Burdett's house to arrest him and take him to the Tower. Willis rode by his coach window all the way and wrote:

> From his house to the Tower we delivered him safe. The Mob were very numerous indeed and still cried Burdett forever. Bricks, stones and mud were flying very quick and a few shots, but we did not receive much injury that day. At the Tower they were so numerous that several of them were forced into the water and drowned . . . [the] military force being so strong, they were forced to disperse, some with their leggs and arms tied up and others with the contents of pistols lodged in them . . . Please do not say this came from a soldier as it is against our orders to write anything of the kind.[17]

The Government was understandably nervous, and although the Life Guards were praised by the King, it made them very unpopular in London where they were nicknamed 'the Piccadilly Butchers'. This incident also resulted in the famous Mansfield judgment. Burdett sued the Speaker of the House of Commons, Abbot, who had ordered his arrest. In his judgment on the case, Mansfield, the Chief Justice, ruled that while soldiers were bound to suppress violence when ordered, they could only do so within the law, and it was wrong 'that an Englishman, by taking upon himself the additional character of a soldier, puts off any rights and duties of an Englishman'. It merely confirmed what the Life Guards had long known, but they had now been reminded, very publicly, of the need to act legally.

Eventually Wellington's desperate need for reinforcements, and prolonged pressure from the two Gold Sticks, Harrington and Cathcart, and the Duke of Northumberland, who had taken over as Colonel of The Blues on Richmond's death in 1806, persuaded the Prince Regent to change his mind. He was not, however, prepared to forgo their services in London and ordered that both regiments of Life Guards be increased from eight to ten troops, and The Blues from six to eight, so detachments could be sent to Portugal, while they still mounted the King's Life Guard and provided escorts. Consequently four troops from each regiment embarked at Portsmouth in October 1812, forming a small Household Brigade under General Rebow, a former Life Guard officer. The expansion of the regiments was not an easy process, and engendered a prolonged battle between the Dukes of York and Northumberland.

Northumberland was an attractive character. He was to reduce his tenants' rents by a quarter in 1815 when agricultural prices fell, and was a popular and effective colonel. He had been a distinguished soldier, serving as a Horse Grenadier in the Seven Years War and then as a general in America, where he had covered the retreat from Lexington to Boston. He took a great interest in The Blues, and spent much of his considerable fortune on the band. A wonderful correspondence exists between him and Hill, the commanding officer, just after The Blues had been told they would be deploying to the Peninsular War, giving an old soldier's advice on kit. He was particularly concerned at the poor quality of the modern jackboot. Modern jackboots, he writes, 'will not answer in the Peninsula for in fact they are not really Jack Boots but a bad imitation of them'; the old ones would 'not only resist wet but are absolutely impenetrable by it'. He was also concerned, correctly as it subsequently transpired, about the cuirasses. 'Col. Elley told me [those] delivered to the Regiment when they went to Flanders were so shamefully bad that they would not even stop a pistol ball at a considerable distance. If this is the case, I should imagine it hardly worth while to apply for them. They are heavy, & cumbersome,' but 'in the Seven Years War it was far otherwise. I remember to have seen the Commanding Officer of The Black Horse, Colonel Stewart . . . with five musket shot sticking in the upper part of his cuirass, every one of which, but for his cuirass, must have killed him.'[18] Northumberland was horrified at the decision for the Life Guards and The Blues to do away with leather breeches and jackboots, except for King's Life Guard and royal escort duties, and to substitute 'blue grey pantaloons, with a scarlet seam down the outside of the leg and short boots for all duties not immediately connected with the Royal Person'. Neither would he have been keen on the new, tight-fitting, short coatees which were introduced to replace the old long-tailed coats, and worn with blue and yellow sashes by the non-commissioned officers and scarlet and gold ones by the officers, although he probably would have approved of the introduction of brass helmets with black horse-hair crests, which, though rather large and ornamental, gave some protection to the head at least.

Northumberland's old-fashioned views also led him to believe, rather more seriously, that the Colonel was entitled to appoint the officers for the new troops and that it was neither for the Duke of York, as Commander-in-Chief, nor the Secretary of State for War, as the Secretary at War had now been redesignated, to presume to post in officers from other regiments to make up his numbers. Consequently he appointed officers from other troops of The Blues on promotion, and recruited his own cornets. The Duke of York argued there was absolutely no precedent for a colonel, even as grand and respectable as Northumberland, to appoint and promote his own officers without sanction from Horse Guards. Northumberland therefore asked Hill to produce some evidence that officers of The Blues had always been appointed by the Colonel. This caused two problems for Hill, as it was blatantly false and there was no accurate record. The Adjutant was promptly told to produce one. His grasp of history must have been quite good, for the resultant book, still in the Household Cavalry Museum, was a brave attempt to prove Northumberland's point, but had too many gaps to be totally convincing. The clerks at Horse Guards demolished the case point by point, and Northumberland backed down and resigned in disgust, decrying what the world was coming to. His place was taken by Wellington, who, whilst rather cool to the honour for some time to come, was quick to ascertain the financial benefits, then standing at £3,000 per year. He did little, initially, to endear himself to Hill and the officers; his first communication asked them to clear their quarters in Lisbon for some hussars. He did not visit them for some considerable time, and he did away with the band, which was costing £900 a year. It was not until after Waterloo, when the regiment had so impressed him and he finally had some time, that he took an active interest.

Chapter Thirteen

DEFEATING NAPOLEON

The Life Guards marched out of Hyde Park Barracks on 19 October 1812 at 4 a.m. and thousands gathered to see them off despite the early hour; the Burdett incident was all but forgotten. 'I shall never forget the thunderous applause,' wrote Lieutenant George Sulivan of the 1st Life Guards in the diary he was to keep throughout the campaign. They marched via Staines, Bagshot, and Alton, where they rested for a day, and arrived at Portsmouth on 23 October. 'Nothing could exceed the enthusiasm with which the Regiment was received through every town and village as it passed, our silver trumpets seem to inspire the fair sex,' Sulivan continued, and it was his involvement with the fair sex that was to be his undoing. 'Oh, how differently did my thoughts and hopes turn out to what I had anticipated at this early period of my life being only 20 years of age,' he bemoans. Sulivan was a fairly typical contemporary Life Guard officer. His father had made a fortune in India, and returned home to die. Sulivan only knew his father for six weeks, perhaps accounting for his lack of self-confidence, but he was left the huge sum of £85,000, as well as his mother and sisters to support in Croydon. Sulivan's problem was that while on duty in London he had fallen for a girl on whom the officer commanding the Life Guard detachment, a Major Camac, also had designs. Captain Edward Kelly, who commanded Sulivan's troop, taunted Camac, and by the time they reached Portsmouth Camac was all for challenging Sulivan to a duel. Sulivan writes that 'the officers of 1st Life Guards were a quarrelsome set of fellows, and much addicted to gambling,' and although he emerges badly from his own journal, he does seem to have had a point. Camac appears as a selfish, rather useless officer, mean towards his comrades and militarily incompetent. On one occasion he formed line from column when the 1st Life Guards were riding along the edge of a cliff, nearly sending the unsuspecting ranks at the rear to a watery grave. Kelly also emerges as a slightly unsatisfactory personality. From Portarlington in Ireland, he came from a large family and seems to have joined the army partly to support them. Originally commissioned into the 2nd Life Guards in 1801, he had left after a year and gone off, unusually, to instruct at the Royal Military Academy, something of a first for a Household

Cavalry officer. In 1808 he had returned, briefly joined The Royals, and then transferred to the 1st Life Guards. We will hear a lot more of him at Waterloo, where he became a national hero, but for the time being we find him stirring up quarrels in the regiment, gambling and stealing kit off Sulivan, with whom he shared a quarter in Portugal. Sulivan may, however, have deserved it, and was rather over-emotional, writing as he sailed from England, 'as we left the fertile and romantic shores, which clearly spoke adieu – when shall we see thee again'.[1] He was also preoccupied with his own quarrel with Camac.

The Life Guard soldiers tended to be slightly older than The Blues. Most prominent among them, and already a national figure, was Corporal John Shaw, the prize fighter. From Wollaston in Nottinghamshire, Shaw was a very well-built man, over 6 feet 3 inches tall and weighing 15 stone. He later became something of a Victorian hero, 'the model of the whole British army in himself . . . I'd give a fifty pound note to be such a figure of a man,' according to Dickens in *Bleak House*. He wasn't above earning extra money by posing as an artist's model for ladies' drawing classes, a very full example of whose handiwork is in the Household Cavalry Museum, but his real fame was in the ring. He had been trained at the Fives Court – a London gymnasium – and had won six out of seven major bouts.

The horses were loaded by 24 October, but then had to wait on board for over two weeks until the wind was right. They finally sailed on 8 November and had a dreadful voyage, hit by storms in the Bay of Biscay and stopped by British frigates blockading French ports. Amazingly, the 1st Life Guards only lost one horse, despite the flat-bottomed Portuguese lighters capsizing while unloading, leaving some of Sulivan's troop swimming up the Tagus. The 2nd Life Guards were less fortunate, landing with only 101 horses fit out of 243. However, there was to be no rush to move, and the brigade spent an agreeable few months in and around Lisbon, strengthening the horses and taking the local colour. They found adequate quarters at Belem, although the food was generally 'filthy beyond description', with 'everything . . . soaked in rancid oil'. The officers saw Wellington at a review of the army. He arrived by boat and was announced by a tremendous peal of cannon. Later Sulivan also saw him at a ball given by the Ambassador, Sir Charles Stuart, where he saw Madame Grassini who 'attends upon all his peregrinations' and 'saw all the Portuguese and many of the Spanish noblesse – such a set!! Their peculiarities and forwardness disgusted me!' The soldiers' preparations for the coming campaign were less glamorous. Sixteen wives who had come out with the 1st Life Guards and eleven with the 2nd Life Guards had to be accommodated. Camp equipment had to be collected, including the newly issued tents and light-weight tin cooking pots to replace the old iron ones, and mules acquired. Every horse was issued with two spare sets of shoes, and 30,000 shoeing nails were carried; the lessons of the retreats of 1810 and 1812 had been learnt. The Blues also acquired a Newfoundland dog called Duke who attached himself to the

Corporal Shaw was not above posing as an artists' model for ladies drawing classes. This rather full example of their work is in The Household Cavalry Museum.

The self-appointed job of Duke, the dog, was to clear the ruined villages, in which the regiment bivouacked, of wolves and strays. The soldiers, rather unkindly, repeatedly sold him to locals in exchange for wine, but Duke always escaped.

regiment. His self-appointed job was to clear the ruined villages in which the regiment bivouacked of wolves and strays before they moved in. The soldiers, rather unkindly, repeatedly sold him to locals in exchange for wine, but Duke always escaped and caught up with them again. Eventually he became a regimental hero and a portrait of him was painted, which still hangs in the mess at Windsor.

The spring of 1813 was late, and not until May was there enough forage to move the Household Brigade forward from Lisbon. They joined the army on the road to Salamanca. Sulivan did not accompany them, having been taken ill, allegedly with sun stroke, and returned to England on Christmas Day. However, this may have been because Camac had stopped him becoming an aide-de-camp. He had an interview with the Gold Stick, Harrington, who implored him to return, as the regiment was so short of subalterns, and Sulivan duly obliged. Private Henry Willis failed to accompany them too. He had died in hospital from fever, and as he lay breathing his last all his personal possessions were stolen by the medical staff; Corporal Sutcliffe wrote to his sister to commiserate, saying, by way of consolation, that such behaviour was common.[2]

Robert Hill had taken over the Household Brigade from Rebow, who had also returned to England, and was now serving alongside his brother, General Sir Rowland Hill, under whose command The Royals had been in Estremadura. Packe, the Major, assumed temporary command of The Blues. The Royals had said goodbye to Slade, with no regrets, and were also freed of Erskine after he jumped out of a window while suffering from a bout of fever. They were now in the brigade commanded by Fane, a competent and experienced officer, together with the 3rd Dragoon Guards. The 4th Dragoons had been so badly depleted in the retreat from Madrid that they had been shipped home, leaving their horses to the grateful Royals who needed them badly. The Royals were issued with new helmets, similar to those worn by the Household Brigade, and had thrown away their old cocked hats. They were in a positive mood, the Secretary records, as they left their winter quarters. 'A new energy sprang up in the army' after news of Napoleon's retreat from Moscow, and on 21 May they 'saw the move start that was to carry Wellington without a check from Portugal to the Pyrenees'.[3]

Wellington knew that the French were in trouble. Joseph Buonaparte and Jourdan had left Madrid to join forces with Clausel, commanding the French army in north-western Spain. His plan was to catch them before they could join together. Using the same old road from Ciudad Rodrigo to Madrid, by Salamanca, as the axis around which his troops were to move, he swept northeast in three columns. His idea was to trick Joseph into thinking he would make his main attack in the centre, while sending men round on his left, northern flank and surprising the French on their right. This 'great turning movement', north of the Douro, caught the French completely by surprise and they never recovered, beginning a slow retreat north-west, away from Clausel's army and towards France. Fane's Brigade was part of the cavalry screen leading the advance in the centre and by the end of May was approaching Salamanca. The French fell back before them, but were now experienced enough to keep tight formation, even when bombarded by the Horse Artillery. They had learnt that once they broke ranks, the cavalry would be in among them and would cut them to pieces. For their part, the likes of Fane had learnt that charging tightly massed infantry was to throw lives away to no purpose, and so The Royals contented themselves by sitting on the French heels, picking off what stragglers they could. In six days Wellington moved his entire army through the mountainous country between Burgos and Vitoria, which the Spanish had solemnly assured him was impassable. He had by this time also opened an alternative logistics hub at Santander, freeing up the large numbers of men and material that had been required to keep the long supply lines back to Lisbon and Oporto open. The Household Brigade was following up in reserve, but would see action when Wellington finally caught up with the slow-moving Joseph, who was hampered by endless baggage trains and his accompanying apparatus of government. They finally met at Vitoria on 21 June 1813. Wellington knew his tactic to bring Joseph to battle would prove decisive in driving the French out of Spain, and it was a master stroke. He outflanked Joseph once more so that when the blow came from the north it was totally unexpected.

The cavalry were not, as a whole, much engaged in the Battle of Vitoria itself, which was essentially a successful British infantry battle. It would normally have been followed by a cavalry pursuit to destroy the remnants of the French army, but the difficulty of the terrain, Wellington's fear of Clausel's army, still intact on his western flank, and the disgraceful looting in Vitoria itself – which lost him control of the infantry – put paid to that. Sir Thomas Graham, within whose corps the Household Brigade was operating, also missed an opportunity as he advanced from the direction of Bilbao. Instead of turning south, where the French had been driven into Vitoria itself, and where he could have trapped their army, he continued east, as ordered, to cut the Pamplona Road. Late in the day, however, by which time Wellington's flanking attacks had forced Joseph and Jourdan to retreat, the Household Brigade, advancing down the Bilbao road with Graham, came across a 'corps of French infantry which had taken up position to cover the retreat of their army. These troops were formed on some heights, their right resting upon the Pamplona Road, and their left communicating with a column of infantry which was endeavouring to hold in check the Allied forces on the right.'[4] Hill decided to attack, but 'whilst advancing to the charge, the progress of the Brigade was impeded by a deep ravine; the two regiments of Life Guards leaped over the obstruction but not without leaving a few men and horses struggling at the bottom, from whence they were, however, extracted without loss of life'. The Blues then wheeled right and crossed lower down without jumping. Hill controlled the manoeuvre well; as the brigade formed line on the far side of the ravine, the Horse Artillery opened up, and as the Household Brigade advanced the French broke and fled, 'leaving the Pamplona Road choked with baggage, cattle and provision'. Graham's orders had been to hold the Pamplona road and so no pursuit was allowed. That experienced French infantry in formation should break and run at the mere sight of the Household Brigade is interesting. It says much for the demoralized and exhausted state of the French army in Spain, but it also shows what an imposing and frightening sight these 6-foot-high soldiers, their height exaggerated by the new brass helmets, mounted on the largest horses in the British army, must have been.

They stayed on the Pamplona Road for two days, bivouacking in a small plantation in pouring rain and with no food as the commissary system tried to catch up after the battle. Meanwhile, the remainder of the French army streamed away to the north, and the majority of the Allied army plundered the huge stock of supplies and valuables that Joseph's army and travelling government had left behind, which included a large number of women. As one embarrassed French general explained to Wellington after his capture, 'Le fait est, Monseigneur, que vous avez une armée, nous sommes un bordel ambulant.'[5] The behaviour of the Allied army in the Peninsula was never particularly good, but at Vitoria it was at its worst, with an almost complete breakdown of discipline as the town was sacked. There was to be little for the cavalry, stuck outside, although there was later an official division of what was left after the looting had stopped, which gave each private 11 dollars, subalterns 20 and captains 90. Both the Household and Fane's Brigades now lingered around Vitoria, protecting the Allied rear from the ever-present threat of Clausel, while Wellington marched first to Pamplona and then north to Tudela. Clausel, having approached near enough to Vitoria to realize that the French had suffered a major defeat, withdrew to Saragossa and then slipped back over the Pyrenees into France. The regiments were critical of Wellington's conduct after Vitoria, believing that he had let a valuable opportunity slip away. 'If Lord Wellington merits the title of a good general on the field of battle, he is universally allow'd to be the most ignorant of following up any advantage gain'd. Instead of closely pursuing an army retreating with only one howitzer left, and harassing it with artillery and cavalry, the enemy was quietly suffer'd to retreat,' complained the Secretary, and whereas Wellington was clearly at home with infantry tactics (being an infantry officer by background) both the artillery and cavalry ended the Peninsular War feeling that he never really understood how to use them.

However incomplete the destruction of Joseph's and Jourdan's army may have been, Vitoria sealed the fate of the Napoleonic regime in Spain. Joseph was sent into retirement and although Soult, placed in overall command in Spain by Napoleon, delayed Wellington on the Pyrenees throughout the summer of 1813, there were no more major battles involving the cavalry on

An artist's impression of what The Blues might have looked like in the Peninsula. The reality was much less glamorous, but the sheer size of the men and their horses caused a French regiment to break at Vitoria before they had even charged.

Spanish soil. They remained in reserve while Wellington took San Sebastián in September and during the battles in southern France as he pressed Soult north to Toulouse. The Household Brigade spent the summer around Pamplona and then in a comfortable convent in Logroño. In October they were inspected by Stapleton Cotton, who said, rather rudely, that the Life Guards were too heavy, and their horses carrying too much weight. He ordered them to give up their carbines – which were very heavy – less six per troop for guard duty, and prescribed a regime of route marches to get everybody fitter. In September Camac's row with Sulivan came to a head, and he placed Sulivan under arrest for alleged disobedience on parade. A court martial was duly arranged, which not only exonerated Sulivan, but found that Camac's behaviour was vexatious and frivolous. Wellington, who approved the findings, added that 'the possession of rank in the service is attended by the necessity for the performance of duty'. It is difficult to feel any sympathy for Camac being so publicly humiliated. He soldiered on in the 1st Life Guards until the 1820s, but was not at Waterloo and never progressed beyond the rank of major. It is also difficult to feel particularly pleased for Sulivan, whose life thereafter took a number of turns for the worse, as he lost most of his money and then fell very ill.

The Household Brigade stayed near Logroño until March 1814 when they crossed the Pyrenees into France. They were present, but not in action, at Toulouse, which fell after Soult evacuated it on 12 April 1814. By that stage the campaign was running out of steam, and it seems to have become clear to the French that the war was lost. Private Smithies of The Royals records that at the front line French and Allied troops negotiated not to attack each other, whatever they were ordered to do, to save lives. 'French, Portuguese and English [also] all plundered at the same time in one house,' he added. 'They plundered in perfect harmony, no one disturbing the other on account of his nation or colour.'[6] Such politically correct plundering would have horrified Wellington, who appears not to have known about it.

Once the armistice was declared, a long march began back to Boulogne, through Cahors, Brives, Limoges, Orleans, Nantes and Abbeville. The troops reached Boulogne on 21 July and were welcomed back to London by the Duke of York on 1 August. The Royals, who were leading the pursuit of Soult from Toulouse, heard of the armistice near Carcassonne. They returned to Toulouse, from where the sick, including the Secretary, were shipped home with the infantry, while the remainder set out for a six-week march to Calais, which they reached on 17 July. Nineteen officers and 371 non-commissioned officers and privates arrived at Dover two days later and marched to the West Country to their headquarters in Bristol. There were still eight prisoners unaccounted for by the time they reached Calais, although Wyndham had now been returned, and they were not heard of again and were eventually assumed to have died in French custody. They had been on active service in Portugal and Spain for just under five years. Many of those who went out to Lisbon in 1809 were still serving; very soon they were to be in action yet again but this time they would not be so lucky.

Napoleon's fall, and exile to Elba, and the restoration of the Bourbon dynasty in France seemed to end, finally, a war that had lasted intermittently since 1793. True to form, the first thing on the Government's mind in London was either to reduce regiments or send them to America, where Britain was at war with the United States. The Royals, who were a strong possibility for service in America, something which they dreaded, did not fare too badly in the reductions. None the less, they still lost two troops, keeping eight which were fixed at a captain, two subalterns, a trumpeter, a farrier and sixty-two men. Ben the Ruler used the reductions to get rid of troublesome individuals, one of whom promptly joined a criminal gang in Birmingham, carried out a major burglary and was hanged before the end of the year. They also had to lose the two junior captains and eight lieutenants (as the third subaltern in each troop had been removed) to the half-pay list, so there were some painful farewells. Both regiments of Life Guards and The Blues also lost their extra troops. While they had been away, the Prince Regent had been considering the future employment of the three regiments. In August 1814 he issued an order that for the foreseeable future there were to be two regiments in London, at Hyde Park and King Street, and one in rotation to be stationed in 'Country-Quarters', which was an accurate description of Windsor in 1814. The regiments in London would answer to the monarch through the Gold Sticks, or, more accurately, the Silver Sticks acting for them, whilst those at Windsor would follow the orders of a general detailed by the Commander-in Chief, a system still partly in use today. Furthermore, he directed that whenever two or more of the regiments were serving together they should be formed into a Household Cavalry brigade. This was to happen rather sooner than he had anticipated.

The regiments themselves seemed to share in the general relief that at last Napoleon had been defeated, and they could return to peacetime routine. This was particularly true for The Royals, and the Secretary tells us that their initial concern was 'the establishment of two very necessary things for a regiment in England, namely a Mess and a Band'. On arrival five months' pay had been issued to the privates, perhaps slightly unwisely, in one lot. 'For some days after the distribution of pay hardly a man was to be found,' notes the Secretary, until 'at last Dorville determin'd to put some order to affairs, and gave out that he should make some severe examples.' The Royals did not care much for Bristol, finding the people unfriendly, especially to officers, and they were pleased to be ordered to Exeter in December 1814, though this soon turned to horror on the realization it might be a prelude to being sent to Canada. 'This,' the Secretary exclaims, 'was a mortal blow to the veteran Royals. Was this their reward for all their long sufferings in the Peninsular? After five years' service in a barbarous land was the repose of barely five months in England to be considered as too great a blessing, only to be expiated by an immediate embarkation to the frozen lakes and black forests of Canada?'

No sooner were the orders to sail cancelled, to everyone's general relief, than the Secretary bemoaned how dull life in Exeter had become. 'Barrack life is everywhere and always the same – uniformly dull and uninteresting. The society of the town is rarely open to the military . . . The billiard table, the pastry cook, the fruitier, or the oyster shop is the general resort of the barrack officer.' Yet the fault was probably not entirely with the inhabitants of Bristol or Exeter, for it is evident that it took a while for those who had gone out to the Peninsula in 1809 to readjust. Relations with women, for example, posed a particular problem for soldiers whose only experience for the last five years had been restricted to the odd accompanying wife or the prostitutes who inevitably hung around the army. The Secretary tells us that to the officer in barracks 'the joys of love are never known; servant girls the very refuse of footmen and hostlers, whores, that prostitute themselves to corporals and privates for a glass of liquor are the officers most obedient attendants'. However, when all the officers were invited to the Exeter Ball, it was our letter-writing friend Heathcote who disgraced himself. There was a Miss Dickinson at the Ball, 'a young innocent girl, who was fond of flirting, handsome, well made, and perfectly adjusted by nature to inspire the softer passion'. Heathcote was introduced to her, and exchanged half a dozen words with her. Later that evening, finding her free, Heathcote went up to her and told her he had something important to tell her. 'The poor child, for she was only sixteen, demanded what it was he could possibly have to say to her. "No," replies Heathcote, "it is something of particular consequence."' He managed to get her into the card room where, putting on a grave face, romantically taking a pinch of snuff that he applied 'abundantly to his nostrils by way of making himself more lovely. He then informed the young trembling girl that she was the favour'd object of his heart; that he was persuaded she had a mutual passion for him and proposed an immediate marriage'. The shocked girl denied everything and prevented him from requesting her hand in marriage from her father. Heathcote made things worse by telling all his brother officers on the way home in the coach of his proposal and his lucky escape. One feels for him, and his shyness born of all those years in camp in Spain, and also realizes just how false some of his letters home to his mother in Hesse Cassel must have been.

Nor was Heathcote, or any of the other Royals officers, to be allowed that period of peace they so badly wanted. In March 1815 Napoleon escaped from Elba and landed at Antibes. 'This however excited no alarm at first, the French papers represented the arch rogue Buonaparte as surrounded on all sides, and as inevitably destin'd to be made prisoner and doubtless to be publicly executed,' recorded the Secretary. However, within three weeks he was back on the throne of France and the Bourbons had fled. Napoleon's escape shook the European powers, still negotiating the break-up of his empire in Vienna, out of their lethargy. Prussia, Austria and Russia agreed to provide 150,000 men each to invade France. The British Government had already reduced its forces so rapidly that it had to promise subsidies instead, but it did offer an expeditionary force in the Low Countries, and Wellington's services as Commander-in-Chief. Napoleon, however, had moved quickly. By May he had 300,000 troops available; once he had put forces on the borders with Italy and Spain and on the Rhine, and sent a force to suppress the Royalists in the Vendée, he still had over 100,000 infantry and 23,000 cavalry, together with 370 guns, with which to invade Belgium and defeat the British, Dutch and Prussian troops assembling there.

At first The Royals were not considered for the army assembling under Wellington in Belgium. Ben the Ruler, already grumpy that his troops, spread throughout Dorset, Devon, Somerset and Cornwall, had little to do, wrote to Horse Guards demanding they be sent, but was told their anti-smuggling duties were too important to spare them. 'Thus were the veteran Royals . . . condemn'd to linger out an inglorious existence in performing the part of excise officers and constables, while regiments which had never left their native shore, which had never bivouac'd before an hostile army, were sent to reap the glory of a short campaign,' thundered the Secretary. But a reprieve was at hand. 'On the 21st. April about nine in the evening as Ben the Ruler had retired sulkily from the Mess . . . someone taps at his door . . . and presents an Adjutant General's letter ordering the Royal Dragoons to proceed to Canterbury and prepare for immediate embarcation.' Landing at Ostend by 21 May, they marched to quarters in Ghent, a journey many of their predecessors had made, and were put alongside the 2nd Dragoons – the Scots Greys – and the 6th Dragoons – the Irish Inniskillings – in what was quickly termed the Union Brigade, commanded by Major General Sir William Ponsonby, who had taken over Le Marchant's heavy brigade after he was killed at Salamanca and commanded it for the rest of the war in the Peninsula.

Similar activity was taking place in London and Windsor. The Prince Regent took little persuading this time, despite serious corn riots in London in March 1815, for which extra troops were called in. The Peninsula model was repeated, with each regiment providing approximately 300 men, organized into two squadrons, or four large troops. Hill commanded The Blues, with Ferrier commanding the 1st Life Guards and Lygon the 2nd Life Guards. Camac and Sulivan were left behind, but Edward Kelly went, commanding a troop, as did Corporal Shaw, who had just beaten the celebrated boxer, Painter, at Hounslow in thirty minutes, which included ten knockdown blows. Changes were made to their uniform, yet again, and the black horse-hair crests on the helmets were replaced with marginally less inconvenient red and blue woollen ones and a white plume added. Rather more practical, and comfortable, sheepskin shabracques, or saddle cloths, were also introduced. There is a good display case in the National Army Museum which shows the uniform worn at Waterloo by Captain William Tyrwhitt-Drake, who commanded a troop in The Blues, and there is an array of helmets in the Guard Chamber at Windsor Castle.

As the men mobilized, the strength of all three regiments was increased to 589 each, proof that, whatever the Secretary might predict, the Government was worried this could prove another long war. The six squadrons were formed, as instructed by the Prince Regent, into a Household Brigade, to which four squadrons – 583 men – of the King's Dragoon Guards were added, all commanded by Major General Lord Edward Somerset, an experienced and competent cavalry commander from the Peninsula. They left England three weeks earlier than The Royals, moved by an order worded in exactly the same format as Blathwayt had moved their forebears to Sedgemoor, and were in Ghent by the first week of May. The Household and Union Brigades were the only two heavy cavalry brigades in the British Expeditionary Force. Tellingly, given the bloodbath that lay ahead, the adjutant posted a notice in barracks, the week the detachment were leaving, asking all those who wished to purchase vacancies to let him have details of which bank could advance their money.[7]

By June the army Wellington was rapidly building up in Belgium consisted of approximately 90,000 men organized in three corps. The 1st Corps was commanded by the Prince of Orange, an incompetent officer who had served in the Peninsula, whose inclusion was diplomatically important, the 2nd by Wellington himself and the 3rd by Hill, now ennobled as Lord Hill, whose youngest brother served as his aide-de-camp while, of course, his middle brother, Robert, commanded The Blues. These corps consisted of a mixture of British, Dutch, Hanoverian, Hessian and Brunswick troops. There were seven British infantry divisions, several of whom were untested, for many Peninsula veterans were in America and the West Indies. There was one cavalry corps, 14,550 strong, under Lord Uxbridge. Uxbridge was not Wellington's first choice. He did not like him, as he had eloped with Wellington's sister-in-law, and had not been on operations since Corunna. Wellington preferred the solid and reliable Stapleton Cotton, but Uxbridge, with powerful friends at Horse Guards, secured the nomination. Instead of forming divisions, Uxbridge decided to command directly the two British heavy brigades and six light brigades, most of which contained a mix of British and German regiments. One of these, the Hanoverian Brigade, contained the Duke of Cumberland's Hussars, manned by wealthy Hanoverian gentlemen who provided their own horses and equipment. They would distinguish themselves at Waterloo by fleeing as one body at the first cannon shot and not stopping until they arrived safely in Brussels.

Wellington knew his force was numerically inferior to Napoleon's, but the Allied strategy was to cooperate with the Prussian army, 100,000 strong, commanded by Field Marshal von Blucher, about half of whose force would ultimately come to their aid at Waterloo. Wellington's operational plan was to let Napoleon make the first move and then react. He knew that large parts of his army were untried, and doubted the reliability of some of his Allied contingents. He therefore planned a defensive battle, and had sketched out in his mind various places where he could make a stand, if, as he suspected, Napoleon's intention was to defeat his army and take Brussels. Napoleon would thereby gain control of French-speaking Belgium, consolidate his position as Emperor, remove the nearest threat to his regime and gain time to prepare for any subsequent threat from Russia or Austria. However, Wellington was unsure whether Napoleon, whose army, the intelligence service reported, was gathering at Charleville-Mézières, would approach Brussels on the more roundabout northern route through Mons, threatening Wellington's supply lines to the Channel ports, or whether he would take the more direct route through Charleroi. Consequently he held his army back, only risking deployment when he was sure of the French moves. He relied, perhaps unwisely, on the Prussians, deployed well west of Brussels on the Belgian–French border, for intelligence of what was happening.

The heavy brigades were quartered near Meerbeck and Ninove, between Ghent and Brussels. Kelly, for one, was pleased to be back on active service, writing to his wife from Ostend on 3 May that 'in my part the disagreeable part of the business is over with me leaving so large and helpless a family behind me, and should I get home safe, which I have little or no doubt of, the event must be more advantageous to me than remaining in London upon the plan we have lately been upon, indeed another year or two would have been fatal to our pecuniary affairs'.[8] Poor Kelly! He was undoubtedly an able officer, whose soldiers respected him. He had approached Wellington for a place on his staff, and, though refused, was at least honoured with a reply. However, the years of peace in London were ruinously expensive for him and he was always short of money, a commodity his adored wife, Maria, and two daughters back home in Marlow seem to have had an insatiable ability to spend. His correspondence is full of details of where the next pound might come from. He even sold a horse to a brother officer, Cox, for £54 when he knew it had been injured on the ship taking them to Ostend and was going blind. Maria does not seem to have been totally sympathetic to his endless protestations of affection, and her replies were mostly demands for yet more funds.

Wellington reviewed the cavalry at Gramont near Meerbeck, on 29 May. Uxbridge, something of a showman, had arranged the day to perfection. 'At twelve precisely The Earl of Uxbridge appeared on the field arrayed in the richest uniform, and took command of the most numerous and precise body of British cavalry that was ever assembled in a body in the annals of history,' wrote the Secretary, clearly warming to the glamour of the occasion. 'Eight and forty squadrons of cavalry exclusive of the artillery were drawn up in review order.' Wellington rode out from Brussels and was late, not arriving until 2.30 p.m. He was greeted by a twenty-one-gun salute and escorted through the ranks by the Life Guards. The Secretary was amused to see Marmont, who had deserted Napoleon, in the ranks of Wellington's retinue, 'distinguishable by a white Arabian horse and the same that he rode at Salamanca, and which form'd a singular contrast with his black face', highlighting his dark skin. Uxbridge had arranged that Wellington should inspect his own regiment, the 7th Light Dragoons, and the light cavalry first, but Wellington, correct to precedent but more probably because he wanted to snub Uxbridge, started with the Household and Union Brigades. 'As Wellington passed The Royals, he gave Ben the Ruler a very friendly nod and ask'd him how he did. The ruler dropped his sword in reply, and cock'd his ugly face in the air and look'd wonderfully happy for a minute or two.'

Napoleon invaded Belgium on 15 June. He had chosen the direct route to Brussels through Charleroi, and planned to defeat first the Prussians and then the Allies. His army, now 107,000 strong, was not quite the magnificent war machine that it had been. Many of the men were certainly his old regulars who had been drafted directly into the Bourbon army when he was sent to Elba, but no money had been spent on them during the past year and there were some critical equipment shortages which even Napoleon's magic could not rectify in the short period between his arrival in Paris and deployment to the Belgian border. There was also a serious shortage of horses, the French having lost 185,000 in Russia, and the cavalry were not well mounted. Nor was French command and control as sharp as it had been. Many of Napoleon's trusted team were with him, such as Ney, who commanded the left wing, Grouchy the right wing and Soult, who was Chief of Staff. The corps were commanded by d'Erlon, whom The Royals had met in Estremadura, Reille, who had commanded at Vitoria, and Lobau, with Drouet commanding the Imperial Guard. However, the staff machinery which Soult supervised was not efficient and Napoleon soon had cause to regret the death of Berthier, who had organized so many of his campaigns. The orders, for example, for the move into Charleroi were confused, leading to endless jams and delays. However, it was taken easily enough, and Napoleon then deployed to face the Prussians at Ligny, a crossroads on the Naumur–Brussels road just north-east of Charleroi. It took Wellington some time to resolve that the Charleroi move was not a feint. Ziethen, commanding the Prussian cavalry screen on the border, neglected to send back regular reports. He sent one at 9 a.m., which only reached Wellington six hours later and then there was no follow-up. Similarly, the Hanoverian General Dornberg, positioned south of Mons, did not think to report that there was no movement in his area. Consequently it was not until the evening of 15 June that orders were sent out for the army to concentrate and deploy on the Prussians' right (i.e. north) at Quatre-Bras, a village on the main road between Charleroi and Waterloo.

The Royals did not receive their orders until 4 a.m. on 16 June, but marched soon after, riding through Gramont and Ath towards Nivelles, where they heard

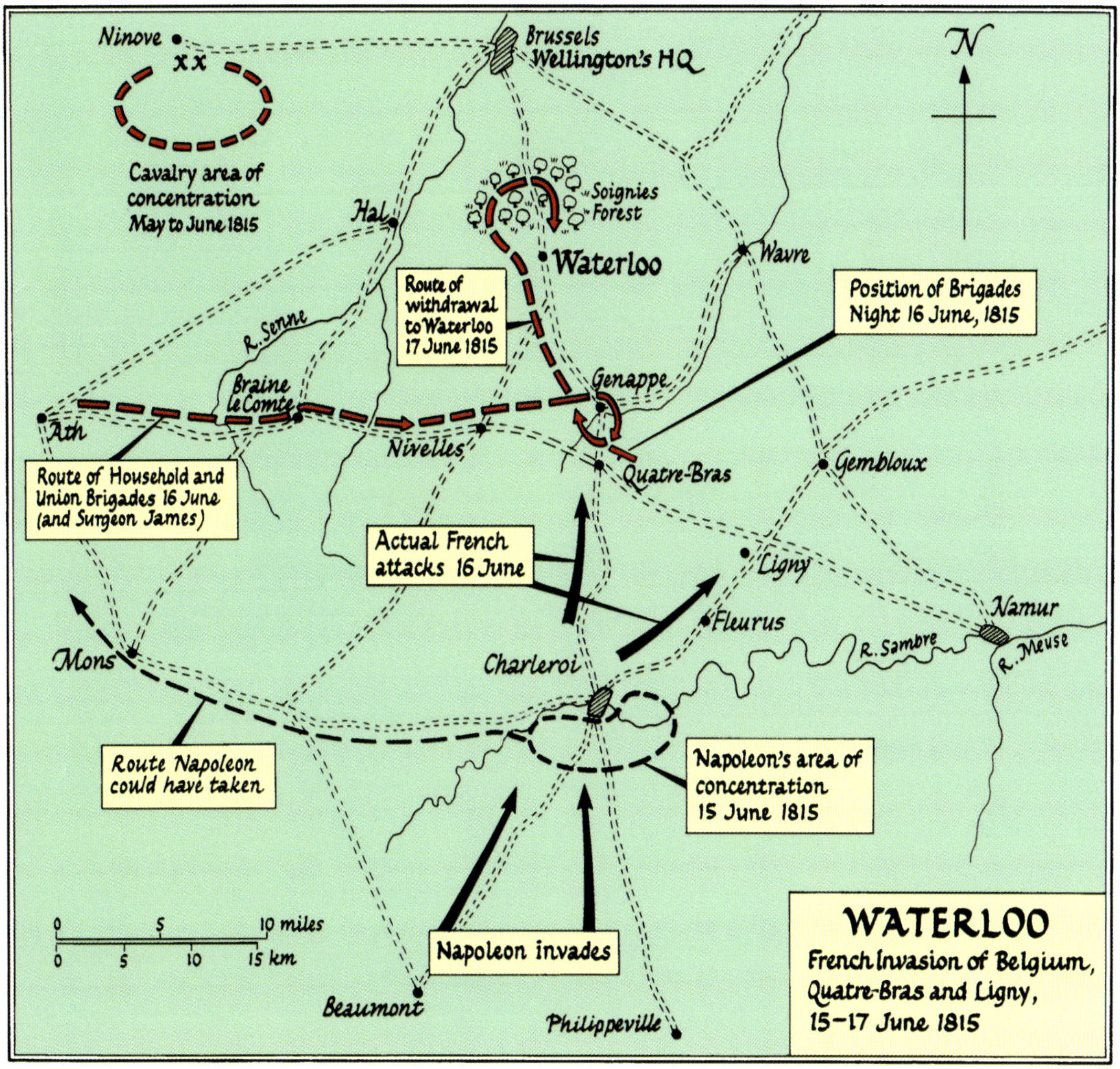

Ninove
xx
Cavalry area of concentration May to June 1815
Brussels
Wellington's HQ
N
Soignies Forest
Hal
Waterloo
Wavre
Route of withdrawal to Waterloo 17 June 1815
Position of Brigades Night 16 June, 1815
R. Senne
Braine le Comte
Genappe
Ath
Nivelles
Quatre-Bras
Gembloux
Route of Household and Union Brigades 16 June (and Surgeon James)
Actual French attacks 16 June
Ligny
Fleurus
Namur
R. Sambre
R. Meuse
Mons
Charleroi
Route Napoleon could have taken
Napoleon's area of concentration 15 June 1815
0 5 10 miles
0 5 10 15 km
Napoleon invades
Beaumont
Philippeville
WATERLOO
French Invasion of Belgium, Quatre-Bras and Ligny, 15–17 June 1815

the cannonade at Quatre-Bras. The Household Brigade had received their orders slightly earlier. It had been a beautiful evening the night before and Dr John James, surgeon to the 1st Life Guards, had walked back to his quarters 'replete with my friends excellent dinner and vintage wine on that fine warm night'. He had probably enjoyed it rather too much, for two hours later he was woken up by Kelly, to whose troop he was attached, to be told that the trumpeters had been sounding 'To Horse' for an hour. 'It was a lovely morning, the sun about to rise and our trumpets sounding in every direction – a tremendous air of bustle, clatter and indeed confusion that was over all.'[9] He bumped into 'two hussars, staggering down the street very drunk and all unconscious of the call to action around them. One said to his companion, "I don't think I shall go to bed now." One of our lads who heard him laughed and called over, "Belike you will be put to bed with a shroud this night, and know nothing about it."' Kelly produced coffee and eggs for breakfast, and put some cold tongue in his haversack for later. The 1st Life Guards prided themselves on being ready by 4 a.m. The orders were to march 'left in front', so the 1st Life Guards, as the most senior regiment and therefore on the right when drawn up in line, were at the rear, with the junior regiment, the King's Dragoon Guards, in front, followed by The Blues and the 2nd Life Guards. They waited in column for four hours, tired, uncomfortable and nervous, until the order to move was finally given at 8 a.m. They rode via Enghien and Braine-le-Comte to Nivelles, just west of Quatre-Bras.

It took all day. The procedure for moving cavalry brigades was that the regiments themselves went on ahead in 'marching order', taking dry rations, in this case three days' biscuit and some hard forage for the horses and hay nets. All the heavy baggage, officers' comforts, any soft forage, like hay and straw, and the balance of the rations followed up behind on the regimental bat horses, or mules in Spain, with the commissary. When the whole army was on the move this inevitably meant that the narrow Belgian lanes quickly became blocked by slow-moving lines of carts, which mingled with the marching infantry battalions, the gun teams and the ammunition trains. James should have ridden with the troop, as surgeons, vets and farriers normally did, but he had been recruited at short notice from St Bartholomew's Hospital and was no horseman. He even found trotting rather difficult, and was riding an unsuitable horse, which soon lost a shoe and left him back behind the regiment, desperately searching for a replacement and to catch up. His servant, Barnes, finally managed to procure a grey pony, and they set off. The roads were full of 'straggling baggage and women following the army'. They came across a battalion of German infantry 'resting from the sun on their mighty packs and singing as they went on a hymn like music'. Then

> We rode over a succession of low hills, and on the summit of one of them I heard a low murmur. I was not certain but might this not be the sound of

distant artillery? As I proceeded further it ceased to be indistinct. The distant battle was announced by another sign. It was an afternoon of clear, blue sky, but in the south there were some clouds. These in one part assumed the form of a pyramid, whose base was a line, straight as if drawn with a ruler. It was the canopy which the combatants had formed for themselves.

Passing through Nivelles, James saw the streets full of wounded Foot Guards from Quatre-Bras but had no instruments to help them. He finally found his regiment that night, bivouacked behind Quatre-Bras, but by then 'the cannon had ceased to roar, and silence had sunk on the land. The conversation amongst the officers was discouraging. At Ninove the most sanguine expectations had been entertained of our marching to Paris almost without resistance. The full news of yesterday's events had been the first to contradict such hopes.'

The events of 16 June had not been good for the Allies. The Prussians had been attacked by Napoleon at Ligny and defeated. Blucher, who had had his horse shot under him, was forced to withdraw north to regroup. Wellington's army had been slow to get to Quatre-Bras. Ney had attacked with Reille's corps. The British infantry had born the brunt of his assault, and, as James tells us, had been 'most damaged, and scores of wounded passed us'. The Duke of Brunswick had been killed and the 69th Foot had lost their colours. Yet, as bad as it seemed to James and the Life Guards, as they ate Kelly's tongue and 'drunk wine out of Cox's little leather bucket', it was the French who had made serious mistakes. Poor staffwork from Soult meant they had not concentrated enough troops against Blucher to defeat him decisively at Ligny. D'Erlon's corps marched all day between Quatre-Bras and Ligny, as it received order and counter-order, and Lobau's corps never arrived at all. So while Blucher had been forced to give ground, the majority of his army was still intact and able to re-engage once it had reorganized. One of Napoleon's mistakes was not to accept this. He was convinced the Prussians had suffered so badly that they had ceased to be operational, and it was not until the morning of Waterloo itself, when he saw through his glass Bulow's corps 6 miles away, advancing to join Wellington, that he realized he had miscalculated. Similarly, although Ney had achieved what Napoleon had intended and 'fixed' Wellington at Quatre-Bras, he had not forced him back, and Wellington withdrew his infantry in good order during 17 June so that he could keep pace with the Prussians' retirement and occupy ground on which he could fight his defensive battle at Waterloo. It was in covering the rear of this withdrawal and redeployment that the Household and Union Brigades were to be first engaged.

The night of 16 June had been uncomfortable for the Household Brigade. The French occupied the woods immediately in front of the 1st Life Guards' bivouac, and shots occasionally whistled over their heads. The soldiers found a barrel of local beer in a farmhouse, but in their eagerness to open it wasted half of it. In the morning Somerset moved the brigade into line and ordered

The regiments were not convinced by Wellington's plan for Waterloo (*left*). They felt he had wanted to fight the main engagement at Quatre-Bras and was outwitted by Napoleon. They blamed him for being at the Duchess of Richmond's Ball, and thought the move from Ninove to Quatre-Bras (*below*) and back to Mont St Jean was chaotic.

hay nets to be emptied. The men dismounted and fifty were sent out as a screen, as an attack was expected imminently. 'It was now most intensely hot, so much so that we perspired copiously as we lay on the ground,' James noted. 'We remained there until the afternoon, watching the retreating army on our left, and an immensely heavy cloud on our right, both of which augured us no good.' No one really knew what was happening, for it was not standard practice to brief orders down to the troops.

> At last the order came to mount, followed soon by that of 'the line will retire', which we now did, passing through intervals in the German cavalry, halting to let them pass through alternately, and riding through fields of rye as tall as ourselves on horseback. We had scarce commenced this movement when the thunderstorm which had threatened us for so long burst over our heads with the most tremendous peal I have ever heard, and a torrential fall of rain soaked us to the skin almost instantly.

What they had in fact witnessed was Wellington's withdrawal of his infantry and artillery in good order, and the cavalry were now falling back in turn, covering the rear against any attempt by Ney to harass them. This he started to do very late in the day, sending light cavalry patrols north up the Brussels road from Quatre-Bras into the village of Genappe. The Household Brigade went into column and passed through Genappe before Ney's lancers got there. Beyond the village they halted on the brow of a hill, still in column. Wellington and his staff rode by looking 'very cheerful and smiling, and were smartly turned out in contrast to us who were beginning to show the signs of two nights in the open, and a violent thunderstorm. The Duke was wearing his usual blue coat, white cravat and low cocked hat, and his air of calm put heart into us all.' Kelly, whose troop was at the rear of the regimental column, rode up to James and asked him if he had any gin left in his flask. As he took a deep swig he said, 'I should not be surprised if we have a bit of a fight here. I believe the Duke is surprised that we have not been more pressed by the French before this.' As he spoke, looking down on Genappe, the Life Guards saw the 7th Hussars and 23rd Light Dragoons, the two light cavalry regiments who had been at the very rear of the cavalry screen, pour out of Genappe in confusion, followed by French lancers, with whom they were inextricably entangled. The 7th Hussars had been caught by the leading French regiment and had fought them off, but were now in danger of being overwhelmed. Uxbridge had ordered the 23rd Light Dragoons to assist them, but they had reacted too slowly, and found their swords were no match for the French lances.

Uxbridge now rode over to the 1st Life Guards, and, finding Kelly's troop first, told him to wheel around and charge, saying 'the Life Guards shall have this honour'. Kelly duly did so in style, turning around immediately and forming line. Trotting down the hill, he lined up on the leading lancers, and his trumpeter blew the charge as they came down to the village. Again, the visual effect of the Life Guards seems to have momentarily paralysed the French. The sheer mass and size of a heavy cavalry squadron must have been terrifying, and, for once, the Life Guards were operating on open ground and over a short distance and could keep formation. The French fought back, causing casualties with their lances, but the overall effect was too much for them. They wavered, Kelly blew for his men to re-form for a second charge, and the French turned and galloped back through Genappe. 'Well done, the Life Guards, you have saved the honour of the British cavalry,' called Uxbridge, as he rode up, something Kelly was not slow to remind people of thereafter.

As the Household Brigade now continued north, Ponsonby's Union Brigade took up the rear, and for a time The Royals were the rearmost regiment. Radclyffe's' squadron was 'thrown out to skirmish', and was pressed by French chasseurs, who were now cautious and 'finding that they could not overpower us by their fire . . . huzzaed and endeavoured to excite each other on with cries of "Vive l'Empereur", but they did not dare put things to the test of a charge'.[10] The Union Brigade's operation that afternoon was very creditable. They withdrew by alternate squadrons, skirmishing and keeping the French at bay so that the rest of the cavalry could follow the infantry back to Waterloo. Uxbridge called it 'the prettiest field-day of cavalry and horse artillery that I ever witnessed'.[11]

The Union Brigade's action forced the French to break contact at dusk, and allowed Uxbridge to manoeuvre the cavalry into position behind Waterloo overnight. He found this difficult to do, for, despite being Wellington's nominal second in command, the man to assume command if he was killed, Uxbridge had no idea what his plan was or of where he was supposed to go. Plucking up the courage to ask, he went to find him that evening in his quarters in Waterloo. He told Wellington of his predicament. Wellington listened in silence and then asked, 'Who will attack the first tomorrow, I or Bonaparte?' 'Bonaparte,' Uxbridge replied. 'Well,' continued the Duke, 'Bonaparte has not given me any idea of his projects: and as my plans will depend upon his, how can you expect me to tell you what mine are?' The Duke then rose, put his hand on Uxbridge's shoulder, and said, 'There is one thing certain, Uxbridge, that is, that whatever happens, you and I will do our duty.'[12] Splendid words, if not a little condescending, but poor Uxbridge went away none the wiser.

Wellington's plan was in fact very simple. He would position his infantry along the Mont-St-Jean ridge in front of Waterloo, blocking the approach to Brussels, and giving them shelter from French artillery fire. Furthermore when the French attacked, they would have to do so up hill. He knew he was not strong enough to defeat Napoleon on his own and realized he had to hold off the French attack for long enough to allow Blucher to join him. The Allied cavalry were placed in reserve behind the infantry, and that is where they took up position in the pouring rain on the night of Saturday, 17 June. It was still light as they rode in, though Colonel Ferrier got lost and overran so the 1st Life Guards ended up temporarily in the forest of Soignies. James surveyed the following day's battlefield from the top of the ridge.

> The view was of the most tremendous description commanding the field of Waterloo and an immense tract of country, dark with woods and coloured with columns of troops, both English and French. The storm was breaking up, leaving patches of light and grey isolated showers in different parts of the landscape. I soon saw the regiment coming, so covered with black mud that their faces were hardly distinguishable, and the colour of their scarlet uniforms invisible. The ground was a quagmire.

And it continued to rain all night. There was no chance to bring up rations or drinking water, and the men slept as best they could, their arms slipped through the reins of their fully saddled horses in the high standing corn, woken intermittently by the still circling storm. 'The strongest thunder rain fell that ever did flow,' wrote Private Peel of The Blues to his sister, 'and the poor soldiers was knee deep in water. It rained all night.'[13] Kelly had finished off James's gin, but the soaking-wet doctor, who had been tending the wounded from the Genappe action, did manage to strip naked under the pouring rain and put on a pair of dry woollen stockings and flannel jacket that he had in his saddlebags. Soon afterwards Captain Haywood walked over to say that his troop had found a cottage and got a fire going. It was so crowded no one could lie down. He got no sleep and 'was glad when the first light of dawn began to lighten the crowded and airless room'. He was not alone, and at dawn the bedraggled Household Brigade immediately started to clean and dry their weapons.

They would not have much occasion to use their pistols or carbines in the coming battle. They would rely on their swords, as the British cavalry had since Marlborough's day, and, wrote Private Smithies, 'For the first time ever known in our army, the cavalry were ordered to grind the backs of their swords, so as our Captain Clark said, we should have to use both sides. It was thought by the men that this order had been given because we had to contend with a large number of French cuirassiers, who had steel armour, and through this we should have to cut.'[14] Corporal Shaw, drawing on his Peninsula experience, advised his troop to swing at the back of the cuirassiers' necks, should they encounter them, as this was where they were most vulnerable.

As daylight came the two heavy brigades were positioned next to each other, about 400 yards behind the ridge, and separated by the main road from Genappe to Brussels. Three hundred yards in front of them, and mostly again just behind the ridge, was the line of infantry. From the map on p. 324 it can be seen that all around the Household Brigade were positioned German and Dutch brigades. Below them, across a sunken lane, lay the farm complex of La-Haie-Sainte, which was fortified and defended by the King's German

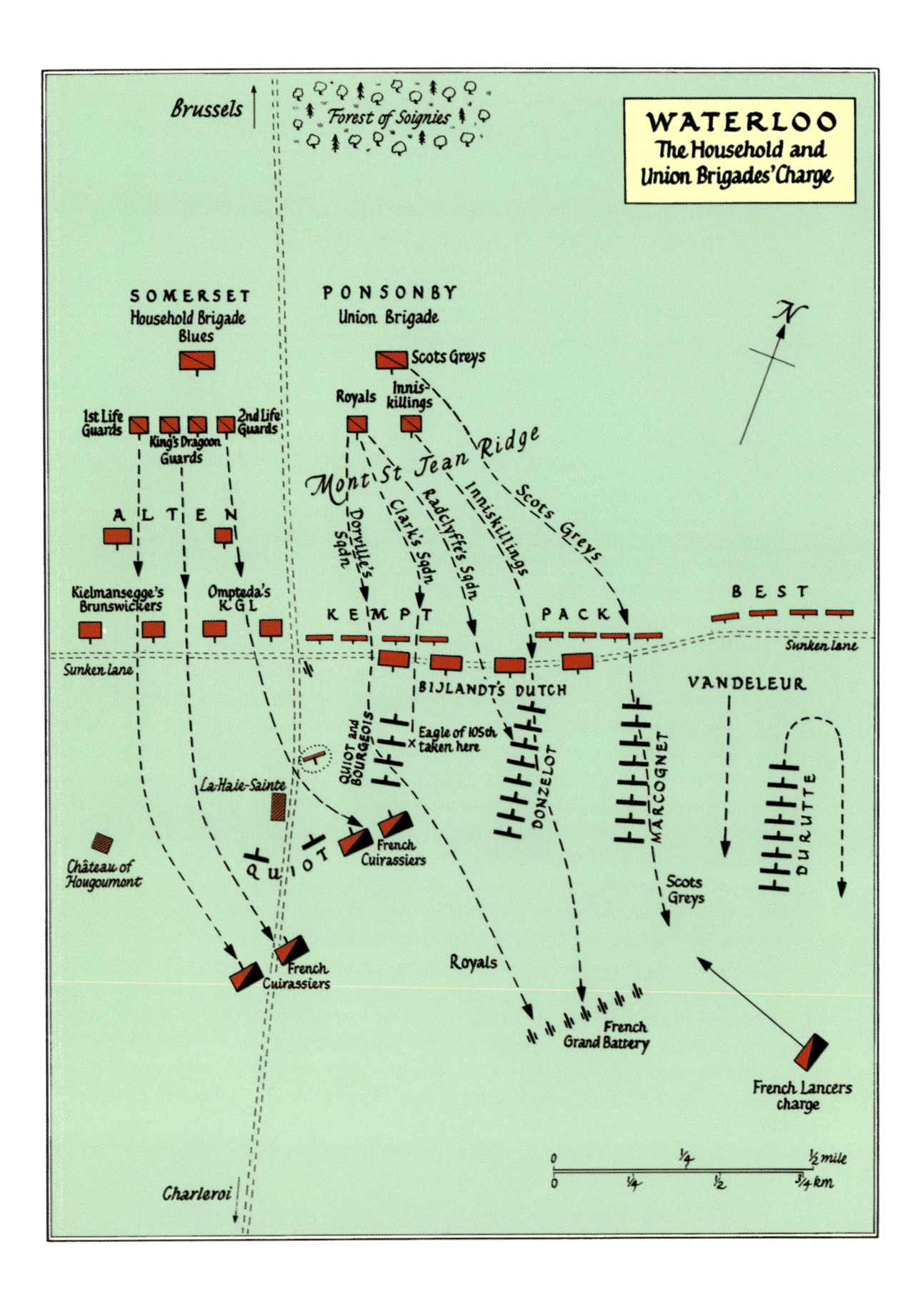

WATERLOO
The Household and Union Brigades' Charge

Legion. The heavy cavalry were therefore at the heart of the Allied army, astride the likely French main line of attack, whilst the light cavalry were mostly off to the left flank. The two brigades sorted themselves out in line formation. In the Household Brigade the front line consisted of the 1st Life Guards on the right, then the King's Dragoon Guards and the 2nd Life Guards on the left; The Blues formed the second line. In the Union Brigade, The Royals, as the senior regiment, were on the right of the front line, with the 6th Inniskillings next to them; the Scots Greys formed the second line.

And there they waited for several hours. The weather improved and the sun came out, so the rain slowly steamed off the men and horses. At 10.30 a.m. a portable telegraph was set up just in front of the 2nd Life Guards, and shortly afterwards Wellington passed along the front 'with his staff looking entirely unconcerned and as smart as if they were riding for pleasure'. James was later very critical of Wellington's plan, as were many cavalry officers, saying that the Mont-St-Jean position was a bad one as the only way back, if the battle went against them, was along the narrow Brussels road through Soignies Forest. James admitted there was a common view that it would have been better to have fought at Quatre-Bras, which they would have, he thought, if Wellington had not been at the Duchess of Richmond's ball on the night of 15 June. A cursory glance at Wellington's battle map suggests that they may have been correct. It was prepared so that it centred on the area south and west of Waterloo, with Mont-St-Jean only in the top right-hand corner, so that it would be difficult to relate the position to the surrounding topography. Nor did it show the area through which Blucher was to manoeuvre, which must have made it difficult to make sense of reports of the Prussians progress during the day. It is preserved in the Royal Engineers Museum at Chatham, complete with spots of blood from his wounded staff officers.

Hidden as they were in dead ground, the heavy brigades could see nothing of what was happening in the great bowl to their front, but at noon they heard a huge din on their right as Reille's corps attacked the Château of Hougoumont, strongly defended by Foot Guards, Hanoverians and Nassauers. Shortly thereafter they heard the French artillery, which had been massed on a ridge and was, with typical French flair, now named the Grand Battery, open fire from its position only 700 yards away, and shots passed overhead and occasionally hit their ranks. In response, Bijlandt's brigade moved back, while most of the French shot passed harmlessly over the Allied infantry protected by the ridge. At 1.30 p.m. the Grand Battery ceased firing, and the massed drums of D'Erlon's corps beat the advance as the main French attack developed against the Allied centre and immediately in front of their positions.

It is sometimes difficult, in these days of high-powered rifles, fighter aircraft, precision weapons and long-range artillery, to appreciate just how short the distance between the armies was at Waterloo, and at what close quarters most of the engagements took place, and also how much of it was bloody,

An oil painting of the Battle of Waterloo that hangs in the present day officers' mess in Knightsbridge Barracks.

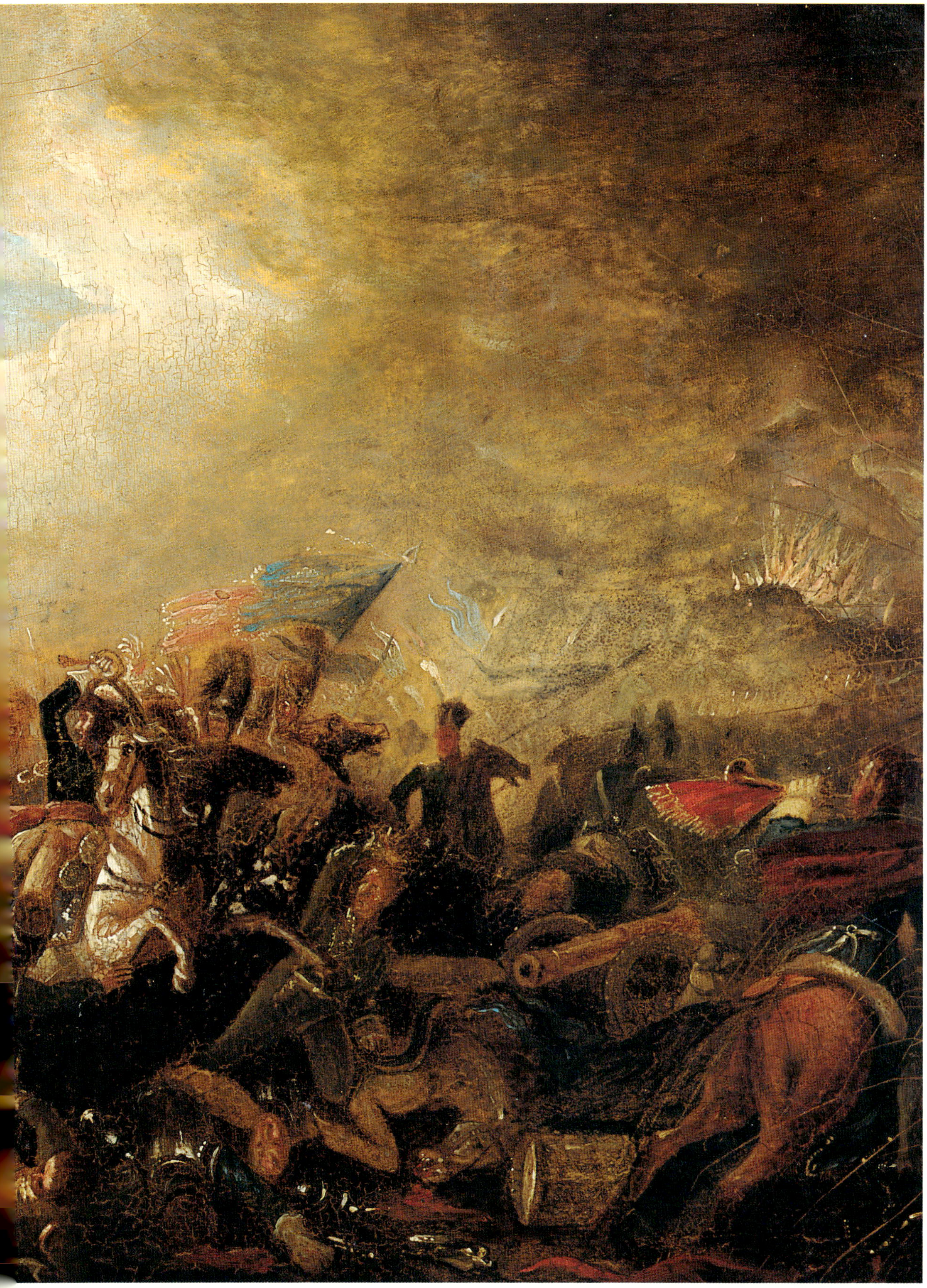

exhausting and terrifying hand-to-hand combat, whether by sword, lance or bayonet. The distance between the opposing armies before the French attack was about 1,000 yards, and the whole battlefield only covered 4 square miles. The average artillery engagement was at 700 yards, with the maximum range of the most effective British guns, the 9-pounders, only 1,700 yards. The effective range of the 'Brown Bess' musket was 80 yards, with the Baker Rifle, issued to some rifle and light battalions, at 250 yards. The cavalry, as we have seen, did not use their pistols or carbines, and all their fighting was hand-to-hand. This was what the two heavy brigades were about to experience as D'Erlon's drums tapped out the 'Pas de Charge', and his four divisions set off for the crossroads at La-Haie-Sainte. For the first 500 yards they moved in file, threading their way through the wagons and limbers of the Grand Battery, but once clear they formed into columns for the attack, with 3,000 skirmishers forming a front line across the corps' front. The four divisions stepped off in echelon by the left, with 400 yards between them, so the furthest left, Quiot's, moved first. They made directly for La-Haie-Sainte. Donzelot's moved next, heading for Kempt's and Pack's Brigades, followed by Marcognet's and, finally, Durutte's on the right. With Quiot's division was Dubois' Cuirassier Brigade, 800 men from the 1st and 4th Cuirassiers, drawn from Milhaud's Reserve Cavalry Corps, there to protect D'Erlon's left flank. These cuirassiers were the elite of the French cavalry. The men, who had to be at least 6 feet tall, had to have served in three campaigns and have twelve years' service to be accepted. Napoleon reckoned they were 'of greater value than any other type of cavalry', and their heavy steel armour and long swords made them formidable. They were designed for use rather like a modern battle tank, en masse, to smash through infantry and exploit weakness. The two regiments now moving forward had fought at Austerlitz, Jena, Friedland, Ulm and in the Peninsula. They had not been used at Ligny or Quatre-Bras, so their horses, heavy weight carriers from Normandy, were fresh.

Wellington had massed his artillery and placed it forward. It was the first to engage D'Erlon's columns, who started to take casualties as they came within range at the foot of the slope. They moved in the traditional Napoleonic formation of battalion columns that were easy to control, which could move quickly into other formations, such as squares, and which preserved mass for a breakthrough when they came up to the enemy. However, it also meant that only about one-fifth of their 500 muskets could be brought to bear. They 'presented three compact phalanxes of a front of 160 to 200 files, with a depth of 24 men',[15] and when they were subject to withering artillery fire, as they now were, they presented an easy target. As they closed with Wellington's line, great gaps were ripped in their columns, and the only cry that could be heard over the din of the guns was 'Close Up! Close Up!' What was particularly demoralizing for them was that they could see nothing on the ridge, as Wellington's battalions were still hidden in the dead ground behind. A French infantryman who survived the advance wrote that 'It was shameful to form our men in such a manner . . . As we mounted on the other side we were met by a hail of balls from above the road. . . . Two batteries now swept our ranks, and the shot from the hedges a hundred feet distant pierced us through and through . . . thousands of Englishmen rose up from the barley and fired their muskets almost touching our men, which caused a terrible slaughter . . . we should have been dispersed over the hillside, if we had not heard the shout "Attention! Cavalry!"'[16]

Around La-Haie-Sainte Dubois' cuirassiers had caught a battalion of Hanoverian infantry sent to assist the defenders of the farm complex and cut them to pieces. More worryingly, although it was horrific inside D'Erlon's columns, once they closed with the Allies' thin line, behind which there were no reserves, there was a serious danger of them breaking through. This was Napoleon's main attack, comprising one-third of his army, and it had to take the ridgeline before the Prussians came up; if it succeeded, the battle was won. Uxbridge, positioned between the Household and Union Brigades on the Genappe road, realized this, and as he saw Donzelot's columns of infantry start to breast the ridge, he realized that now was the time to launch his heavy cavalry. Uxbridge galloped over to Ponsonby himself and quickly briefed him to attack the divisions to his front and to get on with it before they actually crossed the sunken road. He then galloped on to Somerset, directing him towards the area around La-Haie-Sainte, which was then being assaulted by Quiot's left-hand brigade, supported by the cuirassiers who had just cut up the Hanoverians. Placing himself in between his two brigades, the trumpeters blew 'Walk March' and seven regiments moved forward. They should not have done. The Blues and the Scots Greys, both forming the second line, should have stayed a tactical few hundred yards behind to exploit opportunities created by the first line. However, in the excitement Uxbridge forgot to ensure they did so, an omission for which he never ceased to criticize himself later, and as the advance was sounded the two rear regiments came forward so that they were intermingled with the first line.

The Household Brigade moved in line but quickly lost formation as they threaded their way, at a walk, through the infantry and artillery behind the ridge, and then negotiated the sunken lane which ran across their front and parallel to the Wavre road. Once across the road they paused briefly to reorganize, but scarcely had time to do so before sixteen-year-old John Edwards, Somerset's duty trumpeter for the day, sounded the charge.[17] Kelly would have us believe that the brigade then swept down on the unsuspecting French in 'in the most perfect lines he ever saw'. In fact the disruption caused by their move forward, the broken ground and dense smoke meant they were not formed in anything like straight lines as they galloped down the hill. Kelly's troop, on the far right where the going was easier, may well have been better than most, and he, typically, would certainly have us believe so.

As Edwards blew and the regiments surged forward, they immediately came upon the La-Haie-Sainte[18] farm buildings, which acted as a natural channel. The 1st Life Guards, on the right of the line, went to their right, followed by The Blues who quickly came up with them, and the two regiments covered the 100 yards down the hill in a matter of seconds. In the dip to the west of the farm they rode straight into Dubois' cuirassiers. 'A short struggle enabled us to break through them, notwithstanding the great disadvantage arising from our swords, which were a full six inches shorter,' wrote Lieutenant Waymouth,[19] who was later captured, but his confident comments masked the viciousness of the struggle. The cuirassiers were almost stationary when the two regiments hit them, and their horses were blown from their earlier action against the Hanoverians and from climbing the hill carrying their riders' weight. While this undoubtedly helped the British, and the cuirassiers were definitely taken by surprise, they still fought back strongly. Kelly killed Colonel Habert, who commanded the 4th Cuirassiers, in a hand-to-hand combat, and then, rather strangely in the chaos of the battle, claims to have dismounted to cut off his epaulettes as a trophy. Whatever their origin, he certainly produced the epaulettes after the battle, as the unfortunate surgeon, James, was asked to keep them in his suitcase. Kelly also claimed a further ten men to his own sword.

The Blues had a similarly tough fight. Robert Hill was wounded in his sword arm, shot by a line of French chasseurs, light infantrymen who had taken up position in a hollow way by La-Haie-Sainte. He then found himself surrounded by five cuirassiers. At that point his trumpeter, Tom Evans, whom Hill had originally forbidden to accompany the regiment as he was too fat, came to his rescue, killing three of them before breaking his sword blade as he dispatched the fourth. He then used the hilt as a knuckle-duster, just as his forebears had done at Dettingen, and knocked out the fifth. Elley, who it will be remembered was serving on Wellington's staff, had joined in the charge, killing a French officer who had wounded him in the body. He took this man's cuirass and later wore it on regimental parades, in a display of triumphalism which his contemporaries found rather irritating. Major Packe, the officer who had joined the Freemasons back in Nottingham in the 1790s, was killed at this point, run straight through the body by a cuirassier squadron commander and falling dead from his horse. Cornet George Storey was about to do the same to a Frenchman when his victim shouted, 'Don't kill me! Don't you remember me?' Storey, who had originally joined the army in 1792, had been taken prisoner in 1794 and kept at Verdun for seven years where this man was his compassionate gaoler. He duly spared his life.[20] After a few minutes the impact of the combined regiments was too much and the mighty cuirassiers fell back, pursued enthusiastically by the 1st Life Guards into a gravel pit.

Whilst their comrades had gone to the right of La-Haie-Sainte, the 2nd Life Guards and the King's Dragoon Guards were channelled to the left, crossing the Brussels road, which ran alongside the farm wall, and almost immediately

Captain Edward Kelly (*right*), a frustrated and rather enigmatic figure, who felt that his bravery at Waterloo was insufficiently rewarded. He certainly fought with distinction but, rather unusually, dismounted to cut the epaulettes from a French officer's tunic in the middle of the battle (*below*).

Corporal Shaw became a national hero after Waterloo, where he was killed.

Captains Packe and Fenwick in Blues uniform prior to the Peninsula. Packe, who had been one of the first to become a freemason, was killed at Waterloo.

clashed with the right-hand troops of the 1st Cuirassiers, just to the left of the farm, as did the right-hand squadron of The Royals. The cuirassiers' heavy armour gave them a considerable advantage. 'It was desperate work indeed, cutting through their steel armour,' wrote Private Smithies, in Major Dorville's squadron of The Royals, who collided with Dubois' right-hand troops.

> On we rushed at each other, and when we met the shock was terrific. We wedged ourselves between them as much as possible, to prevent them from cutting, and the noise of the horses, the clashing of swords against their steel armour, can be imagined only by those who have heard it. There were some riders who had caught hold of each other's bodies – wrestling fashion – and fighting for life, but the superior physical strength of our regiment soon showed itself.[21]

And no one's physical strength was more apparent than that of the boxer, Corporal Shaw. He had been sent foraging that morning, and had only returned just in time to have a tot of rum and take his position in the left-hand squadron of the 2nd Life Guards, in other words on the extreme left of the Brigade. His first victim was a cuirassier whose face he sliced off 'as if it had been a piece of apple'.[22] He then dispatched a further nine, getting round the problem of his sword being shorter by 'smacking at their faces with the hilt. They'll either topple or turn,' which is exactly what they did, and, when they turned, they were beheaded. Beside Shaw were Privates Dakin and Hodgson, who worked with him. Dakin later recalled that the noise was like 'the ringing of ten thousand anvils' as the swords hit the steel armour. Dakin had his horse killed under him. Crawling out, he found two cuirassiers also dismounted. His fourth stroke divided the head of the first and his fifth did the same to the second. Hodgson, who was 6 feet 4 inches tall, came up against an Irish cuirassier, who roared, 'Damn you, I'll stop your crowing,' but Hodgson sliced off his sword hand and drove his blade through his throat. Private Samuel Godley, who was completely bald and consequently nicknamed 'the Marquis of Granby', also had his horse shot from under him, and lost his helmet as he fell. Struggling to his feet, he attacked the nearest cuirassier, who gave him a terrific blow with his sword across his bald head. Godley collapsed again, but got up on one knee, from which position he killed the cuirassier as he came in for the coup de grâce. Godley then managed to mount his horse and rejoined his squadron to cries of 'Well done, the Marquis of Granby!' His skull was later found to have been fractured by the blow.

The remaining squadrons of The Royals had even less distance to cover and charged straight into the side of the 105th Infantry Regiment of the Line, the left-hand column of Bourgeois' brigade. The French at this point were themselves 'a little deranged' by the effort and the casualties they had taken crossing the sunken road and were taken completely by surprise as The Royals only had to cover less than 100 yards to reach them. They had time to get off one volley at 50 yards, which brought down Captain Windsor and twenty men, but they had been 'quite paralyzed and incapable of resistance'[23] by the British artillery and musket fire, and their tightly packed column formation only allowed the leading two ranks to fire. Within a few minutes they were in a hopeless rout, as were Donzelot's division, who had been charged by the Inniskillings, and Marcognet's troops into whom the Scots Greys rode, ably assisted by the 92nd Highlanders, through whose ranks they had ridden. Captain Clark saw the Eagle, the colour of the French 105th Regiment,

> perhaps about forty yards to my left, and a little in my front. The officer who carried it, and his companions, were moving with their backs towards me, and endeavouring to force their way through the crowd. I gave the order to my squadron 'Right shoulders forward! Attack the colour!' . . . On reaching it I ran my sword into the officer's right side, a little above the hip-joint. He was a little to my left side, and fell to that side, with the Eagle across my horse's head . . . on running the officer through the body I called out twice together 'Secure the Colour! Secure the Colour! It belongs to me!' . . . On taking up the Eagle I endeavoured to break the Eagle off the pole, with the intention of putting it in the breast of my coat, but I could not break it. Corporal Styles said 'Pray Sir! Don't break it' on which I replied 'Very well. Carry it to the rear as fast as you can. It belongs to me!'[24]

French regiments attached immense importance to their Napoleonic Eagles, symbols of the Empire which had been understandably removed in 1814. On his return from Elba Napoleon had reissued them, and presented them in person with much ceremony on the Champs-de-Mars on 1 June before he left Paris. The Scots Greys also captured the Eagle of the 45th, and Lieutenant Tathwell of The Blues took one later in the day, but his horse was shot and he was taken prisoner before he could get it back.

Clark afterwards reckoned that the Union Brigade charge had taken place at exactly the right time. Had it been even a few minutes later the French infantry could have forced their way over the ridge and broken the Allied line. 'In fact,' he wrote, 'the crest of the height had been gained, and the charge took place on the crest, not on the slope of the ridge.' The loss of two Eagles was symptomatic of the plight of d'Erlon's corps. His four infantry divisions were now defeated and Napoleon's main setpiece attack had failed. Dubois' cuirassiers had fled, and the immediate danger to the Allied positions had been removed. Uxbridge's action had been totally successful and both the Household and Union Brigades had good reason to congratulate themselves. Two thousand prisoners had been taken and the French afterwards estimated the charge had cost them 5,000 casualties. However, the brigades now exhibited that lack of restraint for which Wellington so regularly criticized his cavalry.

Instead of withdrawing in relatively good order, and forming the reserve as Wellington intended, both brigades, exhilarated after success, galloped on towards the Grand Battery. Uxbridge himself had by now returned to a happy Wellington and his staff, who, he wrote, 'had from the high ground witnessed the whole affair. The plain appeared to be swept clean, and I never saw so joyous a group as this Troupe d'Oree. They thought the battle was over.' It was at that point that Uxbridge realized that his reserve had gone, and as the heavy brigades arrived at the Grand Battery, their horses were blown.

'In fact,' wrote Major de Lacey Evans, 'our men were out of hand. The General of the Brigade, his staff, and every officer within hearing, exerted themselves to the utmost to reform the men, but the helplessness of the enemy offered no greater temptation to the dragoons, and our efforts were abortive.'[25] In the first minutes after their arrival they did considerable damage to the French artillery. The 2nd Life Guards reached right back to the wagon lines 'where boy drivers sat to be slaughtered, tears streaming down their cheeks', and The Royals and the Union Brigade attacked the artillery men. 'We sabred the gunners, lamed the horses, and cut the traces and harness. I can hear the Frenchmen crying . . . when I struck at them, and the long drawn out hiss through their teeth as my sword went home,' wrote a corporal in the Scots Greys, but although they claimed to have destroyed fifteen guns they had no means of permanently disabling them. As they moved at an exhausted slow trot through the guns and limbers, they were subjected to the inevitable counter-attack by 2,500 fresh French cavalry positioned to their left near the hamlet of Papelotte. These were a mixture of cuirassiers from the 13th and 14th Cavalry Divisions and two light cavalry regiments, the 3rd and 4th Lancers. They now came on the exhausted Union Brigade, with whom the Household Brigade were intermingled, in three waves. The British heavy cavalry were justifiably wary of these French lancers. 'The French fastened the lance to a foot,' wrote Smithies, 'and when we reared them, they sent it out with all their might; and if the man at which they aimed did not manage to parry the blow, it was all over with him.' Ponsonby was killed by a lance, as were so many of his men, speared as they struggled back up the ridge on their exhausted horses. The majority of the casualties each of our regiments suffered during the battle occurred in the next thirty minutes. Shaw was killed at this point. He and Hodgson had allegedly killed another ten Frenchmen, one of whose decapitated heads remained balanced on his knapsack, when Shaw's sword broke and he was back to using the hilt as a club. Thereafter he used his helmet as a flail, and is reputed to have finally succumbed to wounds caused by a drummer boy firing a pistol at him from a ditch. Another Life Guard private who had been knocked out recovered consciousness to find himself in the middle of the Lancers. He threw away his helmet so that he would be less easy to spot as a Life Guard, but was recognized and speared by the lancers anyway. Lying wounded, he had his possessions stolen, something which happened regularly to the wounded, and was dragged to the rear by his feet. He saw several other prisoners being murdered, and was eventually left for dead on a rubbish tip. Coming to, he found himself next to Shaw, passed out again, and when he regained consciousness, after the battle, he found that Shaw had died. Vandeleur's Light Cavalry Brigade eventually moved forward from the Allied left to engage the lancers, and gave some cover in the final few hundred yards, but when the battered remnants of both brigades regrouped behind the ridge at about 3.30 p.m. they numbered about one-third of their strength an hour previously, though more stragglers came in gradually during the evening.

The 2nd Life Guards and The Royals, on the left of La-Haie-Sainte and therefore nearer the Grand Battery, had suffered the worst. Somerset had recovered many of the 1st Life Guards and The Blues before they got too far. Even so, their losses were serious. 'Where is your brigade?' Major General Sir Hussey Vivian asked him as he retook his original post beside the Brussels road. 'Here,' replied Somerset, pointing to a band of horsemen amidst the dead and dying, clad in red, and mutilated and confused horses wandering or circling aimlessly.[26] Yet Wellington himself now rode up and saluted them, which was good of him considering he had always complained he was never himself saluted by the Household Troops, and more especially as he now had no heavy cavalry reserve. The battle was far from won. After the failure of d'Erlon's attack, Ney attacked next with the French cavalry. This was a strange tactic, given that he must have known they could make little impact on the British infantry once they had formed squares. It is possible that as Wellington pulled his battalions back below the crest to shelter from artillery fire, Ney mistook this as a retreat. However, instead of regiments fleeing, his divisions found well-arranged squares, each positioned to give a free field of fire. The French cavalry charged repeatedly and bravely between about 4 and 6 p.m., but made little impact. In between the cavalry attacks the French artillery fired continually at the squares, and at the remnants of the heavy cavalry drawn up behind them. The Royals found this the most trying part of the day, languishing as they took severe casualties from the artillery rounds.

The continual attrition was having an effect all along Wellington's line. La-Haie-Sainte finally fell at 6.30 p.m. when the defenders ran out of ammunition. It gave the French a useful base from which to organize their assaults. At this point Uxbridge moved the remains of the Household and Union Brigades to take up positions further to their left, behind the Brunswick and Hanoverian infantry who were wavering under the onslaught. Here they suffered even more. By this stage The Royals made up only one squadron. Ben the Ruler had now taken over command of the Union Brigade after Ponsonby's death, and Dorville commanded what was left of the regiment. By 7 p.m. the infantry were so weary and battered that the brigades were ordered to charge a regiment of cuirassiers who were making their own last, exhausted attempt to break the Allied line. It was 'not quite so successful as the first, as my ten squadrons were by that time reduced to three,' wrote Somerset, who had nearly been killed himself. 'My favourite mare', he continued, 'was killed by a canon shot, that went through her flank and carried off part of the skirt of my great coat.'[27] 'We charged,' wrote Clark, 'and met half way. We were so tired that the shock was not great and few were killed on both sides, after which we stood within 30 yards, firing our carbines at each other, both parties afraid to move for fear the infantry would give way. At this point the Prussian cavalry came up and relieved our Light Dragoons upon the Left, whereupon the enemy gave way.'[28]

But before they did so, Napoleon tried one last desperate gamble. At 8 p.m., in the gathering dusk, with the Prussian corps now clearly arriving on the battlefield, he sent forward the fourteen battalions of the Old Guard – 4,500 men – in one final attempt to break the Allied line. They were met by the Allied infantry re-formed in line, and were sent reeling back. The remnants of both brigades charged once more in support of the infantry, but once the Old Guard started to retreat they were too exhausted to play any part in their pursuit or in the subsequent general British advance as the whole line moved forward. With this the French army broke, streaming back in chaos towards Charleroi, taking with them Napoleon's hopes of empire, and ending a war that had begun twenty-two years before.

Now was the time to count the cost. Surgeon James had been working behind the ridge all day in a small house. Smoke restricted visibility outside to a few yards and the noise was deafening. 'Our work behind the lines was grim in the extreme,' he wrote in his diary.

> When one considers the hasty surgery performed on such an occasion, the awful sights the men are witness to, knowing that their turn on that blood soaked operating table is next, seeing the agony of an amputation, however swiftly performed, and the longer torture of a probing, then one realizes fully of what our soldiers are made. Most of the wounded were sent back to hospitals in Brussels . . . only to face in so many cases the pain and disgust of spreading gangrene.

In fact he must have done his work well, as did his counterparts, Samuel Broughton in the 2nd Life Guards and David Low of The Blues, for contrary to popular belief very few of those who were wounded on the battlefield and made it back to Brussels actually died. The most common injuries were lance wounds in the body and arms, inflicted during the awful withdrawal from the Grand Battery, and sword cuts to the head and shoulders. Of the sixty-three wounded in the 2nd Life Guards, for example, only four died, with the corresponding figures for the 1st Life Guards being eleven out of forty-five and for The Blues only six out of fifty. But those figures, of course, refer only to those wounded who were able to get back to the Allied lines, and many more died out on the battlefield, undiscovered until too late.

The total number of casualties was horrific. Waterloo is by far the bloodiest battle in which any of our regiments have participated, including the early engagements of the First World war. The 1st Life Guards came off best, with only twenty-one killed, including Lieutenant Colonel Ferrier, whom Sulivan had so badly wanted in command in the Peninsula instead of the awful Camac, and who had made a total of eleven separate charges during the day, most of them after his hand had been cut open and he had been stabbed by a lance. Even Kelly, who heartily detested him, admitted he had done well. The 2nd Life Guards suffered much worse, with eighty-seven killed, including Lieutenant Colonel Fitzgerald, a lieutenant colonel in the army who had, however, fought in his regimental rank of captain as a troop leader, and had been shot by the Chasseurs in the first charge; he and his family had been held in France for twelve years and only allowed home in 1812. The 2nd Life Guards also lost 153 horses. The Blues lost forty-four killed, among them Major Packe and the unfortunate Corporal Major Thomas Bell, one of the oldest men in the regiment, who died of exhaustion. The Royals' losses were proportionately slightly less but also very serious. They had eighty-six killed or missing out of 400 men who had charged d'Erlon's corps, and a further 107 wounded, in other words a casualty rate of around 50 per cent; they also lost 238 horses. Altogether the Household Brigade lost 45 per cent of their strength and the Union Brigade 46 per cent, losses which greatly exceeded the figures for the Light Cavalry. Very few prisoners survived, as most had been killed on capture, and the French behaviour towards those they kept alive was very bad. 'They acted more like barbarians than anything I know,' wrote Private Smithies in his journal, but Lieutenants Tathwell and Waymouth both survived and soon escaped.

The overall casualties at Waterloo were horrendously high: Wellington lost 17,000 men, or about 23 per cent of his army killed, wounded or missing, whilst Blucher lost 31,000 and Napoleon about 30,000. Both the Household and Union Brigades' part in the overall outcome of the battle had been substantial. 'Lord Edward Somerset's Brigade . . . highly distinguished themselves,' Wellington wrote in his dispatch. Having never praised the Household Cavalry in his life, he had now done so three times in as many days. The defeat of the cuirassiers was a particular achievement, given that they were such an experienced elite force and much better equipped. For the much younger and less experienced Household Brigade to beat them so decisively was testament to sound training, good tactical skills and high morale. There was also a determination to prove themselves amongst the Life Guards and The Blues, for they had been disappointed not to play a more active part in the Peninsular War, and to demonstrate they were much more than a ceremonial bodyguard. It was, wrote Gronow, in his *Reminiscences and Recollections*, 'the severest hand-to-hand fight in the memory of man'. It is a pity their endeavours were marred by their headlong pursuit into the Grand Battery, but one has to consider the reality of

A Household Cavalry helmet from Waterloo (*below left*) and the uniform worn by a Blues Officer in the battle complete with Waterloo medal (*right*), together with the field bugle (*below right*) on which sixteen-year-old John Edwards blew the fateful charge at Waterloo.

being among the privates in one of the regiments drawn up behind the ridge. No one had thought to brief them on a plan; indeed, there was no plan. Their corps commander had seized a fleeting opportunity and they had charged, with no idea what their target was or what to do on contact. A natural instinct would be to catch up with those in front and engage as many Frenchmen as possible. Then, in the midst of the smoke, noise and destruction, it would have been fairly difficult to hear trumpets sounding the recall.

Somerset was very upset by this apparent lack of control, writing to his mother that 'as is too often the case with cavalry, particularly the young troops, that they do not know when to stop . . .'[29] The blame for the subsequent loss has been accepted, nobly but unjustifiably, by Uxbridge. He was later to say candidly that he should never have charged with the first line and that he bitterly regretted not holding back The Blues and Scots Greys as a reserve. However, his judgement on the battlefield had otherwise been exceptional, and the poor man was badly wounded at the very end of the day as Wellington ordered the army to advance. As he was beside Wellington in the low ground by La-Haie-Sainte, 'he was struck by a grape shot on the right knee which shattered the joint all to pieces'. 'By God, sir,' he is supposed to have said to Wellington, 'I've lost my leg'. 'By God, sir, so you have,' Wellington is alleged to have replied, reflecting his intense dislike of the man who had eloped with his sister-in-law and whom he could not forgive for not having been part of his Peninsula band. Uxbridge behaved impeccably under the surgeon's knife later that night, when his leg was amputated above the knee. He made a remarkable and complete recovery, and the owner of the house where the operation was performed kept the severed limb and buried it under a weeping willow together with an elaborate epitaph, under which some joker is reputed to have added: 'Here lies the Marquis of Anglesey's limb; the devil will have the remainder of him.'

Waterloo generated many other heroes and all our regiments had their fair share. Many just saw it as part of the job, like Private Peel of The Blues, who wrote straightforwardly to his sister that 'when we was about two hundred yards from the French lines a cannon ball came and took off my horses leg so I was dismounted but looking round I saw a horse that somebody had been killed off so I soon got another. So we continued in that state until night the Prussians came up and began to work and the French began to run and a happy sight it was.'[30] The boxer Shaw's body was buried on the battlefield, but eventually his skull was recovered and returned to England where Sir Walter Scott, excited by the drama and romance of his story, had a plaster cast made of it. Godley remained apparently unperturbed by his fractured skull, until he suddenly collapsed at the stall he ran in his retirement in Baker Street. Hill apologized to Trumpeter Evans, who soon left The Blues to start a pub in Old Windsor, the Oxford Blue, which he ran until his death in 1866.

Others, like Kelly, felt inadequately rewarded, and for him, and more

Lord Uxbridge, later Marquess of Anglesey,
commanded the cavalry at Waterloo, where he lost his leg
at the very end of the battle. His replacement artificial leg
is in the Household Cavalry Museum.

importantly his wife Maria, recognition was very important. He had undeniably done particularly well in the battle before he was wounded badly but not seriously in his leg at about 7 p.m. by a cannon shot. He had also lost three horses, including his favourite bay mare who carried him to safety from the lancers and who was herself wounded in the head by a lance point.[31] He wrote almost daily to Maria and his family from his hospital bed in Brussels, recounting his actions, somewhat immodestly, and speculating on what reward he might get. 'The officers and men of my Regiment are all pleased to bestow kind praises upon me and I consider myself fortunate in having been the first man in with the enemy in every attack we made . . . On our return Lord Uxbridge thanked the Regiment in face of the whole cavalry of the army and said Captain Kelly I have marked your conduct and shall mention you particularly to the Duke of Wellington,' he wrote to Maria. Uxbridge certainly did, but probably never followed it up as he was himself so badly wounded. Maria was evidently not the greatest correspondent, and Kelly's tone with her becomes increasingly offended as she does not send a reply.

Kelly continued to live in hope, writing home to his brother-in-law that he thought he might be given a peerage in recognition of his conduct, and might receive a brevet promotion as he could not, of course, afford to purchase a majority. He was eventually made a Brevet Major, and made a Knight of St Anne of Russia, rather bizarrely, but that was all. The regiment was more generous and subscribed towards a special presentation sword which was given to him after the battle and which is now in the Household Cavalry Museum together with part of his bay mare's tail and the light cavalry pattern service sword with which he dispatched so many Frenchmen. After his recovery he found the continued expense of peacetime soldiering in London too great. He sold his commission to fund Maria and the girls and transferred to the 23rd Light Dragoons, going with them to India. Debts and the cost of his family caught up with him again, and he transferred once more to the much cheaper 6th Foot. He was Assistant Adjutant General to Combermere, as Stapleton Cotton who knew him from the Peninsula had become, and was present at the Siege of Bhurtpore. He died of natural causes in August 1828.

There was also a long and often bitter debate as to whether Captain Clark or Corporal Styles had been responsible for capturing the Eagle of the 105th Regiment. The Secretary and the junior officers claimed that the credit should go to the Warrior Gubbins, who was in Clark's Troop, and who they said acted with Styles, a line strongly supported by Gubbins himself in his private correspondence. Not surprisingly, this interpretation was hotly contested by Clark. Both Clark and Styles were rewarded, Clark by the award of a CB and Styles by being commissioned, although his pleasure at such an advancement must have been mitigated when he heard that it was in the West Indies Regiment. It was not until 1839 that Clark was officially granted the right to display the Eagle on his coat of arms, and at the same time the offending pages of the

Club Book were ripped out, which means that annoyingly, we have no other Waterloo gossip from the Secretary.

On Monday, 19 June both brigades started for Paris. They rode over a battlefield on which lay 3,500 Allied, 7,000 Prussian and an indeterminate number of French dead, together with many thousands more French wounded whom no one had the time or inclination to help. They were buried in

> large square holes about six feet deep, and thirty or forty fine young fellows stripped to their skins were thrown into each, pell mell, and then covered in so slovenly a manner that sometimes a hand or foot peeped through the earth. Some Russian Jews were assisting in this spoliation of the dead, by chiselling out their teeth. Local Belgians went out to shoot the hundreds of wounded horses[32]

so they could eat them. The regiments were glad to ride on to Paris and out of the war.

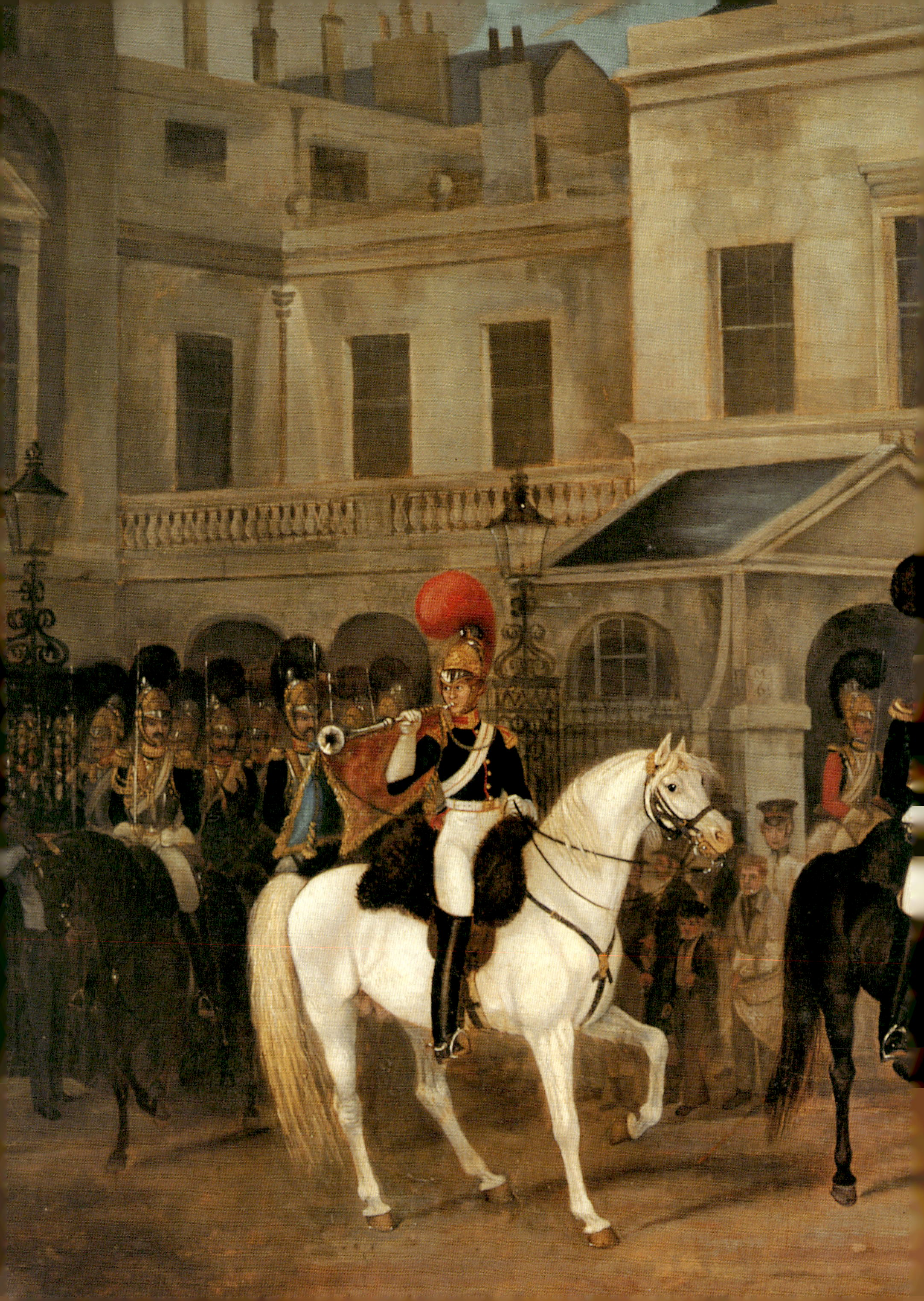

Part Five

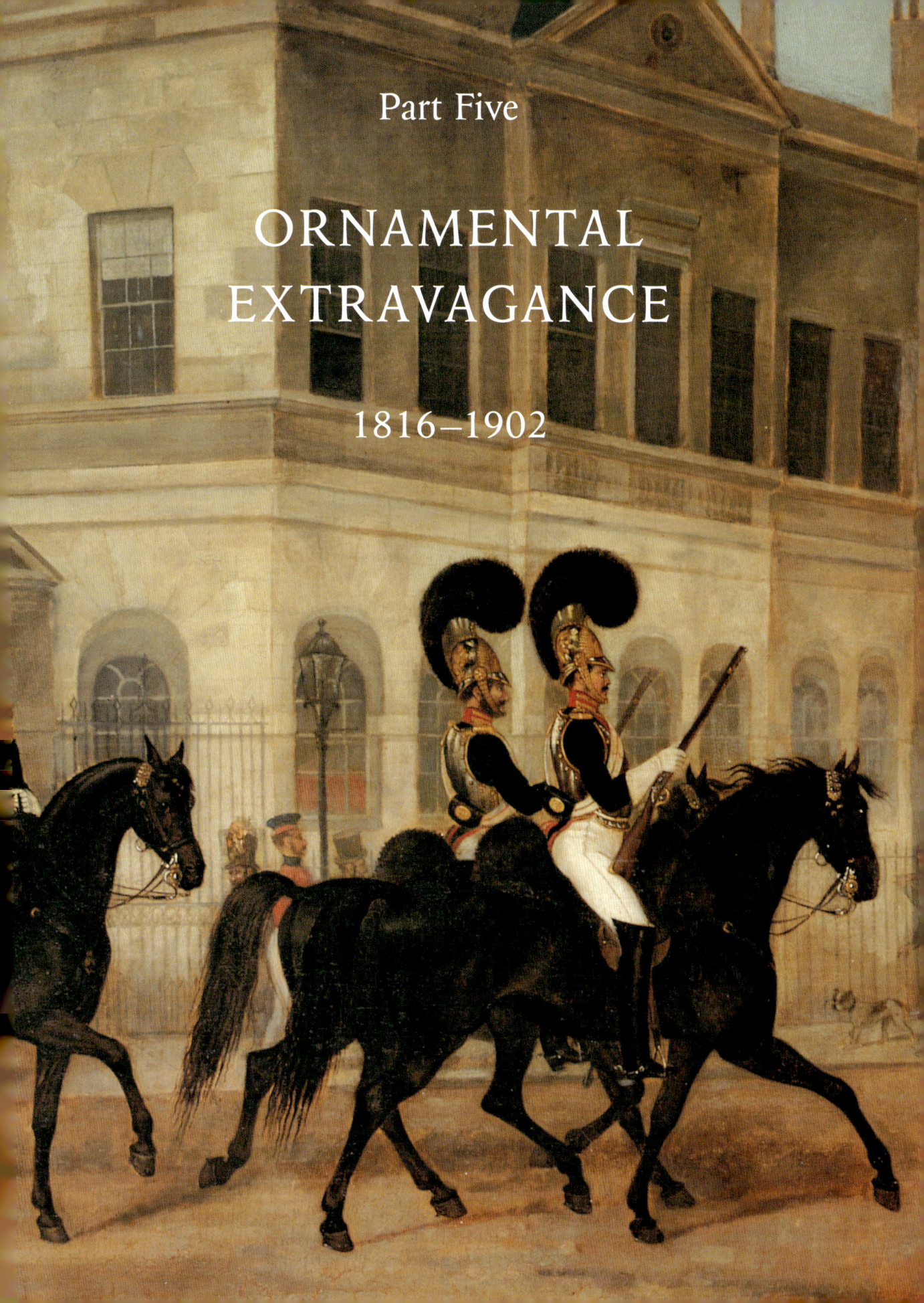

ORNAMENTAL EXTRAVAGANCE

1816–1902

Chapter Fourteen

CEREMONIAL FRUSTRATION

The scale of their victory at Waterloo was not immediately obvious to the regiments, and they marched towards Paris conscious that they might well have to fight again. Wellington was determined to prevent another battle and pressed on to occupy the French capital, so there was little time either to celebrate victory or to mourn losses. Surgeon James complained that 'we have been up every day at three or four o'clock in the morning, marching, halting, and lying about in cornfields all day . . . and to add to this, for ten days we had no baggage up, no writing materials nor any other article of luxury'.[1] Napoleon certainly considered regrouping his army, much of which remained intact – Grouchy's corps, for instance, had played no part in the battle – and some in Paris, like Davout, urged him to do so, but Napoleon had lost the support of the Assembly and on 22 June 1815 he abdicated. By the time the Household Brigade arrived at the attractive town of Boissy, 12 miles from Paris, which the Prussians had already systematically plundered, and the Union Brigade had reached Nanterre, the war was over, and, as James eloquently continued, 'the peace of Europe was won for many years to come'.

Our regiments were part of the army of occupation until early in 1816, and much enjoyed Parisian life, which seemed unaffected by the recent war. The Life Guards particularly liked the French custom of only paying for what you ate in a restaurant, as opposed to what you ordered, and James found the city clean, cheap and full of pleasures. There were a few uncomfortable moments, including the night a number of Life Guard horses were stolen and, on discovery that no guard had been posted, they received Wellington's rebuke that it would be dishonourable for 'the Regiment to make a claim on the French Government for a loss which could not have been sustained had the precautions established by the Service been attended to'.[2] However, by the time they marched north to Boulogne the following January they were nearly up to full strength and the

Page 344 & 345. The Queen's Life Guard leaving Horse Guards c.1840. Through the nineteenth century the Guard remained about fifty strong.

grief at the loss of so many friends at Waterloo had, to some extent, been ameliorated by the satisfaction of those promoted in their place. By February the 1st Life Guards were safely back in Knightsbridge, the 2nd Life Guards in Regent's Park, The Blues in Windsor, and The Royals in Canterbury.

It was only when they arrived home that the full implications of their achievements at Waterloo became apparent. Not only had Wellington's victory finally eliminated the threat of republicanism and French imperialism from Europe, but it had also ended a conflict which had been going on since 1690. As the Prince Regent, the Government and the City came to realize how much had been accomplished, and to appreciate the huge financial benefits of peace, the legend of the battle grew, as did the fame of those who fought there. The charge of the Household and Union Brigades and the consequent defeat of d'Erlon's corps were correctly judged to have been the decisive point in the battle, and for a few short years our regiments enjoyed the status of national heroes. On Lady Day, 25 March, everyone who had fought in the battle was presented with a silver medal with a red and blue ribbon – the first British campaign medal for all ranks awarded since Cromwell struck one for his victory at Dunbar. They were also rewarded with two years' seniority for pay and pension and were to be known as 'Waterloo Men', their names marked out in red on the regimental rolls, though this was more so that the clerks could ensure others did not claim their extra privileges.

The year 1816 also saw a plethora of celebratory dinners. The Royals held their own informal affair at Wright's in Canterbury in January, at which sadly only fifteen officers sat down, all that remained of the regiment which had set off so enthusiastically from Exeter nine months before. In June the Grand Old Duke of York, still Commander-in-Chief and Colonel of the 1st Foot Guards, renamed Grenadier Guards in honour of their defeat of the Grenadiers of the Imperial Guard at Waterloo, came to Windsor where they were stationed and presided over three days of festivities jointly hosted by them and The Blues. On the first day the Grenadiers gave dinner to The Blues, who returned the compliment the following day, also 'entertaining the women of the Regiment with tea and other refreshments in the Riding House'.[3] On the third day the Duke of York provided dinner. Long tables were laid out in the Long Walk in front of Windsor Castle, and both regiments marched up in full dress. There then followed a lengthy sermon by the garrison chaplain, Mr Roper, before quantities of roast beef were served at 2.30 p.m. Eating in full dress has never been the most enjoyable of experiences, and especially not in the glare of the June sunshine after a lengthy sermon, but no doubt the regiments were appreciative of the Duke's good intentions. On the second anniversary of the battle the 2nd Life Guards provided a Guard of Honour for the opening of the new Waterloo Bridge, formed entirely of men who had fought at Waterloo. Even the regimental standards, those cherished symbols of loyalty and achievement, which were reissued in 1815 – two with two guidons for each regiment of Life Guards

The 2nd Life Guards provided the escort for the opening of the new Waterloo Bridge, which was formed entirely from men who had fought in the battle, and was commemorated on this plate, part of the Prussian Service of China, a gift to Wellington from a grateful king of Prussia.

As part of the continuing celebrations after Waterloo the Household Cavalry standards were re-presented, showing just the battle honours connected with Napoleon's defeat.

and five standards for The Blues – now bore in bold letters the names 'Peninsula' and 'Waterloo', almost as if they were the only battles in which the regiments had participated.[4]

The Prince Regent acknowledged the particular part played by the Household Cavalry by making himself Colonel-in-Chief of both regiments of Life Guards and on 29 January 1820, formalized the role of The Blues by making them officially part of the Household Cavalry and becoming Colonel-in-Chief of them as well. It was meant as a compliment, and was certainly taken as one, though The Blues' pay remained lower than the Life Guards' until 1867. From 1821, the regiments now rotated annually between Windsor, Regent's Park and Knightsbridge, so there were always two in London to provide the King's Life Guard and escorts. In 1822 the 1st Life Guards therefore came to Windsor for the first time, breaking The Blues' twenty-year tenure, though The Blues continued to regard it as their home and many of the officers retained their houses there. From now on the term 'Household Cavalry' therefore refers collectively to the two regiments of the Life Guards and The Blues, whilst The Royals continued as the senior line regiment and would not become part of the Household Cavalry for another 149 years.

Yet there were longer-term implications in Surgeon James's acute observation that the peace of Europe was won for many years to come. First were the inevitable troop reductions which came in late 1818. The Gold Sticks were ordered to cut their regiments to thirty-two officers, eight quartermasters, 397 men and 274 troop horses, which meant both Life Guards regiments losing 112 men and The Blues 104. The instruction was 'to select for discharge such of the men who are the least efficient either as to stature or bodily strength', a new idea, revealing the importance now attached to the physical size and strength of the heavy cavalry after Waterloo and also reflecting an increasing emphasis on appearance.[5] This was gradually taken to almost ridiculous extremes over the coming decade. The Prince Regent became obsessed, in particular, with Napoleon's Imperial Guard and with commemorating the defeat of the *grenadiers à pied*, the core of the Old Guard, in those final minutes of daylight as they were sent reeling back from the ridge at Mont-St-Jean. Apart from renaming the 1st Foot Guards as Grenadiers, he now equipped the Household Cavalry with tall bearskin caps for his coronation as George IV on 19 July 1821. They were similar to those worn by the Foot Guards today, but were taller and had a large grenade badge in the centre with a plume of white feathers; grenades were also depicted on the tunics and saddlery. They looked rather ridiculous, and a popular, if unsubstantiated, rumour circulated that the slightly built Duke of Wellington had been blown off his horse while wearing one on parade. William IV subsequently replaced them with a roman-style helmet, but it was not until 1847 that Queen Victoria got rid of them altogether, substituting, on the sound Germanic advice of Prince Albert, the helmets that are still worn today.

George IV also introduced cuirasses for the coronation, something many in

George IV's beautification in the Household Cavalry, particularly his insistence on them wearing absurd headwear, meant that after Waterloo they were increasingly seen as merely ornamental.

An escort of the 2nd Life Guards in 1830 leaving Windsor Castle, led by the trumpeters and kettle drummer in a rather extraordinary red and gold-plumed conical cap.

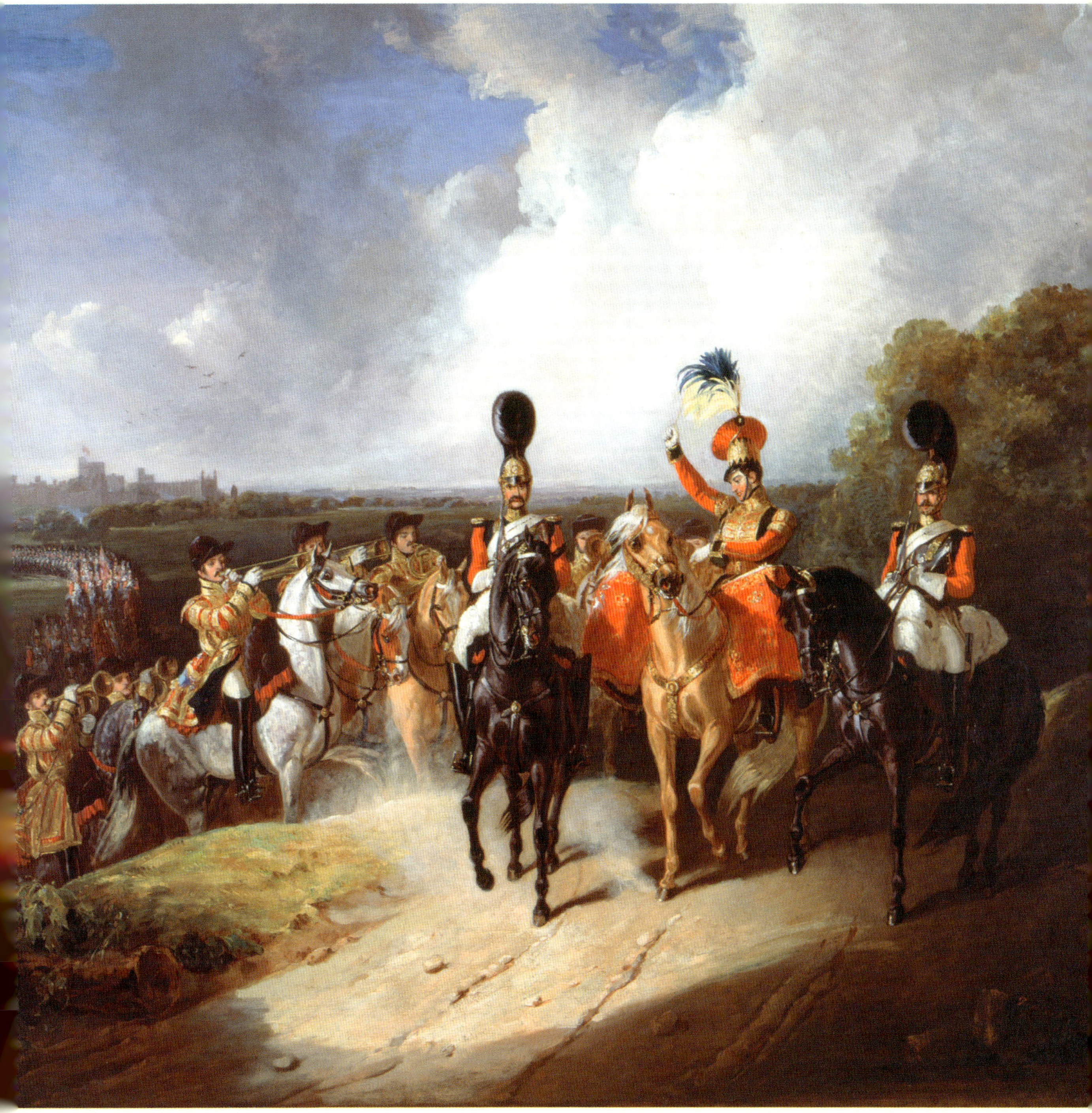

the Household Cavalry felt was a sensible military precaution after their experiences attacking Napoleon's cuirassiers. The King had toyed with the idea in 1814, requiring the Life Guards to wear black cuirasses with gold rims and a large gold star, but decided against them, much to the officers' annoyance as they had been made to buy them at considerable expense.[6] However, the new ones were even more elaborate, and there was a long debate as to whether they should be shiny 'bright iron' or darker 'brazed' iron and whether they should be covered in stars. Eventually it was decided to go for the bright iron version, strongly advocated by Wellington, not least on the grounds that they could be adapted from the old ones issued in 1793 and save expense. The colour of horses was now standardized as black for all the regiments, including the officers, which was not very popular, and it was glumly noted that Lieutenant Colonel Ferrier had been killed at Waterloo at the head of his regiment riding a grey.[7] New and elaborate saddlery was introduced at the same time as the cuirasses. 'An entirely new and curious bridle . . . the most splendid ornament of the above description ever yet seen will be sported by the 1st Regiment of Life Guards, also a real gold bullion rein,' the newspapers announced, tactlessly, on the same day as they carried transcripts of the post mortems of two Londoners killed by the Life Guards during the riots in the course of Queen Caroline's funeral.[8] The King also introduced the acorn motif into the Life Guards' uniform and horse furniture, to commemorate their links with Charles II, who had hidden in an oak tree after escaping from the battlefield at Worcester.

The regimental bands, which had existed informally since the 1790s, were also developed in the period after Waterloo and by 1865 had been established at thirty-two musicians each. Cathcart, Gold Stick for the 2nd Life Guards, had been Ambassador in St Petersburg and was much impressed with the Tsar's Guards' Bands, who played brass instruments. He arranged for the band of the 2nd Life Guards to imitate them when he returned home, bringing with him a set of instruments presented to him by the Tsar in person; apparently the Tsar insisted they could only be brought to England if the playing mechanisms were covered, since when the bands have played with leather covers on the working parts of their instruments. In 1831 the King presented silver kettle-drums to both regiments of Life Guards, to match those which his father had presented to The Blues in 1805, each drum costing the enormous sum of £950. By the 1830s Household Cavalry band concerts were a regular feature of the social scene at Windsor, and in Kensington Gardens, though the urge to dress the musicians excessively became too great. A painting of the Drummer of the 2nd Life Guards in 1830 shows the unfortunate man wearing a uniform more suitable for a carnival than a military musician, with a tall red and gold conical cap and a feather.[9]

All this was very fine, and made the Household Cavalry look spectacular at the coronation, but, as one Life Guard who had been at Waterloo remarked, when asked what he would prefer to wear next time he was asked to fight, it would be easier 'to take off his coat and turn up the shirt-sleeves above the

The bands had grown to thirty-two musicians each by 1865 and were becoming an increasingly important feature of regimental life.

A kettle drummer of The Blues, wearing one of the rather silly helmets introduced by George IV.

elbow!'[10] It was unfortunate that this beautification coincided with the start of a prolonged period of peace. The Household Cavalry were to see no action, other than the odd riot, for sixty-seven years. Furthermore, there was now no European enemy against whom the army could be structured or trained, a service the French had conveniently provided for so long. The absence of any threat gave little incentive for military efficiency, particularly when that came at a cost. Britain was certainly involved in several wars prior to the Crimea in 1854, but these were far away in the colonies, and largely fought by locally raised troops, though the light cavalry regiments did deploy to India. Ironically, the French army suffered the same experience, their emphasis also centred on colonial warfare, and when they next came to fight a European enemy in 1870 they were woefully unprepared.

These factors were gradually to make the Household Cavalry seem an ornamental extravagance,[11] and the glories of Waterloo were soon forgotten. The Cavalry's role as royal guard and London police was to be their main focus in the coming decades, inevitably bringing them once more into dealings with the London mob. Unfortunately this happened relatively quickly after Waterloo, exacerbated by the riots following Queen Caroline's funeral. The wretched Queen, ignored by the Prince Regent throughout their married life, had decided to return to London in 1820 and assert her position as wife of the heir to the throne. She had long been a convenient focus for the radicals and serious rioting broke out against the Government when she arrived in the capital, so that the Life Guards were required to mount continuous street patrols for several days. On 7 August 1821, just after the glories of the coronation, from which she was famously excluded, the Queen died, having previously declared a wish to be buried in her home state of Brunswick. An escort was therefore arranged to take her body to Romford, and on the morning of 14 August a squadron of The Blues under Captain Bouverie drew up in front of her residence, Brandenburg House in Kensington, to meet with a local magistrate, Sir Robert Baker, and take matters forward. The agreed route bypassed the City, where radicals planned to hijack the procession, but as The Blues entered Hyde Park from Kensington a mob slammed the gates in their faces. The Life Guards, exercising their horses in the Park, came to their assistance, and forced the gates open as the mob pelted them. Baker, not the most decisive of men, now decided to go through Knightsbridge to try to reach Tyburn by Park Lane. However, the mob forestalled them and at Hyde Park Corner they found Park Lane barricaded. Baker changed route once more, and went along Piccadilly, whilst the Life Guards finally battered a way into the Park at Cumberland Gate amidst more serious violence. Eventually the beleaguered cortège reached Tyburn, only to find Tyburn Gate, at the end of the Edgware Road, also barricaded. Here matters descended into chaos and the Life Guards shot two men, Honey and Francis, who, as often seemed to be the case in such situations, appear to have been innocent bystanders.

The inquest into their deaths, during which the Life Guards were heavily criticized, was conducted from 17 August and was milked by the radicals. Dr Rogers, a tobacco manufacturer, giving evidence, told the coroner that he 'was at Cumberland Gate and saw a body of Life Guards; [there were] three in front, and the centre man appeared to be an officer from his dress, and the comparative effeminacy of his person, being much thinner and less manly than the other two'.[12] This was Lieutenant Gore, who, poor man, was also described by a second witness as being 'from eighteen to twenty, of an effeminate voice and boyish appearance'. He and Captain Oates both gave evidence and were subsequently convicted of manslaughter. There was, however, considerable public sympathy for them – some papers started a subscription fund for their defence – and nothing was ever done to punish them. There was further rioting as Honey and Francis's funeral procession passed Knightsbridge Barracks, probably planned as a further deliberate provocation. The mob accompanying the procession spied an unfortunate trumpeter riding unaccompanied and promptly beat him up. The Life Guards, who had been confined to barracks, found this too much to take and jumped the wall, setting about his assailants 'with swords and the butt end of carbines', which led to more accusations of criminality. The Sheriff of London, a radical called Waithman, wrote that the Life Guards acted as if they were above the law, and one paper noted that 'it seems apparent to us that the time is come when the people of Great Britain, like their ancestors, will not endure a standing army however small'.

Luckily public attention soon shifted to the case of Sir Robert Wilson, a serving general, who, riding past the Life Guards at Cumberland Gate, had strongly and publicly criticized Oates and was subsequently sacked by the King for inciting mutiny. His case quickly became a radical cause célèbre, and, although he was eventually reinstated, his plight diverted attention at a convenient time. Wilson was an interesting character, who was already in trouble for obtaining false passports to allow a condemned Bonapartist to escape execution under the restored Bourbons; Wellington called him a 'very slippery fellow'. However, he survived this disgrace and ended up as a Member of Parliament and the Governor of Gibraltar.[13]

There were several other occasions when the regiments were used to deal with riots, particularly in Sussex in 1830, when the 2nd Life Guards were sent to Brighton, and during the Chartist Riots in 1838–40, but thereafter not only were disturbances less frequent but the launch of the police force meant much of this disagreeable duty went to them, something Wellington had long advocated. Gradually, therefore, their royal guard and escort duties preoccupied them most and, though not particularly demanding militarily, they were time-consuming and often tiresome. Throughout most of the nineteenth century the King's and, subsequently, Queen's Life Guard involved two officers and forty-nine non-commissioned officers and privates, which meant the duty came along approximately every eight days and included numerous escorts and other ceremonial events. Most of these were now well-established routines, several of which are still current today, whilst a few were peculiar to the time. One of these was the funeral of George IV in St George's Chapel at Windsor in January 1830, conducted at night as royal funerals generally were in the nineteenth century. The entire regiment of Blues escorted the coffin of the King who had done so much for them, while the Life Guards lined the staircases and aisle. They were also to be involved in both the coronation and the funeral of George's short-lived successor, William IV, and the coronation of Queen Victoria in 1838, which was a particularly splendid affair, slightly marred by one London newspaper's nasty comment that two Life Guard officers at Buckingham Palace had dirty boots,[14] but the Household Cavalry particularly enjoyed the accompanying military review. Not only did they have the opportunity of seeing the new Queen, but they enjoyed the added bonus of watching Marshal Soult, Napoleon's Chief-of-Staff at Waterloo, now firmly in the Bourbon camp, and who had decided to use Napoleon's stirrups and leathers for the great day, bucked clean off his horse when one of these revered items broke. In 1852 the 2nd Life Guards escorted Wellington's coffin, the escort commander, Edward Howard, subsequently becoming a cardinal in the Roman Catholic Church, an irony which the staunchly Protestant Anglo-Irish Duke would probably have found unamusing.

Wellington himself continued as Colonel of The Blues, and therefore the first Blues Gold Stick, until 1827. Although he now had the same right of access to the King on regimental matters, such as appointments and promotions, as the two Life Guard colonels, he purposely refrained from exercising it, regarding such matters as more correctly the preserve of the normal army chain of command; in fact he had written to the Duke of York in 1820, when The Blues became part of the Household Cavalry, to say that he deplored the 'extension of this questionable privilege'. Wellington still seemed to regard the position as a largely political one. He expressed considerable surprise when the King appointed Lord Combermere to be Colonel of the 1st Life Guards in 1829 on the death of the aged, but much loved, Lord Harrington, without first consulting the Prime Minister, though he was personally pleased that his old cavalry commander was to be so honoured. When the Duke of York died in 1827 Wellington succeeded him as Commander-in-Chief, becoming at the same time Colonel of the Grenadier Guards, requiring him to resign as Gold Stick. Several senior officers thought that they might be in line to take over from him, including Lord Londonderry, a distinguished former cavalry officer and diplomat, but the King chose his brother Ernest, Duke of Cumberland and later King of Hanover. He did not prove a particularly inspired colonel, and, in true Hanoverian style, firmly believed that the three Gold Sticks-in-Waiting, in other words the Colonels, should have absolute authority over appointments and promotions in their respective regiments without reference to normal army authorities. His views, therefore, reflected those that had led to the resignation of the grand Duke of Northumberland in 1814. By 1830 he had forced the

The Last Return from Duty. Wellington retired as Commander-in-Chief in 1852. He had always complained that the sentries at Horse Guards never bothered to salute him until he became Colonel of The Blues, a post he had handed over to the Duke of Cumberland in 1827.

The Life Guards at the Coronation of William IV.

issue to such an extent that the new King, his brother, William IV, had to make a decision. With Wellington now supreme at Horse Guards, William decided the Household Cavalry should be regarded similarly to any other regiment in the army. The Gold Sticks would continue to be responsible directly to the monarch for matters such as guards and escorts, but in all other matters the Household Cavalry 'should enjoy all the advantages which can be derived from the command and care of the General Officer Commanding-the-Army-in-Chief' and 'should make all their applications respecting promotions, exchanges, leaves of absence etc.' to him. Cumberland was predictably furious and told William IV that 'it appears that your Majesty means to place the Gold Stick merely on the footing of a Court Office, which changes the whole character of the situation, as it ceases to be a pure military one'. And, he thundered on, 'I cannot, as eldest Field-Marshal in the British army, next to his Grace the Duke of Wellington, receive orders from a General Officer junior to myself'.[15] He therefore 'begged most humbly to resign' and was a little aggrieved that this was quickly accepted.

His successor was Rowland, Lord Hill, Wellington's veteran corps commander and elder brother of Robert, who had commanded at Waterloo and resigned in 1823. His youngest brother Clement, who had served as his aide-de-camp, had now taken over as commanding officer, so The Blues remained very much a Hill family preserve.[16] Wellington claimed he had no part in the selection of another of his close favourites, for he did not want political opponents to accuse him of abuse of patronage. It is more likely that the regiment itself asserted pressure on the King to choose Hill, for not only was there the obvious family connection but the Waterloo generation was concerned that military eminence was being lost at the expense of fashionable repute. The appointment of distinguished former operational commanders, as opposed to political appointees, as Colonel might redress this. Queen Victoria, when she acceded in 1837, strongly supported this policy, regarding the Household Cavalry colonelcies as fitting rewards for her most senior officers. In 1842 she selected Uxbridge, now Marquess of Anglesey, to succeed Hill. However, even then politics played a part. Anglesey, happily ensconced as Colonel of his own regiment, did not really want the job. 'A Service of 45 years in the 7th would make me lean to remaining as I am,' he wrote, but 'a house party of some thirty-five Whigs, "all good men and true", expressed their fear that The Blues might "fall into the Tory hands of Lord Londonderry". There was much concern . . . that their party had no representative at the head of any of the Household regiments',[17] and Anglesey accepted. Thereafter all the regiments had distinguished senior officers as colonels for the next fifty years, although some, such as Combermere and Anglesey, were more distinguished than others, such as Lucan, of whom we shall shortly be hearing more.

Life as an officer in the Household Cavalry in the decades after Waterloo was agreeable, if rather dull, and certainly expensive. Commissions remained

After George IV's and William IV's experiments with bearskins and Roman style helmets (*above*), Prince Albert introduced a more sensible German designed helmet for both the Life Guards and The Blues (*right*), which is still in use today.

the most expensive in the army; a sub-lieutenant's place in the Life Guards in 1854 cost £1,260; a captaincy £3,500 and a lieutenant colonel's position £7,250. The figures for The Blues were the same, except that a cornetcy cost only £1,200. On top of that was the considerable cost of uniform, horses and mess life, now way beyond what could be funded from pay, and a private income was essential. Few had the opportunity, or inclination, to serve in India, which offered the only prospect of active service. Some, like Edward Kelly, transferred because they could not afford life in London. He was, however, credited with the success of the eight regiments of cavalry at the siege of Bhurtpore in 1826. Others, like Clement Hill, went to India on promotion. He was made a Major General and given command of the Madras Army in 1841, but died naturally soon after his arrival. Several went into politics, such as Colonel George Reid, commanding officer of the 2nd Life Guards, elected Member of Parliament for Windsor in the controversial 1845 by-election. He was seen as the 'court' candidate, strongly opposed by the local radical, Rupert Kettle, who accused him of using soldiers to intimidate the electorate; the normally supportive Windsor papers reported 'a scandalous breach of public peace and order' with soldiers drunk and running riot, and even *The Times* opined that 'we are not even sure now, that Kettle is not the legal member for Windsor'. Reid felt he had to resign, and during the next general election great care was taken to keep the Household Cavalry in barracks.[18] Otherwise the majority of officers were content to take advantage of the sporting and social opportunities afforded by London and Windsor. Whilst guard and escort duties were time-consuming, they were not exactly mentally taxing. The highly efficient non-commissioned officer corps ran the daily regimental administration under the direction of the Adjutant, still an elderly officer commissioned from the ranks, with few demands on the officers. Several preferred living in Windsor, still seen as something of a refuge from the turmoil of Victorian London and less public; twenty-eight-year-old Captain Hugh Baillie, of The Blues, for example, found it easier to set up house with his forty-seven-year-old mistress, Lady Glintworth, in Clarence Crescent – interestingly, the household also included her twenty-four-year-old niece and a twenty-one-year-old friend of hers. The regiment in Windsor ran its own pack of drag hounds, one of whose best meets was the Crown Hotel in Slough, and the officers and court officials had a theatre company, the Windsor Strollers, who put on regular performances at the Theatre Royal.

Many officers now joined for much shorter periods – much as in the early 1800s – indifferent to any military career, and regarding themselves as only peripherally subject to their commanding officers. There is a wonderful group portrait of the officers of the 1st Life Guards in their mess in 1857 which typifies their attitude midway through this period. It was commissioned by Mervyn Wingfield, 7th Viscount Powerscourt, who joined the regiment in 1854 and left eight years later. He enjoys the central position, together with his friends Viscount Grey de Wilton, who only served seven years, and The Honourable William North, who served for six years. The Commanding Officer, Lieutenant Colonel Parker, whom Powerscourt and the officers much disliked for being too strict and humourless, is depicted in the far corner of the room, his back to his officers, looking very grumpy and referred to as Carter. Each officer is portrayed in a different form of the bewildering variety of uniforms then worn: Powerscourt himself is shown in full dress, with helmet and cuirasses, whilst others are in frock coats, stable dress or, in many cases, civilian clothes which reflect their interests. The concept was repeated in 1988 when the officers of the current Household Cavalry Mounted Regiment had a contemporary version painted and the two portraits now hang together in the Knightsbridge mess.

Powerscourt was also something of an artist himself and kept a sketchbook of regimental life throughout 1857 and 1858. He had a sharp sense of humour, and through his hand we see Quartermaster Hanley saluted by the Foot Guards who mistake him for the Duke of Cambridge, the Commander-in-Chief, and Colonel Parker berating the young officers for looking so scruffy alongside two immaculately turned-out corporals. Most of the sketches are, predictably, devoted to field sports, at which the officers spent most of their leisure and a fair amount of their duty time.

It would be quite easy to misjudge the officers in the group portrait. With their relaxed attitude, cigars, drinks, dogs, endless variety of uniforms and lack of respect for military authority, they may seem detached, even louche. Yet underlying Powerscourt's sketches one senses a happy and cohesive regiment at ease with itself. The Household Cavalry were by no means the only regiment in the army to lack recent operational experience, and the sketches show a self-confident group of officers and soldiers, who thoroughly enjoyed their job, however much they may have disliked their commanding officer. They were, though, serving at a time when the gap between officers and non-commissioned officers and privates in the British army was as wide as it had ever been, and the lack of military action gave few opportunities to develop the mutual respect that comes when all ranks are together in the field for months at a time. This gap was not quite as marked in the Household Cavalry as in other parts of the army, such as the infantry regiments. Fifty-four per cent of Household Cavalry recruits came from skilled or semi-skilled backgrounds, and a few still had private means and the vote, though these were far less numerous than in 1780. However, the lack of Government funding for barracks and welfare meant the lives of the officers were in sharp contrast to those of the non-commissioned ranks. Army and ordnance spending, which had been £49.6 million in 1815, was down to just £8.9 million by 1846, and whilst the King may have been sincere when he spoke of the Household Cavalry enjoying all the advantages derived from the care of the commander-in-chief, these were not immediately apparent to the soldiers in Knightsbridge, Regent's Park and Windsor.

The Powerscourt Painting. The officers of 1st Life Guards in their mess in 1857, painted wearing the wide variety of uniforms then in use or civilian clothes according to their interests. Powerscourt and de Wilton are to the fore, whilst the unpopular commanding officer, Colonel Parker (who is referred to as Carter) is on the far left looking grumpy. A bachelor, he had purchased his captaincy but was promoted beyond that by brevet. Other more popular regimental characters, such as Stead, the mess waiter, and Hugh Hanley, the Irish Quartermaster, who closely resembled the Duke of Cambridge and whose party trick was to get the Foot Guards to 'present arms' when he rode past, are sympathetically portrayed. So are William Hessy, the Riding Master, who joined as a Private four years before Waterloo, and John Limbert, the Adjutant, commissioned from the ranks aged forty-six, and reputedly the best swordsman in the British Army. The only man in the painting with any operational experience was Mr Jex, the vet, who had been a veterinary adviser to Raglan in the Crimea.

Some of Powerscourt's comical sketches of regimental life between 1857 and 1858, which now form part of an ornamental screen in the officers' mess at Knightsbridge.

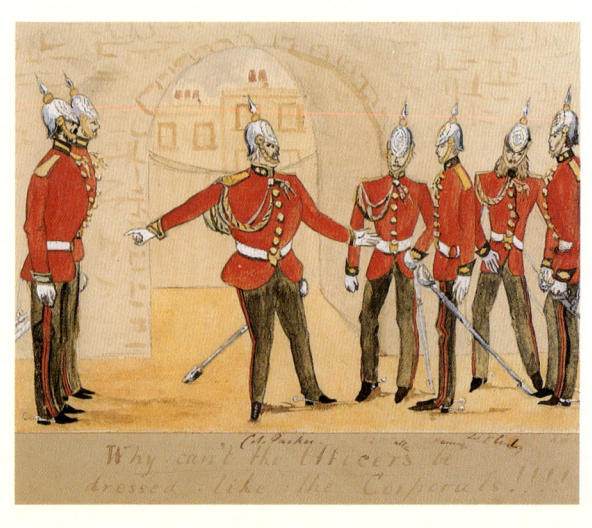

Mounting Guard.

Going round Stables.

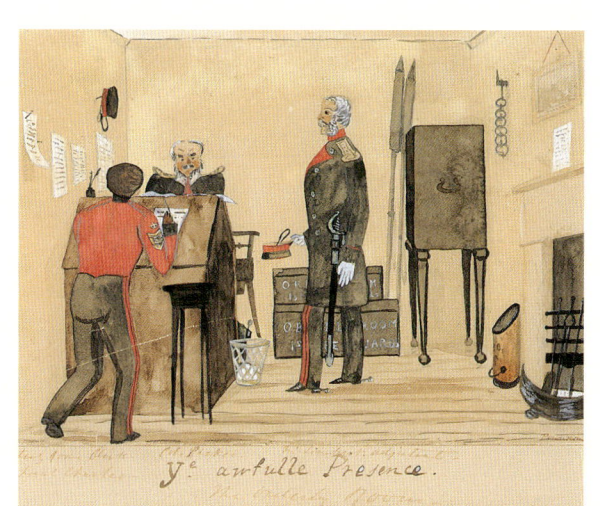

Ye awfulle Presence.

E.J.W. Patten. Esq. Sub Lt.

All three barracks were far too small, with around 300 cubic feet allowed per man, whereas the figure for gaols was 1,000. In Windsor nine soldiers slept, washed, ate, cleaned and stored their equipment in a room measuring 28 by 16 feet. They were allowed one roller towel per week between them, and their bedding – straw stuffed into paillasses – was only changed every two months. Washing facilities included a wooden tub, which stood in the middle of the room and also passed as a urinal at night. There was no running water and no washrooms, and even as late as the 1860s the regiment opposed the introduction of water closets as they became blocked with the bundles of hay issued, instead of lavatory paper. This last commodity was eventually issued on the basis of one sheet per soldier every four days. The death rate in Knightsbridge Barracks was seventeen in every 1,000, against an average for Kensington Parish, to which the barracks belonged, of just three in every 1,000. What amazes now is how long it took anyone to notice. Whilst contemporary conditions throughout England were almost as bad, the situation was not abnormal to Parliament or to Horse Guards, and so it was not until the army reforms after the Crimea that there was any urgency to address the causes. One of the main protagonists for reform was the crusading Regimental Medical Officer of The Blues, Dr Logie, who as late as 1870 was criticized by the Army Medical Department for having written a letter saying that Windsor Barracks were unfit for habitation, having had the water analysed and finding it to contain 'an excess of chlorine, ammonia and organic albuminoid'.[19] The general officer commanding the Home District, to which Windsor belonged, remarked that it was unhelpful for doctors to show such private initiative!

Life for families was even more disagreeable. In the nineteenth century the army had become less tolerant of soldiers marrying, restricting the number of wives permitted to six to a troop. No extra facilities were provided, and married quarters consisted of a curtained-off corner of a barrack room, allowing absolutely no privacy or opportunity to develop family life. However, the relatively settled nature of the Household Cavalry's duties now led more soldiers to marry, and the lack of provision for families began to be seen as not only unhealthy but unacceptable to a society concerning itself with public morality. The Blues led the way by ignoring Horse Guards' regulations and allowing married soldiers to live outside barracks, and by 1841 ninety-six of the regiment's families did so, although on their pay rented quarters were still poor. A regulation in 1836 decreed that soldiers could only marry if they had earned two good conduct badges, as these each carried 1d. extra pay, deemed sufficient to cover a basic rent. As it took on average fourteen years to earn these badges the system rapidly became impractical and in 1849 a married allowance of 2d. a day was introduced, though soldiers still had to get their commanding officer's permission before they qualified. By 1851 all wives had moved out of the barracks, except those of non-commissioned officers, whose families were allotted separate rooms, the original married quarters. Queen Victoria was

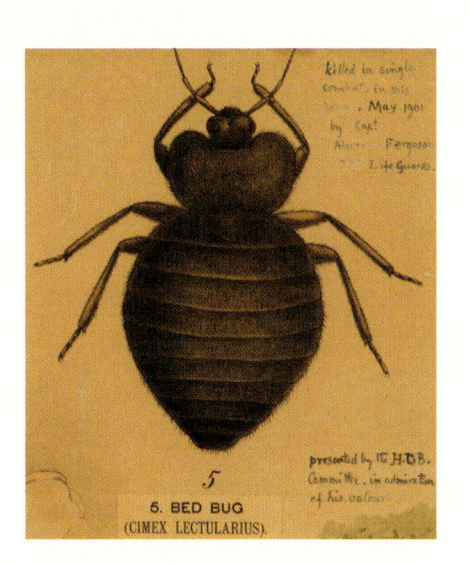

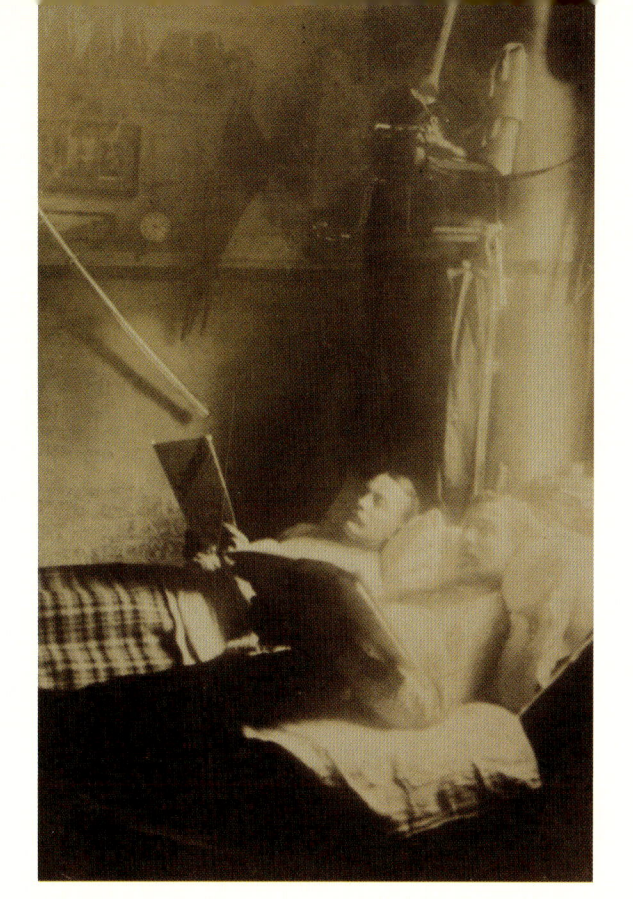

Accommodation was quite cramped (*above right*). The officers' quarters were not much better as this bed bug killed 'in single combat' at Horse Guards in 1901 testifies (*above*).

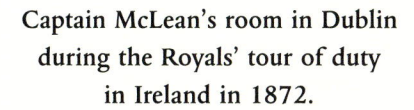

Captain McLean's room in Dublin during the Royals' tour of duty in Ireland in 1872.

horrified when she inspected these in 1864 and ordered them immediately rebuilt, and the following year a purpose-built block for thirty-five families was erected. The regiments ran their own schools, presided over by a corporal major, and many children regarded it as natural that they should follow their father's career, often signing on as boy soldiers, for whom there remained an establishment of two in each troop. Many of the wives and daughters also worked in the regiment, either as waitresses or laundry women, which, given that they had to move every year, was easier for them than holding down civilian jobs. Throughout the century some soldiers preferred, like the officers, to leave their families in Windsor when the regiments rotated. The unfortunate Private Charles Wooldridge did so, installing his attractive young wife in Alma Terrace while he went with The Blues to Knightsbridge in 1895. She started an affair, which led to an inevitable row during which the infuriated Wooldridge stabbed her. He was executed in Reading Gaol while Oscar Wilde was serving his sentence for homosexuality there and has been immortalized in Wilde's 'Ballad of Reading Gaol' as the 'brave man with a sword'.

Military punishments in the Household Cavalry were less severe than in other parts of the army. Whenever a Household Cavalryman was flogged he was immediately discharged. In the Parliamentary debates over flogging at the time of the Burdett riots, The Blues had been particularly praised by Joseph Hume as a regiment where 'flogging never takes place', although it is rather suspicious that when the regiment was inspected in 1815 the relevant pages of its court martial book had been torn out, so this claim could not be verified. Courts martial certainly did take place, but there had never been a tradition of flogging in The Blues, where even fifty years before such degradation would have been considered unthinkable. From 1816 the records show that there were about four floggings a year up until 1827, after which it became extremely rare. The Life Guards made more use of the lash, particularly the 2nd Life Guards, although again they hardly resorted to it after 1827; the last soldier flogged in the Household Cavalry was Private William Atkinson of the 2nd Life Guards, who received 150 lashes in 1843 for doing something rather nasty to a mare with a broom handle; he was also charged with 'ignominy', and, of course, dismissed.

Overall it was not regarded as a bad life, and recruiting remained good. Most served for an average of ten years, although a steady trickle purchased their discharge, or bought their way out of their contracts of service, mainly through boredom. There was little entertainment, apart from the odd band concert or cricket match, and many of the men longed to go on active service. The Waterloo legend still dominated their lives, and the Waterloo men were still regarded as national heroes, though George Clements thought them 'terrible old ruffians. Their language would have shaken the devil on his throne and they drank whisky like water.'[20] However when Private William Westwood, who had charged with the 1st Life Guards, died in 1846, his funeral still made the front page of the papers and a vast crowd turned out to follow his cortège.

The Royals found life after Waterloo equally unchallenging, and unlike the Household Cavalry were not often together in barracks, making their regimental cohesion even more difficult to retain. They too were cut back in 1818, losing two troops, so that Sigismund Trafford had to go on half pay, and, with no action in prospect, little likelihood of re-employment. The remaining six troops were reduced by thirteen men. Ben the Ruler continued in command, taking them from Kent to Ipswich and then to Scotland for a year. From 1818 until 1821 they were on the first of what were to become regular deployments to Ireland, and on their return they were sent to Dorset, then to London, back to Scotland and then to Ireland once more. Policing was their main duty and little opportunity arose for military training. They also suffered from George IV's beautification policy, the officers grumbling at having to find what by 1829 amounted to £140 for full dress which now included a ludicrously impractical Roman-style helmet, complete with horse-hair crest. Gradually the old Peninsula and Waterloo veterans left. Ben the Ruler finally handed over command in 1829, having been in post for nineteen years; sadly he had outlasted the Secretary, who had left in 1826, so we have no record of the subalterns' views of his final years. Dorville retired in 1827, and Clark transferred to the Royal Scots Greys, who had also captured an Eagle at Waterloo; he eventually became their colonel, and one gets the feeling he never really forgave his own regiment for doubting his version of the events in that epic charge. The last Waterloo veteran, Goodenough, retired in 1833. Their replacements tended to be wealthier, easily able to find the £840 required to purchase a cornetcy and, as in the Household Cavalry, less committed to a career. Consequently they did not stay for very long, finding the lack of opportunity for military action frustrating and the rapid succession of postings unsettling. As a result the average age of officers decreased, so that the six captains serving the next time the regiment went on operations in 1854 averaged just less than six years' service. There were exceptions, such as de Ainslie, who took leave to study German and attach himself to the Prussian army, but they were few.

The men found their frequent tours in Ireland depressing, particularly from 1835 to 1838 when they had the unpleasant and sad job of policing the food riots. George Clements, who joined in 1846 as he found his job as a clerk to a firm of land agents in Norwich boring, recorded his impressions of a riot at Rathkeale in County Limerick, when the workhouse, where flour was known to be stored, 'was literally besieged by a frantic mob of peasants clamouring for bread'. The mob 'began to bombard us with heavy stones, bottles and the like' when they realized that all the troops had taken refuge inside the workhouse. Later, as he records in his diary, his troop had to officiate at the public hanging of Ryan Puck and his accomplices, the notorious White Boys, who attracted considerable public sympathy when hung in chains. De Ainslie described their marches through the country as being 'far from journeys of pleasure, generally through a wild and dreary country' with perpetual rain,[21] and they were all relieved to return to Liverpool in 1848. Clements' troop, D Troop, was sent to Halifax where they were quartered in an old hotel. 'The barrack room was used as a living-room by everybody, the married men and their wives as well as the single men. There was not the slightest privacy for anybody.' There were no regular cooks, and each man in the troop took it in turns to prepare meals, so the food was predictably terrible. Clements was promoted fairly rapidly to lance corporal in 1849, and went with his troop to Barnet in 1851, ready should there be any trouble in London during the Great Exhibition; this was a possibility that obviously much exercised Horse Guards, and 1851 was the only year when the annual Household Cavalry rotation was cancelled. In Barnet Clements lived at the Two Brewers, was made a corporal and earned his first good conduct badge, spending the extra penny a day on tobacco. The regiment was very much heavy cavalry.

> When I joined . . . my front rank man, Dicky Lambert, stood six feet six inches high and rode at twenty one stone. Many men rode at eighteen. The only weapon we carried was a very heavy sabre; pistols being abolished some years before. Sabre exercise only included five cuts and one thrust. And there was none of the splendid horsemanship you see . . . nowadays. They relied on weight in the charge. On parade we wore the old pattern brass helmets and every man had to have a moustache. If recruits did not possess one they had to black their upper lip with burnt cork before going on parade.

Clements also describes the attempts by Horse Guards to improve horsemanship, which involved teaching the heavy cavalry to jump, something the officers found natural enough from hunting, but which was not taught to recruits. The order caused something of an uproar, being considered totally unnecessary for heavy cavalry. Clements describes how his friend Fred Shaw, an old soldier of considerable size, was killed in his first lesson when he was thrown after his horse refused at the practice fence.

IN 1854 CLEMENTS RECORDS the first rumours of war with Russia, and The Royals were told to hold themselves in immediate readiness. In 1853 the Tsar had taken advantage of the chronic decline of the Ottoman Sultan's regime to seize Turkey's European provinces of Moldavia and Walachia, in modern-day Bulgaria and Romania. France and Great Britain feared he might not stop there and could come to dominate the Dardanelles and Egypt. The so-called 'Eastern Question', the stability of the ever-vast Ottoman Empire, would remain, as every schoolchild knows, an enduring issue of British foreign policy for many years, and even today the Household Cavalry are suffering from its consequences in Iraq. In October 1853 the Sultan declared war on Russia, and after a winter of fruitless discussion, France and Britain joined him in March 1854. The Crimean War, as it came to be known, was initially popular at home, even though Russia claimed her intervention was to protect the Sultan's Christian subjects and to gain access for them to the Holy Places in Jerusalem, which were under Ottoman control. Public attention focused more on Tsar Nicholas as a despot and 'an enemy of liberty abroad, and an upholder of serfdom at home'.[22] War was seen as potentially advantageous to trade, and even as cleansing British honour after forty years of peace. What neither the British public nor their timid Prime Minister, Aberdeen, realized was that their army was in no fit state to fight. It was now to do so, attended for the first time by a press corps who saw themselves as the guardians of the high standards of public administration the British now expected, and who attracted an increasingly wide readership as a result. The circulation of *The Times*, which was to be foremost amongst those newspapers criticizing the administrative chaos in the Crimea, had been 7,000 copies a day in 1817; by 1851 that figure had risen to 40,000.[23]

The British army that was dispatched to the Black Sea in the summer of 1854 consisted of five divisions of infantry and one of cavalry. This cavalry division was commanded by Lord Lucan, and consisted of a heavy brigade of ten squadrons under General Scarlett, a genial and intelligent man, albeit without any operational experience, and a light brigade, under the infamous Lord Cardigan, who had already attracted criticism for personifying all that was wrong with the British cavalry. As no regiment was strong enough to deploy more than two squadrons at war strength, five heavy regiments produced two each, so in May The Royals embarked 320 men under their new commanding officer, John Yorke, who had joined in 1832 and who was well liked, though Sergeant Major Cruse, who was to write regularly to his wife during the war, thought he looked 'like an old Jew'.[24] Ben the Ruler, having served outside the regiment as a general, had returned as Colonel in 1842, a position he was to hold for twenty-seven years, giving him a total service as commanding officer and colonel of forty-six years. The Secretary would have turned in his grave had he known. Whilst they considered themselves in very good order as a regiment, with fine men and horses, The Royals had not conducted any formation training for thirty-nine years, and they were now part of an expeditionary force led by men like Lucan, with no experience of such operations, and, in particular, with a totally inadequate understanding of logistics. The Commander-in-Chief, Lord Raglan, who succeeded Lord Anglesey as Colonel of The Blues the month he sailed, had in fact enjoyed considerable success as a staff officer under Wellington in the Peninsula and had lost an arm at Waterloo, but he was now sixty-five and had never actually commanded any formation in the field. Brave, charming, but largely incompetent, he was to

Lord Raglan, the charming but ineffective British Commander in the Crimea, who had been one of Wellington's staff officers. He forgot that the French were now his allies, jumping up in alarm when told they had arrived at his headquarters. He was Colonel of The Blues when he died in June 1855.

cause his staff some confusion by jumping up in alarm when told the French had arrived at his headquarters, forgetting that they were now his allies. Little attempt was made to learn from those officers who had fought in India – often cold-shouldered in the smart light cavalry regiments as being in some way socially inferior – though the sensible Scarlett appointed two of them to his staff and listened carefully to their advice.

The army's initial destination was Varna, on the Black Sea coast, north of Constantinople, from where it was to threaten the Russian flank on the River Pruth. The Russians, however, withdrew and there was little for the Allies to do but wait while new plans were discussed in London and Paris. Varna was not a particularly attractive place to wait. Raglan had been warned it would be difficult to supply the army there, not least because Horse Guards had turned down the provision of a transport corps as unnecessary. It was not long before the regiments began to suffer; food and fresh water were hard to find and soon large numbers of soldiers went down with cholera. Captain Stocks, who commanded a troop in The Royals, and who seems not to have concentrated in his English lessons at school, noted in his diary that by 5 August 'Dragoon Guards had 56 empty saddles . . . that will tell a tale of cholera but that is nothing when compared to the French Regts that went up to the Danube they left 6000 strong & lost in a fortnight 3000'.[25] On top of this, the horses suffered from glanders and farey.[26] George Clements was put in charge of the isolation lines. 'We were completely cut off from the rest of the troops and our food was thrown to us over a hedge. The epidemic was very bad, and with my own hand I shot twenty-eight horses.'[27] He thought taking the infected horses swimming in the salty sea water might help cure them, but found it difficult to control them. 'Riding a swimming horse when one is naked is very unpleasant and makes it an awkward job to hang on with the water rushing between one's thighs and the horse's flanks.' He was swimming a horse around a transport in the bay one day when the sailors on board started cheering. The horse panicked, kicked Clements off and made for the shore, leaving him to swim the mile and half inland on his own. He just made it but left off swimming after that.

Stocks rapidly found that 'the beauties of campaigning can only be experienced by being tried its all very well for those at home sitting in a nice cool place in the climate they are accustomed to . . . and say why don't the British army advance and what a glorious thing it must be to be out there . . . let them come and after a month they will alter their tune'. The flies were terrible. In the evening they congregated 'at the extreme top of the tent & then your time to pay them out for all the annoyance they have caused during the day blow them up with gunpowder and down they'll come in scores'. Rations had nearly dried up and Stocks suspected his brother was pocketing his pay instead of paying it into his account at Cox's. He was therefore very relieved when the decision was taken for the army to re-embark and continue down the coast to take Sebastopol, the major Russian city on the Crimean peninsula, a policy decided in London which provided negligible strategic advantage but made the army, dispatched with such publicity, appear to be doing something. The Royals were among the last troops to sail, so missed the Battle of the Alma on 19 September when the Allies, having landed on the Crimea, forced back a Russian force blocking their route inland. Clements, however, was there, as he had been afforded the great honour of being selected to join Lucan's staff as his orderly sergeant. His description of Lucan gives us, probably unwittingly, an interesting insight to his character.

> Early next morning we were astir, and saw before us the heights of the Alma covered with deep masses of grey-clad troops, while on our own side were long lines of twinkling steel where the English and French infantry moved forward to the attack. The cavalry regiments were drawn up by themselves and harangued by Lord Lucan in a very terse and common sense manner. 'Well, my lads,' said he, as he rode down the lines, 'there are the enemy, now you've got to fight 'em.'

As it was, the cavalry were not involved in the battle. Raglan had intended to use them to follow up a Russian retreat, but the French refused. Clements describes riding over the battlefield:

> when the action was over, which was not till close upon night fall . . . Lord Lucan . . . came upon an Englishman who had lost both legs and was slowly bleeding to death . . . The General pulled up and said: 'My poor fellow, I am afraid that you are badly hurt.' The man tried to sit up and gasped out: 'I suppose, sir, they'll give a fellow a medal for it.' He died a few minutes afterwards.

Clements later spent the night of the battle 'under the lee of a wall on the heights of the Alma, with hundreds of corpses, both of friends and foes all round'.

The Royals finally left Varna on 26 September and the storm they experienced on the voyage up the Black Sea made what they had suffered so far seem insignificant. The steamer towing their sailing ship lost control and cut them adrift at midnight on 26 September. The upper deck, where the officers' horses were stabled, collapsed, throwing them down on top of the troop horses below. 'Horses that had cost hundreds lying with broken backs and legs . . . horses and saddles, carbines and swords mixed up,' wrote Stocks. Clements reported the account of a farrier friend:

> it was determined to lighten the vessel by sacrificing some of the horses . . . with this purpose the farrier-sergeants descended to the 'tween-decks

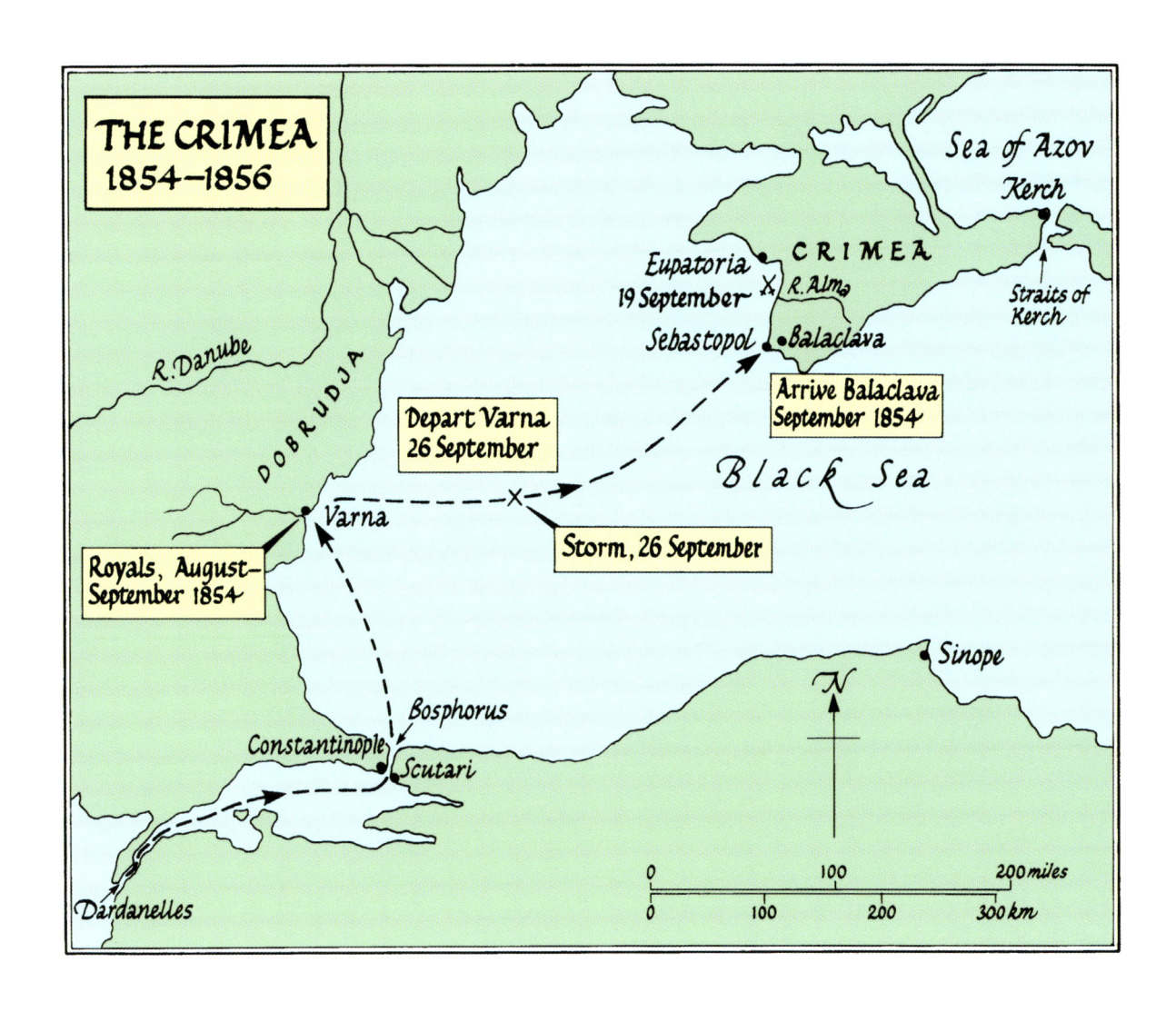

THE CRIMEA 1854–1856

- Sea of Azov
- Kerch
- Straits of Kerch
- CRIMEA
- Eupatoria 19 September
- R. Alma
- Sebastopol
- Balaclava
- **Arrive Balaclava September 1854**
- Black Sea
- R. Danube
- DOBRUDJA
- Varna
- **Depart Varna 26 September**
- **Storm, 26 September**
- **Royals, August–September 1854**
- Bosphorus
- Constantinople
- Scutari
- Sinope
- Dardanelles

0   100   200 miles
0   100   200   300 km

and cut the throat of horse after horse, the carcasses being at once hoisted on deck by the troops and swung overboard. In this manner ninety-nine of the officers' and troopers mounts were killed.

By the time they finally arrived in the Crimea they were down to one squadron. 'On that fearful night . . . the Regiment lost more horses than at Waterloo . . . Total loss, 150,' Yorke wrote to his sister.[28]

Raglan now besieged Sebastopol, a city he could probably have taken in the immediate aftermath of the action on the Alma had he been more forceful with the French. This meant supplying the Allied army by only one tenuous logistic chain, through the wholly inadequate harbour at Balaclava, from where only a rough dirt track led up to the Allies' positions on the heights between the sea and the city. As the weather grew colder, and it became apparent that Sebastopol was not about to fall, the soldiers suffered the consequences of those decades of military ineptitude. The cold became intense. 'Had an awful cold night of it,' Stocks wrote, 'night before last on out lying picket in the direction where there is supposed to be an army the wind had changed into the North & I never felt anything so cold in my life no fire out all night 3 miles from the camp'. The horses developed 'coats like sheep and are never groomed'[29] and Clements suffered from an attack of dysentery 'and was sent into hospital at Balaclava. The conditions in the hospital there were awful. The sick and wounded alike housed in small, unfurnished huts. There wasn't the slightest attempt at sanitation and we were under the fire of the enemies batteries.' Discharging himself, Clements crawled back to the regiment, and just made it to the tent he shared with thirteen others before collapsing. His friend Johnny Lee revived him with rum, and managed to get him to the regimental surgeon, where, as was common, he received much better care than in a base hospital. He was evacuated to Scutari, and spent a month recovering, arriving back on 21 October, and rejoining The Royals as his illness had cost him his place on Lucan's staff.

An attack by the Russians on Balaclava was expected daily, and consequently the cavalry patrolled persistently, often coming across the Russian Cossacks, who, Stocks thought, 'remind you of rabbits only not quite so harmless'. Balaclava was defended by an outer series of redoubts, positioned on the high ground north of the harbour and manned, with varying degrees of effectiveness, by the Turks, and then by an inner line of defences under the competent command of Sir Colin Campbell. At 5 a.m. on 25 October the Russian General Liprandi moved out to capture them with 25,000 men, including thirty-five squadrons of cavalry. When he received news of Liprandi's advance, Raglan ordered an infantry division to move down from its position in front of Sebastopol to reinforce Campbell. Knowing it would take them some hours to arrive, he sent Lucan forward to intercept the Russians around the redoubts. Lucan's brigades had 'as usual turned out half an hour before

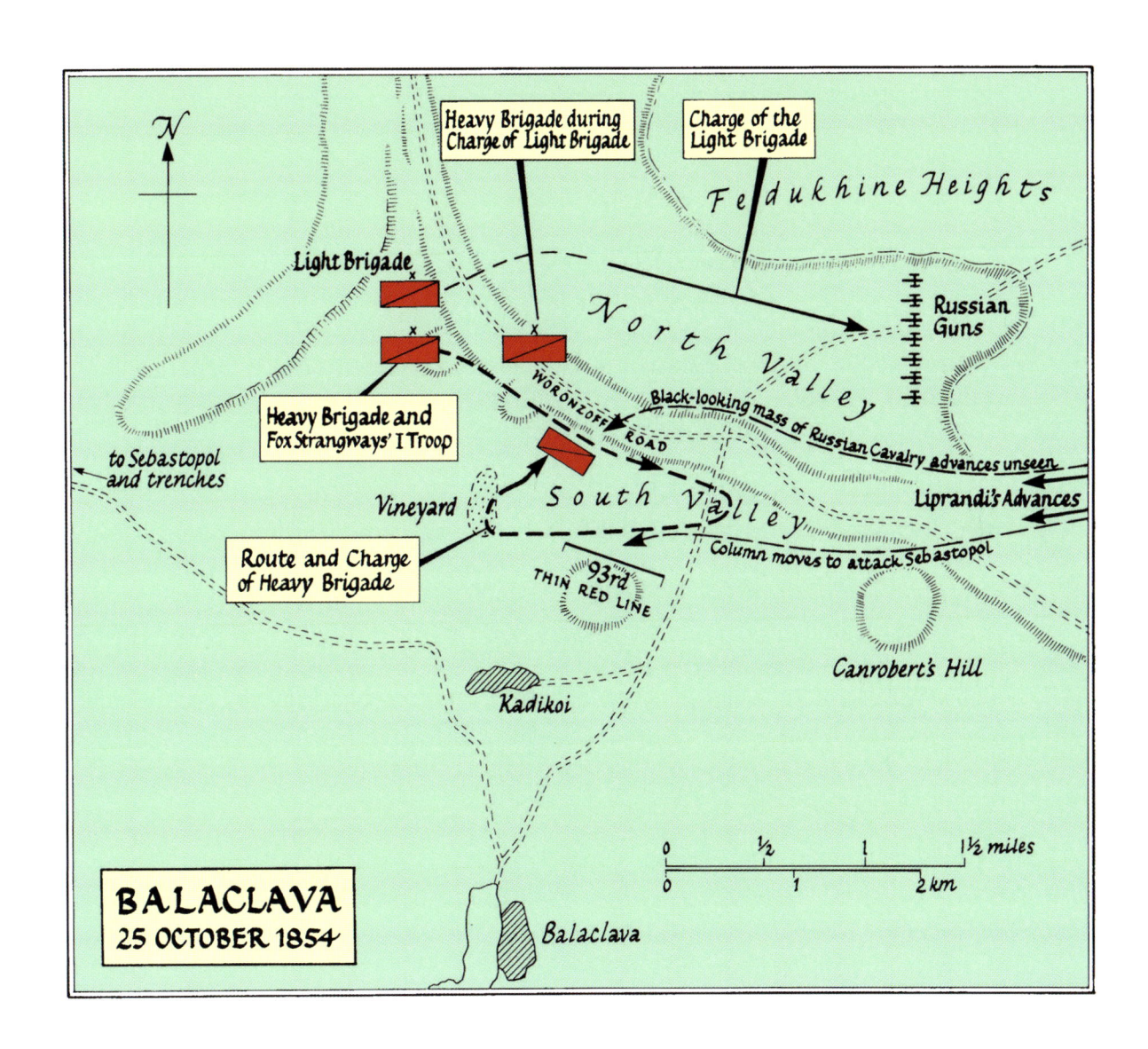

BALACLAVA
25 OCTOBER 1854

- Heavy Brigade during Charge of Light Brigade
- Charge of the Light Brigade
- Feldukhine Heights
- Light Brigade
- North Valley
- Russian Guns
- Heavy Brigade and Fox Strangways' I Troop
- WORONZOFF ROAD
- Black-looking mass of Russian Cavalry advances unseen
- to Sebastopol and trenches
- Vineyard
- South Valley
- Liprandi's Advances
- Route and Charge of Heavy Brigade
- Column moves to attack Sebastopol
- 93rd THIN RED LINE
- Kadikoi
- Canrobert's Hill
- Balaclava

day break'[30] and were ready. Leaving Cardigan and the Light Brigade as a reserve, Lucan took forward Scarlett's Heavy Brigade and some horse artillery. His eye for ground was not good, though to be fair to him the country around Balaclava is difficult to read, and as they came up they were engaged by Russian artillery. 'We were placed,' wrote Colonel Yorke,

> directly in the line of fire . . . All the very large shot that over crowned the heights naturally bowled like cricket balls into our ranks. . . . The officers could easily escape: we only had to move a few yards to let the shot pass which movement I effected frequently, but when the shot came opposite the closely packed squadrons it generally took a front & rear rank horse and sometimes a man. . . . In this foolish manner we lost 7 horses and 2 men.[31]

The horse artillery with them returned fire, but their wagon horses had earlier been sent down to the harbour for supplies so they quickly ran out of ammunition.

Liprandi now successfully occupied some of the redoubts and closed on to the defences of Balaclava itself. Sir Colin Campbell therefore sensibly advised Lucan to retire, which he did, taking all Scarlett's 'Heavies' less The Royals. This allowed Campbell and his famous 'thin red line' of the 93rd Highlanders 'to stand the brunt of it which they did well & sent the [Russian] Hussars to the right about in fine style,' wrote Stocks. 'When the Russian cavalry were almost on top of them, they received their order to fire,' wrote Clements, who witnessed the attack.

> At such close quarters it was awful; the head of the Russian column crumpled up like smoke at the first discharge. They received a second and a third which shook them, that almost on the Highlanders bayonets they wheeled to the left and rode back. As they turned, we could plainly see many men who had been hit tumble out of their saddles. Then the whole body swung round to the right about and retreated.

However, whilst Liprandi was forced back by the Highlanders, his main body of cavalry, 'a black looking mass'[32] of about 2,000 hussars and lancers, with black horses and wearing black oil skin covers over their shakos – non-metallic cavalry hats – with dark grey overcoats, and under command of General Rikoff, had moved steadily up, out of sight of Raglan and Campbell, one valley to the north. As Scarlett's Brigade retraced their steps towards Balaclava, and had in fact just reached the area of the Light Brigade's camp where the ground was broken with vineyards and walls, they suddenly saw the 'black looking mass' as they wheeled left. It is difficult to know who was the more surprised, but Scarlett certainly reacted first. He remained calm, and took what seemed to the men like an age in dressing his squadrons so they

A private in C Troop of The Royals in marching order.

Colonel Yorke, who commanded The Royals in the Crimea. Sergeant Major Cruse thought he looked like 'an old jew'.

were in some sort of order forward of the vineyard walls. Clements reckoned that they were only 300 men in total, and when Scarlett had finished they were drawn up with The Royals' old friends from the Union Brigade, the Inniskilling Dragoon Guards and the Scots Greys in the first line and the 4th and 5th Dragoon Guards in the second. The Royals, whom Yorke had now moved forward, were coming up behind the Greys, when Scarlett rode forward a few yards and had his trumpeter blow the charge. It was a difficult manoeuvre from a standing start, with only 500 yards to cover, but Scarlett's calmness had unnerved Rikoff who had halted his squadrons, and as the first line of the Heavy Brigade hit them they were at a standstill.

> The first line charged and rode straight into the Russian ranks, but they were so outnumbered that they were outflanked, and Colonel Yorke saw the mess they were in and gave us the order to charge. We inclined to the left and rode down on the right flank of the Russians. The charge broke through the enemy's lines and checked his advance and in a few minutes the whole column had retreated,

noted Clements in something of an understatement. It soon became apparent that Rikoff had halted to throw two wings forward to engulf the tiny Heavy Brigade, but the committal of the British squadrons in quick succession meant that he never quite achieved it. From Raglan's vantage point he saw 'First Scarlett and his staff, then the three squadrons of the first line . . . swallowed up, lost and engulfed in the great grey Russian mass, and then suddenly they had not disappeared. Red coats were visible, bright specks of colour against the Russian grey.'[33] It took eight minutes for the 'black looking mass' to break, and neither Lucan nor Cardigan thought to pursue them with the Light Brigade, an obvious opportunity which would have turned a tactical success into an important victory, and for which omission Lucan was afterwards nicknamed 'Lord Look-on'. Casualties in the charge were remarkably light, with only ten British dead and ninety-eight wounded, some only very lightly. This was partly due to the uselessness of the swords on both sides. The British ones were still too easily bent to stick into a man's body, particularly if protected by a thick greatcoat. The Russians appear not to have sharpened theirs at all, and there were several cases of men with cuts, none of which caused serious injury. Mass and weight seem to have been the most important factor in the 'Heavies'' success; the worst Russian casualties were those poor unfortunates cut through their skulls to their chins by a 6-foot man standing in his stirrups and bringing his sword down on their heads. Helmets generally stood up well, but the lack of gauntlets led to several bad injuries to arms and hands. Neither pistols nor carbines were used. In terms of tactics and weapons, there was nothing in Scarlett's action which would have been unfamiliar to the veterans of Waterloo.

The Charge of the Heavy Brigade was a triumph, particularly given what the men and horses had been through in the preceding months, and says much for Scarlett's wisdom in having experienced Indian officers on his staff. It was commemorated by Alfred Lord Tennyson in an unexciting poem, which may be why it remains relatively unknown compared to the Charge of the Light Brigade, which was to follow soon afterwards and which Tennyson captured rather more vividly. The Royals were moved in behind the Light Brigade to support them as they galloped off to their destruction against Russian artillery. Wisely, Scarlett restrained them from becoming embroiled in the ensuing slaughter, but not before Yorke had his leg smashed by a cannonball, Captain Campbell had been shot through the back, Lieutenant Edwards through the calf and Lieutenant Hartop through the thigh – much more serious injuries than they had sustained that morning. Stocks witnessed the charge, writing,

> Lord Raglan was brought to Lucan to attack the enemy which he did by sending the light Cavalry into the greatest trap that ever was made . . . somebody said let the Light Cavalry go on, & on they went . . . they went at a gallop & we saw nothing more of them until we saw them coming back by ones & twos some mounted but mostly dismounted, such a smash never was seen, they were murdered it seems.

There was little relief that night, with the Russians expected to renew their attack; Stocks complained that he got to bed at 1 a.m. but was up again at 3.45 a.m. In fact, the Russians did not try again until 5 November, when they fell on the Allied infantry in their trenches in front of Sebastopol. The cavalry were not involved in the resulting Battle of Inkerman, but by then they were already fighting a battle of survival to keep their horses alive during the Russian winter.

On 14 November the Allies' camp was struck by a hurricane which destroyed all the tents except, annoyingly, Lord Lucan's, which was pitched in a gully. More seriously, it sank ten ships in Balaclava harbour, including the steamer *Prince* which contained all the troops' winter clothing. The storm was followed by heavy rains, making the track up from the harbour impassable, and snow. It was not the coldness of the weather that caused problems, but the complete lack of preparation to spend the winter outdoors. The cavalry division moved their camp nearer to Balaclava on 6 December and, Sergeant Major Cruse wrote to his wife, 'we have every reason to be thankful that our lot is not so bad as the poor infantry in the trenches . . . Take it altogether I do not think the weather has been much more severe than it was in Manchester last January, but only fancy, dearest, a camp life in such weather as that.' The poor horses suffered worst, unable to move, very short of forage and standing in deep mud. They 'have a good roll in the mud and after that a good fall of snow, and then the whole to be frozen on to them, is enough to kill any animal except one cast in

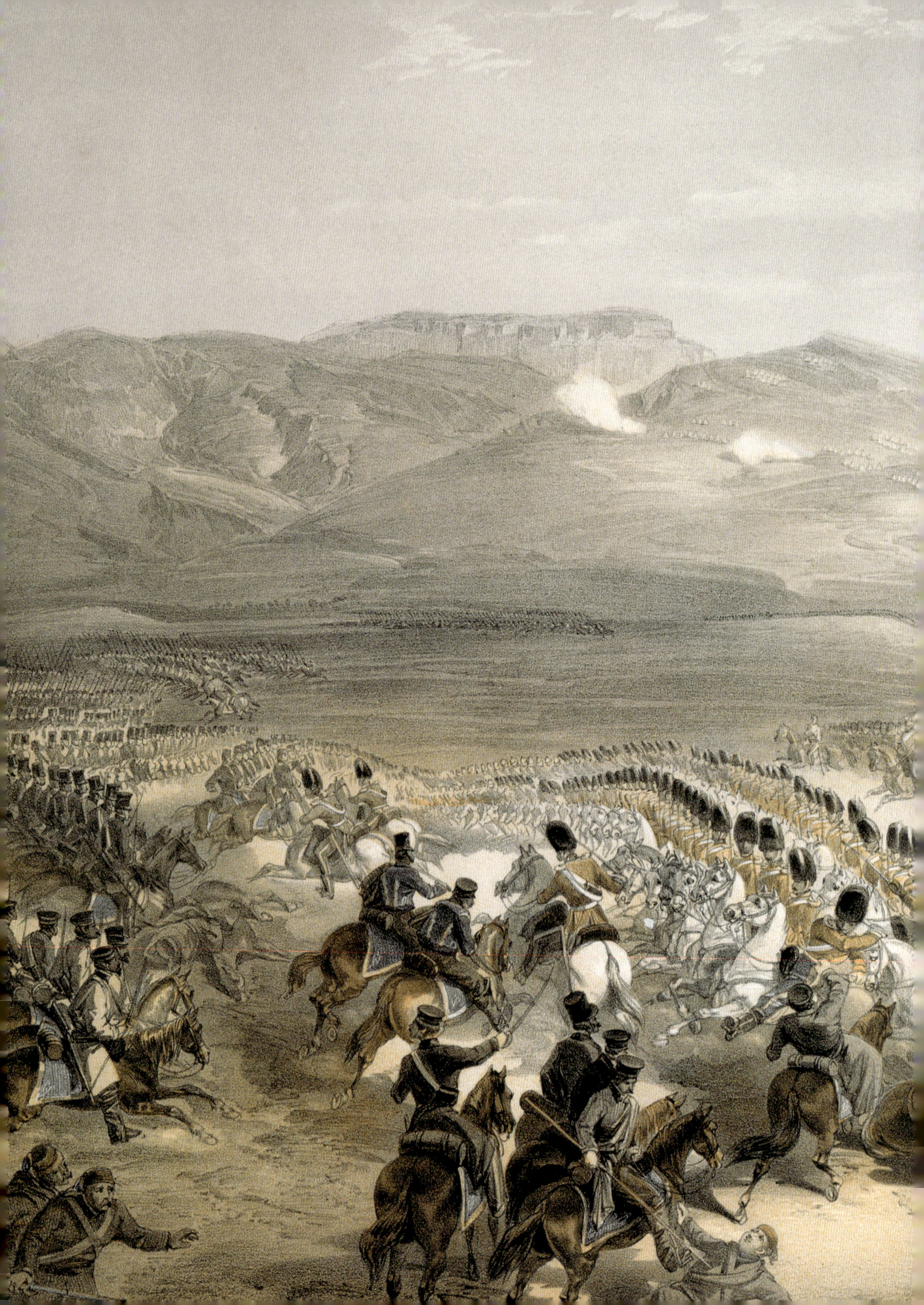

The Charge of the Heavy Brigade at the Battle of Balaclava in October 1854.
'First Scarlett and his staff, then the three Squadrons of the first line . . .
swallowed up, lost and engulfed in the great Russian mass.'

bronze,' Cruse continued in his next letter home.[34] Even worse than the physical hardships was the order of 12 December which required the cavalry to produce 500 horses every day to assist the commissariat in transporting supplies forward to the infantry. Lucan thundered ineffectually that 'the fearful consequence to the cavalry of having to continue in the discharge . . . of duties so totally foreign to their profession'[35] would cause disaffection and result in an unsustainable loss of horses; he was correct in his latter point, with the Heavy Brigade losing 47 per cent of its horses between October 1854 and March 1855 and The Royals losing an average of fifteen per month.[36] 'I calculate that in six weeks more,' Stocks wrote in his journal for 26 November, 'the heavies will be at an end, for the average of deaths in the brigade is ten per day.' Clements found that he would wake in the morning with his beard frozen to his chest and his clothes so rigid that they had to be thawed before he could put them on.

By January most of the cavalry had managed to construct rough wooden huts and life began slowly to improve. 'I am seated writing these notes at a round table', Stocks continued,

> rudely constructed . . . from the head of a rum cask . . . Behind me, are scattered a miscellaneous collection of empty bottles and boxes, and in the corners stand a barrel of cheap coal and a sack of charcoal suspended from the roof is the remains of what was once a ham . . . an oiled bag containing tobacco . . . and the rest of our stock of eatables and drinkables . . . my companion sleeps warm, first a mattress 2 horse rugs folded double, a blanket 5 more on the top of him, his cloak folded in three, his sheep skin then a waterproof sheet and lastly a pilot coat and his unmentionables . . . he sleeps in a welsh wig, a jersey over his shirt, a pair of pyjamas and Turkish slippers.

Conditions improved slightly in February with the construction of a light railway, and the arrival of recruits and remounts from England. Stocks did not think much of them. The remounts were 'cart horses, hearse horses, refuse', and of the recruits, who arrived with ludicrously tight uniforms, of these 'little young bears' half were either hospitalized or dead within ten days. Yet things were slowly improving. The fiasco of Balaclava and the accurate reporting from the attached correspondents had caused an outcry in England. A commission of enquiry was despatched to investigate what was going wrong, and there was a marked improvement in the supply system. The unfortunate Raglan died in June, succeeded by Simpson, who had headed the enquiry into Raglan's staff and who was at least a competent if not an inspiring leader. Campaign medals, to which the army seems to have attributed considerable importance since Waterloo, were also issued in an attempt to raise morale, although many thought them 'a vulgar looking thing and the clasps for the various battles look like decanter labels'.[37]

Sebastopol finally fell in September 1855 with heavy losses to the infantry, and a treaty with Russia was eventually negotiated in March 1856, one of the never-ending Peaces of Paris. The Royals saw no more military action, although they thought they might in August when, back to full strength, they were deployed forward to cover against the final Russian attempt to relieve the siege in a powerful attack at Tchernaya Bridge. There was, wrote Stocks, 'a fine slope of land for a gallop' and 'if [the Russians] had attempted a passage the chances are not many would have re-crossed'. Clements and his colleagues stole down to help the thousands of Russian wounded after the battle, but were shot at by them for their pains. 'More than once some wounded man, after receiving a draught of water, tried to rise up and shoot his benefactor or would attempt to stab him with his bayonet,' Clement wrote. Later, he and his friends rode around the ruins of Sebastopol on Cossack ponies they had bought for 10d. each. 'We wandered through the streets, observing the tremendous havoc played by our shell fire, with houses ruinous, streets torn up and confusion and wreck everywhere. We also explored the bomb-proof cave where the Russian general Todleben had lived. It was merely a dark hole with an earthen roof.' While exploring they discovered the ground was booby-trapped with mines and were shot at by saboteurs. In November they were sent back to winter in Scutari, from where they much enjoyed the pleasures of Constantinople, and in the spring of 1856 they returned home, arriving in Aldershot in May.

Chapter Fifteen

SMALL WARS IN AFRICA

THE FIRST THING THAT CLEMENTS wanted to do when he got home was to drink a pint of beer in an English pub, an aspiration with which future generations would sympathize. That was more difficult than it might seem, for although on arrival in Portsmouth the regiment 'found the whole place illuminated' for their arrival, 'the authorities, fearing that the inhabitants might be led to feast and make much of the soldiers' ordered them to march immediately. Clements was not to be outdone. In the first village they came to he told his friend Farrier Sergeant Stocks that his horse had a loose shoe, and while Stocks affected to inspect it, Clements went into the local and reappeared with two quarts of beer. The loose shoe was quickly fixed, and they 'cantered after the squadron again which we rejoined in a more contented frame of mind'.

The poor, sandy land around Aldershot had been acquired by the War Office just before the Crimea War and had been used for one manoeuvre in 1853, much along the lines of James II's Hounslow Camps. However, it was now decided, in the mood of post-war reform, that a permanent camp would be established there which would accommodate more than one regiment, and which, together with Colchester, Shorncliffe in Kent, and the Curragh in Ireland, constituted the British army's first proper garrisons outside London and Windsor. The Royals rather enjoyed living alongside other regiments, as it offered opportunities for socializing and endless varieties of mounted competitions, but they were not stationed there for very long, and by June were off for another tour in Ireland. Otherwise the reforms were more limited than many thought necessary, and despite various committees of enquiry there were few structural changes to the army until the late 1860s, when they were initiated not because of the lessons of the Crimea but because a Liberal Government saw they were long overdue and soon had the experience of the Franco-Prussian War of 1870, when the newly united Germany invaded and easily defeated the French, to substantiate their case.

In 1871 an anonymous pamphlet, *The Battle of Dorking*, was published,[1] speculating on what might happen to that most English of communities were

The regiments developed a fondness for mascots and pets in the nineteenth century. This bear seen with Private Locke was owned by H. Naylor-Leyland.

For those not fortunate enough to go off campaigning in Africa, the latter part of Queen Victoria's reign was a relatively quiet time. There were few escorts, and the main activity for the regiments in London was to mount the Queen's Life Guard.

A group of rather relaxed non-commissioned officers of 1st Life Guards c.1870.

the Germans to invade England. This introduced two very novel and alarming ideas. First, it effectively said that Germany, not France, was the main European threat to Britain and that, in the event of war, even somewhere as respectable as Dorking might not be safe from invasion. In 1868 Gladstone appointed Edward Cardwell as Secretary for War. A brilliant man, who might otherwise have been Chancellor of the Exchequer, Cardwell set about the first major reform of the army since the 1790s. He faced considerable opposition, not least from the Commander-in-Chief, the Duke of Cambridge, but between 1868 and his retirement in 1874 he effected a series of major reforms which shaped the British army, and, indirectly, the Indian Army, for the next century.

Cardwell is now chiefly remembered for having abolished the purchase system. This had long outlived whatever use it once had and few still supported it, though those that did, led by Cambridge, mounted a spirited defence in Parliament. The impact of its abolition was, however, considerably less than had been anticipated. In any case, it had never applied to gunners or engineers, who were now producing a generation of talented officers, and in the Household Cavalry and The Royals, the sort of regiments which the radicals in Parliament had hoped would be most affected, it made no difference at all, though officers were delighted to be compensated for their initial outlay, the total bill for which was £8 million across the army.[2] The financial barrier to a commission was not so much the purchase price as the high cost of horses, uniform and mess life on what remained very meagre pay. Between 1850 and 1899, seventy-seven peers or their sons served in the Life Guards, and thirty-nine in The Blues, the highest concentration in the history of either regiment, and the Household Cavalry persistently attracted the sons of the new industrialists, such as John Brocklehurst, son of the successful Macclesfield silk miller Henry Brocklehurst, who went on to be a major general.

The abolitionists assumed that the purchase system was responsible for the inadequacies of command in the Crimea, but this did not stand up to analysis. The vast majority of regimental officers had behaved professionally, remarkably few exercising their right to sell out and return home, despite appalling conditions and a lack of confidence in their generals. The problems were with the staff and the generals themselves, who were promoted on brevet, and the lack of training and professional education, more than of inherent privilege. One particular fault of the legislation was that it failed to introduce a robust system of promotion to replace purchase. Consequently regimental promotion now tended to be decided by seniority and influence, and although the Commander-in-Chief theoretically ensured merit also played a part, in practice that seldom happened. Confidential reports on officers' performance and competitive examinations for selection were introduced but were regarded with suspicion by the chain of command and largely ignored, until after the Boer War when the committee established to examine officers' education and advancement reported that in South Africa 'the advancement of the indolent and incompetent was just as rapid as that of conscientious and able officers'.[3] Lastly, in 1872 the system introduced by Charles II whereby Guards and Household Cavalry officers automatically assumed an army rank one above their regimental rank was abolished for all those who joined after August 1871.

Cardwell's other reforms did, however, have a profound effect. The War Office was reorganized and the Commander-in-Chief was now subordinate to the Secretary of State for War, which was to have major repercussions in the First World War. In 1868 Cardwell abolished flogging, and, although by then this punishment was seldom used, the ban on it gave soldiers greater self-respect. Cardwell carried out a major reorganization of the infantry, giving the regiments of the line – those infantry regiments who were not Guards – a geographical affiliation, and creating a battalion system so that each regiment had a foreign service battalion, available to deploy overseas, and a home service battalion, who could recruit and create a reserve. This idea of a rather more efficient reserve than the ancient county militia came from what was perceived, erroneously, to have been the major factor in the Germans' success in 1870 in that they could mobilize reserves quicker than the French. Cardwell also sorted out the artillery, giving them 156 more guns, although even he had to admit defeat when their technical experts managed to argue, against all the rules of scientific logic and military experience, that muzzle loaders were more efficient than the highly effective German breach loaders. Arguably he did less directly for the cavalry, although a number of small reforms, such as introducing rifled carbines, replacing the troop with the squadron as the main administrative unit in peacetime and increasing numbers by 1,700, were significant improvements. However, the chief significance of Cardwell, and something from which the whole army benefited, was that he formalized the status of the private soldier as an individual.

In the cavalry the privates had always been treated more as individuals than they had in the infantry, stemming from the days when they arrived as men of substance who provided their own horse. After Waterloo, and the award of a medal to every soldier who fought there, the attitude of British society had gradually changed, so all soldiers were valued as men in their own right rather than as cogs in a machine that delivered volleys at the correct time on the battlefield. Cardwell gave this growing respect a definite form, introducing terms of service that allowed soldiers to serve for shorter periods, introduced a proper career pattern and an educational programme with formalized record-keeping, and, most importantly, regularized pensions. Living conditions also improved, particularly for families. Whereas those Household Cavalrymen who fell at Waterloo were buried in mass graves, after 1870 every one who was killed in action had a headstone. Cardwell also gave the British army the questionable benefit of a reformed War Office. In 1871 he moved the Commander-in-Chief from Horse Guards to join him, the Financial Secretary

The Cardwell reforms, satirized in this cartoon, were to have a major effect on the British Army – but had little direct impact on the Household Cavalry.

When Lord Zetland left The Blues in 1874 he omitted to give the customary leaving present to the officers' mess. When asked what he was going to do about it, the very rich Zetland casually remarked, 'Oh, buy a piece of silver and put it on my bill'. The officers duly commissioned an enormous and grotesque centrepiece from the firm of Roskell & Hunt that took four to lift and cost the then astronomical sum of £1,000. It is seen here on the dining room table at Regent's Park barracks. The receipt is in the Household Cavalry Museum.

and the Surveyor General of Ordnance in his offices in Pall Mall, and he placed the Quartermaster General's department under that of the Adjutant General, effectively creating a single as opposed to a rival and competing staff, though even he thought that creating a single 'Chief of Staff' was going too far.

THE BENEFITS OF the Cardwell reforms were evident in 1882 in the highly efficient – unless you happened to be an Egyptian – campaign to defeat the revolt of Mohammed Arabi. Despite the defiance conveyed in the Powerscourt painting, there was disquiet among senior Household Cavalry officers that they were seen merely as a ceremonial guard, a role Queen Victoria seemed quite happy for them to fulfil. This had crystallized in 1871 when, during a debate in the House of Commons, a Liberal Member of Parliament, in some very direct remarks, noted that the effective performance of the German Uhlans – light cavalry armed with lances – in the Franco-Prussian War demonstrated the days of the heavy cavalry were over, and that the Household Cavalry, in particular, were merely ornamental, and cost the exchequer £100 per man per year – much of it the needless splendour of their uniforms – as opposed to £80 for a dragoon. He also added that the 'nocturnal revels of Knightsbridge' showed a 'considerable laxity of moral discipline'.[4] His tirade was answered by Captain Reginald Talbot, an officer in the 1st Life Guards and Member for Stafford, who spoke for many of the new generation of Household Cavalry officers in his offended response, which was well received, despite lasting a couple of hours. First, quoting no less an authority than Count Lehndorff, Master of the Horse to the German Emperor, he demolished the arguments against heavy cavalry, pointing out that the Uhlans were, in fact, much more substantial than might be supposed, weighing in at 20 stone 8 pounds against an average of 21 stone 13 pounds for a Household Cavalryman. Second, he reminded the House that a Household Cavalryman cost more because he was paid at a higher rate than his colleagues in the line cavalry, though he still had to purchase his own equipment on joining, which cost him £5. Household Cavalrymen were on duty far more than most soldiers, being on guard one day in four, and Captain Talbot repudiated allegations of 'revels' at Knightsbridge, by quoting military records which showed that civil crime and drunkenness were virtually unknown in the Household Cavalry, although he may have been stretching credulity on the latter point. He finished, in a move which may have been deliberately introduced to infuriate the radicals, by quoting their bête noire, the Duke of Cambridge, who had said recently that the Household Cavalry were, and always had been, the pride of the service.

Talbot may have won the debate, but many officers felt awkward and, throughout the 1870s, remained conscious that, in an army focused on overseas intervention, they were seen as something of an irrelevance. They were not encouraged by newspaper articles claiming that

The Blues were unavoidably prevented from attending morning service the other Sunday at Windsor, owing to a shower of rain. I understand that HRH the Duke of Cambridge has ordered umbrellas for the crack corps . . . and it is felt too risky to send them to church without this insurance against the cold. It might drizzle, you see . . . and the notion of a Blue being rained upon is quite appalling.[5]

When Mohammed Arabi, a nineteenth-century prototype of Nasser, overthrew the pro-British Khedive Tawfiq in Egypt in 1882, massacred the British community in Alexandria, and launched his Egyptian nationalist campaign, and it became obvious that a British force would have to restore order and safeguard the Suez canal, Colonel Keith Fraser, Commanding Officer of the 1st Life Guards, lobbied vigorously to ensure a Household Cavalry contingent was included. That he had to do this instead of the Gold Stick is probably explained by the fact that the Gold Stick was Lord Lucan.

The Household Cavalry owes much to Fraser, who dealt with the Queen's ambivalence, War Office apathy and hostility from other cavalry regiments. It would have been too much for the Queen to agree to any of the three regiments going as a formed unit, as that would have caused unacceptable disruption to the pattern of her guard and escort, so Fraser reverted to the Peninsula and Waterloo concept, lobbying for a squadron from each regiment to be sent, creating a composite regiment, and thus allowing royal duties to continue, but still deploying a coherent military force. His efforts were finally rewarded, and still preserved in the Household Cavalry Museum is the letter on flimsy blue paper from the Adjutant General to the Colonel of The Blues, dated 7 July 1882 and marked 'Most Confidential', saying that 'in the event of an expedition being sent to Egypt a Regiment made up of a squadron from each of the Household Cavalry Regiments will form part of the force' and detailing that the total would be 470 officers and men.[6] Fraser's victory had important implications, and the concept of a 'composite regiment' for overseas deployments became the established method of deploying the Household Cavalry until after 1945.

There was considerable competition to be selected within the regiments. Sadly for Keith Fraser, his tenure in command had just run out, and the composite regiment was to be commanded by Colonel Henry Ewart – known to all as 'Croppy' – Commanding Officer of the 2nd Life Guards. Ewart was, in fact, the senior cavalry officer in the expeditionary force by army rank, having been commissioned prior to 1871, and should therefore have commanded the cavalry brigade, but he chose instead to stay with the regiment, so brigade command devolved to Sir Baker Russell. Our friend Reginald Talbot commanded the 1st Life Guard Squadron and Major Townshend the 2nd Life Guard squadron, whilst command of The Blues squadron went to the regimental second-in-command, Lieutenant Colonel Milne Home, to the great disappointment of the regiment's Commanding Officer, Fred Burnaby, of whom we will hear more shortly. The Prince of Wales, who had been made Colonel-in-Chief by his mother, badly wanted to serve as well, but the risk was considered too great and he had to content himself by giving a dinner for the officers at Marlborough House on the eve of their departure and keeping up a correspondence with Ewart throughout the campaign.

The British expeditionary force was commanded by Sir Garnet Wolseley, one of the most competent of the new generation of generals, already respected for his success in putting down the Red River Revolt in Canada, defeating the Ashantis, and for his Wellingtonian attention to detail, particularly over logistics. He had been ill that summer, and travelled out to Egypt on the same ship as the Household Cavalry where he was restored to health by Surgeon Major Hume Spry of the 2nd Life Guards, thereby starting an appreciation of our regiments which was to last for the rest of his life. The speed with which he assembled his force of 16,400 was remarkable, and shows just how effective Cardwell's reforms had been. Having been warned on 7 July, the Household Cavalry were re-equipped with red or blue serge jackets, Hessian boots and pith helmets, and left London on 1 August. Their ships sailed past Cowes so that Queen Victoria could see them pass from the grounds at Osborne. The Blues sent her an effusive message of loyal greeting as they sailed past, thanking her for 'the extreme sense of interest she has taken of our departure to Egypt on active service'.[7] In fact she had never been very keen on them going, and her own comment for the day is more cryptic: 'took my short walk and on coming back saw from my terrace the first detachment of Horse Guards pass in a transport'.[8] She was, throughout the short campaign, to be more concerned about her son Arthur, Duke of Connaught, whom Wolseley had put politically in command of the Guards' Brigade.

By the time Wolseley's force reached Egypt the Royal Navy had taken control of Alexandria with troops loyal to the Khedive, and Arabi had retreated with his main force to Cairo. Deciding to attack him from the flank, over the shorter desert route from the Suez Canal, Wolseley moved his force on to Port Said. By 20 August they had secured the town of Ismailia as a logistic base, and by 24 August the Household Cavalry were in action for the first time since Waterloo. Advancing from Ismailia inland along the freshwater canal towards Cairo with two guns of the Royal Horse Artillery, they took the town of El-Magfar, defended by a detachment of Arabi's infantry, which Ewart duly charged, scattering them and clearing the way to take Mahsamah and Kassassin Lock, possession of which guaranteed Wolseley's line of communication from the Suez Canal to the Nile delta around Cairo.

It had been an exhausting few days for both men and horses, who had been heavily involved in ceremonial before they sailed and were therefore not particularly fit; two weeks on board ship had not helped, nor had the heat of the Egyptian desert in August. 'We had very rough work at first,' Brocklehurst

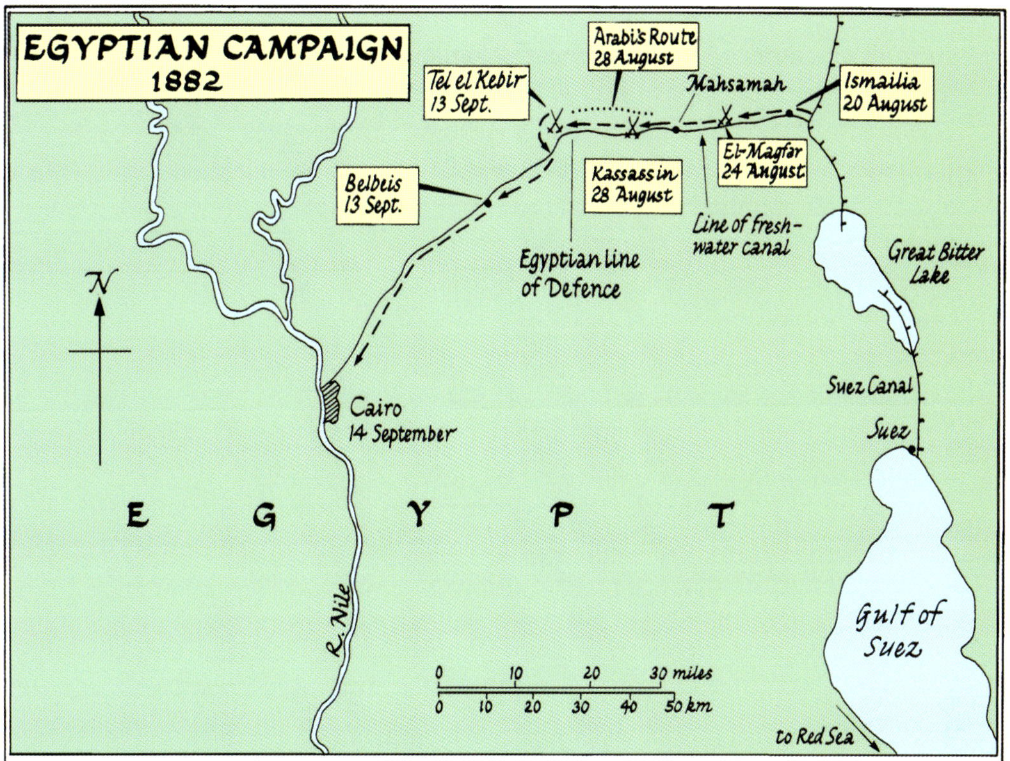

EGYPTIAN CAMPAIGN
1882
Arabi's Route
28 August
Tel el Kebir
13 Sept.
Mahsamah
Ismailia
20 August
El-Magfar
24 August
Kassassin
28 August
Belbeis
13 Sept.
Line of fresh-
water canal
Egyptian line
of Defence
Great Bitter
Lake
N
Cairo
14 September
Suez Canal
Suez
E G Y P T
R. Nile
Gulf of
Suez
0 10 20 30 miles
0 10 20 30 40 50 km
to Red Sea

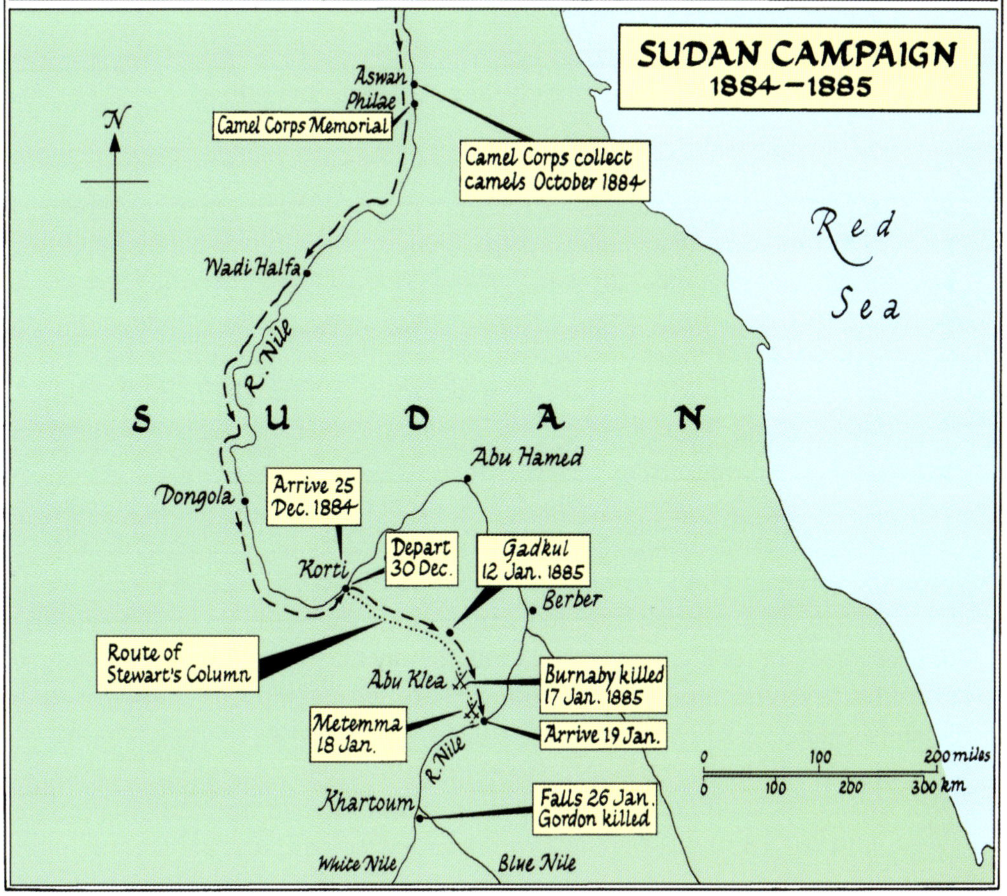

SUDAN CAMPAIGN
1884–1885
Aswan
Philae
Camel Corps Memorial
Camel Corps collect
camels October 1884
N
Red
Sea
Wadi Halfa
R. Nile
S U D A N
Abu Hamed
Dongola
Arrive 25
Dec. 1884
Korti
Depart
30 Dec.
Gadkul
12 Jan. 1885
Berber
Route of
Stewart's Column
Abu Klea
Burnaby killed
17 Jan. 1885
Metemma
18 Jan.
Arrive 19 Jan.
R. Nile
0 100 200 miles
0 100 200 300 km
Khartoum
Falls 26 Jan.
Gordon killed
White Nile
Blue Nile

wrote to his aunt, 'very short of food for men and horses; none at all for 48 hours. When we took Mahsameh Camp Oh such loot, but I was too busy to look after it, and afterwards too dead beat. I'd have given the Koh-I-noor for a water melon.'[9] The *Times* correspondent with the expeditionary force described the regiment as presenting a strange appearance, grimed and semi-bearded, but most noticeable was how they 'absolutely dwarfed other bipeds and quadrupeds into insignificance'.[10] Wolseley himself described the action in a letter to Cambridge:

> In going round the wounded the other day, I asked a Life Guardsman, who had a nasty sabre-cut over his right arm, how he came by it. He said . . . a man on foot shot his horse, and then came up at him with a sword, with which, as he was getting up, the Egyptian cut him over his guard across the arm. 'Well,' I said, 'and what became of your friend?' He replied, without moving a muscle, 'I cut him in two, sir.' In several instances these great giants with their heavy swords cut men from the head to the waist belts.[11]

Although each private was carrying his Martini Henry carbine, and pistols, they were hardly used, and the main weapon was, once again, the sword. The 2nd Life Guards and Blues carried the 1848 pattern whilst the 1st Life Guards were still using the 1820 version brought in after Waterloo, all of which had been allowed to rust on board ship, so they did not glint in the sun.

Wolseley now sent General Graham's brigade to hold Kassassin while he prepared his force for the advance on Cairo, and Graham duly occupied the town on the 27th, while the cavalry remained a few miles to the rear at Mahsamah. On the 28th Arabi himself came forward from his main position at Tel-el-Kebir, approximately half-way between Kassassin and Cairo, and threatened Graham's positions with a force of about 9,000, greatly outnumbering his brigade of 2,000. Graham consequently sent for the cavalry, but finding that Arabi did not look as if he was going to press his attack home, they withdrew again and spent the afternoon looking for such shelter as they could find, many of the men sitting under their horses. 'There was no wind and it was indescribably hot,' wrote Reginald Talbot, but that evening 'we had hardly watered and fed our horses, and the men had not time to get their dinners when the firing recommenced.' Graham now sent word back for them to come up for a second time, but his aide-de-camp, Lieutenant Pirie, who afterwards transferred to the Life Guards, overexcitedly garbled the message to General Drury Lowe, in overall command at Mahsamah, and claimed that Graham was in danger of being overwhelmed. Drury Lowe set out immediately. 'It was just before sunset that we marched off,' Talbot continued,

> this time upon no fruitless errand. It was a full moon, and, after the sun had set, we had brilliant moonlight. The 7th Dragoon Guards led the way, fol-

lowed by our R.H.A Battery, the Household Cavalry in the rear in squadron columns. We marched silently along, getting away to the right, along the line of sand ridges, an occasional order to trot or to change direction alone breaking the silence. We must have marched some five or six miles when the silence was broken by the boom of a gun, followed by the hissing of a shell.

Drury Lowe then ordered his guns to unlimber and reply and the 7th Dragoon Guards to clear their front, thus leaving the Household Cavalry in the front of the column. They had only advanced a little further when

> in a moment became visible a white line of infantry in our immediate front, which opened a tremendous fire upon us. Not a moment was to be lost: 'Front form in two lines. Draw Swords. Charge!' And we were upon them. . . . Until we got within 100 yards they continued to fire, but in one moment, the brilliant light from the firing line, and the rattle of fire, and the whiz of the bullets ceased: the white line had faced about and was in flight. We rode them down in solid rank, but as they dispersed we opened up and pursued. They fell like nine pins, many of them unwounded, who fired and stabbed our horses as we galloped past them. . . . We could give no quarter, for they fired after they were wounded as soon as one's back was turned. . . . We charged for some 300 yards; then Ewart, who had led the first line (Home the second) called out 'Rally' and we set to work to collect our men.[12]

What Drury Lowe had in fact done was to loop round to the right of Graham's position and charge into the left flank of Arabi's infantry, positioned there to protect his guns. They were not actually posing any direct threat to Graham, but because his aide-de-camp had exaggerated his plight, Drury Lowe assumed quite naturally that he had saved the brigade at Kassassin. Tactically the charge did not therefore achieve very much, but it did have two important consequences. First, it severely damaged the already shaky morale of Arabi's troops, and second, it gave the Household Cavalry an enormous boost. They had performed very competently in a complicated night-time manoeuvre within a month of leaving London, and showed that their training and fighting ability were equal to that of any other part of the army. 'I can imagine no more splendid sight than this moonlight charge of our fine fellows on their black horses, against the guns supported by the white line of infantry . . . Then the cheer we gave, then the few seconds of silence, and then the havoc and slaughter,' continued Talbot. Others, like Brocklehurst, saw it rather differently.

> Our Moonlight Charge at Kassassin frightened the Egyptians and gave us some rest; it was all by moonlight and was a weird and ghastly proceeding. We came on some infantry, their left wing, rather unexpectedly, but we

The moonlight charge at Kassassin in 1882. 'In a moment became visible a white line of infantry in our immediate front . . . not a moment was to be lost: "Front form in two lines. Draw swords. Charge!".'

Non-commissioned officers of the Life Guards with their Egyptian Campaign medals – the first awarded to a formed unit of the regiment since Waterloo sixty-seven years earlier.

promptly charged them. For the first few minutes it looked as if they meant to shoot us down; and then it was our men's turn to butcher them.

The cost had been two privates killed in the Life Guards and one in The Blues, Bennet, who was found after the battle with his arms and legs crossed like a Crusader.

After Kassassin, Wolseley was even more effusive in his praise for the Household Cavalry. He wrote again to Cambridge,

> These men of the Household Cavalry are teaching me a lesson, and that is that it would pay us well as a nation to obtain men of a better stamp for our army by offering double the pay we now give. This system of paying the soldiers badly gives us the lowest stamp of man for our ordinary Regiments, whilst the Household Cavalry have such good men that crime is unknown amongst them.

Tom Froude, a private in the 2nd Life Guards, was more direct in the poem he wrote to commemorate the charge:

> The Body Guard of England's Queen have woke to life once more,
> The glories won at Waterloo in stormy days of yore,
> Thus answering without anger the tongues who cast their sneers,
> 'That we are useless, save for show'; let this assail their ears;
> We were foremost in the fight when e'er the conflict raged.[13]

And the fighting was not yet over. The Household Cavalry remained near Kassassin, camped alongside the 2nd Bengal Cavalry. 'It was amusing,' wrote one of their officers,

> to see the big troopers coming into our lines to have their swords sharpened by the sikhligars, and gladly exchanging clasp knives etc. for Indian chupatti to supplement their rations which had been rather short . . . [they] were carefully located near a field of millet. Their officers came and asked us what they were to do for forage, and were astounded when told it was growing at their doors.[14]

By 12 September Wolseley had completed his preparations, with his full force assembled at Kassassin, and was ready to attack Arabi's strongly fortified position at Tel-el-Kebir. He estimated Arabi to have 30,000 troops, including reliable Sudanese men, and seventy guns, and knew that for his much smaller force to be certain of success they had to surprise him. Wolseley's plan therefore was to make a night approach march and, in what became a well-tried British tactic, follow it up with a dawn attack. The army formed up and got what sleep they could. 'We formed up Regms [regiments] posted and each man slept with his horse in line of battle,' Brocklehurst wrote. 'This means tying your bridle round your wrist, lying flat on your back in the sand, with all your arms on, and going to sleep, that is if the nag permits. McGhur [his horse] was much too astonished at the whole affair to admit of my sleeping.' Setting off at 1.30 a.m. on 13 September, Wolseley put in his attack at 5 a.m., taking Arabi completely by surprise. The Household Cavalry went round to the right once again, and turned the enemy's left flank, although there was little direct fighting as most of Arabi's men now ran. That night Ewart's men reached Belbeis, after sixty continuous hours in the saddle, and the following day they were in Cairo and Arabi was captured.

The return home was predictably triumphal, the 2nd Life Guards and The Blues landing at Southampton on 20 October and moving by special train to Windsor, where the Prince of Wales came to meet them. The Blues subsequently moved on to Regent's Park barracks, and were cheered and mobbed by a huge crowd. Queen Victoria, relieved that her son Arthur was safe, noted in her journal that 'They were received in perfect triumph in London and Windsor. It is described as having been a most affecting sight, as the men looked so ill and worn and their clothes so ragged and dirty. The poor horses too, so thin and ill.'[15] She now overcame her annoyance at the War Office having sent 'her Household Cavalry' and became quite enamoured of their story. When Wolseley wrote commending their performance yet again, she replied rather tartly that 'the Queen is glad that Sir Garnet Wolseley entertains such a high opinion of her Household Cavalry as she would remind him that they are the only long service corps in her army'. Croppy Ewart, who claimed slightly disingenuously to have been the first Household Cavalryman wounded since Waterloo after his horse put its foot in a rabbit hole and threw him soon after landing, was invited to Balmoral, where his account of the campaign so stirred the Queen that she proposed his health after dinner herself. He looked 'thin and worn', she wrote in her journal and 'he spoke of the cavalry charge, described their privations as great and the heat as fearful . . . at the dinner I proposed Col. Ewart's health, in these words, "I wish to propose the health of Col. Ewart and the officers and men of my Household Cavalry and I express great admiration for their conduct in Egypt."' She obviously rather relished the details, but worried about the killing. 'The battlefield – a dreadful and never to be forgotten sight. At Kassassin the slaughter was fearful. The men, who were exasperated from privations and harassing attacks, spared no one, but they were justified in doing so, as they were always fired on by the Egyptians on the ground.' And, after Tel-el-Kebir, she continued, 'they were most forebearing, touching no one, as they all threw down their arms'.[16] The Prince of Wales added his congratulations, writing to Ewart from Bad Homburg where he was taking the waters. 'I would have given anything to have seen the whole force including the Indian Troops now in Egypt, but alas that is quite out of the

A helmet worn during the Sudan campaign.

Fifty men from each of our regiments formed a Heavy Camel Regiment (*right*) for the 1884–85 Sudan campaign, captured in sketches by Captain Willoughby Vernier. In January 1885, in what was becoming an increasingly desperate attempt to reach Gordon in Khartoum before the city fell to the Mahdi, Wolseley despatched the Camel Corps across the desert (*below*).

question,' he concluded, showing his evident frustration at being excluded from an active role by his mother.[17]

TWO YEARS LATER, when Gladstone reluctantly agreed to send a second expedition to Egypt, this time to rescue General Gordon, trapped in Khartoum by the Mahdi, the Queen appeared resigned to 'her Household Cavalry' being taken again, although that did not stop her having a letter written to Cambridge saying that 'rumours have reached the Queen of troops being sent to Egypt but although it is reported that some of the Household Brigade are to be sent her permission has not been asked'.[18]

In 1882 an ascetic Sudanese tribal leader, Mahomet Ahmed, had started an Islamic Nationalist movement in Sudan, claiming to be the Mahdi, a prophet sent from God according to Islamic tradition. He proclaimed a jihad against the Egyptian occupation of the Sudan and gained widespread support, which increased still further when he decisively defeated the Khedive's troops under General Hicks, always known as Hicks Pasha, in Kordofan in October 1883. There was little British or Egyptian appetite to take him on and the considered response was to withdraw north up the Nile. General Gordon, who had previously been the Khedive's Governor in Khartoum but was currently in England, was asked to return there and to evacuate the Egyptian garrisons through the Sudanese port of Suakin on the Red Sea coast. Gordon had to spend the day before he sailed being briefed at the War Office and asked whether he might stay with the 2nd Life Guards at Knightsbridge; he had no suitable clothes for dinner so spent his last evening on British soil eating off a tray in the mess ante-room.

On arrival in Khartoum, Gordon, a devout Christian, believed he could restore the situation and was slow to start the planned withdrawal. In the meantime a second Egyptian force, this time under Valentine Baker, was badly defeated just inland from Suakin while they were trying to secure the evacuation route. Of Baker's men, 4,000 were wiped out by the Mahdist General, Osman Digna, increasing the Mahdi's prestige still further. The Government in Cairo now realized they had to act to retake Suakin or the whole evacuation would fail, and General Graham was sent with a joint British–Egyptian force. He duly had his revenge on Osman Digna at two bloody battles, El-Teb and Tamai in February and March 1884 respectively. Thereafter Wolseley, who had returned after his last campaign to resume his duties as Adjutant General, was sent back to Cairo to assemble a force to relieve Gordon. He was determined, despite Graham's victories and strong opposition from the authorities in Cairo, to abandon the coastal route through Suakin in favour of the Nile route. Using his experience of Canadian rivers to transport troops, he assembled a fleet of boats which could be carried across the Nile cataracts, and decided his cavalry should be mounted on camels to operate effectively in the desert. He therefore bravely asked Cambridge to form three Camel regiments: a heavy regiment, made up of men from the heavy cavalry, and to which all three Household Cavalry regiments contributed fifty officers and men, as did The Royals; a light regiment, and, to Queen Victoria's horror, a Guards regiment. 'Although the Queen scarcely understands the object for which re-enforcements for Egypt are being prepared,' her Secretary wrote to Horse Guards on 22 September, 'she will sanction the creation of a camel corps which the government have decided on forming' but 'as her own Life Guards, Horse Guards and Foot Guards are among those selected, the Queen's permission ought to have been specially asked before the government announced their decision'.[19] The Household Cavalry and Royals detachments duly assembled at Aldershot and were shipped to Alexandria on 24 September, travelling up the Nile to Aswan, where they first encountered their strange new mounts in October. By 6 November they had mastered camels, at least to a degree, and reached the Egyptian army's advance post on the Nile at Korti, at the end of the great Nile bend, at Christmas.

The Heavy Camel Regiment was commanded by Reginald Talbot, but several other Household Cavalry officers had been specifically requested by Wolseley to serve on his staff. One of these was Johnny Brocklehurst, who was a friend of Gordon's, and who knew the Sudan, and a second was the Commanding Officer of The Blues, Fred Burnaby, who had been so disappointed not to have been included in the first expedition.

Of all the interesting men who have served in the Household Cavalry, Burnaby must rank among the most eccentric. He was a giant of a man, 6 feet 4 inches tall and weighing well over 20 stone. He was extraordinarily strong, and worked out regularly in a London gym lifting weights, something his brother officers found rather odd. On one occasion he carried two ponies down the stairs at Windsor, one under each arm, and is reputed to have bent a poker around the neck of the Princess of Wales as an after-dinner stunt. He was also said to have been able to hold a billiard cue, outstretched, by the tip between his thumb and forefinger. He had joined The Blues in 1859, paying £1,250 for a cornet's commission, which stretched his family's finances, but he soon found peacetime soldiering rather dull. He first came to public attention by publishing an account of a journey to Khiva, deep in the Tsar's troubled Central Asian territories, during which he employed a Tartar dwarf as his servant. He decided to go because he had read in the papers that all foreigners were expressly forbidden from travelling there. He had, as he would freely admit, from his earliest childhood 'what my old nurse used to call a most "contradictorious" spirit'.[20] After Khiva he went campaigning in Bulgaria with his friend Valentine Baker, got caught up in the Carlist revolt in Spain, crossed the Channel in a balloon, was the *Times* correspondent in Sudan where he went on anti-slavery expeditions and became a firm admirer of Gordon, stood as Conservative candidate in Birmingham against Joseph Chamberlain and helped found the magazine *Vanity Fair*. He did not, unsurprisingly, find much time for his regiment, and was not much liked by the officers, who accused him of passing on stories of their affairs to the press and ultimately refused to speak to him directly, although the soldiers were rather more appreciative of Burnaby's individuality.

Early in 1884 Burnaby went out to Egypt to help his old friend Valentine Baker, and fought at El-Teb, where he was wounded. However, his conduct there did not go down well at home, for it transpired he had fought dressed in civilian clothes, armed with a double-barrelled twelve-bore shot-gun loaded with pig shot that he had borrowed from a naval officer. He boasted of accounting for thirteen Sudanese with twenty-three cartridges, an average of which he was rather proud. Later in the battle, as Baker's force assaulted the Mahdist defences, Burnaby was one of the first on their parapet, firing his shotgun at point-blank range until he ran out of cartridges and had to be rescued by a Highlander when he was wounded. The wound in his arm was serious and he returned home both to get it treated and to contest the Birmingham constituency once more. That autumn Wolseley wrote to him asking him to join his staff on the Nile. Whilst Burnaby was determined to be with his regiment and to help his friend Gordon, he was also aware that his recent anti-Government speeches in Birmingham and his past record would compel Cambridge and the War Office to forbid him to go. He therefore applied for six months' leave in South Africa, and slipped quietly out of England, arriving at Korti in the Sudan in December, whilst the War Office signalled Cape Town that on no account was he to be allowed any active role on his arrival.

The position facing Wolseley that Christmas was a difficult one. Gordon, who had earlier defied all requests to evacuate Khartoum, was now relaying messages that, unless help arrived soon, he was finished. It was for this eventuality that Wolseley had planned his camel corps, and he now detached them under Sir Herbert Stewart to march across the desert from Korti to Metemma, thus cutting off the great Nile bend, while he continued up river with the main force. Gordon had signalled that the mere appearance of 200 redcoats outside Khartoum would jolt the Mahdi and he would retire. The plan was for Stewart's small force to reveal itself outside the city, supported by a small flotilla of steamers on the Nile commanded by Lord Charles Beresford, and reinforce Gordon until the main body came up. Stewart's force set out on 30 December with an initial objective of securing the wells at Gadkul, about half-way to Metemma (see map on p. 393). The Household Cavalry had taken to their camels rather well. A special uniform had been designed for them, consisting of loose-fitting grey serge tunics – the forerunner of khaki – which the Queen described sniffily as a sort of *café au lait* colour, yellow Bedford cord breeches, dark blue puttees, short brown boots and pith helmets with a 'pagri' wound round it, the ends of which were left hanging loose to protect the neck from the sun. Corporal Kerr and Trooper Smith both lost theirs, and both committed suicide when they got home, which the regiment ascribed to sun stroke.

The Camel Corps left Korti on 30 December 1884, riding through the desert (*above*) cutting off the great bend in the Nile, and encountered the enemy at Abu Klea (*below*).

Over their shoulders they wore brown leather bandoliers, and, for the first time, their carbine was their main weapon, swords being of limited use off a camel. In their kit bags they had 'goggles, veil, drawers, cholera belt, Prayer Book, housewife [a small kit for mending things], spurs, spare pair of boots, socks, and all the usual paraphernalia of a man's kit'. It was all very workman-like and 'all Sir Garnet' as they used to say, commending Wolseley's legendary efficiency. Learning to ride was more difficult, but after a few weeks at Aswan they had become moderately proficient. It was a welcome relief that 'stables' now consisted of a leisurely period picking ticks out of the camels' skin. It had been required that all the men were over twenty-two years old and first-class shots and, more difficult than learning to cope with the camels, they were now required to act as mounted infantry, for that is what they had in fact become.

To the tune of 'The Campbells Are Coming' – chosen by some wit as the Camel Corps' march and changed, of course, to 'The Camels Are Coming' – they set off on the 200-mile ride from Korti for Gadkul, which they took without incident on 12 January. The next stage was to seize the wells at Abu Klea, three-quarters of the way to Metemma, and which, once secure, would ensure their water supply. The Mahdi, however, possessed a very good intelligence system and, aware of Stewart's progress from the start, he dispatched a force of 16,000 men from Khartoum to intercept him. Stewart now received reports that they were between his force and Abu Klea. On 16 January he advanced within a short distance of the wells, rested for the night and built a thick thorn hedge, called a zariba, around his position. All that night they could hear the Mahdi's men shouting and beating tom-toms, and they slept uneasily, knowing that they were likely to be attacked.

The following morning they set off on foot for the wells in a square formation, the camels at the centre, led by a strong force of skirmishers including most of the Heavy Camel Regiment. After 2 miles the enemy's flags, which had been shadowing them, changed direction suddenly and a group of 700 warriors broke off from the main body and charged them. The square was moved on to a slight knoll to receive them and became disorganized in the process, leaving many of the camels outside it together with the skirmishers. At the same time the enemy's main body, which had remained hidden in the long grass, charged suddenly as well. The 'Gardner machine-gun, from which wonders were expected, was brought through a gap on the left face, but after firing a few rounds it got jammed and became useless,' wrote George Arthur, who was on Wolseley's staff, rather bitterly. The camels and skirmishers raced for the square before the Mahdists reached them. Several skirmishers had to crawl for the last hundred yards so that their comrades could fire over them. The last man in was Major Byng of the 1st Life Guards, but the man behind him was caught and speared. At this point Burnaby, inside the square, saw a gap develop in the square around the 4th and 5th Dragoon Guards and ran over to warn them. Before he could do so a group of Mahdists rushed the gap and, in the ensuing hand-to-hand fighting, Burnaby was the first to fall, speared through the neck. Corporal Mackintosh of The Blues rushed out to save his commanding officer, driving his bayonet into the back of Burnaby's assailant, but he was overwhelmed and quickly cut down as well. For five minutes the square was a maelstrom of fire. The Heavy Camel Regiment were charged by Baggara horsemen and cut them down with repeated volleys; that not a single enemy penetrated the square from this point on reveals the wisdom in choosing marksmen, although, peevishly, some later claimed their accuracy was not up to infantry standards. As soon as he could, Lord Binning of The Blues

> crept out of the square and gave Colonel Burnaby some water out of his bottle and crept back to the square again on his hands and knees. He was very nearly killed coming in by a man in the Royal Dragoons who blew his gun off so near Lord Binning's head that it actually blew his hat off.[21]

The Royals, slightly further down the square, also had to take the full force of the charge, losing more men than any other regiment in the Camel Corps; Major Gough and thirteen men were killed in the first charge, and Lieutenant Burn-Murdoch nearly followed him by going back to bring a wounded man into the square. Private Steele, who went to help him, won the Distinguished Conduct Medal. The concentration of rifle fire was such that the Mahdist attack withered and soon petered out, and they withdrew. At least 1,100 enemy bodies were counted immediately outside the square and many more were found later. Once it was quieter, Binning ran out again to see whether Burnaby was alive. 'I was not the first to find him', he wrote,

> a young private in the Bays, a mere lad, was already beside him, endeavouring to support his head on his knee; the lad's genuine grief, with tears running down his cheeks, was touching as were his simple words: 'Oh! Sir; here is the bravest man in England, dying and no one to help him.' But he was past help. A spear had inflicted a terrible wound on the right side of his neck and throat, and his skull had been cleft by a blow from a two handed sword.

Whatever his indiscretions had been in peacetime, no one in the Household Cavalry could deny Burnaby was a superlative field soldier. 'It is not too much to say,' continued Binning, 'that in our little force his death caused a feeling akin to consternation. In my own detachment many of the men sat down and cried.'

Burnaby was one of seventy-four men killed that morning, including nine officers, and ninety-four men were wounded.

Cautiously the square moved on to Abu Klea, where they found the wells brackish and of little use, although Beresford still found the water 'cool, sweet and delicious'. Stewart now realized they must reach Khartoum as quickly as possible. Not only were Gordon's messages now more desperate, but the Mahdi obviously knew their exact position and would certainly try to take the city before the British could get there. Stewart therefore decided to march straight on to try to reach the Nile at Metemma the following day. After a dreadful night march – the rigours of which soldiers of all generations know only too well – the men and camels starving and exhausted, the guides lost, and no one really clear what they were doing, the Camel Corps came within sight of the Nile, but had to fight their way down to it. It took until 3 p.m. to restore order after the chaos of the night march and re-form the square, but it was eventually achieved. As soon as they set off they were attacked once more in strength, but this time they had avoided the previous mistake with their skirmishers, and as the Mahdists streamed down an incline towards them they were mown down in hundreds by concentrated rifle fire. Afterwards not a single body was found closer than 100 yards to the British positions. Five minutes after charging, the enemy broke off to the south and vanished back towards Khartoum, to a resounding British cheer.

British casualties were minimal but, tragically, included the dynamic Stewart; on his death, command passed to his intelligence officer, Sir Charles Wilson. Wilson was described by Beresford as a 'small, insignificant looking man, very nice and quiet to talk to, and I believe a wonder at surveying, but no more fit for the position he now found himself in than he would have been for the command of a man-of-war'.[22] Wolseley had intended Burnaby to take over command if Stewart was killed but his plans had now been frustrated and, as he later complained, 'the whole thing broke down'. Wilson reached Metemma on 19 January but spent so long dithering and organizing his force that by the time he was ready it was too late. Gordon had been killed on 26 January and Khartoum captured. The relief expedition had failed.

When news of Burnaby's death reached Windsor, music was banned in the barracks and the privates' and non-commissioned officers' balls were abandoned. The Duke of Cambridge was criticized in the press for continuing with his planned visit to the theatre, and the Queen noted in her diary that the report of the battle 'quite took my breath away . . . amongst the officers killed is Col. Burnaby of The Blues. Poor man, it is a sad ending to his brave and strange life. It must have been a desperate affair, and one feels very anxious.'[23] It was one of her very few journal entries on the Sudan, a war of which she continued to disapprove. Private Cameron of The Blues was slightly more emotional in his memorial poem:

> The soldier's friend, the best of men,
> Beloved of all his corps,
> So mourn you Royal Horse Guards Blues.
> Brave Burnaby no more.

Colonel Fred Burnaby (*right*), who commanded The Blues, was killed at Abu Klea (*below*). An enormous and very strong man, he was also a traveller, explorer, balloonist, journalist and would-be politician. Distrusted by the officers, but lionized by the soldiers, he was not meant to be in the Sudan and had slipped out of England to find Wolseley's force by pretending to the War Office he was going to South Africa.

THE DEATH OF COLONEL BURNABY AT THE BATTLE OF ABU KLEA WELLS, JAN. 17

By 7 March the Heavy Camel Regiment was back at Korti, having lost 115 men in the two months since it left. The Household Cavalry lost five officers and men from enemy action and ten from disease, whilst The Royals lost thirteen and four respectively. They were buried where they fell, including Burnaby. Their names were inscribed on a column in the Temple at Philae; when the Aswan High Dam was built in the 1960s the Temple was moved to an island on the newly created Lake Nasser, where the names can still be seen.

On 10 March they started back down the Nile, intending to spend the summer at Wadi Halfa while Wolseley prepared plans for a renewed attack on the Mahdi in the autumn, but it never happened. There was no appetite for more fighting in London, and in May Wolseley's force was recalled, much to his disappointment. Gordon's death would not be avenged for another fourteen years when Kitchener, who had been present throughout the campaign, would lead another column down the Nile, retake Khartoum, and destroy the Mahdi's son.

Chapter Sixteen

THE BOER WAR

THE HOUSEHOLD CAVALRY were pleased with their performance in the Sudan. Major Lord Arthur Somerset, writing a report on the men in The Blues' squadron, was very gratified their non-commissioned officers were offered senior staff positions, such as regimental corporal major and quartermaster corporal, in the Heavy Camel Regiment. After mentioning many individuals by name he concludes his report by stating, 'Of the other men whose names I have not mentioned I have nothing special to report but they all did their work cheerfully and well on all occasions and from the time I left England Sep 25th till the day I handed over command Feb 20th. I made no entry of any sort in the defaulters book,' which is something of a record for a Victorian regiment on active service.

The problem now was to re-establish a peacetime routine; for those who had withstood the charge of the 'fuzzy wuzzies' at Abu Klea, duties such as the Queen's Life Guard could seem a bit dull. Nit-picking discipline could also sometimes be overbearing, particularly with the heavy ceremonial workload, and was most marked among those who had not seen active service. In 1892, the officer commanding 'C' Squadron the 1st Life Guards, Captain Rawson, dissatisfied with a Saturday kit inspection, ordered his men to 'show again' on the Monday, losing them a weekend. On the Sunday morning twenty-four saddles in one troop were found vandalized and the whole troop was confined to barracks. Returning from church later that morning, the men from the punished troop were cheered and Rawson was hissed, and that evening the squadron gathered in the canteen and sang patriotic songs. On the following Monday morning the newspapers, greatly exaggerating as usual, carried the headline 'Mutiny in the Life Guards'. Trooper Horace Marshall, a man who had served eleven years, cut out one of these headlines, pinned it to the canteen wall, and wrote the words 'Comrades' above it and 'Stick Together' underneath. Corporal of Horse Bayliss rubbed the words out and took the cutting down. Soon after, both he and Marshall were detained, Bayliss for not having previously arrested Marshall. The authorities were nervous of supposed 'mutinies' in 1892, particularly after the Curragh incident in 1887 when the

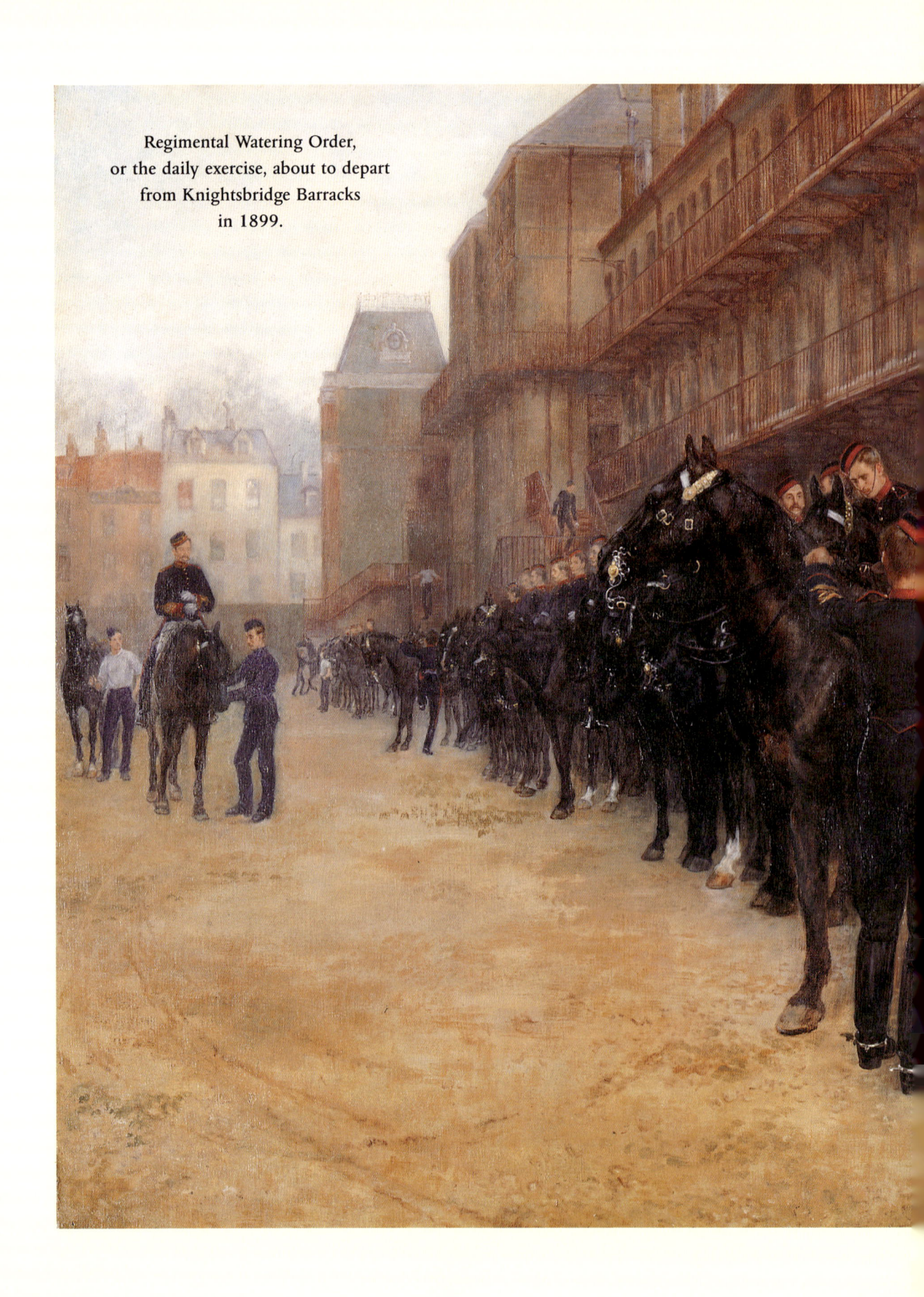

Regimental Watering Order,
or the daily exercise, about to depart
from Knightsbridge Barracks
in 1899.

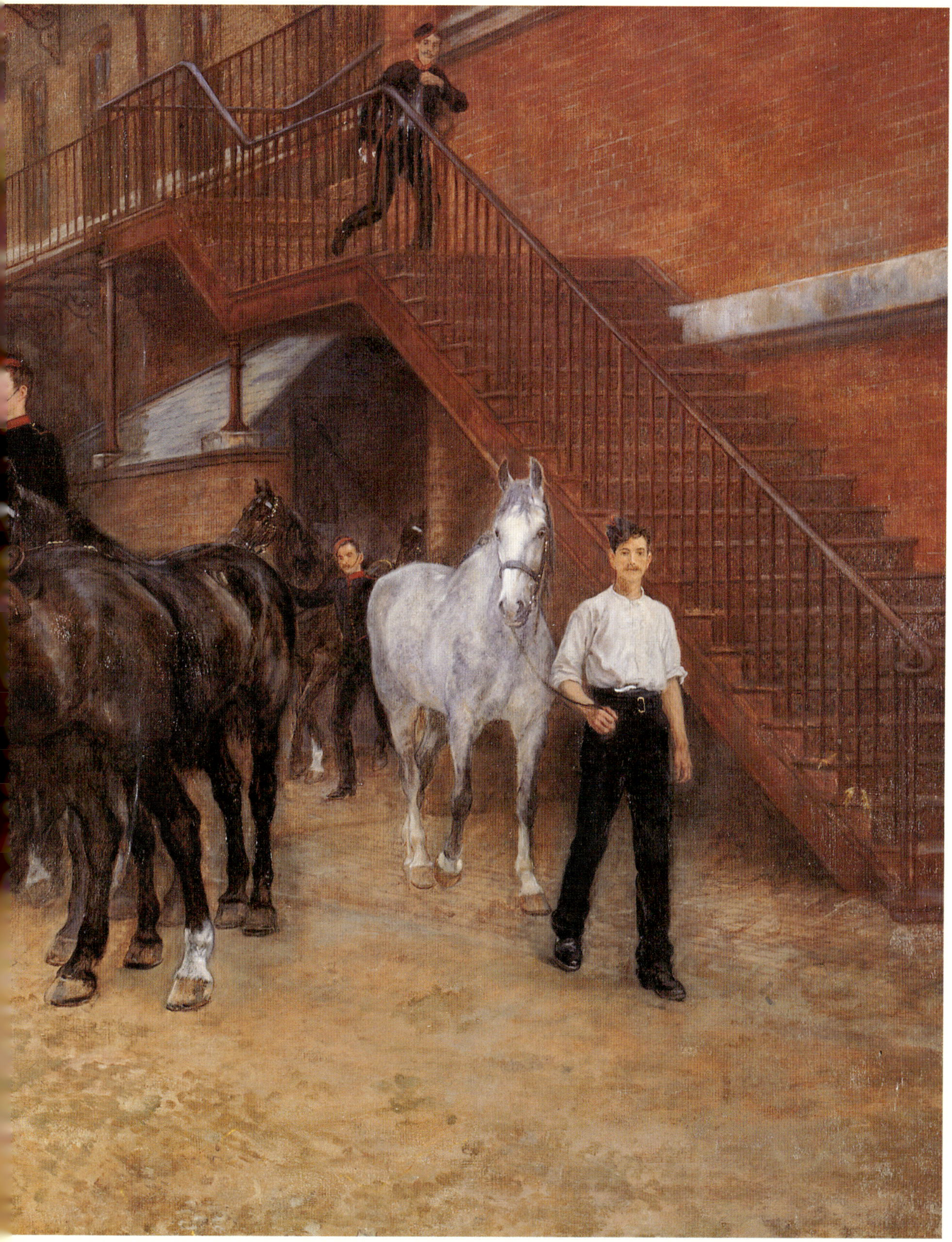

men of the 19th Hussars mutinied against their commanding officer, and they now grossly overreacted. Bayliss was reduced to the ranks and Marshall sent to Brixton Prison for eighteen months. Rawson was put on half pay and posted out. Even worse, in October, Lord Methuen, the general commanding the Home District, paraded the whole regiment in the riding school to tell them they were being posted to Shorncliffe as a punishment – Shorncliffe was considered the worst posting in England – and there they remained until July 1893 when they returned to Regent's Park.

Ironically, Burnaby's influence on officers was greater after his death than it had been when he was commanding. Whilst many still counted days hunting accomplished or dances attended as personal achievements, others were genuinely enthused by Burnaby's example and found plenty of scope for adventure in the late-Victorian empire and, doubtless, many of the high-quality non-commissioned officers would have followed them had they enjoyed the same opportunities. Johnny Willoughby or, more correctly, Sir John Willoughby Bt, who had commanded a troop in Egypt, charged at Kassassin, and had been in the square at Tel-el-Kebir, went to South Africa and took part in the Jameson Raid of 29 December 1895, the ill-fated attempt to initiate a British revolt against the Boers in Johannesburg, as did Charles Villiers. Villiers, who joined The Blues in 1887, unusually from the Royal Military College at Chatham, spoke French, Swahili and Arabic. He took part in the Unyoyo campaign in East Africa, for which he was decorated by the Sultan of Zanzibar, and was then seconded to Rhodes's British Chartered Company in South Africa, from where he joined Jameson. The War Office, embarrassed, denied both his and Willoughby's involvement, but was caught out by a published photograph of them standing with Jameson on the boat back to England. Instead of the prison sentence the Boers demanded for all Jameson's accomplices, Villiers returned to The Blues on promotion, and went out in 1899 to command the South African Light Horse in the Boer War. Burnaby would have been proud of him. Even in 1901, when most cavalry officers were heartily fed up with African campaigns, Major Hanbury-Tracy volunteered to accompany the Abyssinian Expedition into the Ogaden, a most dangerous and uncomfortable adventure, though somewhat ameliorated by the fact that his personal retinue included fifty men and forty-five camels.[1]

For The Royals there were more tours in Ireland. As one of only four 'Heavy' regiments outside the Household Cavalry, they were not considered suitable for service in India, and their lives rotated between Aldershot and its Irish equivalent, the Curragh, where they normally served for six years. They were long years, and though Irish hospitality was generous, they took no pleasure in their frequent policing and protection duties. Casualties were mercifully rare; the only death noted was that of Corporal Wallace, murdered near Gort in 1882 while escorting the local magistrate. Their equipment had not altered much, though in the 1890s they were temporarily issued with lances, a weapon making a comeback in military thinking, and in 1896 they were issued with the new .303 Lee Metford carbine. Whilst sword practice was still the main skill at arms training, musketry was taken more seriously since the Sudan, and was soon to stand the regiment in good stead in South Africa. A major change came in 1887 with the foundation of the Army Remount Establishment; from then on all army horses were purchased centrally by the Inspector-General of Remounts, and issued to regiments as required. The cavalry regiments were deeply insulted by this, as they prided themselves on their horse judgement, and the hurt was compounded when the new Inspector-General refused to issue horses younger than five to any regiment except the Household Cavalry; long gone were the days when troop leaders could buy what they liked from the Remount Fund.

In 1894 another significant change occurred in their lives when the Queen made the German Kaiser, Wilhelm II, Colonel-in-Chief of the regiment. The Royals had never had a Colonel-in-Chief before and had never particularly felt the need for one. However, the Prince of Wales exerted pressure to reciprocate the honour paid to the Queen, who had been made Colonel-in-Chief of the German Garde-Dragoner, an honour that seems not to have moved her unduly. The Kaiser was already an Admiral of the Fleet, which Lord Rosebery, the Prime Minister, felt was quite enough, but the Prince of Wales was insistent, and after a state visit to Windsor the Queen duly conferred the appointment on her grandson, which, she noted, 'seemed to please him excessively'.[2] Although Rosebery still grumpily argued it should only have 'been granted in return for some proof of goodwill which has yet to be exhibited',[3] the Kaiser was clearly thrilled. 'Deeply and sincerely do I thank you for the great honour which you conferred upon me by naming me hon. Colonel of The Royals. I am moved, deeply moved, at the idea that I now too can wear beside the naval uniform the traditional British Redcoat. How many brave and brilliant soldiers have worn it, and', he added, in words which he knew would work with the Queen, 'above all my beloved Grandpapa!'[4] Thereafter he proved to be an interested and generous Colonel-in-Chief, inviting frequent delegations of officers to Berlin, where they were very well entertained. 'Visits to the theatre or the opera and to show places like Potsdam and Charlottenburg were sandwiched in between reviews, field days, inspections of regiments, usually crack corps like the Red Hussars or the First Garde Dragoner, Queen Victoria's regiment, which now became the "sister regiment" of Royals'[5] and on 18 June every year the Kaiser presented The Royals with a wreath to commemorate Waterloo.

In June 1897 the regiment returned from Ireland to Hounslow, just in time to take its place in the Queen's Jubilee celebrations. In 1898 Lieutenant Colonel Burn-Murdoch, whom we last saw in the square at Abu-Klea, took over as commanding officer and led them in the army's summer manoeuvres on the newly acquired Salisbury Plain training ground where they were brigaded alongside the Household Cavalry Composite Regiment, renewing an old friendship. Within a year they were to be deployed on operations together once more. The

Kaiser Wilhelm II became
Colonel-in-Chief of The Royals in
1894 (*left*). He took an active interest
in the regiment, both visiting on his trips
to his grandmother, Queen Victoria (*below*),
and inviting parties back to Berlin.
His appointment, unsurprisingly,
came to an abrupt end in 1914.

British army that mobilized in the autumn of 1899 appeared one of the most prepared for overseas operations that the country had produced since the 1690s, and the cavalry were no exception. There had been an almost continuous series of reforms since Cardwell – based on lessons learned in Africa and Asia – in weapons, equipment, tactics, training, and, particularly, in pay, accommodation and conditions of service. Every soldier in both the Household Cavalry and The Royals now had a 'Soldier's Small Book', which they carried at all times, that recorded their pay, service and attainment of the Army's Certificates of Education. It also carried handy hints for army life with sections on saluting, weapon cleaning, applying for leave, conduct on guard, and, rather injudiciously next to each other, gaining permission to marry and making a will. There was a real sense of pride in promotion, and in the Household Cavalry Museum there are countless carefully posed formal photographs of family groups, wives and children gazing adoringly at their enormous and inevitably moustachioed father as he proudly displays the aiguillettes which denoted his new rank.

The deployable army consisted of what was now termed a corps, being a 35,000-man strong grouping of divisions, commanded from Aldershot by Sir Redvers Buller, VC, an immensely experienced officer who had been Wolseley's Chief-of-Staff in the Sudan, supported by a cavalry division. They had trained together in the summer of 1899 and enjoyed considerable public confidence. The empire was at its height, the Queen had just celebrated her Jubilee, and it was that felt, if there was a need to go to South Africa to teach the Boers some respect, it was a foregone conclusion that the British army would soon triumph. The army had in fact just returned from victory in the Sudan, where Kitchener had taken Khartoum and avenged Gordon's death in a remarkably efficient operation. It was to be an abrupt and unwelcome shock that not only were the Boers a considerably more formidable enemy than the Dervishes, but the British army still had much to learn about command and the logistics of expeditionary operations, particularly in such a harsh environment as South Africa.

There was, once more, considerable pressure from the Household Cavalry to go, not least from Colonel Audley Neeld, Commanding Officer of the 2nd Life Guards, though this time, having been included in Buller's manoeuvres on Salisbury Plain, there never seemed to be much doubt. Wolseley, now both Commander-in-Chief and Colonel of The Blues, took great care to consult the Queen, sending a 'dispatch' to her at Balmoral to ask her permission to send a 'regiment of Household Cavalry to South Africa if the Queen approves. Regiment to be made up by one squadron from each of the three Regiments'.[6] The Queen now not only approved but also paid the newly formed composite regiment the most unusual compliment of travelling all the way to Windsor from the Highlands to see them off. 'They were all in Khaki uniforms,' she wrote in her journal, which seemed to me very practical . . . I addressed them in the following words: 'I have asked you, who have always served near me, to come here that I may take my leave of you before you start on your long voyage to a distant part of my empire . . .' Col. Neeld said he hoped I approved of his having urged the Household Cavalry to go.[7]

The Queen never recorded whether she approved or not, but she was to lose a fair proportion of her Household Cavalry over the next eighteen months. In addition to the 600 officers and men in the composite regiment, the 'Burnaby Factor' meant that a further twenty-four officers, including the Riding Master of the 1st Life Guards, attached themselves either to other regiments or to the staff, so well over half of all serving officers were deployed. In addition, two ex-officers, the Earls of Dundonald and Erroll, commanded brigades. Dundonald, who, as Lord Cochrane, had been the man who brought Wolseley the news of the seizure of the wells at Gadkul and of Gordon's death in 1884, was the antithesis of what, only a few years earlier, was thought to be a typical Household Cavalry officer. During his tenure as Commanding Officer of the 2nd Life Guards, he had concentrated on rifle practice and mounting and dismounting skills. He was also something of a military innovator and had designed a horse-drawn maxim gun, a new system of storing drinking water and, perhaps for more specialized use, a 'waterproof bag in which men could cross rivers while keeping dry'.[8] The regiment sailed in early December and arrived in Cape Town on Christmas Eve 1899. Twenty-one-year-old Private George Freemantle, of the 1st Life Guards, wrote to his mother from the *Maplemore*, a cattle ship with good accommodation for the horses but not the men, that, although he was sorry to miss Christmas, he had never felt better in his life and would surely be back home by the next one.[9] His main concern, shared by most of the British army, was that they should get there before the war was over. The Royals, who had sailed in October, had arrived a month earlier.

Their worry stemmed from the fact that the Government had already sent 10,000 men to South Africa, whose very presence was intended to overawe the Boers and compel them to accept British demands. British policy in South Africa had been dominated for most of the nineteenth century by the struggle of the colonial government in Cape Town against the Low Church Dutch settlers, the Boers, who had been pushed further and further inland as British influence in the Cape expanded. The Boers wanted land and independence, and had established their own states after the Great Trek of the 1830s, during which they had ventured well into the interior, north of the Orange and Vaal rivers, defeating the local African tribes en route. These battles, with such stirring names as Blood River, had been savage and costly, and had further instilled the idea of suffering into the Boer psyche. The British made periodic attempts to annex these new states, the Transvaal and Orange Free State, succeeding briefly in 1877, only to be decisively reversed by President Kruger of the Transvaal when his citizen army defeated the British regulars at Majuba in 1881. Majuba still rankled with those in Cape Town, like the Governor Sir Alfred Milner, and the Colonial Secretary in London, Joseph Chamberlain, against whom Burnaby had stood in Birmingham, who favoured a 'forward' policy, working towards integration of the Boer states with the Crown colony and the expansion of British rule across all southern Africa. Their fervour increased in the 1890s when gold and diamonds were discovered in commercial quantities in the Transvaal, and their cause was reinforced as the Boers refused to grant civil rights to British settlers, the so-called Uitlanders, many of whom were engaged in the mining industry.

At New Year 1896, Johnny Willoughby and Charles Villiers had accompanied the eccentric adventurer Dr Jameson on his raid into the Transvaal that was supposed to start an Uitlander uprising and to overthrow Kruger's government. It was a hopeless venture, encouraged and financed by Cecil Rhodes. Though condemned in London, whence Kruger, as we have seen, cleverly had Jameson, Willoughby and Villiers returned under arrest, it was taken by many Boers as evidence that they would never be free from British interference unless they defended themselves militarily. Encouraged by Milner and the Cape industrialists like Rhodes, Beit and Werhner, British policy became increasingly uncompromising. In October 1899, Kruger, in Pretoria, still President of the Transvaal and Steyn, in Bloemfontein, President of the Orange Free State, issued an ultimatum to the British, mobilized their efficient and well-equipped volunteer army of approximately 40,000 men, organized into large regional 'commando' groups, and moved to occupy key cities in the British-held areas of Cape Colony and Natal. The British reaction was summed up by *The Times*, which commented that it was 'an infatuated step by this petty republic'.[10] The 10,000 men, under General Sir George White, sent specifically to terrify the Boers into never risking such a move, were too ambitious. White decided to defend Natal north of the River Tugela (see map on p. 419), overextending himself and allowing his army to be easily outflanked. They were quickly cut off and besieged by Kruger's and Steyn's men in Ladysmith in north Natal, while other British forces were similarly trapped in the mining centre of Kimberley in Cape Colony, where the garrison included Cecil Rhodes, and nearby Mafeking. This was the situation that confronted Buller's field army when they arrived at Christmas 1899, and so the first phase of the subsequent war was determined by White's dreadful mistake.

Buller's strategy was therefore virtually dictated to him by the time he had arrived in late October 1899. Instead of assembling his mighty corps in Cape Town and 'steamrolling' his way up to Bloemfontein and Pretoria, he had to divide his army in two. He left the Life Guards' old friend Lord Methuen, with 7,000 men, to advance north through Cape Colony to relieve Kimberley and Mafeking, while he steamed on to Durban with the remaining 19,000 men to relieve Ladysmith and take Pretoria. There was little coherence in either force, and despite the careful training on Salisbury Plain, divisions were now broken up and regiments committed according to their order of arrival. The Royals, therefore, never actually landed at Cape Town, steaming on to Durban to form part of Buller's small cavalry force of two brigades, one commanded by Lord Dundonald and the other, soon after arriving in Natal, by Burn-Murdoch. The Household Cavalry, arriving later, disembarked at Table Bay in the New Year, and were committed to Methuen's force. They were soon on trains heading north to join the main cavalry division, under General John French, in the more open country of the Cape, encamped on the River Modder.

Sixty-three hours later their exhausted horses, still unfit from a month on board ship, staggered down the ramps of the cattle trucks at Rensburg. The army they joined was demoralized. Methuen had attempted to cross the River Modder, just south of Kimberley, in November but was forced back with heavy losses. Two weeks later he had seen the Highland Division massacred at Magersfontein, since when he had camped south of the Modder, unsure what to do. He showed the lack of leadership the Life Guards had already experienced and lost his self-confidence too, writing to his wife that his troops 'will never agree to serve under me again'.[11] Buller had suffered a similar reverse at Colenso, trying to cross the River Tugela in Natal. The Household Cavalry therefore arrived in a climate of total stalemate; Buller's armies were unable to advance, while the Boers both blocked them and besieged the trapped British garrisons. Buller had also by now lost the confidence of the cabinet in London and, on 10 January, Field Marshal Lord Roberts, the hero of Afghanistan and Commander-in-Chief in Ireland, arrived to take supreme command with Kitchener as his Chief-of-Staff. While they set about regaining the initiative, the Household Cavalry was put in to the 2nd Cavalry Brigade with the 10th Hussars and 12th Lancers, under General Broadwood, and had little time to acclimatize to the realities of campaigning in the heat of the African summer before they were in action.

Corporal Hugh Hidden, a medical orderly in the 2nd Life Guards, found the ground 'awfully hard to drive pegs into. It appears to be full of iron. We live in a continual state of expecting the tent to be blown away. It's very dusty round here . . . it's dangerous to sit down as the ground is covered with cacti . . . what with the puff adders, blood beatles, etc. and the flies torment the life out of us.'[12] More shocking, he found the graves 'of our poor chaps and the hill at the back of my tent has any amount of them. There is a grave of a man who was killed and buried just outside my tent. In fact, I could put my hand out and touch it. You will think it funny of me writing all this but it will give you a true idea of things.' This cannot have much encouraged his young wife Emily, whom he had married in July, and who produced their first and, as it turned out, only child the very day he was writing. The patriotic Hidden duly had his son christened Rensburg.

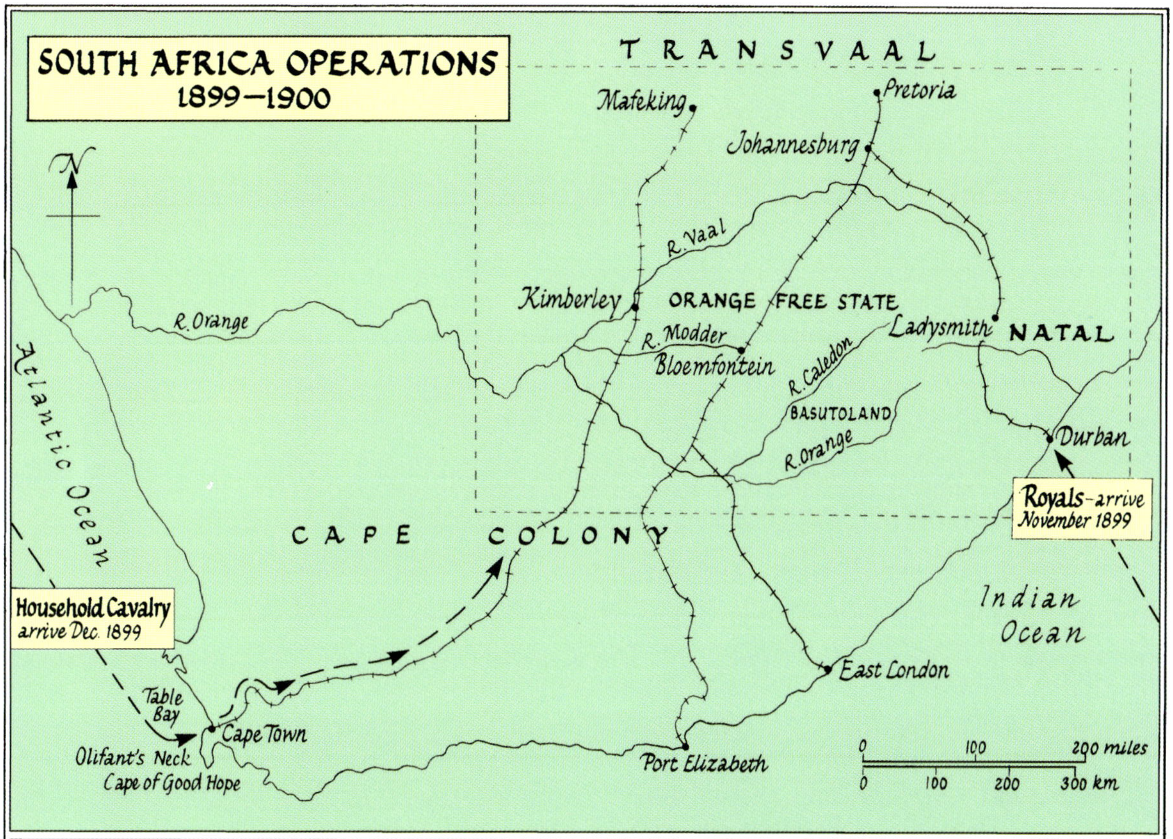
SOUTH AFRICA OPERATIONS
1899–1900
N
TRANSVAAL
Mafeking
Pretoria
Johannesburg
R. Vaal
Kimberley
ORANGE FREE STATE
R. Modder
Bloemfontein
Ladysmith
NATAL
R. Caledon
BASUTOLAND
R. Orange
Durban
Royals – arrive
November 1899
R. Orange
Atlantic Ocean
CAPE COLONY
Indian
Ocean
Household Cavalry
arrive Dec. 1899
Table
Bay
Cape Town
Olifant's Neck
Cape of Good Hope
East London
Port Elizabeth
0 100 200 miles
0 100 200 300 km

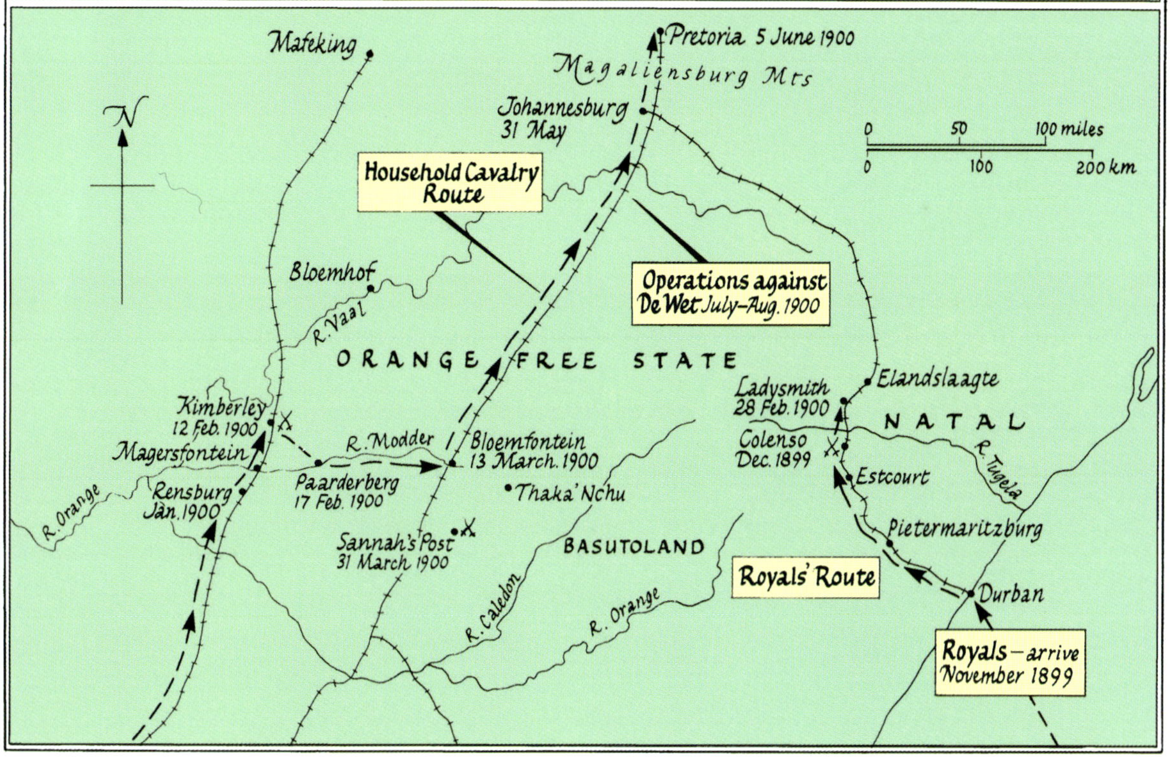
Mafeking
Pretoria 5 June 1900
Magaliensburg Mts
Johannesburg
31 May
N
0 50 100 miles
0 100 200 km
Household Cavalry
Route
Operations against
De Wet July–Aug. 1900
Bloemhof
R. Vaal
ORANGE FREE STATE
Elandslaagte
Ladysmith
28 Feb. 1900
NATAL
Kimberley
12 Feb. 1900
R. Modder
Bloemfontein
13 March. 1900
Colenso
Dec. 1899
R. Tugela
Magersfontein
Paarderberg
17 Feb. 1900
Estcourt
Rensburg
Jan. 1900
Thaka' Nchu
R. Orange
Sannah's Post
31 March 1900
BASUTOLAND
Pietermaritzburg
Royals' Route
R. Caledon
R. Orange
Durban
Royals – arrive
November 1899

They were soon in action, probing the Boer lines, and skirmishes were frequent. On 12 January they were called forward to help another cavalry patrol which had run into Boer outposts.

> It was a good time to get used to the bullets. They were whistling over our heads at a good old rate . . . I don't believe they [the Boers] are all such wonderful marksmen. It's the number of rounds they fire that tell. Several men and more horses were shot. Most men had only minor injuries.

Harry Neil, a private in The Blues, found that

> we had been galloping all morning till my horse was fairly dead beat . . . our men were retiring behind another kopje two miles off, and my horse began to drop behind 'till I was the last one of the lot. Well the poor beast was so dead beat that he dropped into a walk . . . so I turned to watch the Boers following us. I saw one of them get off his horse and begin to fire at me . . . his third shot hit my poor faithful horse in the hind leg and down he dropped.

Neil was taken back to Pretoria, the first Household Cavalry prisoner of the war.

Their first major action came on 12 February when Roberts ordered French to take the cavalry division and 'rush' Kimberley. It was a daring move, crossing through the Boer lines, and relied on speed and surprise. 'I have never been through such an experience,' wrote George Freemantle of the 1st Life Guards to his mother.

> We left our camp Cliff's Drift about 6 in the morning and before we had got a mile we were shelled by the Boers . . . after that we had a gallop for our lives (under shell and rifle fire) for about 21 miles, . . . expecting every minute to be shot or have my horse killed but the 1st was under a charm I should think for we only had one horse wounded. But when we halted you should have seen our poor horses quite done up bad. We still had 15 miles to go so we had to push on. We didn't meet with any more Boers all the way to Kimberley. The people overjoyed to see us . . . One thing I must tell you, the 1st LGs were the first at Kimberley. That is something to be able to say isn't't and I hope that I shall get back alright to wear the Silver Star that Cecil Rhodes is giving us.[13]

It was undoubtedly a triumph, but it came at a cost. It was 'a magnificent march', Lieutenant Colonel Thomas Calley, the regimental second-in-command who would take over as Commanding Officer when Neeld was injured, wrote to his wife, 'but at a fearful cost to horses . . . 15 of our horses died that night

– some more the next day . . . poor brutes they died like flies.' A couple of days later he added 'the poor horses are a pitiful sight after their long marches often without food and water . . . one squadron have lost 44 horses out of the 172 that left England and there are lots that are not fit to go on.'[14]

From the day they left Klip's Drift (or Cliff's as Freemantle called it) the regiment were continuously on the move until 28 August, during which time they covered 1,592 miles in 161 days, with only fifty-seven days when they were not involved in some sort of operation. They had just one day at Kimberley before they were off to Paarderberg, where French succeeded in trapping Cronje and 4,000 men, the first major British success of the war, but again not without cost. Privates Gellatley and McLennan of The Blues were killed and Hugh Hidden and Private Henning severely wounded; Hidden survived, and will reappear in our story, but young Henning died.

From Paarderberg they advanced in Roberts' 'Steam Roller' to Bloemfontein, commanded now by Sir Ian Hamilton, later to be heavily criticized for his failure at Gallipoli in 1916. Bloemfontein fell on 13 March. 'We took it very easily only a few shots were fired no one was hurt on our side I think . . . It is a very pretty spot here amongst the hills . . . It is quite a treat I can tell you to have a rest and to be able to get fresh butter and milk (a thing I haven't tasted since I left England),' wrote Freemantle on 16 March, but two days later they were off again. Broadwood's brigade, sent to secure the Bloemfontein waterworks at Thaba'Nchu, were almost cut off by de Wet's commando at Sannah's Post, where the Royal Horse Artillery won four Victoria Crosses. Broadwood escaped censure for this debacle – Roberts felt he had dash, a quality then highly prized in cavalry officers – even though he had neglected to send out any scouts.[15] On 31 May Roberts took Johannesburg and five days later rode triumphantly into Pretoria as Kruger fled. The British prisoners held there were delighted to see him, but it was just too late for Harry Neill. He was alive and well after his capture, he wrote to his adored father, and he must not worry and he was being well looked after, but in March he went down with fever, probably enteric, and he died on 1 April.

On 28 February Buller finally managed to relieve Ladysmith. The Royals had been discontented under his command for four months. They had, in fact, done very little at all, for two reasons. First, Natal was 'abominable country for cavalry to manoeuvre in', which explains why Buller left the bulk of it under French in Cape Colony, and because 'Buller will not use his cavalry and is frightened to death of his lines of communication. . . . He has made a mess of everything he has touched, and if the truth comes out about the relief of Ladysmith, he will take a back seat.'[16] During the earlier debacle of the attempted crossing of the Tugela at Colenso he had sent his two brigades off to the flanks, Dundonald's to the right and Burn-Murdoch's to the left, but recalled them both as he realized the crossing was failing. Thereafter they sat in camp at Frere until the next attempt at the end of January. The Royals had particular reason to appreciate Burn-Murdoch's qualities during General Warren's ill-fated operation to seize the high ground north of the river.

> Thanks to the Colonel we are still alive, but for him certainly at the very least half of us would be killed or wounded. After our infantry had retired from Spion Kop (which is an enormous hill) and the Boers had taken possession of it again, a staff officer came up to the Colonel and told him to take his regiment up the hill, find out if it was really occupied and, if it was, to retake it. The Colonel said to him 'Am I to take that as an order? Listen carefully to what I say as I may be tried by Court Martial for it, but I refuse to take my regiment up on only your order, but I will go up there myself and find out if the hill is occupied.' He then went to C Squadron which was with him at the time and asked for two volunteers to go with him, and Arty Russell, and went up the hill. On the way up he met the stretcher bearers coming down the hill, who begged him not to go up as the Boers were swarming up there.

When they finally got to Ladysmith The Royals were unimpressed that the garrison had eaten all but 400 of their 2,000 horses, and by that time the officers were complaining they had done 'practically nothing – swords are never drawn, bugles never blown, and seldom do you get within a thousand yards of the enemy, and then either you get away as quickly as you can or they do'.[17] In August 1900 Burn-Murdoch wrote to the Kaiser, updating him on what his regiment had been up to. After describing the operations on the Tugela, he went through all the dead and injured: Captain Hardman had died of enteric, Lieutenant Pilkington had been killed in action, and Majors Lindley and Carr-Ellison, Captain Burns, Lord Charles Fitzmaurice and Lieutenant Godman had all been invalided home. In addition, Captain Hamilton-Russell had been badly wounded in the arm. He concludes, wistfully, by saying that 'we live in daily hope of moving on and getting into a country where cavalry can act as cavalry . . . and the Officers and men join me in thanking your Majesty for your great kindness in sending such beautiful presents to our stall at the National Bazaar'. The Kaiser received the letter a month after it was posted, and, having initialled the top, passed it on to the German General Staff, where, interestingly, it seems to have been scrutinized in detail by every department, each one marking it in turn with a progressively impressive array of stamps.[18]

Both the Household Cavalry and The Royals had discovered this was not the sort of war for which they had prepared on Salisbury Plain. British cavalry practice prepared horses for wars in which they marched, stood in the rear while artillery softened the enemy up and the infantry attacked, and then advanced in one short crescendo of a charge as the enemy retreated. All field days were conducted in this manner at Aldershot, and this was how Buller and Methuen had fought their disastrous actions at the Modder and Colenso. It was

Colonel Audley Neeld, 2nd Life Guards, commanded the Composite Regiment that set out for South Africa in 1899. Queen Victoria travelled from Scotland to Windsor especially to see them off in November 1899. 'They were all in khaki uniforms,' she wrote, 'which seemed to me very practical.'

Spion Kop: the scene that greeted Burn-Murdoch. If he had not been so resolute in questioning his orders The Royals would have suffered the same casualties.

a system that had stood the test of many recent wars, and was well suited to the English hunting psyche, but it was one which the Boers, most unsportingly, ignored by melting away when they should have been convenient targets. There had been some early traditional cavalry successes in Natal, when French had charged a Boer force at Elandslaagte, and also some notable disasters, as when the 18th Hussars were taken prisoner en masse, but it was certainly apparent now that the opportunities for charges were decreasing.

The British were faced, instead, with a war of continuous movement and frequent engagements, where the regiments were unsure whether they were just skirmishing or part of some larger scheme. Gone were the close, almost intimate, battlefields of Balaclava, Kassassin and Abu-Klea, where a man could see everything develop before his eyes. Modern artillery, of which the Boers had a plentiful supply, and rifle fire, shaped battles in South Africa that took place over 20 or 30 miles. Now the real challenge was to adapt to tactics demanded by this new style of fighting and, most importantly, to keep the horses fit, rather than to judge the critical moment for a charge. They were simply unable to march all day and still have the energy to charge. Writing to his wife on 9 March, Calley reflected, 'the infantry attacked in front and we in back . . . If we could have a fresh cavalry brigade we should have cut them off at the river and captured the whole lot of them. But our horses have had so little food that it was impossible – some of the gun trains could hardly raise a trot and toward the end of the day could only walk.'

The traditional British methods of horsemastership were not 'remotely relevant to war in the veldt, where the ideal horse was one which would go twenty-five miles a day, however slowly, on half-rations and one drink of dirty water'.[19] The Boer native ponies, used to the veldt, had been half starved since birth and were broken by being tied to older horses to develop patience and docility. They were also used when shooting lion, deer and elephant, which made them steady to rifle fire. The average Boer carried a rifle, copious amounts of ammunition and little else, living comfortably off the country. The Household Cavalry troopers carried an extensive kit list designed to cope with all eventualities, including enough polish for a snap inspection. The horses, Hugh Hidden wrote to his wife, 'have to carry an enormous weight. My own saddle by itself is a very heavy one and there is the horse blanket and one of my own underneath the saddle . . . My cloak in front with an iron picketing peg. My mess tin and generally two days feed of corn on one side of the saddle, with a surgical haversack on the other side . . . and then on the top of it all is myself with a full water bottle and full haversack'. Captain Horace Hayes, who was to write the most celebrated post-war manual on horse care, noted that the average Boer pony carried 16 stone whilst the average British troop horse carried in excess of 20; in addition the Boer practice was to lead a spare pony and a pack pony alongside,[20] an idea which was quite impossible for the horse-strapped British to copy.

The Boers enjoyed a considerable advantage in that they travelled light
and saved their horses whilst the British cavalry carried extensive kit and fodder
(*above*) to cope with all eventualities. The result was that their horses did not last.
Carrying excessive weight and unused to life on the veldt,
they died in their thousands (*below*).

By the time they returned to England in May 1902, The Royals had lost 3,275 horses, or six for each one they had taken out originally.

Only one Household Cavalry horse that had sailed in 1899 returned home, Freddy, who received a medal in his own right together with a letter from Queen Alexandra.

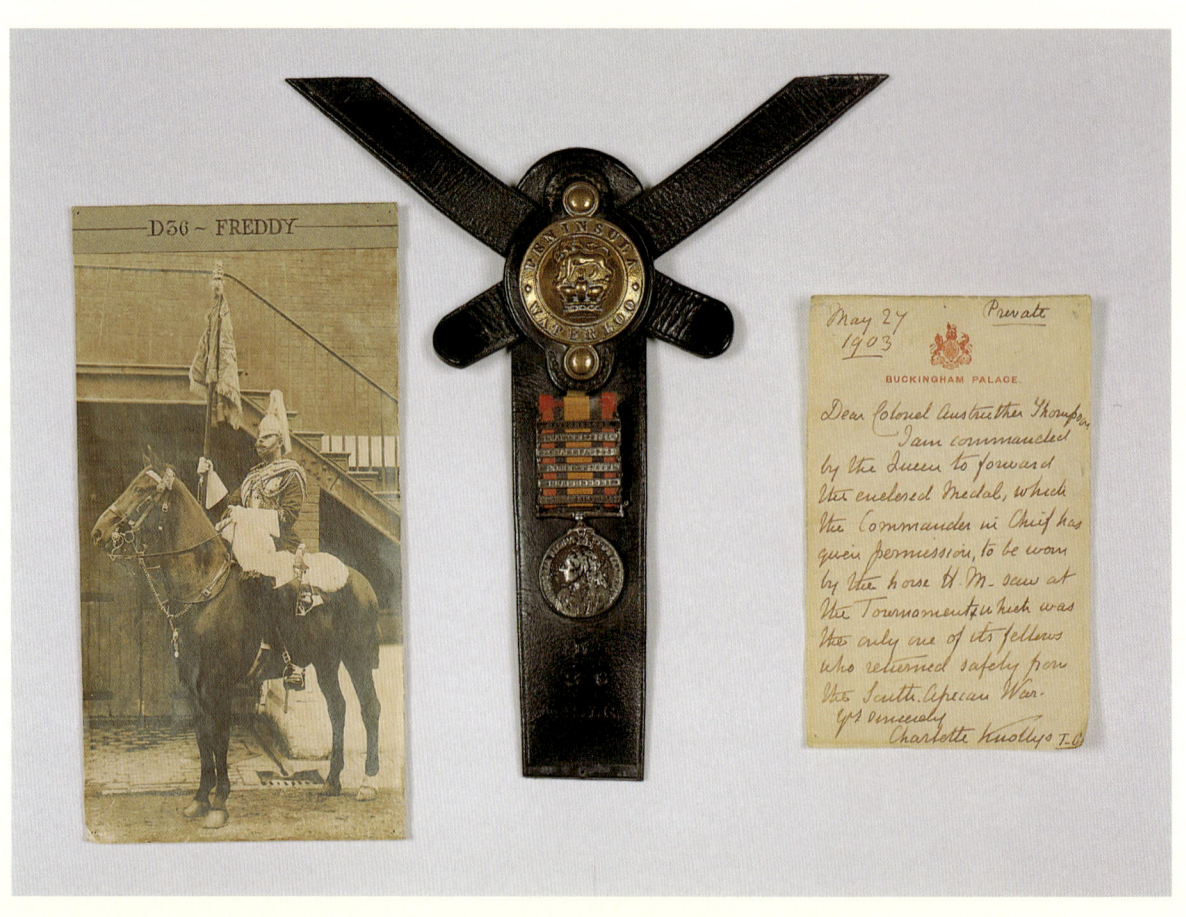

The British supply system, which until February had been run regimentally and worked after a fashion, broke down completely when Kitchener had the apparently good idea of centralizing all the transport at army level. By March, George Freemantle was complaining that 'we have been very badly off for food for a good many days. We had only about one biscuit each about twice the size of a lunch biscuit, so you guess how we got on. It was almost starving us.' 'We have been disgracefully treated,' Calley continued in July as winter was coming, 'the men have never had any winter clothing . . . their underclothing is worn out and their upper clothing in rags . . .' Captain Ernest Clowes of the 1st Life Guards, who also wrote home regularly, told his mother in August that

> one man was picking his shirt out looking for lice the other day and another man asked him what he was doing 'oh, trying to spot a winner', was his answer. Somebody said he saw a man put his hand into his shirt and a thing as big as a hare jumped out and ran across the veldt! They have worn the same shirt now for 3 months . . . Kitchener at the head of it. A worse manager never existed – who ran the Egyptian show for him, I don't know, but if he done there as he is doing here, things would have been a bit different.[21]

Contemporary photographs show that by the autumn instead of the smart figures in their pith helmets, breeches and puttees, portrayed in the press at home, the Household Cavalry were scarcely distinguishable from the Boers, wearing old trousers, slouch hats and riding replacement Australian and Argentinian ponies. Disease, particularly enteric fever, was also killing far more men than enemy action and was markedly prevalent around Ladysmith. Of the total 20,721 British and Imperial troops killed in the war only 7,582[22] were actually killed in action; the remainder died of disease, with little move by Roberts or Kitchener to sort out the army medical services.

There was very direct criticism of the generals now, something the Household Cavalry would never have considered with Wolseley, Stewart or Gordon in Egypt or the Sudan. Their letters and diaries are full of disparaging remarks about such national heroes as Roberts, Kitchener and Buller. 'If one didn't know the stupidity of the staff officers, one would almost imagine they were in the pay of the Boers,' Calley wrote in September. Sadly, the Household Cavalry's own senior officers did not escape censure; Dundonald was nicknamed 'Dundoodle' and Brocklehurst, now also commanding a brigade, 'Pogglehurst'. The attitude is best summed up in a wonderful poem, 'A South African Dream', written by a Household Cavalry officer in camp one night on the veldt, a fragment of which is reproduced here:

> I dreamt that while I struggled with
> Some liver mixed with sand

> There came a laggard orderly
> With a paper in his hand,
> On which was writ in characters
> No mortal man could read,
> 'The force will be in readiness
> To march at frightful speed
> Towards a spot unknown to us
> Which way be best described
> As either in our front or rear
> Or p'r'aps on either side.
> And as the tracks are difficult
> And rather hard to find,
> We think it best that those in front
> Should follow those behind.
> The hour of march is 2 p.m.,
> Or four, or half-past seven,
> Provided that no orders come
> At nine or at eleven . . .

The Household Cavalry's final operations in August and September 1900 involved the 'great de Wet hunt', a complicated plan of Kitchener's designed to trap the most effective of the Boer leaders and his 2,600-strong commando force at Olifant's Neck in the Magaliesberg range of mountains. Everything was in position and Hamilton held the pass for Kitchener to bring up forces to administer the coup de grâce. However, Hamilton then decided to abandon his positions, allowing de Wet to slip through behind him. Whilst the Household Cavalry were to be cheated of their prize, for them the campaign was almost over.

With both the enemy capitals now in British hands, and with the relief of Ladysmith, Kimberley and Mafeking, which fell to Plumer on 28 May 1900, the war would normally have drawn to a close. Roberts put out several hopeful proclamations that had little effect on the Boers, who continued to harass the British with roaming commando groups. But effectively the first part of the war ended with the proclamation of the annexation of the Transvaal in Pretoria in October. Orders were received from London that the regiment should return home. Roberts held a parade to bid them farewell, 'thanking them for their splendid services. He said that, although when next he should see them they would be clad in more gorgeous uniform, they could never don any which should surpass the khaki in its honourable association.'[23] His words, though much appreciated, were greeted with slight cynicism, as the only replacement set of those khaki uniforms the regiment received in its entire time in South Africa was for that very parade.

They arrived home in November 1900 and were received by Queen

What the Household Cavalry looked like for most of their time
in South Africa (*above*) . . . what they looked like when they paraded for
Lord Roberts in Pretoria as they were leaving for home (*below*) – the
only time they received replacement clothing in a year.

Victoria at Windsor Castle, in a private reunion, with just the Royal Family present. The regiment ranked past in fours, which had replaced threes as the arrangement for cavalry in column of march in the 1890s, and then gathered around the Queen's carriage on the lawn in front of the Victoria Tower in the failing afternoon light. 'It is with feelings of great pleasure and deep thankfulness that I welcome you home after your gallant and arduous services,' she said to them. 'Alas, the joy of your safe return is clouded by the memory of sad losses of many a valuable life which I – in common with you all – have to deplore.' Seven weeks later she was dead, and the next time the Household Cavalry escorted her was to her grave.

The regiment's total losses had certainly been sad. Only six men had actually been killed by the Boers but a further fifty-eight had died of either wounds or enteric fever, and a further 100 were either wounded or long-term sick. The death toll among the horses was devastating. Only one horse that had sailed out with them lived to return. That was Freddy, who had joined the 2nd Life Guards as a four-year-old in 1897. He took part in every action in which the regiment was engaged, covered 1,780 miles, always ridden by Corporal of Horse Stephens, and had only forty-eight days off. Unperturbed by his ordeals – the only sign of which was a rather short tail, as his original one had been eaten by flies on the veldt – he became the lead horse in the Household Cavalry Musical Ride and was introduced to Queen Alexandra at the Royal Tournament. She asked why he had no campaign medal, and immediately demanded he be awarded one. A rather stuffy War Office finally agreed and Freddy wore the medal with clasps on his breastplate. He finally retired from duty in 1905, but continued to live in the barracks in Windsor until his death in 1911, when he was buried under the Regimental Square.

There was to be no such homecoming for The Royals. Although the 'formal' part of the war was over, and Roberts returned home in November, handing command to Kitchener, many Boers refused to accept the annexation of their states and fought on as guerrillas. The Royals, fairly inactive throughout 1900, now found themselves in the forefront of Kitchener's counter-insurgency campaign, and were to spend the next eighteen months in cavalry 'sweeps' that were ultimately to force the Boers to surrender. These were not pleasant operations and, indeed, until April 1901, they were also remarkably unproductive – the first one in northern Natal employed over 20,000 troops under French. Success eventually came as a result of Kitchener's strategy of erecting barbed-wire fences and concrete block houses across the veldt and concentration camps in which to imprison Boer families; one in five children in these camps died.

In April 1901 The Royals were moved to eastern Transvaal. Major Carr-Ellison was now in command as Burn-Murdoch had been promoted and the Second-in-Command, Lord Basing, had been invalided home with fever. The first Transvaal 'drive', whereby whole columns swept the veldt, was very successfully led by the eccentric Sir Bindon Blood, capturing 1,500 Boers and

55,000 cattle, and was followed by two similar operations in the Orange Free State. By September 1901 tactics were changed and each regiment was given a particular area on which to concentrate, policing it and conducting the first of what the British army today calls 'Framework Operations'. Basing, now returned fit from sick leave, and The Royals ran an area south of Bloemfontein, centred on the River Caledon, about 30 miles by 15, and up against the Basutoland border. By January the novelty of the drives had worn thin. The return of hot weather brought a fresh outbreak of enteric fever and the sick list grew. Luckily a draft of 129 men and 147 horses reached them to keep their strength up.

Their two last major operations were massive drives in the northern Free State with Captain Ernest Makins commanding the regiment, Basing having been promoted and Carr-Ellison having been invalided home for a second time. Their tactics by this time were so sophisticated they usually outwitted the remaining Boers. 'Night raids and long marches seem to be the most successful form of operation now,' the diarist continues,

> but even that requires a good deal of luck to be successful, as Boer commandos are constantly moving their laagers, and always after dark, besides which they always have special picquits watching our camps, and report any movement in time to warn the commando. The Landrost of Sweitzer-Reineke who we captured said that we were reported to him as quiet in camp at 6 p.m. . . . with no sign of moving, and he could not understand how we had done the journey in the time. Night marching is easier for horses as it enables them to graze all day, avoids marching in the heat, and does away with the necessity of carrying forage. The men carry tea, coffee, and biscuits in their haversacks, depending on captures for meat.

By May 1902 it looked as if peace would soon be signed. Kitchener had brought the Boer leaders together to discuss terms, and Makins noted that 'we have engaged not to molest any commando whose leader is absent at the conference'. They finished the war quietly at Bloemhof on the Vaal on the borders of the Free State and Transvaal. 'Everyone was really very glad to hear that peace had at last been signed, as three years continuous campaigning without a break is enough for the biggest fire eater.' They had, in those three years, lost a total of 3,275 horses – six for each one they had taken out with them in 1899.

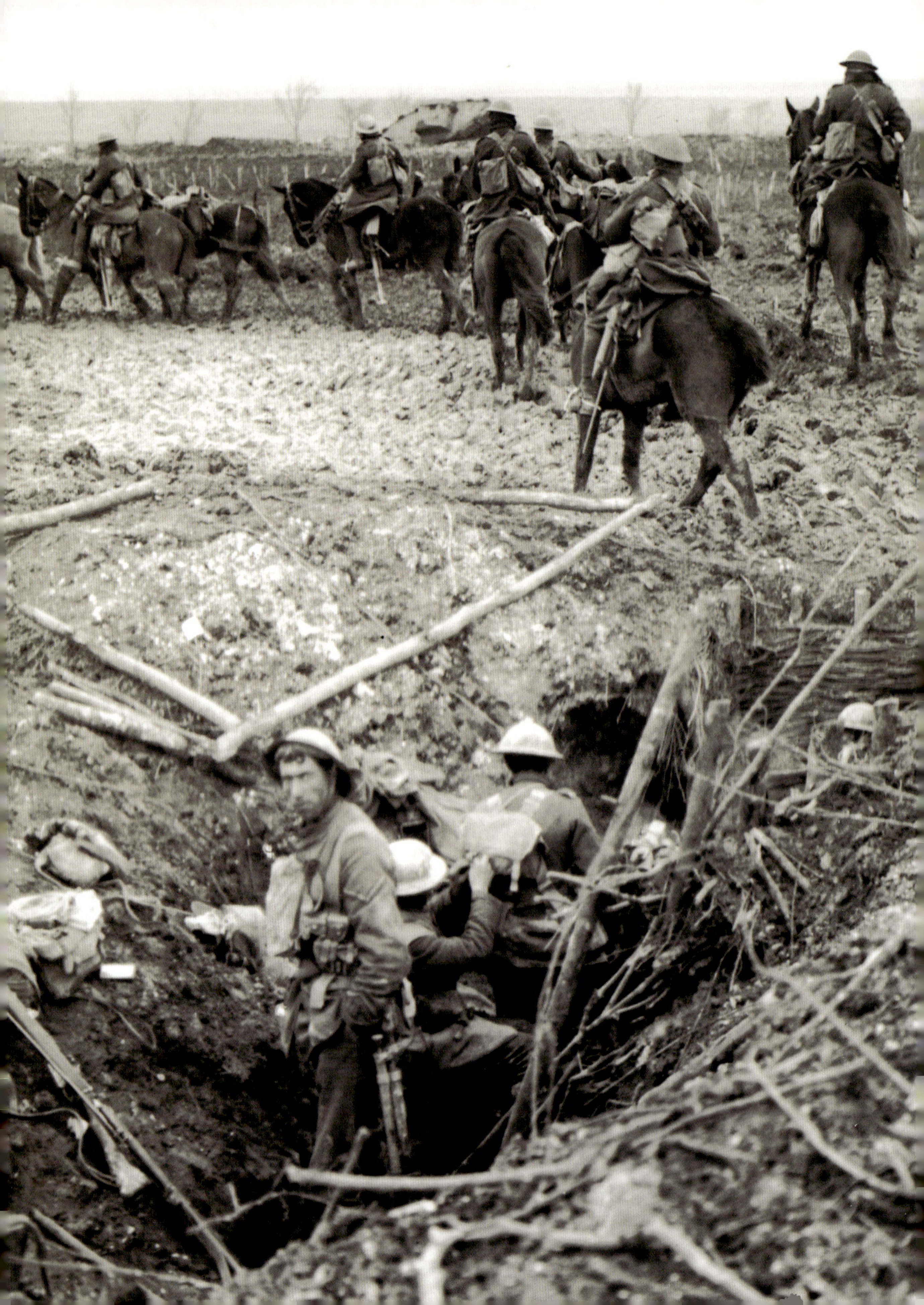

Part Six

'THE ORDERED PAST BEHIND US LIES'

1902–1939

Chapter Seventeen

POLICING THE EMPIRE AND TRENCH WARFARE IN EUROPE

Major Ernest Makins and his squadron were lucky. They had been on the first ship home and represented The Royals at the great victory parade in London on 24 October 1902. By the time they had finished celebrating and returned to Shorncliffe, where the regiment was to be stationed, the rest of The Royals had joined them. Shorncliffe was not exactly their ideal posting, but anything was acceptable after the long years on the veldt, and they had the Kaiser's parade to look forward to. He duly arrived on 8 November and carried out a very detailed inspection in a downpour, only slightly ameliorated by the German awards he presented to several officers and non-commissioned officers; rather more acceptable was the large donation he made to the Regimental Families Fund. However, the excitement of being home was to be short-lived, as so often before. The initial thrill of seeing families, new girlfriends, and the enjoyment of those comforts which had been so conspicuously lacking in South Africa, soon gave way to concerns about the future.

The second phase of the Boer War, when the cavalry had excelled at counter-insurgency operations, was to prove both their triumph and their nadir. It was certainly a triumph, however distasteful Kitchener's tactics, but it also now revealed the archaic nature of the traditional role of cavalry in war. Some argued that the Boer War was an exception, an irritating diversion from the 'normal' wars for which armies should prepare. The Boers' use of artillery and the effect of their rapid, if inaccurate, rifle fire, however, augured a new way of

---

Page 432. The cavalry struggled to find a role in the static trench warfare that characterised the fighting in France from the autumn of 1914. Initially held in reserve to exploit any breakthrough, as the war progressed they were increasingly used as replacement infantry.

fighting, which others recognized; the new Cavalry Drill Book, produced in 1904, confirmed that 'instead of the fire-arm being an adjunct to the sword, the sword must become an adjunct to the rifle'.[1] More horrifying to many, khaki permanently replaced scarlet, except for ceremonial parade use. Those, and there were many, who endorsed the versatility and mobility of the cavalry in South Africa, failed to appreciate that their success had been due as much to the quality and adaptability of their junior officers, non-commissioned officers and troopers, as to their training or the nature of cavalry fighting. The twelve years of peace that followed their return only confirmed this prejudice and, as so often before, the true lessons were masked.

Another, more worrying, trend was the lack of faith in the army's senior leadership engendered in both the Household Cavalry and The Royals by the war's end. The Wellingtonian legacy that viewed British generals as rather annoying, but more or less competent, had until now been an accepted fact of army life. Wolseley, Roberts and Kitchener had, in the years before 1900, restored respect and authority after the damage done by Raglan, Lucan and Cardigan, and the Crimea was seen as a temporary aberration. The tactical and, above all, administrative mistakes in South Africa shattered that trust once more. By 1901 Kitchener was no longer the hero of Khartoum to the army, but 'K of K[ch]aos'. By 1902 the only generals held in any respect in both the Household Cavalry and The Royals were French and Haig. This air of cynicism was to pervade the 'Old Contemptibles' as they struggled to cope with the German advances into Belgium and France twelve years later.

One of The Royals' first tasks was to cut numbers by half. No fewer than 1,102 members of the regiment were on parade for the Kaiser's inspection, of whom only 533 had horses available to them. It was an enormous number, which showed just how much had been expected of the cavalry regiments in 1901–2, and although most of those discharged had been reserves in training, many who had served in Africa also had to go. In 1903 it was announced that the traditional distinction between 'heavy' and 'light' cavalry was to be abolished, which meant that regiments like The Royals – previously categorized as 'heavy cavalry' – were now liable for overseas tours in peacetime, and on 27 January 1904 they marched to Southampton to sail for India. The Kaiser disapproved of 'his' regiment being sent anywhere so uncivilized, and tried to enlist the help of his cousin, Edward VII, to stop the posting, but to no avail. By the end of February they were in Lucknow, where they remained until 1910 when they moved to Muttra, south of Delhi, not far from Agra and the Taj Mahal. Although several of the older generation had no relish for yet another prolonged period outside England, the majority of the regiment enjoyed their Indian service. Even in 1904 India still exercised considerable magic; not only was it the heart of the empire – an enormous country that the British still could hardly believe they ruled – but it fired imaginations with its fabulous images. Both officers and soldiers deliberately joined regiments posted there both for the experience and to escape the boredom of soldiering at home. They were not, in the main, disappointed.

John Cusack, who had run away from the Glasgow slums to enlist, joined the regiment in Muttra.[2] It took him some time to get used to the heat and strange habits, such as latrines 'which were very primitive, the receptacle being a pot in the shape of a Welshman's hat. Behind it crouched a native of the 'untouchable' caste. As soon as you had a motion the native would take the pot away. . . . The old soldiers warned us seriously, "Never go out at night to use the latrines, whatever you do. There'll be natives there with knives, snick-snack, to turn you into geldings."' But once acclimatized, Cusack thoroughly enjoyed himself, riding and swimming, and experiencing a status and way of life superior to anything he could have expected in Aldershot. 'We rode out very early every morning before the flaming heat of the day, and we rode like gentry: each of us had two horses with a syce, an Indian groom, to look after our second horse.' Native servants could be hired very cheaply. 'Hardly before we had got into our tents we were surrounded with "which sounds like Waller" as they pronounce it but it's really "wali",' wrote Trooper Wilsher.

> Wallers selling fruit, tomatoes, butter, milk and also boot, button, helmet, sword cleaners and a host of others too numerous to mention . . . Every morning, before the last note of Reveille had sounded, we were surrounded alive with these Wallers. The first to shout were hot coffee, cocoa wallers . . . then they gradually increased before breakfast to almost 50 of them.[3]

Cusack particularly enjoyed tent pegging, a sport whereby a tent peg hammered in the ground was removed with a lance from a horse at a gallop. It apparently originated as a method for attacking native camps by trapping the enemy in their tents as they collapsed; in fact its origins were quite different, not least because the Indians had an unsporting habit of not sleeping in tents.

Cusack found it odd that the troops hardly ever ventured into Muttra itself and their entire lives were centred in the cantonment, 5 miles outside the ancient city. The only time they came into contact with Indians was either with the traders in the camp or when they went on field days along the Ganges, or the 'Gumpti' as they called it. Female company was very limited; only forty-eight wives were allowed to accompany 641 members of the regiment when they left England and opportunities to increase their number were few. Young Trooper Wilsher – married only four months before they left – was too junior for his wife to accompany him. On the day of his departure, he wrote, 'the day has come when I and my wife must bid farewell for a few years. We arose at 5 a.m. as I had to be on parade by 6.30. We sat talking until it was time for me to depart. I felt that I could have continued the conversation for the best part of the day. After lots of "Good Byes" I left her when it was full time I should be on parade.' On the ship out Cusack had been amused by twenty young women, pen pals of prospective army husbands serving in India. Although they had never met their correspondents, they planned to marry within twenty-four hours of arriving, or else go back home on the same boat. The young husbands-to-be waited on the docks.

> We watched them nervously approaching each other, wondering if they were going towards the right person. . . . They would stare, then give each other a shy kiss or clumsy embrace. As they did so all of us young soldiers would let loose a burst of cheering. They would look horribly embarrassed. Not all the meetings were funny; some were sad. We'd watch a couple gazing at each other dismayed; then tugging photographs from pocket or bag, trying vainly to compare the flattering picture with the stranger's face. They would break loose and start looking desperately round them, praying they had made the wrong contact.

Not all the regiment enjoyed India as much as Cusack did. Operationally there was little to do. There was no credible external threat to India and British regiments stationed there acted more as a deterrent against any repeat of the mutiny of fifty years earlier. Wilsher, thinking constantly of his young wife back in Shorncliffe, found life quite dull. His diary entry for Sunday, 3 April, which reads, 'very quiet – still no church parade', is typical of many. The officers, however, generally found life agreeable. The differences between them and the troopers were superficially stark. Although there were still a few relatively wealthy 'gentlemen rankers', commercial opportunities in Edwardian Britain were such that most troopers tended to come from relatively poor backgrounds, like Cusack, the so-called conscription of hunger. The average officer had a private income and had possibly been raised on an estate where his chief interests were horses and hunting. Well intentioned as Cardwell's reforms had been, forty years later cavalry officers were from much the same background as they had been in 1870 and in relatively the same financial situation. A lieutenant in 1910 was, for example, only paid £230 a year, and the average mess bill, even in India, which was a cheap place to serve, came to nearly £300. However, many troopers were from agricultural backgrounds too, and once they and the officers had been through the rigours of riding school together, social barriers broke down, at least to a degree.

Julian Grenfell joined as a second lieutenant at Muttra at the same time as Cusack joined as a trooper. Grenfell chose The Royals because he wanted to escape the stuffy formality of Edwardian social life in which his parents, Lord and Lady Desborough, played a very full part. Grenfell, who had already established a reputation as a poet while at Oxford, wrote that he favoured The Royals because they were 'a steady, old fashioned regiment without any kingly favour' and that when he arrived he found them 'magnificent and yet friendly . . . I like these people better than the Oxford people. I thought it would be the reverse.' Ernest Makins, now commanding officer, was 'the nicest man in the world'.[4] It was certainly a happy time. Makins and most of the senior officers and non-commissioned officers had fought in the Boer War and, with little left to prove, had the self-confidence to allow men like Grenfell and Cusack some enjoyment without too much regulation. Grenfell found some things irritating, including the amount of time he had to spend changing uniform, and in the Riding School, and the unwelcome attentions of another officer's wife which required his servant to sleep outside his bungalow to forestall her. Yet once through his training he relished the 'freedom from constraint' that India offered and spent his time racing, shooting and playing polo. He also loved the wildlife, writing that on his evening ride he saw '2 real live crocodiles, 18 pigs, 3 black buck, 1 wild cat, 2 foxes, 6 jackal and a bird of paradise'. But his favourite pastime was the dangerous sport of pig sticking, or chasing and spearing wild boar with a lance, the officers' equivalent of the tent pegging that had so gripped John Cusack. Many pig stickers were hurt, either in falls galloping across the rough Indian country, or by the boar itself when cornered, and it was this danger that seemed to appeal in particular to Grenfell and inspired him to write a 'Hymn to the Fighting Boar':

> God gave the horse for man to ride
> And steel wherewith to fight
> And wine to swell his soul with pride
> And women for delight;
> But better gift than all these four
> Was when he made the fighting boar.

Later he was to try even more dangerous sports, revealing a desire to live so dangerously that his life would ultimately become forfeit.

The Kaiser was unable to visit the regiment himself but in January 1911 he sent his eldest son, the Crown Prince, on an official visit, causing even the genial Makins to fuss a bit and the officers and soldiers to complain about the disruption to their lives. 'Old and cunning pigstickers ride and drive the pigs towards him and old and cunning polo players edge the ball gently up to him. . . . We are all quite weary with bowing and scraping . . . my democratic feelings arouse themselves at 11 p.m.; by 12 I am a socialist and by 1 a.m. an anarchist,' Grenfell wrote to his mother. For Cusack and the troopers it meant extra parading and polishing, but they were rewarded when the elephant hired to perform in front of His Imperial Highness 'suddenly had an urgent call of nature; its mighty discharge rattled on the boards like the sound of the midday cannon. We troops shouted and roared with laughter.'

All this was not without some cost. When The Royals were finally posted to South Africa in November 1911, they left forty-nine of their number behind,

The German Crown Prince's visit to the Royals in Muttra. His Teutonic stance gives him away in the group photo. Makins is beside him to the right and Julian Grenfell is behind him to the left.

Sergeant Measures and his wife on the veranda of their bungalow outside Pretoria. 'It is a filthy place, great grass downs studded with rocks and no trees and tin huts everywhere,' complained Julian Grenfell.

many of whom are commemorated on a plaque in Lucknow Church. Of these most died of disease, including Trooper O'Shea, the first to die, who succumbed within a few weeks of arriving. Poor Mrs Fose lost her baby son on the voyage out, and her husband, Sergeant Fose, died from liver failure in November. There were also a few suicides, the first of which was Trooper McIntyre, who blew his brains out with a revolver after only six months. Despite these sad losses, The Royals counted their India tour as happy and successful, and the move to South Africa was definitely unpopular. Grenfell announced that he was going 'to settle at Muttra with a dusky harem', whereas Cusack complained about the dull, routine jobs which included packing all the paintings and silver in the officers' mess, and taking particular care 'of the huge "drag", the very smart carriage which the Kaiser had given to "his" regiment . . . We were repeatedly warned that the slightest damage to the drag would be treated as a terrible offence.' Spirits did not rise much on arrival in Roberts' Heights, their new camp outside Pretoria. 'It is a filthy place, great grass downs studded with rocks and no trees and tin huts everywhere. . . . The mess is made of tin and the quarters are made of tin and everything else is grass and sky. We have one little room to live in and a sort of box joining it where we sleep all made of tin,' Grenfell complained, though he cheered up when he was made Regimental Scouting Officer and was given the opportunity to take his scouts out on to the veldt. Cusack volunteered to be one of these. He respected rather than liked Grenfell and was always rather in awe of him.

> He was a tremendous character, a broad six-footer, always on the go and always with an aggressive, challenging attitude to life. He was rough and boisterous, yet had this very high, la-di-dah voice. He wasn't at all good looking, but had a strong, tough face and I suppose if you saw him in mufti you might guess he was a chucker out. He was an extraordinary mixture. . . . . He wasn't particularly easy to talk to – it was easier, we found, to talk to Mr Sclater-Booth, who had more of an artistic temperament, we thought. Julian Grenfell would listen to our stories, but hardly ever sympathized with us or gave away any concessions.

The scouting patrols were exciting. Cusack was quite challenged by being posted as crocodile scout when crossing rivers, and was surprised to find how little animosity they encountered from the isolated Boer farms. By 1911 few of the young officers or troopers had fought in the war, and Makins organized battlefield tours to educate them. Life in Johannesburg itself remained fairly unpleasant, though there was more contact with locals. The officers struck up a useful partnership with Johannesburg Ladies' College, which compensated to some extent for the lack of female company in India, whilst Cusack reports that Grenfell took him to a brothel. Grenfell certainly maintained that women were attracted to him, and the new Commanding Officer, Steele, warned him from seeing so many and confined him to camp. Grenfell was predictably furious, parodying Steele's lecture to him.

> They [the girls] would come down here and make scenes on the platform which is undignified and degrading for a gentleman; besides, you see, when you are in command of men you must consider what they are thinking, you can't think only of yourself, it is the responsibility which is so sacred.

He also parodied Steele's wife who, he sniped, was 'very over-dressed, driving a lame troop-horse in a second hand buggy'. He sought relief in boxing – beating the reigning South African champion – and in his greyhounds, taking them and the regimental scouts on a three-week trek into Basutoland. 'My long dogs go with us and we practically live off what they kill. The camps are just like gypsy camps: all the men round the fire watching the dinner being cooked and all the horses round outside, watching too. They are jolly men, all the wild spirits, and they love being out. One gets to know them well, living with them – more than one would in years of barrack life.' Cusack agreed that the scouts did love the open air and living off the veldt, and his lasting memory of the trip was Grenfell calling his favourite dog, Pongo. 'I can hear him now,' he wrote, 'across nearly 60 years Julian's high, piping voice like a flute across the veldt: Pongo! *Pongo!*'

In July 1913 The Royals were occupied putting down serious rioting in Johannesburg during the miners' strike. This was unpleasant, and four horses were killed and twenty-two men and fourteen horses were wounded, as many as in some Boer War engagements. Cusack did not have too bad a time. He was in Sclater-Booth's Troop. A large and formidable woman called Mrs Fitzgerald advanced on the troop as they were drawn up across a road. She carried a large red flag and was shouting 'British butchers'. Sclater-Booth tried to reason with her, but she hit his horse over the head with the flag and down it went. The troop Sergeant, Vanson, came to the rescue, advising Mrs Fitzgerald that unless she withdrew swords would be used. She evidently believed Vanson and the crowd dispersed. 'Sergeant Vanson was in his thirties, tall, fair and the absolute picture of a good cavalryman. We guessed that he had been specially posted to our troop to counter Mr Sclater-Booth, who was a very nice officer, interested in theatricals, but not the robust cavalry type.'

The tour in South Africa was due to have continued for longer than it did, but in August 1914 news came that war had been declared in Europe on their Colonel-in-Chief. Initially they thought they had been forgotten. 'It is horrible being tucked away here at a time like this,' wrote an over-eager subaltern, and plans were made for an invasion of German colonial possessions in Africa. It was not to last, and on 23 August they sailed from Cape Town, their families travelling on a separate boat. German naval ships were loose in the Atlantic, and it was an uneasy voyage, escorted home by Royal Navy and French cruisers. From Southampton they went by train to Salisbury Plain to complete mobilization and were put in the 6th Cavalry Brigade with the 10th Hussars; they were to remain in the brigade until 1918. What arrangements were possible were made for the families, many of whom had been away for ten years and some of whose children had never set foot in England; they now had to get used to a strange and much less comfortable life and say goodbye to their fathers, in many cases for the last time.

The regiment brought their Basutoland ponies with them from South Africa, and Colonel Steele, to give him his due, argued strongly with the War Office that they should be allowed to keep them. Kitchener, now Secretary of State for War, thought them beneath the dignity of a British cavalry regiment, but Steele persevered and eventually they went to France and proved much tougher than the British remounts. Corporal Bullock, especially fond of his, had a particular problem as it was a very rare white colour. Knowing it would be taken away, he dyed it brown, which worked until the heavens opened just as he paraded for embarkation and was confronted with a zebra; he tried again and by the time he disembarked in France the pony was a more suitable khaki colour. It was not long before he and the rest of The Royals met up, once again, with their comrades in the Household Cavalry.

Their life since their return from South Africa in 1900 had reverted to the traditional Household Cavalry pattern, alternating between Knightsbridge, Regent's Park and Windsor. The accession of Edward VII, however, brought important changes. First, when awarding South African medals, the King had been disturbed to notice that the enlisted ranks in the Household Cavalry were still referred to as 'privates', being a corruption of the original term 'private gentleman', but now used army-wide to denote the lowest enlisted rank. He thought this rather beneath the dignity of his Household Cavalry, preferring the title of 'trooper', which was already used informally. The War Office, needless to say, objected to the expense of re-engraving medals, but they duly did so, and they were finally issued in the name of each individual 'trooper', which thereafter became the official designation for the junior ranks. Second, it was now acknowledged for the first time that operational and ceremonial roles were different. Whilst the two regiments stationed in London continued to provide the King's Life Guard and royal escorts, and their commanding officers to share the duties of Silver Stick, the composite regiment now became a permanent part of the deployable army, each regiment contributing a squadron, the regimental headquarters provided by whichever regiment was in Windsor. They trained with the Cavalry Division, and spent long hours perfecting their accuracy with the rifle, known throughout the British army as 'musketry practice'. The composite regiment still wore blue field uniforms, unlike the rest of the army who had converted to khaki, and this 'placed them at a considerable disadvantage when manoeuvring against other troops',[5] but it took until the 1913 army manoeuvres for them to change.

The two regiments in London were equally busy. Edward VII was a social monarch and escorts were frequent, making up for the long years his mother had spent in mourning. A Sovereign's Escort was now fixed at 116 men, roughly the same strength as it is today, and the daily King's Life Guard at two officers and thirty-three other ranks, about double the size of its modern equivalent. For once the ceremonial uniform did not change with the monarch, a policy maintained to the present day, so ceremonial uniforms today are virtually the same as they were in 1901. A considerable amount of time was taken up in a somewhat arcane debate with the Foot Guards as to whether they had the right to bear arms in royal palaces, a privilege the Household Cavalry claimed exclusively their own. A similar argument in 1889 had led to a row between the Silver Stick and the senior Foot Guards officer, the grandly titled 'Field Officer in Brigade Waiting', as to who should take precedence. The Master of the Rolls, Lord Esher, had ruled in favour of the Household Cavalry, a judgement since referred to as the 'Esher Award' and still eagerly quoted by those for whom such matters are important. The King's Private Secretary now invited both sides to draw up a 'case', which Colonel Vaughan Lee did for the Household Cavalry in exhaustive detail. These were sent to the long-suffering Lord Chancellor, Lord Halsbury, who 'after sufficient delay to give an additional spice of dignity to his reply' judged that it didn't matter much either way and that it was up to the King to do what he wanted.

For the soldiers, ceremonial duties were more basic and required considerable preparation. Robert Lloyd joined the 1st Life Guards at Regent's Park in 1911. He came from Durrow in Ireland and had a gift for languages. His father had intended him to be a schoolmaster but Robert thought that too boring. Instead he signed on for twelve years, the common engagement at the time, though by 1913 this had become eight years with four on the reserve. He went on his first King's Life Guard from Regent's Park Barracks, an experience 'which was enough to fill the heart of a novice with awe. On evening stable parade the Orderly Corporal read out the names of the men and horses for the following morning.'[6] Having washed his horse's mane and tail, and cleaned his steel collar chain, called a 'bright chain', in wet silver sand, he was up late into the night cleaning his boots, belts and cuirasses.

> After breakfast the saddle and all its appendages were brown-polished; head-kit [bridle] blackened; brow band and girth pipe-clayed; bit and stirrups burnished; brass head-stall and breastplate polished, and all buckles polished inside and out. The horse was then saddled, and sheepskin and cloak placed in position. He was then tied short, and somebody asked to keep an eye on him lest he lie down. There followed a dash

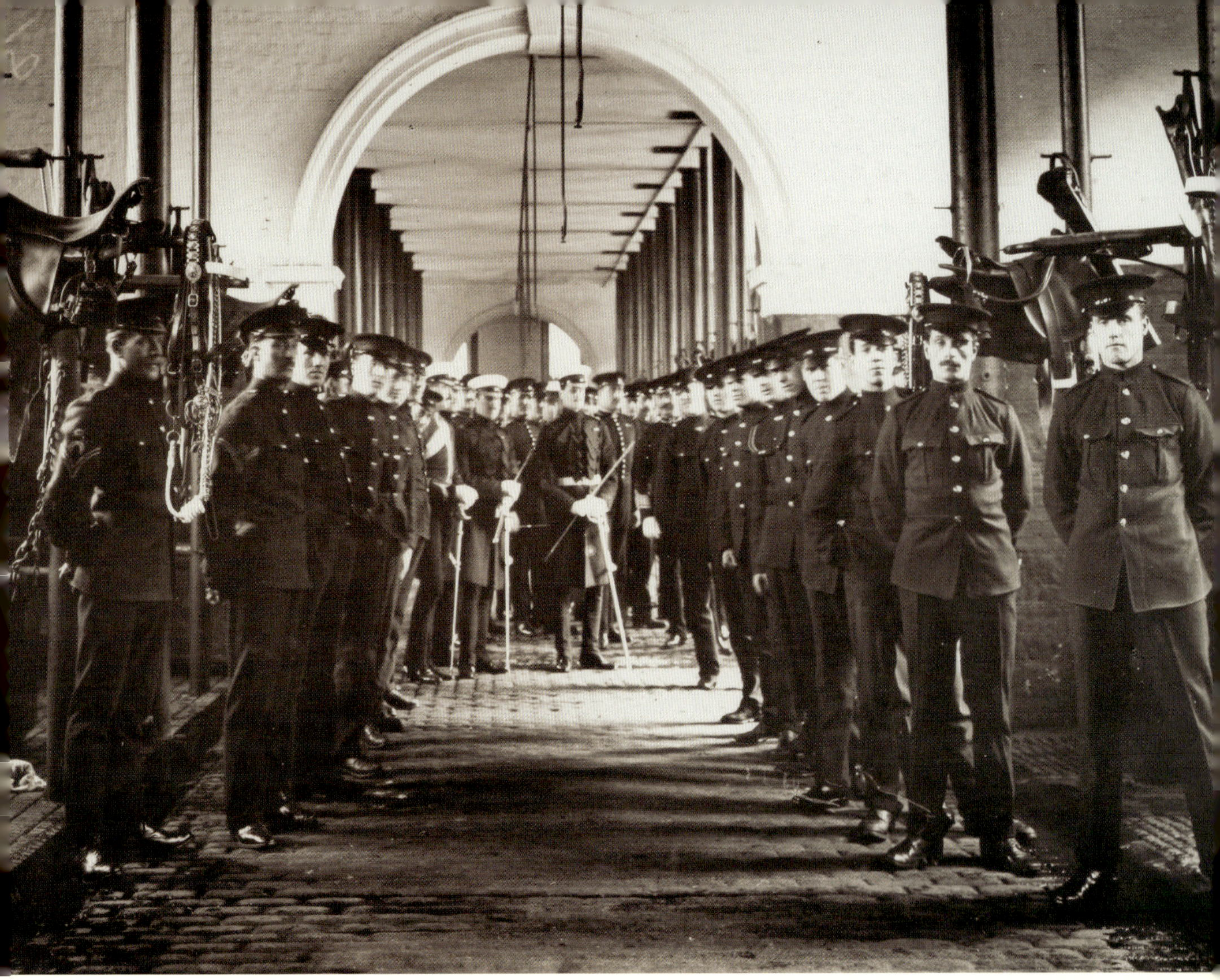

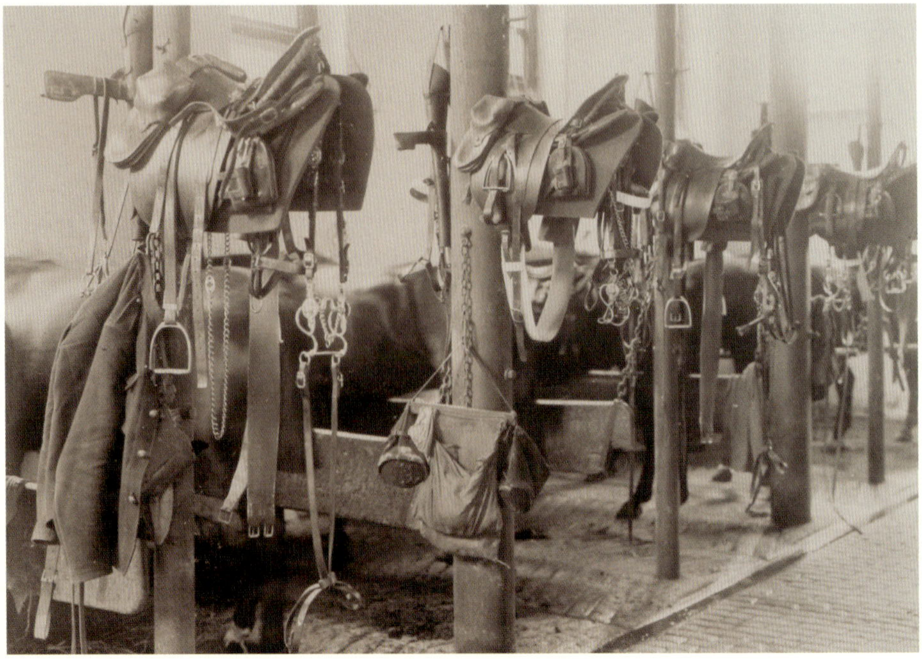

Life in the Household Cavalry between the Boer War and the Great War revolved around ceremonial for the regiments in London, and training for active service when in Windsor. It was a happy and stable time, if rather boring. 'My fellow troopers were excellent men,' wrote Robert Lloyd, 'decent and straightforward, always ready to lend a hand.' Shown here are the troop stables (*left*), the stable yard (*right*) and a trooper watering a horse (*above*).

upstairs to shave, wash, and dress. . . . For the King's Guard there were actually two parades. The first was on foot. We were marched on to the parade ground by squadrons. The inspection which ensued was something of an ordeal. The Adjutant, Quartermaster, and RCM turned everything inside out.

The second inspection was by the Riding Master and

> the mounted inspection was a thousand times worse than that on foot . . . We sat there like so many graven images. When your turn came one would examine your horse's mane; another would pick up a hoof to see if it had been washed out; a third would beat a tattoo with his whip on your sheepskin in the hope of making the dust fly. Perched up in the air as you now were, any of them could look at the insides of your boots and spurs. Unless you had a kicking horse there was not the flimsiest chance of getting away with anything.

The best-turned-out soldiers were rewarded by being given the most coveted positions on Guard, the reliefs in the mounted sentry boxes facing Whitehall. This duty was popular both because it finished at 4 p.m. and because it constantly attracted the attention of passing women, some of whom were known to drop notes in the men's boots suggesting future liaisons. The less glamorous positions were, by contrast, given to those not so well turned-out. These were the 'foot reliefs', the foot sentries who stood under Horse Guards Arch and whose duty lasted well into the night. Lloyd soon got a reputation as a 'Boxman', partly, he maintains, because he inherited a really smart jet-black horse who always looked the part and whose kit was in very good condition. The system of awarding reliefs on today's Queen's Life Guard is remarkably similar.

After the rigours of his initial training and passing through Riding School, and apart from the terror of going on King's Life Guard, Lloyd found life friendly if very formal and strictly hierarchical. He soon felt a great sense of belonging, and found 'the great majority of my fellow-Troopers were excellent men, decent and straightforward, always ready to lend a hand . . . and with few exceptions always good humoured and quick to see the funny side'. However, once he had mastered the intricacies of kit cleaning he soon became bored and found that 'the routine of our lives now appeared to consist almost entirely in soiling articles of equipment and arms in order to clean them again'.

He much preferred the summer months, when the London regiments would take it in turns to ride down to Stoney Castle Camp, near Pirbright, then 'a small island of two green fields set in the midst of pinewoods and gentle heathery slopes. Filled in with neat rows of tents and lines of tethered horses, it made a delightful picture.' There they spent long hours on musketry and would later

Physical training at Windsor (*above*) and sword practice at Knightsbridge (*below*).

train with the Windsor regiment. However, Lloyd's best year was 1912, when the 1st Life Guards moved to Windsor to take their turn to provide the core of the Composite Field Regiment. Not only were the barracks more comfortable and spacious, if bitterly cold in winter, but the field training was much more fun than standing on guard in Whitehall. 'Field days began at once. For a while these were Squadron affairs; but soon the whole Regiment left barracks daily in the early morning and returned covered with dust and sweat about 1 p.m. I found these daily excursions thrilling. There was much galloping. To gallop in the ranks in various formations, but especially in line with the whole Regiment was sheer joy. Horses soon became hard and fit. To see them at work and to work with them made life worth living.' Things did not always go according to plan on these field days. One misty morning in 1909 the composite regiment was manoeuvring against the 1st Cavalry Brigade at Aldershot. 'Simultaneously the scouts of each brigade sighted the enemy. Simultaneously each brigade was ordered to charge. So close were they that men could hear the orders shouted to their opponents. The charge was launched, the men could not be stopped, and they met with a crash. The superior weight of the Household Cavalrymen swept the 1st Cavalry Brigade back to their own side of the hill. Two men of a Lancer Regiment were killed outright, and casualties were numerous.'[7]

Lloyd was soon promoted and took his place in the non-commissioned officers' mess, a privilege he much valued, where he found life considerably more comfortable. He describes taking meals sitting at squadron tables, the senior non-commissioned officer presiding, carving the joint at the table, and the Orderly Corporal handing round plates in the manner of any well-to-do Edwardian household. He liked the officers, the great majority of whom 'were fine fellows, gentlemen and good leaders; but, unlike foreign officers, they were not dependent on the service for their livelihood; they were not obliged to regard the army as a serious profession . . . they simply did what was absolutely necessary and were promoted, as time went on, by seniority'. Lloyd particularly liked his Commanding Officer, Lieutenant Colonel E. B. Cook, 'a thorough gentleman, sympathetic and approachable, though always a stickler for having everything done with absolute correctness'. He was also very fond of Lord John Cavendish, the Second-in-Command, who was known for his generosity. Most of the officers had nicknames; in The Blues, for example, Colonel Vaughan Lee was known as 'Flea', while Lord Londonderry was 'Manse', Lord Arran 'Pudding', Sir Richard Howard-Vyse 'Wombat', Gordon Wilson 'Erasmus' and the Duke of Roxburghe 'Bumble'. Lord Crichton, who would take over command of the composite regiment from Cook in France, was 'Pompey'.[8] The officers remained, as Lloyd pointed out, almost exclusively men of private means, who enjoyed their leisurely life but could be intolerant of those who did not match their standards. In July 1902 four subalterns of the 2nd Life Guards determined they did not like the newly arrived Second

Lieutenant Charles Gregson. After dinner one night they auctioned Gregson's uniform as he wore it, pulling off items one by one. A coal scuttle was emptied over his head, and then he was made to run outside the mess wearing only his boots. They then threw him into a water trough and rolled him in mud, before going upstairs and throwing all his furniture out of the window. Lord Roberts, still Commander-in-Chief, was not amused. Captain Spender-Clay, the senior officer present and a South Africa veteran, was forced to resign.[9]

Although Lloyd's comments may have been accurate when describing the junior officers, they did not necessarily apply to squadron leaders and commanding officers, the majority of whom were South African veterans and took regimental training considerably more seriously than their forebears had ever done. They were all determined that the Household Cavalry would never again be left on ceremonial duties while a British army was deployed overseas, and the permanent inclusion of the composite regiment in the Field Army now guaranteed this. By 1913 the British army, though small by Continental standards, was highly efficient and moderately well equipped, largely due to the pragmatic and far-sighted reforms introduced by Haldane as Secretary of State for War. The men were very well trained individually, particularly when it came to shooting, and although the debate as to how cavalry should be used in a future war was still very much alive, no one seriously doubted that they had a key role to play. The Old Contemptibles, as the British Expeditionary Force that embarked for France in the baking sunshine of August 1914 were called, were probably the most efficient force Great Britain has ever assembled, and they were self-confident. They consisted, wrote John Buchan, of 'perhaps the most wonderful fighting men that the world has seen. Officers and men were curiously alike. Behind all the differences of birth and education there was a common temperament; a kind of humorous realism about life, a dislike of talk, a belief in inherited tradition and historical ritual.'[10] None of them that summer could believe that the war to which they were deploying would last five long and bloody years, and would change for ever their 'ordered past' as Julian Grenfell succinctly described the first decade of the twentieth century.

Only the year before, on 17 June 1913, the new King, George V, who had appointed himself Colonel-in-Chief of the regiments of the Household Cavalry immediately on his accession in 1910, had reviewed the regiments in Windsor Great Park. 'With a bevy of princes and famous soldiers',[11] the King rode on to the ground to find the troops drawn up in line, with The Blues in the centre, and the Life Guards on either side, 'a blue body with red wings flecked with gold and lit up by the twinkling of the sun on many breastplates'. The regiments marched past in column behind their massed mounted bands, led by the Gold Sticks, with Lord Grenfell at the head of the 1st Life Guards; Sir Evelyn Wood, who had 'paid unusual attention to his personal appearance', at the head of The Blues, and the aged Lord Dundonald leading his old 2nd Life Guards. The trot past was followed by a slow gallop past, which somewhat tested

The funeral of Edward VII at Windsor in 1910 with the Coldstream Guards in the foreground and The Blues in two ranks on the green.

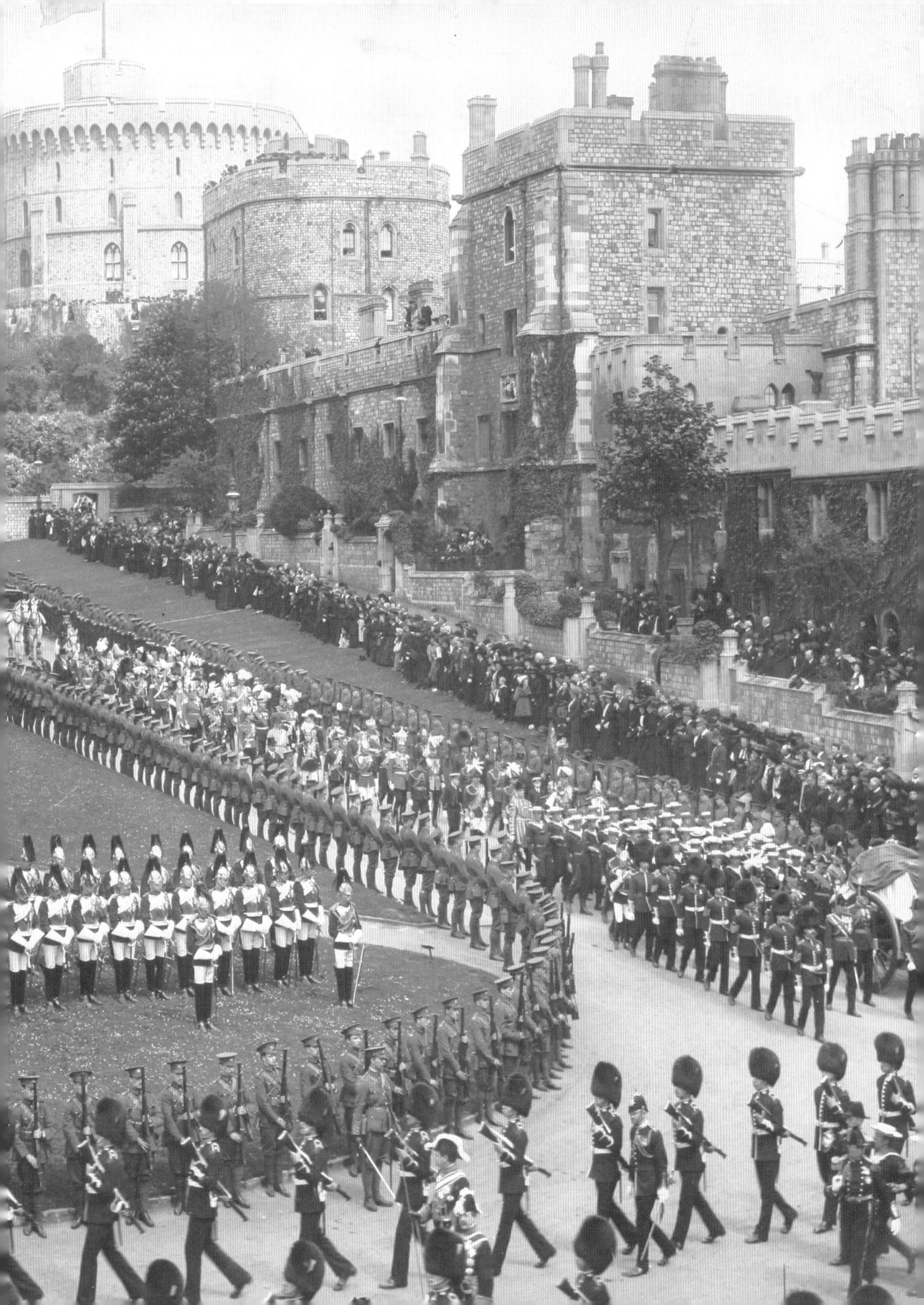

Lord Grenfell's horsemanship, after which the regiments disappeared into the distance. They reappeared at the gallop, moving

> comparatively gently till they were past some outstanding trees. Then with one united and terrifying yell they charged straight down upon the stands. The gallop had been nothing to this. Right across the big level stretch of grass they came with a most thunderous noise; on and on, so that it was something of a relief when they pulled up, still some little way off, and with the long line still beautifully and mathematically straight, the onlookers still untrampled. Taking the time from the Brigadier, Colonel Cook, they gave three tremendous cheers before forming into Brigade mass.[12]

The three cheers were not a resounding success for Cook who, having trained the men to prolong the 'ah' bit of 'hurrah', had forgotten to warn the band. Luckily the King did not seem to notice, and he addressed the assembled regiments and Colonel Cook most warmly. But it was to be the last charge the Household Cavalry were to make for five years, and within a year a quarter of those on parade, including Cook and Cavendish, would be dead.

War was declared on Germany on 4 August 1914, after German troops invaded Belgium. Historians will continue to argue about the underlying reasons for the start of the First World War, as it came to be known, for many years. They are too complex to be analysed here, but most would agree that German commercial and military ambitions, coupled with the chaotic state of the Austro-Hungarian Empire and French resentment at the loss of Alsace-Lorraine in 1870, meant that Europe was inherently unstable by the summer of 1914. All the potential belligerents possessed strong military forces. The assassination of the heir to the Austro-Hungarian throne in Sarajevo in 1914 started a crisis of events that escalated towards mobilization of those forces that respective statesmen seemed unable or unwilling to stop.

The British Expeditionary Force under the Household Cavalry's old friend Field-Marshal Sir John French was mobilized the same day. It consisted of around 150,000 men divided into two corps, one under Douglas Haig and the second, eventually, under Horace Smith-Dorrien. In addition there was a Cavalry Division, consisting of around 10,000 men in four brigades, commanded by Allenby. The Household Cavalry service squadrons were immediately equipped, and on 14 August Queen Alexandra said goodbye to The Blues in Regent's Park while Queen Mary did the equivalent for the 1st Life Guards in Hyde Park. The 2nd Life Guards marched from Windsor and the composite regiment arrived in Le Havre on 16 August. Colonel Cook, who was to command it, went to say farewell to the King and to lodge the standards in Buckingham Palace for safe keeping. Under Cook the 1st Life Guards' squadron was commanded by the genial Cavendish, with Lord Crichton, or

Lieutenant Colonel Cook, who commanded 1st Life Guards and the Household Cavalry Composite Regiment at Knightsbridge Barracks on 19 August 1914, the day they embarked for 'destination unknown'. Lloyd thought him 'a thorough gentleman, sympathetic and approachable'.

Trooper Harry Heard. He had been a waiter and joined up in December 1914. Unlike many, he was to return home in 1918.

'Pompey', commanding The Blues. The 2nd Life Guards' squadron was under Captain Gurney. The composite regiment were to be in the 4th Cavalry Brigade, together with the 3rd Hussars and 6th Dragoon Guards, under Brigadier General The Honourable C. E. Cis Bingham, a former commanding officer of the 1st Life Guards. After two days at Le Havre the regiment marched east into Belgium, taking up positions near Mons by 20 August.

Their campaign equipment, their 'marching order' as it was called, had improved significantly since the Boer War. A serious effort had been made to reduce weight, but the troop horses still carried around 18 stone. However, a new saddle, the 'universal' pattern, introduced in 1902, now spread this weight more evenly across a horse's back. Each man carried the 1913 pattern 'short' .303 Lee Enfield rifle in a rifle 'bucket' on the off (right)-hand side, with thirty rounds of ammunition in a bandolier over his shoulder; a further sixty were carried around the horse's neck. A highly effective new sword was introduced in 1908, designed specifically for thrusting, and was carried on the saddle; the King had taken a violent objection to these, finding them ugly and impractical. Although he finally agreed to his Household Cavalry carrying them on operations, he insisted on retaining the more old-fashioned but elegant 1892 sword for ceremonial, which is consequently still carried on parades today. The soldiers 'wore a stiff-peaked khaki cap, a khaki serge jacket (which buttoned up to the neck), breeches, known as "pantaloons", made of khaki cord with leather strapping at the knees, puttees, black ankle boots and spurs'. They carried a felt-covered water bottle and haversack over their shoulders, whilst strapped to their saddles were mess tins, two feed bags each carrying 7 pounds of oats, spare horse shoes, canvas bucket, greatcoat and cape. Under the saddle were two blankets, one for the man and one for his horse. In addition each regiment had two water-cooled Vickers machine guns, carried in limbers in a troop of twenty-five men, and accurate up to 2,900 yards.[13]

The German intention had been to hold the French in the Ardennes and Lorraine while developing a wide swing through the Low Countries to take Paris, in much the same way von Moltke the elder had in 1870. This plan, the so-called Schlieffen Plan, premeditated in 1905, was now poorly executed by the German Commander-in-Chief, Moltke the younger, who lost his nerve. He was too weak to prevent his powerful subordinates from attacking in Lorraine and failed, at the same time, to mass enough troops for a breakthrough in the north. Nevertheless, the Germans still invaded Belgium in sufficient strength on 20 August to force the French armies to retreat. The British Expeditionary Force, covering the left or northern flank of the French, resisted an attack by six German divisions at Mons on 24 August, but then fell back to conform. For the Household Cavalry 'the retreat from Mons' was a fortnight of almost total confusion, during which no one had any idea of what was really happening. They were involved in skirmishes for four days from 20 August, and then on 27th Allenby ordered them to lead the withdrawal, acknowledging

The Composite Regiment took part in the retreat from Mons in the late summer of 1914. By 1918 possession of the medal awarded for those battles – the Mons Star – was valued more highly than the Military Medal.

A watercolour of two troopers in barrack dress of the day.

that he had no idea of where the Germans were and that they had, very possibly, got ahead of them. It was a pitch-black night as the regiment moved out, guided by a staff officer in a car, primed to turn on his rear lights if the leading squadron were required to dismount and attack. 'The greatest handicap we had to face in those early days was lack of sleep,' wrote Trooper Eason,[14] 'the men slept in their saddles and were wakened at intervals by neighbours; the horses slouched along mechanically on the heels' of the one in front. Lieutenant 'Volley' Heath was known throughout the regiment for needing more sleep than most. One night he arrived at a farm, whose sole occupants were a 'singularly hideous old hag, whose companion was a lanky, half-witted boy'.[15] He was so tired that he fell asleep without establishing his nationality and was woken by the boy trying to stab him, his mother muttering encouragement, convinced Heath was German.

By 30 August they were back in the region of the town of Compiègne. They had not seen much of the enemy, though a squadron of Uhlans had attacked a bridge held by the 2nd Life Guards' squadron the day before. They seemed more exhausted than the Life Guards, who had to shoot the emaciated horses the Germans left behind. Their first serious action was near the village of Néry on 1 September when a more determined German cavalry patrol penetrated their lines. The Blues reported sitting in a field of clover watching German machine guns 'mow a path across their front, the clover falling as though cut by some giant scythe'. Luckily they were out of range. 'Volley' Heath was sent to work around them. His troop surprised them and forced them to retreat, though Heath was badly wounded. He died that afternoon, the first Household Cavalry casualty of the war. On 4 September the regiment were allowed a break at the agreeable château of a chocolate magnate – the first opportunity to groom their horses, clean their kit and write home since quitting Le Havre three weeks before. The German advance reached its apogee on 6 September, the French finally holding them on the Marne, and the regiment was sent to cover the left flank of the French as they counter-attacked.

Whereas the last two weeks of August had been a continuous withdrawal, September, conversely, saw the regiment advance every day from the 4th, reaching Soissons on the 12th, where they found the Germans dug in. The war of movement stopped abruptly and during the two weeks that followed the Household Cavalry experienced static warfare for the first time. The French had failed to gain the high ground beyond the River Aisne, and the Germans predictably counter-attacked, supported by what was now well-coordinated heavy artillery, and the Household Cavalry felt the effect of this for the first time too, with consequent casualties. Among those killed in September was Lieutenant Naylor-Leyland. 'Such a good lad; we were all so fond of him,' wrote his Captain.[16] By late September the war had already developed into stalemate. The Germans had failed to capture Paris, but retained possession of large parts of France and Belgium, and the Allies were too weak to force a counter-

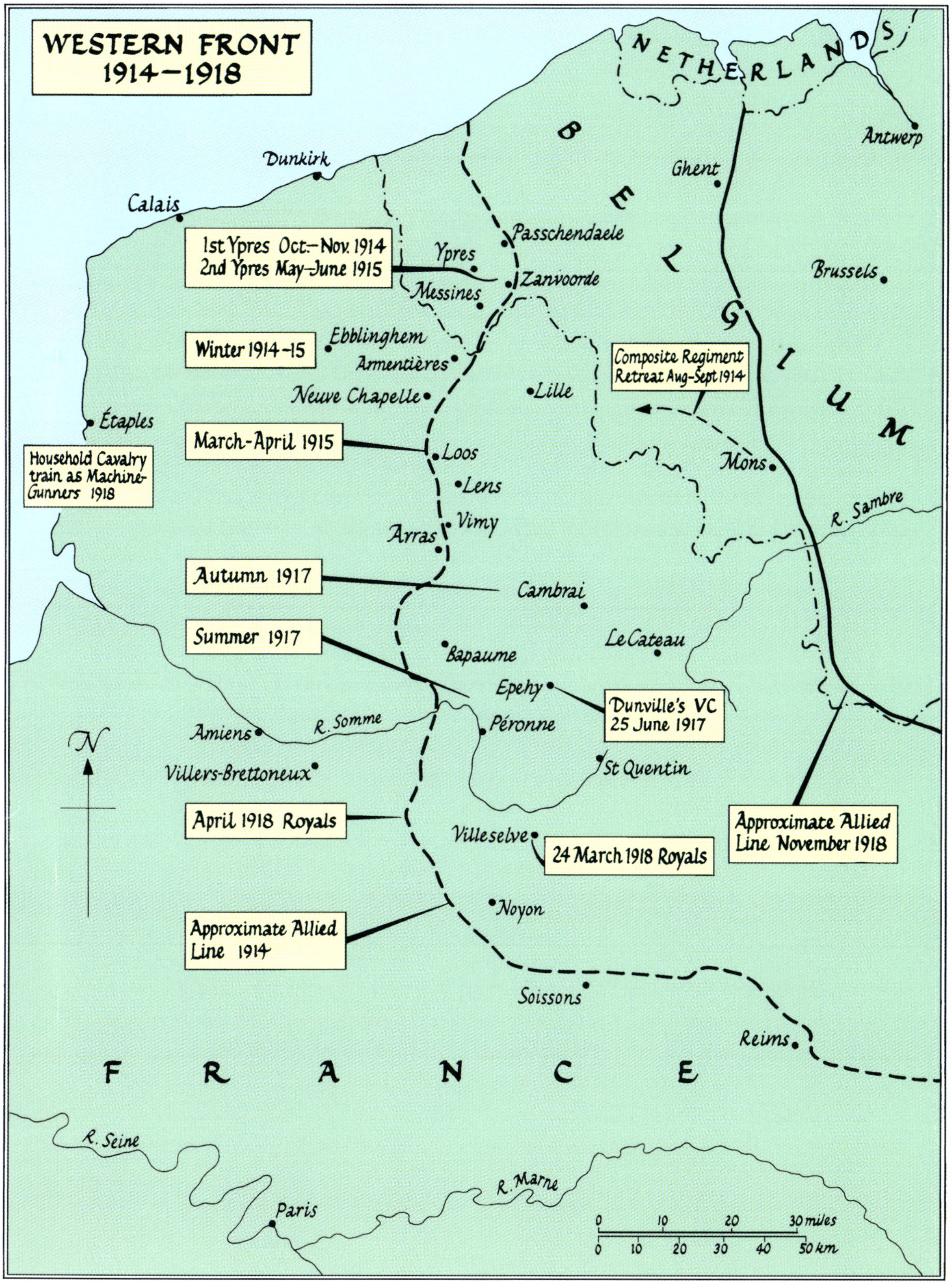

WESTERN FRONT
1914–1918
NETHERLANDS
BELGIUM
FRANCE
Antwerp
Ghent
Brussels
Dunkirk
Calais
1st Ypres Oct.–Nov. 1914
2nd Ypres May–June 1915
Ypres
Passchendaele
Zanvoorde
Messines
Winter 1914–15
Ebblinghem
Armentières
Neuve Chapelle
Lille
Composite Regiment
Retreat Aug–Sept 1914
Étaples
March–April 1915
Loos
Lens
Mons
Household Cavalry
train as Machine-
Gunners 1918
Vimy
Arras
R. Sambre
Autumn 1917
Cambrai
Summer 1917
Le Cateau
Bapaume
Epehy
Dunville's VC
25 June 1917
Amiens
R. Somme
Péronne
N
Villers-Brettoneux
St Quentin
April 1918 Royals
Villeselve
24 March 1918 Royals
Approximate Allied
Line November 1918
Noyon
Approximate Allied
Line 1914
Soissons
Reims
R. Seine
R. Marne
Paris
0 10 20 30 miles
0 10 20 30 40 50 km

offensive and drive them back. This stand-off, initially regarded as temporary, was to last for over four years. In early October it was agreed that the British Expeditionary Force would move north, handing over to the French on the Aisne, and taking over the left, or northern, part of the Allied line, between Ypres and the sea, and closer to their supply lines which ran through the Channel ports. Therefore the composite regiment had taken up position around the village of Messines by 18 October.

It was now clear in London that hopes for a quick war had evaporated and therefore moves were put in place to reinforce the British Expeditionary Force. As a result, all three Household Cavalry regiments were to be sent to France as regiments in their own right, as well, as we have already seen, as The Royals, who arrived in mid-October. The problem for the Household Cavalry was how to make up their numbers, with each regiment short of the squadron they had deployed with the composite regiment. There was no Household Cavalry reserve, previously thought unnecessary given that the composite regiment would always be reinforced from the parent regiments guarding the monarch at home. While this had recently changed – the period of Household Cavalry service had been adjusted from twelve to eight years with the regulars and four in the reserve – there had been insufficient time for the reserve to build up. On 17 August the three commanding officers, the Duke of Teck of the 1st Life Guards, who had replaced Cook and would diplomatically take the additional title of Marquess of Cambridge, Colonel Ferguson and Gordon Wilson were summoned to the War Office to discuss this problem with the Adjutant General. The idea of a second composite regiment was quickly dismissed and the solution that emerged was the creation of a Household Cavalry Brigade, with three fighting regiments and three reserve regiments. The immediate demand for recruits was met by using reservists from other cavalry regiments who were to be rebadged, so the Dragoons were paired with the 1st Life Guards, the Lancers with the 2nd Life Guards and the Hussars with The Blues. They were detailed to produce enough men to make the service regiments up to strength while the reserve regiments were built up. In addition, a new regimental headquarters had to be found for the 1st Life Guards whose headquarters had been deployed to France with Cook. The three regiments were deployed to Ludgershall on Salisbury Plain for training, while the King's Life Guard was reduced to a 'short' guard – normally mounted when the King was away – and was established with those who were too old or sick to deploy, as it was to remain throughout the war.

Throughout September recruits from the Dragoons, Lancers and Hussars duly joined. Lloyd, as a regimental clerk in the orderly room arranging matters, found it all very strange. Most of those who went to the 1st Life Guards were Inniskilling Dragoon Guards, 'all of whom had served together in India . . . for about a year on average they had been at home on the reserve, and had not quite settled down to the comparatively drab existence of civilians. Now they were, quite unexpectedly collected together again in one place, as if by magic. No wonder they felt inclined to make merry.' One immediately obvious difference was in their height – contemporary photographs show 6-foot non-commissioned Life Guard officers alongside 5-foot 'skins', as they were nicknamed. Lloyd soon came to like and admire his fellow Irishmen, many from Liverpool, who so readily adapted to their new circumstances, although he did begrudge the extra work their endless breaches of discipline caused, usually after the canteen, housed in a marquee, had closed at night, when the civilian manager was generally rolled down the hill with his empty beer barrels. By now Lloyd was a Corporal of Horse, and had acquired Herbert, the horse he would ride throughout the war. Herbert was an individual horse, who adjusted to life in the Household Cavalry by developing specific idiosyncrasies. He was the tallest horse in the regiment and thought very smart, but he refused absolutely to go anywhere near 'trains, buses, steam-engines, and all huge things which moved mechanically and made strange noises in their insides'. Consequently he was not popular 'for ceremonial', but Lloyd, whose new role made him regimental 'staff' and who therefore generally rode unaccompanied, took to him immediately.

The newly formed brigade was called the 7th Cavalry Brigade, and with the 6th Brigade, which included The Royals, formed the 3rd Cavalry Division, so, with the exception of the composite regiment, now in Allenby's line at Messines, all our regiments were grouped together. The 7th Brigade was commanded by the popular Brigadier General Kavanagh, of whom Lloyd thought the world. Later in the war he was detailed to take dispatches to him and wrote, 'I was struck by the absence of all the pomp and eyewash one is apt to associate with a general and his suites. Here was one of the finest generals the army had produced up to now, actually sharing quarters, rations and shaving water with a private.' The brigade moved to France on 6 October, and was soon riding east, ordered to assist the Belgians in Antwerp. However, the Germans took the city on 9 October and for eight days from 8 October the brigade retreated, much as the composite regiment had done a month and a half earlier, and provided a rearguard for the Belgians, while staying in touch with Allenby's corps to create a line of sorts between the advancing Germans and the Channel ports. On 16 October French troops relieved them, and they collapsed exhausted into billets in the village of Passchendale, near Ypres. Julian Grenfell, predictably, enjoyed it all hugely. 'The guns go on all day and most of the night,' he wrote to his mother.

> Of course it's very hard to follow what is going on; even the squadron leaders know nothing; and one marches and counter marches without end, backwards and forwards, nearer and further, apparently without object. Only the Christian virtue of faith emerges triumphant. It is all the most *wonderful* fun; better fun than one could ever imagine. I hope it goes on a

nice long time; but pigsticking will be the only tolerable pursuit after this or one will die of sheer ennui.[17]

This short period was to be the only movement the newly formed brigades were to enjoy. 'On 19 October 1914 the war of movement in open country lapsed into a state of trench warfare,' Lloyd wrote prophetically, and both brigades were now entrenched on the lines in front of Ypres, taking turns either to man the trenches or act as an immediate reserve.

By 20 October the Cavalry Corps, as it now became when the 3rd Division joined up with Allenby's force, was responsible for a section of the 35-mile front that the British Expeditionary Force was holding in Flanders. Each cavalry brigade held approximately 600 yards of a semicircle east of Ypres that would later become known as the Ypres Salient. As ill luck would have it, their part of the line was exactly where the Germans intended to concentrate their next offensive, designed to seize the Channel ports and cut off and destroy the British army. The resulting battle of Ypres, called the First Battle at Ypres, was the bloodiest in the history of the Household Cavalry after Waterloo.

When regiments were in the trenches they left their horses a mile or two back, cared for by men detailed as horse holders, responsible for five or six horses each. When they came out of the line they were reunited with their horses, saddled up in reserve. Autumn rapidly gave way to an early winter with driving rain and sleet which turned the low-lying country around Ypres into a quagmire. 'All idea of time was lost,' wrote Lloyd.

> Nobody could have named the date or the day of the week, and nobody cared. The only factors which reminded us of the passing of time were daylight and darkness. Our horses ceased to be employed as cavalry horses. Their role was . . . the rapid conveyance of rifle-and-bayonet soldiers to the line. The exciting scampering along country roads and through villages gave place to an existence comparable only to that of a water-rat in a swamp.

'The Horses stand about all over the place looking miserable,' added Sir Morgan Crofton, a Boer War veteran who had rejoined the 2nd Life Guards on mobilization (he always spelt Horses with a capital 'H'). 'They have had no hay for a month and they gnaw everything they can get hold of. There is not a tree which has not had its bark gnawed off . . . and a waggon stands just outside our door which is half eaten by them.'[18] Grenfell, predictably, relished the life, writing,

> I've never been so fit or nearly so happy in my life before; I adore the fighting and the continual interest which compensates for every disadvantage. . . . I *adore* war. It is like a big picnic without the objectlessness of a

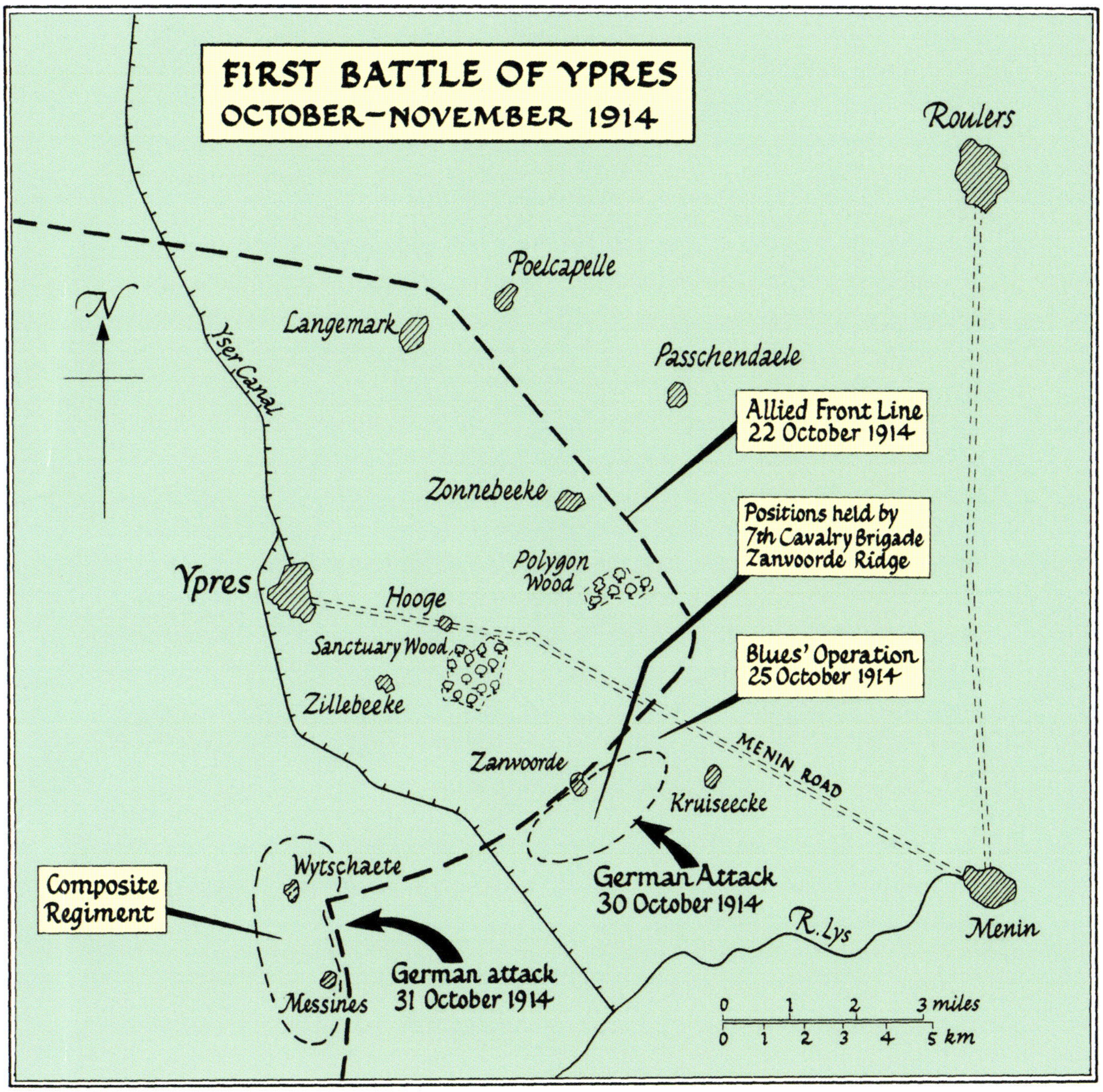
FIRST BATTLE OF YPRES
OCTOBER–NOVEMBER 1914
Roulers
Poelcapelle
N
Langemark
Yser Canal
Passchendaele
Allied Front Line
22 October 1914
Zonnebeeke
Positions held by
7th Cavalry Brigade
Zanvoorde Ridge
Polygon
Wood
Ypres
Hooge
Sanctuary Wood
Blues' Operation
25 October 1914
Zillebeeke
MENIN ROAD
Zanvoorde
Kruiseecke
German Attack
30 October 1914
Wytschaete
Composite
Regiment
R. Lys
Menin
German attack
31 October 1914
Messines
0 1 2 3 miles
0 1 2 3 4 5 km

picnic. . . . No one grumbles at one for being dirty. I've only had my boots off once in the last ten days, and only washed twice.

This was despite losing his troop sergeant when a group of Germans opened fire on them after showing a white flag, when even Grenfell admitted that being under fire was 'bloody'. But he was pleased with his troop who behaved very well despite using 'the most filthy language'. Second Lieutenant St George of the 1st Life Guards took a rather different view, writing, 'We have been in the thick of it last four days, solid fighting day and night . . . You can't imagine what it's like. Words can't describe the hell it is.'[19]

Life in the trenches in October 1914 was not the well-regulated affair that it later became. The trenches themselves were not a continuous line but a series of pits dug in the sandy soil, each holding about a dozen men. Lloyd describes going up with reinforcements on 25 October. 'The night was as black as the pit. . . . There was no continuous line. The trenches were a series of holes, for all the world like large graves, not connected, and running zigzag across the hillside. At the point where we struck each trench was chock-full of men who absolutely refused to admit us.' Once in a trench, it was very difficult to move without being shelled or sniped at and rations could only be delivered at night, though 'the men creep out to make tea in the quiet intervals'. The worst strain was the shelling, which reached a crescendo before an actual attack. Casualties occurred daily from 20 October onwards and bodies, recovered during the night, were buried behind the lines. On 25 October Sir Richard Levigne was shot and buried that night in a village churchyard. The following day it emerged he still had the squadron's pay in the inside pocket of his jacket. He was duly disinterred and the money recovered.

On 25 October The Blues staged a daring mounted operation, riding across the front of two German cavalry regiments to cover the retreat of the 20th Infantry Brigade from Kruiseecke. 'We were ordered to move about mid-day', wrote Corporal Millin.

> We moved cautiously up to a road and started galloping to draw German fire and shells which we succeeded in doing to such an extent that we lost 10 more men in my troop, including 2 or 3 dead. I don't know how I escaped the shrapnel. Shells were bursting all around me, and men and horses were falling right and left of me. My horse was forced to jump over several men and horses in the road. I could hear the horses groaning, but I do not seem to have a clear remembrance of what I saw; it was simply hell. All that I do remember is seeing the men and horses on the ground with lots of blood about.[20]

Lord Tweedmouth's (known universally as Beef) was shot in the leg. 'I had to stop,' he wrote, 'and get into Hugh Grosvenor's trench. Got out presently and shot my horse with my revolver and saved all my kit. We were very lucky considering the fire we came in for.'[21]

Yet much worse was to come on 30 October when the main German attack began. Six new German divisions, supported by four elite Jaeger regiments, and 260 guns, had been brought up. The assault fell against the Household Cavalry at Zanvoorde Ridge, their position on the perimeter of the Ypres Salient, just east and south of the town. Haig, who was rarely sympathetic to the Household Cavalry, described that awful day, after the war.

> They were in narrow trenches on the forward slopes before us in full sight of the enemy. Their trenches were soon blown in, and at 8 a.m. after one and a quarter hour's bombardment, the whole of the 39th German infantry division and three battalions of Jaegers attacked their shattered position. The time had come to slip away, and orders were issued for retirement to the second line; but the greater part of the two squadrons of Life Guards on the left and the Royal Horse Guards machine guns could not get away and were cut off and died to a man, except for a few wounded prisoners.[22]

Corporal Millin survived once more but 'had a very narrow shave, having a bullet pass right across my chest, through all my clothing and scraping my skin'. Later a shell burst 20 yards from him. 'I was covered with a shower of dirt and debris and almost fell over, but I was not hit. I shall never forget 30 October 1914.' Lloyd survived because he was in the rear. He describes the survivors staggering back, 'weary to death as they marched in. Both A and D squadrons had sustained losses but C squadron had, with the exception of Charlie Wright and six or seven men, been absolutely wiped out.' Many of the casualties had occurred early on, from the shelling, when men were either blown to pieces or buried alive. Many of the remainder were bayoneted in the hand-to-hand fighting once the German infantry came up.

The second major attack came the following day, 31 October, and fell against the composite regiment manning the trenches between Wytschaete and Messines. Cook had been wounded by an artillery shell on 20 October, and Cavendish killed, and command had passed to Lord Crichton, who gave the impression of being everywhere as the German attack developed. It began with an assault by a Bavarian division, the brunt of which fell on the composite regiment's neighbours, and during the evening noise and singing could be heard from the German lines. At 7 p.m. there was a lull, but at midnight the main attack fell directly on the Household Cavalry.

> Under the rays of the moon the Germans, open mouthed and heavy handed, came, as it seemed, straight for the composite regiment, line after line and shoulder to shoulder. At 200 yards the regiment opened fire and poured in round after round, and at any rate saw live men climbing over their dead

colleagues simply to fall themselves. The Germans swung left-handed short of The Blues' trenches to engage in hand-to-hand fighting. Twice B and C squadrons were driven out, and twice they came back to regain what they had lost against overwhelming odds.

Eventually they could hold on no longer and the Germans worked their way round behind The Blues' squadron, now under Bowlby, who were attacked from three sides. Crichton ordered them to fall back, and as they did so the Lincolns came to their aid. By 9 a.m. the following day the Germans were in Messines and could not be driven out, despite a strong French counterattack, but they got no further. They never reached Wytschaete, and the line held, but at a dreadful cost. Crichton was dead, and when Bowlby mustered what was left the regiment could only muster thirty men of the 1st Life Guards' squadron, three from the 2nd Life Guards and thirty Blues. It was their last action, for, the following week, the survivors rejoined their parent regiments at Ypres.

The next major blow fell at Klein Zillebeke on 6 November. Millin was wounded again: 'a bullet struck me on the side of my head as I was firing – I turned round exclaiming "I'm hit, I'm hit", but it was only a scratch and a bruise. This bullet passed through my woollen cap. I don't want to have any more narrow shaves. They are getting too frequent! I'm sure my luck is in.' It was; although he subsequently suffered from frostbite and jaundice, he survived the war. Lieutenant St George was less lucky. He survived at Zillebeke, writing sadly to his parents that 'an awful lot of people are going home owing to their nerves going though constant shell fire. I admit it's trying. A lot of good fellows killed here last two days. Poor Willie Cadogan [killed on the] 10th.' St George was killed himself just after writing this last letter when the battle was judged to be at its crisis point.

While the Household Cavalry took the brunt of the cavalry casualties at the First Battle at Ypres, The Royals also suffered badly. They had handed over to the Household Cavalry Brigade at Zanvoorde on 29 October, so missed the main attack, but the following day they were rushed to the nearby château at Hollebeke where a secondary German attack was in progress. Each man who went forward into the narrow and sandy trenches there fired 350 rounds that day, and the horse holders behind the lines were constantly shelled, having been spotted by German artillery observers in aeroplanes. Julian Grenfell delighted in patrolling right up to the German lines when he could. On 17 November he crawled forward to the nearest trench which seemed empty. Jumping into it, he found a solitary German whom he shot. Sensing something was not quite right, he sat and waited. Twenty minutes later he saw a large group of Germans approaching. He shot the officer and ran back to The Royals' trenches at what he described as a galloping crawl, and warned the brigade that a new German attack was developing. He was right, and when the Germans attacked the brigade was ready. Grenfell was subsequently awarded the Distinguished

Service Order, but the soldiers sensed he was after a Victoria Cross. John Cusack described later how Grenfell ordered his new troop sergeant, Pat Mortimer, a veteran of South Africa, to gather the troop and follow him in a clearly suicidal attack on a group of Uhlans. Mortimer took no notice.

The regiments remained on the line until late November and although there were no more major German attacks, they continued to take casualties from snipers and shellfire. Sir Morgan Crofton describes what it was like coming forward to the trenches.

> We now dismount to continue to march on foot, and hand over our Horses to one of our No. 3's [the grooms, farriers and regimental staff who acted as horse holders] who will return. . . . I remove my spurs and prepare for a muddy wet filthy walk. It is now dark as pitch and we stumble along a lane until we reach a partially destroyed village called Zillebeke. Not a light nor a living soul appears. Silhouettes of ruined houses mark our dismal journey through the rain and mist. On entering the village we suddenly come under machine gun fire and a stream of bullets whiz over us. We rush to the battered wall to take cover for a short time while it lasts . . . After about 10 minutes it dies away as suddenly as it began . . . We move on . . . By now the night has become fine and frosty and it is about 6 p.m. There has been a considerable fight during the afternoon and we have to wait at the sloppy mouth of the entrance to the trench while the casualties are being removed. A group of 10 dead Somersets were laid in a line next to the Ration Dump which was going to be issued to us. We stumbled down the trench making slow progress, as it was very narrow and half way up was blocked by a dead man, over whom we tripped and fell in the darkness. At the end of about 50 yards of trench we came to our front line of trenches which stretched away to the left and right of the communications trench up which we had come. A man lay across the front trench badly wounded, I think in the lungs, for he moaned a lot, and as he breathed he hissed like a punctured tyre . . . As our men filed away to the right they found it blocked by 2 dead men who had been left behind by the Somersets . . . It was horrible, for the corpses were dragged and pushed along like sacks of potatoes, anyhow, to get them clear of the trench. The German trenches were about 50–100 yards off. About 20 yards out beyond our trenches we heard wounded Germans, the result of ineffective attacks in the afternoon, calling out in a plaintive and mournful manner. They were like Banshees. Then one by one the cries ceased presumably as the men died.

Crofton later described 'Trooper Boyce, an extremely good and reliable youth . . . came along with 2 jars of rum, carrying one in his hand and one on his shoulder. Boyce was a very lighthearted individual, with a supreme contempt for the Germans.' Part of the trench parapet, about four foot of it, was broken

Lord Hugh Grosvenor. Lord Tweedmouth took refuge in his trench when he was wounded at 1st Ypres. Grosvenor was killed five days later on 30 October 1914.

Julian Grenfell (*left*), who detested Colonel Steele (*right*). They were both killed within days of each other at 2nd Ypres in May 1915.

Sir Morgan Crofton by his dugout at Brielon. What primarily upset men like Crofton, a very traditional regimental officer, was that their old well-ordered pre-war world was disappearing.

down and a German sniper was annoying the regiment by firing at people for the few seconds they were exposed as they passed this section.

> We warned Boyce of this man, when he got to the other end of the trench with the rum jar on his shoulder to bob down higher up the trench as it was very exposed. He however didn't think it worthwhile to do so, and he hadn't passed us 20 seconds when we heard a 'phut' followed by a thud and a white face looked around the corner of our dugout and said 'They've got him, Boyce is hit'. We crawled up to him. He was making terrible noises, but we found that nothing could be done. He had been shot clean through the chest, and died in about five minutes.

By 21 November the cavalry regiments were withdrawn from the front line and taken back to billets in the rear so that they could refit. The British strategy was to dig in during the winter, building up numbers and supplies, and use the infantry to break through the German lines in the spring, creating a gap which the cavalry corps could exploit. The Royals were happy as it gave them time to take stock and make sense of their losses. Cusack wrote that 'we hadn't taken off our boots or puttees, let alone our underclothes, for the last eight weeks, and when we did get back to the billets we were absolutely filthy. All of us were footsore, some of us had frozen feet and most of us had trench-feet.' Leave was granted, and most of the regiment got home for a few days. Cusack made it to Glasgow to see his mother. 'I don't think any of us returned with fear,' he wrote, 'or that we were scared to go back again, but our spirits had altered since those first days in August. We realized now it wasn't going to be easy, and though we still had thoughts of victory coming with the spring, we were making excuses about the British army.'

The Household Cavalry pulled back 30 miles west of Ypres, to billets grouped around the village of Ebblinghem. By December the 1st Life Guards had been reduced to only 150 men and badly needed to recuperate and get reinforcements, which duly arrived from England. Sir Morgan Crofton kept a detailed diary throughout the winter. He noted that of the forty officers who had either left England with the composite squadron in August or who had been deployed with the main regiment in October, nine had been killed, eleven wounded, three were missing or prisoners and five evacuated through illness; only twelve of them remained. Crofton's diary reveals many emotions. One of the most striking is his belief that the British cavalry, so carefully trained and nurtured, was being sacrificed needlessly. He complained that staff officers 'who must be totally ignorant of the cavalry' did not realize that once you had taken away 25 per cent of a cavalry regiment for horse holding, they could only put 240 men in the line, so a whole brigade was needed to achieve the same number of rifles found in an infantry battalion. The cavalry were being wasted and the reserves who turned up in France were 'immature and untrained youths. This cannot be wondered at, for it takes at least two years to make a cavalryman. If the cavalry are to be used as infantry, or in trench work, it is being uselessly frittered away and as it is the most expensive arm, it is useless extravagance to waste it.'[23]

Crofton also struggles to make sense of how the war is affecting his familiar world. Whereas the Boer War was bloody and prolonged, it was easy to comprehend because ordered life at home was unaffected and the British would 'inevitably' win. This war was different. There was no clear end in sight, and no easy vision of what the post-war world might look like. 'For us on the ground,' wrote Cusack, 'the war was full of uncertainties and confusion.' The regiments jumped on any rumours suggesting there might be a quick resolution and way out of the netherworld in which they found themselves. They believed anything, from the Kaiser dying to the Russians inflicting a massive defeat on the Germans in the east or a great victory at Gallipoli, but they found it difficult to grasp that they could be fighting for years. This was a total war, not an excursion, which demanded not one, but a seemingly endless series of supreme efforts. It required either considerable optimism or extreme faith for men to trust that they would not soon be mown down as so many of their friends had been. It was also particularly difficult to deal with the contrasts between the trenches and the relative normality of life behind the lines, such as the regiments enjoyed for much of that winter. They were relatively comfortable, able occasionally to go home on leave, and mostly bored.

The King came to inspect the Household Cavalry on 2 December. All three regiments turned out mounted, and, as far as possible, clean, lining a narrow country lane. Lloyd and his horse, Herbert, were on the far left. They had to wait for some time before the King arrived so Herbert got cold and bored waiting. As the King finally made his appearance he suddenly plunged forward, span round 'six times like lightning and dashed the rank all to bits'. Luckily this faux pas was overshadowed by the Colonel of the Leicesters, next in line to be inspected, whose bored horse went to sleep just as the King greeted him, collapsing in an untidy heap in front of the royal party. Lloyd, now fed up with recovering Herbert each morning after he had broken his head collar and gone foraging around the local countryside, records a seventy-two-hour leave pass during which he determined to see his parents in Ireland. By a convoluted route he managed to get home to his parents at 4 a.m. on the day after he left France, still in his service uniform, and clasping his rifle, having walked through woods and 'on rides and paths I had often trod in the old days'. That evening he cycled 40 miles back to Waterford in four hours. Once back on the train he realized that his leave 'was now to all intents and purposes over, and all too quickly, and I was once more in the grip of the machine against which there was no use struggling'.

'The worst of war,' Crofton noted, 'is that one is either bored stiff in billets, or scarified out of one's existence by high explosive shells. There is no happy medium.' There were periodic spells in the trenches during the winter, either in the front line or as part of digging parties. The men were now taken up to the line by London buses and the horses left in the rear. In April the cavalry left their comfortable billets to prepare for the great breakthrough that was supposed to occur at Neuve Chapelle, but never materialized. Instead they were committed once more to the Ypres Salient to plug gaps as the Germans launched their own offensive. They opened a 4-mile gap in the Allied lines using mustard gas for the first time. On 12 May the 3rd Cavalry Division moved up at dusk to take over a section of the line near Hooge, very close to where they had lost so many friends in October and November. 'Marched into Ypres,' wrote Lieutenant Murray Smith, 'the town burning fiercely and smelling horribly, extraordinary state of ruins.' The plan was for The Royals to be on the left of the line, with both regiments of Life Guards on the right and The Blues in reserve. The forward trenches were mostly blown in, and when the Germans began a massive artillery bombardment at dawn on 13 May, the Household Cavalry took casualties straight away. The subsequent German infantry attack was half-hearted and held off relatively easily, though the British artillery could only muster one gun in support because of the chronic shortage of ammunition. However, Colonel Steele of The Royals felt a counter-attack would now drive the Germans back, so the reserve was told to prepare.

Murray Smith was enjoying

> a good drink of rum and water. Just finished and feeling quite gay when Innes-Ker looked in and said we had orders to make a counterattack at 2.30 p.m.; not very pleasant news. Got back to the trench and told men to take off coats and equipment, only rifle and bayonet and bandolier to be carried; one man a squadron to be left behind to look after our belongings . . . About 12.45 p.m. we filed out to the right, a slight dip till we got to the railway, but as soon as we got across it and through some farm buildings we were spotted . . . Doubled to a high bank with trees, from where the attack was to be launched, huddled together close under it, with some remnants of The Royals, who had had a bad time, several badly wounded and some gory sights. The men seemed to realize we were 'for it', everybody soaked and cold; this was the worst part of the day.

At 2.20 p.m. the Colonel stood, whistle in hand, while the men were ordered to fix bayonets and dry the butt plates of their rifles 'to prevent slipping when placing bayonet in Hun'. At 2.30 p.m. the Colonel blew his whistle, and the men jumped forward in open files, rushing across 600 yards of open ground in front of the German lines. Men fell at once.

> Seemed to be nothing but machine guns on every side, also every sort of shell. Got to a shell hole; seemed to be very few of our men left; found most

of my collar and shoulder strap shot away without wounding me; another rush; Bowlby shot dead just in front of me; lay close to him for a time; looked wonderfully peaceful considering what was going on.[24]

On the left The Blues reached the German trenches and the occupants immediately fled. On the right they got 'hung up with cross machine-gun fire, and did not reach the trench; however the object was attained as the Germans bolted'.[25] Though successful, the cost was terrible. 'But for sheer, unmitigated hell I have never imagined such shell fire as we received from all kinds of guns, big and small, shrapnel and high explosive shell; it really is a mystery to me why anyone got away clear.'[26] An airman who observed the attack said that it looked like a parade movement. The whole of the 3rd Division was now in the front line, where they remained until 14 May. Casualties for the two days amounted to seven officers and over 100 men of the 270-odd who had started.

The Royals had suffered very badly from shellfire during 13 May. Julian Grenfell, as usual, was in his element. During the winter he had acquired a telescopic sight for his rifle, and continued to make daring patrols into No Man's Land trying to snipe Germans. About an hour before The Blues' counter-attack he reconnoitred the positions of their neighbouring regiment, the North Somerset Yeomanry, dragging a reluctant Cusack with him along a communication trench, much of which was blown in and open to German view. 'It was absolute hell,' Cusack wrote, 'the bullets were flying and the shells were crushing the parapets flat. I ducked and crouched as low as I could . . . but as I dodged and darted along, there was Julian Grenfell striding along, upright, in front of me.' They reached the lines safely. Grenfell duly completed his task and called to Cusack to go back. 'When we were only fifty yards from the railway cutting the ground was entirely flat and as I was crawling across it, I heard Julian being hit. I heard a thump and he grunted. I looked round; he hadn't fallen; he was kneeling. I saw blood flowing from a wound in his temple.' Grenfell died in a base hospital on 26 May.

The Royals and The Blues were back in the line on 24 May, in Sanctuary Wood, where the trenches were only 300 yards from the German front line. No actual attack developed this time, but they again took heavy and continual artillery fire. By the time The Royals were finally withdrawn at the beginning of June they had lost thirteen officers and 123 men, mostly from shellfire; of these seven officers and twenty-one men were killed, including Colonel Steele, who died from wounds three days before Grenfell.

The remainder of 1915 was to be relatively quiet for the cavalry. They moved back from Ypres in mid-June to billets behind the lines, and though they were brought forward again in September for the battle of Loos, they were never actually committed, though they did take a few casualties supporting the Foot Guards. After the Second Battle of Ypres the disillusionment that had emerged the previous winter became more widespread. Crofton, whose comments about the staff in the winter had been relatively restrained, now became openly critical of the British generals. 'There is no doubt that the Salient at Ypres is simply an inferno. It is not war, but murder pure and simple. The massacre which has been going on there since 22 April is not realized at home.' Grenfell also detested the staff. Although there were many brave and respected generals like Kavanagh, there were still those who were perceived, unfairly in most cases, to live behind the lines in châteaux, isolated from the bloodiness of the trenches. One of Grenfell's most biting poems is his 'Prayer for Those on the Staff'. One extract of this runs:

> The Staff is working with its brains
> While we are sitting in the trench;
> The Staff the universe ordains
> (Subject to Thee and General French).
>
> God help the Staff – especially
> The young ones, many of them sprung
> From our high aristocracy;
> Their task is hard, and they are young.
>
> O Lord, who mad'st all things to be
> And madest some things very good
> Please keep the extra ADC
> From horrid scenes, and sights of blood.[27]

The human cost of the war did not move Grenfell, who appeared to live by a Homeric ideal, no doubt inculcated in him at school. His last great poem, 'Into Battle', is almost unique for 1915 in that it still praises war and the noble emotions it inspires. The last three verses of this run:

> And when the burning moment breaks,
> And all things else are out of mind,
> And Joy of Battle only takes
> Him by the throat, and makes him blind.
>
> Through joy and blindness he shall know,
> Not caring much to know, that still
> Nor lead nor steel shall reach him so
> That it be not the Destined Will.
>
> The thundering line of battle stands,
> And in the air Death moans and sings
> And Day shall clasp him with strong hands,
> And Night shall fold him in soft wings.

His views were not commonly shared, and the continuing human cost was more painful and prosaic to men like Crofton for whom the regiment was almost his family. 'A rifle grenade fell into our trench,' he wrote on 6 June,

> and hit one of our best Corporals, Wilkins, on the left thigh, a man who did most awfully well on the Retreat from Mons, and got the DCM. The grenade exploded, nearly blew his leg off and severely wounded him on the other leg, in all making forty wounds. He was in dreadful pain and very hard to move out of the trench. I hope his life will be saved but it is doubtful. Anyhow he will lose his leg at the hip joint. He was engaged to such a pretty young woman in the dress department of Marshall and Snelgrove.

Corporal Wilkins died ten days later.

Chapter Eighteen

THE END IN FRANCE AND REORGANIZATION

The winter of 1915–16 was a particularly difficult one for the cavalry. Haig had replaced French as Commander-in-Chief, and was facing pressure to use the cavalry more as infantry. In February each cavalry brigade had to provide a battalion for the trenches; The Royals' squadron sent up were positioned at the Hohenzollern redoubt and again suffered heavy casualties from shelling, with seventeen killed and forty-seven wounded. Cavalrymen were also being used as Military Policemen and for traffic control. Furthermore, the recruits joining the new reserve regiments at home were emerging as a particular problem. Although casualties were heavy, they were still lighter than in the infantry, and once the service regiments in France were brought up to strength, the reserve regiments were left with an embarrassment of numbers at a time when the infantry needed everyone they could get. There was no military inclination to enlarge the cavalry, but an ingenious scheme was developed to create, from Household Cavalry recruits, cyclist companies for the Guards Division. The idea was that cyclists could work at liaison tasks in the rear areas, but, inevitably, they were quickly assimilated into the front line. The first Life Guards' cyclist company that arrived in France was in the trenches with the Foot Guards within two weeks. Although generally deemed a success, the experiment did not last, and only two companies were ever raised. The second was ultimately absorbed into the Life Guards.

In July 1916 the cavalry had closed up to the Somme to exploit the breakthrough thought inevitable after the assault by Kitchener's newly raised armies, now finally adequately supported by artillery. It never happened, and the reserves, ready to be deployed from London and Windsor, were not needed. Consequently the question of what to do with them became more urgent and a suggestion was made that they could be formed into a Household Cavalry infantry battalion. This was duly raised in September, crossing to France in November under the command of Lieutenant Colonel Portal. It was first in action on 8 December on the Somme, and was, from then on, fairly permanently engaged all winter. By mid-January 1917 it had already been reduced to 276 effective men. Brought up to strength with more reservists, it took part in the Arras offensive with the 4th Division, at a cost of a further four officers and 166 other ranks. In May, once brought up to full infantry strength, they took part in the assaults on the River Scarpe, winning nine military medals at the Battle of Roeux Cemetery.

Many of those who signed up as troopers in 1915, hoping to join the Household Cavalry, were from better educational and social backgrounds than those who joined before the war. University and professional men chose the Household Cavalry because, they felt, it offered them a chance to serve their country in a slightly superior milieu without the pressure of officer selection. Ironically many were commissioned, including many from the Household Battalion, forty-six of whom had been gazetted as officers into other regiments by 1918. Crofton noticed the increasingly high educational standard of Household Cavalry reservists as early as 1915. 'One of the corporals is a Bachelor of Science at London University,' he noted with surprise in his diary on 10 February, and 'an official out of the Mummy Department in the British Museum is in our Cavalry Field Ambulance.' An exceptional number of men in The Royals went forward for commissions. Fifty-three non-commissioned officers from the regiment were commissioned during the course of the war, the vast majority into other regiments as there were so few vacancies in The Royals themselves.

In April 1917 the 3rd Cavalry Division was again brought forward to exploit the anticipated breakthrough at Vimy and Arras. By this stage they were fairly desperate to be involved, both to prove their worth and because their hatred of the Germans had deepened to such an extent. The Divisional Commander issued an order prior to their move-up which read:

> Officers must impress on men that when our chance comes we must go 'all out' to make it good. Cavalry is the arm to complete a victory, and so rewards the other arms for their sacrifices and labour. Killing Germans is not advocated if it is easier and quicker to accept their surrender. Men should, however, be reminded that Germans sink hospital ships, poison wells, and commit every possible atrocity, and that the only good Germans are dead Germans.

At first it looked as though this time they would have their chance. The initial assault took the Germans' first and second lines by surprise and the cavalry moved forward behind the infantry into Arras itself, but once more the attack petered out and they were frustrated, though both the Household Cavalry and The Royals were in action in May as they were put into the line to free the infantry to prepare for further assaults.

A proud couple at Waterloo Station in August 1916. The casualties in the Household Battalion would be horrific.

Lieutenant Colonel Portal, who raised and commanded the Household Battalion in September 1916 from reservists at Windsor. 'In the confusion the Colonel could not find his respirator and called for his orderly to bring it. It couldn't be found but in a few seconds he came back with one in his hand and said "Here it is, Sir!" Colonel Portal put it on. When we came to take them off 20 minutes later, the orderly was seen dead with nothing on.'

A Household Cavalry cyclist company was created from recruits during the winter of 1915–16. Here they are seen passing through the village of Vraignes in March 1916.

Waiting for the breakthrough. By 1917 the role of the cavalry on the Western Front had become intensely frustrating.

From 12 May The Royals were in the trenches between Épehy and Vendhuile, where it was imperative to dominate No Man's Land and deny any initiative to the Germans. One way of doing this was to raid the enemy trenches, and one such raid was ordered for 25 June. John Cusack was in the party, commanded by Lieutenant Bickersteth, as was a new second lieutenant, Johnnie Dunville. As Bickersteth later wrote to Johnnie's mother,

> I think perhaps you may be glad to hear about Johnnie. I was on the same raiding party as he was and though I did not actually see him hit, I was only a few yards behind. . . . Throughout the whole affair he was as brave as a lion and extraordinarily competent. He led the party on a compass bearing over an extremely difficult piece of country straight to the German wire. We had 850 yards to go and he never made a mistake. Our barrage was accurate, but not enough to do in the Boches who received us with a heavy rifle fire. Johnnie ran forward directly . . . the barrage lifted and he helped the sappers put the torpedo under the wire to blow it up. The sappers are full of the bravery he showed in trying to protect them with his own body while they were doing their work. Then he was first through the gap and almost at once got wounded. He ran back calling to me in the cheeriest way that he was hit.

By the time the engineers had finally finished all surprise was gone and Bickersteth decided the only option was to withdraw, which they did, dragging the badly wounded Dunville with them. Dunville died in hospital the following day. In his letter Bickersteth continues:

> I hardly dare to offer any words of sympathy. It seems so cold and formal. To me his death is a tremendous blow. He joined the same day at York as I did, and many are the days hunting and cheery evenings we had together. Of course in the regiment he was a general favourite from the day of his arrival – and I don't think there was a dry eye yesterday when the last post was sounded at his graveside. It must be a comfort to you to know that he died as he did, the whole regiment admiring his pluck and mourning his loss.[1]

Dunville was awarded a posthumous Victoria Cross, the only such award ever won by The Royals.

From June the 3rd Cavalry Division was rested in the area around Péronne and Bapaume. Those who experienced these months described them as both bizarre and extraordinarily peaceful, as if the war was worlds away. 'It was an idyllic time, after three years hell and hammering,' wrote Cusack. 'Midsummer 1917 was a lovely time. There had been no crops off the country for the

Lieutenant Johnnie Dunville, VC 'I hardly dare to offer any words of sympathy. It seems so cold and formal. To me his death is a tremendous blow. He joined the same day at York as I did, and many are the days hunting and cheery evenings we had together.'

previous three autumns and the grass was rich and the horses summered well on it. We still had quite a number of our fifteen hand Basuto ponies which we had brought from South Africa.' The Household Cavalry turned their horses loose after morning exercise, with the duty troopers 'loping around in the fashion of cowboys on range duties'. In July there was even a skill-at-arms competition and a divisional mounted sports event.

While they enjoyed this unexpected break, the Household Battalion was preparing for what was to be its most testing engagement yet at Passchendaele, a small village where The Royals had collapsed after their retreat from Antwerp in 1914. The Third Battle of Ypres, as the 'Passchendaele Push' was called, started in July 1917, continued well into the autumn and was among the bloodiest battles of the war. The Household Battalion celebrated its first birthday on 1 September in a somewhat macabre fashion by burying Captain Pember, who had been killed in May but whose body had just been recovered. After his interment there was a festival tea and inter-company sports – the men had obviously become very accustomed to death in just twelve months. Within six weeks many of those celebrating followed him. On 12 October the battalion, still part of the 4th Division, took part in their attack on Poelcappelle. Lieutenant Colonel Portal realized the key to success lay in seizing and holding an area around Requette Farm. Advancing at 5.30 a.m. on 12 October, the battalion seized the farm in an hour, discovering that the term 'farm' was misleading for there was only a pillbox. The cost in men was horrific. By 9.30 a.m. there were only three officers left in action and all their Vickers machine guns had been made scrap iron by German fire. Captain Cazalet was in command when, at around 3 p.m., surrounded on all sides, and with only a narrow passage to the north as an escape route, he finally gave the order to retire. They fell back just 50 yards, revealing just how close engagements were by this stage in the war. Only two officers were left when relief finally arrived, and the 'Households' had lost 400 men. They were reinforced with a draft of 500 reservists but, despite their extraordinary record, in the spring of 1918 they were disbanded – one of the reasons being that they were more expensive than normal infantry battalions as they were still paid at Household Cavalry rates. The men were taken into Foot Guard battalions.

What is so touching about the extraordinary achievements and sacrifice of the Household Battalion is how they identified with the ethos and traditions of the Household Cavalry although they never actually served in their parent regiments. They were loyal to an idea, passed on to them during very brief training at Windsor, which instilled a sense of duty, honour and reputation that they were determined to uphold. Padre Haines, a clergyman who joined as their chaplain towards the end of their service, wrote regularly to his wife, always making light of the casualties and difficulties. 'We squatted on the fire step wrapped in every article of clothing we could lay hands on,' he wrote of his Christmas in the trenches in 1918,

> feeling quite certain that had the Bosch tried to poke bayonettes into us, he could never have got through the clothes . . . it is rather difficult to do much in the way of services on the frontline, but I managed to arrange a very small celebration between 2 and 3 on Xmas morning in a small sap running out of the trench. There was room for twenty-five men at a time and I managed two services. It was very weird to scan the snow all around and not hear a single shot fired.

The portable altar he used for this service is in the Household Cavalry Museum. Later he describes the spirit of service and sacrifice he found, and so admired, in the battalion.

> The Bosch began shelling us with his beastly gas shells and everyone dashed for his respirator. In the confusion the Colonel could not find his and called for his orderly to bring it. It couldn't be found but in a few seconds he came back with one in his hand, and said 'Here it is, Sir'. Colonel Portal put it on. When we came to take them off 20 minutes later, the orderly was seen dead with nothing on. He had deliberately given his own respirator, which he was perfectly justified in keeping to himself, to the Colonel, knowing that it meant death for him in a few minutes. Isn't it wonderful?[2]

In November 1917 the Allies came nearest to achieving a breakthrough when they attacked at Cambrai, using a predicted artillery bombardment and massed tanks effectively for the first time and achieving so much surprise that in places the Germans were forced back 5 miles – an enormous distance in a war where progress was usually measured in bloodstained yards. The cavalry came forward very late in the day when daylight was fading, ready to exploit the openings made by the tanks. Lloyd still 'had old Herbert, whom nothing short of a tank could stop'. But the swift German response and the difficult going meant they never got much beyond the first line of German trenches. It was bitterly frustrating. The church bells had already rung out in London celebrating the anticipated victory, but, despite the odd successful charge, the cavalry were largely employed once more as emergency infantry.

For the Household Cavalry the consequences were to be profound. In February 1918 it was decided to reduce the cavalry by two divisions. The Indian Cavalry who had been serving in France were sent to the Middle East, where they would no doubt be warmer, and one cavalry division in France was disbanded. Although The Royals and the 6th Cavalry Brigade remained mounted, the decision was taken temporarily to convert the Household Cavalry regiments and the Yeomanry into machine-gun battalions.

There were several reasons for this apparently strange decision. First, the Germans' successful re-establishment of their battered line at Cambrai had been partly the result of effective grouping of their machine guns into battalions, which enabled them to concentrate fire quickly and flexibly. Second, the Allied method of holding trenches now involved a thin, forward line of machine guns, usually housed in pillboxes, and the infantry concentrated further back, in comparative safety, so they could react en masse to any German attack. These forward lines had to be manned without disruption to the infantry's cohesion, a role which required competence and an ability to act independently, qualities well demonstrated by the Household Cavalry. It may seem strange that the oldest and most traditionally horsed regiments were chosen. Some asserted that Haig's apparent dislike of the Household Cavalry had something to do with it, possibly stemming from resentment that they had been sent home after only a year in South Africa, whilst he and the bulk of the cavalry stayed on to fight the guerrilla war throughout 1901 and 1902. Haig was also influenced by Kavanagh, now commanding the cavalry corps, who went to see him regarding the reductions. 'The 7th Cavalry Brigade is composed of 3 Household Cavalry Regiments,' Haig noted in his diary on 15 January 1918,

> Kavanagh says it is a weakness in the Division; the men are very heavy and use up a large number of horses; also these regiments are not getting as good officers as the others. Kavanagh wishes the regiments set free from the Indian cavalry Division to be organized as a Brigade to replace the Household regiments. The latter to be reduced to one Composite regiment as was the case at the beginning of the war.[3]

There was no doubt that finding enough officers to replace the casualties in the Household Battalion had left the parent regiments short of officers, a problem not faced by other cavalry regiments who did not also have to support an infantry battalion. Ironically, the change was popular within the regiments, and they actually welcomed a more positive role. In January 1918 several non-commissioned officers had volunteered for service in West Africa rather than continue with the cavalry's artificial life in France; six were actually deployed and returned safely after the Armistice, except for Lance Corporal Head who died of natural causes. Lloyd himself wrote:

> not that we minded being machine-gunners or anything else. We had a taste of most things in the campaign; but parting with our horses who were almost part of ourselves, and who had shared everything with us for three years, was a heavy blow. We had never been given a chance as cavalry. The opportunity occurred more than once, but it had been allowed to slip, as at Cambrai, and we had been left in the lurch.

Kavanagh, so lionized by men like Lloyd, emerges from the whole episode as rather two-faced; in March he is writing to the Gold Sticks of his regret over

The Frenchman Paul Maze served in the British army in two world wars and made his home in England after the First World War. Known as 'the last impressionist', he first met the British Cavalry in France in 1914 and was to have a long association with our regiments, photographing and illustrating many scenes from their activities.

A photo by Maze of a service held in the ruins at Cambrai Cathedral led by Abbé Thuilles, 13 October 1918. The Battle of Cambrai, launched in November 1917, was the first time tanks were used in significant force.

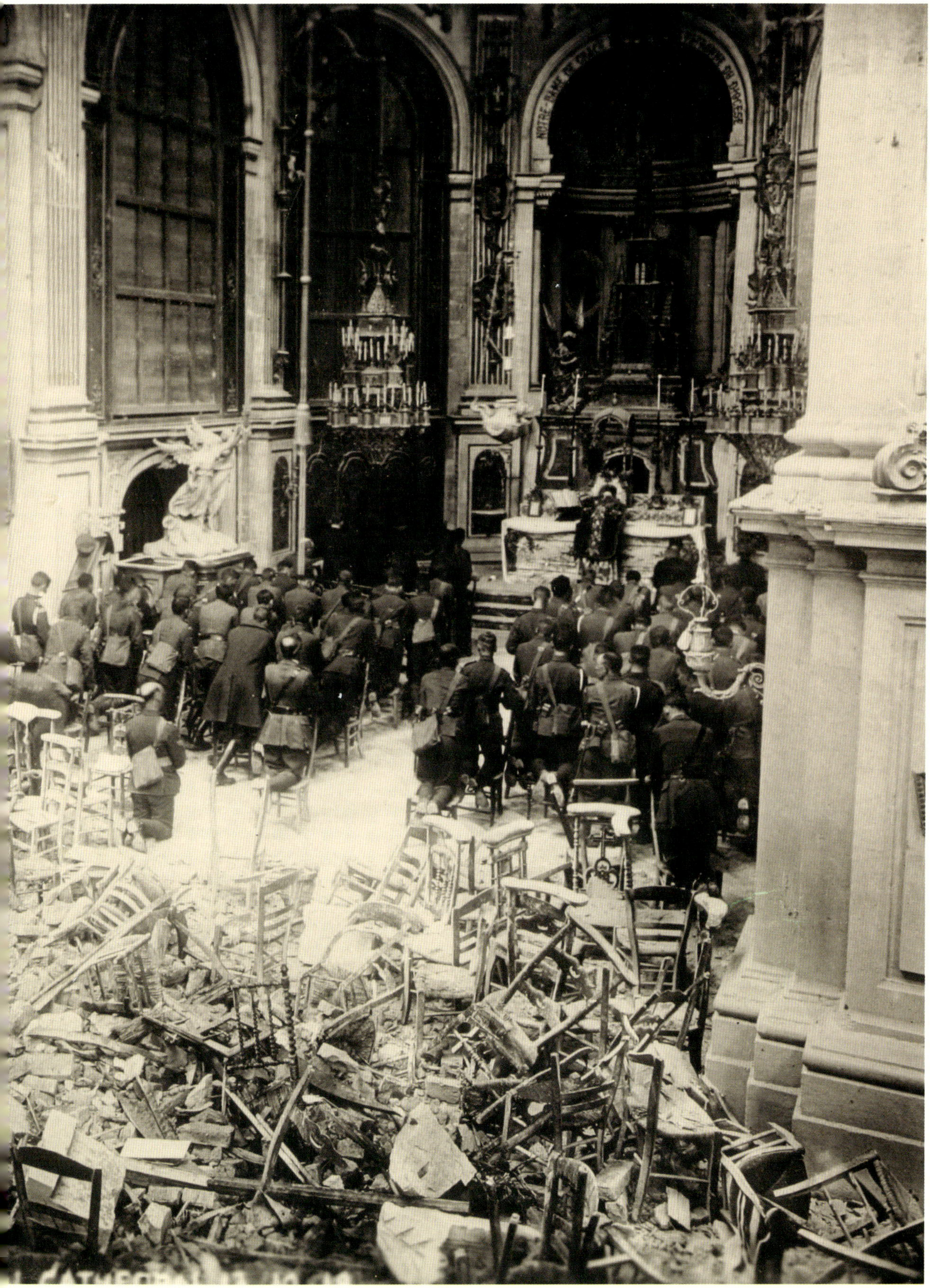

the changes, when he had advocated them. He did not fool Sir Evelyn Wood, that scruffy but splendidly independent Colonel of The Blues, who wrote back saying, 'You can picture my pleasant thoughts when I contrast the spirit of the BLUES turning to the duties of Machine Gunners, and the false swagger of the men . . . in a Light Dragoon Regiment.'[4]

Between March and May 1918 the three regiments, as opposed to the one composite suggested by Kavanagh, retrained as machine gunners at Étaples, and were issued for the first time with what was then called 'motorized transport'. This period of relative calm was spoilt by two things: first, the War Office, typically, tried to impose infantry rates of pay on the regiments, claiming they were now infantry, and, more seriously, an air raid at Whitsun killed forty-two of the 1st Life Guards and wounded a further eighty-two. The 1st Life Guards had been known as 'God's Own' as they had suffered so lightly compared to the 2nd Life Guards and Blues, but now that changed, horribly, to their disadvantage. Lloyd was one of the injured.

> At about 11 p.m. a warning came that enemy planes were on the move overhead, so lights were extinguished and we moved away to our tents. . . . All was quiet so far, and we were just comfortable in our blankets when old Beasneys came scratching round our tent asking for a match. The drone of planes could be distinctly heard overhead, so somebody told him to run off to bed. But he must have got a match from somewhere, for the next instant he actually struck a light outside our tent. A fraction of a second later I heard the hiss of a falling bomb; there was a blinding flash, and then silence, except for a groan here and there among the wreckage of the tents. I felt nothing in the way of pain. I tried to stand up, but discovered I could not. My left leg was smashed.[5]

The regiments had not finished their conversion in time to participate in the defence against the great German attack of March 1918 when they broke through the British 5th Army and penetrated 40 miles within a week, the furthest they had reached since 1914. In the chaotic fighting which followed, Lloyd's horse, Herbert, was captured and The Royals, who had been moved forward to Pontoise-les-Noyons, were split up. One group of about fifty, including mostly horse holders, farriers and headquarters staff, found themselves together with similar groups from the 3rd Dragoon Guards and the 10th Hussars in a sunken road near the village of Villeselve when some companies of German infantry appeared out of the woods on their flank. It was the opportunity the cavalry had been waiting for since Mons. Farrier Sergeant Bert Turp described what happened next.

> A major of the 10th Hussars gave us the order to draw swords and to hold them down over our horses' shoulders so that the enemy would not catch

the glint of steel . . . a moment later, we wheeled into line, and then, with a loud yell, it was hell for leather for the enemy! We had of course been taught that a cavalry charge should be carried out in line, six inches from knee to knee, but it didn't work out like that in practice and we were soon a pretty ragged line of horsemen at full gallop . . . I can't remember if I was scared, but I know that we were all of us really excited and so were the horses. The Germans had taken up what positions they could in the open, and I remember seeing three or four machine guns, and each of them seemed to be pointing straight at me as they opened up! Men and horses started going down but we kept galloping and the next moment we were in amongst them. Oddly enough, at this moment of the real thing, I remembered my old training and the old sword exercise. As our line overrode the Germans I made a regulation point at a man on my offside and my sword went through his neck and out the other side.[6]

The official history of the 6th Cavalry Brigade put the enemy dead at 'between 70 and 100 sabred', and 107 were made prisoner; the machine guns, though, had done their work, and seventy-three of the 150 who charged were casualties, and although few of these were killed, the officer who led The Royals, Lieutenant The Honourable W. H. Cubitt, was mortally wounded. It was a splendid episode, which demonstrated the continuing utility of cavalry and was the last time The Royals ever charged on horseback in anger. It was, however, only one small incident in the Allied response, which eventually stopped the German offensive near Amiens, and in which The Royals were used, once more, mostly as infantry. By late summer Haig was himself ready to attack, and the '100 Days' that took the Allies from their positions in front of Amiens up to the borders of Germany and the Armistice of 11 November began on 8 August. This should have been the army cavalry's golden opportunity, pursuing a broken enemy as they fell back, but it did not work out like that. 'Opportunities for cavalry work were decidedly restricted . . . the ground was a mass of shell-holes, old trenches and wire, often covered and concealed by long grass and weeds, and utterly unsuitable for cavalry action.'[7]

It was a different story for the Household Cavalry, who now realised the full benefits of their conversion and mechanization. The '100 Days' offensive was one of the most sophisticated ever mounted by a British army, which saw for the first time the coordinated use of tanks, aircraft, cavalry and infantry, although its success tends to be invalidated by historians who concentrate more on the horrors of what went before. The machine-gun battalions, each now equipped with sixty-four Vickers machine guns, played a most important role. The Blues were directly in support of the 47th London Infantry Division and were highly valued by them for their ability always to appear in the right place at the right time, whilst the 1st and 2nd Life Guards formed a machine-gun brigade. 'The [blank] battalion gets wiped out,' wrote an infantryman in a letter home, 'and these blokes from London wot wears tin tummies comes and does it,' when describing the Life Guards' support for an attack in which he took part. But the casualty rate increased, and the new role put the regiments in dangerous and exposed positions. Eighty-one of them were killed during those 100 Days, many from artillery fire when their positions had been located. Some were killed by gas, which the Germans were still using, and, bizarrely, the 2nd Life Guards lost several men who ate vegetables which had been saturated with mustard gas from repeated shelling.[8]

When the Armistice was finally declared on 11 November 1918, the 1st and 2nd Life Guards were at Lille, The Blues on the Sambre Canal and The Royals on the old battlefield of Willems. Trooper Stanley Butler recalled what was almost an anticlimax.

> We all lined up in the orchard, all my regiment. There were no celebrations then – we didn't even get a rum ration that night . . . some civilians provided us with coffee but there were no celebrations as such. Next day the Colonel came along and addressed us, telling us what was going to happen, that the war was over. We had a rum ration the next night and that's when we started the jollifications, when they brought up the rum to us. I've forgotten what happened that night![9]

An officer in The Blues suddenly noticed

> the SILENCE – the absolute silence. It was a most extraordinary sensation. One had, I suppose, ceased to hear the ordinary noises, drowned by the din of battle. When that ceased there was nothing. In a moment our world had tottered and been swept away. We had to orient ourselves. There was no more of the war routine; our minds went blank; what on earth were we to do? That was the feeling, and you know it took a very long time to get back to peace-time mentality.[10]

It was also time to count the cost. Eighteen officers and 163 men of the 1st Life Guards were killed prior to the formation of the machine-gun battalions; for the 2nd Life Guards the figures were nineteen and 209 and for The Blues thirty-three and 140. In addition eighteen officers and 420 were killed in the Household Battalion. For the Royal Dragoons the figures were twenty-four officers, approximately one in four of every officer who had served with the regiment between October 1914 and November 1918, and 141 other ranks, being about 10 per cent.

On 22 March 1919 the Household Cavalry, 'on foot, in drab khaki, with no glitter or glory of accoutrements', marched past King George V at Buckingham Palace together with the Foot Guards. On 19 April a requiem was held

Operational and ceremonial: a contrast in Household Cavalry uniforms in 1918.

Two non-commissioned officers in ceremonial uniform
wearing the prized Mons Star.

The unveiling of the Zanvoorde memorial by Field Marshal Earl Haig
on 4 May 1924.

at Westminster Abbey, in the presence of the King. The Queen and the Queen Mother, both of whom had seen the regiment off only five years before, were also there. The anthem was 'Though I Walk through the Valley of the Shadow of Death', to music by Arthur Sullivan, who had always been a particular favourite of the Life Guards. Five years later a Household Cavalry Memorial was built at Zanvoorde, chosen because it epitomized the worst of the suffering they had endured, and unveiled by a now somewhat chastened Field Marshal Earl Haig, who spoke warmly of their achievements. Slowly their world returned to normal. The 1st Life Guards gradually reassembled at Knightsbridge, where their reserve regiment had been throughout the war, the same for the 2nd Life Guards at Windsor and for The Blues at Regent's Park. It was not until May 1921 that the old rotation system restarted, and then it was only to be for one short year.

It was remarkable, but sad, just how quickly the regiments began to lose their identity after the Armistice. Men had suffered for the duration of the war out of a sense of duty, rather than conscription, but after their experiences in the trenches many of them longed for the routine of civilian life and from 1918 a general exodus occurred, including many of the pre-war regulars, who might have been expected to stay on. The Royals were stationed in Cologne immediately after the Armistice, as part of the Army of Occupation. The disintegration of their solidarity was palpable, as reservists were demobilized and regular officers, who had been attached to various staff, and other extra-regimental appointments now returned. They retained the same number of horses, despite their reductions, and there was little to do but muck out stables, exercise and groom. In August 1919 they returned to Hounslow, leaving the horses in quarantine in Luton.

Reductions in the enormous army of 1918, the largest British army ever fielded, were inevitable. 'At the Armistice there were twenty-eight regular cavalry regiments in the British Army, over fifty yeomanry and forty-five Indian native regiments.'[11] It was obvious some had to go, but the debate as to who took some time. The colonels of our regiments rejected out of hand a War Office suggestion that they should be converted en masse into mechanized units. Ultimately a programme of amalgamations was determined, which ensured that no regiment was actually disbanded, although four came perilously close to it. The Royals, as the senior cavalry regiment still, at this stage, outside the Household Cavalry, survived with only some reductions in their establishment, but the Household Cavalry was not deemed exempt. After fierce debate it was agreed that the 1st and 2nd Life Guards would amalgamate, retaining two squadrons from each regiment. Neither Gold Stick, Allenby for the 1st Life Guards, nor Sir Cecil Bingham for the 2nd Life Guards, was inclined to step down, and so the new regiment was known as The Life Guards (1st and 2nd), with 'A' and 'B' squadrons being the 1st Life Guards and 'C' and 'D' squadrons the 2nd Life Guards. This arrangement continued until September 1928, when they became known purely as The Life Guards, although Allenby served on until 1936 and Bingham until 1934. William Mullan, Clerk of Works at Knightsbridge Barracks, who considered himself very much a member of the Household Cavalry, noted in his diary:

> a number of men were given the option of going into civilian life. So quite a number went out to look for jobs. Some were snapped up by the Liverpool mounted police, but a good many tried the Met[ropolitan] Fire Brigade – they all got the offer of employment providing they could produce at least a second class school certificate of education. As the war had not been long over, school had not produced many 2nds so it was a bit of a problem.

The actual amalgamation was deeply unpopular. The two regiments seemed to have drifted apart in the four years since the war, and many serving then had since left. Robert Lloyd recalls arriving back from hospital to Knightsbridge in 1923 and finding 'the barrack-rooms housed a brand-new generation of men, and in the stables were horses which were complete strangers. In the same old corner stood the canteen. It was as dead as a doornail. . . . Some four or five old troopers were the only clients, the last survivors of two dead regiments and of a regime that had passed away for ever.' Lloyd left the regiment in 1925, taking a job as a modern languages teacher in a secondary school. Hugh Hidden, the young medical orderly who had found camping on the River Modder during the Boer War so uncomfortable, left as Captain Hugh Hidden MC, having been quartermaster of the 2nd Life Guards throughout the war. The 2nd Life Guards' officers had in fact developed such a loathing for their counterparts in the 1st Life Guards that they gave all their silver to the new non-commissioned officers' mess rather than have to share it with them.

Thereafter the two Household Cavalry regiments, The Life Guards and The Blues, rotated initially between Windsor and Regent's Park and then, as Regent's Park became too cramped, from 1932 between Windsor and Knightsbridge. Their operational role was preserved with a new composite regiment which developed into the cavalry regiment for the 3rd Infantry Division. It was rather a depressing time for them, for, although state ceremonial soon resumed and only a minority of officers and non-commissioned officers had wartime service by the mid-1920s, the pomp and pageantry were still undermined by the awful losses. The Royals, after their return from Cologne in 1919, were sent almost immediately to Ballinasloe in Ireland. After an equally depressing time standing in as police against the Irish Republicans, they returned to their old haunt of Curragh Camp once the Treaty of 1921 was signed, before being posted back to Aldershot. In September 1927 they were dispatched to Egypt, and after two years there, on to Secunderabad, next to Mysore in southern India.

Presentation of standards to the Household Cavalry by King George V on Horse Guards Parade in 1927. In his address he remarked to the Life Guards that 'if no regiment has varied its title as often as yours, no regiment has preserved its character more closely . . .'

Part of George V's full dress uniform.

Spike Mays joined The Royals in Aldershot in March 1924 as a 'band rat', a trainee bandsman, regarded as the lowest form of life in the regiment. He came from an impoverished farming family in East Anglia, and his main motivation for joining was to earn enough money to eat properly and to break out of the deadening agricultural trap. For him it was 'that post war period of malnutrition and human misery'.[12] He was initially sent to the cavalry depot at Canterbury for basic training – a fairly horrific experience as many of the instructors were non-commissioned officers considered unsuitable for service in their own regiments. Those who had venereal disease, and there were many, were required to wear a blue tie, and 2s. per day was deducted from their pay to cover the cost of their treatment. Mays eventually arrived in The Royals, only to pass out one night after a concert in the officers' mess and be admitted to hospital with diphtheria. On the verge of death in a military hospital, he had a surprise visit from a small, very military figure, who said to him, 'What is all this nonsense about dying? It is an offence for a Royal Dragoon to die in bed. Get better at once, that's an order. When you do, get a haircut!' This imperious figure turned out to be Lieutenant Alfred Wintle, an officer who had won an MC with the 18th Hussars in France and transferred to The Royals in 1920. Wintle was one of those curious characters who appear periodically throughout the history of our regiments, whom the soldiers tolerate for being fairly professional, but whose somewhat studied eccentricities their fellow-officers find hard to take. When Mays was finally discharged from hospital, and transferred to the troops from the band, he found Wintle was his troop leader. He immediately impressed Mays by discontinuing the unpleasant habit whereby more experienced and stronger troopers made the weaker cut chaff – a tough job reducing hard bales of hay to forage by grinding it on 'a great chaff-cutter on which were mounted mammoth blades'. If the poor weakling on the blades failed, he was made to man the handle the following day, and so on until he could do no more. Wintle challenged the strongest bully to a chaff-cutting contest and beat him easily, making him man the wheel for a whole week as a penalty.

Mays went to Egypt in Wintle's troop, a posting he and his fellow troopers thoroughly enjoyed. Prior to their deployment Wintle had given his troop lectures on Egyptian mythology, and was therefore much impressed on his first stable inspection to see that Trooper Capstick had named the horse he had inherited from the departing 3rd Hussars after the Egyptian God Horus.

'Capstick,' enquired Wintle, 'are you really interested in Egyptian mythology?'

'Jest a bit, sir . . . jest a bit,' replied an embarrassed Capstick.

'Have you been reading about it?' continued Wintle.

'Nossir!'

'Has there been much talk of it in the barrack rooms since my lectures? About the sphinx, the pyramids, the gods?' asked Wintle hopefully.

'Not as I've noticed, sir.'

Spike Mays, who joined The Royals as a 'Band Rat' in 1924 to escape grinding rural poverty in East Anglia.

Jack Hamilton-Russell won the Kadir Cup, the Indian Army pig-sticking championship, in 1934 on Lindy Loo. He was later a Squadron Leader at Alamein and was killed in a traffic accident in Sicily. His son and grandsons all served in the Household Cavalry.

The tradition of satirical sketches begun by Powerscourt in the mid-1800s continued. The billiards player – 'Haw! I shall win this game as sure as God made little apples' – is from the 1920s, while Captain R. L. H. Jenkinson – 'Ring that b—y bell! (Sniff.)' – is from the late 1940s.

'Tell me then, why the devil did you name your horse Horus?' demanded Wintle.

'Ah, I see what you mean, sir . . . old Horace here, I named him after me brother, he's a corporal in The Life Guards.'

The life that Mays describes once they reached India was remarkably similar to that Cusack had experienced twenty years before. There wasn't much to do militarily, and in Secunderabad the soldiers were forbidden from going into Mysore, much to their annoyance, as it was for 'officers only', a regulation imposed by the Indian Army rather than the regiment. They saw much of their Indian colleagues in the native regiments, with whom they got on very well indeed, and, restrictions aside, everyone had a thoroughly enjoyable time, employing cheap Indian labour and taking full advantage of the sporting opportunities. In 1934 Lieutenant Jack Hamilton-Russell won the much-coveted all-India pig-sticking trophy, the Kadir Cup, which still sits on the dining-room table of the officers' mess. Mays himself found there was little to keep him occupied, and resigned, much missed by Wintle with whom he had struck up something of a rapport. One day Wintle summoned him to his quarters to announce that he had been selected by the commanding officer to run a paper chase for the officers and their wives, a sort of mounted treasure hunt, when they followed a trail of clues which were intended to lead them gently back to the mess for well-earned drinks. Wintle and Mays concocted clues of such fiendish 'obscurity, ambiguity and incomprehensibility that not only were all the ladies late for tea but search parties had to be mustered'. Wintle was delighted but it is easy to understand why he was less than popular with his brother officers.

In the autumn of 1938 the regiment were ordered to Palestine to take part in the counter-insurgency campaign against the Arabs who were threatening the burgeoning Jewish settlements in the Holy Land. By the time they arrived they were one of only two mounted regiments left in the British army outside the Household Cavalry, the other being the Royal Scots Greys, who were also posted to Palestine where there was a continuing role for horsed units. The Life Guards and The Blues were both, of course, still mounted, but they were still actively engaged in ceremonial and with the 3rd Division and were not to arrive in Palestine for another year. The difficult debate over mechanization continued. General Sir Ernest Makins, who had become Colonel of The Royals in 1931, pursued a vigorous campaign for the regiment to retain their horses. He lobbied just about everybody, including the King, arguing that The Royals were the oldest and most senior regiment outside the Household Cavalry. He objected to the fact that the Scots Greys had started a press campaign to support their case to remain mounted, in which they argued they were the equivalent of the Household Cavalry in Scotland, a spurious argument given the history of the 4th Troop of Life Guards and the Scottish Troop of Horse Grenadiers who had become the 2nd Life Guards, but one that nevertheless found some resonance in the media. Makins argued that if the Scots Greys were to keep their horses, then so should The Royals as the senior English regiment, and his tenacity succeeded. On 1 November 1937 it was announced that both The Royals and the Scots Greys would remain mounted and this was cause for much celebration. 'Your telegram,' Major Reggie Hayworth wrote to Makins from India, 'arrived after dark and I had it posted up in the Sergeants Mess, Corporals Mess and Institute [Troopers' Mess] and everyone was delighted. The men had just left stables, otherwise would have read it out. All the men that I have talked to are very pleased about it and fully appreciate the honour. In the officers' mess a great many bottles of champagne were drunk that night.'[13] Yet maybe not all the regiment were quite as pleased as Hayworth and Makins supposed. There were those still serving who could remember the long years of frustration in France and the sudden, undignified, re-rolling as infantry. Some wondered whether they might not have done better to accept the inevitable, and convert as soon as possible to armoured cars and play a full role in the next war, which was now imminent. Within two years of his great victory Makins would be writing to the King in a very different tone, and when the horses finally went it tended to be only the sentimentalists who regretted their passing; the majority of troopers found armoured cars to be much less work and they did not miss the endless rounds of stables and kit cleaning.

It was much the same in the Household Cavalry. There was an acceptance, of course, that horses remained an indispensable part of ceremonial and, even in the late 1930s, an important element in royal security, but they saw no reason why the composite regiment could not be mechanized. Exercising in 1931, Humphrey Wyndham, who later commanded The Life Guards for four years, complained that

> when the leading [mounted] patrols reach the summit they see on the opposite ridge across the valley before them a line of hostile armoured cars . . . One man takes from the rifle bucket on his saddle a wooden stick about four feet long, with a piece of bunting wrapped round it. He plants the stick in the ground, and unwraps the bunting, revealing a green and white flag. This flag represents the anti tank gun with which the British Army is not yet equipped. In each of the three sections of the troop one man is carrying a policeman's rattle. These rattles represent the light machine guns with which the British cavalry, less fortunate than their comrades in the infantry, are not yet equipped. . . . When the leading patrols on their horses came up and looked across the valley to the armoured cars on the opposite ridge, the scene before their eyes was a vision of the future. The horse, after serving as a medium of mobility in war from the earliest times, was in process of supersession by the internal-combustion engine across the valley.[14]

Wyndham, who had commanded a machine-gun squadron in France, records a conversation with Winston Churchill in 1918, in which he stated his preference that the Household Cavalry had become tank, rather than machine-gun units. Wyndham had replied that he preferred machine guns; in 1939 he ruminated bitterly that Churchill had been right. 'Then The Life Guards and Blues would have led the way in the mechanization of the cavalry, instead of being made to follow it.' As it was, they were to mobilize with their horses in 1939, and though four of the officers in The Blues were serving masters of fox hounds, the vast majority wished they could have been in armour from the very beginning.

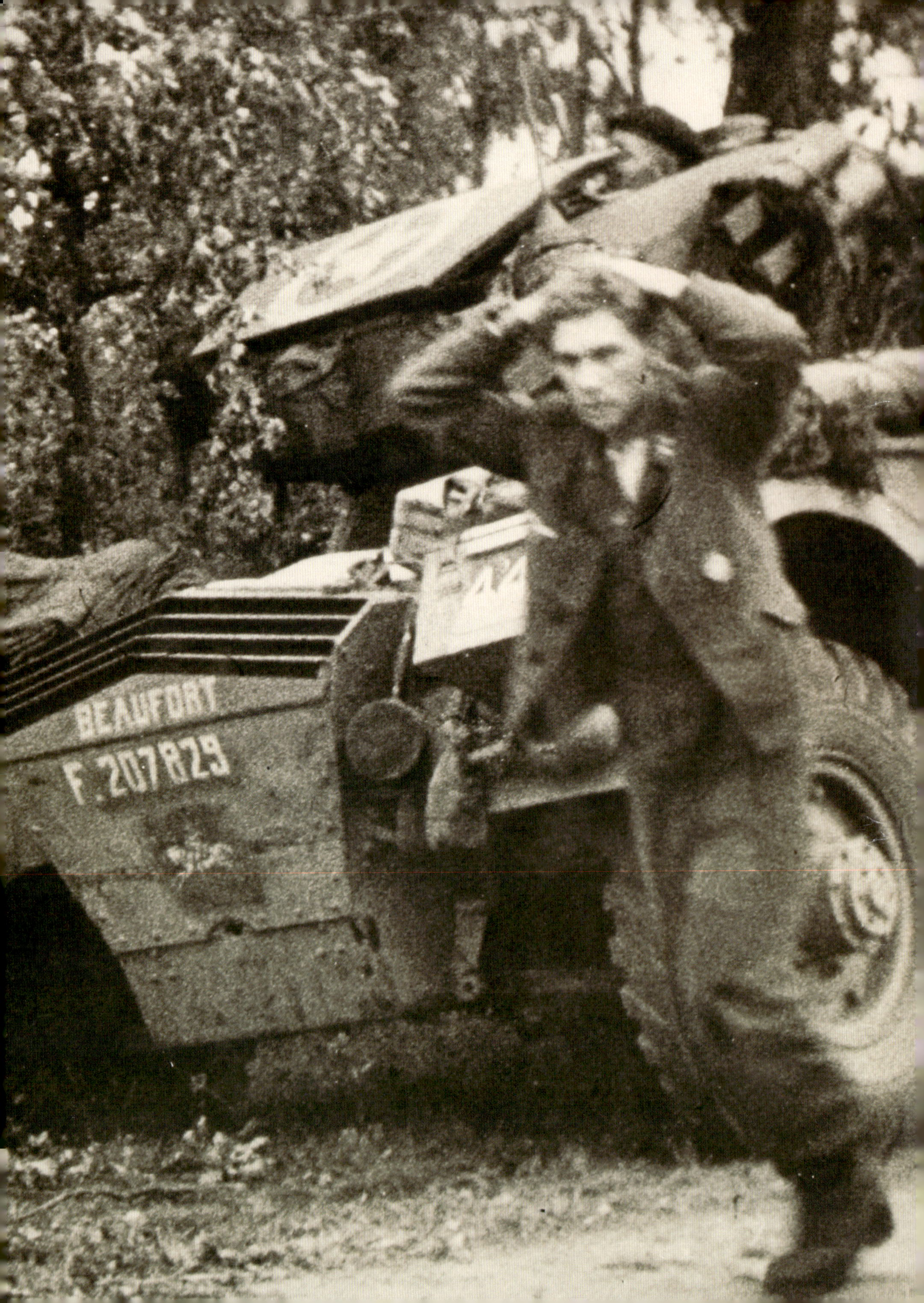
BEAUFORT
F 207829

Part Seven

THE SECOND GREAT CHANGE

After 1939

Chapter Nineteen

THE SECOND WORLD WAR: THE MIDDLE EAST

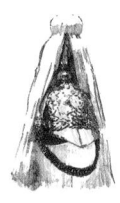

Tim Bishop joined The Life Guards at Windsor in 1934. He had been educated at Stowe, where he spent so much time hunting that he failed his school certificate, a requirement for Sandhurst entry and subsequent commissioning into the army. He decided he must therefore try the alternate route to becoming an officer, completing a period of soldier service, becoming a non-commissioned officer and being recommended by his commanding officer. On arrival at Windsor with 'four pleasant-faced, phlegmatic, tall and lanky South Country boys', he was put into a barrack room which was

> spacious with a high ceiling and directly above the stables. A hideous black stove, out in the centre, was guarded all round by a bleak little curb of whitewashed concrete. A dreadful black pipe rose from the stove to disappear through a hole in the ceiling. There was a trestle table and forms [benches]. Against the walls, closely aligned, stood diminutive iron bedsteads, without mattresses or blankets, folded to chair size. Three pegs and an empty locker served each bed. The floor was of bare boards. . . . Worse was the adjoining 'ablution room', with stone floor, urinal, and cold-water taps – cold water only. Even if one had joined out of desperation, as perhaps some boys had, it was a poorish welcome.[1]

Later he describes entering the troopers' mess for the first time.

> Somewhat timidly we entered this crowded and noisy room and found ourselves placed on benches at trestle tables with a plate of fried egg and chips.

Page 498. Normandy, 1944 – a German prisoner doubling to the rear past Lieutenant David Tabor's Daimler armoured car. The soldiers gave all their vehicles familiar names, partly for ease of reference. Those in 'A' Squadron began with A, those in 'B' Squadron began with B, as seen here.

> Still clad conspicuously in our civilian suits we were surrounded by cheerfully curious and rowdy soldiers in canvas dungarees that reeked of stables. Their every word, it seemed to me, was the same four-letter one, even inserted quite often into the middle of ordinary two-syllable words. It was used as a verb, noun or adjective without inhibition.

Many more things were to make Bishop's life a misery as he went through training: the non-commissioned officers shouting at the recruits to get out of bed in the morning; mucking out stables with bare hands; having to remove grease from spur straps by leaving them in the urinal; shaving in cold water wearing ankle boots with nailed soles, and the disgusting food. 'A slab of yellow, soap-like cheese and one large white and pungent slice of raw onion,' he wrote, 'was frequently the last meal of the day and a breakfast of bacon smothered in fried onions could surely stymie the hungriest.' He and his fellow recruits used to joke, 'Join the Army and see the world; join The Life Guards and sweep it.'

Yet Bishop survived Riding School and was soon promoted and came to appreciate the rather strange world into which he had been cast, and in which it was still de rigueur to grow a moustache. He took part in King Edward VIII's review of the Household Cavalry in 1936, when the King reported that even as the regiments galloped past the ranks 'were as inflexibly straight as blocks of wood'. 'At the parade's conclusion,' Bishop wrote, 'we were played back to barracks down the sun-flooded Long Walk to the strains of "Colonel Bogey" ... With the King riding at our head it soon began to sound grander than all the symphonies. An aura of splendour surrounded one, from the glossy black quarters of the horses in front to the gilt and silver royal ciphers emblazoned here, there and everywhere around.' Although Bishop was immensely proud to be a Life Guard, and would later write, even after a distinguished war record as an officer in the 12th Lancers, 'The Life Guards set standards for me which nothing could ever match', his description of riding back behind Edward VIII is remarkably reminiscent of those eyewitness accounts of George V's review of 1913, and the regiments that were about to deploy to fight Hitler were arguably more deficient in terms of materiel and training than their forebears had been twenty-five years before.

The problem the British army faced in the 1930s was that it was unsure of its purpose. It was certainly there to police the empire, which it continued to do moderately effectively, as shown by The Royals' service in Egypt and India. However, the rise of fascism should have led it to prepare for a second major war in Europe – something for which the politicians had neither equipped nor funded it, and, to be fair to that much-maligned generation of British statesmen, even within the regiments themselves people could not bring themselves to comprehend the possibility of another war against Germany. They were dominated psychologically by the 1914–18 war, partly mourning the loss of so many friends, partly relieved that their old world had, though battered and changed, survived. The lack of any army initiative to react to German rearmament made it easy for individuals to seek refuge in the safe and ordered world of drill, kit-cleaning and field days where the machine gun was a rattle and the anti-tank gun non-existent. Some, like Wyndham, accurately predicted the awful reality that would lead to Dunkirk, but there was little they could do in the face of prevailing political apathy. Bishop's comments on Life Guard officers are interesting in this regard. Although they were liked and respected, with the odd exception such as the lieutenant whose greyhound lifted its leg against the immaculate jackboots of one of the men he was inspecting, they were not much in evidence. One of them said to Bishop long after the war that the commanding officer ran the regiment through his adjutant, his warrant officers and non-commissioned officers. It was considered a futile waste of time for anyone else to put in an appearance. The commanding officer preferred his officers to 'busy themselves with hunting, race-riding and polo rather than have them hanging about in Knightsbridge'. That is an over-simplification. There was a hard core of officers, men like Robert Laycock and Henry Abel-Smith, who, in the tradition of Compton and Granby, took a keen military interest and who realized that, if properly equipped early on in the inevitable war, the Household Cavalry's core values would ensure them operational success. They were to be proved absolutely correct, although getting hold of the proper equipment was to be a minor war all of its own.

The 1918 Treaty of Versailles had failed to provide a lasting solution to peace in Europe. Hitler and his Nazi Party had seized power in Germany, determined to reverse what they saw as an unnecessarily humiliating peace forced on them when, in their view, they had not actually been defeated militarily, and which deprived Germany of much of what they regarded as her rightful territory. Germany had rearmed throughout the 1930s, and Allied disunity meant that Hitler was able to occupy the Rhineland, Austria and Czechoslovakia without opposition. It was not until he invaded Poland in September 1939 that Britain declared war on Germany for the second time in twenty-five years. The Life Guards were in Knightsbridge and The Blues in Windsor when mobilization was ordered. With the lessons of 1914 in mind, a complicated mobilization scheme had been drawn up which saw the Household Cavalry forming three regiments: a composite regiment, which was to deploy; a reserve regiment in London to continue ceremonial duties, and a training regiment to be formed in Windsor. It took some days to sort out where everyone should go, but eventually the regimental headquarters of The Life Guards and two squadrons made their way from London to Windsor. It was rather crowded as two regiments were trying to form in space previously deemed suitable for one; furthermore, many reservists had rejoined, swelling numbers significantly. Eventually 'B' Squadron found accommodation in the Royal Hotel in Ascot and 'C' Squadron went to the Old Etonian Club at Clewer. Overall the regiments, once formed, were short of soldiers, and, as in 1914, about 100

Edward VIII on parade in 1936. 'With the King riding at our head it soon began to sound grander than all the symphonies. An aura of splendour surrounded one, from the glossy black quarters of the horses in front to the gilt and silver royal ciphers emblazoned here, there and everywhere around.'

The King's Life Guard in the early days of the Second World War. Full ceremonial uniform had been soon abandoned.

reservists from other cavalry regiments were drafted in to make up numbers. On 30 September King George VI inspected the composite regiment, who paraded on foot with steel helmets, and he then visited each squadron in turn. Of all the monarchs to have a close affiliation with the Household Cavalry, George VI ranks as one of the most interested and the most genuinely well liked. Later in the war his intervention led to the current arrangement whereby the regiments can continue both to provide state ceremonial and fulfil a worthwhile operational role. In late October the composite regiment went off to train in the Midlands, before deploying to join The Royals in Palestine as part of the 1st (and only) British Cavalry Division. We will now follow their progress in the Middle East, not returning to those left behind at Windsor until 1944 when they entered the war in earnest.

Once brought up to their war establishment, the composite regiment found they were short of horses, and were issued with more by the Remount Depot. Many of these were 'conscripts' purchased in 1939, who found adjusting to army life quite demanding, particularly those who had been private hunters. 'It was noticeable,' wrote Wyndham, almost as if he were speaking of soldiers, 'that the better the home they came from the more difficult they found it to adjust themselves to the changed conditions.' And very soon these were to change dramatically, as in January 1940 they received orders to deploy to Palestine. Travelling via France, where they lost their first soldier, Trooper Richardson, killed in a railway accident at Montélimar, they loaded the horses in Marseilles, arriving in Haifa on 22 February. They were destined to spend most of the next year training or occasionally assisting the Palestine Police, much as The Royals were doing. The Royals had now been there since the autumn of 1938, and had enjoyed some success in their counter-insurgency role, though they were finding life generally unexciting. They had been particularly incensed that their new divisional commander had taken the view that their horses were unnecessary and ordered them to guard a railway line on foot, saying he might even send their horses home. Lieutenant Colonel Heyworth, the new commanding officer, wrote to General Makins complaining at the outrage. 'Montgomery is the gentleman's name, and I am told he is one of the brains of the Army,' added the disbelieving Heyworth.[2]

As the war in Europe developed throughout 1940 The Royals experienced an uncomfortable feeling of being irrelevant, similar to their forebears in Johannesburg in 1914, and it became evident to both them and the composite regiment, now renamed the 1st Household Cavalry Regiment, or 1 HCR as they were universally known, that they had to mechanize quickly or risk becoming totally irrelevant, perhaps as garrison troops in India. Heyworth wrote to Makins in a very different vein early in September 1940 saying, 'We have all been worried at our uselessness to date . . . If there should be any intention of retaining our horses merely to carry out internal security duties in this country, I know that I shall find it extremely difficult to keep officers and men

The Composite Regiment, renamed 1 HCR, sailed with its horses for Palestine in January 1940 (*above*), where they joined The Royals in the 1st Cavalry Division. It was to be the last cavalry division ever deployed by the British Army. The horses were exercised in the sea once they were there (*below*).

happy.' Makins now started reverse lobbying, requesting they 'mechanize' as soon as possible.[3] Later that month the War Office agreed not only that The Royals should mechanize, but that they could also choose between being a tank regiment or an armoured car regiment. Logically, having been used in the last two centuries as heavy cavalry to overwhelm the enemy by weight and mass, they should have chosen tanks, fulfilling a similar role on the modern battlefield. Palestine in 1941 was, however, full of rumours of the success of General Wavell's armoured cars against the Italians in Cyrenaica, as Mussolini had so romantically renamed the parts of North Africa he occupied. The role of armoured car regiments was to reconnoitre well ahead of a division, acting as its eyes and ears, giving warning of enemy movements, and to raid vulnerable enemy positions when they could. It was, in effect, the role traditionally performed by light cavalry, particularly hussars. Normally one regiment was allocated to each division and, later, to each corps. This daring and independent role appealed more to The Royals than the slower and heavier life of tanks, and, they argued, as armoured car troops spent much of their time on their feet (when manning observation posts, for example), it was similar to their original role as dragoons, so they chose armoured cars.

In December 1940 they handed over their horses to the Remount service in Rehovoth. Various colonels from other regiments 'came down and the horses were paraded for them, as if at an old-fashioned slave market', wrote Lieutenant the Earl of Rocksavage. 'We all felt a bit depressed. . . . One felt that another historic milestone had passed, and we all wondered what our new mounts would be like.'[4] These were Mark 3 Marmont Harrington armoured cars, and by February 1941 The Royals had moved to the newly formed Royal Armoured Corps centre at Abbasia outside Cairo to learn all about them. This was to be their base for the next two years.

The Marmont Harrington was a curious machine. Manufactured in South Africa, and procured in a hurry as the War Office had omitted to develop any alternative in the 1930s, they were high and unwieldy. The term 'armoured' was relative, as they carried only 9 millimetres of armour which was easily penetrated. They were only armed with a pretty useless Boyes anti-tank rifle, popularly supposed to be unable to penetrate anything but the Marmont Harrington itself. They were, however, mechanically reliable, and not too uncomfortable; besides, there was nothing else available. By March 'A' Squadron had completed its conversion, after a fashion, and was deployed forward into the North African desert.

1 HCR were not to be so fortunate. In October 1941 they were moved up to Tiberias, like some ancient crusader army, to guard the frontier with Syria, now ruled by the Vichy French, and took part in 'the last great mounted exercise ever to be undertaken by British cavalry in the Plain of Esdraelon, which has a nice Biblical sound and involved about two thousand horses'.[5] Life was fairly depressing for the men that winter. Not only had they received no mail

Middle East during the Second World War

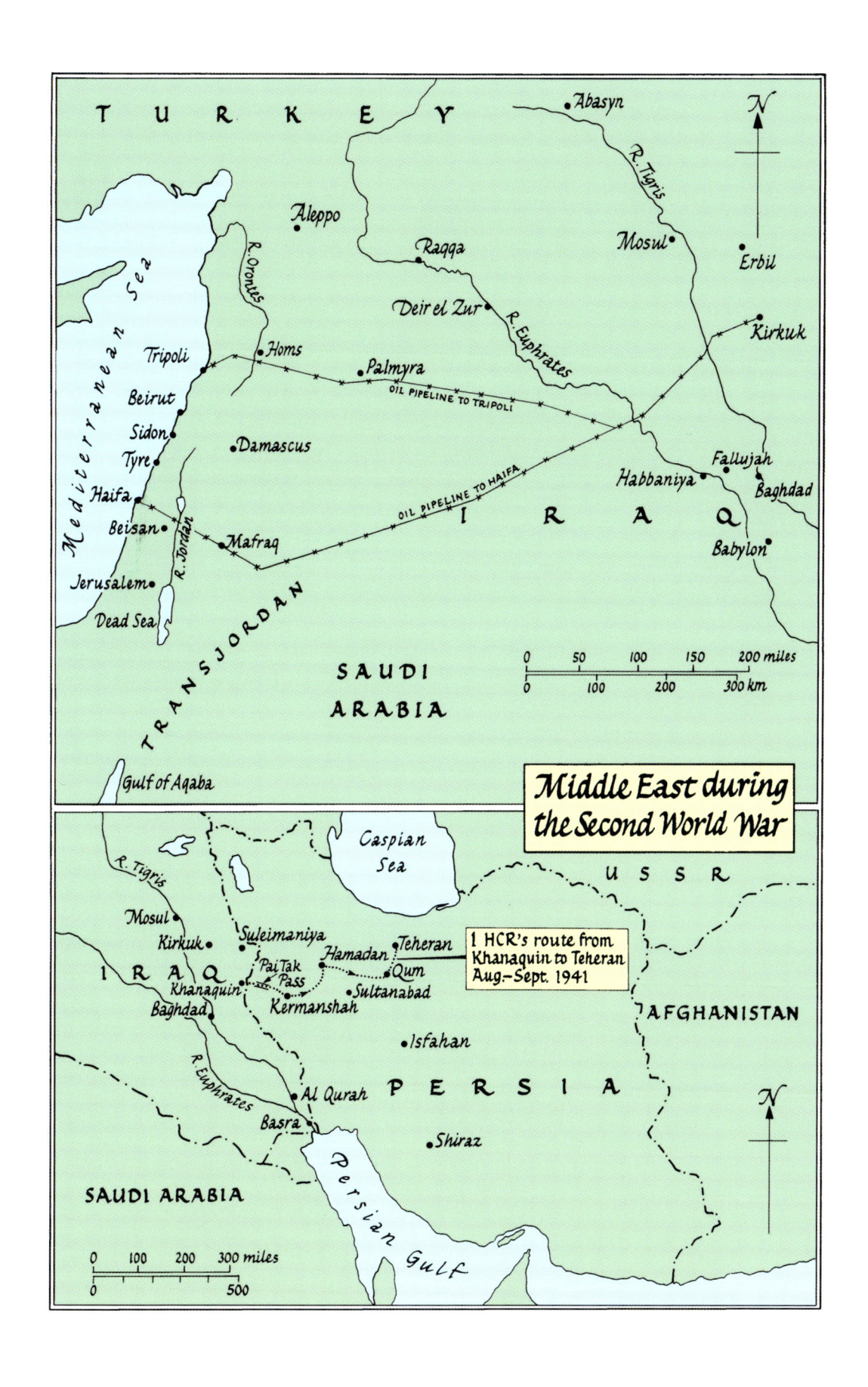

for three months, and so had little idea what was happening to their families in England, but they were also fairly sure that the Cavalry Division was never actually going to participate in operations. Despite the reported success of the recent exercise, the regiment's divisional horse artillery was taken away and, at a demonstration of the eagerly awaited anti-tank rifle, they were told there were only two rounds available to the whole division. It was obvious to them that it was now only a matter of time before they lost their horses, and they began to prepare themselves for that inevitable day with mixed feelings: sadness at losing old friends and excitement at what the future might hold. In fact Lord Athlone, who had become Colonel of The Life Guards in 1936, had gone with Lord Birdwood, Colonel of The Blues, to lobby General Lord Ironside, the Chief of the Imperial General Staff, for a mechanized role at the beginning of the war, even suggesting they reform as machine-gun battalions, but Ironside had been unable to offer any opportunities. The order to mechanize finally came through in February 1941, specifying that all horses over fifteen years old were to be destroyed and the younger ones drafted to horse transport companies in Egypt. It was, wrote Wyndham, 'for many a conflict between the head and the heart', and the best way to look on it was, as Major Legge-Bourke wrote, that 'war and horses should have no association with each other'.[6] The practicalities were more difficult, and for Lieutenant Valerian Wellesley 'one of the saddest days I can ever remember was when . . . I had to take fourteen old horses of my troop into the Judean Hills and shoot them. Those lovely old black horses, which had taken part in all the great state occasions of the last ten years or so including the 1936 Coronation, ended their days on a bare, bleak Palestinian hill to become fodder for vultures and jackals.'[7] In their place 1 HCR were issued with thirty-five 15-cwt trucks, being one per troop. These would give them some experience of driving and vehicle maintenance – skills then very foreign to them – in preparation for the issue of armoured cars when they became available. They already saw themselves as an armoured car regiment in waiting, but the reality, as so often happens in the British army, was to be rather different, and within two months they were off to war with their training transport.

The reason for this sudden transformation in the fortunes of 1 HCR was the developing situation in Iraq, a region with which their modern successors were to become all too familiar. In March 1941 the pro-German and Italian Rashid Ali, who drew support from Vichy Syria, ousted the pro-British Regent in Iraq in a coup. Iraqi oil, and the twin pipelines from Kirkuk that transported it through Syria to the Mediterranean terminals at Haifa and Tripoli, was vital to the Allied war effort, and in April 1941 a British brigade from India landed in the Persian Gulf to secure the main southern Iraqi city and port of Basra. Meanwhile, British families from Baghdad were evacuated to the Habbaniya Air Force Base, on the Euphrates, west of the capital, which then contained 2,200 military, mostly Royal Air Force personnel, and 9,000 civilians, and was promptly besieged by Rashid Ali's forces. The 1st Cavalry Division was rapidly transformed into the Habbaniya Task Force, or 'Habforce' as it was universally known, and told to rescue them. 1 HCR were put into a small advance-striking column within Habforce, commanded by Brigadier Kingstone and called 'Kingcol'. Although they had been training with their new trucks for some weeks, the speed with which the force was assembled took them by surprise and called for some rapid reorganization. Lord Roderic Pratt, who was already Motor Transport Officer, and who had apprenticed himself to the foreman at the Haifa Ordnance Depot to try to learn something of his new responsibilities, now became Technical Adjutant charged with the repair and provision of items such as radiators and tyres. A motley collection of vehicles was requisitioned to supplement the ancient lorries; the only one available for the commanding officer was a Haifa taxi, a low-slung Plymouth saloon painted a vivid green. The regimental barber became the assistant armourer overnight and the exotic collection of animals, which had attached themselves as regimental pets since their arrival in Palestine, were farmed out, less Trooper Dan's rabbit, which he managed to smuggle into regimental headquarters. Radios were issued on the scale of one per squadron. Water was clearly going to be a serious problem; the ration was to be half a gallon per man per day, although much of this leaked away from the 7-pint 'chargules' in which it was carried. Jewish buses were hired to carry the extra stores and equipment required – hired by the day, it was in the owners' interests to ensure frequent breakdowns. On 9 May 1 HCR were put on two hours' notice to move, and were issued with one 2-inch mortar per troop with no time to practise using them. These were the only extra weapons they received, otherwise carrying just what they had on their horses – rifles and the now ancient Hotchkiss machine guns. They had been issued with Bren guns in England but these had subsequently been withdrawn. They were then given Brens latterly captured from the Iraqis, but had to return these after the Iraqi surrender, thus ending the Iraq campaign armed almost exactly as the composite regiment had been on the retreat from Mons.

On 12 May, in a heatwave that saw the highest temperatures in the Middle East for twenty-five years, and with frequent khamsins, or sand storms, the strange collection of old lorries, taxis and buses crossed the River Jordan and headed east. The first day they covered 140 miles, following the Kirkuk–Haifa oil pipeline, temperatures rising to 130°F and the men packed in the back of the trucks sporting their blue- and red-fringed sun helmets. It proved too much for Trooper Dan's rabbit, which died that evening, the first regimental casualty of the campaign. The following day they made it to the oasis of Rutba, well inside Iraq, where they met up with Glubb's Arab Legion, who had just taken it. They made an immediate impression, the men jealously eyeing their Ford trucks, and nicknaming them Glubb's Girls because 'they wear long curly hair and sing continuously'.[8] After Rutba they were subjected to air attacks, though Mr Wolland, the regimental Corporal Major, objected vigorously when told he had been machine-gunned, insisting the sound was merely knocking in his engine. The heat got worse. 'The hours from 11 o'clock till 4 o'clock were practically unbearable,' wrote Captain Summers, the Intelligence Officer, 'the Second in Command decided that one shouldn't drink water while the sun was up, as a result of which he arrived frothing at the mouth in a state of collapse.' By 16 May they had reached the Euphrates and turned south, only to find the road impassable. They struck off into the desert to find a way round. 'This adventure was a failure,' Summers continued, 'the apparently hard desert had only a hard crust and all the heavy vehicles stuck. The temperature in the shade was over 120 degrees. It was a memorable day that we spent in digging out these vehicles up to the axles and lying exhausted under our trucks until the evening . . . Few men will ever forget that day.' But on 18 May, having covered 700 miles in six days 'along the same route as Alexander the Great had taken', as Summers added, romantically if inaccurately, they reached Habbaniya to find the enemy had fled. That evening they were told they could bathe in the lake, and Wellesley remarked, 'I shall never forget the sight of hundreds of men tearing off the clothes they had been wearing for the best part of a very hot and exhausting week and racing stark naked, like a crowd of excited schoolboys, into the cool waters of the lake.'[9]

There was not much time to recover. The first problem they encountered was that the sand 'bund' along the Euphrates, which carried the road to Fallujah and Baghdad, had been damaged, and it had to be repaired under daily air attack. Meanwhile, 'C' Squadron were deployed to Fallujah, a hotbed of Iraqi resistance then as now, to hold the Euphrates Bridge against any counter-attack by Rashid Ali while work to repair the bund progressed. They had to abandon their trucks and, ferrying their weapons and equipment on rafts made of old oil drums, crossed the floodwater along the river, literally wading their way into Fallujah.

By 27 May Habforce was ready to advance on Baghdad. For this operation the regiment was split in two, the main part under the commanding officer, Andrew Ferguson, 'with his mournful dark eyes and dark head of hair',[10] going north, and 'C' Squadron and the main body of Kingcol going south. Ferguson's force crossed the Euphrates by ferry and headed north of the city, establishing a position across the Baghdad to Mosul railway, before turning south towards the city itself. At this point they were told, much to their consternation, that there was an enemy division in front of them, a regiment on their flank, and an armoured train to their rear. In fact initially there was little opposition. Regimental headquarters was attacked, unsuccessfully, and the Iraqis left behind a Ford truck with which Ferguson promptly replaced his Haifa taxi.

But there were some sharper engagements as they probed south towards the city, where 'B' Squadron were held up outside the mosque at Al-Khadimain. 'We were caught in the open – in the middle,' wrote Lieutenant 'G' Leigh. 'We

Lieutenant 'G' (Gerard) Leigh during the advance on Baghdad in May 1941 with a wrecked Messerschmitt in the background.

Part of the floating advance to Baghdad led by Andrew Ferguson on the Euphrates.

had to run for shelter about a hundred yards away. Trooper Shone, who had been drafted to my troop from the cookhouse the day before, got hit and fell. We made it to a mud hut which gave us a certain amount of shelter from machine-gun fire.' Trooper Shone had been killed. Wellesley was sent with his troop to recover his body, but was pinned down by accurate Iraqi fire and decided to fall back. He ordered his troop Corporal of Horse, Maxted, to move first. Maxted had never been under fire before but 'when there was a pause,' Wellesley wrote,

> I gave Maxted the signal to move. I then witnessed something which I shall always regard as one of the most courageous acts I have ever seen. Most men under the circumstances would have run back to the ridge, doubled up and as fast as their legs would carry them. Laden with rifle, fifty rounds of ammunition and equipment, they would have arrived puffing and panting and in no fit state to take command of a situation let alone aim a rifle in the right direction. Not Maxted – he stood up all six feet three inches, brushed himself off like a good soldier and marched erect and straight with his rifle at the short tail across that hundred yards of desert as if he was on the parade ground at Windsor. It was a magnificently defiant gesture. He was the old soldier amongst us all and he knew that behind him on the ground lay some very frightened men. Whatever his own feelings were and he must have been as afraid as we were, he wasn't going to show it. The movement triggered off more firing and I watched him go back to the ridge as the bullets flicked up sand all round him with a full heart and a prayer on my lips.[11]

The southern force, with 'C' Squadron, got from Fallujah to the outskirts of Baghdad without incident, but as they came near the city they were held up by wide ditches which the Iraqis had dug and flooded, using isolated groups to cover them with machine guns, who melted away before they could be attacked. Again they were part of a division and in places offered stiff resistance, and a few Italian and German pilots were still active, one of whom baled out and was captured by Lieutenant Somerset de Chair. It was a difficult position for the regiment, with the men packed in lorries on roads with flooded ditches on both sides and no space to manoeuvre. Just as they were preparing themselves for a final push into the city, word came of an armistice, and the regimental trumpeters duly sounded the 'cease fire'. By 31 May 'C' Squadron were billeted in Baghdad railway station.

The next stage in the operation, which again has a certain familiarity for the regiment today, was to put down the ensuing insurgency by those who did not accept the armistice, and in particular to capture the insurgent leaders, the Nazi agent, Dr Grobba, and El Fawzi el Rashid. El Fawzi was a curious man, who had been educated at St-Cyr, fought as a Turkish officer against Allenby's forces in the First World War, led the Arab revolt against the Jewish settlers in Palestine thereafter and then became Rashid Ali's war minister. Rabidly anti-English, he was a competent, if unpleasant, soldier, and his insurgents had a nasty habit of picking off single vehicles or small groups, and mutilating the crews before shooting them. A task force, or 'column', was put together from the regiment to round him up, based on 'A' Squadron and commanded by Major Merry, and inevitably known as Mercol. Merry, 'that grey-haired, dark skinned Red Indian of a man, who was known to the troops as "Old Misery"',[12] was an able officer possessed of much charm beneath his rather dour exterior. He moved towards El Fawzi's base at Abu Kemal, on the Syrian frontier, on 9 June, stopping en route to bivouac on the Euphrates where his troops found old ration tins from 1916. When he got near he decided to send three troops forward to try to draw Fawzi out, and succeeded rather too well as two of them were ambushed as they approached. Merry then sent for reinforcements while Wellesley's troop was sent to try to work round to the south of Abu Kemal to establish an observation post. Radio communications in Habforce were at that stage fairly rudimentary, and a troop was unlikely to be able to communicate back to its squadron headquarters much over about 15 miles. When Wellesley found an ideal position for his task about 30 miles out in the desert he therefore resigned himself to operating without support. He was consequently astonished, when making the routine communications check, that he

> heard a faint signal asking my position, which I gave. I wondered what on earth had happened. Had squadron HQ set up a relay station after all? Or was my signal bouncing off the ionic layer and vice versa in freak conditions? It was mysterious and I could not help feeling faintly uncomfortable and was impatient to see what happened when I called at midday. Bang on 12 noon I called again. This time the reply came loud and clear asking for my position. I gave it but again I was decidedly uneasy. Something was happening which I didn't understand. It was about five minutes later when I was staring at the desert to the west that I thought I saw a cloud of dust 'no larger than a man's hand' to borrow a biblical expression. A minute later it was quite clear that it was dust and moving fast in my direction. I told Maxted to give the order to prepare to move at short notice.[13]

It was Fawzi, who had captured an old armoured car off the RAF at Habbaniya before they could destroy their codes, and had been listening in to Mercol's radio frequencies. Wellesley's troop got away just in time, racing Fawzi's vehicles over the desert, and not pausing to think what would happen if he caught up with them.

The operation to capture Grobba was led by Major Eric Gooch, and was based on 'B' Squadron. They had moved from Baghdad to Mosul and by 3 June were occupying Mosul airfield from where the Germans had been mounting air attacks. General Clarke, Habforce's commander, then told Gooch to assemble a force to capture Grobba, who was thought to be hiding in the Syrian village of Kameschle. The plan was to mount an audacious night raid into Syria, returning to Iraqi territory before the French were aware. Having learnt a few lessons about radio security from Wellesley's exploit, Clarke and Gooch agreed a code based on hunting terms which they would both understand but which would hopefully baffle any listening Iraqis. Even El Fawzi might have been forgiven for failing to understand the finer points of one message which ran, 'Made twenty mile point on stale line, covert blank, hounds unable to draw covert satisfactorily owing to very thick briars. Local inhabitants report fox leaving covert day before.'[14] Gooch's raid went in on 7 June but ran into problems on the frontier where they bumped into a French outpost. Trumpets sounded and the French garrison turned out to enquire politely what the British were doing invading French territory. Gooch explained they had missed their way in the dark and withdrew, swinging wide of the post, crossing the border well below it and looping back to cut its telephone wires. Next they ran into a French patrol as they tried to cross a wadi. Lieutenant Gerard Leigh, who spoke fluent French, persuaded them they were themselves another French patrol, and the French non-commissioned officer in charge agreed to help them find their way to Kameschle. By the time they finally arrived it was daylight and they were met by the French commandant, immaculate in boots and breeches, who asked them courteously what they wanted. Gooch decided to come clean and admit they were after Grobba. The French captain said he had been there and had left the day before, so he would be grateful if Gooch would stop invading French territory and return to Iraq. Gooch, noticing sizeable French forces in the village, agreed to do so. His squadron were escorted back to the frontier via the same border post from the previous night, where it was requested of them, even more politely, should they pass that way again, to refrain from vandalizing the telephone wires.

Unknown to both Grobba and the French in Kameschle was the fact that the British advance into Syria had begun as they conversed, and on 20 June columns had moved to Damascus from Palestine. Habforce's role now was to make the French believe the main Allied thrust would come from Iraq by advancing up the Euphrates, taking Palmyra – a base for German aircraft – and harassing enemy communications between Damascus and Homs. The main body of 1 HCR originally went to help Mercol against El Fawzi, but by this stage he had retreated into Syria, from where he would attack Habforce's flank as they moved west. Once reunited, they crossed into Syria on 21 June, reinforced with a troop of guns and some Royal Air Force armoured cars. Ferguson had gone down with malaria, so command devolved to Gooch, who was now told to move 230 miles west along the Kirkuk–Tripoli pipeline, capturing two pumping stations on the way. The first pumping station, called T2, was about 50 miles over the border. Summers scribbled a demand in schoolboy French for the garrison to surrender and the RAF armoured cars were sent forward

David Smiley behind a bullet-ridden windscreen. He would later leave to fight with the Special Operations Executive in the Balkans where he would win two Military Crosses.

During the search for Dr Grobba 1 HCR find a crashed car full of Iraqi officers.

'B' Squadron encounter French troops having crossed the Syrian border in an attempt to capture Dr Grobba at Kameschle.

with a white flag to deliver it. The French garrison commander replied apologetically in immaculate English that he could not comply as he was from the Foreign Legion and must do his duty. The Foreign Legion was rather a different matter to Iraqi levies, and 'A' Squadron was left behind to watch them while the rest pressed on. They were about to attack the next pumping station, T3, when they encountered the rest of their brigade and were ordered to continue straight to Palmyra itself. From this point on enemy activity increased markedly. The ground forces were mostly Foreign Legion and they were now subjected to continual air attacks. They did not mind the bombers so much as the fighters, who flew a few feet above the trucks, machine-gunning them as they passed. Trooper Reeve, a remarkably strong man, downed one by firing his heavy Hotchkiss machine gun – which normally took two men to carry – from the shoulder. On the third day six French bombers circled lazily over their heads, dropping bombs at will, when six RAF fighters miraculously appeared and shot down every one of them. Despite the frequency of the attacks, overall casualties were remarkably low. Later a French airman claimed they had destroyed 200 vehicles, but the real figure was a fraction of that.

The regiment moved into the foothills north-east of Palmyra, where they were marginally better protected from air attack, and from where they mounted reconnaissance patrols to ascertain the extent of the enemy defences. These were long and dangerous missions, partly in trucks and partly on foot, bringing in much valuable information that led directly to the fall of Palmyra on 3 July. Both Lieutenants John Shaw and Valerian Wellesley were awarded Military Crosses for their part in this operation. Sadly for the regiment, they did not enter Palmyra itself but, as the city surrendered, were sent on westwards, still following the pipeline. On 8 July they attacked a ridge defended by the Foreign Legion in front of the village of Djerboua, which they then occupied. As they prepared for the advance on Homs itself, news of a cease-fire arrived. The French regime surrendered on 10 July and three days later the regiment drove peacefully down to Aleppo where they were comfortably billeted in an old school with a wonderful view of the city. On 15 July Winston Churchill, clearly enamoured with the romance of the setting if misinformed about 1 HCR's equipment, and also desperate for some good war news, announced to the House of Commons that he hoped it would soon be possible to 'give further accounts to the public . . . of the Syrian fighting, marked as it was by so many picturesque episodes, such as the arrival of His Majesty's Life Guards and Royal Horse Guards, in armoured cars, across many hundreds of miles of desert, to surround and capture the oasis of Palmyra'.[15]

Once again their peace was not to last. While they had been invading Syria, Hitler had invaded Russia, and it was now felt in London that there would be merit in opening an alternative supply line to Stalin through Persia. Approaches to the Shah, who was noticeably pro-Axis, failed to produce the desired results, and the decision was taken to occupy Teheran. Elated by the success and ease of the Iraq and Syrian campaigns, Churchill and Stalin agreed on a two-pronged attack, with the British forces invading from Iraq, approaching Teheran via Kermanshah, Hamadan and Qum, while the Russians moved down from the north. The 1st Cavalry Division was now optimistically renamed the 10th Armoured Division – despite the fact that it had hardly any armour – and was moved from Syria back to Iraq and then up to the Persian frontier. 1 HCR left Aleppo on 5 August, retracing their route along the Tripoli–Kirkuk pipeline to the Euphrates, and then to the border town of Khanaquin, where the Kermanshah road crosses into Iraq on the border about midway between Baghdad and Kirkuk. There they lingered while various ultimatums were rejected by the Shah, and amused themselves by fishing with hand grenades in the river. They only caught a few fish, but the local inhabitants did rather better, as they retrieved many stunned fish downstream and sold them back to the regiment. On 27 August they moved forward into Persia, reaching the Pai Tak Pass in the Zagros Mountains the same day. There was no defence, which boded well for it was a natural position, and indicated there wasn't much Persian will to fight. So it proved, and by 17 September they had reached Teheran. A careful plan had been agreed with the Russians that both armies would enter the city together at 3 p.m. that day, but 'in accordance with the methods with which the world has since then unfortunately become all too familiar'[16] the Russians moved in at 6 a.m., and when the regiment moved forward they found themselves passing Red Army checkpoints. There followed ten very agreeable days in the sophistication of Teheran – despite the old German armaments factory in which they were billeted – interspersed with joint parades with the Russians, who sweltered in thick green uniforms. None of them spoke anything but Russian, whereas most of the Persians spoke French, and proved most accommodating hosts. 1 HCR left on 27 September, driving roughly 1,000 miles back to Jerusalem in two weeks.

It was the end of an extraordinary campaign, which secured Persia for the remainder of the war and had cost the British Army just twenty-two killed and forty-two wounded. In the six months since they had handed over their horses, 1 HCR had taken part in the successful occupation of three countries, and troopers whose lives had previously revolved around stables and sword drill and who had only a few hours' driving experience when they left Rehovoth in May, had now covered an average of 6,300 miles each. Casualties had been almost incredibly low, despite the frequency of air attack; nine members of the regiment had been killed in action and nineteen wounded, with a further five killed in accidents and seven dead from disease or heart failure.

The Royals, or at least part of them, had, of course, been fighting the desert war for eighteen months and were old hands at that confusing series of advances and retreats up and down the Mediterranean coastline to Tobruk that reflected the respective fortunes of the 8th Army and the Afrika Korps. However, two squadrons had been withdrawn to assist in the invasion of Syria from

David Rocksavage – later the Marquess of Cholmondeley – who fought throughout the war in The Royals, won a Military Cross, and wrote a very good account of what life was like in armoured cars in the desert.

One of the dummy tanks from Tony Murray Smith's 'Smithforce', which had successfully deceived the Luftwaffe.

The German gun factory in Teheran where 1 HCR were billeted in September 1941.

Palestine and, while 1 HCR had been advancing from Iraq, they had been involved in operations south of Damascus, entering that city the day it surrendered. Thereafter they had spent an enjoyable few months patrolling the Turkish frontier and did not rejoin 'C' Squadron, who had remained in the desert, until October 1941. They then became the armoured car regiment for the famous 7th Armoured Division and moved up to join them south of Tobruk in the pursuit to Benghazi.

In this first phase of the desert war, that is, the period up until the Battle of Alamein in October 1942, the role of the armoured car regiment was very much a troop leaders' and car commanders' war. Typically the regiment would be given a front of about 30 miles to watch, with two squadrons forward and one resting several miles back. There were five troops in each squadron, and they, in turn, would have three forward and two back, meaning that six troops would effectively cover the regimental area, each responsible for about 5 miles of desert. A troop, which consisted of three armoured cars and twelve men, normally went forward for three days at a time. The area of the Western Desert in which they operated was the coastal strip between the Mediterranean Sea and the Qattara Depression, 200 feet below sea level, and the northern arm of the great sand sea of the Sahara. Movement through the Depression was impossible for more than one or two vehicles and it was the preserve of groups like the Long Range Desert Group and the Special Air Service. Conventional forces were therefore restricted to the harder sand and rock of the coastal plain. On the Libyan border, south of Tobruk, this was several hundred miles wide, but it narrowed as it neared the Nile so that at Alamein, 50 miles from Cairo, it had reduced to only 30 miles.

Life in the desert for the isolated troops acquired a distinctive pattern. The main activity was observation, with car commanders spending long hours scanning the empty desert through their binoculars for any sign of movement. There was little local life apart from the odd Bedouin family and a few birds, and it could be a solitary and tedious job. When vehicles did appear it was difficult to tell how far away they were and whether they were friendly or enemy. 'It was very confusing', wrote Lord Rocksavage, a troop leader in The Royals,[17]

> but previous experience helped one on those sort of occasions. In our columns there were certain features to be looked for. . . . All the lorries were quite square, and if the sun caught them they shone bright yellow. In fact the whole party would have an unmistakably British look . . . The enemy columns had equally distinctive characteristics. Most of their transport was mixed Iti and Jerry pattern of a very unmilitary kind as compared with ours. They were long and low, often looking like charabancs.

It was usually baking hot and the shortage of water made the heat hard to bear. The allowance was half a gallon per man per day, which meant one mug for washing and shaving, leaving enough for three cups of tea unless the radiator was leaking, which it often was, and in which case its needs came first. The tea was invariably liberally laced with Ideal sweet tinned milk, and after the war many desert veterans could not face a cup of tea again. 'Men spent the hours of daylight dreaming of babbling brooks and limpid mountain pools,' wrote Julian Pitt-Rivers.

> Petrol on the other hand was plentiful and was used for washing clothes . . . nor was it possible to encourage economy in this regard when so much was seen to drip into the sand. For the type of tin used to carry petrol to the forward areas, a flimsy square affair, was quite unfit for the rough journey and was found as often as not to have lost its contents by the time it reached the front.[18]

Flies were a particular menace, swarming wherever the troops went, and showing an unpleasant predilection for the desert sores which often covered the men's faces and hands. Disease was quite common, including a bad outbreak of jaundice just before Alamein.

In these conditions the troops got to know one another very well indeed and established a camaraderie that was to last for the rest of their lives. At regimental reunions veterans of North Africa would still sit in their same troop group up until the mid-1990s when age and infirmity prevented them from attending. Car crews ate together – the driver usually did the cooking – and the officers only messed together when they were back in a squadron leaguer or the regiment was together in camp. The social gulf between officers and men – so apparent to men like Spike Mays and Tim Bishop in the 1920s and 1930s – quickly dissolved in the intimacy of months on end in the very close proximity of an armoured car.

There was also the shared risk, and The Royals were not spared casualties. They were always vulnerable to air attack, particularly before the Desert Air Force chased off the Luftwaffe. Just after Christmas 1941, when the whole regiment was, unusually, grouped together for replenishment and maintenance at Haseiat in the desert south of Benghazi, word came of a strong enemy column approaching. As they prepared to move they were caught by seven Stukas who bombed them. They hit regimental headquarters, killing three men outright and wounding Colonel Heyworth and his second-in-command, Major Joy. With the German tanks approaching there was little that could be done and the casualties were bundled into the backs of the ambulances as they drove east. Heyworth died that night and command passed to Major Pepys.

There were more casualties in May and June 1942 as Rommel attacked British positions south of Gazala – the famous 'boxes' or defended areas in the desert – captured Tobruk and forced Auchinleck to withdraw 700 miles back to the east, until he finally found a defensive position. This was at Alamein,

NORTH AFRICA DURING THE SECOND WORLD WAR

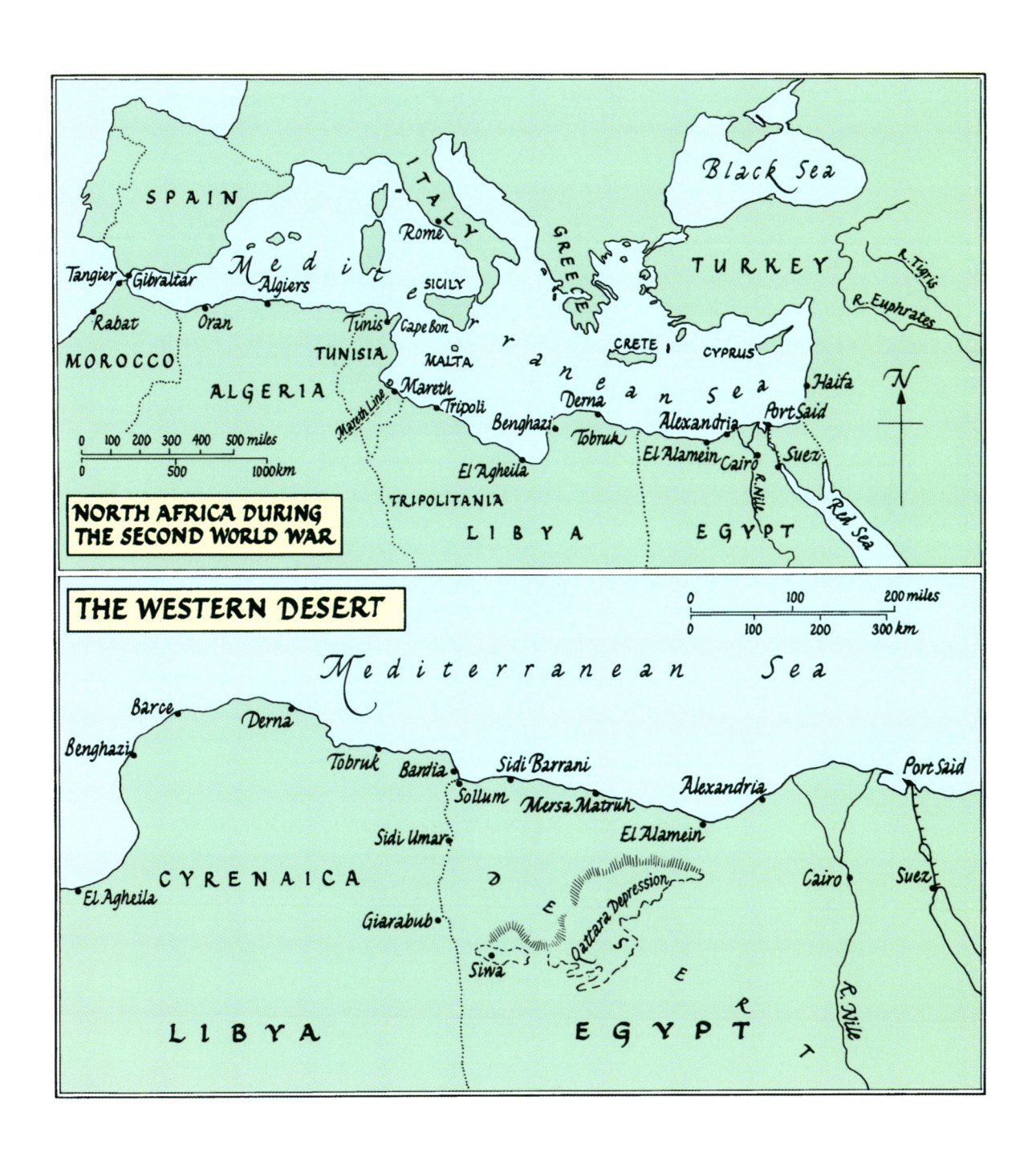

THE WESTERN DESERT

where the Qattara Depression came sufficiently far north to narrow the gap between it and the sea and create a space small enough to be defensive and block the advancing Afrika Korps. Auchinleck's position was established just in time and, despite several attacks, held, so that by early July it was clear that Rommel could advance no further and Cairo was safe, at least for the time being. The Royals remained on the Alamein Line for a further month, manning observation posts, but at the end of July were pulled back to a rest camp near Alexandria. After the initial novelty of showers and beer had worn off, the squadrons soon became restive, irritated by the drill and parades which seemed inevitable whenever the regiment was grouped together and missing their independent life in the desert. They would not have long to wait.

Fond as 1 HCR had become of their mixed and battered transport, there was general relief when it was announced in January 1942 that they were to become an armoured car regiment like The Royals. This had not been a straightforward decision. As late as November plans were being discussed to create two Guards armoured divisions, with The Life Guards forming the armoured car regiment for one and The Blues for the second. This would have required 1 HCR to be split into its constituent squadrons – which were by now completely intermingled with Life Guards and Blues – and return to England for more training. They felt they had more than proved themselves in Iraq and Syria and were keen to get into action in North Africa. Fortunately for them the scheme was finally dropped, and the regiment's role as the armoured car regiment for the 10th Division looked secure. Training schools were set up and courses commenced. Because the establishment of an armoured car regiment was smaller, they had some people spare. These were put under Major Tony Murray-Smith and sent off early to Egypt to man a dummy tank force. Inevitably this was called 'Smithforce', and ran a fleet of old Morris lorries covered with canvas mock-ups of tanks. From the air these were indistinguishable from the real thing, and were placed at selected sites in the desert either to deceive the enemy into making expensive attacks on them or to give the impression that an area was more heavily defended than it was. It was a remarkably successful detachment, which those involved rather enjoyed, and while most eventually rejoined the regiment when it finally arrived in Egypt, some remained with the dummy force throughout the war.

Just as it seemed that everything was finally going to plan, out of the blue 1 HCR received a signal telling them to move to Cyprus, leaving their vehicles behind. This was unpopular as it appeared they were to be sidelined once more, much as they had been in 1940. Actually the order resulted not from some malign influence in the War Office but from a genuine fear the Germans would invade Cyprus, much as they had other Mediterranean islands. Auchinleck, the Allied Commander-in-Chief in the Middle East, had already infuriated Churchill by diverting the 50th Division, intended as reinforcements for North Africa, to Cyprus. They had been sent out from England at some cost to counter the then prevalent notion that Dominion troops were doing most of the fighting, so their diversion was politically difficult. 1 HCR's armoured car training was interrupted and they were destined to spend the six months from March 1942 patrolling the mountains and beaches of Cyprus. It was an uneventful period, enjoyed for the relative comfort of the island and the hospitality of its British settler community, but still immensely frustrating as it seemed to take them away from the real war.

However, by August Montgomery's rejuvenation of the 8th Army was well underway and he needed reconnaissance regiments. They were in Egypt by September, camped on the old battlefield of Kassassin, converting to armoured cars in earnest. 'The 25th September [1942] was a red-letter day. For the first time in its history 1 HCR paraded as an armoured car regiment with the full war establishment of vehicles.'[19] The following day they were in the desert, just as Montgomery finalized plans to drive Rommel and his German and Italian armies out of Africa once and for all.

By October 1942 Montgomery, who had assumed command of the 8th Army after Churchill had sacked Auchinleck, decided he was strong enough to attack Rommel's positions beyond the Alamein Line and to force him back through Libya and into Tunisia. During the summer reinforcements and new equipment had been flowing into Egypt so that Montgomery now enjoyed a considerable advantage in both numbers and supplies. The German and Italian lines of communication across the Mediterranean were, on the other hand, fragile, subject to constant attack by the Royal Navy and Royal Air Force, and Rommel was short of fuel, ammunition and, above all, tanks. This new British equipment included more modern armoured cars. Some of these were Humbers, which had better weapons, thicker armour, a turret that could traverse properly and, most importantly of all, a radio in each car. The others, the Daimlers, were even better, having all these advantages but also a much more powerful 2-pounder gun. The Royals were given two Humbers and one Daimler per troop whilst 1 HCR were given one Daimler but kept two old Marmont Harringtons.

Montgomery's plan was simple. He would make Rommel think he was going to attack in the south, up against the Qattara Depression, the traditional area for breakthroughs in the desert war, and where he would place XIII Corps. However, his real intention was to break out in the north along the coast, where he massed two corps; XXX Corps would make two breaches in Rommel's defences, which had extensive and sophisticated minefields, and then X Corps would pass through and exploit. The Royals now took over 1 HCR's old role as the armoured car regiment for the 10th Armoured Division in X Corps and so had the demanding role of leading the breakout once the breaches had been made. 1 HCR went as armoured car regiment to the 7th Armoured Division in the south, and would start the battle manning a line of observation posts just north of the Qattara Depression.

For the first nine days of the battle there was little for The Royals to do other than wait while the infantry and engineers broke into the enemy positions. The waiting was difficult. Major Jack Hamilton-Russell used another hunting metaphor to give his wife Diana, to whom he wrote whenever he had the chance throughout his time in the Middle East, an idea of what they were about to do which would pass the censor's pencil.

> I am just off to Kirby Gate . . . my coat is smart, my top-boots polished, my horse's mane plaited and lovely . . . but, as usual, I am pushed, and just bustling round looking for gloves and whip. The scent is good, the Country the cream . . . the whole pack of bitches & dogs & riding our best horses. It must be a good day and then we shall be satisfied. Lastly, I am told there are a nice strong lot of foxes about too.[20]

For the first two days they were held well to the front, in what had originally been the German and Italian forward positions, but when it became clear that the breakthrough was going to take longer than anticipated, they were pulled back to just behind the artillery lines, where what rest they could get was shattered by constant gunfire. By 1 November, when the infantry had penetrated as far as a position known as Kidney Ridge, Montgomery and General Lumsden – commander of X Corps and himself an ex-commanding officer of an armoured car regiment – decided it was worth infiltrating The Royals forward through the crumbling German and Italian lines both to report back on what was really going on and to cause panic by appearing in the rear of their positions. Only two squadrons were to be sent as they had more chance of success than the whole regiment with its headquarters and echelon, and, should the worst happen, at least a core would remain from which the regiment could be rebuilt. Montgomery envisaged the squadrons operating in the main enemy positions, but Pepys insisted on going much further, deep behind enemy lines where, he argued, they would not only have a greater chance of survival but would have an effect disproportionate to their size. Montgomery grumpily agreed, remarking that most regimental commanders had been happy to do what he told them.

On the night of 1 November 'A' Squadron, under Jack Hamilton-Russell, and 'C' Squadron, under Major Roddy Heathcoat-Amory, moved forward as quietly as they could behind the 51st Highland Division who cleared a final belt of mines to their front. Then,

> they reached the end of the marked tracks and knew that they were through the prepared defences. The night ahead was full of flashes and the sounds of battle but to the south, where their course lay, all seemed quiet. A late moon was rising. The column threaded its way through tanks and anti-tank guns which waited, with engines throbbing, to go forward.' The first two

armoured cars fell into abandoned trenches but eventually they found a track that the enemy had been using. 'Soon they were aware of troops either side of the track. Sleepy guards sat rubbing the backs of their hands, or ran over to consult with one another about the strangers passing through their position. They could not be enemy, these Germans thought, so far from the battle and arriving in column of march . . . The track led them through a battery of howitzers. They could see the gun-crews sleeping by their guns. The guards watched them through bleary eyes and stamped their feet. Already the east was green behind them and the waning moon hung like a toy in the sky, but by the time it was light the two squadrons were fleeting through open desert.[21]

As dawn broke they passed a man actually in bed in his pyjamas, automatically assumed to be an Italian quartermaster, who was woken by having a Very light fired into his blankets. Now it was time to turn and create what havoc they could. In the next four days they destroyed a total of 181 vehicles, three tanks, forty-one guns and an aeroplane. They also cut the telephone lines leading to the enemy's forward headquarters. 'The columns of smoke climbing up from the lorries we burned attracted the attention of tanks and aircraft,' *The Times* reported Jack Hamilton-Russell as saying.

> We managed to dodge the tanks but the aircraft pestered us throughout the next four days. One German pilot adopted a novel form of bombing. He had probably grown tired of aiming at the small target offered by an armoured car and, attaching a bomb on a piece of rope suspended from his Me 109, flew over us hoping to bump the bomb into our turrets. After twenty-four unsuccessful attempts the bomb hit the ground,

and, he added, 'caused irreparable damage to his piece of rope!'[22] The operation was not, sadly, without cost, and two crews were lost to anti-tank guns whilst several others had to abandon their vehicles and try to regain their own lines on foot; one crew took thirty Italian prisoners between them en route. By the evening of 5 November the Battle of Alamein was won. Regimental headquarters came forward and the regiment was reunited and now prepared itself for the pursuit to Tunis that would drive the Germans and Italians out of North Africa as Montgomery had so confidently predicted.

Although life had not been quite so exciting for 1 HCR it had been busy enough. The regiment had moved into position covering about 6 miles of the southern part of the Alamein line on 4 October, which included the main enemy defensive position on the Himeimat feature, a rocky desert outcrop. Their technique was to take their armoured cars forward through gaps in the British minefields at first light and establish observation posts about a mile in front of the main British positions. At night they would withdraw back through the minefield gaps that were guarded by the infantry. The Italians mortared them fairly regularly, and on 21 October they received news that the battle was to start on 23 October.

Neither The Royals nor 1 HCR were particularly taken by Montgomery's style, and The Royals still smarted from his comments about their horses in Palestine, but they did at least trust him. 'Alexander,' wrote Hamilton-Russell, referring to the new commander-in-chief in the Middle East, '& Montgomery of course have everyone's confidence & we are all very pleased with them. They have mustered almost as much respect as Archie Wavell out here.'[23] They were also aware they were witnessing a turning point in the war. One of the 1 HCR officers described watching the initial attack going in.

> At 2140 hours the barrage began. It looked like the flash-lamps of batteries of photographers who had lain hidden in the desert until that moment. Perhaps a minute later the angry chun-chun-chun from the gun lines came down the breeze, to be followed from across the valley by the kerun-kerun-kerun-kerun and four vivid flashes of exploding shells, but very soon the series of fours overlapped and merged into a continuous rumble and crash.[24]

Although the attack in the south was intended as a feint it seemed very like the real thing to the regiments who took part, many of whom were killed and wounded on the minefields in front of the Himeimat which the Germans were defending strongly. It took three days to break through the minefields, code-named January and February, but by 25 October a bridgehead had been established. There was not much for 1 HCR to do at this stage and Wellesley was sent forward to offer support to the infantry battalion to their front. He found the Commanding Officer 'distinctly rattled and I could hardly blame him. His battalion was spread out in small slit trenches all over a forward slope and was being mortared regularly and accurately every few minutes'. Nearby he saw 'a sad little line of shallow graves, each marked by a steel helmet or a rifle stuck in the ground by its bayonet'[25].

The 7th Armoured Division was pulled out to the north but 1 HCR stayed put, and on 4 November the infantry in the south finally broke through at much the same time as the main thrust in the north and 1 HCR

> got the chance it had been waiting for – to take up the pursuit. I shall never forget the feeling of elation as we got through the last gap in the minefields and fanned out four troops up with miles of open desert and good going stretching ahead of us apparently forever. We pushed on quickly but very soon were having to stop constantly to deal with hundreds of dejected prisoners, mainly Italian, streaming eastwards, weaponless and with only one thought in mind – to become prisoners of war as soon as possible . . . Only the officers retained their pistols and some were most unwilling to

hand them over as they said they needed them to protect themselves from their own troops! I remember at the end of the day there were so many pistols on the floor of my armoured car that I was standing on a pile of them.[26]

On the first day they advanced 30 miles and captured over 1,000 prisoners, including the odd German, among whom was Major Burckhardt, a German parachute officer who had achieved notoriety in Crete, and was a colossal snob, constantly telling the regiment what an honour it was to be taken prisoner by the Household Cavalry. There were odd occasions when Germans organized temporary resistance, such as two Mark IV Panther tanks hiding in a transport column Wellesley's troop were shooting up, forcing them quickly to withdraw. However after two days they had penetrated 60 miles, neutralized any threat from the south, and captured almost the entire Italian Folgore Division, a total of around 10,000 men.

Despite the success of this operation and the relish with which the regiment looked forward to following up the retreating Germans and Italians into Libya, on 13 November they were called back. An armoured car regiment was required on the Syrian border with Turkey as part of the 9th Army, charged with protecting Turkey in the event of German attack, and they had been selected for the task. This really was a bitter blow. Having finally been properly equipped, and having more than proved their worth at Alamein, they were to be sidelined once more. 'Although the reasons were logical I, and all those who were there, feel bitter even to this day. We had done all and more than had been asked of us . . . It was with a feeling of deep disappointment and even humiliation after the euphoria of the last few weeks that, after a few days rest, we retraced our steps to a base south of Cairo,'[27] wrote Wellesley fifty-five years later. Montgomery, thought to have little time for the Household Cavalry, was blamed, and many recalled his visit to the regiment before Alamein when he had worn his Australian hat festooned with different cap badges, but no one had offered him one of theirs.

The next fifteen months were perhaps the most unsatisfactory period in the whole history of 1 HCR, stuck on a very quiet border near Raqqa on the upper Euphrates, in a miserable camp and with very wet weather for the rest of the winter. They were not permitted to enter Turkey, which was neutral, and their task was to patrol her borders as a deterrent and to enable a quick move to occupy Anatolia if a German attack did materialize. Eric Gooch, who had taken over command from Andrew Ferguson just after Alamein, tried to cheer everyone up by making a rousing speech at Christmas dinner. Trooper Hunt, the oldest soldier in the regiment and the only one by then who had fought in the First World War, replied, saying things were not as bad as they had been then, and between them they raised morale a little, but it was a dull job and what little news they received was full of the exploits of the 8th Army as they drove

Valerian Wellesley, left, watches as two German prisoners are searched after El Alamein.

Italian prisoners of war during the capture of Tunis between January and May 1943.

on into Tunisia. There was the odd exciting moment, such as when Greek troops in Syria mutinied in July 1943 and had to be disarmed, but it was poor compensation. They were relieved in late September 1943, and were sent back to the Red Sea to take up an issue of new Daimlers on which they were to retrain in preparation for the move to Italy, which the 8th Army had now invaded. Just as they arrived they heard the French had mutinied and a force under Major Ferris St George was sent racing back to Syria to deal with them. In January training was resumed and the remaining Marmont Harringtons were finally sent away. By February they were back outside Alexandria, and on 5 April 1944 embarked for Italy, landing in Naples a week later.

The Royals, however, who were to play a very full role in the pursuit after Alamein, must have wished at times that they were on the Syrian border. The role of armoured cars in the pursuit was to lead, establishing where the enemy was defending. Consequently they were usually the first to be shot at. Up until Christmas 1942 they operated in familiar desert, with the wrecks from earlier battles much in evidence, 'the tanks on the ridge which they had failed to hold, the lorries in the wadi where the stukas found them, the scout-car cooked up on the minefield's edge'.[28] Rocksavage noted that 'some were a year old, Honeys and Valentines from last year's flaps, but others were two years old, obsolete looking vehicles from Wavell's day. I felt very modern in my Daimler, which fairly roared over the heavy going.'[29] After Christmas they operated in rockier, mountainous country with deep wadis that offered good defensive positions to the withdrawing enemy. In mid-December they took part in an operation to outflank the enemy position south of Agheila, the furthest point any British forces had previously reached in North Africa. The position was protected on its southern flank by a salt marsh, and skirting it took three days along treacherous tracks, though by the time The Royals made contact most of the Germans had withdrawn. The Luftwaffe was more active the further west they reached and they were under constant air attack by both the dreaded Stukas and fighters. Mines were also a menace, particularly as the wind had often blown away the markings on the old minefields. Colonel Pepys was blown up when he drove into one by mistake. 'I am very angry with myself,' he wrote, 'as I've blown myself up on a mine, & lost a bit of my left leg; however I am full of hope that I shall manage very well on these new ones they give you & shall be back with the regiment before long'.[30] He was, rejoining them in Normandy in 1944.

Montgomery visited the regiment on 7 January and told them that they would soon capture Tripoli, still 200 miles away, and would enter through the west gate. They were annoyed to find that when Tripoli did duly fall, on 29 January, they were otherwise engaged on the flank of the army entering Tunisia – the first 8th Army troops to do so. Tripoli had been their goal since 1941, and they were disappointed to miss Churchill taking the Victory Parade. A few groups managed to get there on leave, but they still had a long and difficult advance to Tunis. Between January and May 1943, when Tunis fell, they functioned in different country again, now fertile and populated, which nullified their normal desert tactics. They lost their Daimlers and were given some Humbers and a much heavier armoured car called an AEC. They needed frequent assistance from the Royal Engineers and now operated in mixed groups of armoured cars, engineer vehicles, some infantry, a troop of artillery and some anti-tank guns, which proved effective in dislodging the German positions from the Tunisian Hills and in the battle to force the Mareth Line in March. This was a strongly defended line of prepared positions between the coast and Matmata Hills at the bottom of the Gulf of Gabes. It fell in a week, and with it went Rommel's last chance of holding up the 8th Army. The Allies had landed successfully in Algeria in November 1942 and he was now squeezed between converging armies. Yet again The Royals were to be disappointed, for they were withdrawn from the line as Montgomery neared Tunis and they were denied entering their second capital, but that was only a minor setback. They had already, so near the end in North Africa, lost Captain Desmond Hamilton-Russell, killed by a shell as he drove away from a visit to his brother's squadron headquarters, and now they were bombed by the Americans as well, a fate which seems to stalk the Household Cavalry. At 8 a.m., while the crews breakfasted beside their cars, thanking God they had made it to the end without injury, a fleet of Baltimore Bombers laid a pattern of bombs across the regimental leaguer. Regimental Sergeant-Major Low and two other men were badly wounded and Trooper Sanders was killed outright. It was a bitter end to two years of distinguished service in North Africa.

Chapter Twenty

THE SECOND WORLD WAR: EUROPE

MEANWHILE, IN TUNIS, a quarter of a million Germans and Italians surrendered. Churchill and Roosevelt had agreed at the Casablanca Conference in January 1943 that Sicily would be invaded as a means of securing the Mediterranean. Planning was well underway and Jack Hamilton-Russell's 'A' Squadron was withdrawn from the regiment, before the fall of Tunis, to be part of the amphibious invasion force that was assembling. As the excitement of desert war faded, Hamilton-Russell realized just how much he missed his beloved Diana. 'Oh! Darling,' he wrote on 14 June, 'it does seem almost too long to count now. It gets no easier – but we shall bear it, and it will be terrific in the end with the sounding of all the trumpets. It reminds me of a verse from a trooper's prayer:

> I love a game; I love a fight,
> I hate the dark, I love the light,
> I love my child, I love my wife.
> I am no coward. I love life.[1]

The censor would not, of course, permit him to say where he and his squadron were heading.

They arrived off the Sicilian coast on 10 July after a dreadful crossing, feeling very seasick, but that was the least of their worries. There was no role for them on land until the bridgehead was secured, so they had to wait at sea in their transports while the initial assault went in. This was unpleasant. German bombers sank three out of the six ships in their group (the last one), just as they went ashore. 'By the light of the anti-aircraft guns and its own flames, men could be seen leaping into the sea from it when its stern rose into the air for the final plunge. As they watched this awesome sight the men of "A" Squadron rubbed the shingle gratefully under their feet,' wrote Pitt-Rivers.[2] A large-scale amphibious operation like Husky, as the invasion of Sicily was codenamed, was demanding for an army that had never done anything similar before and was particularly problematical in the cooperation required between the Royal Navy, the army and the Royal Air Force and also between the British and Americans. Consequently the ground troops had to endure a difficult three weeks' fighting, moving slowly up the east coast towards Catania, which fell on 5 August. 'A' Squadron was now equipped with two flat-topped Daimler scout cars, and two of the larger Daimler armoured cars, painted green and brown to match the Sicilian landscape instead of the familiar sand colour of North Africa. They had to adjust their tactics quickly to adapt to the close terrain, with its hills, woods and dips, and they spent as much time on their feet as they did mounted. 'It is a very dirty country this, and instead of nice clean sand, like the desert, it is black dirt and consequently one can't stay clean for two minutes,'[3] Hamilton-Russell complained. Their memories of those weeks are of stifling heat, the stench of rotting farm animals killed by shelling, of Germans hiding behind every farm building or hay stack, of overenthusiastic villagers celebrating their liberation before the Germans had actually left, and, finally, once Catania was taken, of brief relaxation in appropriated villas, drinking local wine and being very well cared for by the grateful Sicilians. 'We are still resting by the sea,' Jack Hamilton-Russell wrote in a much more cheerful mood to his wife on 14 August, 'in among the olive groves and vineyards. I eat on average about 6 bunches of grapes a day with masses of figs (fresh off the tree), loganberries, plums and peaches. We get some nice Massala wine (sherry) also white wine and we captured a mass of Munich lager beer the other day, which is most pleasant.'[4]

On 19 August he reflected that 'this campaign was an extra good one really – 37 days over the cream of the country in a nice dart'. He had just returned from a dinner with Montgomery. Discovering it was the anniversary of Montgomery's assuming command of the 8th Army, he took along a peahen as a present, Montgomery apparently having a particular liking for them, and 'Monty was tickled to death (not literally!)'.[5] It was the last letter he wrote. On his way back to his squadron from the Brigade Headquarters later that month his jeep overturned and he was killed, the third of three brothers to be lost in the war.

The Allies landed in the toe of Italy on 3 September and the Italian Government surrendered on 8 September. The following day the Allies made landings just south of Naples at Salerno and the Germans began to withdraw to more defensible positions astride the Apennines. 'A' Squadron crossed the Straits of Messina, driving across Calabria to join the 78th Division, who had been landed on the Adriatic coast at Bari, where they arrived on 22 September and helped to clear the remaining Germans out of the area around Foggia, near the Adriatic coast almost opposite Naples. Their one particular task was to clear the Manfredonia Peninsula, the 'spur' to the Italian boot. This they accomplished remarkably quickly with the help of the mayor in the first village they came to. He quickly rang all his fellow-mayors in the peninsula villages, who advised him that the Germans had gone. They were struck by the poverty of the countryside, the ragged state of the disbanding Italian army and the bitter hatred for the Germans. When they reached the small coastal town of Termoli they found a party of Germans who had been slow to leave and had been blasted with shotguns and left to die in the square for everyone to spit at as they passed. But by now they were encountering more prepared German positions, and they were withdrawn south to rest and await the remainder of the regiment.

They had been having a dull and uncomfortable summer, camped on a particularly dusty strip of desert on the Libyan coast about 100 miles from Tripoli. Apart from a great deal of training, boredom was relieved by horse races against the local Bedouin and exploring the ruins of nearby Leptis Magna. They had also been cheered by a visit from the King, who enquired if there was anything he could do for the regiment. There was, as it happened, as they were having a battle with the War Office to retain their grey berets. When they had moved from Palestine they had given up their sun helmets, or solar topees, and had been issued with black berets, black being the prescribed colour for the Royal Armoured Corps that was now the parent organization for the mechanized and armoured cavalry regiments. The Royals rather preferred grey, and duly ordered a regiment's worth, to the fury of Whitehall. The King readily agreed to intervene, but the bureaucrats, who reminded him, smugly, that he had already signed an order saying that everyone should wear black, ultimately beat him.

In September 1943 they moved to Taranto, on the heel of Italy, to take part in the coming offensive. They had a depressing journey as their kit was rifled by the ship's crew, and on arrival they spent forty very wet days in an olive grove just outside the town. In November they finally moved up to join 'A' Squadron near Manfredonia, but not for long. They were now required for another task, and by 22 December they had left Taranto, heading back to England to prepare for the invasion of Normandy. They spent Christmas at sea, docking in the Clyde on 4 January 1944, the first time they had been in Britain for six years. They moved to Durham, went briefly on leave, and then returned to start training for D Day.

Whilst The Royals returned to England, 1 HCR were completing their preparations for service in Italy. They sailed on 8 April 1944, Easter Saturday. John Shaw kept a diary during the coming year. He was particularly pleased to have a cabin on the top deck, near the lifeboats, and was even more pleased at the food on board. 'Excellent breakfast this morning,' he noted on Good Friday. 'The first time I've seen a kipper for three or four years and a damn good kipper too.'[6]

The situation that confronted them on arrival in Naples was one of stalemate. The German defences had been consolidated during the winter. They had fortified the high ground running across the country roughly half-way between Naples and Rome, particularly around Monte Cassino. The Allies had attempted landings in the German rear, at Anzio, just south of Rome, but these had failed to break through to the south and the troops there were now stuck in a 10-mile bridgehead, still 50 miles away from the main Allied armies. The 8th Army's plan in the summer of 1944 was to concentrate between the Mediterranean and the Monte Cassino positions to force back Kesselring, the German commander, link up with the Anzio bridgehead and liberate Rome.

1 HCR collected new Daimlers in Naples, and were briefed by Colonel Gooch. 'The Colonel told us what he knew of what we were going to do in the future,' Shaw noted on 4 May, 'fairly interesting and not too dangerous, though one never knows.' It was a wise rider. What they were going to do was to support 4th Indian Division on the River Sangro, facing strong German positions on the still snow-capped Mount Amaro in the Della Maiella Mountains, where most of the activity was on foot and their new vehicles would get litttle use for some months. On arrival they took over a series of isolated positions, from which they would observe and probe the German defences. Much of this patrolling was above the snow line, and was dangerous and demanding. Shaw took out a particularly successful patrol on 9 May. 'At 1700 Lamb came in from a patrol down the road with a mass of information,' he wrote.

> At 2030 hours I set out with Cpl Hawkins, Martinelli & Dode & Laws, a rare mixture. We were all very tired and I for one very nervy. We went slowly down the road halting often when we all dozed in spite of the cold damp of the fog which had come down. We confirmed Lamb's report as we came to 17 various points. At 0230 we lay up off the road to await first light. At first light [on 10 May] we moved on uphill to get an OP [Observation Post] if possible to see the Staz. di Palena [Palena Station]. We got one but not to see the station, but we could see the German sentry at the cross roads and also an OP on the opposite hill. We stopped there an hour and then went on to try and gain the ridge ahead from which we should have seen the station. In getting there we were shelled inaccurately and having been seen we went back to Palena to report. I thought it was an unsatisfactory patrol but we got congratulated for good work.

Life for the regiment in front of Mount Amaro was, as so often in the Second World War, a combination of a few nerve-racking days and many quite dull ones. When not patrolling, they dealt mainly with routine military matters, their comfort, extra food and drink to supplement their rations – with which they were now pretty bored – and staying in touch with friends in other troops and squadrons. Shaw's diary entry for 24 May is fairly typical. 'Went to Bomba to buy wine with Valerian [Wellesley]. On the way called in on Nick to settle a few things and shot a rat. Got forty litres of fairly good wine in Bomba and met George Murray Smith on the way back. Hoped to see the mortar experts

Trooper Funnel receiving the latest reports of fighting in his sector during the occupation of Fano in the Marches region of Italy 1944.

An armoured car of 1 HCR approaching the Della Maiella Mountains in Abruzzo, where they were to support the 4th Indian Division in May 1944.

as well but they had moved. Arrived back to find a ration of whisky and gin in, an excellent development.' They had now been on operations for nearly four years, and although by mid-1944 the majority of the troopers were from a post-1940 intake drafted in from the training regiment at Windsor, there was a remarkable degree of continuity among the officers and non-commissioned officers. They realized they were winning the war, and overall there was a definite atmosphere of optimism about both the 8th Army and 1 HCR in particular. They were by now very experienced, good at working with other arms, particularly the artillery with whom they got on very well and whose services armoured car regiments always valued. They realized they would inevitably lose more people in the months ahead but were determined that lives would not be wasted, although there was still the occasional individual, like Domski Revertera, who had something to prove. Revertera was an Austrian who had lost his family in the Anschluss and therefore loathed the Nazis. He took out a patrol on 7 June high up on Mount Amaro, went too close to enemy positions and was shot in the stomach. Ironically he was shot by a ski patrol, which was probably Austrian too and could have loathed the Nazis as much as he did.

By early June the Monte Cassino battle had been won, the link-up with Anzio achieved and Rome liberated. The Germans withdrew north again, consolidating their defence first on a line running through Tuscany and Lake Trasimeno, but by August they had been forced even further, to the so-called Gothic Line which ran across Italy from Pesaro to La Spezia. 1 HCR were consequently pulled back from Mount Amaro, did a quick period of refresher training at L'Aquila and then moved north, driving through the battlefield of Cassino, to work, now firmly with their vehicles, under General Dick McCreery's X Corps around Perugia, and then, on 2 August, for Major General Gerald Templer, who would later become Colonel of The Blues. The fighting was demanding, the regiment at times holding a front of 20 miles, and casualties kept coming. It was a particularly wet summer and the roads were almost impassable and bridges over the Arno washed away. A week later they were moved again, this time over to the Adriatic coast to support the 2nd Polish Corps who were trying to force a passage across the River Cesano and take the port of Fano. They got on very well with the Poles, and particularly the Carpathian lancers who came to their assistance in Fano. Shaw was the regimental liaison officer to the headquarters, where he found the common languages were French and whisky. 'All seems to be going well here,' he noted, 'although an immense amount of time is spent in clicking heels and other courtesies.' He thought them 'very charming people', and, he added, in contrast to his experiences at some British corps headquarters 'very helpful'. They ran an excellent mess, particularly so when General Anders 'and some American general' visited. On a more depressing note, the Polish officers seemed to be able to predict what would happen to their country after the war, although nobody believed them. The attachment of 1 HCR was such a success that Anders subsequently invited the regiment to wear the Polish Army badge, the Mermaid of Warsaw, which they duly did, sewn to their sleeves, for the rest of the war.

The next problem to confront 1 HCR came from the War Office, who, concerned at the effect long periods of continuous duty was having on morale, had designed a scheme called, incongruously, Operation Python, whereby any soldier who had served less than six months in the United Kingdom in the last four and a half years was to be returned home. That meant the vast majority of 1 HCR officers and non-commissioned officers would have to leave, which, with 2 HCR now providing an alternative fighting focus for The Life Guards and The Blues in France (more of which later), would mean that 1 HCR would effectively be disbanded. Fortunately, earlier in 1943, the two Gold Sticks had already been putting their minds to the post-war focus for the Household Cavalry, and had appointed Andrew Ferguson to a new post as 'Regimental Lieutenant Colonel'. Ferguson now arrived in Italy, armed with the Gold Sticks' instructions, and negotiated with the 8th Army that 1 HCR should be transferred en masse to England to be trained for subsequent operations in north-west Europe. Although some in the regiment feared they were being withdrawn from an active operation yet again, just as the fighting on the Gothic Line was developing, they realized that the only alternative was disbandment. Leaving the Poles in late August, they moved first back to Perugia, and did another spell in the line in front of Carpegna, before being pulled back via Arezzo and Rome to Naples from where they sailed on 13 October. Shaw was pleased to find lots of old friends on board, particularly the Wiltshire and the Warwickshire Yeomanry from Habforce days, but also 'a lot of bloody women – always a bore on a troop ship'. Ferris St George thought the ship, the *Monarch of Bermuda*, was vaguely familiar, and then remembered that it was the one on which he had returned from his honeymoon. They landed on 24 October and went straight to barracks in Aldershot.

Of all the emotions that exercised the Household Cavalry as a corporate body during the Second World War neither casualties nor separation from wives and families – bad as they were – dominated their thoughts, as did their role as the core of the standing, or regular, army, as it was now called. They wanted a full and central part in the conflict, something which most of them felt personally that their position required. However irritated 1 HCR may, at times, have been, their frustration was nothing compared to that felt by some Household Cavalrymen left behind in 1940. The 1939 mobilization plan had established three Household Cavalry groupings: the Composite Regiment, or 1 HCR, whom we have been following, a Training Regiment at Windsor to provide remounts and recruits and a Horsed Reserve Regiment at Knightsbridge. This last organization was intended to provide the King's Life Guard and whatever other ceremonial was required during the war, but such activities rapidly became impractical and it was put into abeyance and the horses were put out to grass at the Remount Depot in Melton Mowbray. In its place a royal armoured car protection troop was formed, known as 'Morris Mission', commanded by Major The Honourable Arthur Baillie, a veteran Life Guard who had fought in France and Mesopotamia in the First World War and, unusually, served on the staff. It was based at Windsor, although it followed the Royal Family wherever they went.

It became evident quite quickly that the Training Regiment at Windsor did not have a full-time job supporting 1 HCR, particularly when there was a limited requirement for horses. They therefore took on a local defence role around Windsor, including long mounted patrols in Windsor Great Park – where it was feared the Germans might stage a parachute landing – and, less glamorously, guarding the Water Board reservoirs at Staines and Laleham. An example of their activities took place in September 1940, when the code word 'Cromwell' was issued, which indicated that invasion was imminent. The Adjutant, Arthur Collins, was surprised, on being called into barracks, to find the Duty Officer from the neighbouring Foot Guard battalion there, asking what it meant as all their code words had been carefully locked away in the safe and no one had a key. The duty squadron was dispatched to its mobilization location at Langley Airfield, where the squadron leader, Major Bowes Daly, who had joined in the final days of the First World War, saw a strange shape that failed to answer his challenge. He shot it with his pistol, only to find he had dispatched a carthorse. This was not really a very worthwhile role. Furthermore, it had become difficult to recruit officers and soldiers who comprehended that horse-mounted regiments would no longer play a full part in the war.

The Gold Sticks with the War Office made the plan, therefore, that the Training Regiment would become a motor battalion like 1 HCR, and train in lorries until armoured cars were available. They would then join 1 HCR in the Middle East where they could re-form as The Life Guards and The Blues. Events, as always, did not quite work out like that, and 1 HCR were soon too involved in Iraq to consider reorganizing, but the Training Regiment, now renamed 2 HCR, sent its horses off to join the others at Melton Mowbray and enthusiastically set about training on their lorries around Windsor and Burnham Beeches. Even that was a fairly limited role, and they still, like 1 HCR, regarded themselves as an armoured car regiment, just without their armoured cars. However, in the summer of 1941 it was decided to form a Guards' armoured division, putting some of the Foot Guard battalions in tanks, and the Division needed an armoured car regiment. The King signed the order on 19 September 1941 and 2 HCR exchanged the relative comforts of Windsor for the 'dreariness of wind-swept Nissen huts'[7] on Salisbury Plain as they strove to master their new equipment.

2 HCR was to be commanded by Henry Abel-Smith, who had fought with 1 HCR in the Middle East and returned to take up his appointment in July

1941. Abel-Smith is one of the handful of exceptional Household Cavalry commanding officers in our story, like Francis Compton, who trained and then commanded his regiment for a prolonged period on operations. Universally respected, if not always liked by those who did not match his standards, and known in 1 HCR as 'Auntie' because he was so fussy, Abel-Smith was a dedicated and energetic man who understood the demands of modern warfare and how horsed regiments had to adapt to it. On the first day he arrived he ordered a 'maintenance parade' when the whole regiment had to parade with their vehicles for inspection to ensure they were battle-ready. Captain Hubert Duggan, the Member of Parliament for Acton, made the mistake of turning up in his khaki service dress complete with polished shoes, as opposed to the regulation denims, and was unable to explain why his truck appeared to be joined to its garage wall by a large cobweb. Abel-Smith, or Colonel Henry as he was universally known, trained 2 HCR as part of the Guards' Armoured Division throughout 1942 and 1943 and by the time they deployed to Normandy, just after D Day in July 1944, they had the reputation of being one of the best armoured car regiments in the army. Overall, one of his greatest achievements was to produce such a well-officered and manned regiment in Normandy.

Three years, however, was a long wait. The novelist Evelyn Waugh transferred from the Commandos to The Blues in 1942, through the good graces of his friend Robert Laycock, and served until 1945, although he was never actually employed within the regiment. He appeared not to have enjoyed his time at Windsor much, remarking that the officers were 'middle-aged, embittered subalterns' with 'good pictures, poor conversation'.[8] He was perhaps wide of the mark on both counts, as The Blues' picture collection at that time consisted largely of martial portraits and his companions were men whom Colonel Henry deemed better at training recruits than out in the field with 2 HCR. In private Waugh was more complimentary, writing to his wife in some excitement that 'The Blues have accepted me so I can now grow my hair long and wear a watch chain across my chest, and you can have a suit made of their check tweed',[9] and his time in the regiment did not stop him thereafter wearing his Guards' tie possibly more regularly than most, or prevent his son, Auberon, from joining The Blues in his wake. Yet Waugh did have a point, and one of Colonel Henry's greatest challenges was retaining able officers and non-commissioned officers who might otherwise transfer to regiments where the possibility of active service seemed greater. As a partial response, Laycock had already started a Household Cavalry commando troop, which initially trained at Windsor under Lord Sudeley; altogether fifteen members of The Life Guards and Blues were to become casualties serving with the Commandos. Nine more were to be either killed or wounded serving with the Special Forces, where their armoured car reconnaissance skills were highly valued, and David Smiley was to depart to play a vital role in the Balkans.[10] However, over time a combination of their new role, the Household Cavalry tradition and the inevitability of the Allies opening a 'second front' in Europe meant that by 1943 2 HCR was now able to attract some highly able men, who liked the challenge of service in armoured cars, though it took some time to sort out their respective qualifications. One day a soldier asked to see Colonel Henry, complaining that in civilian life he had run 150 Walls' Ice Cream stalls, but since he had been in the regiment he had done nothing except sweep the barrack square.

However, those who thought they might have missed out on the war so far were now about to get a continuous year's service in its most operationally demanding theatre. By June 1944 2 HCR consisted of fifty-five officers and 778 other ranks organized in four squadrons of armoured cars, called 'A', 'B', 'C' and 'D' and termed 'sabre squadrons', and an administrative 'headquarters' squadron. The main fighting unit was the troop, ten men under a lieutenant with two small, two-man Daimler scout cars, armed only with a machine gun and no turret, and two bigger, four-man Daimler armoured cars, with a turret and a bigger 2-pounder gun which could take on lighter German armoured vehicles but which would be lucky to destroy a tank. Each squadron also had a 'heavy troop', equipped with Matador armoured cars, with a bigger 75-mm gun that could destroy tanks, and also a 'support troop', who basically performed the role of infantry.

They landed on the Normandy beaches on 12 July, well after the main D Day invasion where there had been no role for armoured cars, to find the situation in stalemate. The initial assault had been successful in establishing a bridgehead, but despite three weeks of bitter fighting which had seen infantry casualties on a First World War scale, the British and Canadian armies had failed to break out. Caen, a major objective of D Day, had not been taken. There was pressure from the Americans to draw some of the German effort away from them in the west, on the Cherbourg Peninsula, and, finally, the bridgehead itself was also becoming overcrowded. Montgomery planned to address these three problems in Operation Goodwood, which envisaged using armoured divisions, including 2 HCR, to cross the River Orne between Caen and the sea, then swing south and advance to the Bourguébus ridge. They were to be preceded by a massive aerial bombardment, which, it was hoped, would surely flatten all opposition. Goodwood was only partially successful; it did draw German forces away from the Americans, setting them up for their own break-out, and it did lead to the fall of Caen, but the armoured divisions failed to gain their objectives. There was not enough room for them to manoeuvre and so they presented mass targets for the German tanks and anti-tank guns that had miraculously survived the aerial bombardment. The resulting cost in tanks and crews was enormous. 'A' and 'B' Squadrons of 2 HCR were involved, operating under the Guards' Armoured Division, but the lack of space prevented them from carrying out their main reconnaissance role. Instead they

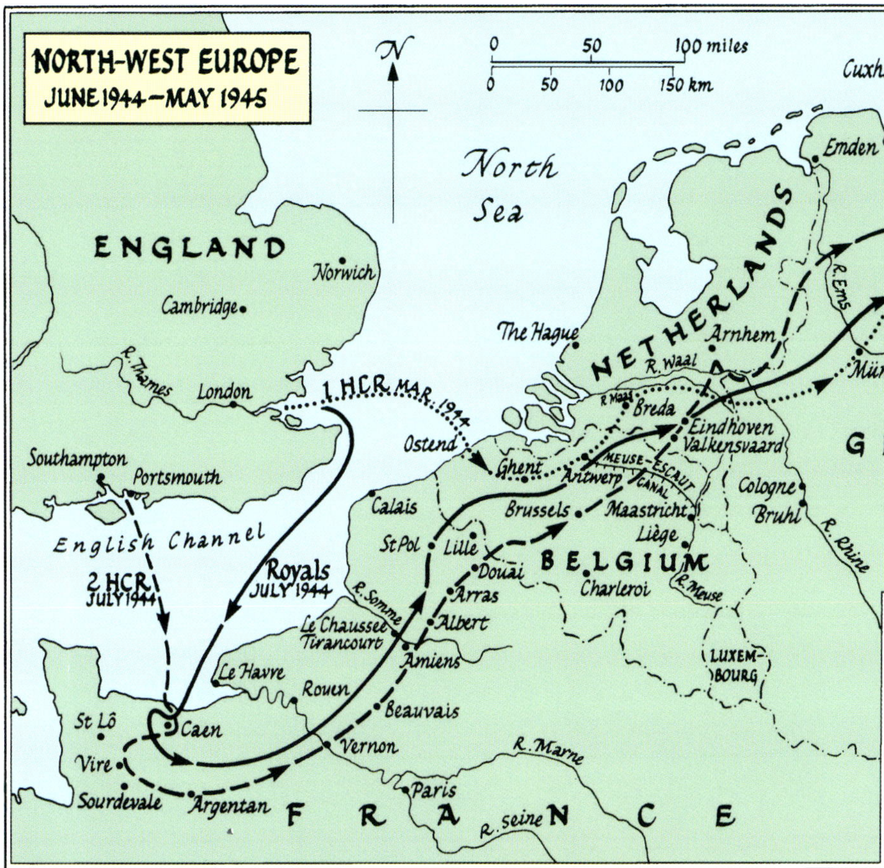
NORTH-WEST EUROPE
JUNE 1944–MAY 1945
0 50 100 miles
0 50 100 150 km
N
North Sea
ENGLAND
Norwich
Cambridge
R. Thames
London
Southampton
Portsmouth
English Channel
2 HCR JULY 1944
Royals JULY 1944
1 HCR MAR. 1944
Ostend
Ghent
Antwerp
MEUSE-ESCAUT CANAL
Calais
St Pol
Lille
Douai
Arras
Albert
R. Somme
Le Chaussee Tirancourt
Amiens
Le Havre
Rouen
Beauvais
Vernon
St Lô
Caen
Vire
Sourdevale
Argentan
Paris
R. Seine
R. Marne
FRANCE
The Hague
NETHERLANDS
R. Waal
R. Maas
Breda
Eindhoven
Valkensvaard
Arnhem
Brussels
Maastricht
Liège
BELGIUM
Charleroi
R. Meuse
LUXEMBOURG
Cologne
Bruhl
R. Rhine
R. Ems
Münster
Osnabrück
R. Weser
Hanover
Harz Mountains
GERMANY
Emden
Bremen
Stade
Cuxhaven
Hamburg
R. Elbe
Lübeck
SCHLESWIG HOLSTEIN
1 HCR
2 HCR
Royals

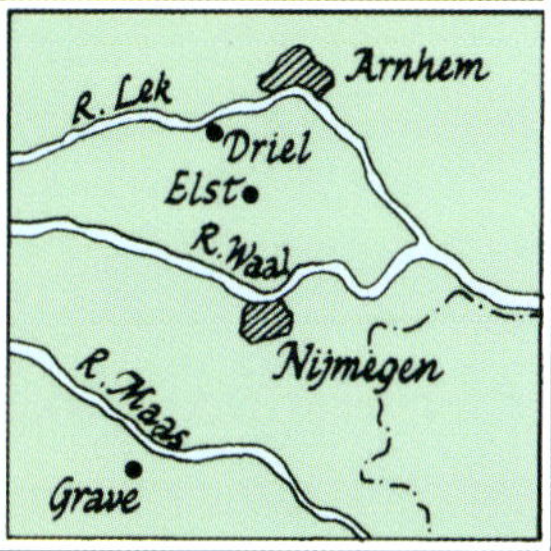
Arnhem
R. Lek
Driel
Elst
R. Waal
Nijmegen
R. Maas
Grave

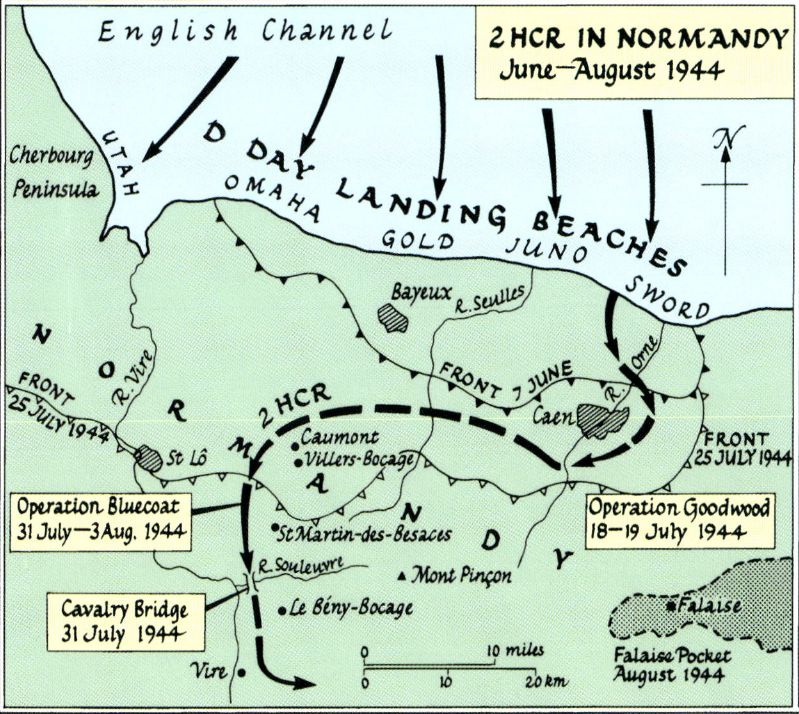
2 HCR IN NORMANDY
June–August 1944
English Channel
Cherbourg Peninsula
UTAH
D DAY LANDING BEACHES
OMAHA
GOLD
JUNO
SWORD
N
Bayeux
R. Seulles
R. Orne
Caen
FRONT 7 JUNE
FRONT 25 JULY 1944
R. Vire
NORMANDY
2 HCR
St Lô
Caumont
Villers-Bocage
FRONT 25 JULY 1944
Operation Bluecoat 31 July–3 Aug. 1944
Operation Goodwood 18–19 July 1944
St Martin-des-Besaces
R. Souleuvre
Mont Pinçon
Le Bény-Bocage
Falaise
Cavalry Bridge 31 July 1944
Falaise Pocket August 1944
Vire
0 10 miles
0 10 20 km

ITALY
1943–45
0 100 200 miles
0 100 200 300 km
N
La Spezia
Gothic Line
Apennine Mts
R. Arno
Florence
Arezzo
Pesaro
Fano
L. Trasimeno
Perugia
Rome
Anzio
Monte Cassino
R. Sangri
Termoli
Manfredonia Peninsula
Foggia
Bari
Naples
Salerno
Taranto
Straits of Messina
Calabria
Palermo
SICILY
Catania

British column held up on the Vire to Caen Road following D Day. This long straight stretch was a nightmare for the leading scout cars until the Household Cavalry penetrated the line east of Le Bény-Bocage.

The Royals sticking maps together after a heavy downpour of rain near Lisieux.

General Montgomery at Sourdevalle on 16 August 1944. Having visited the 2 HCR's infantry positions on the Burcy ridge, he explained the latest situation to Colonel Henry, some of his officers, and men of the Royal Northumberland Fusiliers.

were used for traffic control – an important, though unglamorous job – as the tanks rumbled over the Orne bridges, and for liaison. Sadly, they still took casualties, with six members of the regiment being the first killed, all from artillery or German air attack.

The regiment now retired to the villages between Caen and Bayeux to await Montgomery's next attempt to break out and the start of the war of movement he so desperately sought. They immediately took to the battered Norman countryside which, they felt, 'with its prolific cider orchards and waving cornfields, was the last place in the world to be created for war, and the draped coils of signal wire wrapped round the telegraph poles, the discarded petrol tins and empty shell cases all struck a note of horrible incongruity'.[11] They were well looked after by the locals and Camembert and Calvados were plentiful. By the end of July General Dempsey, commanding the British 2nd Army in Montgomery's army group, was ready to launch his second attempt to break out, Operation Bluecoat. His main effort was planned with XXX Corps attacking south towards Villers-Bocage and Mont Pinçon. At the same time VIII and XII Corps would try to break out in the west, south of Caumont, trying to establish crossings over the Rivers Vire and Souleuvre while protecting XXX Corps' flank. 2 HCR were transferred for the operation to Major General Pip Roberts' 11th Armoured Division in VIII Corps, and, packing up their bivouacs in the comfortable farms, drove west in baking hot weather and clouds of dust to their assembly areas. The VIII Corps' attack was launched from Caumont towards St-Martin-des-Besaces on 30 July by the 15th Scottish Division, and parts of the Guards' and 11th Armoured Divisions, but did not get very far. German resistance was determined. XXX Corps, further east, made similarly slow progress, so that by the morning of 31 July it looked very much as if the second British attempt to break out would end in failure as well.

It was at this point that Lieutenant Dickie Powle managed to get a radio message through to regimental headquarters to advise that he had seized an intact bridge over the Souleuvre and was observing it. He had left the area around St-Martin-des-Besaces early that morning and had soon lost one of his armoured cars which got stuck in one of the narrow lanes of the hedgerow country of the *bocage*, and its accompanying scout car which got stuck behind it. Pressing on with just two cars, he found a gap in the German lines, through which he slipped. He was soon in the Forêt l'Evêque, and 6 miles behind enemy lines he found the bridge, guarded by a solitary sentry who was quickly and silently dispatched by Trooper Read. If he could be quickly reinforced there was an opportunity to get forces across the Souleuvre, swing behind the Germans around Le Bény-Bocage and unhinge their defence. The 11th Armoured Division reacted quickly, sending a brigade down the same route – which, it transpired, was a German divisional boundary that poor planning had left uncovered – within six hours, followed by most of the 11th Armoured Division. The seizure of Cavalry Bridge, as it came to be called, was 'unquestionably a turning point in the campaign in France', says the official history of the 11th Armoured Division,[12] and it made 2 HCR's name. All Colonel Henry's training was paying off and 'Souleuvre' is now a battle honour of The Blues and Royals.

For the next two weeks 2 HCR were to be continually in action around Le Bény-Bocage and Burcy as VIII Corps battled south to close the western end of what would become the Falaise Pocket, where Montgomery intended to trap and the destroy the German forces in western France. For a period they had to emulate 1 HCR, fighting as infantry. Montgomery came to visit them, clearly tickled that the Household Cavalry should be fighting on their feet. The first person he spoke to was Lieutenant Peake, who was occupying an old Irish Guards' trench at Sourdevale. 'How do you like being infantry?' he asked. 'I hate it, sir,' replied Peake, 'and the sooner I am allowed to get back to my armoured cars, for which we have been trained, the better.'[13] It was clearly not the answer the Field Marshal had been expecting. In fact his first visit to 2 HCR on Salisbury Plain had gone little better. He had greeted Colonel Henry rather superciliously as he approached with the comment 'What have we here?' to which Colonel Henry quite logically replied 'The Household Cavalry, sir.' Montgomery also disliked the fact that the Household Cavalry, despite careful briefing by his staff, refused to rush up and gather around his car as he arrived and as the media image required, and would only move when ordered so to do by their non-commissioned officers. It was nearly the end of the war and the only man from our regiments who had so far made a good impression on him was Jack Hamilton-Russell with his peahen.

Yet unlike their forebears in France a quarter of a century before, 2 HCR felt completely confident in their chain of command from Colonel Henry upwards, and whilst they did not much warm to Montgomery's public persona, they did trust him. Morale throughout was remarkably high, as noted by Lieutenant Johnny Seyfried, who served in 2 HCR from Normandy until the end of the war, and doubts such as those that so assailed Morgan Crofton and his contemporaries were non-existent. Men who fought with 2 HCR recount it as a formative experience. Seyfried felt it was one of the happiest periods of his life, sharing a sense of common purpose and working in an organization which they all thought truly excellent. Each troop of ten men was a cohesive unit, where the enforced intimacy of an armoured car meant they got to know one another as well as The Royals had done in the desert. They were usually on their own, either in squadron or troop groups, and niceties such as uniform – the awful thick serge battle dress – were quickly discarded. Seyfried spent the whole summer in a V-neck sweater, army trousers, brown shoes and a silk scarf to keep out the ubiquitous dust. They were also, by this stage in the war, well administered, so they did not want for petrol, ammunition or, importantly for them, rations, though the packs always arrived with the tinned fruit salad – the most popular item – removed, which regimental headquarters was accused of stealing. There was a canteen system, operated by the NAAFI, and they could get beer and spirits, unlike the Americans who were dry; Seyfried managed to swap a bottle of whisky for a US Army jeep, which he kept until well after the war.

They were certainly nervous, especially as they turned their engines in the half-light of dawn wondering what the day would bring. Infantrymen they passed said they would not want their role for anything, dangerously exposed on their own in front of a division, but they felt they had a much better deal than the infantry. Casualties – an accepted part of life, bad luck if they happened but not something to dwell on – were, nevertheless, severe, with seventy-eight killed between the regiment's founding and the end of the war; of these twenty-three were accidents. They particularly hated the close *bocage* country with its narrow lanes and high hedges in which the Germans hid ambush groups. There was no room to manoeuvre and if caught it was impossible to get away. They also hated working for those infantry divisions who tried to use them as light tanks, much preferring to be with the Guards or the 11th Armoured, or, especially, with XXX Corps. They rarely used their weapons, the eye and the radio being their main assets, and if engaged by the Germans would immediately discharge the smoke grenades attached to the outside of their cars and try to pull back. They became experts at calling for artillery fire and aircraft support, the latter provided through the RAF detachment that travelled with each squadron. Mines were a particular threat, which they got round to some extent by putting sand bags on the floor of their cars, although by the middle of August they had lost over forty vehicles to them. They felt they could smell the Germans, and many car commanders maintain that they owe their lives to pausing and sniffing the air; Seyfried thought it was a mixture of their gun oil, synthetic petrol and rations. They soon got used to some pretty horrible sights, although what upset them particularly was the stench of animal carcasses. The German army was still largely dependent on horses for transport and around Falaise their bodies were everywhere, often being hacked at by the local French for meat.

German resistance in Normandy collapsed at Falaise, and as their defeated troops streamed back across France it was 2 HCR, working now directly under Lieutenant General Sir Brian Horrocks, commanding XXX Corps, and The Royals, who had landed in late July, who led the pursuit. There was no front line as such and the roads were a mass of French refugees, German stragglers and advancing Allies. It was a chaotic, exciting and confusing time. At 1 a.m. on 31 August, Horrocks asked 2 HCR to seize three bridges over the Somme behind which he was afraid the Germans were making a stand. 'The ensuing advance,' in Horrocks' own words

> must have been a nightmare; the men were already tired before they started, it was pouring with rain, and the roads were blocked with every

sort of traffic including German tanks. Nevertheless the leading troops, commanded by Groenix van Zoelen, Rupert Buchanan-Jardine and Tom Hanbury on the right and Peake on the left pushed on relentlessly and the seemingly impossible was achieved – the bridges were all captured intact.[14]

They were never quite sure when they entered towns whether they would be greeted as liberators or fired on by the SS, which is what happened to Lieutenant Bradstock and his troop of Royals when they entered La Chaussée-Tirancourt and found themselves instantly surrounded. Withdrawing to the central square, they resorted to firing their Sten guns from their turrets, and when they finally managed to break out they left twenty dead fanatics lying on the cobbles.

On the evening of 2 September they had reached Douai, and Major General Alan Adair, commanding the Guards' Armoured Division, announced his intention to liberate Brussels the next day. Things were going extraordinarily well and it appeared that German resistance was collapsing. Leaving early in the morning, 2 HCR crossed the battlefields of the First World War, covering in twenty minutes the distance it had taken their forebears four years. By the evening Lance Corporal of Horse Dewar, from Aberdeen, and Trooper Ayles, from London's Walworth Road, were the first Allied troops into the centre of Brussels. As the rest of the regiment arrived it seemed the entire population was out on the streets offering every kind of hospitality. Seyfried told his driver over the intercom that now was the time for a breakdown; unfortunately he was, by mistake, broadcasting on the regimental net and Arthur Collins, the Adjutant, heard his message and quickly curtailed his plans for a comfortable night.

The fall of Brussels took the Germans by surprise and Horrocks' instinct was that the next stage would not be quite so easy. He needed to know the German positions up on the Belgian/Dutch border, particularly along the Meuse–Escaut Canal, so that he could plan what to do next. No Allied troops had yet entered Holland, so he asked 2 HCR to have a look. He knew it was a risky request, and Rupert Buchanan-Jardine, whose troop were given the task, decided that 'the only possibility of getting through the German positions was to drive down the main road which ran through the centre of their line, trusting to surprise to get him through'.[15] Taking only two scout cars, Buchanan-Jardine set off.

> It seems incredible now but this daring manoeuvre succeeded. The two scout cars drove straight through the German line, then sent back valuable reports of the situation in the rear, and subsequently returned the way they had come. By the time they got back everything on the outside of the cars was punctured and broken by small arms fire.

The German garrison in Valkenswaard, where Buchanan-Jardine had stopped, were so infuriated that the local Dutch had talked to him that they shot three of them in revenge.

What Buchanan-Jardine's daring reconnaissance had told Horrocks was that the Germans were determined to defend Holland and that the next stage would be more difficult. Operation Market Garden was consequently planned to try to prevent a long and bloody slog through Holland. Montgomery has been heavily criticized for Market Garden but its concept was a very good one. The idea was to seize the bridges over the three big rivers that divide Holland – the Waal, the Maas and the Rhine – with airborne troops, drive XXX Corps forward to link up with them and effectively cut through to the north German plain – ideal ground for the Allies' multitude of armour – and obviate the need for a long slog though the Ruhr. Had it worked, it is entirely possible that it could have ended the war in 1944 and that the post-war map of Europe would have been very different. The problem came in the execution, and, in particular, through a misapprehension of the strength of German defences and the nature of the terrain that left XXX Corps with no room to manoeuvre. The plan was that US airborne troops would drop at Grave and Nijmegen to secure the bridges over the Maas and Waal; the Polish Airborne Brigade would then drop at Elst, between Nijmegen and Arnhem, whilst the British 1st Airborne Division dropped at Arnhem to seize the bridge over the Rhine. Both 2 HCR and The Royals were heavily involved in the ensuing operations, which started on 17 September. The Guards' Armoured Division did not manage to take the Nijmegen Bridge until 21 September, by which time the airborne troops had already been holding out at Arnhem for four days. Two troops of 'C' Squadron of 2 HCR managed to get across the Waal that day, and, using a thick morning fog, steal past the waiting German panzers. Captain Wrottesley managed to link up with the Poles and Lieutenant Young reached Driel, just across the Rhine from Arnhem, but two troops of armoured cars did not constitute a relief and there was little they could do on their own. Young's experience at Driel was, however, instructive. While trying to fight off the attentions of the major part of a panzer division, he found himself the focal point for seemingly every senior officer in the 2nd Army. The Commander Royal Artillery wanted to know what effect his guns were having, whilst the senior Royal Engineer had endless questions from the state of the bank approaches to a detailed recce of every possible ferry site. Young drew the line when he was asked to measure the gap in the railway bridge, which was then being overlooked by two panzer divisions.

Arnhem was only a partial failure. Admittedly, it had failed to open the back door into Germany, but it had given the Allies control of large parts of Holland. They now needed to pause and to consolidate, both to clear the remaining resistance and to open Antwerp as a supply base, given that currently their supplies were still coming forward from Normandy. Consequently both 2 HCR and The Royals were now put on the defensive, watching the line of the River Maas, or Meuse, and the German border, occupying, at one stage, a section from just south of Maastricht right down through Liège and Huy to Charleroi, places with which so many of their forbears would have been very familiar. It lasted longer than they expected, and the war of movement did not get underway again until the following spring. In the interim, 2 HCR were involved in the preparations to counter Hitler's final offensive in the west in December 1944, the so-called Battle of the Bulge, should he succeed in breaking through towards Antwerp. Luckily he did not.

In February and March 1945 they had to wait while the infantry fought the hard battles of the Reichswald, but by late March they were on the move again and all looking forward to a swift end to the war. It was at this stage that 1 HCR landed in Ostend, and moved through Ghent and Breda to take control of a section of the Meuse, watching over the German border. Before they had left England the aged Lord Birdwood, Colonel of The Blues, had been to say goodbye to them. He had asked whether a group of officers could be assembled in the mess so that he could give them a few words of advice before they sailed. Even in 1945 Birdwood was still a legend, a much-respected soldier, one of the few who had made a success of high command in the First World War, and famous for his command of the Anzac Corps at Gallipoli where he had managed to pull off their withdrawal in the face of the cream of the Turkish army. He had also proved a conscientious and popular Gold Stick, who cared deeply about the regiment. The officers consequently awaited his words of wisdom attentively. There were, he said, only three things they had to remember in combat. These were his cardinal points and he had stood by them all through his career. They were easy to remember as they all began with 'c'. The first was obvious enough – it was 'cunning'. The officers all diligently scribbled 'cunning' into their pads. The second cardinal point was 'concealment', but by far the most important was the third. If they forgot this, his third 'c', then they were as good as dead. The officers waited with pencils poised. 'I must emphasize,' Birdwood continued in his high-pitched voice, 'that if you forget my third and most important "c" you will most certainly fail.' There followed an uncomfortably long dramatic pause. 'Oh dear!' he finally said, 'I've completely forgotten what it was. Never mind, let's go and have lunch!'

Lieutenant Roy Redgrave had just joined the regiment from Sandhurst. He had originally hoped to join 2 HCR, 'which had just completed a magnificent dash from the French frontier into Brussels and were in my opinion the finest reconnaissance regiment in the Army'.[16] In fact he was posted to 1 HCR, which he had heard were 'a bunch of elderly pre-war soldiers who had lived in a different world and wished they still had horses . . . It was as if a long forgotten Roman legion had at last returned from a distant province.' He very soon realized that he was mistaken, and came to value 1 HCR's 'practical experience, versatility and team spirit' and the extraordinarily high quality of their soldiers,

A Guards Armoured Division vehicle exploding after being hit during Operation Market Garden, September 1944.

The liberation of Denmark. The Royals were sent there to supervise the German surrender. They stayed for six months and were very well looked after by the relieved and hospitable Danes.

over sixty of whom would be given commissions in other regiments before the end of the war. His first assignment was to take over a section of the line along the river from a regiment whose parting words to him were 'Don't show yourselves much by day because their artillery fire can be quite accurate, and do watch out for mines', a point made blatantly obvious by the bloated bodies of two cows in a nearby orchard. German attacks had been frequent, and he found the continual alertness exhausting. 'The nights became a strain as we peered into the mist and listened out for the grating of a boat's keel on the shore and the squelch of a boot in the mud.'[17]

After ten days on the Meuse, 1 HCR crossed the Rhine into Germany. The Royals, who had provided bank control for the main assault crossings on 23 March, had gone on ahead, as had 2 HCR who were now advancing deep into northern Germany. Although there was an air of imminent victory, there were still casualties caused by pockets of SS and, bizarrely, Hitler Youth, some of those captured being as young as ten. In the last six weeks fifteen members of 1 HCR were killed or wounded in action, and in 2 HCR, twenty-seven wounded and eight killed. A bazooka hit Redgrave's armoured car on 1 May near Stade just south of the Elbe. Whilst Redgrave himself was wounded, his driver was killed and his operator, Corporal Smith, who had been in the regiment since the desert, was severely wounded. Redgrave rescued him from his turret under fire and was awarded a Military Cross. It was a muddling time, with many conflicting emotions, summed up by an officer in 2 HCR who wrote that 'There was no doubt that the chatter of machine guns, sudden head on encounters, the cheering crowds of liberated towns, the orders and counter orders all tended to build up a nervous exhilaration quite hard to define yet almost impossible to suppress.'[18] They did not feel any particular antagonism to the German population as a whole, and at times even felt quite sorry for what the Nazis had done to them. 'In this village where we now are the war casualties so far have been 104 killed against 33 in the last war,' wrote Colonel Henry on 3 May. However, they were less than sympathetic to the odd groups who still held out, even when it was clear that the war was over. A group of Hitler Youth who killed Corporal Allen of 1 HCR on the penultimate day of the war, 3 May, received 'short shrift'.

Between 4 and 7 May the Germans surrendered, and VE day was 8 May. 'There were no scenes of wild rejoicing' in the regiments although there were 'mild celebrations in all the messes'.[19] It took a long time for the news to sink in and, much as in 1918, people wondered what would happen next. The war had been their life, for many of them their entire adult life. 2 HCR were amused to see that the *feu de joie* fired by their divisional artillery, and carefully targeted into the middle of the Elbe estuary, bracketed a German cargo vessel moored there by the Royal Navy.

1 and 2 HCR ended the war next door to each other in the flat country on the south of the Elbe estuary not far from Cuxhaven. 1 HCR were soon moved

to Bremen to assist in rounding up German prisoners, and later down to the Harz Mountains with their headquarters at Goslar. 2 HCR were ordered to supervise the surrender of the 7th German Parachute Division near Cuxhaven. That accomplished, they were moved back south-west to Brühl, just outside Cologne, driving en route through the rubble of the Ruhr. The Royals were told to concentrate near Lübeck, prior to being sent to supervise the surrender in Denmark. They were to stay there for six months, very well looked after by the relieved and hospitable Danes, and with regimental headquarters ensconced in a comfortable country house, before moving south into Schleswig-Holstein where they were put into ex-German barracks at Eutin. The frustrations of 1940 and 1941 now seemed very far away, and in the last year of the war both the Household Cavalry and The Royals had distinguished themselves as large, modern reconnaissance regiments at the centre of the most demanding operation mounted by the British army. They were also experienced in armoured warfare, which it was already clear would form the core of the West's defence against Russia. The trick would now be to maintain that position.

Chapter Twenty-One

WITHDRAWAL FROM EMPIRE

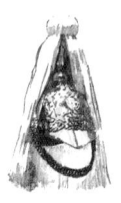

Work had been going on since 1943, when Andrew Ferguson had been appointed to the new position of 'Lieutenant Colonel Commanding the Household Cavalry', to decide on the post-war structure of the Household Cavalry. Of the two Gold Sticks, Lord Athlone, the former Prince Alexander of Teck, was a much-liked officer who had served with the 2nd Life Guards throughout the First World War, and who renounced his German titles in 1917. His daughter, May, was married to Colonel Henry. Athlone was, however, now Governor General of Canada in Ottawa, whilst Lord Birdwood was eighty and living in retirement at Hampton Court. The bulk of the work therefore fell to Ferguson, who held an initial meeting with the commanding officers in the Turf Club in October 1943 where it was agreed the main principle must be that the Household Cavalry were operational regiments who also did ceremonial rather than ceremonial regiments who occasionally sent a composite regiment to war. They therefore decided to re-examine their role from scratch and see what solutions that study came up with.[1] The King was consulted first, and made it absolutely clear that he required both mounted ceremonial to restart after the war and to have a Household Cavalry regiment in Windsor. Sir George Arthur, the venerable Household Cavalry historian who was generally regarded as the keeper of the Household Cavalry's historical conscience, was then asked to prepare a paper on the roles that the Household Cavalry should perform. Arthur, it will be remembered, had fought at Kassassin. Since then he had filled a number of important appointments, including acting as Military Secretary to Kitchener when he was Secretary of State for War from 1914 until 1916, but he was now a little elderly although, as always, a great optimist. His central point was that Queen Victoria had harmed her reputation by not being seen enough in public with a Household Cavalry escort, and to avoid this happening again he recommended a comprehensive increase in mounted ceremonial, a premise he based on the possibly slightly dubious assumption that 'the British taxpayer is a cheerful giver and never more so than when he is subscribing to the expenses of the monarchy'.[2]

In the end it came down to two basic options: either one regiment would stay on armoured cars and one on horses or else there would be two armoured car regiments, with each regiment providing one squadron, in other words about 100 soldiers, to perform ceremonial duties in a mixed regiment in London. Ferguson, a Life Guard, who favoured the second option, then put it to the King before the likes of Colonel Henry and The Blues had thought about it, which led to a prolonged and slightly acrimonious correspondence between Hampton Court, Ottawa and 2 HCR, with Colonel Henry saying that Ferguson's position was only temporary and he should not be making Household Cavalry policy. But ultimately Ferguson's solution was adopted, with his post as Commander of the Household Cavalry being permanently established and upgraded to Colonel, though always to be known, most confusingly, as 'Lieutenant Colonel Commanding the Household Cavalry'. He was also to take on permanently the duties of Silver Stick and command of the ceremonial regiment, which before the war had of course been filled by the commanding officer of whichever regiment had been in London. Colonel Henry ultimately calmed down, accepting this as the best solution, and in 1946 he actually took on Ferguson's old job. But the key change was that the Household Cavalry would now have two operational regiments which would be fully equipped and deployed in peacetime, with ceremonial being provided by a smaller regiment in London, called the Household Cavalry Mounted Regiment, with a squadron apiece of Life Guards and Blues. Regular soldiers would go first to mounted duty in London and then on to their respective regiment, whilst conscripts would go direct. This was the second great change in the Household Cavalry's history, just as significant as that of 1788 when the private gentlemen were replaced by regulars, and it was to serve monarchy, the nation and the regiments themselves very well indeed for the next half-century.

All this high politics meant that in late 1945 a group of officers was sent back to London to generate two mounted squadrons in Knightsbridge to restart the King's Life Guard. Johnny Seyfried – one of those sent to The Blues' squadron – recalls Knightsbridge Barracks as being rather like a museum. On his first walk round he found two old soldiers who had spent the whole war sharpening the operational swords for when they were needed in the final push into Germany. Some horses were brought back from Melton Mowbray and a further thirty Dutch Blacks were presented by Queen Wilhelmina of the Netherlands, just as William III had done; these were 'very heavy common horses . . . and very uncomfortable to ride'.[3] Initially the Guard was mounted wearing khaki, but in September 1947 the pre-war ceremonial dress was reintroduced, being first worn for the wedding of the present Queen and the Duke of Edinburgh. In 1950 the King, alarmed at talk of his Household Cavalry regiments being placed under the Army's Director of the Royal Armoured Corps, expressed his desire for them to be incorporated with the Brigade of Guards to form a 'Household Division', which was to be commanded by the

The first King's Life Guard after the war. It was mounted in khaki until September 1947.

A touch of galmour in post-war Germany – the Dortmund Military tattoo in 1947, with Valerian Wellesley, later Duke of Wellington, and the musical ride performing for the first time since the war.

Major General in London from the Household Cavalry's spiritual home in the Horse Guards building. In practice this arrangement only applied to ceremonial, administrative and regimental issues as the two operational regiments would obviously answer to whoever commanded the theatre where they were deployed, and, to start with, this was firmly in Germany.

In June 1945 the Guards' Armoured Division was disbanded, and 1 and 2 HCR were split up and recast. 1 HCR, still at Goslar in the Harz Mountains, on the new border between East and West Germany, became The Life Guards and 2 HCR, at Brühl, became The Blues. It was an unhappy time. Many had to say goodbye to friends they had served with for six years, indeed the only friends that many of them had in the regiments, for only the more senior officers and non-commissioned officers had pre-war service. There was also a sense of anticlimax after the relief at the end of the war, and it was apparent that rather than going home to parades and medals, the regiments would have to serve on as part of the Army of Occupation in a country largely destroyed, which offered little by way of entertainment or relaxation. About half the soldiers in both regiments were still conscripts waiting to be demobilized – replaced in 1947 by National Servicemen – the difference being only in timing and terminology. The old regulars did not like National Service, feeling that the lack of continuity made the regiments inflexible and high standards difficult to achieve. Many National Servicemen were distinctly unenthusiastic – their training had been repetitive and over-long – and they were also unhappy at being paid so much less than their regular counterparts. Roy Redgrave found service at this time depressing. 'I soon realized that the daily routine of an occupation army was going to be no fun at all. There were far too many parades and petty regulations, with countless inspections of vehicles, equipment and stores', and, he complained, 'the officers' mess was dominated by a number of bored, hard-drinking, gambling officers.' Only those officers over twenty-five and soldiers over twenty-one were allowed to have their wives with them, and to cap it all the officers who could not ride – and in the wartime regiment there were a lot – were all made to do a purgatorial equitation course.

The Royals were at Wolfenbüttel, near The Life Guards, until 1950. Many of their wartime officers were now leaving. The eccentric Wintle, whom we last heard of in India in the mid-1930s, had been got rid of much earlier. He had found a novel way of annoying his brother officers at that time by sending regular Christmas cards to their ex-Colonel-in-Chief, Kaiser Wilhelm, in exile in Holland, and then displaying those the Kaiser sent in return prominently in the mess. In 1940 he had lost a lot of equipment in Palestine, which he compounded by getting heavily into debt, committing the heinous crime of owing the Regimental Polo Fund £100. In December 1940 he took the opportunity of mechanization to resign, much to Colonel Heyworth's relief, asserting that he was too old to retrain. But they had certainly not heard the last of him. In a bid to contribute to the war effort he tried to commandeer an aeroplane

The Queen's Coronation 1953 – the rehearsal (*above*) and the day itself (*below*).

Paul Maze painting the Trooping the Colour on a stand especially constructed for the purpose. Shown below is a study for the final painting.

to fly to France, where he had been an instructor at the French staff college, thinking that he could help the Resistance. He was put in the Tower of London as a result, which appealed to his romantic English instincts, and was court-martialled, surprising the Judge Advocate by suggesting they kissed and made up. After his release he made it to France, where he was promptly incarcerated by the Vichy regime in Toulon and kept in solitary confinement for thirteen months. During this period he struck up a very good relationship with his guard, Molia, who wanted to marry but could not get time off to visit and propose to his intended, since Wintle refused to give an undertaking not to escape. When he heard about his predicament, Wintle agreed a parole for a short period so that Molia could try his luck, but made him promise not to take no for an answer, to marry by Saturday and be back by Sunday. Molia agreed, and was married and back on time. Wintle later claimed to have been the only wartime prisoner who gave his gaolers time off. Released from France, he continued to court controversy in London after the war, debagging a solicitor who opposed him in the case of his sister's will, and was arrested for the third time. He became something of a national character in the 1950s, broadcasting radio interviews and writing for the *Evening Standard*, the original Colonel Blimp. He stayed in touch with Spike Mays, who sang at his funeral.

Despite the gloom, matters were no worse than those suffered by any other regiment in Germany at the time. The key achievement of the Ferguson plan was that for the first time there were now two operational Household Cavalry regiments stationed overseas in peacetime, and as the withdrawal from Empire – which we will discuss below – gathered pace, they were given more exciting jobs. The Life Guards moved to Berlin in March 1946 and later that year to Egypt, where they were some of the last troops out of Cairo when, under pressure from Egyptian nationalists, the British pulled out of the capital and Alexandria, although by the provisions of the Anglo-Egyptian Treaty of 1936 Britain still had the right to maintain defence forces in the Suez Canal Zone. They then spent a year in the Canal Zone and Palestine helping to administer the ill-fated British mandate to facilitate a Jewish homeland, in place since the 1920s. They helped the Palestinian police keep the peace between Arabs and Zionists – a difficult and unrewarding role which they only relinquished in May 1948 as the mandate expired – and were bombed by the Egyptian air force, supporting the Palestinian Arabs, as they left for Windsor. Two years later, in 1950, The Royals followed them to the Canal Zone, where they were to spend four years, protecting it from insurgent attacks, a familiar life to those who could remember Palestine in 1938. The Life Guards were to return to the Canal Zone again in 1954, and had a squadron in reserve for the Suez operation of 1956, although it was never actually deployed.

Attention in the mid-1950s was switched to Cyprus, still controlled by Britain, where the Greek-backed resistance movement, EOKA, led by Archbishop Makarios and an ex-Greek Army colonel called Grivas, was threatening

The Blues departing for Cyprus in 1956, to quell a rebellion against British rule lead by Archbishop Makarios.

This group picture was taken in 1956 at Government House in Cyprus. In the front row (left to right) are Lady Dorothea Head, Field Marshal Sir John Harding (Governor of Cyprus, later to become Colonel of the Life Guards), Lady Harding and Sir Antony Head (Secretary of State for War). Also about to enjoy a game of croquet are Valerian Wellesley and his wife, standing behind Lady Harding who that morning had discovered a bomb under her bed.

Trooper Grice on jungle patrol in Borneo.

Five regiments represented in a Borneo patrol in the Sungai Plieran area near the Usun Apau plateau, including Trooper Hodgson of The Life Guards in the front on the left and Captain Lord Patrick Beresford on the right.

British rule. The Life Guards first sent a squadron there in 1955, but from 1956 until 1959 The Blues were deployed as a regiment and found themselves fully committed in combating EOKA. They took over a motley collection of old Daimlers on arrival, but were soon equipped with the new four-wheeled, two-man Ferret scout cars, and deployed with squadrons in Nicosia, Famagusta and Limassol. It was a campaign with some notable successes against Grivas's terrorists, but also some sad losses. The Regimental Medical Officer, Captain Gordon Wilson, was murdered soon after arrival, as he was visiting families in Nicosia. In 1958 the campaign intensified after talks broke down. A troop of The Blues was attempting to arrest an EOKA man in a village when the troop leader's Ferret scout car was attacked by a youth throwing stones. The troop leader shot him, and a ricochet from his gun also killed a woman. Grivas threatened revenge, and three days later Cornet Stephen Fox Strangways and Trooper Procter, both National Servicemen, were shot in the back in Famagusta. By 1959 The Blues were as involved in preventing clashes between the Greek and Turkish Cypriots as they were in suppressing EOKA. That year 'A' Squadron noticed that EOKA men were escaping from villages as all the dogs barked in warning of their approach. Their solution was to hire donkeys – unworthy of Cypriot dogs' attentions – which led to notable successes in arresting EOKA couriers. There were, sadly, further casualties. Trooper Birch was killed when his Ferret was blown off a mountain track by a mine, and Cornet Auberon Waugh, son of Evelyn, was wounded when he accidentally shot himself with the Browning machine gun on his Ferret. His Troop Corporal of Horse, Chudleigh, not being as well versed in British history as his Troop Leader, was a little surprised to be asked to kiss the semi-conscious Waugh. The Blues remained on the island until 1959, when the London–Zurich Agreement provided a political way forward, though many of their successors would return to continue their efforts to keep the peace between Greeks and Turks.

By the mid-1950s the British Government was also dealing with unrest in the Aden Protectorate, on the southern coast of the Arabian Peninsula, which, at its largest, consisted of twenty Arab tribal states. The neighbouring Yemenis, supported by Russia and Egypt, fomented trouble. The Life Guards were deployed there in 1958 and The Royals followed them in 1959. The squadrons escorted convoys from the port up country on what became well known as the Dhala Road. One squadron was detached to Sharjah on the Persian Gulf where it operated under the Sultan of Oman's forces, then commanded by David Smiley of The Blues. Although on first arrival Aden 'looked just like a penal settlement',[4] and there were few facilities for families, so many of the men were unaccompanied, both regiments found they enjoyed both the job and the country, particularly when they were away from the town of Aden itself.

From Aden The Royals went to Malaya, towards the end of the Communist insurgency that had sprung up after the Second World War. It was less stimulating than Aden, and most of their duties, like manning checkpoints and providing communications, were routine. They came under the command of the infamous General Walter Walker of the 17th Gurkha Division who was surprised to be told confidentially by the commanding officer, Philip Fielden – a distinguished amateur jockey who found these frequent tours to the world's trouble spots interrupted his racing – that horses came before soldiering; thereafter the unfortunate Royals were 'kicked all around Malaya' by the indignant Walker.

By the early 1960s, within fifteen years of the end of the war, all three regiments had therefore had plenty of interesting things to do, and the Household Cavalry had demonstrated that it could easily provide mounted ceremonial to a high standard while still providing two operational regiments. Demanding as these imperial excursions were, the majority of the British army remained committed to defending Central Europe from the threat of invasion from Communist Russia, and both the Household Cavalry and The Royals had to play their part in this somewhat intense theatre. Until 1962 all three regiments remained on armoured cars, first the old wartime Daimlers, which were then superseded by a combination of Ferret scout cars and large six-wheeled replacements for the Daimler armoured cars, called Saladins. From the early 1960s it was decided that all ex-cavalry regiments in the Royal Armoured Corps would alternate tours between tanks and armoured cars, and in 1963 The Royals duly converted to Centurions at Tidworth on Salisbury Plain before heading off with their new tanks to Germany. Once The Blues returned from Cyprus, the Household Cavalry, who remained on armoured cars, also established a pattern, with one regiment in Germany committed to the Central Front and one in Windsor as part of the strategic reserve who still had opportunities worldwide, with squadrons in the mid-1960s deploying to Hong Kong, Singapore, Borneo and Cyprus again, this time as part of the newly established United Nations force.

The people were also changing, and by the early 1960s there were only a few left who had seen wartime service. The last National Servicemen, who at times had constituted two-thirds of a regiment, left in 1962, which was a general relief both to them and to the regiments, who could now concentrate on training professional career soldiers as they had prior to 1939. National Service had led to some strange casting, with some who might normally have tried for commissions serving as troopers; The Blues had a McAlpine, from the building firm, as non-commissioned officer in charge of the post and a Rothschild as the bedding store man. Other National Servicemen included the comedian Tommy Cooper, and Jack Charlton, who captained the successful Blues' football team. The terms upon which people served also changed. Up until the end of the war the old Household Cavalry contract of eight years' regular service followed by four with the reserve, which had started in 1913, was still in force for regulars. Now soldiers served for twenty-two years, based on an average age, on joining, of eighteen. By the 1970s officers' education was standardized and they were all sent through Sandhurst. Lord Harding of Petherton, who had been Governor in Cyprus, had taken over as Gold Stick and Colonel of The Life Guards after Lord Athlone's death in 1957, and in 1965 Earl Mountbatten, in turn, succeeded him. Lord Birdwood of The Blues had died in 1951, and Sir Richard Howard Vyse took his place. In 1962 Field Marshal Sir Gerald Templer, under whom 1 HCR had served in Italy and who had recently distinguished himself as potentate in Malaya, replaced him.

The officers seemed to change rather less. There were those, often the non-commissioned officers, who complained that the rapid expansion in the size of the regiments in wartime meant officers no longer came with exclusively lengthy blood lines, large private incomes and landed estates, but then they never had done. There was certainly a period after about 1800 when many of them did, and up until 1939 a private income was necessary to pay for uniforms, mess bills and the expense of living in London or Windsor. Two things, however, did change from 1945. First, there were far more officers, the modern armoured car establishment being much bigger than that of the old horsed cavalry regiments and, second, the change in lifestyle, with the regiments mostly in Germany or on operations, meant that life was a lot cheaper and, unless people chose to pursue expensive pastimes, there was no actual need for them to do so. That did not necessarily mean that officers (or the non-commissioned officer in charge of the post or bedding store man for that matter) did not have private means. Many did, and Roy Redgrave complained that in Germany just after the war the mess was still dominated by those who could afford a lifestyle beyond the reach of those who lived off their pay.[5] Yet once life settled down to its peacetime routine there was no real appreciable difference between those serving in the Household Cavalry and the Royal Dragoons in 1950s and their pre-war forebears. The majority of officers were still public school- or university-educated and had some link to the regiment, many being the sons or grandsons of past officers. The difference was that, in common with many others in the austere years of the 1950s and early 1960s, what had counted as a private income before the war was now insufficient to live on, and possession of a landed estate could be argued to be something of a financial liability.

The greatest change was to come at the end of the 1960s. With the withdrawal from empire more or less complete by the mid-1960s, the Labour Government instigated a defence review, which recommended a reduction in the armed forces and a renewed concentration on the Central Front. It was clear once the review was complete that too many tank and armoured car regiments existed and reductions or amalgamations in the cavalry were necessary. Three regiments had never amalgamated, two of ours, The Blues and The Royals, and the Scots Greys. There was a strong argument that neither The Blues, as a Household Cavalry regiment, nor The Royals, as the most senior cavalry regiment of the line should amalgamate, but The Life Guards had already gone through that

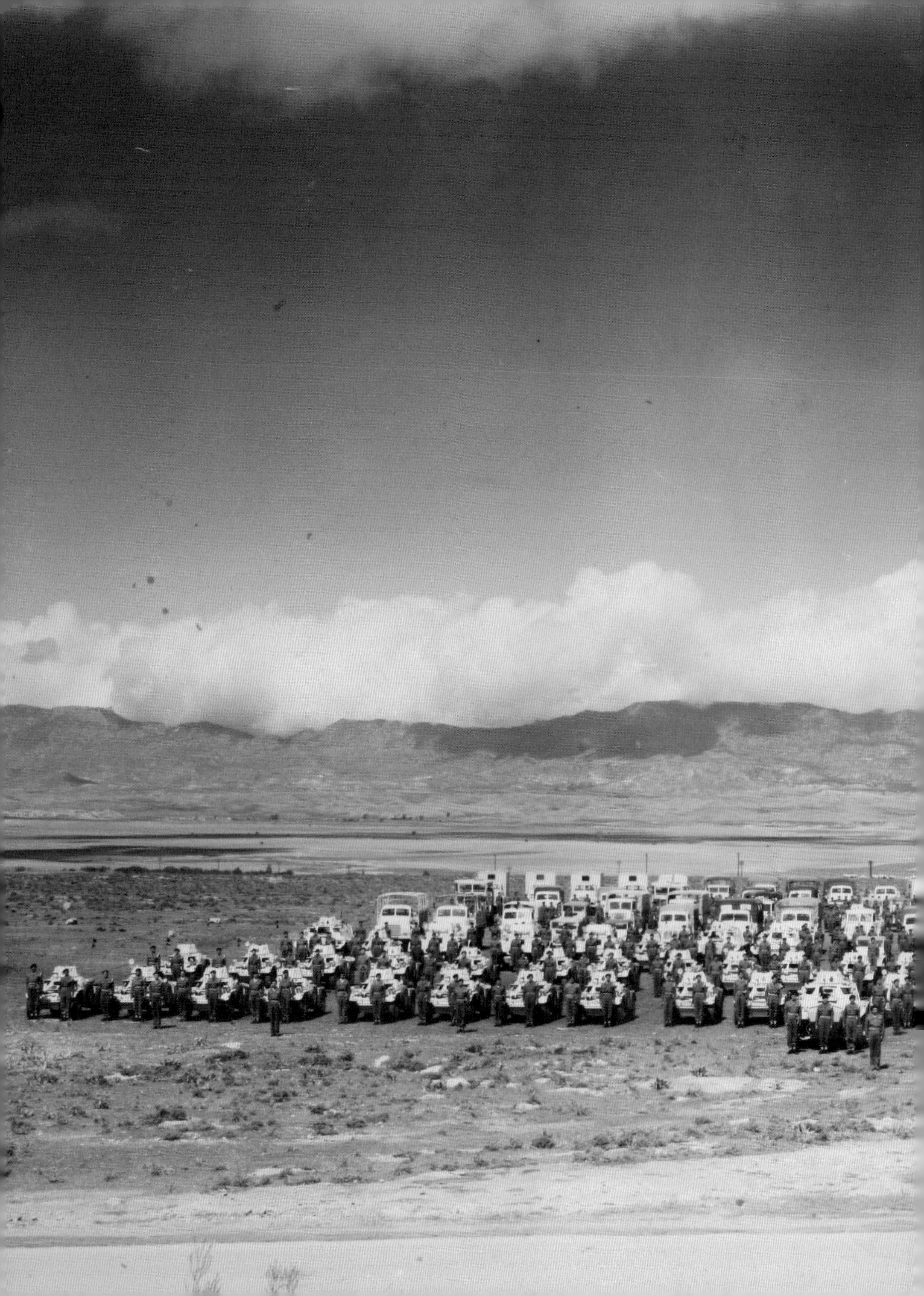

In the mid-1960s the Household Cavalry was deployed once more to Cyprus as part of the newly established United Nations force.

painful process in 1922 and army politics at that stage would not allow other regiments who had already amalgamated to do so again. Initially The Royals thought an amalgamation with their old comrades from the Union Brigade, the Scots Greys, would work well, but on reflection decided it would be difficult for such a very English regiment to become part Scottish. As both The Blues and The Royals had fought so often alongside one another, had the same ethos and outlook and had always got on very well together, it was decided that they would amalgamate and become The Blues and Royals as a regiment of the Household Cavalry. It was not an easy decision, particularly for The Royals who, as they were becoming part of the Household Cavalry, had to accept what was essentially Blues' uniform, and some of their soldiers did not relish the thought of riding horses in London when they had joined the army to fight in armoured vehicles. For The Blues there was a disadvantage in that they would have to convert to tanks, on which The Royals were already serving, and, in due course, so would The Life Guards when The Blues and Royals returned to Windsor and it was their turn to serve in Germany. The amalgamation duly took place in Detmold in West Germany on 29 March 1969, the salute being taken by Field Marshal Sir Gerald Templer who was to be the Colonel of the new regiment. Everyone put a brave face on it, but there was no disguising that many found the day difficult and sad. The new commanding officer, Lieutenant Colonel Richard Vickers, was an officer from the tank regiment and was brought in so that he could start the new regiment without prejudice, although he had already been commanding The Royals for a year.

In the space of 300 years the Household Cavalry had therefore progressed from being three troops of Life Guards to four, then to four troops with two troops of Horse Grenadiers. It had been reduced by two troops in the 1760s, and in 1788 it lost its private gentlemen and became two regular army regiments whose main role was to guard the monarch and carry out state ceremonial. This was the first great change in its history. In 1820 The Blues joined The Life Guards, making three Household Cavalry regiments until 1922 when the 1st and 2nd Life Guards amalgamated, which left two. By 1945 it was clear that ceremonial mounted duties could best be provided by a composite regiment in London, the Household Cavalry Mounted Regiment, allowing the two core regiments of The Life Guards and The Blues to take on a fully operational role in the army's order of battle. This was the second great change but one which in fact re-established the concept of Charles II's regiments as the core of the standing army. In 1969 the amalgamation of The Blues with The Royals did not alter this basic structure, which was to endure until 1992, when more defence cuts were to create one composite operational regiment from The Life Guards and The Blues and Royals. Today the Household Cavalry is therefore two regiments, The Life Guards and The Blues and Royals, organized in two composite units, one in London providing state ceremonial much as it has since 1945, and an operational regiment in Windsor.

Epilogue

THE HOUSEHOLD CAVALRY TODAY

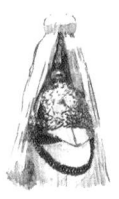

FOR NEARLY TWENTY-FIVE YEARS, from 1969 until 1992, The Life Guards and The Blues and Royals were to alternate every four years between serving on tanks in Germany and armoured cars at Windsor. For the majority of this period their station in Germany was the small and not unattractive Westphalian town of Detmold, between the Teutoburg Wald and the River Weser, which offered at least some opportunity of living in the community and was generally considered one of the better garrisons of the British Army of the Rhine, as the Army of Occupation had tactfully been restyled. While they were there the regiments were part of the British Corps dedicated to NATO to defend West Germany and, by implication, Western Europe, from any Soviet attack over the border from East Germany. The idea was that, as soon as there were any indications of Soviet aggression, they would move rapidly up to the border and deploy to pre-agreed positions hopefully before the Soviets came. Clear as this role may seem, and politically vital as it was, it was not altogether convincing for those involved. In the early days the new Chieftain tanks were unreliable, and the soldiers were not sure they would work if the awful day came, and later, once the equipment had improved, it looked increasingly unlikely that the declining Soviet Union would be in a position to invade Western Europe, even if it wanted to.

At the same time life in Germany by the late 1960s had taken on its own slightly claustrophobic identity, a microcosm of British society with its own institutions and vocabulary, more separate from the Germans than it should have been and with soldiers' freedom curtailed by the need always to have a high percentage in barracks in case they were called out. Overall it was not a particularly enjoyable time, and produced few opportunities for officers to acquire operational experience. The years were dominated by practice 'crash outs', which meant deploying at short notice out of barracks to a nearby wood, usually in the middle of a pouring wet night, gunnery camps, exercises either across German farmland, known as '443 areas', reconnaissance trips along the

Princess Anne escorted by Andrew Parker Bowles during the amalgamation
of The Blues with The Royals in 1969 in Germany.

A tank parade in the 1960s. The Household Cavalry had become tank soldiers
for the first time. It was a frustrating period with few opportunities for
operational service and the Chieftain tanks were initially unreliable.

border between East and West Germany – the 'IGB', as it was called in Rhine Army speak – and endlessly working on the tanks to keep them battleworthy. Individuals' focus consequently remained in England, which was only a few hours' drive away, although there were compensations, such as hunting with a pack of bloodhounds started by the Quartermaster of the newly formed regiment in 1969, Major Bill Stringer, and called the Weser Vale Hunt. Goering had made hunting illegal in Germany in 1934, so instead of hunting foxes they pursued a runner, following his line across the local farmland. This proved very popular with both the army and the local German community, and made full use of the black horses kept in Detmold to provide training for those moving on to the mounted regiment in London. The hounds did not, however, always behave within the rather strict German social norms, and several honest Fraus enjoying their daily constitutional were surprised to be surrounded by slobbery dogs and Englishmen in red coats. The Masters also had to spend long hours discussing compensation for the untimely demise of the odd ornamental duck. The Masters of the Household Brigade Drag would have sympathized. It was at times also difficult to get well-meaning German farmers to understand that the object was to jump their hedges, and that it rather destroyed the point of the exercise if they left all their gates open, which, they argued with faultless Teutonic logic, was much the simplest way of getting from one field to another. Over the years the Weser Vale became a very well-established Anglo-German institution and when the Household Cavalry finally left Germany in 1992 it was taken over by a group of its German supporters who still run it most successfully.

Windsor was a much more popular posting, partly for family and social reasons but mainly because it offered a more satisfactory operational role. This role was changed in the early 1970s from an 'armoured car regiment' to an 'armoured reconnaissance regiment', which was essentially the same thing but with new vehicles. The Saladins and Ferrets were replaced by a family of lightweight tracked vehicles all beginning with 'S'. The main work-horses for the sabre squadrons were the Scorpion, which had a 76-mm gun, and the Scimitar, which had a 30-mm cannon, although some Ferrets, being wheeled and therefore useful for specific internal security operations, were retained. These versatile and air-portable vehicles offered opportunities for both training and the odd operational deployment outside the confines of the north German plain, of which the most significant came in 1982 when two troops of The Blues and Royals, commanded by Mark Coreth, now a well-known sculptor, and Lord Robin Innes Kerr, took part in the Falklands War, operating with both the Airborne and Marine Commando Brigades. It was a most successful short deployment, with the vehicles covering 400 miles over the rough and boggy Falklands terrain and proving to be an invaluable asset. There had always been a strong link between the Household Cavalry and the airborne forces since they were founded in the Second World War, but these were

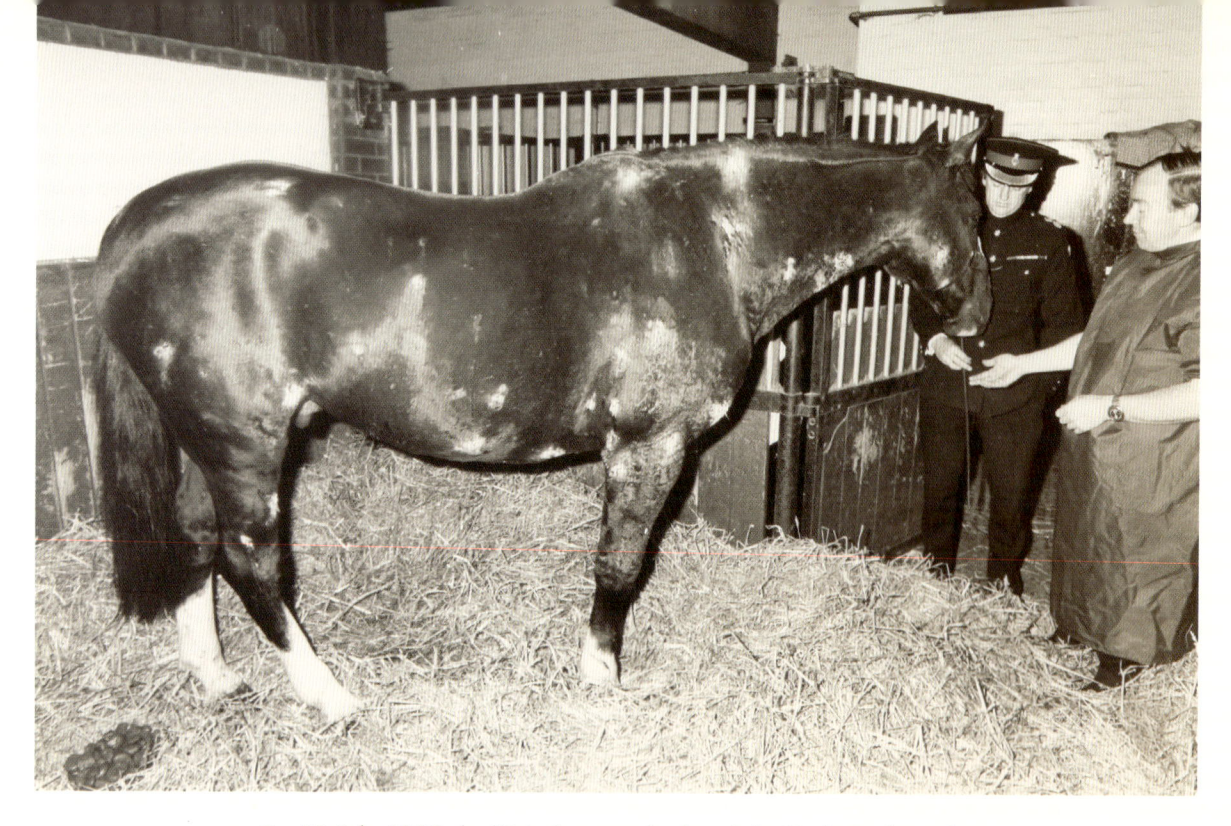

On 20 July 1982 the IRA detonated a bomb in Hyde Park as the Queen's Life Guard was passing. Four members of The Blues and Royals and seven horses were killed, while Sefton, shown here, survived, despite the fact that he was severely injured. The largest donation to help the families came from the Royal Dublin Society.

In 1982 two troops from The Blues and Royals took part in the Falklands War. They entered Port Stanley after covering 400 miles.

consolidated in the Falklands and thereafter the regiment at Windsor became the focus for airborne operations for armoured vehicles, with a squadron and at times the whole regiment dedicated to support the Airborne Brigade, and with a troop kept ready to parachute with its vehicles at short notice.

Two other operations running during the 1970s and 1980s were supported from Windsor. The first of these was the provision of an armoured car squadron to the United Nations Force in Cyprus which, although originally established soon after The Blues had left in 1959, had been substantially restructured since the Turkish invasion of 1974 and whose job was now largely patrolling the 'no go' area between Greek Cypriot and Turkish forces, the so-called Green Line which divided the capital, Nicosia, in half. This was an interesting, if operationally undemanding, tour that the majority of squadrons completed on rotation. The second operation was support to the police in Northern Ireland. Later tank and armoured reconnaissance regiments were exempt from this but for the first decade or so of the 'troubles' they were deployed throughout Ulster, either on Saladins or Ferrets or on their feet. It was a squadron of The Blues and Royals, commanded by Major Andrew Parker Bowles, which first went into the 'no go' areas in Derry in 1972. During a tour in West Belfast, mounted unusually from Germany, in 1976, The Blues and Royals lost four soldiers killed in four months.

The end of the rotation between Germany and Windsor came about because of the collapse of the Soviet empire and the reduced number of tank regiments needed in Germany. However, it also led to defence cuts per se, and there was a fresh round of cavalry amalgamations. While this debate was going on Saddam Hussein invaded Kuwait, and, ironically, the only time the Household Cavalry deployed to fight with tanks after all that training in Germany was as part of the Allied force that ejected his army. A squadron of The Life Guards, equipped by this time with the much more reliable Challenger tanks, was sent to Saudi Arabia in 1991 and participated in Operation Desert Storm. Within months of the end of that very successful short campaign it was announced that The Life Guards would return to Windsor to create a composite armoured reconnaissance regiment with The Blues and Royals; 'A' and 'B' Squadrons would be Life Guards and 'C' and 'D' Squadrons would be Blues and Royals. That decision led inevitably to big reductions in the size of both regiments, and meant that the Household Cavalry was now essentially two composite regiments: the Household Cavalry Mounted Regiment in London with a squadron of Life Guards and one of The Blues and Royals, and the new, larger regiment at Windsor, known as the Household Cavalry Regiment, or HCR, with two squadrons of each.

Frustrating and disappointing as the loss of one of the two operational regiments and the redundancy of so many friends was, it was some compensation that HCR immediately found itself very busy. The decision in September 1992 to commit British troops to the Balkans, first as part of the United Nations and

The decision to commit British troops to the Balkans in the early 1990s meant that the Household Cavalry would become very familiar with Bosnia.

then with NATO, gave them an interesting role keeping the peace initially between Bosnians, Croats and Serbs in Bosnia, and, later, between Serbs and Albanians in both Kosovo and Macedonia, or the former Yugoslav Republic of Macedonia as we should correctly refer to it. Whereas those who had joined the Household Cavalry in the 1960s and 1970s found they were to spend long months in German pine woods changing tank engines and contemplating how they might defeat the Soviet hordes that seemed increasingly less likely to fill the horizon in front of them, their successors had a much more fulfilling time administering the satrapies of the former Yugoslavia. By the beginning of the present millennium the operational opportunities widened even further, with several Household Cavalrymen deploying into Afghanistan when the British-led force established control in Kabul after the defeat of the Taliban in 2002, and 'D' Squadron of The Blues and Royals supported 16 Air Assault Brigade in the American-led invasion of Iraq to oust Saddam Hussein's regime in 2003. This was a most distinguished deployment, which at one time found the small squadron of twenty-odd lightly armoured vehicles up against an Iraqi armoured division, which they defeated, but not without the loss of 10 per cent of their people and a quarter of their vehicles, some, regrettably, to an accidental strike by an American aircraft. Amongst the dead were Lieutenant Alexander Tweedie, step-grandson of David Smiley, Lance Corporal of Horse Matty Hull and Lance Corporal Karl Shearer. In the resultant operational awards Trooper Finney won a George Cross, the first ever awarded to a Household Cavalryman; the squadron leader, Major Richard Taylor, won a Distinguished Service Order, and Corporal of Horse Flynn a Conspicuous Gallantry Cross. They returned home in July 2003, since when successive squadrons from HCR have been deployed as part of the ongoing mission to keep the peace in south-eastern Iraq.

HCR today remains structured much as 1 and 2 HCR were in 1945, with four sabre squadrons and an administrative headquarters' squadron, although it is much smaller. Each sabre squadron has four reconnaissance troops, a 'heavy' troop now equipped with a vehicle that fires anti-tank missiles and a support troop. One squadron is dedicated to supporting the Army's Air Assault Brigade, the successor to the Airborne Brigade and which combines the parachute capability with the newly acquired Apache attack helicopters. Combermere Barracks in Windsor still fills the same site that George III bought for The Blues, although the nineteenth-century barracks, complete with Queen Victoria's new married quarters, was sadly torn down and replaced with some curious and very ugly flat-topped buildings in the 1960s, which, in common with much of the building from that period, were so badly constructed that they are now having to be replaced again.

The mounted regiment in London has changed only very slightly since it was set up in 1945, its size and structure being determined by the ceremonial requirements of providing the daily Queen's Life Guard and escorts for state

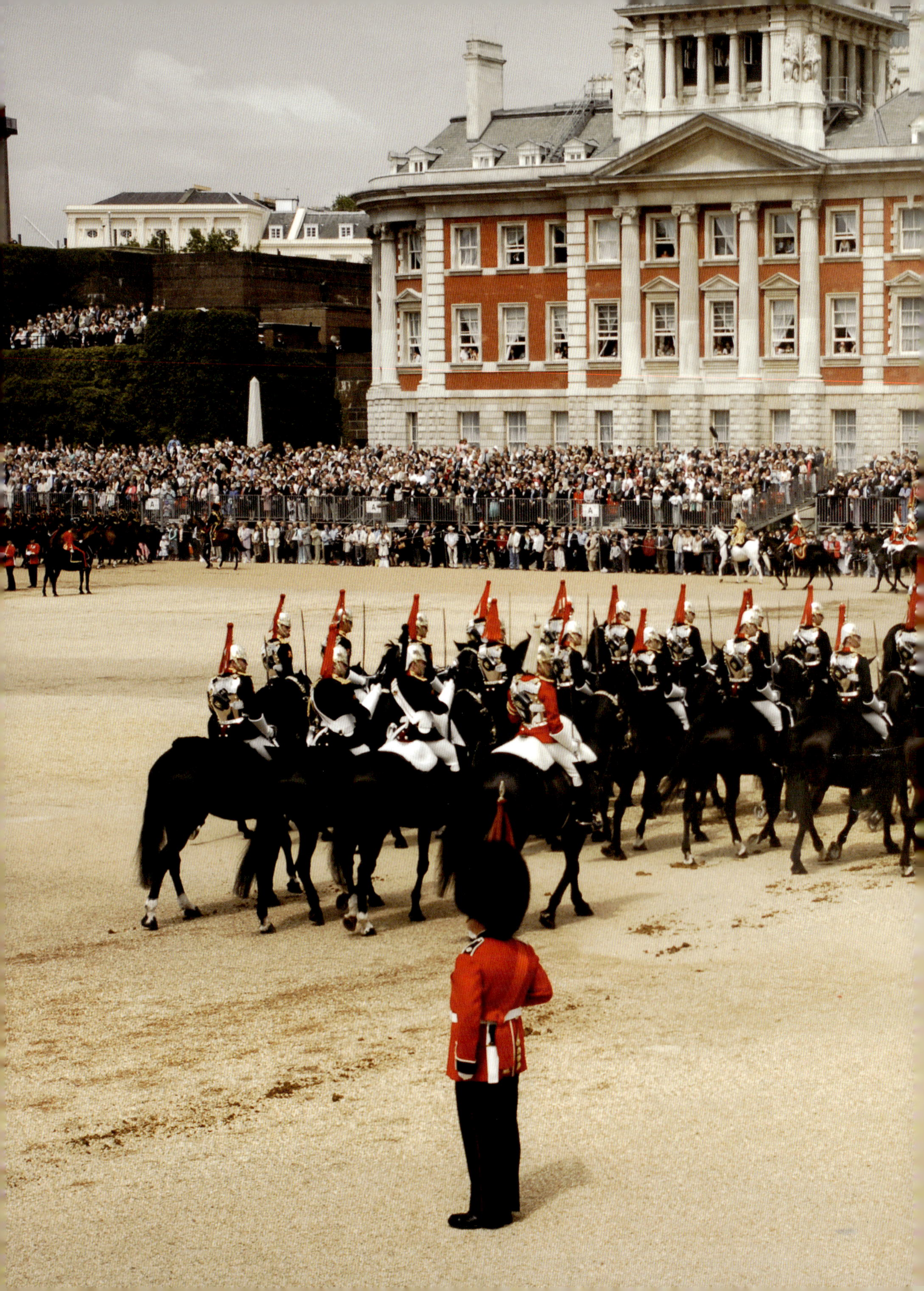

The Queen's Birthday Parade showing HRH The Princess Royal as Colonel of The Blues and Royals, 2005.

occasions. It would, in fact, with its black horses, its farriers busy in the forge, its trumpet calls, its saddlers, tailors and 'rough riders' making young horses, also feel very familiar to Granby or even Marlborough were they to stray into Knightsbridge Barracks through the large new gate off Hyde Park. Regent's Park barracks was never used as a cavalry barracks again after The Life Guards moved in the 1920s and it is now Knightsbridge that is the only Household Cavalry barracks in London. The old building, which so upset the radical Members of Parliament before Waterloo and from where the troopers threw stones at the mob, was also pulled down in the 1960s and replaced with the current concrete pile whose tall tower, which houses flats for families, dominates the Knightsbridge skyline. Its ugliness, lack of proportion and triumph of concrete could be forgiven if it was comfortable and practical to live in, but it was not, and has recently had to be refurbished. Sir Basil Spence designed it, and at the opening, excitedly told Field Marshal Sir Gerald Templer, Colonel of The Blues, that some of his students had helped with the design, to which the acerbic reply was, 'So I can see.'

Life at the mounted regiment today certainly would not be unfamiliar to Robert Lloyd or even to John Cusack of The Royals. The day starts with stables at 6.30 a.m., although mucking out is now down an electrically operated chute rather than by hand, and the horses are then exercised around the London streets before the traffic gets too bad. After breakfast work concentrates on turning out the Queen's Life Guard, which changes daily between The Life Guards and The Blues and Royals and has to be ready by 10 a.m. for inspection before it leaves barracks at 10.30 a.m. When the Queen is in London this is a 'Long Guard' with an officer, a corporal major carrying one of the standards, a trumpeter, a corporal of horse, a junior non-commissioned officer and ten troopers. When she is away only a 'Short Guard' is mounted, commanded by a corporal of horse with a junior non-commissioned officer and ten troopers. Whichever it is makes little difference to the amount of preparation required, which starts the previous evening and involves long hours cleaning and polishing both the horses and personal kit, using much the same methods as Lloyd did. The Guard is, however, now only inspected once, by the Adjutant, and, as of 2005, 'reliefs' are allocated as opposed to being awarded depending on turnout, but the positions, either in the mounted sentry boxes in Whitehall or under the Horse Guards' arch, which was so ridiculed when Kent unveiled it, are still identical. The new Queen's Life Guard arrive at Horse Guards at precisely 11 a.m. and find the Old Guard drawn up either on the Horse Guards Parade Ground in the summer, or in the Tilt Yard on the Whitehall side of the archway in winter. On 20 July 1982, as a Long Guard commanded by Lieutenant Anthony Daly was riding through Hyde Park en route to Horse Guards, the IRA set off a car bomb which murdered him, Corporal Major Roy Bright, who was carrying the standard, Lance Corporal Jeffery Young and Trooper Simon Tipper, together with seven horses. The public response to this outrage was enormous, the horses' suffering seeming to make people particularly indignant, and Sefton, who was one of the worst injured, became a national figure. Of particular note was that the Royal Dublin Society contributed £30,000 to the fund established for the bereaved families.

The Horse Guards building, the official gateway to Buckingham Palace and St James's Palace, no longer houses the War Office staff or the commander-in-chief who moved long ago to bigger offices. It is now home to the Headquarters of the Household Division and of the army's London District, and the Headquarters of the Household Cavalry, and will soon house the Household Cavalry Museum as well. The Queen's Life Guard stables and quarters are in the northern wing, and can be seen from the museum. There is a list of important people, such as members of the Royal Family and politicians, who still carry an 'Ivory Pass', which allows them to drive from Whitehall to Horse Guards Parade Ground through the archway, a very useful privilege given the congestion in central London, although Charles II probably did not quite have that in mind when deciding who should be allowed access to his park. Whenever the Queen, the Duke of Edinburgh or the Prince of Wales passes through the arch the Guard 'turns out' and a salute is blown on the trumpet. Once when Queen Victoria drove through, the Captain of the Life Guard forgot she was coming. It was an occasion when she was genuinely 'unamused' and thereafter the Guard was required to turn out at 4 p.m. every day, something which still happens, and when a Short Guard is on the Orderly Officer from Knightsbridge rides down to inspect it.

The year at Knightsbridge also follows a well-established pattern. December, January and February are dominated by training, of both horses and soldiers, but in March the squadrons start drills in preparation for the coming ceremonial season, the 'silly season' as it is always called. This involves deciding who will ride where, which horses go best in the outside ranks and which – generally the younger ones who may still take exception to the louder bands or more enthusiastically waved flags – should be put in the covered slots on the inside. New 'standard horses' are always required; the standards are carried by corporal majors in the Household Cavalry, rather than by officers as in much of the rest of the army, and they are lowered in salute when an escort passes the Queen, so steady horses are needed who do not mind having a large flag lowered past their heads. Reliable horses are always also in demand for the bands. One of the two bands, either The Life Guards' or The Blues and Royals', is always in Knightsbridge, with the other in Windsor, but are also often required to turn out mounted as a 'massed band'. To ride a horse while playing a musical instrument is not easy, so the bandsmen tend to be mounted on the older and more sedate animals. The trumpeters all ride greys, as they have since James II introduced the custom. The drum horses, which carry the silver kettle-drums presented to The Life Guards by William IV and to The Blues and Royals by George III, now have to be big and heavy enough to carry them.

Since the mid-nineteenth century they have also usually been skewbald, piebald or roan, and are named after classical figures. When playing in the presence of the Queen or other senior members of the Royal Family, the bands wear the gold tunics emblazoned with the royal cipher and black jockey caps, a uniform that has hardly changed since Maugeridge wore it to play for Charles II.

By April the regiment comes together for regimental drills and is inspected in Hyde Park by the Major General Commanding the Household Division to ensure that everything is in order for the coming months. The parade follows the same format as those countless reviews to which the Household Cavalry has been subject in its history, and has changed very little since Charles II's original review of May 1662. The regiment is drawn up with the squadrons in line together with the mounted bands. The General rides down the ranks inspecting the men and horses before retiring to a reviewing post. The bands then take up position and start to play, while the regiment wheels round from its inspection line, and walks and then trots past. Re-forming, they canter forward in line to halt right in front of the General and say goodbye to him with a general salute, hopefully creating much the same effect as the massed regiments did in Windsor Great Park in 1913. Thereafter the summer is a seemingly unending stream of parades and escorts, with the main events being the Queen's Birthday Parade, the Garter Service at Windsor when the regiment parades dismounted, and any state visits. By July both men and horses are ready for a break from the heat of London and the whole regiment moves to Norfolk for three weeks' 'summer camp' where the emphasis is on military training and improving horsemanship. At this time the Queen's Life Guard is temporarily provided by the King's Troop of the Royal Horse Artillery. In September, after leave, they reassemble for the autumn round of escorts, which usually includes the State Opening of Parliament and at least one state visit.

The black horses, and the grey trumpet horses, are now mostly bought in Ireland and generally come as four- or five-year-olds. After a period at the Army's Remount Depot, which is still at Melton Mowbray, and where, like everything else in the army, the horses are given a number which is stamped on their hind hooves, they go to Windsor to start their training. Some take to being cavalry horses very quickly but others find the change from the green fields of Meath and Kildare to the noise and clatter of ceremonial life rather hard to take. When they are in a fit state they are paraded for selection by the squadron leaders of The Life Guards and The Blues and Royals, each one choosing in turn. They are then named according to the year they joined, each year's batch starting with a successive letter of the alphabet, so, for example, the class of 2005 are all 'F'. There is no master list of names, and the same historical figures and events tend to recur, such as Monmouth and Mons, Wellington and Waterloo, or, in 2005, Ferdinand and Falkland. The names are often quite random, so a very badly behaved horse was called Galtieri after the

Falklands War. Once selected, the horses have squadron numbers stamped by the farriers on their front feet, the practice of clipping regimental numbers under their saddle having been phased out. The theory is that when a horse was killed in a campaign the farrier cut its foot off with an axe – which the Household Cavalry farriers still carry on parade – so that the commanding officer could present evidence, when demanding a new one, that the old one was indeed dead, a plausible theory for which I can find little evidence, given that horses were regimental rather than Government property until very late in our story.

Today's ceremonial uniform, known as 'state kit', is essentially that introduced by Queen Victoria and Prince Albert in the 1850s, Edward VII having resisted the temptation to which so many of his forebears succumbed of changing it for his coronation. However, a few minor changes were made in the late nineteenth century, such as doing away with elaborate epaulettes, and the Queen's Life Guard and Royal Escorts ceased carrying carbines. One of the most common points made by those watching ceremonial events today is that they 'wouldn't have wanted to fight wearing that lot', to which, of course, the simple answer is that they didn't. We have already examined the debate over cuirasses, and the modern helmets have never been used in war. The only items carried now which are based on an operational model are the swords – used in Egypt, the Sudan and South Africa – the white 'cartouche' belts with a red cord running through them, which were originally ammunition belts – the 'flash cord' was used for firing grenades and is derived from the Horse Grenadiers – and the long black 'jackboots', which have descended from the design which so vexed the old Duke of Northumberland.

The saddlery is based more on an operational blueprint. The current saddles, individually fitted to each horse and invisible on parade when they are covered with sheepskins, are the post-Boer War type which were introduced to distribute weight more evenly across a horse's back, and are good for carrying a heavy man in his 'state kit'. The officers' and drum horses' saddles have elaborate saddle cloths, called shabracques, blue for The Life Guards and red for The Blues and Royals, on which are embroidered their respective battle honours. Bridles, always known in the army as 'head kits', have a mixed provenance, both operational and ceremonial. They are all double bridles, in other words with two bits in the horse's mouth, one a light bridoon, and the second a heavy curb bit, based on the post-Waterloo model which was introduced in an effort to prevent a recurrence of the dash to the Grand Battery. They are now all also made of black leather, the old red morocco traditionally used by The Life Guards having gone in the last century, with elaborate brass 'head stalls' clipped on to them over the top of the horse's head. This is a vestige of the protection put there to stop a downward sword stroke severing the top of the head kit, which meant that you would lose all control, though the current designs are again nineteenth-century. Life Guard officers still have the gold bridoon reins,

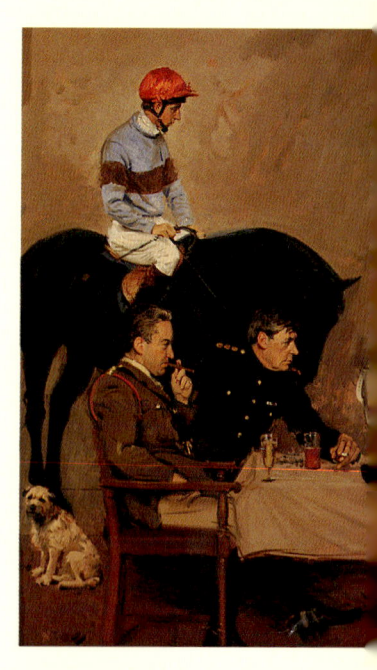

The Festing Painting (*above*). In a direct homage to the Powerscourt Painting of 1857, the officers serving with the Household Cavalry Mounted Regiment in 1988, commissioned Andrew Festing to paint a similar group portrait that now hangs in the officers' mess in the Knightsbridge Barracks.

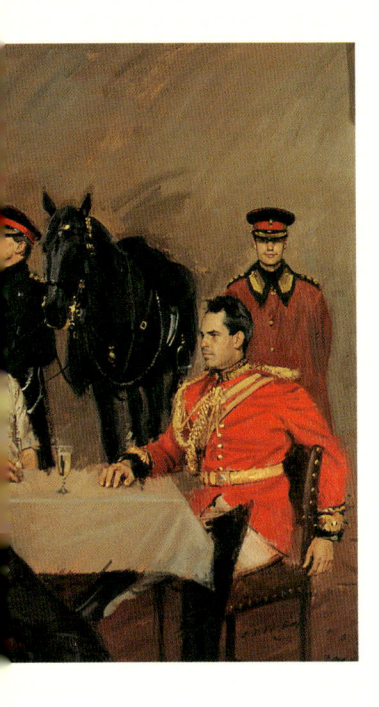

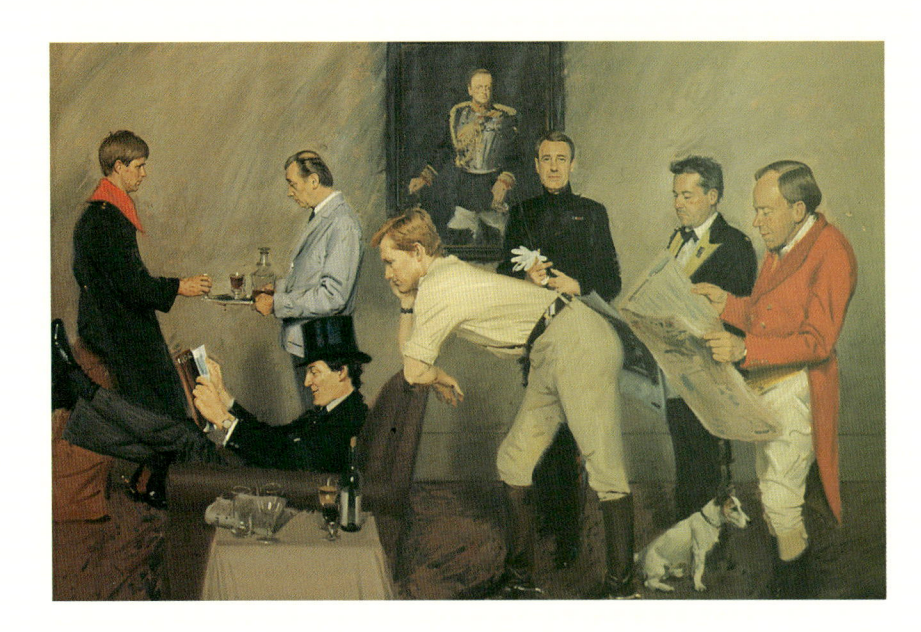

The tradition of portraiture also continues. Here (*below right*) we see
Lucian Freud at work in 2003 on a portrait of Andrew Parker Bowles – suggested
by the subject also as a direct homage to the famous painting of Fred Burnaby
by Jacques Tissot (*below left*).

whose introduction was so unfortunately announced on the same day as the deaths of the onlookers when Queen Caroline's cortège passed through Hyde Park. The Blues and Royals officers' horses also carry a black 'beard', a plume which dangles in front of their chests from the bridle, and whose original purpose may have been to offer some protection to that vulnerable area. This is a Royals' tradition, and was introduced after Dettingen to mark the defeat of the Mousqetaires Noirs.

The Household Cavalry standards are now kept at Knightsbridge, and carried on the Queen's Life Guard and escorts. Each regiment has a sovereign's standard and three squadron standards, and The Blues and Royals also have The Royals' guidon. They are all made of red damask, and have been for some time, James II's vulgar yellow having long since gone. All battle honours are now embroidered on them, instead of just the Peninsula and Waterloo, though not all the battles in which the regiments fought are listed, as various War Office committees have over the years ruled on what does and does not constitute a battle for which an honour can be awarded. The Royals' campaign in Spain in the War of the Spanish Succession does not, for example, get a mention, and they were allowed to include only ten of their First World War battles. The Queen presents new standards to the Household Cavalry every ten years, celebrated by a major parade and regimental get-together, and the guidon is replaced every twenty-five years.

But the most important and continuing element of the Household Cavalry, whether serving with HCR at Windsor, or with the mounted regiment, remains the people, the officers, non-commissioned officers and troopers who make it the institution it is. The two Gold Sticks are now General Lord Guthrie, Colonel of The Life Guards, a former Chief of Defence Staff and a distinguished soldier, and HRH The Princess Royal, Colonel of The Blues and Royals. Their routine responsibilities are executed by the Silver Stick, a serving officer who has his headquarters in Horse Guards and who, on the Ferguson model, commands the Household Cavalry on a daily basis, although HCR is under operational command of whichever formation it is supporting. Soldiers are recruited into the regiments from all over the United Kingdom and Commonwealth, many being relations of past Household Cavalrymen; when I was commanding HCR we estimated that 25 per cent of our soldiers had a family connection. Conversely, we also had a welcome and increasing number of soldiers from ethnic minorities whose families had only come to the United Kingdom relatively recently. After initial training at Pirbright, they are encouraged to go first to the mounted regiment, again on the 1945 model, where they serve around eighteen months before completing training on armoured reconnaissance vehicles and posting to HCR. Some choose not to do this and go directly on armoured training, although they may go back to mounted duty later in their careers. Those posted to Knightsbridge then start riding school at Windsor, not quite as terrifying as it seemed to Robert Lloyd and Tim Bishop, but still a demanding course, which it is a substantial achievement to pass. A few join specifically to ride, and will remain at mounted duty all their careers, becoming riding instructors and, if they are good enough, part of the elite 'riding staff' who work under the Riding Master, instructing recruits, training young horses and generally overseeing equitation standards. Others may become farriers, tailors or saddlers. But the vast majority will go on to serve at HCR, and the strength of the Household Cavalry is that while its men can perform mounted ceremonial to an impeccable standard, they are primarily operational soldiers. They can serve for twenty-two years, although in practice many leave before then, and a few will become commissioned and can serve on until their mid-fifties.

The officers now all join after a year at Sandhurst – a policy which has applied army-wide since the 1960s when the old officer cadet schools were closed – and most now have degrees. They will all go on to the armour centre at Bovington in Dorset where they train in specialist armoured reconnaissance and then become troop leaders at HCR. Some will leave after four or five years, some will go on to serve at mounted duty, and some will try other aspects of military life such as service with the Special Forces. The majority will return to HCR again as captains, probably in their late twenties, to fill roles such as second in command of squadrons or regimental staff appointments. A lucky few will go on to be majors and squadron leaders and later to command HCR or the mounted regiment as lieutenant colonels. What sort of people are they? A broad church, much as they have always been, and by background more similar to those whom Oxford or Granby would have recruited than those you would have found in the Household Cavalry of the mid-nineteenth century. There is the odd silly one, who abuses their position near the Royal Family much as Monmouth's cronies did; then they were executed, but now they sell their stories, and a few other things, to the tabloids. There are some whose families have been in the regiments for generations, particularly in The Royals, but many who have no previous connection at all. There are those who have been educated at some of the best universities and those who have no degree. There are those who live for horses, and those for whom horses are anathema. There are those who join with a field marshal's baton in their knapsack and those who are happy to serve for a few years and then leave. Those who have left recently include successful artists and sculptors as well as bankers, farmers and businessmen. One is a successful pop star, whose first album made it to the top of the charts in 2005.

All those who have left, of whatever age or rank, become members of the regimental associations, which exist to look after their interests and to keep them in touch both with those still serving and with one another. They each arrange an annual dinner hosted either by HCR or the mounted regiment so they can catch up with friends and hear the regimental news. There are no veterans left from the First World War now and sadly very few from the Second,

'D' Squadron of the Household Cavalry Regiment in Iraq in 2003. During the operation the squadron defeated an Iraqi armoured division and won a George Cross, a Conspicuous Gallantry Cross, a Distinguished Service Order and a Military Cross, but sadly lost an officer and two non-commissioned officers.

although both 1 and 2 HCR had thriving lunch clubs until very recently. One thing they all remark on is how busy the present Household Cavalry is. There have been periods of frustration in the story of the Household Cavalry, particularly in the nineteenth century, but though it is now smaller than it has ever been, it is still, 345 years later, successfully discharging those two roles for which it was originally established, being both Royal Guard and the core of the Standing Army.

List of Illustrations

ii The Horse Guards by W. Marlow. *(Officers' mess, Household Cavalry Regiment, Combermere Barracks, Windsor. Photograph © Household Cavalry Regimental Collection Trust)*

viii Mrs Albert Brown in her photographic booth in 1916 at the Exhibition of Women at War Work, Princes's Skating Rink, Knightsbridge. *(Courtesy of Michael Shillabeer)*

Part One – Royal Guard and Standing Army

2 Portrait of King Charles II in 1674 in his Garter robes by artist unknown. *(Officers' mess, Household Cavalry Regiment, Combermere Barracks, Windsor. Photograph © Household Cavalry Regimental Collection Trust)*

5 Equestrian portrait of Louis XIV of France by Charles Le Brun and Adam van der Meulen. *(Musée des Beaux-Arts, Tournai, Belgium/Giraudon/Bridgeman Art Library)*

— Carousel given for Louis XIV in the Court of the Palace of the Tuileries, 5 June 1662 by French School (17th century). *(Chateau de Versailles, France/Bridgeman Art Library)*

10 An English cuirassier at the time of Charles I. *(Private Collection)*

— Helmet, 'front and back' (breast and back plates) and gauntlet from the English Civil War period. *(Household Cavalry Museum. Photograph © Household Cavalry Regimental Collection Trust)*

12 The battle lines before the Battle of Naseby, June 1645. *(Private Collection)*

15 Portrait of Oliver Cromwell by Thomas Wyck. *(Private Collection/© Philip Mould, Historical Portraits Ltd, London/Bridgeman Art Library)*

19 George Monck, 1st Duke of Albemarle, studio of Sir Peter Lely. *(National Portrait Gallery, London)*

21 James, Duke of York, dressed as Mars, God of War by Henri Gascar. *(© National Maritime Museum)*

24 Charles II dancing at a ball at court (at The Hague) by Hieronymus Janssens. *(The Royal Collection © 2006 Her Majesty Queen Elizabeth II)*

— Catherine of Braganza dressed as a shepherdess and seated by a stream by Jacob Huysmanns. *(The Royal Collection © 2006 Her Majesty Queen Elizabeth II)*

25 Barbara Palmer (née Villiers), Duchess of Cleveland by John Michael Wright. *(National Portrait Gallery, London)*

— Louise Renée de Penancoct de Keroualle, Duchess of Portsmouth and Aubigny by Philippe Vignon. *(The Royal Collection © 2006 Her Majesty Queen Elizabeth II)*

— Anne Hyde, Duchess of York (1637–71) from *Lodge's British Portraits* (1823) by English School (19th century). *(Private Collection/Ken Welsh/Bridgeman Art Library)*

32 Captain Thomas Lucy by Sir Godfrey Kneller (c. 1680) at Charlecote House. *(© National Trust Picture Library)*

34 Charles II's cavalcade through the City of London, 22 April 1661 (1662). *(© Museum of London)*

45 Mural of the Defence of Basinghouse by Charles Westcope. *(Palace of Westminster Collection)*

— Mural of Monck with Parliamentarians, 1660, by Edward Matthew Ward. *(Palace of Westminster Collection)*

49 Aubrey de Vere, Earl of Oxford, and first Colonel of The Blues, detail from a copy of an original at Welbeck Abbey. *(Officers' mess, Household Cavalry Mounted Regiment, Hyde Park Barracks, Knightsbridge. Photograph © Household Cavalry Regimental Collection Trust)*

— Sir Francis Compton, Henry Compton and Sir Charles Compton, sons of the 2nd Earl of Northampton and officers in the 5th Troop of Blues, illustrations from *The Story of the Household Cavalry* (vol. 1) by Sir George Arthur. *(Photograph © Household Cavalry Regimental Collection Trust)*

52 Charles the Great, an engraving from 1754. *(Hulton Archive/Getty Images)*

55 James, Duke of Monmouth and Buccleuch (1649–85) in Garter robes by studio of Sir Peter Lely. *(Private Collection/© Philip Mould, Historical Portraits Ltd, London/Bridgeman Art Library)*

LIST OF ILLUSTRATIONS – 587

— James Scott, Duke of Monmouth and Buccleuch by Jan van Wyck. *(National Portrait Gallery, London)*

58 The Four Days' Battle, 1–4 June 1666, by Pieter Cornelisz van Soest. *(© National Maritime Museum)*

63 Mary of Modena by Simon Verelst. *(The Royal Collection © 2006 Her Majesty Queen Elizabeth II)*

— Titus Oates (1649–1705) in the Pillory, 1687, by English School (17th century). *(© Museum of London/Bridgeman Art Library)*

68 View of Old Horse Guards Parade from St James's Park attributed to Thomas van Wyck. *(Private Collection/© Christie's Images/Bridgeman Art Library)*

69 William Blathwayt by Michael Dahl in the Great Hall at Dyrham Park. *(© National Trust Picture Library/Ian Blantern)*

76 Siege of Tangiers by artist unknown (17th century). *(© National Trust Picture Library/John Hammond)*

82 King Charles II attributed to Thomas Hawker. *(National Portrait Gallery, London)*

Part Two – Divided Loyalties

84 William III Landing at Brixham, Torbay, 5 November 1688 by Jan Wyck. *(© National Maritime Museum)*

89 Louis Duras, 2nd Earl of Feversham by Isaac Beckett, after John Riley. *(National Portrait Gallery, London)*

94 Woodcut of the Rout of 1000 of the Rebels at the Battle of Sedgmoor, 6 July 1685, by English School (17th century). *(Private Collection/Bridgeman Art Library)*

— Woodcut of the Battle of Bridgwater, 6 July 1685, by English School (17th century). *(Private Collection/Bridgeman Art Library)*

— Woodcut of the Defeat of the Rebels at the battle of Sedgmoor, 6 July 1685, by English School (17th century). *(Private Collection/Bridgeman Art Library)*

97 An incident at Sedgemoor. A private gentleman of the Life Guards, 1685, illustration from *The Story of the Household Cavalry (vol. 1)* by Sir George Arthur. *(Photograph © Household Cavalry Regimental Collection Trust)*

— Mural of the Destitute from the Battle of Sedgemoor being comforted by Alice Lisle by Edward Matthew Ward. *(Palace of Westminster Collection)*

100 Standards of the 3rd Troop of Horse Guards in James II's time. *(Photograph © Household Cavalry Regimental Collection Trust)*

— The Royal Dragoons guidon and troop standards – with devices modelled on the symbols of successive kings of England. *(Photograph © Household Cavalry Regimental Collection Trust)*

— A red damask standard from the period of William and Mary. *(Photograph © Household Cavalry Regimental Collection Trust)*

102 Engraving of the camp on Hounslow Heath, illustration from *The Story of the Household Cavalry (vol. 1)* by Sir George Arthur. *(Photograph © Household Cavalry Regimental Collection Trust)*

107 Negro Trumpeter, 1st Troop of Horse Guards by David Morier. *(The Royal Collection © 2006 Her Majesty Queen Elizabeth II)*

109 James Fitzjames, 1st Duke of Berwick, illustration from *Portraits des grands hommes, femmes illustres, et sujets memorables de France* by Antoine Louis Francois Sergent-Marceau. *(Private Collection/Stapleton Collection/Bridgeman Art Library)*

— An early London coffee house, signed A. S. *(British Museum/Bridgeman Art Library)*

114 Departure of William III from Hellevoetslouis, 19 October 1688, in the style of Abraham Storck. *(© National Maritime Museum)*

120 Unidentified Woman, formerly Edward Hyde, Lord Cornbury by American School (18th century). *(© Collection of the New York Historical Society, USA/Bridgeman Art Library)*

122 A Portrait of a Gentleman, possibly Patrick Sarsfield, attributed to John Riley. *(National Gallery of Ireland Collection. Photograph © National Gallery of Ireland)*

128 The Battle of the Boyne by Jan Wyck. *(National Gallery of Ireland Collection. Photograph © National Gallery of Ireland)*

133 Mezzotint of Frederick Armand de Schomberg, 1st Duke of Schomberg, by Sir Godfrey Kneller. *(National Gallery of Ireland Collection. Photograph © National Gallery of Ireland)*

— Godert De Ginkel by Sir Godfrey Kneller. *(National Gallery of Ireland Collection, Photograph © National Gallery of Ireland)*

— Richard Talbot, Earl of Tyrconnell, by artist unknown. *(National Gallery of Ireland Collection. Photograph © National Gallery of Ireland)*

138 Mezzotint of the Siege of Limerick, 9–31 August 1690 by Henry MacManus. *(Photograph © National Library of Ireland)*

143 James, Second Duke of Ormond, illustration from *The Story of the Household Cavalry (vol. 1)* by Sir George Arthur. *(Photograph © Household Cavalry Regimental Collection Trust)*

147 General Hugh Mackay, 1690, killed at the Battle of Steenkirk in 1692 during the Nine Years' War by Sir Godfrey Kneller. *(© Courtesy of the Council, National Army Museum, London/Bridgeman Art Library)*

— John Churchill, 1st Duke of Marlborough by Sir Godfrey Kneller. *(National Portrait Gallery, London)*
152 William III, c. 1690, by artist unknown. *(National Portrait Gallery, London)*
— The Treaty of Ryswick, 30 October 1697, by French School (17th century). *(Ministère des Affaires étrangères, Paris, France/Archives Charmet/Bridgeman Art Library)*
155 A View from Windsor Castle by artist unknown. *(The Royal Collection © 2006 Her Majesty Queen Elizabeth II)*
— A View of Windsor Castle by Leonard Knyff. *(The Royal Collection © 2006 Her Majesty Queen Elizabeth II)*

Part Three – A Pattern Established

158 Private, Royal Horse Guards (The Blues) and Grenadier by David Morier. *(The Royal Collection © 2006 Her Majesty Queen Elizabeth II)*
162 Queen Anne in the House of Lords by Peter Tillemans. *(The Royal Collection © 2006 Her Majesty Queen Elizabeth II)*
163 Queen Anne and the Knights of the Garter (includes Queen Anne; Henry Somerset, 2nd Duke of Beaufort; Henry Grey, 1st Duke of Kent; Robert Harley, 1st Earl of Oxford; Charles Mordaunt, 3rd Earl of Peterborough; John Poulett, 1st Earl Poulett; Charles Talbot, 1st Duke of Shrewsbury) by Peter Angelis. *(National Portrait Gallery, London)*
— Charles Mordaunt, 3rd Earl of Peterborough by Sir Godfrey Kneller. *(National Portrait Gallery, London)*
168 St James's Park and the Mall by artist unknown. *(The Royal Collection © 2006 Her Majesty Queen Elizabeth II)*
169 Engraving of the Bubblers Bubbl'd, 1720, by James Cole. *(© Guildhall Library, City of London/Bridgeman Art Library)*
— The Election IV Chairing the Member, 1754–55, by William Hogarth. *(Courtesy of the Trustees of Sir John Soane's Museum, London/Bridgeman Art Library)*
179 Mezzotint of the Battle of Almanza, 25 April 1707, engraved by Jean Baptiste Morret. *(Private Collection/Stapleton Collection/Bridgeman Art Library)*
— King Philip V (1683–1746) of Spain Making Marshal James Fitzjames, Duke of Berwick, a Cavalier of the Golden Fleece by Jean Auguste Dominique Ingres. *(Collection of the Duke of Berwick and Alba, Madrid, Spain/Lauros/Giraudon/Bridgeman Art Library)*
186 George I by John Vanderbank. *(The Royal Collection © 2006 Her Majesty Queen Elizabeth II)*
191 John Campbell, 2nd Duke of Argyll and Duke of Greenwich, by William Aikman. *(National Portrait Gallery, London)*
193 Prices for commissions in the Life Guards (1st Troop of Horse Guards) 1719. *(© Public Record Office)*
201 Trooper in The Blues, c. 1742. *(Regimental Albums, Household Cavalry Museum. Photograph © Household Cavalry Regimental Collection Trust)*
— King George II at the Battle of Dettingen, with the Duke of Cumberland and Robert, 4th Earl of Holderness, 27 June 1743, by John Wootton. *(© Courtesy of the Council, National Army Museum, London/Acquired with assistance of National Art Collections Fund/Bridgeman Art Library)*
206 A View of the Glorious Action of Dettingen, 16–27 June 1743, between the Forces of the Allies Commanded by the King of Great Britain and the French Army under the Marshal Noailles, by F. Daremberg, engraved by I. Pane, printed by Robert Wilkinson. *(Private Collection/ Bridgeman Art Library)*
210 Private, Regiment of Hussars 'Karoly' by David Morier. *(The Royal Collection © 2006 Her Majesty Queen Elizabeth II)*
213 William Augustus, Duke of Cumberland, by David Morier. *(Private Collection/Bridgeman Art Library)*
— An Encampment of British Troops under the command of the Duke of Cumberland attributed to David Morier and John Wotton. *(The Royal Collection © 2006 Her Majesty Queen Elizabeth II)*
214 The Battle of Fontenoy, 11 May 1745, by Pierre Lenfant. *(Château de Versailles, France/Lauros/Giraudon/Bridgeman Art Library)*
— A view of the magnificent structure erected for the fireworks to be exhibited for the solemnization of the General Peace *(British Library, London/Bridgeman Art Library)*
218 Old Horse Guards and the Banqueting Hall, Whitehall from St James's Park, 1749 by Canaletto. *(Private Collection/© Christie's Images/Bridgeman Art Library)*
— New Horse Guards from St James's Park by Canaletto. *(Private Collection/Bridgeman Art Library)*
221 A dragoon horse. *(Regimental Albums, Household Cavalry Museum. Photograph © Household Cavalry Regimental Collection Trust)*
— A View of the West Front of Horse Guards with the Treasury and Downing Street beyond, c.1758, by Samuel Wale. *(© Courtesy of the Council, National Army Museum, London/Bridgeman Art Library)*
225 Horse Grenadiers c. 1742, 1747 and 1760 by David Morier. *(The Royal Collection © 2006 Her Majesty Queen Elizabeth II)*
230 John Manners, Marquis of Granby, by Sir Joshua

Reynolds. *(The Royal Collection © 2006 Her Majesty Queen Elizabeth II)*

231 Marquis of Granby relieving a sick soldier, c. 1765, by Edward Penny. *(© Courtesy of the Council, National Army Museum, London/Bridgeman Art Library)*

— The Dorking and London Royal Mail leaving the 'Marquis of Granby', 1854, by H. W. Allfrey and C. C. Henderson. *(Private Collection/© Bonhams, London/Bridgeman Art Library)*

235 The Battle of Minden, 1 August, copper engraving by artist unknown. *(akg-images)*

— Henry Herbert, 10th Earl of Pembroke by Samuel William Reynolds, after Sir Joshua Reynolds. *(National Portrait Gallery, London)*

246 George III's procession to the Houses of Parliament attributed to John Wotton. *(The Royal Collection © 2006 Her Majesty Queen Elizabeth II)*

— Trumpet banner, one of a pair called the Homeyer Banners. *(Photograph © Household Cavalry Regimental Collection Trust)*

Part Four – The First Great Change

250 Equestrian portrait of Arthur Wellesley, 1st Duke of Wellington by Francisco de Goya. *(Wellington Museum, Apsley House Collection/Victoria and Albert Museum)*

254 Riot in Broad Street, 1780. A mob looting a house, cheered on from the windows of nearby buildings, is confronted by a disciplined formation of soldiers. This riot on 7 June 1780 formed part of the Gordon Riots. *(© Museum of London)*

— 2nd West Yorkshire Light Infantry Militia: inspection of Old Montague House, London, 1780. *(The Royal Collection © 2006 Her Majesty Queen Elizabeth II)*

258 Henry, 10th Earl of Pembroke, and his son George Augustus, Lord Herbert, by David Morier. *(© Collection of the Earl of Pembroke, Wilton House, Wiltshire/Bridgeman Art Library)*

263 George III and Queen Charlotte driving through Deptford, c. 1785, by Thomas Rowlandson. *(Private Collection)*

— Horse Grenadiers watching a parade by Thomas Rowlandson. *(Private Collection)*

270 French Troops in North Holland by J. A. Langendyk. *(The Royal Collection © 2006 Her Majesty Queen Elizabeth II)*

— The Death of Major General John Mansel, at Beaumont, 26 April 1794, by Charles Hamilton Smith. *(The Royal Collection © 2006 Her Majesty Queen Elizabeth II)*

274 Life Guards in ceremonial dress after 1788. *(Regimental Albums, Household Cavalry Museum. Photograph © Household Cavalry Regimental Collection Trust)*

— Troops Watering Horses, c. 1788. *(Regimental Albums, Household Cavalry Museum. Photograph © Household Cavalry Regimental Collection Trust)*

— Major T. O'Loghlin. *(Regimental Albums, Household Cavalry Museum. Photograph © Household Cavalry Regimental Collection Trust)*

281 'The Point of Honour Decided', drawing by Robert Cruikshank. *(British Library, London/Bridgeman Art Library)*

— 'The Interior of Modern Hell. Vide the Cogged Dice', drawing by Robert Cruikshank. *(British Library, London/Bridgeman Art Library)*

283 Officer of the Royal Dragoons 1804 by Robert Dighton. *(The Royal Collection © 2006 Her Majesty Queen Elizabeth II)*

— Henry Bernard Chalon, an officer in 1st Life Guards, 1796. *(Private Collection)*

287 George III, in the uniform of the Royal Horse Guards (The Blues), c. 1800, by Robert Dighton. *(The Royal Collection © 2006 Her Majesty Queen Elizabeth II)*

— Engraving of the view on the River Tagus near Villa Velha, Portugal, by L. Clarke. *(Bibliothèque des Arts Décoratifs, Paris/Bridgeman Art Library)*

297 Viscount Rowland Hill, who commanded a corps in the Peninsula and at Waterloo and was later a Colonel of The Blues. *(Private Collection)*

— Robert Hill, who joined the Blues in 1794 and commanded the regiment at Waterloo. *(Private Collection)*

— Clement Hill, who was Rowland's ADC at Waterloo and was also in The Blues, rising to the rank of Major General in the Madras army. *(Regimental Albums, Household Cavalry Museum. Photograph © Household Cavalry Regimental Collection Trust)*

— Gold and Silver Sticks, including Robert Hill's stick inscribed to commemorate his actions at Waterloo. *(Household Cavalry Museum. Photograph © Household Cavalry Regimental Collection Trust)*

305 Corporal John Shaw, former boxing champion, posing as an artists' model. *(Regimental Albums, Household Cavalry Museum. Photograph © Household Cavalry Regimental Collection Trust)*

— Portrait of Colonel Thoyt with Duke, the black Labrador, during the Peninsular War by R. B. Davis. *(Officers' mess, Household Cavalry Mounted Regiment, Hyde Park Barracks, Knightsbridge. Photograph © Household Cavalry Regimental Collection Trust)*

309 Officers, Royal Horse Guards (The Blues) by Dennis Dighton. *(The Royal Collection © 2006 Her Majesty Queen Elizabeth II)*

320 Wellington's Orders, Battle of Waterloo, 1815. *(Private Collection/Bridgeman Art Library)*

— The Duke of Wellington on the road to Quatre Bras, 16 June 1815, by Robert Alexander Hillingford. *(Private Collection/Bridgeman Art Library)*

326 The Battle of Waterloo, painting by O'Clenell. *(Officers' mess, Household Cavalry Mounted Regiment, Hyde Park Barracks, Knightsbridge. Photograph © Household Cavalry Regimental Collection Trust)*

331 Portrait of Captain Edward Kelly by artist unknown. *(Household Cavalry Museum. Photograph © Household Cavalry Regimental Collection Trust)*

— The Horse Guards at the Battle of Waterloo. One of the officers having killed a French colonel, cuts off his epaulette in triumph, by Dubourg Heath. *(British Library, London/Bridgeman Art Library)*

332 Corporal John Shaw, who became a national hero after Waterloo, where he was killed. *(Private Collection)*

— Captains Packe and Fenwick in Blues uniforms, prior to the Peninsular War. *(Regimental Albums, Household Cavalry Museum. Photograph © Household Cavalry Regimental Collection Trust)*

339 Uniform worn by a Blues officer at Waterloo complete with Waterloo medal. *(Household Cavalry Museum. Photograph © Household Cavalry Regimental Collection Trust)*

— The field bugle on which sixteen-year-old John Edwards blew the charge at Waterloo. *(Household Cavalry Museum. Photograph © Household Cavalry Regimental Collection Trust)*

— Cavalry Helmet from Waterloo. *(Household Cavalry Museum. Photograph © Household Cavalry Regimental Collection Trust)*

341 Lord Uxbridge, later Marquess of Anglesey by artist unknown. *(Household Cavalry Serving Officers' Trust, Windsor. Photograph © Household Cavalry Regimental Collection Trust)*

— Lord Uxbridge's wooden leg. *(Household Cavalry Museum. Photograph © Household Cavalry Regimental Collection Trust)*

Part Five – Ornamental Extravagance

344 The Queen's Life Guard leaving Horse Guards, 1867, by A. G. Boult. *(Officers' mess, Household Cavalry Regiment, Combermere Barracks, Windsor. Photograph © Household Cavalry Regimental Collection Trust)*

348 Plate commemorating the opening of Waterloo Bridge, London, from the Prussian Service. *(Wellington Museum, Apsley House Collection/Victoria and Albert Museum)*

— Household Cavalry standards showing only the battle honours connected with Napoleon's defeat. *(Household Cavalry Museum, Windsor. Photograph © Household Cavalry Regimental Collection Trust)*

350 'Monstrosities of 1821' etching by George Cruikshank. *(Collage/City of London Collection © Corporation of London)*

— Band of the Second Regiment of Life Guards leaving Windsor, 1830, by John Frederick Tayler. *(© Courtesy of the Council, National Army Museum, London/Bridgeman Art Library)*

353 Musicians of the Household Cavalry, painting attributed to Edward Bird. *(Lord Fairhaven Collection)*

— A kettle drummer of The Blues. *(Private Collection)*

357 The Last Return from Duty by J. W. Glass. *(Wellington Museum, Apsley House Collection/Victoria and Albert Museum)*

— The Life Guards at the Coronation of William IV, painting by R. B. Davis. *(The Royal Collection © 2006 Her Majesty Queen Elizabeth II)*

359 Portrait of a mounted trooper, c. 1830s, by Daybraya. *(Officers' mess, Household Cavalry Mounted Regiment, Hyde Park Barracks, Knightsbridge. Photograph © Household Cavalry Regimental Collection Trust)*

— Portrait of a mounted trooper, c. 1845, by A. G. Boult. *(Officers' mess, Household Cavalry Mounted Regiment, Hyde Park Barracks, Knightsbridge. Photograph © Household Cavalry Regimental Collection Trust)*

362 The officers of 1st Life Guards in their mess, 1857, by artist unknown, commissioned by Mervyn Wingfield, 7th Viscount Powerscourt. *(Officers' mess, Household Cavalry Mounted Regiment, Hyde Park Barracks, Knightsbridge. Photograph © Household Cavalry Regimental Collection Trust)*

— Six sketches of regimental life from 1857 to 1858 Mervyn Wingfield, 7th Viscount Powerscourt. *(Officers' mess, Household Cavalry Mounted Regiment, Hyde Park Barracks, Knightsbridge. Photograph © Household Cavalry Regimental Collection Trust)*

365 Troops' sleeping quarters, c. 1900. *(Regimental Albums, Household Cavalry Museum. Photograph © Household Cavalry Regimental Collection Trust)*

— Illustration of bed bug killed 'in single combat' at Horse Guards, 1901. *(Regimental Albums, Household Cavalry Museum. Photograph © Household Cavalry Regimental Collection Trust)*

— Captain McLean's room in Dublin during the Royals' tour of duty in 1872. *(Regimental Albums, Household*

LIST OF ILLUSTRATIONS – 591

Cavalry Museum. Photograph © Household Cavalry Regimental Collection Trust)

370 Portrait of Fitzroy James Henry Somerset, 1st Lord Raglan, by artist unknown. *(Officers' mess, Household Cavalry Regiment, Combermere Barracks, Windsor. Photograph © Household Cavalry Regimental Collection Trust)*

377 A private in The Royals in marching order after the Crimea. *(Regimental Albums, Household Cavalry Museum. Photograph © Household Cavalry Regimental Collection Trust)*

— Colonel Yorke, who commanded The Royals in the Crimea. *(Regimental Albums, Household Cavalry Museum. Photograph © Household Cavalry Regimental Collection Trust)*

380 Engraving of the Charge of the Heavy Cavalry Brigade at the Battle of Balaclava, 25 October 1854, by William Simpson. *(Private Collection/Bridgeman Art Library)*

385 A bear with Private Locke, owned by H. Naylor-Leyland. *(Regimental Albums, Household Cavalry Museum. Photograph © Household Cavalry Regimental Collection Trust)*

386 A group of troopers in full ceremonial dress, with a trumpeter to the left, c. 1865. *(Regimental Albums, Household Cavalry Museum. Photograph © Household Cavalry Regimental Collection Trust)*

— A group of non-commissioned officers, c. 1870. *(Regimental Albums, Household Cavalry Museum. Photograph © Household Cavalry Regimental Collection Trust)*

389 Cartoon satirising the Cardwell reforms in *Punch Magazine*. *(Regimental Albums, Household Cavalry Museum. Photograph © Household Cavalry Regimental Collection Trust)*

— The Zetland solid silver centrepiece on the dining room table at the Regent's Park barracks officers' mess. *(Regimental Albums, Household Cavalry Museum. Photograph © Household Cavalry Regimental Collection Trust)*

396 Illustration of the moonlight charge at Kassassin. *(Regimental Albums, Household Cavalry Museum. Photograph © Household Cavalry Regimental Collection Trust)*

— A group of non-commissioned officers of the Life Guards with their Egyptian Campaign medals. *(Regimental Albums, Household Cavalry Museum. Photograph © Household Cavalry Regimental Collection Trust)*

399 Illustration of a member of the Heavy Camel Regiment from *Sudan Sketches* by Captain Willoughby Vernier of the Rifle Brigade. *(Regimental Albums, Household Cavalry Museum. Photograph © Household Cavalry Regimental Collection Trust)*

— Pith helmet from the Sudan Campaign. *(Household Cavalry Museum, Windsor. Photograph © Household Cavalry Regimental Collection Trust)*

— Illustration of the Camel Corps crossing the desert from *Sudan Sketches* by Captain Willoughby Vernier of the Rifle Brigade. *(Regimental Albums, Household Cavalry Museum. Photograph © Household Cavalry Regimental Collection Trust)*

403 Illustration of the Camel Corps crossing Bayuda from *Sudan Sketches* by Captain Willoughby Vernier of the Rifle Brigade. *(Regimental Albums, Household Cavalry Museum. Photograph © Household Cavalry Regimental Collection Trust)*

— Illustration of the enemy encounter at Abu Klea from *Sudan Sketches* by Captain Willoughby Vernier of the Rifle Brigade. *(Regimental Albums, Household Cavalry Museum. Photograph © Household Cavalry Regimental Collection Trust)*

407 Portrait of Colonel Fred Burnaby by Ethel Mortlock. *(Officers' mess, Household Cavalry Mounted Regiment, Hyde Park Barracks, Knightsbridge. Photograph © Household Cavalry Regimental Collection Trust)*

— Illustration of the death of Burnaby at Abu Klea from *Sudan Sketches* by Captain Willoughby Vernier of the Rifle Brigade. *(Regimental Albums, Household Cavalry Museum. Photograph © Household Cavalry Regimental Collection Trust)*

410 Regimental Watering Order – or the Daily Exercise About to Depart from Knightsbridge Barracks in 1899 by artist unknown. *(Officers' mess, Household Cavalry Mounted Regiment, Hyde Park Barracks, Knightsbridge. Photograph © Household Cavalry Regimental Collection Trust)*

414 Portrait of Kaiser Wilhelm II of Germany, Colonel-in-Chief of The Royals, 1894, by artist unknown. *(Officers' mess, Household Cavalry Mounted Regiment, Hyde Park Barracks, Knightsbridge. Photograph © Household Cavalry Regimental Collection Trust)*

— Kaiser Wilhelm II visiting Queen Victoria, c. 1900. *(Regimental Albums, Household Cavalry Museum. Photograph © Household Cavalry Regimental Collection Trust)*

423 Queen Victoria seeing off the troops in November 1899. *(Regimental Albums, Household Cavalry Museum. Photograph © Household Cavalry Regimental Collection Trust)*

— Spion Kop. *(Regimental Albums, Household Cavalry Museum. Photograph © Household Cavalry Regimental Collection Trust)*

425 A British cavalry horse loaded with kit and fodder,

— c. 1901. *(Regimental Albums, Household Cavalry Museum. Photograph © Household Cavalry Regimental Collection Trust)*
— Distressed British cavalry horse, c. 1901. *(Regimental Albums, Household Cavalry Museum. Photograph © Household Cavalry Regimental Collection Trust)*
426 Dead horses being dispatched at sea, c. 1901. *(Regimental Albums, Household Cavalry Museum. Photograph © Household Cavalry Regimental Collection Trust)*
— Freddy, the only horse who sailed in 1899 and returned home, together with his medal and citation. *(Regimental Albums, Household Cavalry Museum. Photograph © Household Cavalry Regimental Collection Trust)*
429 Members of the Household Cavalry, c. 1900. *(Regimental Albums, Household Cavalry Museum. Photograph © Household Cavalry Regimental Collection Trust)*
— The Household Cavalry parading for Lord Roberts in Pretoria, 1900. *(Regimental Albums, Household Cavalry Museum. Photograph © Household Cavalry Regimental Collection Trust)*

Part Six – 'The Ordered Past Behind Us Lies'

432 Cavalry behind the front line in the First World War. *(Imperial War Museum, Image no. Q 6412)*
439 The German Crown Prince's visit to the Royals in Muttra. *(Regimental Albums, Household Cavalry Museum. Photograph © Household Cavalry Regimental Collection Trust)*
— Sergeant Measures and his wife on the veranda of their bungalow outside Pretoria. *(Regimental Albums, Household Cavalry Museum. Photograph © Household Cavalry Regimental Collection Trust)*
444 Two Photographs of the stables and saddlery, c. 1905. *(Regimental Albums, Household Cavalry Museum. Photograph © Household Cavalry Regimental Collection Trust)*
— A 1st Life Guard watering his horse, c. 1903. *(Regimental Albums, Household Cavalry Museum. Photograph © Household Cavalry Regimental Collection Trust)*
— The stable yard, c. 1905. *(Regimental Albums, Household Cavalry Museum. Photograph © Household Cavalry Regimental Collection Trust)*
447 A physical training session, c. 1905. *(Regimental Albums, Household Cavalry Museum. Photograph © Household Cavalry Regimental Collection Trust)*
— Sword practice, c. 1905. *(Regimental Albums, Household Cavalry Museum. Photograph © Household Cavalry Regimental Collection Trust)*
450 The funeral of Edward VII at Windsor, 1910. *(Regimental Albums, Household Cavalry Museum. Photograph © Household Cavalry Regimental Collection Trust)*
453 Lieutenant Colonel Cook, 19 August 1914. *(Regimental Albums, Household Cavalry Museum. Photograph © Household Cavalry Regimental Collection Trust)*
— Trooper Harry Heard, December 1914. *(Regimental Albums, Household Cavalry Museum. Photograph © Household Cavalry Regimental Collection Trust)*
455 The Retreat from Mons, 1914 by Lady Elizabeth Butler. *(© Royal Hospital Chelsea, London/Bridgeman Art Library)*
— A watercolour of two troopers in dress uniform of the day by artist unknown. *(Household Cavalry Museum, Windsor. Photograph © Household Cavalry Regimental Collection Trust)*
466 Lord Hugh Grosvenor, October 1914. *(Mrs Albert Broom, Household Cavalry Museum, Windsor. © Household Cavalry Regimental Collection Trust)*
— Julian Grenfell and Colonel Steele, c. 1915. *(Private Collection)*
— Sir Morgan Crofton by his dugout at Brielon, c. 1915. *(Private Collection)*
475 A proud couple at Waterloo Station, August 1916. *(Mrs Albert Broom, Household Cavalry Museum, Windsor. © Household Cavalry Regimental Collection Trust)*
— Lieutenant Colonel Portal, who raised and commanded the Household Battalion in September 1916 from reservists at Windsor. *(Mrs Albert Broom, Household Cavalry Museum, Windsor. © Household Cavalry Regimental Collection Trust)*
476 The Household Cavalry cyclist company passing through the village of Vraignes, following the German retreat to Hindenburg, March 1916. *(Imperial War Museum, Image no. Q 1879)*
— Cavalry resting in a bomb hole, 1916. *(Imperial War Museum, Image no. Q2032)*
478 Portrait of Lieutenant Johnnie Dunville, VC, by W. Carter. *(Officers' mess, Household Cavalry Regiment, Combermere Barracks, Windsor. Photograph © Household Cavalry Regimental Collection Trust)*
482 Paul Maze, 'the last impressionist', c. 1914. *(By kind permission of The Hon Mrs Robert Spencer Churchill)*
— A service in the ruins at the cathedral in Cambrai, c. 1916. *(Paul Maze/By kind permission of The Hon Mrs Robert Spencer Churchill)*

LIST OF ILLUSTRATIONS – 593

487 Operational and ceremonial war uniforms. *(Mrs Albert Broom, Household Cavalry Museum, Windsor. © Household Cavalry Regimental Collection Trust)*

488 Ceremonial uniforms with the Mons Star. *(Mrs Albert Broom, Household Cavalry Museum, Windsor. © Household Cavalry Regimental Collection Trust)*

— The unveiling of the Zanvoorde memorial by Field Marshal Earl Haig, 4 May 1924. *(Regimental Albums, Household Cavalry Museum. Photograph © Household Cavalry Regimental Collection Trust)*

491 Presentation of standards by King George V on Horse Guards Parade, 1927, by Sir Alfred Mummings. *(Officers' mess, Household Cavalry Regiment, Combermere Barracks, Windsor. Photograph © Household Cavalry Regimental Collection Trust)*

— King George V's full dress uniform. *(Household Cavalry Museum, Windsor. © Household Cavalry Regimental Collection Trust)*

493 Spike Mays, who joined The Royals as a 'Band Rat' in 1924. *(Private Collection)*

— Jack Hamilton-Russell, winner of the Kadir Cup, the Indian Army pig-sticking championship in 1934, on Lindy Loo. *(By kind permission of Colonel James Hamilton-Russell)*

494 A satirical sketch – 'Haw! I shall win this game as sure as God made little apples!', c. 1920. *(Regimental Albums, Household Cavalry Museum. Photograph © Household Cavalry Regimental Collection Trust)*

— A satirical sketch of Captain R. L. H. Jenkinson – 'Ring that b—y bell! (Sniff.)', c. 1948. *(Regimental Albums, Household Cavalry Museum. Photograph © Household Cavalry Regimental Collection Trust)*

Part Seven – The Second Great Change

498 A German surrenders and in the background is Lieutenant David Tabor's Daimler armoured car named Beaufort. *(Regimental Albums, Household Cavalry Museum. Photograph © Household Cavalry Regimental Collection Trust)*

503 King Edward VIII on parade in 1936. *(Regimental Albums, Household Cavalry Museum. Photograph © Household Cavalry Regimental Collection Trust)*

— The King's Life Guard in the early days of the Second World War. *(Regimental Albums, Household Cavalry Museum. Photograph © Household Cavalry Regimental Collection Trust)*

505 The Composite Regiment, renamed 1 HCR departing for Palestine with horses, January 1940. *(Regimental Albums, Household Cavalry Museum. Photograph © Household Cavalry Regimental Collection Trust)*

— Horses exercising in the sea in Palestine. *(Regimental Albums, Household Cavalry Museum. Photograph © Household Cavalry Regimental Collection Trust)*

511 Lieutenant 'G' (Gerard) Leigh during the advance on Baghdad in May 1941 with a wrecked Messerschmitt in the background. *(By kind permission of Colonel David Smiley)*

— Part of the floating advance to Baghdad led by Andrew Ferguson on the Euphrates. *(By kind permission of Colonel David Smiley)*

515 David Smiley behind a bullet-ridden windscreen. *(By kind permission of Colonel 'G' (Gerard) Leigh)*

— During the search for Dr Grobba 1 HCR find a crashed car full of Iraqi officers. *(By kind permission of Colonel David Smiley)*

— 'B' Squadron encounter French troops having crossed the Syrian border in an attempt to capture Dr Grobba at Kameschle. *(By kind permission of Colonel David Smiley)*

518 David Rocksavage – later the Marquess of Cholmondeley. *(Private Collection)*

— One of the dummy tanks from Tony Murray Smith's 'Smithforce'. *(By kind permission of Colonel David Smiley)*

— The German gun factory in Teheran where 1 HCR were billeted in September 1941. *(By kind permission of Colonel David Smiley)*

528 Valerian Wellesley, later Marquess of Douro and Duke of Wellington, left, as two German prisoners are searched after El Alamein. *(By kind permission of Colonel David Smiley)*

— Italian prisoners of war during the capture of Tunis between January and May 1943. *(Regimental Albums, Household Cavalry Museum. Photograph © Household Cavalry Regimental Collection Trust)*

535 Trooper Funnel receiving the latest reports of fighting in his sector during the occupation of Fano in the Marches region of Italy 1944. *(Regimental Albums, Household Cavalry Museum. Photograph © Household Cavalry Regimental Collection Trust)*

— An armoured car of 1 HCR approaching the Della Maiella Mountains in Abruzzo, where they were to support the 4th Indian Division in May 1944. *(Regimental Albums, Household Cavalry Museum. Photograph © Household Cavalry Regimental Collection Trust)*

542 British column held up on the Vire to Caen Road following D Day. *(Regimental Albums, Household Cavalry Museum. Photograph © Household Cavalry Regimental Collection Trust)*

— The Royals sticking maps together after a heavy downpour of rain near Lisieux. *(Regimental Albums,*

Household Cavalry Museum. Photograph © Household Cavalry Regimental Collection Trust)

— General Montgomery at Sourdevalle on 16 August 1944. *(Regimental Albums, Household Cavalry Museum. Photograph © Household Cavalry Regimental Collection Trust)*

549 A Guards Armoured Division vehicle exploding after being hit during Operation Market Garden, September 1944. *(Imperial War Museum, Image no. B 10124A)*

— The liberation of Denmark, 1945. *(Regimental Albums, Household Cavalry Museum. Photograph © Household Cavalry Regimental Collection Trust)*

554 The first King's Life Guard after the war, 1945. *(Regimental Albums, Household Cavalry Museum. Photograph © Household Cavalry Regimental Collection Trust)*

— The Blues at tattoo in 1947 in Germany led by Major Valerian Wellesley, Marquess of Douro. *(By kind permission of the Duke of Wellington)*

556 The Queen's Coronation 1953 – the rehearsal. *(Regimental Albums, Household Cavalry Museum. Photograph © Household Cavalry Regimental Collection Trust)*

— The Queen's Coronation 1953 – the day itself. *(Regimental Albums, Household Cavalry Museum. Photograph © Household Cavalry Regimental Collection Trust)*

557 Paul Maze painting 'The Trooping the Colour' on a stand especially constructed for the purpose. *(By kind permission of The Hon Mrs Robert Spencer Churchill)*

— A study for Paul Maze's 'The Trooping the Colour'. *(By kind permission of The Hon Mrs Robert Spencer Churchill)*

559 The Blues departing for Cyprus, 1956. *(Regimental Albums, Household Cavalry Museum. Photograph © Household Cavalry Regimental Collection Trust)*

— Government House, Cyprus, 1956. Front row, left to right: Lady Dorothea Head, Field Marshal Sir John Harding (Governor of Cyprus), Lady Harding and Sir Anthony Head (Secretary of State for War). The Marquess and Marchioness of Douro are standing behind Lady Harding. *(By kind permission of the Duke of Wellington)*

560 Trooper Grice on a jungle patrol in Borneo. *(Regimental Albums, Household Cavalry Museum. Photograph © Household Cavalry Regimental Collection Trust)*

— A Borneo patrol in the Sungai Plieran area near the Usun Apau plateau. *(By kind permission of Captain Lord Patrick Beresford)*

564 The Household Cavalry deployed to Cyprus as part of the United Nations force, c. 1965. *(Regimental Albums, Household Cavalry Museum. Photograph © Household Cavalry Regimental Collection Trust)*

568 Princess Anne escorted by Andrew Parker Bowles during the amalgamation of The Blues with The Royals in 1969 in Germany. *(Regimental Albums, Household Cavalry Museum. Photograph © Household Cavalry Regimental Collection Trust)*

— A tank parade in the 1960s. *(Regimental Albums, Household Cavalry Museum. Photograph © Household Cavalry Regimental Collection Trust)*

570 Sefton, the horse who survived a bomb detonated in Hyde Park by the IRA on 20 July 1982. *(By kind permission of Brigadier Andrew Parker Bowles)*

— The Blues and Royals in the Falklands War, 1982. *(Private Collection)*

572 'A' and 'B' squadrons, Gorny Vakuf, July 1994, by Major Harry Holcroft. *(Officers' mess, Household Cavalry Regiment, Combermere Barracks, Windsor. Photograph © Household Cavalry Regimental Collection Trust)*

574 The Queen's Birthday Parade, 2005. *(© Philip Vile)*

580 Officers of the Household Cavalry Mounted Regiment, 1988, by Andrew Festing. *(Officers' mess, Household Cavalry Mounted Regiment, Hyde Park Barracks, Knightsbridge. Photograph © Household Cavalry Regimental Collection Trust)*

— Portrait of Colonel Fred Burnaby by Jacques Tissot. *(National Portrait Gallery)*

— Lucian Freud working on a portrait of Andrew Parker Bowles, 2003. *(© David Dawson)*

584 'D' Squadron on nighttime manoeuvre, 2003. *(Photograph © Household Cavalry Museum)*

— 'D' Squadron at prayer, 2003. *(Crown Copyright)*

Period headress illustrations on chapter title pages by Jason Askew.

Bibliography

GENERAL

The most detailed history of The Life Guards and The Blues is Sir George Arthur's three-volume *The Story of The Household Cavalry*. The first two volumes were published by Constable in London in 1909 and the third, which covers 1914–18, by Heinemann in 1926. Arthur joined 2nd Life Guards in 1880, served on the staff in Egypt in 1882, and was present at Kassassin. He was on Wolseley's staff in Egypt and the Sudan in 1885, and thereafter retained close links to Wolseley and Kitchener, both of whose biographies he wrote, and was Kitchener's Private Secretary during the First World War. More recent historians have said that his work is inaccurate but I do not agree. There is, certainly, the odd mistake, which is hardly surprising in such a full work, but most of his research appears to me to be accurate and it is certainly painstaking.

The History of The Royal Dragoons by C. T. Atkinson, a historian rather than a regimental officer, is an outstanding book. Very thoroughly researched, and immensely detailed, it was published privately for the regiment in 1934, in a limited edition of 125 copies, by Robert Maclehose at the Glasgow University Press and paid for by subscription.

There have also been several shorter histories. J. N. P. Watson's *Through Fifteen Reigns* (Spellmount Publishing, 1997) is an excellent example. All three regiments' histories were also written by Lieutenant Colonel R. J. T. Hills for Leo Cooper's Famous Regiments series in 1972. An earlier version of these, *Historical Records of the British Army*, published as part of a Government initiative by Horse Guards in the 1830s and 40s, contains good volumes on the Life Guards and The Blues by Edmund Packe, son of Major Packe who was killed at Waterloo (*A Historical Record of the Royal Regiment of Horse Guards or Oxford Blues*, Parker, Furnival & Parker, London, 1847). Another work of which I have made extensive use is the very well-researched eight-volume series, *A History of the British Cavalry 1816–1939* by the Marquess of Anglesey, and published by Leo Cooper in London between 1973 and 1997. This covers the period from Waterloo until the beginning of the Second World War. Anglesey served in the Household Cavalry in the Second World War.

There are then three very good histories of the Second World War. The stories of 1 and 2 HCR are covered in detail in companion volumes, *The Household Cavalry at War*. Colonel The Hon. Humphrey Wyndham's *First Household Cavalry Regiment* was published by Gale & Polden in Aldershot in 1952 and Roden Orde's *Second Household Cavalry Regiment* in 1953.

These are both very thorough, well illustrated and have clear maps. *The Story of The Royal Dragoons 1938–1945* by Julian Pitt-Rivers, published privately for the regiment by William Clowes & Son in London in 1955, is also excellent and a very good read in its own right.

The contemporary history of the regiments is also well covered. Two books cover the post-1945 period in detail: Willie Lloyd's *Challengers and Chargers: A History of The Life Guards 1945–1992* and Johnny Watson's *The Story of The Blues and Royals*, published by Leo Cooper in 1993.

UNPUBLISHED SOURCES

Many of the sources I have used are unpublished diaries and letters in the Household Cavalry Archive, part of the Household Cavalry Museum in Windsor. They are all available to researchers and can be seen by arrangement with the Archivist by writing to The Household Cavalry Museum, Combermere Barracks, Windsor, Berks, SL4 3DN. These are all detailed in the notes and do not need repeating here. Otherwise I have made extensive use of the Public Record Office War Office (PRO WO) and National Army Museum (NAM) papers. These are, again, all detailed in the notes.

Other non-published sources which have been invaluable are the following private papers (arranged chronologically):

The Stuart Papers: The Royal Archive at Windsor Castle (RA SP).
The Compton Archives at Castle Ashby.
The Cumberland Papers: The Royal Archive (RA CP).
The papers of John, Marquess of Granby at Belvoir Castle.
'The Problems of a Garrison Town: Windsor 1815–1855': a PhD synopsis by Dr Brigitte Mitchell submitted to the University of Reading in 2001.
Victorian Archive: The Royal Archive (RA VIC) including Queen Victoria's Journal (QVJ).
'Soldier of the Queen: The Life of John Brocklehurst, Lord Ranksborough' by Jean Bray, Librarian at Sudeley Castle. A most valuable unpublished manuscript.
Lord Birdwood's letters and papers 1943–45, kindly copied to me by Lieutenant Colonel Gordon Birdwood.
The Private Papers and Diary of the Duke of Wellington (1941–2).
The Diary of Major John Shaw, MC, in possession of Major Johnny Shaw.

Notes by Captain David Summers, in possession of Major Johnny Shaw.
The letters of Major John Hamilton-Russell, MC, and miscellaneous papers relating to the Royal Dragoons in the Second World War, in possession of Colonel James Hamilton-Russell.

PUBLISHED SOURCES
(arranged alphabetically by author and all published in London unless otherwise stated)

Adkin, Mark, *The Waterloo Companion* (Aurum, 2001)
Ainslie, Charles P. de, *The Royal Regiment of Dragoons* (Chapman and Hall, 1887)
Alexander, Michael, *The True Blue: The Life and Adventures of Colonel Fred Burnaby* (Rupert Hart-Davis, 1957)
Anglesey, Marquess of, *One Leg: The Life and Letters of Henry William Paget, First Marquess of Anglesey* (Jonathan Cape, 1961)
Anglesey, Marquess of, *A History of the British Cavalry 1816–1939* (Leo Cooper, 1973–97):
  Volume One *1816–1850*
  Volume Two *1851–1871*
  Volume Three *1872–1898*
  Volume Four *1899–1913*
  Volume Five *Egypt, Palestine and Syria, 1914–1919*
  Volume Six *Mesopotamia, 1914–1918*
  Volume Seven *The Curragh Incident and the Western Front, 1914–1918*
  Volume Eight *The Western Front, 1915–1918* and *Epilogue, 1919–1939*
Arthur, Sir George, *The Story of the Household Cavalry*, vols 1 and 2 (1660–1902) (Constable and Co., 1909). Vol. 3 (1914–1918) (William Heinemann, 1926)
———, *Not Worth Reading – Memoirs* (Longmans, Green and Co. Ltd, 1938)
Asquith, Stuart, *New Model Army* (Osprey Publishing, 1981)
Atkinson, C. T., *The History of The Royal Dragoons 1661–1934* (Robert Maclehose at University Press, Glasgow, 1934)
Baker, Granville, *Old Cavalry Stations* (Heath Cranton Ltd, 1934)
Bickersteth, Lieutenant Colonel J. B., *History of the 6th Cavalry Brigade 1914–1919* (Baynard Press, 1920)
Bishop, Tim, *One Young Soldier: The Memoirs of a Cavalryman*, ed. Bruce Shand (Michael Russell, Norwich, 1993)
Bruce, Anthony, *The Purchase System in the British Army 1660–1871* (Royal Historical Society Studies in History Series, 1980)
Burnaby, Colonel Fred, *A Ride to Khiva* (Cassell, Petter and Galpin)
Carlton, Charles, *Going to the Wars: The Experiences of the British Civil Wars 1638–51* (Routledge, 1876)
Carver, Field Marshal Lord, *Alamein* (Batsford, 1962)

———, *The National Army Museum Book of the Boer War* (Pan, 2000)
Chenevix-Trench, Charles, *A History of Horsemanship* (Doubleday & Co., 1970)
Childs, John, *The Army of Charles II* (Routledge and Kegan Paul, 1976)
———, *The Army of James II and The Glorious Revolution* (Manchester University Press, 1980)
——— *The British Army of William III 1698–1702* (Manchester University Press, 1987)
Clarendon, Edward, Earl of, *The History of the Great Rebellion*, ed. W. D. Macray (6 vols, 1888)
Clark, Sir George, *The Later Stuarts* (Oxford History of England Series, OUP, 1934).
Cooper, Leo, *British Regular Cavalry 1644–1914* (Chapman & Hall, 1965).
Crutchley, C. E. (ed.), *Machine Gunner 1914–1918* (Mercury Press, Northampton, 1973)
Curtayne, Alice, *Patrick Sarsfield* (Noted Irish Lives Series, Talbot Press, 1934)
Cusack, John and Herbert, Ivor, *Scarlet Fever: A Lifetime with Horses* (Cassell, 1972)
Daglish, Ian, *Operation Bluecoat* (Leo Cooper Pen and Sword Books, 2003)
———, *Operation Goodwood* (Leo Cooper Pen and Sword Books, 2004)
Dawnay, Major N. P., *The Standards of the Household Cavalry* (Gale & Polden, Aldershot, n.d.)
———, *The Badges of Warrant and Non-Commissioned Rank in the British Army* (Society For Army Historical Research, Special Publication No. 6, 1949)
De Chair, Somerset, *The Golden Carpet* (Faber and Faber, 1944)
Dutton, Ralph, *English Court Life* (Batsford, 1963)
Emerson, William, *Monmouth's Rebellion* (Yale, 1951).
Ensor, R. C. K., *England 1870–1914* (Oxford History of England Series, OUP, 1936).
Esdaile, Charles, *The Peninsular War* (Penguin, 2002)
Firth, Sir Charles and Davies, Godfrey, *Cromwell's Army*, 2 (OUP, 1940).
Fraser, General Sir David, *Frederick the Great* (Penguin, 2000)
Frearson, Fritz, *To Mr Davenport* (Society for Army Historical Research, Special Publication No. 9, 1968)
Gilmour, Ian, *Riots, Risings and Revolution* (Hutchinson, 1992)
Glover, Michael, *A Very Slippery Fellow: Life of Sir Robert Wilson* (OUP, 1977)
Goulburn, Edward, *The Blueviad* (J. Maynard, 1805)
Green, David, *Queen Anne* (History Book Club, 1970)
Hague, William, *William Pitt the Younger* (HarperCollins, 2004)
Harvey, Gerald William, *The Diary of a Forgotten Battalion: The Household Battalion in the First World War 1916–1918* (Shalford Publishing, Bradford-on-Avon, 2004)

Hastings, Selina, *Evelyn Waugh: A Biography* (Minerva, 1994)
Hibbert, Christopher, *The Destruction of Lord Raglan* (Penguin, 1961)
———, *Waterloo* (Wordsworth Military Library, 1967)
———, *The English: A Social History* (Guild Publishing, 1987)
———, *Wellington: A Personal History* (HarperCollins, 1998)
———, *George III: A Personal History* (Penguin, 1998)
———, *The Marlboroughs* (Penguin, 2002)
———, *King Mob* (Sutton Publishing, 2004)
Hill, Joanna, *The Hills of Hawkstone and Attingham: The Rise, Shine and Decline of a Shropshire Family* (Phillimore, Chichester, 2005)
Hills, R. J. T., *Something about a Soldier* (Lovat Dickson, 1934)
———, *A Short History of The Royal Horse Guards* (Leo Cooper, 1970)
———, *A Short History of The Life Guards* (Leo Cooper, 1971)
———, *A Short History of The Royal Dragoons* (Leo Cooper, 1972)
Holmes, Richard, *Wellington* (HarperCollins, 2003)
Horsley, John, *The Case of John Horsley Esq.* (Published privately in London in 1805. Copy in National Army Museum (NAM 20301/92 HCR))
James, John, *Surgeon James' Journal 1815*, ed. Jane Vansittart (Cassell, 1964)
Lawn, George, *Music in State Clothing* (Leo Cooper, 1995)
Lees-Milne, James, *The Last Stuarts* (Hogarth Press, 1983)
Liddell Hart, Basil, *History of the First World War* (Pan, 1972)
Linaker, David and Dine, Gordon, *Cavalry Warrant Officers' and Non-Commissioned Officers' Arm Badges* (Military Historical Society Special Publication, 1997)
Lloyd, R. A., *A Trooper in the Tins* (Hurst & Blackett, 1938)
Lloyd, W., *Challengers and Chargers: A History of The Life Guards 1945–1992* (Leo Cooper, 1992)
Lucas Phillips, C. E., *Alamein* (Heinemann, 1962)
Macaulay, Lord, *The History of England* (Penguin, 1968)
Manners, Walter Evelyn, *John Manners, Marquis of Granby* (Macmillan Co., 1899)
Mansel, Philip, *Pillars of Monarchy* (Quartet Books, 1984)
Marston, Daniel, *The Seven Years War* (Osprey Publishing, 2001)
Martyn, Charles, *The British Cavalry Sword from 1600* (Leo Cooper Pen and Sword Books, 2004)
Mays, Spike, *Fall Out the Officers* (Eyre & Spottiswoode, 1969)
Mosley, Nicholas, *Julian Grenfell: His Life and the Times of his Death 1888–1915* (Weidenfeld & Nicholson, 1976)
National Army Museum, *The Glorious Revolution* (1988 Exhibition Catalogue)
Orde, Roden, *The Household Cavalry at War: Second Household Cavalry Regiment* (Gale & Polden, Aldershot, 1953)
Packe, Edmund, *An Historical Record of the Royal Regiment of Horse Guards or Oxford Blues* (1847)

Pakenham, Thomas, *The Boer War* (Futura, 1979)
Pitt-Rivers, Julian, *The Story of The Royal Dragoons 1938–1945* (William Clowes & Sons, 1956)
Redgrave, Major General Sir Roy, KBE, MC, *Balkan Blue* (Leo Cooper Pen and Sword Books, 2000)
Roberts, Andrew, *Waterloo* (HarperCollins, 2005)
Rocksavage, Earl of, MC, *A Day's March Nearer Home: Experiences with the Royals 1939–1945* (John and Edward Bumpus Ltd, 1947)
Roynon, Gavin, *Massacre of the Innocents: The Crofton Diaries 1914–15* (Sutton Publishing, 2004)
Schama, Simon, *A History of Britain* (BBC Worldwide, 2003)
Skrine, Francis, *Fontenoy and Great Britain's Share in the War of the Austrian Succession 1741–1748* (William Blackwood, Edinburgh, 1906)
Smiley, David, *Irregular Regular* (Michael Russell, 1994)
———, *Albanian Assignment* (Chatto and Windus, 1984)
Sykes, Christopher, *Evelyn Waugh: A Biography* (Penguin, 1975)
Symonds, Richard, *The Complete Military Diary* (Partizan Press, 1989)
Tincey, John, *Soldiers of the English Civil War* (Osprey Publishing, 1990)
Tomalin, Clare, *Samuel Pepys: The Unequalled Self* (Penguin, 2002)
Trevelyan, G. M., *England Under Queen Anne* (Collins Fontana, 1965)
Tyndale, Major, *Treatise on Equitation* (A Subscription Book published privately in 1797. Copy in National Army Museum)
Urban, Mark, *Generals* (Faber and Faber, 2005)
Warner, Philip, *The British Cavalry* (Dent and Sons, 1984)
Watson, J. N. P., *Guardsmen of the Sky* (Michael Russell, 1997)
———, *The Story of The Blues and Royals* (Leo Cooper Pen and Sword Books, 1993)
———, *Through Fifteen Reigns* (Spellmount, 1997)
Watson, Steven, *The Reign of George III* (Oxford History of England Series, OUP, 1960)
Wauchope, Piers, *Patrick Sarsfield and the Williamite Wars* (Irish Academic Press, Dublin, 1992)
Wharton, Jeremiah, *The Letters of Jeremiah Wharton* (Tercio Publishing, 1983)
Williams, Basil, *The Whig Supremacy* (Oxford History of England Series, OUP, 1939)
Woodham-Smith, Cecil, *The Reason Why: Behind the Scenes at the Charge of the Light Brigade* (Penguin, 1953)
Woodward, E. L., *The Age of Reform 1815–1870* (Oxford History of England Series, OUP, 1938)
Wright, Thomas, *The Life of Colonel Fred Burnaby* (Everett & Co., 1908)
Wyndham, Colonel, The Hon. Humphrey, *The Household Cavalry at War: First Household Cavalry Regiment* (Gale & Polden, Aldershot, 1952)

Notes and References

Full bibliographical details of works cited are given in the Bibliography.

One – The King's Life Guard

1. Samuel Pepys, *Diary*, 25 May 1660.
2. Ibid.
3. Mansel, *Pillars of Monarchy*, p. 13.
4. John Evelyn, miscellaneous writings quoted in Arthur, *The Story of The Household Cavalry*.
5. Ibid.
6. Symonds, *The Complete Military Diary*.
7. Firth and Davies, *A Regimental History of Cromwell's Army*, 1, p. 42.
8. Edward, Earl of Clarendon, *The History of the Great Rebellion*, 4, p. 19 and quoted ibid., 1, p. 42.
9. Edmund Ludlow, *Diaries*, 1, pp. 39–41.
10. Quoted in Chenevix-Trench, *A History of Horsemanship*, p. 145.
11. John Vicars, quoted in Firth and Davies, 1, p. 43.
12. Ibid., p. 44.
13. John Lillburne, *The Second Part of England's New Chaines Discovered*, quoted ibid., p. 50.
14. *Cromwelliana*, p. 62, quoting *The Moderate Intelligencer*, quoted ibid., p. 51.
15. Clarendon, *Rebellion*, quoted ibid., p. 54.
16. A full, and juicy, account of the Venner Riots is published in the *Mercurius Publicus*, 3 January 1661.
17. Rugge's Diurnal, quoted in Arthur.
18. Ibid., p. 16, quoting Clarke.
19. From Hibbert, *The Marlboroughs*, p. 15.
20. Pepys, *Diary*, 19 May 1668.
21. Figures taken from Gregory King's estimates of 1696, printed in George Chalmers' 'Observations', and reproduced in Clark, *The Later Stuarts*, pp. 25–6.
22. The Royal Wardrobe Books in RA SP.
23. For a full study of the purchase system see Bruce, 'The Purchase System in the British Army 1660–1871'.
24. PRO WO 26/1, f. 33.
25. These prices are taken from an order placed for the Royal Mews on 7 December 1681: RA SP/86335.
26. Examples of front and back armour, hat, pot and sword can all be seen in the Household Cavalry Museum at Windsor.
27. Property of the National Trust at Charlecote Park in Warwickshire.
28. Sir Ralph Verney to his brother Edmund Verney, 12 July 1677.
29. PRO WO 26/3.
30. PRO WO 5/1 No. 55, dated 3 April 1684. There are countless similar orders.
31. Quoted in Hills, *The Life Guards*.
32. *Mercurius Publicus*, 27 September 1662.

Two – Unton Croke's Regiment of Horse

1. From Firth and Davies, *A Regimental History of Cromwell's Army*, p. 6.
2. Ibid., p. 28.
3. Quoted in Thurloe State Papers, ibid.
4. Quoted in Berry's entry in *Dictionary of National Biography* (*DNB*).
5. Firth and Davies, 1, p. 247.
6. Sir Alexander Croke, *Genealogical History of the Croke Family*, 1823, vol. 2.
7. *Mercurius Publicus*, 29 December–5 January 1659, pp. 996–7, quoted in Firth and Davies.
8. Quoted in Firth and Davies, 1, p. 253.
9. Clarendon, *History of The Great Rebellion*, Book VIII.
10. Said to be from Macpherson's Original Papers, *The Life of James II*, vol. 1, and quoted in Packe, *An Historical Record of the Royal Regiment of Horse Guards or Oxford Blues*. I cannot verify the source, but Packe, whose father served in the regiment at Waterloo, is generally fairly accurate.
11. Arthur, *The Story of the Household Cavalry*, 1, p. 51.
12. Earl of Ailesbury, *Memoirs*, p. 72, quoted ibid., p. 52.
13. British Museum (BM), Landsdowne MSS., No. 805, ff. 83–9, 'A Biographical and Highly Sarcastical List'; quoted in Childs, *The Army of Charles II*, p. 37.
14. PRO WO 5/1, No. 58. There are many similar orders in this series.
15. PRO WO 26/3, No. 185. Order dated 10 July 1673.
16. PRO WO 5/1 series has frequent orders worded like this.
17. From *The Travels of Cosmo III in England*, quoted by Arthur, 1, p. 82.
18. From Childs, *The Army of James II and the Glorious Revolution*, p. 5.
19. Figures taken from Clark, *The Later Stuarts*, p. 76.
20. Pepys, *Diary*, 28 April 1669.
21. Clark, p. 100.
22. PR WO 26/2, No. 34, dated 30 March 1674.

23 PRO WO 26/2, No. 373, dated 3 August 1674.
24 Arthur, *The Story of the Household Calvalry*, 1, p. 92.
25 Ibid., p. 90.
26 The twelve are named in PRO WO 26/2, No. 298, dated 19 May 1674.
27 Hatton, *Correspondence*, 1, p. 71, quoted in Childs, *The Army of Charles II*, p. 178.
28 They are listed ibid., p. 234.
29 Arthur quotes the Quest in full, 1, p. 121.
30 From Chamberlayne, *Angliae Notitia*, reproduced in Arthur, *The Story of the Household Cavalry*, 1, p. 116.
31 Actually grenades were not a new invention, and were mentioned by Samuel Pepys as being used by the army as early as 1659.
32 Arthur, *The Story of the Household Cavalry*, 1, p. 117, quoting 'Treatise on Military Discipline', 1684.
33 Memoirs of the Verney family, quoted ibid.
34 John Evelyn, *Diary*, 29 June 1678.
35 The Quartering Order is dated 20 August 1683; PRO WO 5/1, No. 1.
36 John Evelyn, *Diary*, 21 August 1674.
37 Earl of Ailesbury, *Memoirs*, p. 82, quoted in Watson, *Through Fifteen Reigns*.
38 Arthur, *The Story of the Household Cavalry*, 1, p. 149.

Three – The Tangier Horse

1 For a full list of holders of these offices and a more detailed explanation of their duties see Childs, *The Army of Charles II*, pp. 260–1.
2 Carefully preserved in the PRO series WO 4, WO 5 and WO 26.
3 PRO WO 30/48; this extends to some 635 pages and is an extremely thorough piece of military staffwork.
4 PRO WO 4/1, No. 146, dated 20 August 1689.
5 BM, Harleian MSS. 1595, p. 10, quoted in Atkinson, *The History of the Royal Dragoons*.
6 Fairborne's Report to London, quoted ibid., p. 23.

Four – Sedgemoor and James II's Reforms

1 PRO WO 5/1, f. 60 is the Mobilization Order dated 19 June 1685.
2 PRO WO 5/1, f. 56, dated 15 June 1685.
3 PRO WO 5/1, ff. 53 (Blues) and 61 (Royals), dated respectively 15 and 19 June 1685.
4 An unidentified captain in The Blues writing in 1718; Kennett's *History*, 3, p. 432, quoted in Arthur, *The Story of the Household Cavalry*.
5 *The Journal of Edward Dummer*, BM, Harleian MSS. Add. MSS. 31956.
6 Feversham's dispatch to the Earl of Sunderland, Secretary of State, in Stopford Sackville MSS. I.21, quoted in Atkinson, *The History of the Royal Dragoons*, p. 46.
7 See note 4 above.
8 Evelyn's diary, quoted in Arthur, *The Story of the Household Cavalry*, 1, p. 166.
9 *Biographical History of England*, 1, p. 35, quoted ibid.
10 See note 5 above.
11 The Scots Greys and The Queen's Regiment of Horse.
12 The best reference for details on the size of the army in this period is Childs, *The Army of James II and The Glorious Revolution*.
13 Ibid., p. 13.
14 Frazer's *Anonymous Letters* v. 62, 14 February 1687, quoted ibid., p. 34.
15 Arthur, *The Story of the Household Cavalry*, 1, p. 206.
16 Earl of Ailesbury, *Memoirs*, p. 130, quoted ibid., p. 202.
17 PRO WO 5/2 contains most of the movement orders for the period.
18 PRO WO 26/6, f. 102 is the Parade State for the 1686 Hounslow Camp.
19 Sandford, quoted in Arthur, *The Story of the Household Cavalry*, 1, p. 167.
20 Childs, *The Army of James II and the Glorious Revolution*, p. 45.
21 The term squadron first appears in WO papers in 1683 and is used frequently thereafter. See PRO WO 5/1 and 5/2.
22 Childs, *The Army of Charles II*, p. 63.
23 Childs, *The Army of James II and the Glorious Revolution*, p. 97.
24 PRO WO 26/6, f. 8.
25 PRO WO 26/6, f. 79 is the Hounslow Camp Regulations.
26 W. Y. Carman, 'A Trumpeter of the 1st Horse Guards', *Journal of the Society for Historical Research*, LIX, p. 191.
27 There is a magnificent portrait of a black trumpeter in the Life Guards, painted by David Morier in 1751, in the Royal Collection.
28 See Clark, *The Later Stuarts*, p. 39.
29 Calendar of Treasury Papers, VII, Pt 2, p. 1482 for the Tangier System and p. 1204 for Mary Helme's entry.
30 Childs, *The Army of James II and the Glorious Revolution*, p. 35.
31 WO Order dated 28 May 1686, signed by Blathwayt.
32 Childs, *The Army of James II and the Glorious Revolution*, p. 44.
33 Ibid., p. 102.
34 Macaulay's *History of England*, 8, p. 316.
35 *The Diary of Abraham de la Pryme*, ed. Charles Jackson (Surtees Society, 1870), pp. 43–4, and quoted in Childs, *The British Army of William III*, p. 5.
36 The Circular was meticulously entered by Blathwayt's clerks in the WO records; PRO WO 4/1, f. 82.

Five – The Glorious Revolution and War in Ireland

1. The best biography of Sarsfield is Wauchope, *Patrick Sarsfield and the Williamite Wars*. The description of the Battle of Wincanton is on pp. 36–9.
2. Arthur, *The Story of the Household Cavalry*, 1, p. 219.
3. James II, *Life*, 2, p. 217, quoted ibid., p. 217.
4. Ibid., p. 233.
5. Childs, *The Army of James II and the Glorious Revolution*, p. 43.
6. Arthur, *The Story of the Household Cavalry*, 1, p. 231.
7. George Bancroft, writing in the nineteenth century.
8. Hibbert, *The Marlboroughs*, p. 48.
9. Ibid., p. 48.
10. Later casualties in the Irish campaign are recorded in some detail.
11. Arthur, *The Story of the Household Cavalry*, 1, p. 243.
12. Childs, *The Army of James II and the Glorious Revolution*, p. 157.
13. The incident did not appear to harm Poultney's military career. He later transferred to the Life Guards and became a Brigadier General. William III is reported to have said that the loss would have been irreparable had Meesters been captured.
14. WO 5/5, f. 278, dated September 1689, appears to be the first attempt to divide England into different regimental recruiting areas.
15. Atkinson, *The History of the Royal Dragoons*, p. 65, quoting Treasury Records Out Letters General, 26, p. 13.
16. The best description of contemporary medical arrangements in both Ireland and Flanders is Childs, *The Army of James II and the Glorious Revolution*, pp. 158–9.
17. Quoted in Arthur, *The Story of the Household Cavalry*, 1, p. 253.
18. Andreas Claudianus' account is taken from Wauchope, p. 232.
19. Ibid., p. 253.

Six – Flanders Fields

1. Auvergne's description from his narrative of the 1695 campaign, quoted in Arthur, *The Story of the Household Cavalry*, 1, p. 286.
2. Noble, *A Biographical History of England*, 2, p. 34, also quoted in Arthur.
3. RA/GEO 86878, dated 29 April 1696.
4. Childs, *The British Army of William III*, p. 141.
5. Ibid., p. 158.
6. Captain Henry Mordaunt, MP, speaking in the House of Commons, 26 November 1692.
7. From a narrative of the 1693 campaign by d'Auvergne, quoted in Arthur, *The Story of the Household Cavalry*, 1, p. 275.
8. Compton Archives at Castle Ashby, FD 1186(2).
9. Childs, *The British Army of William III*, p. 45.
10. *Post Boy*, 11 November 1699.
11. *London Post*, 9 November 1699.

Seven – Policing London and War in Spain

1. Packe, *An Historical Record of the Royal Regiment of Horse Guards or Oxford Blues*, p. 72.
2. The best description of this incident is in Gilmour, *Riots, Risings and Revolution*, pp. 50–51, from where these quotes are taken.
3. The account of the Life Guards' actions that night is taken from the transcripts of Purchase's trial, recorded in Howells' *State Trials* and reproduced in Arthur, *The Story of The Household Cavalry*, 1, p. 315.
4. Details of their various moves are in PRO WO 5/20.
5. PRO WO 26/14, f. 56 contains the detailed orders.
6. Raby's voluminous correspondence is contained in the Stafford MSS. in the British Museum, but has been well summarized in Atkinson, *The History of the Royal Dragoons*, throughout chapters 6–10.
7. A copy of *The Journal of a Royal Dragoon in the Spanish Succession War* is held in the Household Cavalry Museum, Miscellaneous Papers Box 7, f. 16. It was prepared for publication by the Society for Army Historical Research by The Royals' historian, C. T. Atkinson, and was published as 'A Royal Dragoon in the Spanish Succession War' (SAHR Special publication No. 5).
8. Atkinson, *The History of the Royal Dragoons*, p. 85.
9. PRO WO 4/2, f. 66.
10. The complete list is at PRO WO 26/12, f. 164.
11. Quoted in Atkinson, *The History of the Royal Dragoons*, p. 89.
12. Ibid.
13. Ibid., p. 91.
14. Ibid., p. 92.
15. Ibid.
16. Ibid.
17. Ibid., p. 101.
18. Ibid., p. 105.

Eight – Germanic Order

1. Arthur, *The Story of the Household Cavalry*, has a whole chapter quoting press reports of various lurid misdemeanours, 1, pp. 332–47.
2. Dr Johnson, writing in *The Idler*, quoted in the biography of Cumberland in the Royal Archives.
3. The details of the warrant to re-equip the troop are in PRO WO 26/17, f. 38.
4. PRO WO 4/13, f. 311 refers.
5. PRO WO 30/25, f. 102, dated 25 May 1722, is the

full transcript of the investigation and recommendation which includes an analysis of every Life Guard commission awarded since 1660.
6. PRO WO 30/25, f. 172 is the transcript of the trial.
7. Hibbert, *The Marlboroughs*, quoting Stuart Reid, *John and Sarah, Duke and Duchess of Marlborough, 1650–1744* (1915), p. 429.
8. Hervey, quoted in *Dictionary of National Biography*.
9. PRO WO 26/17, f. 109 is the order regulating Life Guard pensions.
10. PRO WO 26/17, f. 4, dated 4 May 1724.
11. Childs, *The British Army of William III*, p. 146.
12. There are numerous examples of courts martial and the sentences they imposed in PRO WO 30/25. Thorne's case is at f. 141. Details of Horse Grenadier exemptions are at f. 172.
13. PRO WO 26/17, f. 308 is the complete instruction, dated 20 November 1729.

Nine – The War of the Austrian Succession

1. Richard Davenport's letters have been published by the Household Cavalry Museum: 'To Mr Davenport', SAHR, Special Publication No. 9, 1968.
2. Dr Buchanan's diary is kept in the Household Cavalry Museum. It has not, to the author's knowledge, been published, but copies are also held by the Royal Army Medical Corps Museum and by the Wellcome Institute.
3. Edmund Cox's journal is in the National Army Museum (NAM 8208-195-1).
4. Smollet, *Continuation of Hume's History of England*, 3, p. 137, quoted in Skrine, *Fontenoy*, p. 84.
5. Skrine, p. 75.
6. Ingleton's letter, dated 20 June 1743, was published in *The Gentleman's Magazine* and is reproduced in full in Arthur, *The Story of the Household Cavalry*, 1, p. 384.
7. Edmund Cox's journal, 16 July 1743.
8. Quoted in Arthur, *The Story of the Household Cavalry*, 1, p. 373.
9. Skrine, p. 82.
10. Ibid.
11. Dr Buchanan's diary.
12. Cumberland's order was dated 6 May and is quoted in full in Skrine, p. 144.
13. RA CP 2/167.
14. Lord Egmont's speech to the House of Lords, 27 November 1751.
15. Detailed costs are in RA CP, vi: 19:3.
16. Onslow remained in Plymouth until his untimely death in 1760, when he suffered an apoplectic fit at a court martial. Annoyingly, I cannot find out what heinous offence had caused such a violent reaction. Onslow's descendants still serve in the Household Cavalry.

Ten – The Seven Years War

1. PRO WO 4/40, f. 312 is a copy of the letter.
2. PRO SP 44/142, f. 437 refers.
3. From Evan Charteris, *William Augustus, Duke of Cumberland, 1721–48* (Edward Arnold, 1913), p. 84.
4. The only published biography of Granby I can trace is *John Manners, Marquis of Granby*, by his descendant Walter Evelyn Manners. It is difficult to find and I am much indebted to the Duke of Rutland for lending me his copy. Otherwise Granby's papers are to be found in several different archives, of which the Belvoir Castle and British Museum collections are the fullest.
5. Granby Papers at Belvoir.
6. It was the only one of its type to achieve its recruiting target of 780.
7. Atkinson, *The History of the Royal Dragoons*, p. 182, quoting an unidentified source.
8. Letter to John Davenport dated 3 January 1759.
9. In a letter sent to Granby, 25 April 1760. Rutland MSS., 2, p. 207 and quoted in full in Manners, p. 116.
10. Rutland MSS., Miscellaneous Papers, Box 69 contains much of Granby's correspondence on the trial, including copies of The Blues' officers' statements.
11. Quoted by Arthur, *The Story of the Household Cavalry*, 2, p. 445, from Belvoir Castle Papers, although I could not find this reference.
12. To Lord Charlemont; quoted by Manners, p. 136.
13. St Germain had resigned his command when the French armies joined on 10 July because he considered himself superior in rank to de Broglie, and handed his responsibilities over to de Muy.
14. Entry for 1 August in journal of Edmund Cox; NAM 8208/95-1.
15. De Mauvillon, translated by Carlyle, and quoted by Manners, p. 139.
16. Ibid., p. 144.
17. Davenport letters, No. 56, dated 1 August 1760.
18. Rutland MSS., Miscellaneous Papers, Box 163. Letter to Storer dated 21 January.
19. Arthur, *The Story of the Household Cavalry*, 2, p. 456.
20. Ibid., p. 455.
21. Manners, pp. 187–8.
22. Ibid., p. 204.
23. Quoted ibid., p. 220.
24. Granby to Ligonier, 6 July 1762: Rutland MSS. Manners, p. 245.

Eleven – The King's Peace and the Revolutionary's War

1. This is very well covered by William Hague in *William Pitt the Younger*, p. 181.
2. Quoted in Arthur, *the Story of the Household Calvary*, 2, p. 473.

3   Ibid., p. 474.
4   Ibid.
5   The best description of the Gordon Riots is in Christopher Hibbert, *King Mob*, from which this and many of the following quotes are taken.
6   Ibid., p. 57.
7   Ibid., quoting Frederick Reynolds, an eyewitness, on p. 57.
8   Ibid., p. 104.
9   Ibid., p. 128.
10 *Historical Record of The Life Guards*, Household Cavalry Museum, p. 136.
11 An example is in Captain Edward Kelly's case for his pair of Manton pistols in the Household Cavalry Museum.
12 From *England Under The House of Hanover*, 2, p. 106 quoted by Arthur, *The Story of the Household Cavalry*, 2, p. 475.
13 Ibid., p. 476.
14 Christopher Hibbert, *George III: A Personal History*, p. 111.
15 Walpole, *Reign of George III*, quoted in Arthur, *The Story of the Household Cavalry*, 2, p. 479.
16 Floyd's correspondence with Lord Pembroke has been published as *The Pembroke Papers (1780–1794)*, ed. by Lord Herbert (Jonathan Cape, 1950). This extract is taken from a letter written by Floyd to Lord Herbert on 9 November 1780 when Floyd was commanding the 19th Light Dragoons at York.
17 Quoted by Arthur, *The Story of the Household Cavalry*, 2, p. 480.
18 These figures are taken from Mansel, *Pillars of Monarchy*, p. 78, and names can be obtained from the *Army Lists*, a complete copy of which is held by the National Army Museum, amongst other places.
19 Quoted by Hague, p. 333.
20 Atkinson, *The History of the Royal Dragoons*, p. 228.
21 Hague, p. 339.
22 *The London Gazette*.
23 Duke of York's dispatch dated 25 April 1794 from Cateau, quoted in full by Arthur, *The Story of the Household Cavalry*, 2, p. 520.
24 Quoted by Atkinson, p. 220.
25 Quoted by Packe, *An Historical Record of The Royal Regiment of Horse Guards or Oxford Blues*. Packe's father was in the regiment and killed at Waterloo. He joined The Blues in 1799 and probably passed historical material on to his son.
26 Atkinson, p. 225.
27 Harcourt, quoted ibid., p. 232.

Twelve – Fashion in Windsor and War in Spain

1   Hibbert, *George III: A Personal History*, p. 359.
2   *The Pilot*, 17 June 1812, quoted by Arthur, *The Story of the Household Cavalry*, 2, p. 541.

3   It is still in use today as a transport and administrative centre for London.
4   Northumberland to Hill, 26 August 1812 (NAM, 6309-138).
5   RA GEO/21136; Harrington to Colonel McMahon, the Prince Regent's Military Secretary, 14 November 1813.
6   *The Military Panorama*, 1812, reproduced by Arthur, *The Story of the Household Cavalry*, 2, p. 527.
7   All this information is taken directly from *Royal Horse Guards Standing Orders* issued at Windsor in 1802; Household Cavalry Museum, AB2546.
8   Tyndale's *Treatise on Military Equitation* was published privately as a Subscription Book in 1797. There is a copy in the National Army Museum.
9   Some of Hill's correspondence, including this letter, is in the National Army Museum (NAM 6309-18).
10 *The Blueviad* was published by J. Maynard in Haymarket in 1805; copies are in the Household Cavalry Museum. Horsley's defence, *The Case of John Horsley*, was also published in London in 1805. There is a copy in the National Army Museum (NAM 20301-92 HOR).
11 Heathcote's letters were published by his granddaughter in London in 1910 as *Ralph Heathcote, Letters of a Young Diplomatist and Soldier during the Time of Napoleon*. Atkinson, pp. 243–4, quotes them freely.
12 The organization of Wellington's force did not change much after the winter of 1809; he had five infantry divisions, plus the Light Division, and four cavalry brigades.
13 Atkinson, p. 249, quoting Wellington, *Despatches from the Peninsula*, 5, p. 215.
14 Slade's diaries are held in the Cavalry Museum, AB2366, f. 17.
15 Cornet Francis Hall, 14th Light Dragoons, brigaded with The Royals. His *Peninsular Recollections* were published in the Royal United Service Institute journal in 1911.
16 Atkinson, *The History of the Royal Dragoons*, p. 259.
17 The Willis letters are in the Household Cavalry Museum, Box 13, f. AB2643. This one, written to Miss Slater, was dated 21 April 1810.
18 Northumberland's correspondence with Hill is in the National Army Museum (NAM, ff. 6309-138). This extract is taken from a letter written from Alnwick Castle in August 1812.

Thirteen – Defeating Napoleon

1   Sulivan's journal is in the National Army Museum (NAM, f. 7504-17).
2   The hospital at Belem was notorious for its poor standards and for the number of malingerers who kept themselves there. Wellington ultimately sorted it out.

3   Atkinson, *The History of the Royal Dragoons*, p. 286.
4   Ibid., p. 150.
5   From *Notes on Conversations with the Duke of Wellington* quoted by Arthur, *The Story of the Household Cavalry*, 2, p. 575.
6   See note 14 below.
7   Part One Orders, 1st Life Guards, 26 April 1815.
8   A complete set of Kelly's correspondence during May and June 1815 is in the Household Cavalry Museum, Box 1, f. 1.
9   *Surgeon James' Journal* was edited by Jane Vansittart and published by Cassell, London, in 1964.
10 Radclyffe kept a journal, which Atkinson quotes on p. 303.
11 The Marquess of Anglesey, *One-Leg, the Life and Letters of Henry William Paget, First Marquess of Anglesey*, p. 132.
12 Ibid., p. 133.
13 Peel's letter is in the Household Cavalry Museum, f. 22/572/2.
14 James Smithies (1787–1868) served in The Royals throughout the Peninsular and Waterloo campaigns. His own account of his experiences was published in the *Middleton Albion* in January 1868 and an abridged version, based on an article in *JSAHR*, is in the Household Cavalry Museum, Box 7, f. 7.
15 Hibbert, *Waterloo*, p. 203.
16 Taken, along with much of the information on French tactics, from Adkin, *The Waterloo Companion*, a really excellent new battlefield guide and history.
17 Edwards had already been in the Life Guards for seven years, having joined as a boy musician only 4 feet tall; he never grew above 5 feet 6 inches. He served on until 1841, and when he retired kept his trumpet with him. On his death it was donated to the Household Cavalry Museum where it still hangs. His son also joined the Life Guards, aged ten, in 1832.
18 La-Haie-Sainte means 'The Sainte family copse' and had once been in the hands of the local Sainte family. The buildings were, surprisingly, not that badly damaged in the battle and are still occupied by descendants of the same family who lived there during Waterloo.
19 Quoted by Adkin, p. 233.
20 Storey was subsequently commissioned into the 21st Light Dragoons and only transferred to 1st Life Guards in April 1815; at thirty-seven he was the oldest subaltern in the regiment.
21 Adkin, p. 220.
22 Quoted in Hills, *The Life Guards*, p. 65.
23 Atkinson, p. 305.
24 From Captain Clark's own account, held in the Household Cavalry Museum, Box 14, Item 8.
25 Quoted by Atkinson, p. 306.
26 Arthur, *The Story of the Household Cavalry*, 2, p. 612, quoting from *The Life of Lord Vivian*.
27 See note 29 below.
28 Atkinson, p. 309.
29 A copy of Somerset's letter to his mother, written on 23 June, is in the Household Cavalry Museum, Box 14, f. 15.
30 Private Robert Peel's letters are in the Household Cavalry Museum, No. 22/572/2.
31 Her rather mouldy tail is in the Household Cavalry Museum.
32 'Waterloo – An Account by an Eye Witness after the Battle', *United Service Journal*, 1829, Part One, pp. 84–92.

Fourteen – Ceremonial Frustration

1   His letter to Mr Fuller from Boissy, dated 2 July 1815.
2   Quoted by Arthur, *The Story of the Household Cavalry*, 2, p. 623.
3   Ibid., p. 625.
4   Major N. P. Dawnay has written a very full history of the standards and guidons, *The Standards of the Household Cavalry 1660–1967*, a copy of which is in the Household Cavalry Museum.
5   The order came from the Prince Regent on 24 October 1818 and is reproduced on p. 23 of *The Historical Record of The Life Guards* in the Household Cavalry Museum.
6   There are examples of these in the Household Cavalry Museum.
7   The King's order on horses is in PRO WO 3/364.
8   The cutting from *The Morning Paper* is in the Household Cavalry Museum, Box 16, AB2130.
9   *Music in State Clothing* by George Lawn, the third generation of his family to serve in the Band of The Life Guards, is a very well-researched history of Household Cavalry music, from which some of this detail is taken.
10 Arthur, *The Story of the Household Cavalry*, 2, p. 634.
11 In the army debate in Parliament in 1871 a radical MP described the Household Cavalry as 'merely ornamental'.
12 The newspaper cuttings covering the trial, from which these quotes are taken, are in the Household Cavalry Museum, Box 1, f. 16 AB2130.
13 There is a very good biography of this extraordinary man by Michael Glover, entitled *A Very Slippery Fellow*.
14 *The Annual Register*, 1840, p. 6.
15 Cumberland's letter to the King on 30 July 1830, quoted in full by Arthur, *The Story of the Household Cavalry*, p. 648.
16 There is a very good history of the Hill family, *The Hills of Hawkstone and Attingham*, by Joanna Hill.
17 From the Marquess of Anglesey, *One Leg*, p. 311.
18 Details taken from Mitchell, *Problems of a Garrison Town: Windsor 1815–1855*, a PhD thesis submitted to the University of Reading in September 2001 and

available in the Household Cavalry Museum with full notes on sources.
19 Ibid., p. 71.
20 George Clements's diary, a copy of which is in the Household Cavalry Museum: Box 7, f. 23 AB2569.
21 Atkinson, *The History of the Royal Dragoons*, p. 319.
22 E. L. Woodward, *The Age of Reform*, Oxford History of England, 13, p. 251.
23 Ibid., p. 601.
24 Marquess of Anglesey, *A History of The British Cavalry: Volume 2 1851–1871*, p. 42.
25 A copy of *The Diary of Captain Stocks of the Royal Dragoons, Crimea 1854/5* is in the Household Cavalry Museum, Box 7, Item 28 AB2377.
26 A highly infectious skin disease.
27 See note 20 above.
28 See note 24 above. Yorke's correspondence is in the possession of Lord Anglesey and is reproduced in his book.
29 See ibid., p. 59, quoting Cornet Fisher of the 4th Dragoon Guards.
30 Stocks, entry for 25 October 1854.
31 Woodward, p. 63.
32 A very good description of the visual impact Rikoff's horsemen made by Lieutenant Strangways, of C Troop RHA, who supported the Heavy Brigade in their subsequent charge. Used by Anglesey, p. 65.
33 From Cecil Woodham-Smith, *The Reason Why*, p. 224.
34 See note 24, pp. 113–14. Sergeant Major Cruse's correspondence is in the possession of Lord Anglesey.
35 See ibid., p. 115.
36 Atkinson, p. 333.
37 See Woodward, p. 124. There are examples in the Household Cavalry Museum.

Fifteen – Small Wars in Africa

1 Thought to have been written by General Sir George Chesney, Head of the Indian Civil Engineering College.
2 Bruce, *The Purchase System in the British Army 1660–1871*, p. 126.
3 Ibid..
4 Arthur, *The Story of the Household Cavalry*, 2, p. 659.
5 From *The World*. I am much indebted for this quote, and the ensuing quotes from the letters of Johnny Brocklehurst, to Jean Bray, Librarian at Sudeley Castle, whose as yet unpublished manuscript on Brocklehurst's life has been an invaluable source.
6 Household Cavalry Museum, Box 2, f. 21 AB138.
7 This entry, and many of those following, is taken from Queen Victoria's papers in the Royal Archives; this entry is RA VIC/Add O 14/177.
8 From *Queen Victoria's Journal* in the Royal Archives: QVJ, 2 August 1882.
9 See note 5 above.
10 Arthur, *The Story of the Household Cavalry*, 2, p. 674.
11 Ibid., p. 675. Wolseley made much of this story, telling it frequently after the campaign, partly, one suspects, because he had heard it greatly pleased the Queen.
12 Talbot's description is from the Marquess of Anglesey, *A History of the British Cavalry*, pp. 286–7.
13 From a poem in the Household Cavalry Museum.
14 See ibid., p. 291.
15 RA QVJ, 21 October 1882.
16 Ibid., 26 October 1882.
17 The Prince of Wales's letters to Ewart are in the Household Cavalry Museum, Box 10, f. 28.
18 RA VIC/Add O 23/14, 17 September 1884.
19 RA VIC/Add E 62/36, 22 September 1884.
20 *A Ride To Khiva* became a minor bestseller and has seldom been out of print since.
21 Letter dated 27 April 1885 to his Commanding Officer from Major Lord Arthur Somerset, who commanded The Blues Squadron in the Heavy Camel Regiment until he was wounded. Household Cavalry Museum, AB 2659.
22 From Alexander, *The True Blue*, pp. 206–7.
23 RA QVJ, 21 January 1884.

Sixteen – The Boer War

1 His account, the *Staff Diary of Brevet-Major Hon. A. H. C. Hanbury-Tracy, Royal Horse Guards, Attached to Abyssinian Forces Operating In The Ogaden*, was published by the Intelligence Division of the War Office, a copy of which is in the Household Cavalry Museum.
2 RA QVJ, 21 April 1894.
3 RA VIC/Add P21/69, 13 June 1894.
4 RA VIC/Add I60/64, 24 April 1894.
5 Atkinson, *The History of the Royal Dragoons*, p. 346.
6 RA VIC/Add P2/224, 28 October 1899.
7 RA QVJ, 11 November 1899.
8 The Marquess of Anglesey, *A History of the British Cavalry Volume 4: 1899–1913*. Biographical details of Lord Dundonald are on p. 75.
9 George Freemantle's letters are in the Household Cavalry Museum, Box 2, AB2177.
10 *The Times*, 10 October 1899, quoted in Pakenham, *The Boer War*, the best history of the conflict, and most enjoyable to read, p. 109.
11 Ibid., p. 313.
12 Hugh Hidden's letters are in the Household Cavalry Museum, Box 16, f. 2. This one was sent from Cape Town on Boxing Day 1899.
13 See note 9 above.
14 Lieutenant Colonel Calley wrote to his wife at least once a week throughout the war in his almost illegible spidery writing. His letters are in the Household Cavalry Museum, Box 2, AB2185.

15 Pakenham, p. 390.
16 Diary of an anonymous officer in The Royals in the Household Cavalry Museum, Box 7, AB2351.
17 See ibid.
18 A photocopy of the original of Burn-Murdoch's letter is in the Household Cavalry Museum, Box 2, f. 25. It was written from Ingagane, Natal, on 9 August 1900 and arrived in Berlin on 26 September 1900.
19 Chenevix-Trench, *A History of Horsemanship*, p. 176.
20 Horace Hayes wrote several well-known books on horse mastership, including *Among Horses in South Africa*, published in 1900. His most famous book, which is still in print, is *Veterinary Notes for Horse Owners* and is still used as a course book on the Army's Riding Instructors' Course.
21 Ernest Clowes's letters are in the Household Cavalry Museum, Box 2, AB2181. This one, from Brakfontein, is dated 17 August 1900.
22 Lord Carver, *National Army Museum Book of the Boer War*.
23 Arthur, *The Story of the Household Cavalry*, 2, p. 764.

16 Ibid., p. 67.
17 See Mosley, p. 237.
18 See note 10 above, p. 22.
19 The letters of 2nd Lieutenant H. A. B. St George to his parents are in the Household Cavalry Museum, Box 10, AB2667.
20 Corporal A. C. Millin's diary is in the Household Cavalry Museum, Box 3, AB2220.
21 Lord Tweedmouth's diary is in the Household Cavalry Museum, Box 10, AB2637. This entry is for 26 October 1914.
22 Field Marshal Earl Haig's speech at the dedication of the Zanvoorde Memorial on 4 May 1924; see Arthur, *The Story of the Household Cavalry*, 3, p. 247.
23 See note 10 above, p. 84.
24 Murray Smith's diary is quoted in full by Arthur, *The Story of the Household Cavalry*, 3, pp. 129–33.
25 Lord Tweedmouth describing the action, quoted ibid., p. 133.
26 Ibid.
27 See note 4 above; copied from p. 248.

Seventeen – Policing the Empire and Trench Warfare in Europe

1 Cavalry Drill Book 1904, quoted in Atkinson, *The History of the Royal Dragoons*, p. 381.
2 Cusack's memoirs, *Scarlet Fever*, co-written with Ivor Herbert.
3 Trooper Wilsher's correspondence is in the Household Cavalry Museum, inserted in the Sergeants' Mess Scrap Book of the Royal Dragoons.
4 These and subsequent quotes are taken from Nicholas Mosley, *Julian Grenfell – His life and the Times of His Death 1888–1915*.
5 Arthur, *The Story of the Household Cavalry*, 3, p. 12.
6 Lloyd's reminiscences of his time in the 1st Life Guards were published as *A Trooper in the Tins*.
7 See Arthur, *The Story of the Household Cavalry*, 3, p. 10.
8 A list of nicknames is preserved in the Household Cavalry Museum, Box 13, f. 1.
9 The story is told in full in the Marquess of Anglesey, *A History of the British Cavalry*, 4, p. 456.
10 From *The King's Grace, 1910–1935*, quoted in Gavin Roynon (ed.), *The Massacre of the Innocents: The Crofton Diaries, Ypres 1914–1915*, p. 277.
11 See Arthur, *The Story of the Household Cavalry*, 3, p. 26.
12 Described by a journalist from *The Times* who was present and recorded ibid.
13 The Marquess of Anglesey, *A History of the British Cavalry*, 7, pp. 61–4.
14 Corporal A. W. Eason's papers are in the Household Cavalry Museum, Box 5, AB2252.
15 See Arthur, *The Story of the Household Cavalry*, 3, p. 47.

Eighteen – The End in France and Reorganization

1 The correspondence relating to Johnnie Dunville's VC is in the Household Cavalry Museum, Item 626, AB2560.
2 Padre Haines's letters to his wife are in the Household Cavalry Museum, Box 3 AB2207.
3 Haig Diaries, Acc. 3155, National Library of Scotland; entry for Tuesday, 15 January 1918.
4 For Kavanagh's correspondence with the Gold Sticks see Arthur, *The Story of the Household Cavalry*, 3, pp. 196–7.
5 Lloyd, *A Trooper in the Tins*, p. 303.
6 As recounted by Bert Turp to John Cusack the next day; see Cusack, *Scarlet Fever*, pp. 73–4.
7 Atkinson, *The History of the Royal Dragoons*, pp. 461–2.
8 Noted by Trooper Stanley Butler at Vaux Andigny; see Arthur, *The Story of the Household Cavalry*, 3.
9 Trooper Stanley Butler's letter is in the Household Cavalry Museum, Box 18, Item 1.
10 These words were contained in an address he gave to The Blues on Armistice Sunday 1931; see Household Cavalry Museum, Box 6, AB2321.
11 The Marquess of Anglesey, *A History of the British Cavalry*, 8, p. 315.
12 From Spike Mays's memoirs, *Fall Out the Officers*, p. 53.
13 Ernest Makins' complete correspondence is in the Household Cavalry Museum, Box 7 AB2380. The Scots Greys' dealings with the media are covered in this in some detail, including an article in the *Daily Telegraph* on 31 October 1937.
14 From Wyndham, *The Household Cavalry at War: First Household Cavalry Regiment*, pp. 2–3.

Nineteen – The Second World War: the Middle East

1. From Bishop, *One Young Soldier: The Memoirs of a Cavalryman*, p. 3.
2. From Pitt-Rivers, *The Story of the Royal Dragoons 1938–1945*, p. 4.
3. The Makins–Heyworth correspondence is in the Household Cavalry Museum, Box 7 AB2380.
4. The Earl of Rocksavage, MC, *A Day's March Nearer Home: Experiences with The Royals 1939–1945*, his personal account of the war, p. 19.
5. From a private diary kept throughout operations in Iraq and Syria by Lieutenant Valerian Wellesley, who later, as Marquess Douro, commanded The Blues from 1954 to 1958 and subsequently, as the Duke of Wellington, was Deputy Colonel of The Blues and Royals.
6. Quoted in Wyndham, *The Household Cavalry At War: First Household Cavalry Regiment*, p. 11.
7. See note 5 above.
8. From Captain J. D. Summers, *Nine Weeks In The Desert*, a private account of 1 HCR's campaign written in Aleppo in 1941 and never published, as far as I can tell. It was in the possession of the late Major John Shaw who won an MC with the Regiment at Palmyra, and I am indebted to his son, also Major John Shaw, for being allowed to use it.
9. See note 5 above.
10. From Somerset de Chair, *The Golden Carpet*, p. 22. De Chair was an MP for Norfolk, and an officer in 1 HCR who was attached to the Kingcol brigade staff.
11. See note 5 above.
12. See Summers, p. 20.
13. See note 5 above.
14. See Rocksavage, p. 33.
15. See De Chair, p. 6.
16. See Wyndham, p. 48.
17. See Rocksavage, p. 48.
18. See Pitt-Rivers, p. 11.
19. See Wyndham, p. 78.
20. Major Jack Hamilton-Russell's letters are in the possession of his son, Colonel James Hamilton-Russell; this one was written on 22 October 1942.
21. See Pitt-Rivers, p. 60.
22. 'Behind Rommel's Lines', *The Times*, 4 January 1943.
23. See Note 20, letter of 19 November 1942.
24. See Wyndham, p. 83.
25. Taken from notes from a talk given by the Duke of Wellington to the contemporary HCR in October 1997 when they were exercising in Egypt near the Alamein battlefield.
26. See note 25.
27. See note 25.
28. See Pitt-Rivers, p. 65.
29. See Rocksavage, p. 147.
30. Lieutenant Colonel Pepys to Lady Boyne, 6 December 1942. In possession of Colonel James Hamilton-Russell.

Twenty – The Second World War: Europe

1. See ch. 19, note 20: letter dated 19 June 1943.
2. See ch. 19, note 2: Pitt-Rivers, p. 83.
3. See ch. 19, note 20: letter dated 27 July 1943.
4. Ibid.: letter dated 14 August 1943.
5. Ibid.: letter dated 19 August 1943.
6. John Shaw's diary is in the possession of his son, also Major John Shaw, to whom I am much indebted for being allowed to quote from it.
7. From Roden Orde, who served with 2 HCR, *The Household Cavalry at War: The Second Household Cavalry Regiment*, published by Gale & Polden in Aldershot in 1953, p. 13.
8. From Christopher Sykes, *Evelyn Waugh: A Biography*, p. 314.
9. From Selina Hastings, *Evelyn Waugh: A Biography*, p. 441.
10. David Smiley's excellent book on his experiences, *Albanian Assignment*, was published by Chatto & Windus in 1984.
11. See Orde, pp. 62–3.
12. Ibid., pp. 102–3.
13. Ibid., p. 161.
14. Ibid., p. viii.
15. Ibid., p. ix.
16. From *Balkan Blue*, an autobiography by Major General Sir Roy Redgrave, KBE, MC, p. 71.
17. Ibid., pp. 78–9.
18. Quoted ibid., p. 84.
19. Ibid., p. 526.

Twenty-One – Withdrawal from Empire

1. The paper, *Historical Note by Sir George Arthur*, is with the Birdwood papers; these are in the possession of Lieutenant Colonel Gordon Birdwood who very kindly made them available to me.
2. For the minutes of this meeting see previous note.
3. From a letter from Captain Sir Rupert Buchanan-Jardine Bt, MC, to Major J. N. P. Watson and quoted in Watson, *The Story of The Blues and Royals*, p. 46.
4. See Lloyd, *Challengers and Chargers*, p. 134.
5. See Redgrave, *Balkan Blue*, p. 107.

Index

Note: page numbers in **bold** refer to illustrations.

'100 Days' offensive 485–6

Abbasia 506
Abbot 300
Abdul Ghailan 75, **76–7**, 78
Abel-Smith, Henry 'Auntie' (Colonel Henry) 502, 538–40, 544, 550, 552, 553
Abel-Smith, May 552
Aberdeen, Prime Minister 369
Abrantes 172
Abu Kemal 513
Abu Klea **403**, 404, 405–6, **407**, 409, 413, 424
Abyssinian Expedition 412
Act of Settlement 1701 160
Act of Union 1707 28, 164
Adair, Maj-Gen. Alan 546
Adderley, Capt. 93, 119
Addington, Henry 278, 279
Addington, Justice 255
Addison, Cornet 181
Aden Protectorate 561
'Adjutant General' 70, 390
AEC armoured cars 530
Afghanistan 573
Afrika Korps 517, 522
Agra 435
Agueda 299
Ailesbury, Lord 98, 99
16 Air Assault Brigade 573
Airborne Brigade 569–71, 573
1st Airborne Division (Second World War) 547
Al Rashid dynasty 75, 78
Alamein, battle of 1942 519, 520–5, 527
Alamein Line 522, 523, 525
Albanians 573
Albemarle, 1st Duke of *see* Monck, Gen. George, Duke of Albemarle
Albemarle, 1st Earl of *see* van Keppel, Col. Arnold Joost, 1st Earl of Albemarle
Albert, Prince 349, 579
Albuera 298
Alcantara 299
Aldershot garrison 383, 384, 401, 412, 415, 422, 448, 490, 537
Aleppo 516, 517
Alexander the Great 510
Alexandra, Queen 401, 430, 452, 489

Alexandria 391, 392, 401, 529, 558
Algeria 530
Algiers 74
Allen, Cpl 550
Allenby, Sir Edmund 452, 454–6, 459, 460, 489, 490, 512
Allied forces
    and the Austrian War of Succession 200–17, 220
    and the Crimean War 371–9
    and the First Gulf War 571
    and the First World War 456–8, 469, 480, 481, 485
    and the Peninsula War 288, 290, 292–6, 299, 308, 310
    and the Revolutionary Wars 265, 266–72
    and the Second World War 530, 532–4, 539–40, 545–7
    and the Seven Years War 234, 237, 239–44, 248
    and the Spanish War of Succession 171, 176–8, 180, 182–3
    and Waterloo 314–16, 319, 322–40, 343
    under William III 123, 144, 146, 149, 150–1, 157
Alma, battle of 372, 374
Almanza, battle of **179**
Almanza 178
Almaraz 295
Almeida 288, 292, 294
Almenara 180–1
Amelia, Princess 300
America 224, 232, 249, 301, 311
American War of Independence 252, 260
Amherst, Col. Lord 255, 256, 264, 265
Amiens 485
Anabaptists 14, 16, 27
Anatolia 527
Andalusia 286, 298–9
Andalusian horses 175
Anders, Gen. 536–7
Anglo-Dutch Brigade 113, 116
Anglo-Egyptian Treaty 1936 558
Anne, Princess 111, **568**, 582
Anne, Queen 48, 81, 118, 119, 154, 160, 161–6, **163**, 167, 187, 188
    Court of 161, **162–3**
Anthoing 212
Anthony, Edward 216
Antibes 312
Antwerp 459, 479, 547, 548

Anzac Corps 548
Anzio 534, 536
Apache attack helicopters 573
Apprenticeship Laws 18
Arab Legion 509
Arabs 75–9, **76–7**, 495, 558, 561
Aragon 176
Aremberg, General Duc d' 202, 204, 208, 209
Argyll, 2nd Duke of *see* Campbell, John, 2nd Duke of Argyll
Argyll, 9th Earl of *see* Campbell, Archibald, 9th Earl of Argyll
Armistice 1918 481, 485, 486, 489
armoured cars 506, 508
Armoured Divisions (Second World War)
    7th 519, 523, 526
    10th 517, 522, 523
    11th 543–4, 545
Armstrong, Sir Thomas 31, 47, 48, 61, 65–6
Armstrong, William 56
2nd Army (Second World War) 543, 547
5th Army (First World War) 484
8th Army (Second World War) 517, 523, 527–30, 532, 534, 536
9th Army (Second World War) 527
Army Board 70
Army Medical Department 364
Army of Occupation 489, 555
Army Remount Establishment 413
Army's Certificates of Education 415
Arnhem 547
Arran, Lord 188
Arran, Lord 'Pudding' 448
Arras 474
Arronches 294
Arthur, Duke of Connaught 392, 398
Arthur, Sir George 404, 552
'Articles and Rules of War' 1666 51
'Articles of War' 1718 194
Arundel, Lt 180, 181–2
Aschaffenberg 204
Ashantis 392
Ashburnham, Lord 189
Assembly 346
Aswan 404
Aswan High Dam 408
Ath 216, 217, 316
Athlone, Lord (formerly Prince Alexander of Teck) 508, 552, 563
Athlone 134, 137
Atkinson, Pte. William 366
Atterbury Plot 167

Auchinleck 520–2, 523
Aughrim village 134, 135, 137, 140, 141
Austria 195–6, 224, 226, 265, 313, 315, 502
Austrian army 209, 212, 215, 268, 269, 271–2
Austrian Netherlands 265
Austrian Succession, war of 188, 197–222, **199**
Austro-Hungarian Empire 452
Axminster 87–8, 113, 119
Ayles, Trooper 546

Badajoz 291, 294, 295
Baggara horsemen 405
Baghdad 510, 512, 513
Baille, Maj. Arthur 538
Baille, Capt. Hugh 360
Bainham, Adam 9
Baisieux 271
Baker, Sir Robert 354
Baker, Valentine 400, 401, 402
Baker Rifles 328
Balaclava 374–6, **375**, 379, **380–1**, 382, 424
Balkans 539, 571–3, **572**
Ballinasloe 490
Balmoral 398, 415
Baltimore Bombers 530
Bank of England 164, 165, 255
Bapaume 477
Barbary pirates 74
Barcelona 175–6, 177
Barnes 318
barracks 274–6, 361–4, **365**
Barrett, Quartermaster 175
Barri Wood 215, 216
Barrington, Lord 224, 238, 253
Basing House, siege of **45**
Basing, Lord 430, 431
Basutoland 441
Bath 36–7, 39
Bavaria 265
Bavarian troops 463
Baxter, Richard 40, 44
Bayeux 543
Bayliss, Cpl of Horse 409, 412
Bayuda **403**
Beachy Head, battle of 130
Beake, Col. 208
Beake, Capt. 14
Beaumont 269, 271, 277
Beckwith, Col. 240
Beeston Castle 47
Beit 417
Belbeis 398
Belem 288, 304
Belfast 571
Belgium 265, 279, 313–40, 343, 435, 452, 454
Bell, Cpl Maj. Thomas 338
Bell, Thomas 278

'Ben the Ruler' see Clifton, Lt Col. ('Ben the Ruler')
2nd Bengal Cavalry 397
Benghazi 519
Bennefield, Capt. 146
Bennet 397
Benson, Capt. 176, 180, 183, 184
Berber troops 75
Beresford, Sir Charles 402, 405–6
Beresford, Capt. Lord Patrick **560**
Bergen op Zoom 220
Berkeley, Sir Charles (Lord Fitzhardinge/Earl of Falmouth) 26–7, 56
Berlin 413, 558
Berry, Captain Lieutenant (later Maj-Gen.) James 40–2, 43, 44
Berry's Horse 14
Berthier 316
Berwick, Duke of (James FitzJames) 47, **109**, 110, 113, 121, 127, 130, 134, 137, 140, 146, 149, 167, 172, 177–8, **179**, 180
Béthencourt 269
Bhurtpore, siege of 342, 360
Bickersteth, Lt 477
Bijlandt 325
Bill of Rights 1689 118
Bills of Attainders 153
Bingham, Brig-Gen. C. E. (Cis) 454, 489, 490
Bingham, George Charles, 3rd Earl of Lucan 369, 372, 374–6, 378, 379, 382, 391, 435
Bings, Richard 61
Binning, Lord 405
Birch, Trooper 561
Birdwood, Lord 508, 548, 552, 563
Birr Castle 131, 132
Bish, Edward 153
Bishop, Tim 500–1, 520, 582–3
Bishop's War 1639 7
black soldiers 105–6, **107**, 113
Blackguards 257
Blackheath Reviews 260
'Blacks', the, tradition of 157
Blake, Admiral 74
Bland, Humphrey 195
Blathwayt, Thomas 188
Blathwayt, William **69**, 71, 72, 87, 101, 108, 112, 117–18, 119, 123, 130, 141, 146, 151, 154, 166, 188, 314
Blenheim, battle of 157, 164, 170, 172
Blimp, Col. 558
Bloemfontein 417, 421, 431
Blood, Sir Binden 430–1
Blood River, battle of 416
Bloody Assizes 95
Blucher, Field Marshal von 314, 319, 322, 325
'Blues and Royals, The' 566, 573
Blues, The see Royal Regiment of Horse Guards

Board of General Officers 192
Board, Lt 266
Boer War 387–8, 415–31, **419**, **423**, **425–6**, 434–5, 438, 441, 454, 468, 490
Boisselau, General 130
Boissy 346
Bolton, Duke of 190
Bombay 18, 73
Bond, George 151
Booth, Sir George 46
Borneo **560**, 562
Bosnia 573
Bosworth, battle of 7
Boteler, Noel 43
Bothwell Bridge, battle of 65, 66
Bouchain 268
Boulogne 310, 346–7
Bourbons 171, 172, 176–83, 216, 261, 311, 312, 316, 355
Bourgeois 333
Bouverie, Capt. 254
Bovington 583
Bowlby 464, 470
Bowles, Andrew Parker **568**, 571, **581**
Boyce, Trooper 465–7
Boyne, battle of the 123–30, **128–9**, 141
Bradford 90
Bradstock, Lt 546
Brahe, Count 38
Bren guns 509
Brett, Sir Edward 48
Bridges, Maj. Tobias 74–5, 78
brigades, introduction of 104
'Bright Chain' 280
Bright, Corporal Major Roy 576–7
Brighton 355
Brissac, Duc de 233
Bristol, Earl of 46
Bristol 88
Britain 224, 311, 313
 and the Crimean War 368–9
 and France 261, 264–5, 278–9, 285–6, 387
 and Germany 387
 and the Second World War 502
British army 184, 192, 228, 229, 384
 and the Austrian War of Succession 198–202, 204, 209, 212–15, 216, 220
 and the Boer War 415, 416, 417, 431, 435
 and the Boer-First World War interwar period 449
 Cardwell Reforms 29, 387–90, 392, 415, 437
 contemporary 567
 and the Crimean War 369, 371, 376
 cutbacks 220–2, 223, 249, 252, 279, 489
 discipline 185–7, 194
 and the Egyptian campaign 1882 397–8

and the First World War 452–72, 473–89
Framework Operations 431
and George I 185
and George III 265, 273–4, 286, 295, 296–8
musketry practice 442
non-commissioned officers 30
and the Peninsula War 286, 295, 296–8, 308–10
post-Crimean reforms 364
post-First World War 489, 501
post-Second World War 562
and the post-Waterloo peace 361
purchase system abolished 387–8
and the Revolutionary Wars 268, 271, 272
and the Second World War 517, 531–2, 537, 538, 551
and the Seven Years War 232–6, 239, 243–4, 245, 248, 252
uniforms 202
venereal disease 200
Waterloo 314, 319
weaponry 202, 273–4
and Wellington 273, 286
wives/families 198–200, 203, 364–6
British Empire 249
withdrawal from the 558, 563
British Expeditionary Force (BEF) (Egyptian campaign 1882) 392
British Expeditionary Force (BEF) (First World War) 449, 452, 454, 458, 460
British Expeditionary Force (BEF) (Peninsular War) 285
British Expeditionary Force (BEF) (Waterloo) 314
British fleet 177
British Heavy Cavalry brigades 268
'Britons, Strike Home' (song) 282
Brixton Prison 412
Broadwood, Gen. 418, 421
Brocklehurst, Henry 387
Brocklehurst, John 387, 392–4, 395–7, 398, 401, 427
Broome, Lord (Lord Cornwallis) 232
Broughton, Samuel 337
'Brown Bess' musket 328
Brown, Trooper 208
Browning machine guns 561
Brucker Holz 248
Brunswick, Duke of 319
Brunswick (state) 354
Brunswick Corps 294
Brunswick troops 314, 336
Brussels 142, 144, 200, 203, 209, 211, 212, 217, 220, 314, 315, 316, 321, 322, 337, 342, 546
Buchan, John 449
Buchanan, Dr John 198, 200, 203, 208, 211, 216
Buchanan-Jardine, Rupert 546–7

Buckingham, Duke of 47
Buckingham Palace 486, 577
Bulgaria 41, 368
Bulge, battle of the 548
Bullange (Life Guard trumpeter) 189
Buller, Sir Redvers (VC) 415, 417–18, 421, 422, 427
Bullock, Cpl 442
Bulow 319
Burckhardt, Maj. 527
Burcy 544
Burdett, Sir Francis 274, 300, 303
Burdett Riots 1810 256, 300, 303, 366
Burke, Lt 121
Burn-Murdoch, Lt 405, 413, 418, 421–2, 430
Burnaby, Fred 392, 401–2, 404–5, 406, **407**, 408, 412, 417
'Burnaby Factor' 416
Burns, Capt. 422
Burton, Francis 198
Busaco, battle of 288
Bute, Third Earl of 248, 257
Butler, Lt George 101
Butler, Trooper Stanley 486
Buttevant, Thomas 14–16
Byng, Admiral 236
Byng, Francis 190
Byng, Maj. 404

Cadogan, Willie 464
Caen 540, 543
Cairo 392, 394, 398, 400, 558
Calley, Lt Col. Thomas 420–1, 424, 427
Calvinists 164
Camac, Maj. 303, 304, 306, 310, 313, 338
Cambert, Robert 106
Cambrai 269, 271, 480, 481, **482–3**
Cambridge, Duke of 361, 387, 390, 391, 400, 401, 402, 406
Cambron 144
Camel Corps 401, 402–8, **403**
Camel Guards Regiment 401
Cameron, Pte. 406
Campbell, Archibald, 9th Earl of Argyll 87, 88, 90
Campbell, Sir Colin 374, 376, 379
Campbell, John, 2nd Duke of Argyll 167, 190, **191**
Campbell, Lt 116
Canada 243, 311, 392
Canadian Army 540
Cape Colony 417, 421
Cape of Good Hope 278
Cape Town 416, 417, 418, 441–2
Capstick, Trooper 492–5
carbines 273–4, 290, 394, 413
Cardigan, Lord 369, 376, 378, 435
Cardwell, Edward 387, 388, 392
Cardwell Reforms 29, 387–90, **389**, 392, 415, 437
Carlisle, Earl Charles of 14

Carlisle, Earl of 153
Carlyle 228
Carnaby, Sir Thomas 50
Caroline, Queen 33, 352, 354, 582
Carpegna 537
Carpenter, Gen. Lord 180, 188
Carr, William 30, 53–4, 73
Carr-Ellison, Maj. 422, 430, 431
Cartel of Frankfort 216
Carter 361
Carteret, Lord (Earl Granville) 196, 198, 202, 209, 211
Casablanca Conference 1943 531
Caslee, Stephen 31
Cassel, Hesse 285
Castillon 176
Castlemaine, Lady 23, 30
Catalonia 178, 182, 183, 189
Catania 532
Cathcart 300, 352
Catherine of Braganza 23, **24**, 36–7, 73
Cathness, Lt 16
Catholic Relief Act 1778 253
Caudete 178
Cavaliers 4–6, 18, 22–3
Cavalry Bridge, Normandy 543–4
1st Cavalry Brigade (First World War) 448
2nd Cavalry Brigade (Boer War) 418
4th Cavalry Brigade (First World War) 454
6th Cavalry Brigade (First World War) 442, 459, 480, 485
7th Cavalry Brigade (First World War) 459, 481
Cavalry Corps (First World War) 460, 467, 481
Cavalry Division (First World War) 442, 452
1st Cavalry Division (Second World War) 504, 508, 509, 517
see also 10th Armoured Division; Habbaniya Task Force
3rd Cavalry Division (First World War) 459, 469, 470, 474–7
13th Cavalry Division (French – Waterloo) 335
14th Cavalry Division (French – Waterloo) 335
Cavalry Drill Book (1904) 435
Cavendish, Gen. Charles 40
Cavendish, Lord John 448, 452, 463
Cazalet, Capt. 479
Centurion tanks 562
Ceylon 278
Challenger tanks 571
Chalon, Henry Bernard **283**
Chamberlain, Joseph 401, 417
Chandler, Francis 185
Chappell, John 99
Chapuy, Gen. 269–71
Charleroi 56–7, 217, 315, 316, 337, 548
Charles Albert, Elector of Bavaria 195, 196
Charles, Archduke 171, 175, 177

Charles I, King of England 6–9, 11, 14, 20, 23, 29, 44, 60, 65
Charles II, King of England 2, 4, 6, 9, 14, 16–18, 20, 22–3, 26–9, 31, 39, 44, 46–8, 50, 56–66, 70–2, 87, 104, 106, 188, 352, 388, 566, 577–8
   coronation 1661 33–6, **34–5**
   court **24**
   death 67, 83, 95
   escorts 36–7
   and Monmouth 53, 54, 56, 64–5, 65–6, 86
   and Parliament 51
   progresses 36–7
   propaganda war of **52**
   and the Rye House Plot 1683 65–6
   and Sedgemoor 92
   and Tangier 73–4, 79, 80–1
Charles V, Emperor 195, 197
Charles, Prince of Wales 577
Charles of Lorraine, Prince 209
Charles (ship) 80
Charleville-Mézières 315
Charlotte, Queen 262, **263**
Charlton, Jack 562
Chartist Riots 1838-40 355
Chasseurs 338
Château of Hougoumont 325
Chatterton, Quartermaster 181
Chedzoy 86, 90
Chelsea Hospital 256–7
Cheney, Cornet 243
Cherbourg 228
Chesterfield, Countess of 44
Chieftain tanks 567, **568**
Chitham, Capt. John 98
Choiseul, War Minister 245
Cholmondeley, Capt. George 126, 146, 189
Chudleigh, Troop Cpl of Horse 561
Church of England 156, 160, 164, 165
Churchill, Arabella 110
Churchill, Brig. George 149
Churchill, Col. John, 1st Earl and Duke of Marlborough 72, 80–1, 83, 87–8, 90, 93, 95, 99–101, 110, 113, 116–19, 121–3, 132, 137, 141, 144, **147**, 157, 160–1, 164, 167, 170–2, 175, 177, 182, 185, 188–90, 192, 197, 202, 217, 220, 229, 576
Churchill, Sarah 161
Churchill, Winston 497, 516–17, 522, 523, 529, 531
Ciudad Rodrigo 177, 288, 291, 292, 295, 306
Civil Service 245
Clairfayt 271, 272
Clarendon, Edward Hyde, 1st Earl of 9, 26, 37, 44, 48, 119
Clark, Capt. 292, 299, 323, 334, 337, 342–3, 367
Clarke, Gen. 513–14
Clarke, Pte. William 14

Claudianus 136
Clausel 306–7, 308
Clayton, General 204, 205, 208
Clements, George 366, 367, 368, 371, 372–4, 376, 378, 382, 383, 384
Cleveland, Duchess of **25**, 46, 95
Clewer Barracks 279, 286
Clifford, Robert 99
Clifford, Thomas 113, 121, 124, 137, 140
Cliff's/Klip's Drift 420, 421
Clifton, Lt Col. ('Ben the Ruler') 291, 299, 311, 313, 316, 336, 367, 369
Clinton, Maj-Gen. Henry 298
Clowes, Capt. Ernest 427
Coburg 265–8, 269, 271
Colchester, Lord 110, 113, 116, 144
Colchester garrison 384
Coldstream 16
Coldstream Guards (2nd Regiment of Foot Guards) 18, 22, 39, 40, 237, 245, **450–1**
Colenso 418, 421, 422
Collier, Mrs 79
Collins, Arthur 538, 546
Cologne 489, 490
Combermere, Viscount Stapleton Cotton 286, 310, 314, 342
Combermere 358
Combermere Barracks 573
Commandos 539, 569–71
Commissary General of the Musters 67, 72
Committee of the Army 17–18
Committee of Public Safety 266
Commonwealth 4, 14, 36, 39, 43, 44, 47, 48, 67, 74–5
Commonwealth troops 17
Communism 561, 562
Compiègne 456
Composite Field Regiment (Household Cavalry – First World War) 448, 454, **455**, 463
Composite Regiment (Household Cavalry – Second World War) 502, 504, **505**, 537
see also 1st Household Cavalry Regiment
Compton, Capt. Sir Charles 47–8, **49**
Compton, Cornet (Earl of Northampton) 116, 151
Compton, General Sir Francis 48, **49**, 86, 87, 90, 92, 93, 95, 110, 111, 112, 116, 119, 124, 132, 134, 135, 141, 153, 190, 202–3, 502, 539
Compton, Bishop Henry 48, **49**
Compton, Lt Hatton 149
Compton House, Warwickshire 47
concentration camps, of the Boer War 430
Congregationalists 40
Coningsby, Thomas 96–8
'conscription of hunger' 437
Constantinople 383
Contades 233, 234, 236, 237, 239

Cook, Lt Col. E. B. 448, 452, **453**, 458, 463
Cooper, Tommy 562
Cope, Lt John 174, 180, 217
Corbach 239
Corbet, Col. 20
Coreth, Mark 569
Cork 132, 134
Corn Riots 1766 253
Corn Riots 1815 313
Cornbury, Lt Col. Lord 81, 95, 101, 110–11, 113, 116, 118, 119–21, **120**
Cornwall, Henry 121
Cornwallis, Earl 261
1st Corps (Battle of Waterloo) 314
2nd Corps (Battle of Waterloo) 314
3rd Corps (Battle of Waterloo) 314
VIII Corps (Second World War) 543, 544
X Corps (Second World War) 523, 524, 536
XII Corps (Second World War) 543
XIII Corps (Second World War) 523
XXX Corps (Second World War) 523, 543, 545, 547
Corps of Gentlemen at Arms 7
Corunna 285, 314
Cosmo, Prince of Tuscany 50
Cotton, Stapleton (Viscount Combermere) 286, 310, 314, 342
Council 74, 75, 78
Council of War (Glorious Revolution) 116
County Associations 132
Court of Chancery 8
courts martial 108, 211, 237, 238, 310, 366
Coutrai 209
Covenanters 28
   Rebellion of 65
Coventry, Sir John 26, 53, 60
Coventry 256
Coventry Act 53
Coventry riots 1662 48
Cox 315, 319
Cox, Edmund 200, 209–11, 242–3
Coy, Capt. John 79, 80, 86, 99–101, 121
Craufard, Lord Robert 205, 211, 215, 216, 292
Craven, Col. Lord 70
Crawley, Lt 121
Crichton, Lord 'Pompey' 448, 452–4, 463, 464
Crimean War 354, 364, 368–83, **373**, 384, 387, 435
Croats 573
Crofton, Sir Morgan 460, 465–9, **466**, 471, 472, 474, 544
Crofts, Capt. 154
Cromwell, Oliver 4, 6, 9, 14, **15**, 16, 17, 27, 36, 40–1, 44, 46, 48, 66, 67, 74, 81, 132, 347
Cromwell, Richard 16, 43
Cronje 421
Crooke, Edward 106

INDEX

Cropper, Lt Col. Thomas 31
Cruse, Sgt. Maj. 369, 379–82
Cubitt, W. H. 485
Cuirassier Brigade 328
cuirassiers 274, 329, 330, 335, 336
    George IV's 349–52
1st Cuirassiers 328, 333
4th Cuirassiers 328, 330
Cullera 178
Culloden, battle of 160, 211, 217, 220, 226, 232
Culpepper, Col. John 108
Cumberland, Duke of 202, 203, 204, 211–12, **213**, 215, 216, 217, 220, 222, 224, 226, 228, 232, 314
Curragh garrison 384, 412, 490
Curragh incident 1887 409
Cusack, John 436, 437, 438, 440, 441, 465, 467, 468, 470, 477, 495, 576
custom duties 252–3
Cutherlough, Lord John Fane 188, 194
Cyprus 522, 523, 558–61, 562, **564–5**, 571
Cyrenaica 506
Czechoslovakia 502

D Day 533, 539, 540
Daimler armoured cars 523, 525, 530, 532, 534, 562
Daimler scout cars 532, 540, 561, 562
Dakin, Pte. 333
Daly, Maj. Bowes 538
Dalyell, Sir Thomas 83
Damascus 514, 519
Dan, Trooper 509
Danby 60
Danish army 96
Dardanelles 368
Dartmouth, Lord 79, 80, 110
Davenport, John 198, 243
Davenport, Richard 197–8, 200, 203, 205, 209, 211, 216, 217, 222, 233, 234, 237, 239, 243, 262
Davies, Moll 53
Davout 346
de Ainslie 367–8
de Banck, Beatrice 46
de Broglie 233–4, 239, 240, 243, 244, 245
de Chair, Lt Somerset 512
de Faubert, Solomon 98
de Grey, Lt Col. 288
De La Noy, Mr 53
de Muy 240, 242, 243
De Stainville 248
de Tesse, Marshal 177
De Vaudemont, Princesse 146
de Vere, Col. Aubrey, 20th Earl of Oxford 44–7, 48, **49**, 50, 57, 70, 71, 86, 104–5, 110, 111, 119, 121, 124, 141, 151, 153, 154, 189, 202, 229, 583
de Walden, Col. Lord Howard 262

de Wet 421, 428
De Wilton, Viscount Grey 360–1, **362–3**
Declaration of Breda 17
Delawarr, Lord John 189, 256
d'Elboeuf, Duc 149
Delhi 435
Dempsey, Gen. 543
Denmark, liberation of **549**
Derbyshire Militia 282
d'Erlon, Comte 296, 316, 319, 325, 328, 329, 334, 336, 338, 347
Derry 571
Dervishes 415
Desbourough, Lady 437
Desbourough, Lord 437
Desert Air Force (Second World War) 520
Detmold 566, 567, 569
Dettingen, battle of 204–9, **206–7**, 211–12, 216, 220, 226, 273, 330, 582
Dewar, L. Cpl of Horse 546
D'Humieres, General 123
Dickens, Charles 304
Diemel River 239–40, 242
Digna, Osman 400
Diocese of Peterborough 26
3rd Division (First World War) 460
3rd Division (post-First World War) 495
4th Division (First World War) 474, 479
7th Division (Peninsular War) 292
50th Division (Second World War) 522–3
78th Division (Second World War) 532
Dixon, Robert 64
Djerboua 516
Dodd, John 238
Dode, Cpl 534
Doleman, Sir Thomas 37
Dominica 249
Donzelot 328, 329, 334
Dornberg, Gen. 316
Dorrien, Lt Col. 282, 284
Dorrington, General 136
Dorville, Maj. 288, 294, 298, 311, 333, 336, 367
Douai 546
Doughty, Capt 20
Douglas, General 127
Dover, 'secret' treaty of 1670 51
Downes, Mr 142
Dowsson, Manuel 40
d'Oyley, Charles 11
Dragoon Guards 223, 237, 371, 458
    1st (The King's) Dragoon Guards 149, 223, 242, 260, 314, 318, 325, 330–3
    2nd Dragoon Guards (Scots Greys) 83, 150, 228, 313, 325, 329, 334, 335, 340, 367, 378, 495, 496, 563–6
    see also Union Brigade
    3rd (Prince of Wales's) Dragoon Guards 205, 223, 268, 269, 291, 295, 296, 298, 306, 484

4th (Royal Irish) Dragoon Guards 295, 306, 404
5th Dragoon Guards 121, 184, 228, 334, 378, 404, 458–9
    see also Union Brigade
6th (Inniskilling) Dragoon Guards 313, 325, 454
7th (The Princess Royal's) Dragoon Guards 394–5
10th Dragoon 243
Driver, Maj. 188
Drogheda 126
Drouet 316
Drury Lowe, Gen. 394, 395
Dublin 127, 130, 134
Dublin Review 132
Dubois 328, 329, 330, 333, 334
duelling 108, 151–3, 185, **281**, 282–4, 290, 303
Duggan, Capt. Hubert 539
Duke (Blue's dog) 304–6, **305**
Dumas, Alexandre 7
Dumbartonshire Regiment 93, 95
Dummer, Edward 90
Dunbar 347
Dundalk 284, 285, 290
Dundas, Ralph 271
Dundee, 1st Viscount of 124
Dundee, pillage of 1651 40
Dundonald, Earl of (Lord Cochrane) 416, 418, 421, 427, 449
Dunes, battle of the 17
Dunkirk 4, 17, 18, 22, 26, 56, 74, 150, 266, 502
Dunster 47
Dunville, Johnnie (VC) 477, **478**
Duras, Lord (Marquis de Blanquefort/Earl of Feversham) 56, 70, 87, 88, **89**, 90, 92, 93, 95, 104, 112, 116, 117, 118–19
Durban 417, 418
Durham 7
Durutte 328
Dutch army 198, 209, 212, 215, 217, 220, 266, 314, 323
Dutch Blue Guard 113, 118, 123–4, 156
Dutch Life Guard 113, 117, 118, 124, 130, 142, 150, 151
    4th Troop 142, 156
Dutch War 1666 27

Earl of Peterborough's Horse 98
Eason, Trooper 456
East Germany 567–9
East India Company 195, 262
Easterby, Mr 279
Eastern Question 368–9
Ebblinghem 467
Eckersley 296, 299
economic reform 260–1
Edgehill, battle of 6, 8, 11, 23
Edict of Nantes 134

Edward VII, King of England (formerly Albert Edward, Prince of Wales) 392, 398–400, 413, 435, 442, 443, 579
funeral **450–1**
Edward VIII, King of England 501, **503**
Edwards, John 329–30
Edwards, Lt 379
Egerton, Randolph 23
Eglinton, Earl of 40
Egypt 278, 368, 400–2, 490, 492–5, 501, 506, 508, 522–3, 558, 561
Egyptian campaign 1882 390, 391–400, **393**, **396**, 412, 427
Egyptian air force 558
Egyptian army 401
El Fawzi el Rashid 512–13, 514
El-Magfar 392
El-Teb 400, 402
Elandslaagte 424
Elba 311, 312, 316, 334
Elbe estuary 550–1
elections **169**, 256–7
1711 166
1714 166
1741 196
Eliott, George 226, 228, 239, 243, 260
Elizabeth I, Queen of England 72
Elizabeth II, Queen of England 553, 577, 578, 582
coronation **556**
Ellenborough, Lord 284
Elley, Col. 301, 330
Elley, Maj. John 276–7, 282, 284
Ellison 183
Elton, Richard 104
English army 28, 44, 160–1
administration 73
artillery 'train' 130–1
and the Glorious Revolution 1688 112–13, 116–18
and James II 98
pensions 106
and the Royal Regiment of Horse Guards 39–40
and William III 118–37
English civil wars 7, 26, 28, 31, 44, 46, 47, 81
English merchant shipping 74
English navy 67, 74
Enniskillen Regiment 127
EOKA 558, 561
Épehy 477
Ernest Augustus, Duke of Cumberland and King of Hanover 356–9
Erroll, Earl of 416
Erskine 295, 306
Escrick, Lord Howard of 16
Esher Award 443
Essex, 3rd Earl of 9, 11
Estremadura 295, 298–9, 306, 316
Étaples 484
Euphrates Bridge 510

Evans, Maj. de Lacey 335
Evans, Tom 330, 340
Evelyn, Arthur 16
Evelyn, John 7, 64, 95
Evening Standard (newspaper) 558
Ewart, Col. Henry 'Croppy' 391, 392, 395, 398–400
Excise Bill 1733 190
Exclusion Crisis 1679 23, 28, 65, 92
Exeter 252

Fairborne, Lord 78–9
Fairfax, Lord 150
Fairfax, Sir Thomas 11, 14, 40
Falaise 545
Falklands War 569–71, **570**, 578–9
Fallujah 510, 512
Famagusta 561
Fane 306, 307
Fane, Lord John 188, 194
Fano 536
Farrier, Andrew 216
fascism 501
Fawkes, Guy 165
Fenton, Lavinia 190
Fenwick, Capt **332**
Fenwick, Edward 40
Fenwick, Col. Sir John 96, 117, 153
Ferdinand 578
Ferdinand, Archduke 269
Ferdinand of Brunswick, Prince 228, 229, 232, 233, 234, 236, 237, 238, 239–40, 243, 244, 245, 248, 269
Ferguson, Andrew 510, 514, 527, 537, 552, 553, 558, 582
Ferguson, Col. 458
Ferret scout cars 561, 562, 569, 571
Ferrier, Lt Col. 313, 323, 338, 352
Festing painting **580**
Fetherstonhaugh, Philip 31
Fetherstonhaugh, Sir T. 31
Feversham, Earl of *see* Duras, Lord
Fidget (horse) 294
Field Army 449
Fielden, Philip 562
Fielding, George 190
Fifth Monarchists 14, 20
Finney, Trooper 573
First World War 48, 338, 388, 449, 452–72, 473–89, 513, 527, 538, 548, 552, 582, 583
outbreak 441–2, 452
Fitzgerald, Lt Col. 338
Fitzgerald, Mrs 441
FitzJames, James, Duke of Berwick 47, **109**, 110, 113, 121, 127, 130, 134, 137, 140, 146, 149, 167, 172, 177–8, **179**, 180
Fitzmaurice, Lord Charles 422
Flanders 74, 75, 121, 130, 132, 137, 141–51, **145**, 154, 157, 160, 170, 171, 172, 175, 180, 197, 209, 211,

217, 220, 232, 265, 274, 278, 301, 460
Fleet prison 232, 255
flogging 366, 388
Floyd, John 260, 280
Flynn, Cpl of Horse 573
Foggia 532
Folgore Division (Italian – Second World War) 527
Fontenoy, battle of 212–17, **214**, 220, 226, 232
Foot, Regiments of (Infantry)
33rd Foot Guards 273
69th Foot Guards 319
Foot Guards 18, 26, 28, 36, 37, 39, 48, 61, 257, 443
bureaucracy 73
and the First World War 470, 473, 479
in Flanders 149
and George I 167
and George II 223, 238
and James II's reforms 96
musicians 28–9
post-Waterloo peace 361
public order duties 50, 253–5
and Queen Anne 161, 165
and the Second World War 538
and Sedgemoor 86, 90, 95
and the Seven Years War 244
and the War of Austrian Succession 208, 215
and Waterloo 319, 325
and William III 154
1st Foot Guards 22, 64, 347, 349
see also Grenadier Guards
2nd Foot Guards 22, 39, 70
see also Coldstream Guards
6th Foot Guards 342
Grenadier companies 62
'foot reliefs' 446
Foreign Legion 516
Forester, Lord 189
former Yugoslavia 573
Fose, Mrs 440
Fose, Sgt. 440
Fox 256, 257
Fox, Sir Stephen 30, 73
Fox-Strangways, Cornet Stephen 561
Framework Operations 431
France 121, 123, 142, 157, 171, 172, 195–6, 209, 222, 224, 226–8, 249, 264–6, 273, 480, 496
Allied liberation of 539, 540–6
and Britain 261, 264–5, 278–9, 285–6, 387
and the Crimean War 368–9
and the First World War 435, 456–8, 467–8, 473, 481
and Germany 384, 388, 390
and the Peninsular War 308, 310, 311, 313
and Waterloo 346–7

Frances, Duchess of Tyrconnell 127
Francis, Hapsburg Emperor 268, 272
Francis, Mr 354, 355
Franco-Prussian War 1870 384, 390
Frankfurt 202, 244
Fraser, Col. Keith 391
Freddy (horse) **426**, 430
Frederick, King of Prussia 195, 196
Frederick, Duke of York 261, 265, 266, 268–9, 271, 272, 274, 301, 302, 310, 356
Frederick the Great 197, 204, 224, 228
Freemantle, Pte. George 416, 420, 421, 427
Freemasonry 260, 330
French, Field Marshal Sir John 418, 420, 421, 424, 435, 452, 473
French army 67, 123, 134, 144–6, 150–1, 354
    and the Crimean War 372, 374
    and the First World War 454, 456–8, 464
    and Napoleon 273–4, 278–9, 286–8, 290–9, 316, 319–40
    and the Peninsula War 286–8, 290–9, 306–10
    and the Revolutionary Wars 266–72
    and the Second World War 514–16, 529
    and the Seven Years War 232, 233–6, 237, 239–43, 244, 245–8
    and the War of Austrian Succession 171, 172, 182–4, 198, 202, 203, 204–8, 209, 212–15
    and the War of Spanish Succession 167–70, **173**
    and Waterloo 316, 319–40, 343
French deserters 203
French fleet 177
French Republic 265
French Royalists 272
Fretchville, Lord John 48, 50
Freud, Lucian **581**
Friday, Quartermaster 180
'friendly fire' 530
Frome 90
Frondes (1648–53) 7
Froude, Tom 397
Fuentes de Oñoro 291, 292–4, **293**
Funnel, Trooper **535**

Gadkul 402, 404, 416
Gainsborough, battle of 1643 40
Gallipoli 421, 468, 548
Galloping Hogan 131
Galtieri (horse) 578–9
Galway, Lord 175, 177–8, 180
Galway 137
gambling 26, **281**, 284
Garde-Dragoner 413
First Garde-Dragoner 413
Gardes Françaises 205
Gardner machine guns 404
Garrard, Sir Samuel 164–5

Garth 257, 268
Gascoyne, David 43
Gazala 520
Gelderland horses 157
Gellatley, Private 421
Genappe 321–2, 323
General's Life Guard, The 16
George I, King of England 30, 160, 166–7, 185–94, **186**, 217
George II, King of England 187, 189, 194, 196, 197, 217, 222, 223, 238
    death 244
    and the Seven Years War 236–7
    and the War of Austrian Succession **201**, 202, 203–9, 212, 228
George III, King of England 238, 244–5, 255–61, **263**, 264, 271, 272, 274–6, 280–2, 284, 285, **287**, 573, 577
    coronation **246–7**
George IV, King of England (Prince Regent) 277, 299–301, 311, 313, 314, 347, 349, 349–54, 355, 367
    coronation 349–52, 354
    funeral 356
George V, King of England 449, 452, 454, 468, 486, 489, **491**, 495, 496, 501
George VI, King of England 349, 504, 533, 538, 552, 553–5
George, Prince of Denmark 111, 119, 160
Gerard of Brandon, Lord (Earl of Macclesfield) 4, 18, 23, 26, 30, 33, 53–4, 72, 80
Gerard, Sir Gilbert 26
German army 203, 236, 323
    and the First World War 456–8, 460–70, 474–7, 479–81, 484–6
    and the Second World War 513, 523–7, 529–30, 531–6, 540, 543, 545, 546–8, 550
German pilots 512
Germany 170, 200–9, 228, 232–49, 279, 388
    Allied invasion of 547–51
    and the First World War 452, 454–6
    and France 384, 388, 390
    identified as main European threat to Britain 384–7
    post-Second World War 555, 558, 562, 563, 566, 567–9, 571
    rearmament 502
    and the Second World War 501–2, 547–51
Ghent 198, 217, 266, 313, 314, 315
Ginckel, Marshal Godert de 131, 132, **133**, 134–5, 136, 137, 140
Gladstone, William 387, 400
Glintworth, Lady 360
Glorious Revolution 1688 23, 47, 112–21, **113–14**, 165
Gloucester, Duke of 160
Glubb 509
Godfrey, Robert 90, 93

Godley, Pte. Samuel 333, 340
Godman, Lt 422
Goering, Hermann 569
Gofsett (Life Guard trumpeter) 189
Gold Sticks 62, 92, 96, 116, 117, 185, 189, 223, 244, 261, 264, 300, 306, 349, 352, 356, 358, 391, 449, 481–4, 489, 537, 538, 548, 552, 563, 582
Goldsworthy, Lt 243, 257, 266, 268
Gooch, Maj. (Later Col.) Eric 513–14, 527, 534
Goodenough (Waterloo Veteran) 367
Gordon, Gen. 400, 401, 402, 406, 408, 415, 416, 427
Gordon, Lord George 253
Gordon Riots 1780 253–6, **254**
Gore, Lt 355
Gort 412
Gothic Line 536, 537
Gough, Maj. 405
Goulburn, Edward 282–4
Grafton, Duke of 116
Graham, Gen. 394, 395
Graham, Sir Thomas 307, 308
Gramont, Duc de 204
Gramont 315, 316
Granby, Marquis of *see* Manners, John, Marquis of Granby
Grand Alliance, treaty of the 121, 171, 265
Grand Battery (French artillery - Waterloo) 325, 328, 335, 336, 337, 338, 579
Grand Tour 1775 260
Grassini, Madame 304
Gray, Thomas 64
Great Exhibition 1851 368
Great Fire of London 1666 61
Great Trek 1830s 416
Greek troops 529
Green, Capt. 172
Green Line 571
Gregson, Charles 449
Grenada 249
Grenadier Guards (1st Foot Guards) 64, 347, 349
grenadiers à cheval 62
Grenadines 249
Grenfell, Julian 437–8, 440–1, 449–52, 459–62, 464–5, **466**, 470, 471–2
Grenville 257
Grey, Lord 66, 90, 92, 93, 96
Grice, Trooper **560**
Griffin, Col. Edward 66, 92, 111
Grivas 558, 561
Grobba, Dr 512, 513–14
Gronow 338–40
Grosvenor, Lord Hugh 462–3, **466**
Grouch, Gen. 316, 346
Guards' Armoured Division (Second World War) 538, 539, 540, 546, **549**, 555
Guards Division (First World War) 473
Gulf War 1990-91 571
Gumball, Rev. Thomas 27

Gunning, Lt George ('Warrior Gubbins') 292–3, 296, 299, 342
Gunter, Quartermaster 181
17th Gurkha Division 562
Gurney, Capt. 454
Gustav Aldolphus 181
Guthrie, Gen. Lord 582
Gwynne, Nell 53

Habbaniya Air Force Base 508–9, 510, 513
Habbaniya Task Force ('Habforce') 509–16, 537
Habert, Col. 330
Hague, The 46, 112
Haig, Field Marshal Earl Douglas 435, 452, 463, 473, 481, 485, **488**, 489
Haines, Padre 479–80
Haldane 449
Hales, Sir Edward 99
Halifax, Lord 174
Hall, Betty 27
Hall, Michael 51
Halsbury, Lord 443
Hamadan 517
Hameln 233
Hamilton, Gen. 136
Hamilton, George 127
Hamilton, Sir George 56
Hamilton, Col. Richard 121
Hamilton, Sir Ian 421, 428
Hamilton-Russell, Diana 524, 531
Hamilton-Russell, Lt (later Maj.) Jack 422, **493**, 495, 524, 525, 526, 530, 531, 532, 544
Hampton Court 161
Hanau 202, 204
Hanbury, Tom 546
Hanbury-Tracy, Maj. 412
hand grenades 62
Handel, George Frideric 209
Hanley, Quartermaster Hugh 361, **362–3**
Hanover 196, 224–6, 228, 232, 233, 237, 239, 243, 245, 248, 249, 272, 277
Hanoverian Brigade 314
Hanoverians 202, 204, 209, 212, 217, 228, 233, 234, 265, 266, 268, 314, 316, 325, 329, 330, 336
Hanship, Sgt. 296
Hapsburgs 176, 178, 195
Harcourt, Gen. 271
Harding, Lord 562–3
Hardman, Capt. 422
Harrington, Lord (Col.) 256, 277, 300, 306, 356
Harris, Lt 175
Hartop, Lt 379
Harvey 172, 174, 177, 180
Harwood, Oxenbridge 106
Haseiat 520
Haselrig, Sir Arthur 11, 40, 43, 44
Hawkins, Cpl 534
Hawley, Col. 211, 217–20, 226, 228

Hawley, Lt Col. Lord Francis 47, 50, 56
Hayes, Capt. Horace 424
Hayes, Sir James 142
Haywood, Capt. 323
Hayworth, Maj. Reggie 496
Head, L. Cpl 481
Health, Lt 'Volley' 456
Heard, Trooper Harry **453**
Heathcoat-Amory, Maj. Roddy 524
Heathcote, Ralph 285, 286, 288, 299, 312
Heavy Brigade (Crimean War) 376, 382
Charge of the 378–9, **380–1**
Heavy Camel Regiment **399**, 401, 404, 405, 408, 409
Helliar, Pte. 288
Helme, Mary 106
Henning, Private 421
Henry VII, King of England 7
Henry VIII, King of England 7, 105
Herbert (Robert Lloyd's horse) 468, 480, 484
'Hereditary Prince' 233, 240, 242, 243
Hess, Prince of 200
Hesse 233, 239, 244, 248
Hessian troops 202, 209, 228, 265, 266, 268, 314
Hessy, William **362–3**
Hester, William 29
Heyford, Col. Anthony 64, 119, 130, 132, 170
Heyworth, Lt Col. 504–6, 520, 555
Hick, Gen. 400
Hicks Pasha 400
Hidden, Emily 418
Hidden, Cpl (later Capt.) Hugh 418, 421, 424, 490
Hidden, Rensburg 418
Highland Division (Boer War) 418
51st Highland Division (Second World War) 524
Highlanders 211, 220, 226
92nd Highlanders 334
93rd Highlanders 376
highwaymen 48
Hill, Clement **297**, 314, 358, 360
Hill, Lt Col. Robert 276, 277, 284, 295, **297**, 306, 314, 330, 358
Hill, Gen. Lord Rowland 295, 296–9, **297**, 302, 306, 307–8, 313, 314, 340, 358
Himeimat feature 525, 526
Hitler, Adolf 501, 502, 516, 548
Hitler Youth 550
Hodgson, Pte. 333, 335
Hodgson, Trooper **560**
Hodsall, Mr 188
Hogarth, William 161, 223
Hohenzollern redoubt 473
Holdsworth, Joseph 277–8
Holland 17, 23, 57–61, 65–6, 92, 121, 123, 144, 150, 151, 156, 209, 248, 264–5, 272, 273, 277, 279, 546–7

Hollebeke 464
Holy Land 495
Home District 412
Home, Lt Col. Milne 391–2
Homs 516
Honey, Mr 354, 355
Honeywood, General 197
Hong Kong 562
Honiton 113
Hood, Admiral 256, 257
Hooge 469
Hopkins, Lt 121
Hopton Heath 47
Horrocks, Lt Gen. Sir Brian 545–7
Horse Artillery 240–2, 307–8
Horse Grenadier Guards 62–4, **63**, 243, 301, 566, 579
and the Austrian Wars of Succession 197, 208, 209, 211
election work 256–7
and George I 167, 187, 189, 192
and George II 197, 208, 209, 211, 222, 223, 244
and George III 256–7, 261, 262–4
peacekeeping duties 164, 165–6, 167
pensions 262
and Queen Anne 164, 165–6
rivalry with the Life Guards 187
uniforms **225**, 264
and William III 142, 146, 148, 149, 150, 154
1st Troop of 185, 188, 189, 197, 222, **225**, 256, 262, 264
2nd Troop of 164, 165–6, 197, 205, 226, 256, 262, 264
Horse Guards building
new **221**, 223–4, 553–5, 577
old 61, 67, 106, 161, 223
Horsed Reserve Regiment (Household Cavalry – Second World War) 537–8
Horsey, Capt. 253
Horsey, Capt. Samuel 165, 166
Horsley, John (Bluster) 282–4
Horus (horse) 492–5
Hoscht 200–2
Hotchkiss machine guns 509, 516
Houchard, Marshal 266
Hounslow Heath army camps 101, **102–3**, 104, 105, 106, 108, 111, 112, 113, 132, 384
House of Commons 17–18, 31, 60, 161, 165, 167, 390, 516
House of Lords **172**
Household Battalion 474, 479, 486
Household Brigade (Napoleonic Wars) 301, 306–8, 310, 314, 316, 318, 319–21, 322, 323, **324**, 325, 329, 334–5, 336, 338, 343, 346, 347
Household Cavalry 14, 29, 39, 62, 64, 67, 73, 83, 96, 222, 224, 228, 232, 400, 413

bands 352, **353**, 577–8
and the Boer War 415–16, 418–20, 422, 424, 427–30, **429**, 435
and the Boer–First World War interwar period 442–8, **444–5**, 449–52
burials 388
and the Cardwell Reforms 387–8, 392
as ceremonial guard 390–1
contemporary 567–84
converted into machine-gun battalions 480–1, 484, 485
cutbacks 489–90
and Edward VII 442
and Edward VIII's review 1946 501, **503**
and the Egyptian campaign 1882 391–400
evolution 566
and the First World War 452–64, 467–71, 473–4, 477–84, 485, 486, 489
and George III 273, 280, 282
and George IV (Prince Regent) 300, 349–54
horses 424, **425–6**, 430, 578–9
and Iraq 369
mechanisation 496–7, 504–6, 508, 509
military punishments 366
in Palestine 504
peace-keeping duties 354
post-First World War 489–90, 495, 496–7, 502
post-Second World War 552–5, 558–62, 563–6, **564–5**
and the post-Waterloo peace 356, 358–9, 360–4, 366, 367
and regimental drills 578
role in the army (Second World War) 537
saddlery 579–82
and the Second World War 502–13, 514, 515, 516, 517, 519, 522, 525–30, 533–51, **535**
and the 'Soldier's Small Book' 415
standards 582
and the Sudan campaign 1884–85 401, 402, 405, 408, 409
uniforms 349–52, 350, 442–3, **487–8**, 579
and Victoria 358
and Waterloo 338, 349
weaponry 579
and William IV 358
Household Cavalry Brigade (Austrian War of Succession) 211, 215
Household Cavalry Brigade (First World War) 458, 464
Household Cavalry Brigade (Peninsular War) 311
Household Cavalry commando troop 539
Household Cavalry Composite Regiment 413

Household Cavalry Field Ambulance 474
Household Cavalry infantry battalion 473–4
Household Cavalry Memorial, Zanvoorde **488**, 489
Household Cavalry Mounted Regiment 361, 553, 566, 571
Household Cavalry Museum 188, 302, 304, 342, 391, 415, 480, 577
Household Cavalry Musical Ride 430
Household Cavalry Regiment (HCR) 571–3, 582–4
  structure 573
1st Household Cavalry Regiment (1 HCR) 504–12, 514, **515**, 516, 517, 519, 522–3, 525–9, 533–7, **535**, 538, 539, 544, 548–51, 555, 563, 584
  'A' Squadron 513, 516
  'B' Squadron 510, 512, 513, **515**
  'C' Squadron 510, 512, 519
2nd Household Cavalry Regiment (2 HCR) 537, 538–48, 550–1, 555, 584
  'A' Squadron 540–3
  'B' Squadron 540–3
  'C' Squadron 540, 547
  'D' Squadron 540, 584
Household Division 553–5, 577, 578
Houses of Parliament 253, 255
Howard, Capt. Charles, Earl of Carlisle 14
Howard, Capt. Sir Philip 6, 16, 27, 54, 70, 95
Howard, Edward 356
Howard, William, Lord of Escrick 16
Howard-Vyse, Sir Richard 'Wombat' 448
Howarth, Mr 279
Hucker, Capt. 93
Huguenots 98, 99, 106, 113, 126, 127, 134, 136, 148, 156, 175, 178, 188
Hull, L. Cpl of Horse Matty 573
Hulton 296–8, 299
Humber armoured cars 523, 530
Hume, Joseph 366
Hunt, Trooper 527–9
Hussars 268, 458
  3rd Hussars 454, 492
  7th Hussars 321
  10th Hussars 418, 442, 484–5
  18th Hussars 424, 492
  19th Hussars 412
  see also Red Hussars; Russian Hussars
Hussars (of Archduke Ferdinand) 269
Hussein, Saddam 571, 573
Hutton, Robert 40
Huy 148, 150
Huygens, Constantine 117–18
Hyde, Anne **25**, 26, 60, 160
Hyde, Edward, 1st Earl of Clarendon 9, 26, 37, 44, 48, 119
Hyde Park Barracks 303
Hyde Park Review
  1699 157
  1763 248

Imperial Guard 262, 316
  Old Guard 337
    Grenadiers 347, 349
Inchiquin, Lord 78
Independent Company 101
India 224, 243, 249, 342, 354, 360, 371, 412, 435–40, 490, 495, 501, 504
Indian Army 387, 495
Indian Cavalry Division 480
4th Indian Division (Second World War) 534
Industrial Revolution 278
20th Infantry Brigade (First World War) 462
3rd Infantry Division 490
39th Infantry Division (German – First World War) 463
105th Infantry Regiment of the Line 333–4, 342
Ingleton, Pte. Edward 203
Ingoldsby, Brig. 215
Inkerman, battle of 379
Innes-Ker 469
inns **231**, 276–7, 340
Invalid Fund 72
Iraq 369, 508–14, **511**, 516–17, 519, 573, **574–5**
Ireland 14, 121, 123–37, 142, 154, 180, 265, 367–8, 384, 412–13, 490, 571
Ireton 14
Irish army (following the Restoration) 28
Irish army (of James II) 118, 126, 130, 131, 134–40
Irish Brigade Horse 182
Irish Brigades 137, 140
Irish Republican Army (IRA) 576–7
Irish Republicans 490
Ironside, Gen. Lord 508
Ironsides 40, 41, 44
Islam 75
Islamic Nationalism 400
Ismailia 392
Italian troops 506, 512, 523–7, 531, 533
Italy 278, 313, 529
  Allied liberation of 532–7, **541**
Iveagh, Lord 126
Ivory Passes 577

Jacobite Revolt 220
Jacobite Rising 1708 164
Jacobites 112, 124, 130, 136, 140–1, 150, 153, 157, 160–1, 165–7, 196, 217, 220, 222, 253
James I, King of England 160
James II, King of England (earlier Duke of York) 4–5, 17, 18, 20–2, **21**, 23, 26–7, 28, 29, 30, 31, **34–5**, 36, 38, 39, 47, 48, 51, 53, 54, 56, 60, 61, 65–6, 67, 70, 81, **82**, 87, 92, 95, 96, 384, 577, 582
  army reforms 98–110, 153, 154, 157
  campaigns in Scotland and Ireland 121, 123, 124–30
  death 160

616 – INDEX

James II, King of England (*cont.*)
    exile in France 130, 131, 136, 140, 142, 153, 160
    ousted 108–11, **109**, 112–19
James, Dr John 318–19, 321, 323, 325, 330, 337, 346, 349
Jameson, Dr 417
Jameson Raid 1895 412
Jason, Capt. 172, 175
Jeffard, Trooper 211
Jeffreys, Judge 93, 95
Jenkinson, Maj. Charles 205, 215
Jenkinson, Capt. R. L. H. **494**
Jennings, Sarah, Duchess of Marlborough 56
Jermyn, Henry, Lord Dover 99
Jervoise, Maj. 291, 298
Jesus Christ 20
Jewish homeland 558
Johannesburg 421, 440–1, 504
Johannesburg Ladies' College 440
Johnson, Dr 167, 187, 253
Johnston, Lt Col. James 'Irish' 208, 236, 240, 242, 243
Jones, Sir Henry 48, 56, 57, 79, 80, 86, 99
Jordan, Capt. 146
Joseph Bonaparte, Impostor King 285, 286, 295, 299, 306, 307, 308
Jourdan 306, 307, 308
Joy, Maj. 520
'Judge Advocate General' 67–70

Kabul 573
Kadir Cup (all-India pig-sticking trophy) 495
Kalle 240
Kameschle 514
Kassassin 392, 394, 395–7, **396**, 398, 412, 424, 523, 552
Kassel 233, 239, 240, 243, 244, 248
Kavanagh, Brig. Gen. 459, 471, 481–4
Kelly, Capt. Edward 303–4, 313, 315, 318, 319, 321–2, 323, 329, 330, **331**, 338, 340–2, 360
Kelly, Maria 315, 342
Kelso 7
Kempt 328
Kendal, Mr 208
Kensington Palace 161
Kent, William 223
Ker, John, Earl of Dundonald 187, 189
Kermanshah 517
Keroualle, Louise de, Duchess of Portsmouth 23, **23**
Kerr, Cpl 402
Kerr, Lord Robin Innes 569
Kesselring 534
Kettle, Rupert 360
Keyes, Thomas 153
Keynsham 88
Khanaquin 517
Khartoum 400, 402, 406, 408, 415, 435

Khiva 401
Kidney Ridge 524
Kilcommodon Hill 134–5, 136
Killigrew, Lt Col. 170, 172, 175, 177, 178
Kilmainham Hospital, Dublin 72, 192
Kilmarnock, Lady 220
Kimberley 420–1, 428
'Kingcol' 509–12
King's Bench prison 255
King's German Legion 323–5
King's Playhouse 27
'King's and the Queene's Troopes, The' 7
Kingstone, Brig. 509
Kipling, John 271
Kirke, Col. Sir Percy 79–80, 99–101, 116–17, 131, 132
Kirke, Capt. George 153
Kirkuk-Tripoli pipeline 514–16, 517
Kitchener, Lord 408, 415, 418, 427, 428, 430, 431, 434, 435, 442, 473, 557
Klein Zillebeke 464, 465
Klosterseven 224, 228
Kneller, Sir Godfrey 33, 105
Knights of the Garter **163**
Knights of St John 278
Knightsbridge Barracks 361–4, 390, 400, **410–11**, 442, 489, 490, 502, 537, 553, 576, 582–3
Kolin 224
Konigsegg, Count 211–12
Kordofan 400
Korti 401, 402, 404, 408
Kosovo 573
Krefeldt 228
Krotzka 205
Kruger, President 417, 421
Kruiseecke 462
Kuwait 571

La Chaussée-Tirancourt 546
La Roque, Capt. 154, 156
La Rue, Lt 121
La-Haie-Sainte farm complex, Waterloo 323, 328, 329–33, 336, 340
Labour Government 563
Ladysmith 417, 418, 421, 422, 427, 428
Lafsall, Mr 188
Lake Nasser 408
Lallemund 296
Lamb 534
Lambert, Dicky 368
Lambert, John 16, 43
Lamott, Capt. 288
Lancers 448, 458
    12th Lancers (Boer War) 418
    3rd Lancers (French – Waterloo) 335–6
    4th Lancers (French – Waterloo) 335–6
Land Tax 164
Landen 150, 154, 170
Landrecies 266, 268, 269, 271
Landrost of Sweitzer-Reineke 431
Langston, Thomas 79, 80, 87, 99–101, 110

Lanier, General Sir John 112, 113, 124, 126, 132
Larden 150
Lascelles, Capt. 238
Lathan House 26
Latour, Col. 292
Laufeldt 220, 232
Lauzun 124, 127
Laws, Cpl 534
Lawson, Philip 99
Laycock, Robert 502, 539
Le Bény-Bocage 543, 544
Le Havre 452, 454, 456
Le Marchant 296
Le Quesnoy 266
Lee, Col. Vaughan 'Flea' 443, 448
Lee Enfield rifle, .303 454
Lee, Johnny 374
Lee Metford carbine, .303 413
Legg-Bourke, Maj. 508
Lehndorff, Count 390
Leicester, battle of 1645 7
Leicesters (regiment) 468
Leigh, Lt 'G' 510–12, **511**, 514
Leighton, Maj. 188
Lepell 183
Leria 290
Leslie, Cornet 78
Lester, Cavendish 244
Leuse 144
Leuse, battle of 141
Levellers 14, 16, 27
Levigne, Sir Robert 462
Liberal Government 384
Liberals 390
Libya 533
Lichfield, Earl of 7, 8–9
Liège 171
Life Guards 4–38, 39, 41, 48, 50–3, 56–66, 67, 70–2, 83, 110, 346
    armour 33
    and the Austrian War of Succession 197–8, 200, 203, 204, 205, 208, 209, 211, 216, 217
    bases 36
    and the Boer War 415, 416, 418–21, 427, 430
    and the Boer–First World War interwar period 442–52, **445**
    Byzantine rank structure abolished (late 1700s) 264
    and the Cardwell Reforms 387–8
    Catholic membership 98–9
    commissions 30
    communications 70–1
    contemporary 567–71, 576, 577–82
    Corporals of Horse Guards 224
    cutbacks 349, 489–90
    cyclist companies 473, **476**
    damaged reputation 50–4
    discipline 366
    drummers 28–9, 33, 282, 352

duelling 284
Egyptian campaign 1882 391, 394, 396, 397, 398
election work 256
false musters 54, 188–9
and the First World War 452–4, 456, 458–64, 467, 469, 473, 484–6, 489, 552
in Flanders 141–2, 144, 146–51
form composite regiment with The Blues and Royals 571
gambling 284
and George I 167, 185, 186–92, 195
and George II 197–8, 200, 203, 204, 205, 208, 209, 211, 216, 217, 222, 223–4, 228, 244
and George III 252, 253, 255–6, 261–4, 263, 265, 273–4, 276, 277, 279–82, 284
and George IV (Prince Regent) 299–301, 349–53, 356
horses 157
and James II's overthrowal 108, 113, 116–17
and James II's reforms 96, 98–9, 101, 104, 105–6, 108
and the law 51–3
mechanisation 496, 497, 508, 522
musicians 28–9, 29, 33, 105–6, 107, 278, 282, 352
'mutinies' (late 1800s) 409–12
nicknamed the 'Piccadilly Butchers' 300
over-subscription of 31
pay 27–8, 73, 106, 108, 261–2, 264
peace keeping duties 164–6, **169**, 253, 255–6, 265, 300–1, 303, 354–5
and the Peninsula War 299, 300–1, 303–4, 307–8, 310, 311
pensions 72–3, 106, 192, 222
and politics 30–1
post-First World War 489–90, 496, 497, 500–1, 502
post-Second World War 553, 555, 558–61, **560**, 563, 566
and the post-Waterloo peace 349, 354–6, 358–61, 366–7
quartermaster corporals 224
and Queen Anne 161–4, 165–6
reviews 37, 157
rivalry with the Horse Grenadier Guards 187
and the Second World War 502, 508, 510, 512, 516, 522, 538
and Sedgemoor 86–7, 88, 92, 93, 95
and the Seven Years War 244
standards 29, 101, 347–9
and the Sudan campaign 1884–85 404
system of purchase 29–30, 71, 98–9, 192, **193**, 359–60, 387
and the Tangier Horse 79
trumpeters 28–9, 33, 105–6, **107**, 278

uniforms 33, 101, 157, 264, 274, **275**, 280, 301, 352–4, **357**, 454, 554
and Waterloo 313–14, 316, 318, 319–23, 325, 330–3, 335–40, 347–9
weaponry 105, 273, 394, 454
and William III 118–19, 121–6, 130, 132, 140, 141–2, 144, 146–51, 153–4, 156–7
wives 304
1st Life Guards 260, 262, 264, 274, 277, 279–80, 299–300, 303–4, 310, 313, 318–23, 325, 330, 336–8, 347, 352, 360, **362–3**, 366–7, **386**, 390–1, 394, 409, 415–16, 420–1, 427, 443–6, 445, 448–54, 458–9, 462, 464, 467, 484–6, 489–90, 554
1st Troop (His Majesties own Troope of Guards) (King's Troop) 22–30, 33, 36–7, 44, 47–8, 53–4, 56, 61–2, 64–7, 81, 95, 101, 113, 117–19, 124, 151, 154, 156–7, 189, 197, 217, 222, 223, 264, 274, 280, 301, 349, 355, 442, 443–6, 458, **503**, 537–8, 553, **554**
2nd Life Guards 260, 262, 264–5, 274, 279, 284, 299–300, 303–4, 313, 318, 325, 330–3, 335–8, 347, **350–1**, 352, 355–6, 360, 366, 391, 394, 397–8, 404, 415–16, 418–20, 430, 448–9, 452–4, 456–8, 460, 484–6, 489–90, 495, 552, 566
2nd Troop (His Highness Royall the Duke of Yorke his Troope of Guards) 17, 18, 22, 26–7, 29, 33, 36, 37, 38, 54, 64, 86, 101, 113, 117, 118, 121, 123, 124, 130, 154, 157, 167, 188, 189, 197, 217, 222
standard 100
1st and 2nd Life Guards combined 489–90, 495–7, 500–2, 508, 510, 512, 516, 522, 538, 553, **554**, 555, 558–61, **560**, 563, 566–71, 576–82
'A' Squadron 489
'B' Squadron 489, 502
'C' Squadron 489, 502
'D' Squadron 489
3rd Troop (His Grace the Duke of Albemarle his Troope of Guards) 22, 27, 33, 36, 37, 87, 95, 101, 113, 117, 118, 119, 124, 131, 132, 141, 142, 144, 154, 157, 161, 166, 189, 197, 204, 208, 222
see also Queen's Life Guard
4th Troop (pre-1707) 98–9, 110, 113, 118, 124, 134, 143, 149, 151

4th Troop (1707 onwards) 164, 165, 166, 187, 189, 192, 197–8, 222, 495
His Majesty's Troop of Guards in Scotland (Scots Troop) 28, 62, 65, 112, 113, 121, 144, 154, 164
'The King's Life Guards of Horse' 7, 8, **12–13**
'The King's and the Queene's Troopes' 7
Lord General's 11, 27
Monck's Troop of 6, 18, 20, 22, 44
Parliamentarian 9–14, **10**, **12–13**, 27
Queen's Life Guard 27, 29, 38, 54, 61, 64, 355, 409, 446, 569, 573–7, 579, 582
Long Guard 576–7
Short Guard 576, 577
see also Household Cavalry Mounted Regiment; Household Cavalry Regiment; 1st Household Cavalry Regiment; 2nd Household Cavalry Regiment
Light Brigade 376, 378
Charge of the 379
Light Camel Regiment 401
Light Cavalry Brigade 336
Light Division (Peninsular War) 292, 294
7th Light Dragoons 316
14th Light Dragoons 286, 291, 294
15th Light Dragoons 226, 239, 248, 260, 268
16th Light Dragoons 269
21st Light Dragoons (Royal Foresters) 238
23rd Light Dragoons 321, 342
Ligny 316, 319
Ligonier, Gen. 209, 211, 220, 224, 228, 229, 232, 244
Lillburne, John 14
Lille 486
Limbert, John **362–3**
Limerick 130, 131, 134, 137, **138–9**
Limerick, treaty of 137, 141
Lincoln's Inn Fields riots 165–6
Lincolns (regiment) 464
Lindley, Maj. 422
Lindsay, Lord 46
Lion (ship) 217
Liprandi, Gen. 374, 376
Lisbon 171–2, 175, 285, 286, 298, 302, 304, 306, 307
Littleton, Maj. Walter 99, 113, 119
Littleton, Maj. William 56, 87
Livingston, Charles, 2nd Earl of Newburgh 88
Livingston, Sir James, 1st Earl of Newburgh 28
Llera 296, 298
Lloyd, Robert 443–8, 458–9, 460, 462, 463, 468, 480, 481, 484, 490, 576, 582–3

Lloyd, Rowland 106
Lobau 316, 319
Locke, Mathew 70, 71
Logie, Dr 364
Logroño 310
London 165–6, 253–6, 261–2, 265, 299–301, 310, 313, 352, 354–6, 360, 442–6
47th London Infantry Division (First World War) 485
London Post, The 157
London-Zurich Agreement 561
Londonderry, Lord 356, 358
Londonderry, Lord 'Manse' 448
Long 295
Long Range Desert Group 519
Loos, battle of 470
Lord High Admiral's Regiment 70
Lorraine 452, 454
Lothian, Col. Lord 262, 264
Loughborough 256
Louis XIII, King of France 6
Louis XIV, King of France 5, 6, 7, 17, 18, 29, 31, 51, 56, 57, 60–1, 62, 67, 71, 96, 104, 118, 121, 126, 127, 137, 142, 144, 151, 156, 171, 177, 180
Louis XV, King of France 195, 215, 245
Louis XVI, King of France 265
Lovelace, Francis 26
Low Countries 123, 265, 313
Low, David 337
Low, Regimental Sgt-maj. 530
Lowestoft, battle of 56
Lucan, 1st Earl of *see* Sarsfield, Patrick, 1st Earl of Lucan
Lucan, 3rd Earl of *see* Bingham, George Charles, 3rd Earl of Lucan
Lucknow 435
Lucknow Church 440
Lucy, Capt. Thomas 32, 33, 105, 131
Ludgershall 458
Ludlow, Edmund 9, 11
Luftwaffe 520, 529
Lumley, Col. Richard (Earl of Scarborough) 119, 151, 156
Lumsden, Gen. 524
Luttrell, Henry 116, 118, 124, 134, 135, 140
Luxembourg, Marshal 142, 144, 146, 148, 149, 150, 182
Lygon 313
Lynch, Michael 284
Lyttelton, Sir Charles 70

Maas River 547, 548
Maastricht, battle of 1673 56, 57
Maastricht, sieges of 46, 60, 64, 79
McAlpine (of the Blues) 562
Macaulay 46
McCreery, Gen. Dick 536
Macedonia 573
McGhur (horse) 398

McIntyre, Trooper 440
Mackay, Maj-Gen. 135, **147**
Mackenzie, Cornet 78, 79, 80, 83, 87, 121
Mackintosh, Cpl 405
McLean, Capt. **365**
McLennan, Private 421
Macnamara, Capt. 284
Madan, Capt. 20
Madras Army 360
Madrid 292, 295, 298, 299, 306
Mafeking 417, 428
Magaliesberg 428
Magersfontein 418
Maguilla 296–8
Mahomet Ahmed (Mahdi) 400, 402, 404, 406, 408
Mahsamah 392, 394
Main River 232
Maine, Lt Col. Edmund 117
Mainz 202
Maison Militaire du Roi 5, 62, 71, 144, 146, 149, 205, 262
see also Imperial Guard
Majoribanks, Lt 255, 256
Majuba 417
Makarios, Archbishop 558
Makins, Capt. (later Gen.) Ernest 431, 434, 438, 440, 495–6, 504–6
Malaya 561–2, 563
Malis Ismail 78, 79
Malplaquet, battle of 157, 170
Malta 278
Manfredonia Peninsula 532–3
Manners, John, Marquis of Granby 228–32, **230–1**, 233, 234, 236, 237–40, 242–9, 257, 502, 576, 583
Manners, Robert 232
Manners, Russell 238
Mansel, Maj-Gen. 268–9, **270**, 271
Mansfield Judgement 300
Maplemore (cattle ship) 416
Mar, Lord 167, 190
Marcognet 328, 334
Mareth Line 530
Maria Theresa 195–6, 209
Marie Antoinette 265
Marine Commando Brigade 569
Marlborough, Duchess of 189
Marlborough, 2nd Duke of 228
Marlborough, 1st Earl of *see* Churchill, Col. John, 1st Earl of Marlborough
Marlborough, Sarah Jennings, Duchess of 56
Marlborough House 392
Marmont 294, 295, 316
Marmont Harrington armoured cars, Mark 3 506, 523, 529
Marsack, Mr 284
Marsh, Ralph 198
Marshall, Trooper Horace 409, 412
marshals 108
Marston Moor, battle of 44
Martinelli, Cpl 534

Martini Henry carbines 394
Marvell, Andrew 53
Mary II, Queen of England 47, 60, 81, 111, 130, 144, 150
Mary of Modena 60, **63**
Mary of Teck 452, 489
mascots/pets, regimental **385**, 509
Masham, Abigail 161
Massena 286, 288, 290, 291, 292, 294, 295, 296
Matador armoured cars 540
Matthews, Col. Edward 130, 150, 170
Mauggeridge, John 29
Maurice, Prince 7
Maxted, Cpl of the Horse 512
Mayence 202
Mays, Spike 492, **493**, 495, 520, 558
Maze, Paul **482**
Measures, Sgt. **439**
mechanization 495–7, 504–6, 508, 509, 522
Meerbeck 315
Meesters, Willem 131
Melton Mowbray Remount Depot 538, 553, 578
Mercol 513, 514
Mermaid of Warsaw (Polish army badge) 537
Merry, Maj. 513
Messines 458, 459, 463, 464
Metemma 402, 404, 406
Methuen, Lord 412, 417, 418, 422
Metropolitan Police 37
Meynell, Godfrey 282
Middle East 504–19, **507**, 524
Middleton, Lord 78
Milhaud 328
military courts 108
see also courts martial
Miller, Maj. 282
Millin, Cpl 462, 463, 464
Mills, Peter 33
Milner, Sir Alfred 417
Minden 229, 233, 234–6, **235**, 237, 260
mines 529, 545
mining industry 417
Ministry of Defence 67
Minorca 224, 236, 249
Modder 422
Mohammed Arabi 390, 391, 392, 394, 395, 397, 398
Moldavia 368
Molia (guard) 558
Mollins, Mr 99
Mollwitz 195
Moltke the Elder 454
Moltke the Younger 454
Mompesson, Thomas 44
Monarch of Bermuda (ship) 537
Monck, Christopher, 2nd Duke of Albemarle 53
Monck, Gen. George, 1st Duke of Albemarle

4, 6, 16, 17, 18, **19**, 20, 22, 27, 28, 36, 38, 39, 40, 41, 43, 44, **45**, 54, 65, 66, 67, 70, 87–8, 95, 156
Monmouth and Buccleuch, Duke of 23, 28, 29, 30, 47, 53–4, **55**, 56–7, 62, 64–6, 67, 70, 71, 86, 87–93, 96, 108, 578, 583
Mons 142, 144, 212, 217, 315, 316, 454, 484, 578
   retreat from 454–6, **455**, 472, 509
Mont-St-Jean 322, 325, 349
Montagu, Duke of 189
Montagu, Capt. (later Lt Col.) Edward 174, 183, 184
Montague, Edward, Lord Sandwich 74
Monte Cassino 534, 536
Montgomery, Gen. 504, 523, 524, 525, 526, 527, 530, 532, 540, **542**, 543, 544, 547
Montmorency, Duc de 149
Montrose, Duke of 65
Moore, Sir John 285
Moore, Lt 174
Moors 75–9, 83
Mordaunt, Charles, 3rd Earl of Peterborough **163**, 175, 176–8, 180, 189–90
Mordaunt, Henry, 2nd Earl of Peterborough 74, 75
Morris Mission (Household Cavalry – Second World War) 538
Mortimer, Pat 465
Mosul 513
Mount Amaro 534–6
Mountbatten, Earl 563
Mountjuich 176
Mouscron 271
Mousqetaires de la Garde 6–7
Mousqetaires Gris 7
Mousqetaires Noirs 7, 205, 208, 582
Mullan, William 490
Munnocks, Mr 104, 105
Munnocks, Lt Philip 88, 105
Munster 228, 232, 233
Murray-Smith, Maj. Tony 522
Mussolini, Benito 506
mustard gas 469, 486
Mutiny Act 1689 51, 118
Muttra 435, 436
Mysore 495

Naples 533–4, 537
Napoleon Bonaparte 216, 262, 273, 278–9, 334, 352, 355, 356
   abdication 1815 346
   escape from Elba, remobilisation 312–13
   exile to Elba 311
   and the Peninsula War 285, 286, 292, 295, 299, 306, 308
   and Waterloo 314–16, 319, 322, 324, 329, 334, 337
Napoleonic Eagles 334, 342–3
Naseby, battle of 8–9, 11, **12–13**, 44, 81

Nassauers 325
Natal 417, 418, 421, 424, 430
National Army Museum 188, 313–14
National Servicemen 555, 562
Naturalization Act 1698 156
Naumur 144, 149–51, 217
Nave De Haver 292
Navy, Army and Air Force Institutes (NAAFI) 545
Naylor-Leyland, Lt 456
Nazis 502, 512, 536, 550
Nedby, Charles 79, 80
Neeld, Col. Audley 415, 416, 420, **423**
Neerwinden 148, 149
Neil, Trooper Harry 420, 421
Néry 456
Neuve Chapelle 469
new model army 11, 14, 16, 40, 41
Newburgh, 1st Earl of *see* Livingston, Sir James, 1st Earl of Newburgh
Newburgh, 2nd Earl of *see* Livingston, Charles, 2nd Earl of Newburgh
Newburn 7
Newbury, battle of 41, 44
Newcastle, 1st Duke of *see* Pelham-Holles, Thomas, 1st Duke of Newcastle
Newcastle 7
Newgate Prison 153
Ney 316, 319, 321, 336
Nicholas, Tsar 368, 369
Nicosia 561, 571
Nieuport 217
Nightingale, Florence 146
Ninove 315, 319
Nivelles 318, 319
Noailles 202, 204, 205–8, 209
Nock, Henry 273–4
Nock Pattern Heavy Cavalry Carbine 273, 290
Normandie Regiment 243
Normandy 533, 539, 540–6, **541–2**, 547
North Africa 506, 517, 519–27, **521**, 529–30, 533
North Atlantic Treaty Organization (NATO) 567, 573
North, Lord 256
North Somerset Yeomanry 470
North, William 361
Northampton, Cornet Compton, Earl of 116, 151
Northampton, Earl of 47
Northumberland, 1st Duke of (George Fitzroy) 95–6, 117, 119, 123, 185, 189, 190
Northumberland, 2nd Duke of (Col. Hugh Percy) 262, 277, 300, 301–2, 356, 579
Norwegian army 96
Nottingham 256
Nottingham Riding School (of the Blues) 260
Nules 176

Oates, Capt. 355
Oates, Titus 62, **63**, 92
O'Brien (Life Guard) 53, 57
O'Brien, Catherine 111
O'Bryan, Lucius 232
Ogle, John 40
Oglethorpe, Maj. Theophilus 66, 86, 87, 88, 90, 92, 93, 95, 104, 117
oil 508
Okey, Colonel 9, 81
Old Montague House camp **254**
Oldbridge 126, 127
Olifant's Neck 428
O'Loghlin, Maj. T. **275**
Oman, Sultan of 561
O'Moore 116
One Day's Pay scheme 192
O'Neill, Col. Daniel 44–6, 47
O'Neill, Sir Neal 126, 127
O'Neill, Owen 44
Onslow, Maj-Gen. Richard 211, 222
Operation Bluecoat 543
Operation Desert Storm 571
Operation Goodwood 540
Operation Husky 531–2
Operation Market Garden 547
Operation Python 537
Oporto 295, 307
Orange Free State 416, 417, 431
Ordnance 33, 70, 132, 229, 273–4
Orford, Cpl 216
Ormonde, Duke of 119, 130, 142–4, **143**, 148, 149–50, 153, 156, 167, 174, 189
Orrel, Capt. 166
Orrery, Earl of 104
Osborne, Charles 50
Oschsendorf 240, 243
O'Shea, Trooper 440
Osnabruck 244
Ossory, Lord 79
Ostend 197, 217, 266, 271, 313, 315
Otto, Lt Gen. 268
Ottoman Sultan (1853) 368–9
Ottomans 368–9
Oudenarde, battle of 157, 164, 170, 189
Our Owne Royall Regiment of Dragoones (aka Royals; King's Own Royal Regiment of Dragoons; Royal Regiment of Dragoons; 1st Royal Dragoons; Royal Dragoons) 81–3, 96, 110, 111, 160, 190, 222, 224, 304
   adopt black as regimental colour 208
   amalgamation with the Blues (post-Second World War) 563–6
   anti-smuggling work 252, 257
   and the Austrian War of Succession 197, 200, 204, 205, 208, 209, 211, 215, 217
   and the Boer War 416, 418, 421–2, **426**, 430–1, 434, 435

Our Owne Royall Regt of Dragoones (*cont.*)
  and the Cardwell Reforms 387
  Catholic membership 99
  contemporary 567–71, 576, 577–83
  and the Crimean War 369, 371, 372–4, 376–8, **377**, 379, 382, 383
  cutbacks 249, 367, 435, 489
  female relationships 312
  and the First World War 441–2, 458, 459, 467, 469, 470, 473, 474–9, 480, 484, 485, 486
  forms composite regiment with the Life Guards and the Blues 571
  and George I 192–5
  and George II 197, 200, 204, 205, 208, 209, 211, 215, 217
  and George III 252, 257, 260, 261, 266, 268, 269, 271, 272, 273, 276, 284–5, 286, **287**, 288–98
  horsemanship 260
  horses 174–5, 260, 372–4, 377, 382
  in India 435–40, **439**, 490, 495, 501
  in Ireland 384, 412–13, 490
  and James II's overthrowal 108, 112, 113, 117
  and James II's reforms 96, 98, 101–4, 105, 106, 108
  Kaiser Wilhelm II awarded Colonel-in-Chief of 413
  mechanisation 495–6, 506
  in Palestine 495, 504, 506, 519
  pay 105, 106, 192–4, 311, 437
  and the Peninsula War 286, **287**, 288–98, 306, 307, 310–12
  pensions 106, 130
  post-First World War 489, 490–6
  post-Second World War 555, 558, 563–6
  and the post-Waterloo peace 367–8
  and the Prince Regent 349
  and the Revolutionary Wars 266, 268, 269, 271, 272
  and the Second World War 506, 517–22, 523–6, 529–30, 531–2, 533, **542**, 544, 545, 547–8, 550, 551
  and Sedgemoor 86, 87, 88, 90, 93, 95
  and the Seven Years War 228, 239, 240, 243, 245, 248, 249
  in South Africa 1911 438–42
  and the Spanish War of Succession 167–84
  standard 100
  Sudan campaign 1884-85 401, 405, 408
  uniforms 178, 285, 294–5, 367, 533
  and Waterloo 313, 314, 316–18, 322, 333–4, 335, 336, 347
  weaponry 178, 412–13
  and William III 119, 124, 126, 127, 130, 132, 134, 137, 140, 141, 150, 154, 156, 157
  wives 436–7, 440, 441–2
  'A' Squadron 506, 524, 531–2, 533
  'C' Squadron 524
  'D' Troop 368
  Light Troop 226–8, 249
  see also Household Cavalry Regiment; Union Brigade
Overkirke, Monsieur 142, 151, 156
Oxford, 20th Earl of *see* de Vere, Col. Aubrey, 20th Earl of Oxford
Oxford Blues, The *see* Royal Regiment of Horse Guards

Paarderberg 421
Packe, Cornet (later Capt. and Maj.) 260, 276, 306, 328, 330, **332**
Paderborn 232, 238, 239, 244, 248
Painter (boxer) 313
Palestine 495, 504, 506, 509, 513, 514, 519, 526, 555, 558
Palestine Police 504
Palmyra 514, 516
Pamplona 308, 310
Pamplona Road 307–8
Panther tanks, Mark VI 527
Panton, Col. Thomas 26
Papelotte 335
7th Parachute Division (German – Second World War) 551
Paris 346
Parker, John 64
Parker, Lt 88, 90
Parker, Lt Col. 361, **362–3**
Parliament 6, 8, 11, 14, 16–17, 18, 28, 31, 36, 39, 43, 44, 51, 54, 67, 79, 80, 87, 98, 110, 118, 119, 121, 196, 277, 364, 366, 387
  Coventry Act 53
  dissolution 1660 20
  prorogued by James II 98
  Quest of Grievances 57–60
  State Opening 578
  under Charles II 57–61, 62, 65, 70
  under George I 192
  under George II 222, 224
  under George III 245, 261
  under the Prince Regent 300
  under Queen Anne 161, 164
  under William III 144, 146, 148, 150, 151, 153, 154, 156, 161
  see also House of Commons; House of Lords
Parliamentarian Life Guard 9–14, **12–13**, 27
  armour **10**, 11
Parliamentarians 40
Parry (Life Guard) 53
Parson 87
Parsons, Sir Laurence 131
Passchendale 459, 479
Paymaster General 67, 73
Peace of Aix-la-Chapelle **214**, 220, 224
Peace of Amiens 278, 279

Peace of Paris 1856 383
Peace of Ryswick 141, 151, **152**
Peake, Lt 544, 546
Peavey, Capt. 146
Peel, Pte. 323, 340
Peers, Lt 174
Peke, Capt. 172
Pelham-Holles, Thomas, 1st Duke of Newcastle 165, 220–2, 223, 237, 238, 239, 244–5, 257
Pember, Capt. 479
Pembroke, Earl of **235**, 239, 240, 245, **258–9**, 260, 268, 280
Pembroke, Lord 90
Peninsular War (early 1800s) 269, 274, 277, 280, 285, 286–99, **289**, 300–2, 303–12, 313, 338, 369, 391, 582
Penruddock 14
Pepys, Maj. (later Col.) 520, 524, 529
Pepys, Samuel 4, 18, 27, 33–6, 37, 46, 51, 54, 67, 74, 79–80, 99, 110
Péronne 477
Perrin, Marshal Victor 286
Persia 516–17
Perugia 536, 537
Petre, Father 98
Philae Temple 408
Philip V, King of Spain **179**
Philip of Anjou 171, 180, 182
Philip, Prince, Duke of Edinburgh 553, 577
Philipson 257
Pichegru, Marshal 266, 271, 272
Pierson, Col. 238, 244
Pilkington, Lt 422
Pilot, The (newspaper) 274
Pirbright 582
Pirie, Lt 394
Pitt the Elder 202, 222, 224–6, 228, 229, 245, 252
Pitt the Younger 252, 256, 261, 264, 265, 266, 272, 285
Pitt-Rivers, Julian 520, 531–2
Plumer 428
Poelcappelle 479
Poitiers, battle of 1356 216
Poland 265, 502
police 48–50, 101–4, 300–1, 354, 367
Polish Airborne Brigade 547
2nd Polish Corps (Second World War) 536–7
Pompadour, Madame de 245
Pongo (dog) 441
Ponsonby, Maj-Gen. Sir William 313, 322, 329, 335, 336
Pontoise-les-Noyons 484
Pope, Alexander 161, 190, 282
'Popish Plot' 62
Port Said 392
Portal, Lt Col. 473, **475**, 479, 480
Porteous, Capt. 166
Portland, Lord 126, 189
Portsmouth Six 111

INDEX – 621

Portugal 73–4, 75, 171–5, 177, 182, 285, 286, 290, 292, 295, 299, 301, 304–6, 310–11
Portuguese troops 181, 182, 288
Potter, Richard 64
Poultney, Capt. Thomas 131
Powerscourt painting 360–1, **362–3**, 390
Powle, Lt Dickie 543
Pozo Bello 292
Praetorian Camp 274
Pratt, Lord Roderic 509
press-gangs 239
Preston 167
Prestonpans 174, 217
Pretoria 417, 418, 420, 421, 428
Prince of Orange 266, 314
Prince (steamer) 379
Princess Anne's Regiment of Horse 110
prisoners of war **528**
Privy Council 18, 51
prostitution 106
Protestant Association 253, 255
Protestantism 46–7, 57, 60, 66, 74, 92, 110, 253, 255, 256
Prussia 224, 226, 228, 232, 237, 248, 249, 265, 272, 313
Prussian army 226, 239, 314, 316, 319, 325, 329, 337, 343, 346, 367
Puck, Ryan 367–8
Pulford, Cornet 175
Purchase, George 166
puritans 47, 57, 92
Putney Heath Review 1684 83, 87, 101
Pyrenees 182, 308, 310

Qattara Depression 519, 522, 523
Quackerism 43, 47
Quatre-Bras 316, 318, 319, 321, 325
Queen's Birthday Parade 37, 578
Queen's Life Guard 27, 29, 38, 54, 61, 64, 355, 409, 446, 569, 573–7, 579, 582
    Long Guard 576–7
    Short Guard 576, 577
Queen's Regiment 101
Quiberon Bay 237
Quiot 328, 329
Qum 517

Raby, Lord 170, 171, 174, 177, 180, 183, 184
Radclyffe 296, 299, 322
Raglan, Lord 369–71, **370**, 374, 376, 378, 379, 382, 435
Ramilles, battle of 157, 170, 177
Randall, Thomas 43
Ranelagh, Paymaster General 192
Raqqa 527
Rashid Ali 508, 509, 510, 513
Rathkeale riot 367
Ravine of the Dead 181
Rawson, Capt. 409, 412

Read, Trooper 543
Rebow, General 301, 306
Red Hussars 413
Red River Revolt 392
Redgrave, Lt Roy 548–50, 555, 563
Redmaine, Hugh 31
Redmaine, Sir T. 31
Redoubt d'Eu 215
Reeve, Trooper 516
Reeves (Life Guard) 53
Regency Bill 264
Regent's Park Barracks 274, 412, 442, 443, 489, 490, 576
45th Regiment (French – Waterloo) 334
Regiment of Light Horse 79, 80
Regimental Families Fund 434
Regimental Polo Fund 555
Rehovoth 506, 517
Reichswald 548
Reid, Col. George 360
Reille 316, 319, 325
Remington, Mr 53
Rendarvy, Nicholas 56
Rensburg 418
Requette Farm 479
Reresby, Sir John 101, 104
Reserve Cavalry Corps 328
Restoration 16–17, 22, 26–8, 31, 36, 39–41, 43–4, 46, 48, 110
Reus 178
Revertera, Domski 536
Revolutionary Wars 265–72, **267**, **270**, 273
Rhine River 232, 237, 313, 547, 550
Rhineland 502
Rhodes, Cecil 417, 420
Richard, Duke of Gloucester 4
Richards, Henry 51
Richardson (Life Guard) 166
Richardson, Trooper 504
Richelieu, Cardinal 224
Richmond, Duchess of 325
Richmond, Duke of 257, 272, 284, 300
Rikoff, Gen. 376, 378
Riot Act 165, 166, 256, 300
Rivers, Lord 178, 189
Roberts, Field Marshal Lord 418, 420, 427, 428, 435, 449
Roberts, Maj-Gen. Pip 543
Roberts' Heights camp, nr Pretoria 440
Rocksavage, Earl David (Marquess of Cholmondeley) 506, **518**, 519
Rocoux 220
Roeux Cemetery, battle of 474
Rogers, Dr 355
Roman Catholicism 6, 48, 51, 54, 56–7, 80–1, 92, 98–9, 110–11, 113, 116, 121, 142, 226, 253, 290
Romania 368
Rome 534, 536
Rommel, Field Marshal Erwin 520–2, 523, 530
Roos, Lord 243

Roosevelt, Franklin D. 531
Roper, Mr 347
Roscarrick, Edward 26
Rosebery, Lord 413
Rothschild (of The Blues) 562
Roubaix 272
Rowton Heath 23
Roxburghe, Duke of ('Bumble') 448
Royal Air Force (RAF) 508–9, 514–16, 523, 532, 545
Royal Armoured Corps 506, 533, 553, 562
Royal Artillery (Austrian War of Succession) **213**, 547
Royal Commission 1683 79
Royal Dublin Society 577
Royal Engineers 530, 547
Royal Engineers Museum, Chatham 325
Royal Escorts 579
Royal Horse Artillery
    and the Boer War 421
    and the Egyptian campaign 1882 392, 395
    Bull's Troop 286, 291, 294
    King's Troop 569
Royal Horse Guards *see* Royal Regiment of Horse Guards
Royal Hospital, Chelsea 72, 106, 180, 192
Royal Marines 70, 288
Royal Marriages Act 257–60
Royal Mews, Charing Cross 64
Royal Military Academy 303–4
Royal Military College, Chatham 412
Royal Navy 220–2, 237, 264, 279, 392, 442
    and the Second World War 523, 532, 550
Royal Piedmont regiment 240
Royal Regiment of Horse Guards (The Blues) 22, 39–66, 67, 70–4, 83, 190, 352, 412
    amalgamation with the Royals (post-Second World War) 563–6
    anti-smuggling work 252, 257
    and the Austrian War of Succession 197–8, 200, 203, 204, 205, 208, 209, 211, 212, 215, 216, 217
    become part of the Household Cavalry 1820 349, 356
    and the Boer War 420, 421
    and the Boer-First World War interwar period 448, 449
    and the Cardwell Reforms 387–8
    as ceremonial guard 391
    communications 70–1
    contemporary 567–71, 576, 577–82
    cutbacks 249, 349
    deserters 211, 278
    discipline 366
    drummers 352, **353**
    duelling 282–4
    and the Egyptian campaign 1882 391, 392, 394, 397, 398

Royal Regiment of Horse Guards (*cont.*)
   and the First World War 452–4, 456,
      458, 462–4, 469, 470, 484, 486,
      489
   forms composite regiment with The Life
      Guards and Royals 571
   Fretchville's Troop 50
   functions 48–50
   gambling 284
   and George I 167, 185, 188, 192, 194, 195
   and George II 194, 197–8, 200, 203–5, 208–9, 211–12, 215–17, 223–4, 238
   and George III 252, 257, 260–2, 264–6, 268–9, 271–80, 282–4
   and George IV (Prince Regent) 299–301, 356
   horse management 41
   horse rations 105
   horses 157, 203, 260
   and James II's overthrowal 108, 112, 113
   and James II's reforms 96, 98, 101–5, 106, 108
   mechanisation 497, 508, 522
   mobility of 50
   officer training 277
   pay 73, 106, 194
   peace keeping duties 164, 165–6, 167, 256, 257, 300–1
   and the Peninsula War 299, 300–2, 304–8, **309**, 311
   pensions 72–3, 106
   post-First World War 490, 495, 497
   post-Second World War activity 553, 555, 559, 561–6
   and the post-Waterloo peace 349, 354, 356, 358, 360, 364, 366
   and Queen Anne 161, 164
   and the Revolutionary Wars 265–6, 268, 269, 271, 272
   and the Second World War 502, 508, 516, 522, 538, 539, 544
   and Sedgemoor 86, 87, 88, 90, 92, 93, 95
   and the Seven Years War 228, 229, 233, 234–7, 239, 242–3, 244, 245, 248, 249
   standards **348**, 349
   and the Sudan campaign 405, 406, 409
   system of purchase 71, 276, 360, 387
   and the Tangier Horse 79
   uniforms 104–5, 194, 201, 301, 313–14, **332**, **339**, **357**, 454
   and Waterloo 314, 318, 323, 329–30, 336, 337, 338–40, 347, 349
   weaponry 105, 394, 454
   and William III 119, 121, 123–4, 127, 130, 132, 134, 135, 136–7, 141, 148, 151, 153, 154, 157
   wives 364, 366

3rd Troop 47
4th Troop 47, 50
5th Troop 47
7th Troop 87
8th Troop 87
Oxford's Own Troop 47, 135, 151
'A' Squadron 561
see also Household Cavalry Mounted Regiment; 1st Household Cavalry Regiment; 2nd Household Cavalry Regiment; Household Cavalry Regiment
Royal Wardrobe 29, 222
Royalists 6, 7–9, 11, 14, 23, 26, 31, 39, 41, 46
   army 17, 23, 44, 47, 86–7, 90, 93–5
   artillery 87
Rufford Abbey plot 41
Rumbold, Richard 65
Rumsdorp 149
Rupert, Prince 7, 8, 23, 47
Russell, Arty 422
Russell, Sir Baker 391
Russell, Col. 208
Russell, Col. John 22
Russell, Lt Col. Francis 117
Russell, Lord 66, 96
Russell, Theodore 56
Russia 265, 295, 299, 313, 315, 316, 561, 562
   and the Crimean War 368–9, 372, 383
   and the First World War 468
   and the Second World War 516, 551
Russian army 372, 374–9, 383, 517
Russian Cossacks 374
Russian Hussars 376
Rutba 509
Rutland, Duke of 229, 232
Ruvigny 175
Rye House Plot 1683 65–6, 92, 96

Sacherverell, Dr 161, 164–5, 166
Sacheverell Riots 1710 253
Sackville, Lord George 228, 229, 233, 234, 236, 237, 238
St George, Maj. Ferris 529, 537
St George, Second Lt 462, 464
St Germain 239
St James's Palace 161, 224, 577
St James's Park **168**, 224, 245
St John Lodge 260
St Pierre, Lt Col. 170, 172, 174–5, 177, 178, 180
St Ruth 134–5, 136
St Vincent 249
Saladins 562, 569, 571
Salamanca 292, 296, 306, 307, 313, 316
Salerno 532
Salisbury Plain 112, 113
Salisbury Plain training grounds 413, 415, 418, 422, 442, 458–9, 538, 544, 562

Sambre Canal 486
San Sebastian 310
Sanctuary Wood 470
Sanders, Trooper 530
Sanderson, Major 40
Sandhurst 500, 563, 583
Sandys, Capt. (The Blues) 87, 93, 111
Sandys, Lt Sir Thomas 20, 23–6, 53
Sannah's Post 421
Santander 307
Santarem 290–1
Saragossa 181–2
Sarajevo 452
'Sarcastical List' 47
Sargossa 308
Sarsfield, Patrick, 1st Earl of Lucan 66, 88, 92, 99, 113–15, 118, **122**, 124, 126, 127, 130, 131, 134–5, 136, 137, 140, 146, 149
Saudi Arabia 571
Saunders, Ed 216
Savage, Richard 110
Saxe 209, 212, 215, 216–17, 220, 224, 232
Scarlett, Gen. 369, 371, 376–9
Schartenbach 175
Schlieffen Plan 454
Schomberg, Marshal Count 118, 123, 124, 127, 131, 132–4, **133**, 187, 265
Schwarzenberg, Gen. 269
Scimitars 567
Sclater-Booth, Mr 440, 441
Scorpions 567
Scotland 16, 18, 28, 40, 65, 124, 154, 164, 217, 220, 222, 232
Scots Greys *see* Dragoon Guards, 2nd Dragoon Guards
Scott, Anne, Countess of Buccleuch 53
Scott, Sir Walter 340
Scottish army 28
15th Scottish Division (Second World War) 543
Scout Master General 70
Scrimshaw, Charles 26
Scutari 374, 383
Sebastopol 372, 374, 379, 383
Second Dutch War 1665 56, **58–9**
Second World War 501–30, **507**, 531–51, **541**, 583
Secretary at War 67, 70, 71–2, 117, 150, 171, 172, 174, 192, 197, 223, 224, 238, 245, 253, 262, 301
Secretary of State for War 301–2, 387, 388, 442, 449
Secunderabad 490, 495
Sedascue, Adjutant Gen. George 43
Sedgemoor, battle of 56, 66, 86–96, **91**, **94**, **97**, 98, 101, 104, 106, 110–12, 119, 132, 180, 188, 314
Sedley, Catherine 26
Sefton (horse) **570**, 577
Seignier, Mr 161

Septennial Act 1716 167
Serbs 573
Serch, Edmund 106
Seven Years War 196, 223–49, **227**, 252, 260, 261, 265, 273, 301
Seyfried, Lt Johnny 544–5, 546, 553
Seymour, Algernon, Earl of Hertford, 7th Duke of Somerset 167, 189
Seymour, Conway 153
Seymour, Frances 229, 237–8
Seymour, Lord 37
Seymour Conway, Gen. Henry 211, 228, 229, 248, 257–60, 264, 272
Shadwell, Thomas 123
Shaftesbury 51, 62, 65, 67, 92
Shah of Persia 516, 517
Shannon, Lord 187, 189
Sharjah 561
Shaw, Fred 368
Shaw, Lt John 516, 532, 534–6, 537
Shaw, Cpl John 304, **305**, 313, 323, **332**, 333, 335, 336
Shearer, L. Cpl Karl 573
Sheldon, Capt. Lt 170
Sheldon, Maj. Dominic 134
Sherrifmuir 167, 190, 217
Shipman, Capt. 211
shire drum horses 282
Shone, Trooper 512
Shorncliffe garrison 384, 412, 434
Shovell, Admiral Sir Cloudesley 175
Shrewsbury 23
Sicily, invasion of 1843 531–2
Siderfin, Mrs 99
Sidney, Algernon 66, 96
Silesia 195
Silver Sticks 62, 66, 92, 111, 442, 443, 553, 582
Simpson 382
Singapore 562
Slade, Gen. Sir John 284–5, 286, 290, 294, 295–6, 298, 306
slavery 74, 95
Slingsby 87
Smiley, David **515**, 539, 561, 573
Smith, Cpl 550
Smith, Capt. Thomas 142
Smith, Edmund 188
Smith, George Murray 534
Smith, Lt Murray 469–70
Smith, 'Marshal' Peter 104, 108
Smith, Trooper 402
Smith-Dorrien, Horace 452
'Smithforce' **518**, 522
Smithies, Pte. 310, 323, 333, 335
Smollet 202
smuggling 252–3
Soignies Forest 325
Soissons 456
'Soldier's Small Book' 415
Solmes, Count 117, 144–6, 149
Somerset, Maj. Lord Arthur 409

Somerset, 7th Duke of *see* Seymour, Algernon, Earl of Hertford, Duke of Somerset
Somerset, Maj-Gen. Lord Edward 314, 319–21, 329, 336, 337, 338, 340
Somerset regiment 465
Somme 473–4
Sooles, Brig. 146
Sophia of Hanover 160
Sorez 299
Soubise, Prince 245, 248
Souleuvre River 543–4
Soult, Marshal 286, 295, 296, 298–9, 308–10, 316, 319, 356
South Africa 388, 412, 413, 415, 416–31, 435, 438–42, 481, 504
South African Light Horse 412
South Molton 41
South Sea Bubble crisis 167, **169**
Sovereign's Escort 443
Soviet Union 567, 571
Spain 73, 80, 285, 286–8, 291, 292, 295, 299, 306, 307, 308, 310–11, 313
Spanish guerrillas 299
Spanish Succession, wars of 156, 157, 161, 167–84, **173**, 582
Spanish troops 14, 17, 288
Special Air Services (SAS) 519
Special Forces 539, 583
Spence, Sir Basil 576
Spencer, Diana 189
Spender-Clay, Capt. 449
Spion Kop 422, **423**
Spry, Surgeon Maj. Hume 392
SS 546, 550
St-Malo 228
Stahremberg 180–1, 182, 183
Stair, Lord 198, 200, 202, 203, 204, 209
Stalin, Josef 516–17
Standing Orders 1674 54
Stanhope 180–1, 182, 183
Stanley, Edward 26
Staples, Col. 146
Stapleton, Sir Philip 9
Steed, Mr 288
Steele, Col. 441, 442, 469, 470
Steele, Pte. 405
Steenkirk, battle of 62, 140, 144, 146, 149, 150, 170
Stephen, Sir 30
Stephens, Cpl of Horse 430
Stewart, Col. 301
Stewart, Sir Herbert 402, 404, 406, 427
Steyn 417
'stinck pots' 79
Stisted, Henry 290, 291
Stocks, Capt. 371–2, 374, 376, 379, 382, 383
Stocks, Farrier Sgt. 384
Stohwasser, Herr 278
Stoke, battle of 7
Stoney Castle Camp, nr Pirbright 446–8, **447**

Storey, Cornet George 330
Story, Rev. Doctor 135
Stringer, Maj. Bill 569
Stuart, Bernard, Earl of Lichfield 7, 8–9
Stuart, Charles 43
Stuart, Sir Charles 304
Stuart, Charles Edward, the Young Pretender (Bonnie Prince Charlie) 160, 164, 217, 220
Stuart, James, the Old Pretender 160, 167
Stuart monarchy 17, 61, 66, 67, 92, 96, 111, 167
Stuart army 72
Styles, Cpl 334, 342
Suakin 400
Sudan campaign 1884–85 **393**, 399, 400–8, **403**, **407**, 409, 413, 415, 427
Sudeley, Lord 539
Suez canal 391, 392, 558
Suffrage 256
Sulivan, Lt George 303, 304, 306, 310, 313, 338
Sullivan, Arthur 489
Summers, Capt. 510, 514–16
Sunderland, Earl of 46
Sunderland, Lord 165
Sutcliffe, Cpl 306
Swiss Planta regiment 242
Switzerland 279
swords 273, 394
Symonds, Richard 8–9
Syria 506, 508, 514–19, 529

Table Bay 418
Tagus valley 288, 299
Taj Mahal 435
Talavera 285, 286
Talbot, Capt. Reginald 390, 391, 394–5, 401
Talbot, Richard, Earl of Tyrconnell 124, 127, 130, 131, **133**, 134
Taliban 573
Tamai 400
Tangerines 110
Tangier 18, 73–80, **76–7**, 83, 99, 101, 104, 106, 180, 194
Tangier Horse 67–83, 86, 98
and James II's reforms 96, 99–101
widow's pensions 106
and William III 132
tanks 485
Taranto 533
Tathwell, Lt 334
Taunton 88, 252
Tavernor, Mr 188
Tawfiq, Khedive 391, 392, 400
Taylor, Maj. Richard 573
Tchernaya Bridge 383
Teck, Duke of (Marquess of Cambridge) 458
Teheran 516–17
Tel-el-Kebir 394, 397–8, 412

Temple Fire 1679 87
Templer, Maj-Gen. Gerald 536, 563, 566, 576
Ten Year Diary approach 200
Tenison, Dr (Archbishop of Canterbury) 98
Tennyson, Alfred Lord 379
tent pegging 436
Termoli 533
Territorial Army 73
Test Acts 56, 98, 111
Teviot, Lord 75–8, 83
Thaba'Nchu 421
Theatre Royal 360
'thin red line' 376
Third Dutch War 56, 104
Thirty Years War 11, 46, 181
Thompson, Alexis 284
Thorne, John 194
Thynne, Sir James 37
Tiberias 506–8
Tidworth 562
Times, The (newspaper) 360, 369, 394, 401, 417, 525
Tipper, Trooper Simon 576–7
tobacco 50
Tobago 249
Tobruk 517, 519, 520
Todleben, Gen. 383
Toleration Act 1689 164
Topham, Capt. 253, 255
Topham, Lt 174
Tories 164, 167
Tormes 299
Torres Vedras 286–8, 290, 294
Torrington, Lord 238
Tortosa 176, 180
Tothill Fields (now Vincent Square) 39
Toulouse 310
Tournai 142, 212, 217, 271–2
Townshend, Harry 248
Trafford, Cornet Sigismund 291–2, 299, 367
Training Regiment (Household Cavalry – Second World War) 537
Transvaal 416–17, 428
  'drives' 430–1
Treason Club 110–11
Treasury 73
Trelawney, Charles 110
trench warfare 456–8, 460–72, 473–86
Triennial Act 1694 164
Trinidad 278
Tripoli 529
Troopes of Guards 22
Trooping of the Colour 37, **557**
Troughback, John 27
Tsar's Guards 352
Tudela 308
Tunis 530, 531
Tunisia 529–30
Turberville, Troilus 8
Turenne, Marshal 17, 56, 81

Turf Club 552
Turkey 368, 527, 571
Turkish army 374, 548
Turner, Lt Col. 187
Turner, Lt Col. Sir Charles 266
Turnham Green plot 11, 153
Turp, Farrier Sgt. Bert 484–5
Tweedie, Lt Alexander 573
Tweedmouth, Lord 'Beef' 462–3
Tyndale, William 280
Tyrwhitt-Drake, Capt. William 314

Uhlans 390, 456, 465
Uitlanders 417
Union Brigade (Waterloo) 313, 314, 316, 319, 322, **324**, 325, 329, 334–5, 336, 338, 343, 346, 347, 378, 566
United Nations (UN) 571–3
United Nations Force 562, 571
United Provinces 171
Unton Croke, Col. 18, 22, 40, 43–4
Unton Croke's Regiment of Horse 18, 22, 39–66
  see also Royal Regiment of Horse Guards
Upcott, Capt. 86, 87, 93, 96
US Air Force 530
US troops 532, 540, 545, 547
Utrecht, treaty of 183
Uxbridge, Earl of (Marquess of Anglesey) 314, 315, 316, 321–2, 329, 334, 335, 336, 340, **341**, 342, 358, 369

Valencia 176–7, 298
Valenciennes 266
Valkenswaard 547
van Keppel, Col. Arnold Joost, 1st Earl of Albemarle 156, 187, 189, 208
Vandeleur 336
Vandervand (Life Guard drummer) 189
Vanity Fair magazine 401
Vanson, Sgt. 441
Varley, Troop Corporal Major 279
Varna 371, 372
Vaughan 90
Vaughan, John 64
VE Day 550
Vellinghausen 245, 249
Vendée 313
Vendhuile 477
Vendôme, Marshal 182, 183, 184
Venner riots 18–20, 22, 39, 98
Venner, Thomas 18–20
Verdun 330
Verney, Sir Ralph 33, 64
Versailles, Treaty of 1918 502
Vezon 215
Vicars, John 11
Vichy regime 506, 508, 516, 558
Vickers, Lt 181
Vickers, Lt Col. Richard 566
Vickers machine guns 454, 479, 485

Victoria, Queen 349, 358, 364–6, 413, **414**, 443, 552, 573, 577, 579
  and the Boer War 415–16, 428–30
  coronation 356
  and the Egyptian Campaign 1882 390, 391, 392, 398
  jubilee 413, 415
  and the Sudan Campaign 401
Villeroi, Marshal 150
Villers 268
Villers, Col. 131
Villeselve 484
Villiers, Charles 412, 417
Vilvorden 220
Vimy 474
Vitoria, battle of 307, 308, 316
Vivian, Maj-Gen. Sir Hussey 336
von Ziethen 226
Vyse, Brig. 269
Vyse, Sir Richard Howard 563

Waal River 547
Wade, Field Marshal George 209, 211
Wadi Halfa 408
Wagstaffe Rebellion 41
Waithman, Sheriff of London 255
Walachia 368
Waldeck, Prince 123, 144, 212
walis 436
Walker, Gen. Walter 562
Wallace, Cpl 412
Walpole, Horace 167, 190–2, 195, 196, 238, 243, 244, 245, 257
Walsh, Lt 236
Wagenheim, Gen. 233
War Office 65, 117–18, 172, 184, 384, 388–90, 391, 398, 400, 402, 430, 442, 458, 484, 489, 506, 522, 533, 537, 538, 577, 582
Warburg 240–3, **241**, 244, 248, 273
Ward, Thomas 98
Warminster Declaration 43
Warren, Gen. 422
Washington, George 232
Waterford, Governor of 130
Waterloo, battle of 39, 252, 260, 274, 276, 277–8, 290, 302, 304, 310, 313–43, **317**, **320**, **324**, **326–7**, **331–2**, **339**, 346–9, 354, 366–7, 369, 388, 391, 413, 460, 578, 579, 582
Waterloo Bridge 347, **348**
Waugh, Auberon 539, 561
Waugh, Evelyn 539, 561
Wavell, Gen. 506, 526
Waymouth, Lt 330
Weaver's Riots 1765 253
Wedderburn, Attorney 255
Weigh, Roger 220
Wellesley, Lt Valerian 508, 510, 512, 513, 514, 516, 526, 527, **528**, 534
Wellington, Duke of 229, **250**, 269, 273, 276, 277, 280, 285–8, 290–1, 292,

294, 295, 296, 298, 299, 300, 302, 349, 352, 355, **356**, 358, 369, 578
   funeral 356
   and Waterloo 304, 306–7, 308–10, 313, 314–16, 321–2, 325, 328, 330, 334–5, 336, 340, 342, 346, 347
Wentworth, Lord 18
Wentworth, Cornet Thomas 170, 171, 174
Werhner 417
Wesel 243
Weser River 232
Weser Vale Hunt 569
West Africa 481
West Country 87–95, 101, 108, 112, 252
West Germany 567–9
West Indies 224
West Indies Regiment 342
Western Desert 519–27, 529
Western Front **457**
Westminster, treaty of 1674 57
Westminster, treaty of 1755 224
Westmorland, Earl of 188
Westonzoyland 86, 87, 90, 92, 93
Westphalia 243, 272
Westwood, Pte. William 366–7
Whetham, Nathaniel 43
Whigs 65, 67, 92, 121, 153, 164–5, 166–7, 232, 256, 261, 358
White Boys 367–8
White, Gen. Sir George 417
White, Pte. Joseph 271
Whitehall Palace **155**, 161
Wild Geese 137–40
   1st Troop 140
   2nd Troop 140
Wilde, Oscar 366
Wilhelm II, Kaiser 413, **414**, 422, 434, 435, 438, 440, 468, 555
Wilhelmina, Queen of the Netherlands 553
Wilhelmstahl 248
Wilkes Riots 1768 253

Wilkins, Cpl 472
Willems 271–2, 277, 486
William III, King of England 23, 29, 47, 60, 61, 92, 96, 108, 111, 112–32, 137, 140, 141–51, **152**, 153–7, 160, 161, 165, 170, 171, 188, 192, 194, 202, 249, 553
William IV, King of England 349, 356, **356**, 359, 577
Williamites 124, 126, 127, 131, 134, 135–6
Willis, Pte. Henry 300, 306
Willoughby, Sir John 412, 417
Wilsher, Trooper 436–7
Wilson, Sir Charles 406
Wilson, Capt. Gordon 561
Wilson, Gordon 'Erasmus' 448, 458
Wilson, Sir Robert 355
Wiltshire and Warwickshire Yeomanry 537
Winchester, Bishop of 93
Windsor, Capt. 291, 298, 334
Windsor 161, 280, 282, 284, 286, 306, 311, 313, 314, 347, 349, 352, 356, 360, 361, 364, 366, 398, 406, 413, 415, 430, 442, 448, 479, 489, 490, 500, 502, 504, 536, 537, 538, 539, 552, 562, 566, 567, 569, 571, 573, 577, 578, 582–3
Windsor Great Park 64, 276, 279, 280–2, 449–52, 538, 578
Windsor Strollers 360
Windsor Uniform 280
Winkfield Plain 279
Wintle, Lt Alfred 492–5, 555–8
Witham, Edward 78
Wolfe, James 220, 224, 229
Wolfenbüttel 555
Wolland, Corporal Major 509–10
Wolseley, Sir Garnet 392, 394, 397–8, 400, 401, 402, 404, 408, 415, 416, 427, 435
Wood, Henry 72

Wood, Maj-Gen. Henry 148
Wood, Sir Evelyn 449, 484
Wooldridge, Pte. Charles 366
Worcester, battle of 1651 4, 44, 47, 352
Worcester, Marquess of 37
Wray, Sir Baptiste 98
Wray, Sir Cecil 256–7
Wright, Anthony 151
Wright, Charlie 463
Wroth, Sir Henry 48
Wrottesley, Capt. 547
Wurtemberg, Duke of 148, 150
Wyndham 288–90, 291, 310
Wyndham, Charles 47
Wyndham, Sir Francis 47, 48, 50, 87
Wyndham, Humphrey 496–7, 502, 504, 508
Wytschaete 463, 464
Wyvilles, John 190

Yemen 561
Yeomanry 480–1, 484
Yeomen of the Guard 7, 57
Yonge, Sir William 197
York, Grand Old Duke of 347, 356
York 50
Yorke, Col. John 369, 374, 376, **377**, 378, 379
Young, L. Cpl Jeffery 576–7
Young, Lt 547
Ypres 458, 460, 464, 469, 470
   first battle of 460–4, **461**
   second battle of 470–1
   third battle of 479
Ypres Salient 460, 463, 469, 471

Zanvoorde Ridge 463, 464
Zetchwitz's Regiment 269
Zetland Trophy **389**
Ziethen 316
Zionists 558
Zoelen, Groenix van 546

THE HOUSEHOLD CAVALRY MUSEUM

This new Museum, scheduled to open in June 2007, will give visitors a unique view of the proud history of the Household Cavalry, its modern day operational role as well as a privileged 'behind the scenes' insight into their famous ceremonial duties.

Located within the historic building and working stable at Horse Guards, London, the museum will chart the Household Cavalry's history from the time of Charles II, through Waterloo, to its modern deployment in Iraq. The story is told with the help of fascinating objects from its extensive Regimental collection and archives and will be brought to life through captivating personal stories and accounts.

The existing Regimental Museum at Combermere Barracks, Windsor, is also scheduled to re-open in September 2007, as a collection and education facility that will support the London operation.

For more information and opening times see the
Household Cavalry Museum website at
www.householdcavalry.gvon.com